P9-DDN-689

FINLAND

Helsinki

Leningrad

Stockholm

Tallin

ESTONIA

EDEN

BALTIC
SEA

Riga

LATVIA

Moscow

Moskva R.

Oka R.

Dnieper R.

hagen

Memel

LITHUANIA

Kaunas

Danzig   Königsberg

BYELORUSSIA

Minsk

nemünde

EAST
PRUSSIA

Tannenberg

tettin

POLISH
nburg   CORRIDOR

U.S.S.R.

berswalde

cienwalde

Vistula R.

Warsaw

rlin

tsdam

Don R.

len

POLAND

Oder R.

gue

Kiev

Katowice

Lwów

UKRAINE

MIA AND   Cracow

ORAVIA   Teschen   Krosno

Dnieper R.

Brno   SLOVAKIA

Vinnitsa

na   Trnava   Uzghorod

RIA   Bratislava   RUTHENIA

Budapest

HUNGARY

RUMANIA

Bucharest

Belgrade

BLACK SEA

YUGOSLAVIA

Danube R.

BULGARIA

Sofia

ALBANIA

Durazzo

Ankara

THE DARDANELLES

GREECE

TURKEY

Athens

CRETE   CYPRUS

BOOKS
BY LEONARD MOSLEY

DUEL FOR KILIMANJARO: *An Account of the East African Campaign 1914–1918*

THE LAST DAYS OF THE BRITISH RAJ

THE GLORIOUS FAULT

THE CAT AND THE MICE

REPORT FROM GERMANY: *1945*

GIDEON GOES TO WAR: *The Story of Wingate*

DOWNSTREAM: *1939*

CASTLEROSSE

SO FAR SO GOOD

HAILE SELASSIE: *The Conquering Lion*

FACES FROM THE FIRE: *The Biography of Sir Archibald McIndoe*

Novels

THE SEDUCTIVE MIRROR

SO I KILLED HER

WAR LORD

EACH HAD A SONG

NO MORE REMAINS

ON
BORROWED
TIME

ON
BORROWED
TIME

How
World War II Began

LEONARD MOSLEY

RANDOM HOUSE   NEW YORK

Copyright © 1969 by Leonard Mosley
All rights reserved under International
and Pan-American Copyright Conventions.
Published in the United States
by Random House, Inc., New York.

Library of Congress Catalog Card Number: 69–16427
Manufactured in the United States of America
by the Book Press, Brattleboro, Vermont
Designed by Andrew Roberts
Maps by Rafael D. Palacios

Special thanks and acknowledgment are hereby extended to the following for permission to reprint extracts from the works listed below:

Houghton Mifflin Company—*The Memoirs of Anthony Eden*, Vol. III, *The Reckoning*, by the Earl of Avon.

Alfred A. Knopf, Inc.—*1940: The Fall of France*, by André Beaufre. Trans. by Desmond Flower. © Copyright 1967 by Cassell & Co. Ltd.

Houghton Mifflin Company—*The Life of Lord Halifax*, by Lord Birkenhead.

Librairie Plon—*De Munich à la guerre*, by Georges Bonnet.

Houghton Mifflin Company—*The Second World War*, Vol. I, *The Gathering Storm*, by Winston Churchill.

E. P. Dutton & Co., Inc.—*Ciano's Hidden Diary*, by Count Galeazzo Ciano. Trans. by Andreas Mayor. Copyright 1953 by E. P. Dutton & Co., Inc.

Chicago Daily News—*Ciano's Diaries 1939–1943*, by Count Galeazzo Ciano. Ed. by Hugh Gibson.

Houghton Mifflin Company—*The Light of Common Day*, by Diana Cooper.

Librairie Hachette, Editeur—*De Staline à Hitler*, by Robert Coulondre.

Miss Lena Wickman—*The Last Attempt*, by Birger Dahlerus.

Simon & Schuster, Inc.—*Mission to Moscow*, by Joseph Davies. Copyright 1941, © 1969 by Joseph E. Davies.

Her Majesty's Stationery Office—*Documents on British Foreign Policy 1919–1939*, 3rd Series, and *Documents on German Foreign Policy 1918–1945*, Series C, Vols. I–II, and Series D, Vols. I–XI.

E. P. Dutton & Co., Inc.—*Old Men Forget*. The autobiography of Alfred Duff Cooper, Viscount of Norwich.

Routledge & Kegan Paul Ltd.—*World Finance 1938–1939*, by Paul Einzig.

Macmillan & Co. Ltd.—*The Life of Neville Chamberlain*, by Sir Keith Feiling.

Curtis Brown Ltd.—*The Fallen Bastions*, by G. E. R. Gedye.

E. P. Dutton & Co., Inc.—*Panzer Leader*, by Heinz Guderian. Trans. by Constantine Fitzgibbon.

Raymond Savage Ltd. (Literary Executors for the late Sir Nevile Henderson)—
    Failure of a Mission, by Nevile Henderson.
Simon & Schuster, Inc.—*The Secret Diary of Harold Ickes*, Vol. II, *The Inside
    Struggle: 1936–1939*. Copyright 1954 by Simon & Schuster, Inc.
Stein and Day, Inc.—*The Memoirs of Field-Marshal Keitel*. Ed. by Walter Görlitz.
    Copyright © 1961 by Musterschmidt Verlag. Translation copyright © 1965
    by William Kimber and Co., Ltd.
Union Verlag Stuttgart—*Nicht aus den Akten*, by Erich Kordt.
David Higham Associates, Ltd.—*The Memoirs of Captain Liddell Hart*, by B. H.
    Liddell Hart.
Harvard University Press—*The Moffat Papers*. Ed. by Nancy Harvison Hooker.
Howard Fertig, Inc.—*Diplomatic Prelude*, by Sir Lewis Namier.
Lady Namier—*Europe in Decay*, by Sir Lewis Namier.
Orbis—*New Documents on the History of Munich*.
The New York Times Company—material from articles which appeared in several
    1938 and 1939 issues of the *New York Times*. Copyright 1938/1939 by
    The New York Times Company.
Collins Publishers—*Diaries and Letters*, Vol. I, *1930–1939*, by Harold Nicolson.
    Ed. by Nigel Nicolson.
Cassell & Co. Ltd.—*The Central Blue*, by Sir John Slessor.
Editions Robert Laffont—*Témoignage pour l'histoire*, by Paul Stehlin.
André Deutsch Ltd.—*At Home and Abroad*, by Lord Strang.
The World Publishing Company—*The Founding Father*, by Richard Whalen.
René Julliard—*Souvenirs et solitude*, by Jean Zay. © René Julliard.

TO D.
WITH MY LOVE

Acknowledgments

Any writer of a book of this kind who says that he has done his own research should immediately explain what is meant by that statement. In my case, it means that every document and every book referred to in the narrative was read and checked by me, and that every person whose new material or opinions are quoted either was interviewed personally by me or gave me the information in the course of correspondence. But I hasten to add that at every stage of my work, in every country I visited, I had an indefatigable fellow worker at my side, and there were always others—experts, librarians, researchers, statesmen, soldiers, civil servants, eyewitnesses—ready to proffer information or advice.

I would like to say how grateful I am for the groundwork which has been done by the historians of the period who have already written about these sad days. I have been particularly influenced and helped by the late Sir Lewis Namier, Sir John Wheeler-Bennett, General Telford Taylor, Professor Alan Bullock, Mr. A. J. P. Taylor, Mr. William Shirer and Professor Hugh Trevor-Roper, as well as by the writings about the period by Mr. Malcolm Muggeridge, who vividly recalls the febrile atmosphere of the time.

For helping me through the great mass of German documents I owe much to scholars and researchers in the United States, where the bulk of the documents of the Nazi regime went at the end of World War II. Under the auspices of the American Historical Association Committee for the Study of War Documents a guide has been prepared from which a researcher can pick his way through a veritable jungle of information, and historians owe a heavy debt to Dr. Boyd C. Shafer, the executive secretary of the AHA, and to his subcommittee consisting of Drs. Fritz T. Epstein, George W. F. Hallgarten (chairman), C. Easton Rothwell, Witold S. Sworskowski and Gerhard L. Weinberg.

In the field of German military documents, a similar debt is owed to Philip P. Brower, who edited the *Guides to German Documents* in the National Archives, Washington, with the assistance of Anthony F. Grassl, Howard H. Puckett and Richard Scharf, and to Donald E. Spencer and Dr. Willard Allen Fletcher. My old friends at the National Archives, Robert Wolfe (Specialist in German Records), his assistant, Richard Bauer, and John E. Taylor (of the Military Records Department) helped me find my way through the *Guides* before letting me loose in the jungle, and smoothed my passage between the Archives, the Library of Congress and the warehouses at Alexandria, Virginia.

No less helpful to me in my search for information were Miss Judith A. Schiff, head of the Historical Manuscripts and University Archives Department of Yale University Library at New Haven, Connecticut, and Miss Dorothy Bridgwater, acting head of the Reference Department. I am indebted to Miss Agnes F. Peterson of the Hoover Library at Stanford University for spending so much of her time compiling the references to the vast number of documents in which I was interested.

In England that distinguished scholar of Japanese history, Dr. Richard Storry, introduced to me the documents and resources in the German section of the library at St. Antony's College, Oxford; and, as usual, I found the Public Record Office and the Wiener Library invaluable.

I am sorry that my old and good friend, the late Randolph Churchill, will not be reading these words, for I would have liked him to know how appreciative I am for the help he so willingly gave me. He made me a welcome guest at his home in East Bergholt and went through his father's documents with me over the period with

xii

which I was dealing, and ill though he was, he was never too tired to answer any of my questions.

I am also deeply grateful to Mr. Laurence Cotterell, a good friend of Poland and the Poles, for putting me in touch with those Poles in exile who could help in tracing the course of events in their homeland just before and after the German invasion of their country. These included Captain E. Lubomirski, of the Sikorski Institute, London, and Major E. Hinterhoff, a veteran soldier and flier of wide experience. I have also been in touch with Colonel A. Sawczynski, General Joseph Jacklicz, Colonel M. Prothsewicz, Colonel St. Fabiszewski and Mr. J. Carlinski. In Poland itself Mr. Stanislaw Kostarski, of the Foreign Office, was of most help, particularly in directing me to the Western archives at Cracow.

A diplomat of great charm and prescience, Professor Dr. Erich Kordt (who might well be called the father of the present-day German foreign service) not only answered all my questions and let me study all his documents, but also put me in touch with Dr. Helmuth Krausnick, curator of the Institut für Zeitgeschichte in Munich, where I was made welcome and whose files were opened to me.

Thanks to Dr. Miroslav Had of the Czech embassy in London, I was given all facilities for research in Czechoslovakia at the Institute for International Politics and Economics in Prague. Under difficult circumstances (the political situation was tense; when is it otherwise in Prague?), Dr. Karel Kratky went out of his way to be of help, as did Mr. Jaroslav Pospisil of the Army Museum and a number of others whose names, at the time this is written, it might be unwise to specify.

In France I was grateful for the willing help of the Bibliothèque Nationale and the Collège Européen des Sciences Sociales et Economiques. I wish that I had received equal co-operation from the U.S.S.R., but though I received no direct refusal of help, neither did I receive any reply to my requests. Because of my experience of some years as a foreign correspondent, I was not surprised by this, but I was disappointed. Until the Russian files are thrown open, exactly what motivated the Kremlin in its negotiations with Germany in 1939 and why Stalin put such faith in the pact with the Nazis once it was signed will not be fully known.

As to individuals, I am most grateful to Sir Horace Wilson for giving me his time and so frankly answering all my questions. There were many others who saw me or answered by correspondence or both. These include the Earl of Avon; the Honorable Charles E. Bohlen (now in the State Department in Washington but ambassador to France when I saw him); General Karl Bodenschatz; General André Beaufre; the Earl of Birkenhead; Lord Coleraine; M. Edouard Daladier; Mme. Dryak of Cheb (Eger), Czechoslovakia; the late Mr. Paul Emrys-Evans, Lord Harvey; the Earl of Hardwicke; General Franz Halder; the late Senator Robert F. Kennedy and his aides; the late Viscount Kemsley of Dropmore; the office of Mr. Joseph P. Kennedy; Dr. Brigitte Lohmeyer; Mr. Alvar Liddell; Lord Strang and General Paul Stehlin.

This book has been read before publication by three distinguished historians who are experts on the period: Mr. Christopher Thorne, Mr. Geoffrey Warner and Mr. Hans L. Trefousse. I am most grateful to them for their diligent reading of the manuscript and for correcting factual mistakes. But as is the case with all others who have been consulted about this book, they have no responsibility for the opinions I have expressed; these are entirely my own.

Finally, a word of thanks to my agent in New York, John Cushman, who has been associated with this book from its inception. It is he who made it possible for me to begin the long research in so many countries, over so many miles and over so much time. He was most loyally backed by Graham Watson in London, who has always been one of my most trusted advisers. George Weidenfeld and Anthony Godwin also have encouraged me and been available whenever I needed help.

There are two others to whom I would like to express my particularly warm thanks for their good advice and expert guidance, but one of them has adamantly refused to allow me to name him. He has my gratitude just the same. The other is my copyeditor in New York, Barbara Willson, who really ought to be in charge of the information-sifting center of Interpol. She has the keen mind of a great detective and has allowed no loosely worded statement nor questionable date to slip through the narrative. If there is any documentation still missing from this book, it is not her fault. I thank her for being such a hard taskmistress.

L.M.

Contents

Contents

xvi

ONE

Aide-mémoire

I
Incident at Eger

Just after dawn on the morning of September 13, 1938, two Czech policemen on bicycles rode slowly down the main street of the ancient Sudetenland city of Eger and stopped outside the Victoria Hotel. Propping their cycles against a pillar at the entrance, they mounted the steps to the hotel's main door; and while one pulled a button which presently set a bell clanging inside the building, the other took a piece of paper from his leather pouch. It was a search warrant signed by Dr. Anton Dryak, military judge for the district of Cheb (as the Czechs called Eger), which instructed the two policemen to make a thorough search of the Victoria Hotel on the grounds that it was being used as headquarters by the Sudeten German National Socialist party and because a store of small arms was believed to have been smuggled into it during the previous twenty-four hours.

It was a damp, cool, misty morning and the streets were deserted. "Ring again," said one policeman to the other, and once more the bell jangled. But still there was no sound within, while outside, in the streets, it seemed to have grown quieter than ever.

Exasperated and perhaps made nervous by the silence, the first policeman suddenly raised a huge fist and began to hammer heavily on the door, while his companion fumbled at his belt for his revolver.

3

It was then that a faint creaking noise was heard from above, and the first policeman stepped back and glanced upward just in time to receive a bullet in the head which spun him around and down the steps on to the cobbled roadway, where he jerked and groaned for a few seconds and then lay still. In the silence which followed it was possible to hear his companion breathing hard, and then he clattered down the steps to his bicycle, tried to mount it, failed, and let it fall into the road as he ran around the nearest corner. Then there was silence again: no sound or movement from the Victoria Hotel; no stir in the surrounding streets. The body of the Czech policeman lay sprawled on the cobbles in a coagulating pool of blood, an untidy heap in a neat, well-swept street.

After a quarter of an hour there was the sound of an opening door, and from the side of the Victoria Hotel there appeared a young man in breeches, boots and khaki shirt with a swastika armband. Running to the dead Czech, he turned him over with his boot, and then divested him of his belt and pistol, which he slung over his shoulder as he returned, rather more cockily and slowly now, to the hotel. A sudden noise galvanized him, and he regained the hotel at a run.

It was the noise of two motorcycles threading the streets from Eger's police (and temporary military) headquarters on their way to the scene of the shooting. They came to a halt at the corner, their engines still running, their helmeted riders astraddle with pistols in their hands, waiting. A few minutes later, in a flurry of revving engines, Czech armored cars poured in from all angles, their Bren guns pointing at the Victoria Hotel. They edged in and then, with a sudden burst, shattered a row of windows on the second floor.

Through a megaphone, a voice spoke in German with a Czech accent: "Come out with your hands on your heads and you will be unharmed. If you stay inside, we will destroy you."

There was a ping as a bullet bounced off the side of the leading armored car, followed by several other ragged shots. A grenade flew from an upstairs window, landed on the cobbles in the square and then exploded as one of the policemen gunned his motorcycle forward and scooped it up. The man and his machine were blown in flaming pieces against the side of one of the armored cars and set it momentarily ablaze. The Bren gun kept up a steady stream of fire throughout the incident.

4

Now small groups of Czech soldiers edged around the corners of the old buildings with mortars, calmly sighted them and began lobbing in bombs. Their accuracy was uncanny; the missiles crashed down on the roof, several through the highest windows, one through a water tank.

Not that it was all over quickly. The firing from inside the building went on all morning, and it was not until midday that a white flag appeared through one of the windows. Presently the same young man who had stolen the dead Czech policeman's pistol came out of the door, hands behind his head in surrender while simultaneously he tried to rub his tear-gassed eyes with his forearms. He was one of two survivors.

There were eight dead men in the rooms upstairs, all of them Sudeten Germans. The other survivor was Karl Hermann Frank, second-in-command of the Sudeten Nazi party; he had climbed out of a back window at the start of the battle and made his way through back streets to the house of another member of the party. From there he was driven to party headquarters in Asch, and gave his chief, Konrad Henlein, the news of the battle; despite the fact that eight of his comrades had been killed, he looked hugely pleased.

He had reason to be. Henlein, a less complicated and more sympathetic character, openly showed disapproval of his subordinate's lack of sorrow, but he too felt that this incident might just be what they needed. He said, "Our comrades have fallen in the battle for freedom, killed by the Czechs, but they will not be forgotten. They could not have chosen a better time." He shouted for his secretary to come into the room. "I must inform the Führer at once. Adolf Hitler can now demonstrate to the world that Sudetens and Czechs can never live together, that it is useless to go on negotiating, that the only place for the Sudeten Germans is back home in the Reich!"

That same afternoon Henlein's description of the attack on the Victoria Hotel—in which, of course, the brutal Czech police had murdered eight unarmed Sudetens—was sent by courier across the Czech frontier to Bayreuth and teletyped to Adolf Hitler's retreat at Berchtesgaden in Bavaria.

For Adolf Hitler's purposes, the news of the killings couldn't have been better timed. On September 15 Prime Minister Neville Chamberlain was flying out from London to meet him. He was coming to see Hitler in a desperate effort to solve the problem that was now worrying the whole of Europe: how to settle the demands of the Sudeten Germans living inside the democratic state of Czechoslovakia without plunging Britain and France, and possibly the rest of the world, into a war with Germany.

The battle of the Victoria Hotel in Eger that September of 1938 has never until now received more than a passing mention in the history books. And why should it, when so few people were involved and only ten men were killed? Yet its influence on subsequent developments in the Western world was in fact both decisive and tragic. A shot at Sarajevo in 1914 is said to have started World War I. The mortar bombs at Eger did not start World War II, but they did alter the situation in Czechoslovakia at a crucial moment when two statesmen, Hitler and Chamberlain, were discussing its future. For one thing, they persuaded the Czechs to move in against Henlein, and Henlein to move his activities temporarily to Germany.

This book is an account of the last turbulent days of peace and the first brutal days of battle when World War II began in Europe in 1939, and it will not dwell on the melancholy events of the year before. But to understand the nature of the situation in Europe during the final months of peace, a summary of the events preceding those months is needed.

In the summer of 1938 the Western democracies in Europe— or at least the men who governed them—were paralyzed with fear of one man and what he might do to them. That man was Adolf Hitler of Germany. Great Britain was still the ruler of the greatest empire the world has ever known, with a powerful navy and vast riches in food supplies, raw materials and gold. Her ally, France, had Europe's largest army, and even some of her potential opponents believed at that time that it was the most efficient. Yet by an inspired combination of propaganda, threats and bluff Adolf Hitler had succeeded in convincing these two nations that they were well-nigh helpless, and that if they denied him what he wanted he would descend on them with the inevitability of an avalanche and crush them.

There had been a time, shortly after he came to power in 1933 and turned Germany into a National Socialist state, when the dictator of Germany had feared the might of the British Empire; he

6

dreaded the prospect of its fleet blockading Germany from her food supplies and starving her into surrender, as had happened during the World War. But in 1935 Italy defied the civilized world by attacking Abyssinia, one of the last independent nations in Africa. This act of aggression by the Italian dictator, Benito Mussolini, not only aroused the indignation of all liberal-minded people, especially in Britain; it also seriously threatened the lines of communication and strategic future of the British Empire. It was a moment for Britain to demonstrate that she would react in no uncertain fashion to such a threat to her security, with the certain knowledge that the British people were behind their government, though more for moral than political reasons.

Adolf Hitler waited for the showdown. To the head of the Political Department of his Foreign Ministry, Baron Ernst von Weizsäcker, who had brought him a message asking for the loan of ships for Italy's East African operation, he said, "Let the Italians have a hundred ships! We'll go back, undamaged. They will go through the Suez Canal, but they will never go further. The British navy's battleship *Repulse* will be waiting there and signaling: 'Which way are you going?' 'South,' the Italians will reply. 'Oh no, you're not,' the *Repulse* will reply. 'You're going north!' and north they will go."

To his personal adjutant and old wartime comrade, Fritz Wiedemann, Hitler said, "If I had a choice between the Italians and the English, then I would take the English. Mussolini is closer to me, but I know the English from the last war. I know they are hard fellows. If Mussolini thinks he can chase away the English fleet from the Mediterranean with his own, he is very much mistaken."

But Mussolini was *not* mistaken. With a badly trained and undermanned fleet (which a British admiral was later on to compare with "a squadron of paper boats which start to sink if you blow on them"), the Italians bluffed the British into keeping their own ships in harbor. Britain could have closed the Suez Canal without, as it turned out, any possibility of the Italians doing anything to force them into opening it again. The Italian armies in Abyssinia would have been cut off from their home bases in Italy and withered away from lack of support. Instead, the Canal remained open because of British fear of reprisals, and the Italian troop transports, supply ships and war vessels which eventually hammered the Abyssinians into defeat continued to pass through.

To Adolf Hitler these events were a revelation of how the mighty British lion had diminished into a mouse, and from that moment on he was increasingly inclined to exploit the fact. In 1936 he gave orders for his army to march into the Rhineland, which had been demilitarized by the Allies as part of the Treaty of Versailles, but he told his commanders that the operation would be canceled immediately should the British navy order mobilization and assemble the fleet. The British did nothing of the kind, and this reinforced the Führer in his growing suspicion of the nature of their malaise. On February 4, 1938, Hitler reorganized the military establishment and declared himself Supreme Commander of the Armed Forces. A week later he summoned the Chancellor of Austria, Kurt von Schuschnigg, to a conference at Berchtesgaden and then proceeded to bully and threaten him because he had tried to suppress National Socialist agitation in his country. Schuschnigg signed an ultimatum giving considerable concessions to the Nazis in Austria, but a month later, after Schuschnigg had announced a plebiscite giving his people a choice over the question of autonomy, Hitler marched his armies over the frontier and followed them in triumph into Vienna. He had brought his first independent country under the control of the German Reich, confident that neither Britain nor her French ally would do more than voice a faint protest. In fact, they stood shamefacedly by while the Nazi storm troopers took over in Vienna, while the murders and beatings began, and while the Jews and democrats were rounded up and herded into the concentration camps.

Since they were both still so rich and powerful, why were the British and French so afraid?

The simple answer is that in the main, the ordinary people of Britain and France were not afraid at all. They had watched the growth of the Nazi movement in Germany and they did not like what they saw. They had read of the persecution of men, women and children on racial and political grounds; they had heard talk for the first time of concentration camps; they had watched and heard the swaggering Nazi leaders boasting and threatening in the newsreels. On the whole their reaction was one of distaste and a suspicion that one of these days such people would become a threat to life and comfort and would have to be put down. To the British people the

Germans were proving what willing tyrants they could become under the wrong sort of leaders; to the French, *les sales boches* were beginning to act up again.

It was among the elected rulers that panic ran through the veins and atrophied the thinking processes of government whenever they thought of German power. In France a series of political crises and temporary administrations, mostly of a left-wing character, all destroyed by right-wing intrigue, had given way to a middle-of-the-road government presided over by Edouard Daladier, a hard-drinking, solid politician of little inspiration but much honesty and good will. But his administration had one great menace—along with several minor ones—to its stability. The most influential post in the government, that of Foreign Minister, had been given by Daladier under political pressure to Georges Bonnet, one of the most equivocal characters in the history of French politics.

The people who quaked with fear over Germany in each of these countries were what could still, in those days, be called "the ruling classes": the men and women of title, money or position who, whether in the government or not, were members of the Establishment and knew how to use their influence. In France this clique was riddled with corruption and defeatism; hagridden by the menace of Nazi Germany from outside their borders and by the threat of domestic Communism within, many of them were increasingly ready to make an accommodation with Germany in the hope that accord with National Socialism would throttle the threat of Red revolution. Bereft of real leadership, the men who mattered in France in 1938 had begun to doubt their country's role as a great power; they had neither faith in themselves nor in their people, and the stronger the aggression from Germany, the more they were inclined to stick their heads in the sand and hope that the menace would go away. Though their army was still considered the most powerful in Europe, and though they had a series of alliances designed to protect them from the very threat which Hitlerian Germany presented, their mood was self-destructive. In the meantime, they had passed the responsibility for protecting themselves and for preserving peace and stability in Europe to their principal ally, Great Britain.

■

Prime Minister Neville Chamberlain had succeeded Stanley Baldwin as head of the Tory party the year before, and a less happy selection for such trying times can hardly be imagined. The world in 1938 was changing rapidly for the worse, and the British Empire was menaced by hungry enemies in all parts of the globe. It was time for a leader with a sense of mission and of urgency, one capable of rallying the British people to an understanding of the dangers facing them. Among the members of the ruling Tory party there was a small group of Members of Parliament who realized only too acutely the perils of Britain's situation, and they urged a program of rapid rearmament at home and a stern and positive Anglo-French policy toward the German and Italian dictators. Chief among them was Winston Churchill, and it is typical of the mood of the times that his repeated prophecies that trouble was coming moved even his friends to call him "a bit of a Jeremiah." Neville Chamberlain disliked him and firmly refused to have him in his Cabinet. He would have liked to keep out of his administration anyone who believed that National Socialism was anathema, or that war with Germany was inevitable, and though he did not entirely succeed—at least two of his Cabinet ministers were well aware of the German menace—he did manage to keep them in the background and in ignorance of his intentions until it was too late for them to protest.

Neville Chamberlain has variously been presented by British historians as a misguided statesman, a victim of circumstances, a disastrous political simpleton or a brave antagonist against impossible odds, but all have gone on to add that he was only doing his best and was a good, simple man, straightforward and sincere. The facts show that these are hardly the appropriate adjectives for him.

As so often is true in British politics, Chamberlain had risen to the leadership of his party more because of the mediocrity of his achievements than for any brilliance in his career. Joseph Chamberlain, his father, was a famous Victorian statesman, and his half brother Austen had been a distinguished Foreign Secretary in the twenties, but Neville, as one of his political opponents once remarked, had only the qualities to be "Lord Mayor of Birmingham in a bad year."* These qualities had, in fact, gained him several

* Birmingham, the industrial capital of the English Midlands, had always been a Chamberlain stronghold.

10

ministerial posts in the Tory governments of the twenties and thirties; he had filled them all efficiently if not with distinction.* He believed in low taxes and a balanced budget, and the idea that money should be frittered away on guns and planes instead of on peaceful purposes irked him. He did not think that rearmament was necessary; he believed that peace was attainable by reasonable discussion rather than through military strength. Winston Churchill wrote later of the struggle waged by Chamberlain's Secretary of State for Foreign affairs, Anthony Eden, to persuade the Prime Minister of the need to present a bold front to the dictators. "Eden became increasingly concerned about our slow rearmament," wrote Churchill. "On the 11th [November, 1937] he had an interview with the Prime Minister and tried to convey his misgivings. Mr. Neville Chamberlain after a while refused to listen to him. He advised him to 'go home and take an aspirin.' "

The surprising thing that developed from Neville Chamberlain's promotion to the prime-ministership in 1937 was the change it brought about in his character. As long as he had been a minister in the government or the Cabinet, his colleagues had found him shy and reserved, always willing to listen to advice from his experts, and a strict noninterferer in the affairs of other departments. To a certain extent, he continued to act in this fashion as far as domestic affairs were concerned, but it soon began to emerge that the post he felt himself better able to control than the minister filling it at the time was the Foreign Ministry. He was convinced that up until the time that he assumed office, the professional direction of Britain's foreign policy had been badly conceived and wrongly oriented, and that the fault lay mainly with the professionals who advised the Foreign Secretary on his policy. It quickly became apparent that he believed that only a "fresh approach" to the Nazi and Fascist regimes in Europe could bring them into line with the democracies and thus secure peace for the Continent, and he made it clear that there were elements in the Foreign Office who stood in the way of such a policy. He was convinced that the permanent department chiefs were too pro-French at a time when the French were the sick men of Europe, racked by internecine political squabbles, and that it was this leaning toward

---

* In fairness, it has been pointed out by one reader of this manuscript that this hardly does justice to Chamberlain's performance as Minister of Health, where he displayed ideas in advance of his time.

11

Paris and antipathy toward the stronger and more realistic elements in Berlin which were responsible for the wrong direction of British foreign policy.

The personality in the Foreign Office who he felt most strongly —and wrongly—influenced British policy toward Europe was the Permanent Undersecretary of State, Sir Robert Vansittart, a professional of great prescience whose prognostications of what would eventually happen in Europe a few years hence were to prove startlingly correct. But for Chamberlain, he was too pro-French and anti-German. The Prime Minister decided that he must go, and in true British tradition Vansittart was "kicked upstairs" to become Chief Diplomatic Adviser to the British government, a high-sounding appointment with no power behind it. He was also fobbed off with a baronetcy and henceforth kept out of all the principal negotiations concerning foreign policy.* Vansittart was succeeded by Sir Alexander Cadogan, a less forthright adviser who was, in any case, more in sympathy with Chamberlain's policy of coming to an arrangement with the dictators.

Vansittart's emasculation as foreign policy adviser to the British government could have been avoided had not the Foreign Secretary been Anthony Eden, one of the most popular young political stars of the day. Forty years old, handsome, charming and intelligent, Eden was well aware of the dangerous storms blowing up in Europe, and was a strong believer in standing up to both Hitler and Mussolini. Unfortunately, Vansittart was not; he believed that the menace to the peace of Europe was in Germany, and though he was lukewarm about Italian Fascism, he believed its leaders should be appeased in order to get Italy on the side of the democracies in the inevitable war with Nazism. Therefore he had been willing to condone Mussolini's invasion of Abyssinia, whereas Eden vehemently opposed it. The two men split on this. When Chamberlain decided that Vansittart must go, Eden's opposition to the departure of such a percipient adviser could have forced the Prime Minister to back down, for this was his first show of strength, and he was uncertain whether it would succeed. But when Eden held back and let his associate depart with-

---

* Chamberlain also had a personal reason for getting rid of Vansittart. He had discovered that the Secretary was seeing Winston Churchill privately and briefing him on foreign policy moves. Henceforth secret service agents tailed Vansittart, and had instructions to report back on all his meetings.

12

out a fight, Vansittart said to him sepulchrally, "It will be you next."
Indeed it was.

It is not difficult to understand the antipathy which existed between
Neville Chamberlain and his Foreign Secretary, for they were generations and worlds apart. Chamberlain's career had been slow, even
plodding, until he was elected to Parliament, with some family help,
at the ripe age of forty-nine. Eden had been elected at the age of
twenty-six and became Foreign Secretary at thirty-eight. He was
always in the news, and not simply because of politics. He wrote well;
he was not only a connoisseur of art but had sowed his wild bohemian
oats with the artists whose paintings adorned his wall: Dunoyer de
Segonzac, Signac, Picasso, Ben Nicholson, Chagall, and others. He
exasperated Chamberlain by his insufferable habit of interrupting
with remarks like "But, Prime Minister, I take it you can't know the
Franconians when you say that. Now, when I was living in Nuremberg . . ."

One of the principal bones of contention between these two men
was Italy. Chamberlain maintained that Benito Mussolini of Italy
was a powerful factor in European politics, and one whom Britain
should do everything to appease and satisfy; Anthony Eden maintained that he was a paper tiger. Chamberlain was prepared to go to
such lengths to appease Mussolini that he had refused to allow his
Foreign Office to protest the sinking of British ships in the Mediterranean by Italian submarines during the Spanish Civil War lest the
Italians be offended. He believed that he had a "special relationship"
with Dictator Mussolini because the Italian and his half brother
Austen had been close friends in the nineteen twenties. He had sent
his sister-in-law to Rome with messages of friendship, and promises
that his government would soon manipulate public opinion in England and recognize the Italian conquest of Abyssinia. This action he
took without even informing Eden or the Foreign Office.*

This was serious enough, but a move Chamberlain made early in
1938 was a much graver error in the view of those who hoped to

---

* "Lady Chamberlain wears a Fascist badge," wrote Italian Foreign Minister
Ciano in his diary on December 22, 1937. "I am too much a patriot to appreciate
such a gesture in an Englishwoman at such a time . . . I went with Lady Chamberlain to the Duce, to whom she showed an important letter from Neville Chamberlain . . ."

13

mobilize the world against the Nazi menace to peace. It had always been the ambition of the British Foreign Office to involve the American government in their engagements in Europe in the hope that it would help to dissipate U.S. isolationism and bring American aid, material if not military, to the European democracies in the event of war. In 1938 America showed every evidence of remaining behind its Atlantic wall while the Europeans quarreled among themselves. Except for President Roosevelt: although he did not want to be involved either—for political reasons it would have been unwise for him and the Democratic party—his emotions were engaged by the menace of National Socialism and Fascism, and he could not resist the hope of becoming a mediator from the New World in the quarrels of the Old.

On January 12, 1938, Roosevelt wrote a message to Britain (he planned to send it to other countries subsequently), proposing a conference in which the United States would join. This conference would examine the political aims and claims of certain European states—meaning primarily Germany and Italy—to see if these "hungry states" would be satisfied with an equal access to the world's raw materials. The President's message was handed to the British ambassador in Washington, Sir Ronald Lindsay, by Undersecretary Sumner Welles with a warning that it be treated as a top-secret communication until the views of the British government had been made known.

The significance of Roosevelt's message was obvious, and it might seem natural that any British statesman would have called for a celebration. Here was the United States, whose Congress was so determined to be neutral in Europe's quarrels and whose isolationism was being more firmly proclaimed than ever in 1938, about to involve itself through its President in the political contentions which divided the European democracies and totalitarian powers. Of course it was only a toe in the water, but it was a hopeful sign that America might be persuaded to become actively involved.

Alas, this harbinger of hope for Britain could not have arrived at a worse time. Anthony Eden, who would have understood its vital significance at once, was on the French Riviera conferring with Winston Churchill and former Prime Minister David Lloyd George, both perfervid opponents of Chamberlain. In the Foreign Secretary's absence, the President's letter went directly to the Prime Minister,

14

who read it and failed to appreciate its importance; he in turn sent it on to the new Permanent Undersecretary of State for Foreign Affairs, Sir Alexander Cadogan, with instructions that he discuss it with the Prime Minister's chief adviser, Sir Horace Wilson.

Though few members of the general public knew his name, Sir Horace Wilson had become a power in the land by 1938. A civil servant formerly attached to the Ministry of Labour, where he became adept at negotiating with trade unionists, he had first come in contact with Chamberlain when he was Chancellor of the Exchequer, and they became mutual admirers while working together at the Ottawa Tariff Conference in 1934. "We were seasick together on the boat going over," Sir Horace has said. "It established a bond." He was one of the chief advisers to Prime Minister Stanley Baldwin, and when Chamberlain succeeded him, Wilson was retained and given an office at No. 10 Downing Street. He was soon the principal source of advice upon which Chamberlain relied; the newspapers called Wilson "the *éminence grise* in a homburg hat." Like his chief, he spoke no foreign language, had rarely been outside England, had met few foreigners and had no experience of foreign affairs. "But what did that matter?" he was to say later. "Foreigners are people, just like trade unionists. Chamberlain was a practical man, I was a practical man. What more did we need?"

It was in the hands of this cool, professional civil servant that the fate of President Roosevelt's message was now resting. It did not help that like his master, Wilson disagreed with the policy of Anthony Eden and suspected that the Foreign Secretary would have sent a joyful message of acceptance to the presidential communication. In any case, the sort of conference which Roosevelt was proposing would only interfere with plans which Wilson and Chamberlain were working out together—in secret, without informing Eden or other members of the Cabinet—for a rapprochement with Fascist Italy.

On Wilson's advice, Chamberlain ordered Cadogan to send a reply to Roosevelt turning down the offer, on the grounds that he had much more fruitful prospects of his own. Cadogan was instructed to say nothing of the message or of the reply to either Eden or the other members of the Cabinet. (In fact, Cadogan had already desperately tried to reach the Foreign Secretary by telephone and had dispatched a copy of the President's message to him by courier, but it missed Eden by five minutes as his train passed through Marseilles.

15

He did not hear what had happened until he reached Folkestone on January 15, where Cadogan was waiting for him with the bad news.)

The next morning Eden burst into Sir Horace Wilson's office at No. 10 Downing Street, his face flushed. "You damn fool!" he burst out. "Do you realize what you've done?"

Sir Horace Wilson looked at him with the icy calm of a civil servant well used to keeping cool while being sworn at by an angry miners' leader. "I beg your pardon, Minister. Is there something amiss?"

"Roosevelt's message," said Eden. "You persuaded the P.M. to reject Roosevelt's message! How dare you? Don't you see how vital it was for us to accept?"

"Oh that," replied Wilson. "Surely you wouldn't have taken that seriously, would you, Minister? Woolly nonsense, you know, just woolly nonsense."

Eden then went to the Prime Minister's office and offered his resignation unless Chamberlain canceled the rejection of Roosevelt's overture and substituted an acceptance.

"But you can't resign, my dear Anthony," said Chamberlain smoothly. "The President particularly asked that his message to me be kept secret." How could he resign over something that was supposed to be kept secret?

"It was plain that no resignation by the Foreign Secretary could be founded upon the rebuff administered by Mr. Chamberlain to the President's overture," wrote Winston Churchill. "Mr. Roosevelt was indeed running great risks in involving the United States in the darkening European scene. All the forces of isolationism would have been aroused if any part of these interchanges had transpired. On the other hand, no event could have been more likely to stave off, or even prevent, war than the arrival of the United States in the circle of European hates and fears. To Britain it was a matter almost of life and death. No one can measure in retrospect its effect upon the course of events in Austria and later at Munich. We must regard its rejection—for such it was—as the loss of the last frail chance to save the world from tyranny otherwise than by war."

It was Neville Chamberlain's hand, as Churchill says, which waved it away, and the decision "leaves one, even at this date, breathless with amazement. The lack of all sense of proportion and even of self-preservation, which this episode reveals, in an upright, competent, well-meaning man charged with the destinies of our country and all who depended upon it, is appalling. One cannot today even reconstruct the state of mind which would render such gestures possible."

By this time, however, both Chamberlain and Wilson were determined that the Foreign Secretary would have to go; he was interfering with their plans. Three weeks later they had worked out a scheme between them by which Eden's removal was secured. It was a devastating example of the deviousness of Chamberlain's mind, and of the character of the leader of a democracy, for the maneuver entailed a conspiracy between him and the Italian ambassador behind his own minister's back.

Ever since his return from France (he had gone back to Paris to consult the French government on January 25), Eden had been trying to corner the Italian ambassador in London, Count Dino Grandi, to find out exactly how Mussolini was reacting to Nazi pressures on Austria. But on instructions from the Duce, Grandi had contrived never to be alone with Eden and thus lay himself open to hostile questioning. The Foreign Secretary saw the Italian on February 10, but Chamberlain was there too and he saw to it that the conversation was kept strictly to the question of an Anglo-Italian rapprochement. But on February 15 came the announcement that Chancellor Schuschnigg had agreed to Hitler's demand that the chief Nazi agent in Austria, Arthur Seyss-Inquart, be included in his Cabinet. This was a grave step which obviously threatened Austria's independence, and Eden wanted more than ever to find out how Italy (which had always supported Austrian integrity) would react to it. Was there a secret agreement between the two dictators? But Grandi dodged a meeting on such a dangerous subject—or did so until Chamberlain set the wheels of his intrigue in motion.

Now an emissary of Chamberlain's (an unscrupulous Tory party fixer named Sir Joseph Ball) met Grandi and asked him to accept Eden's invitation "because it will take place at Downing Street and the Prime Minister will be there." The emissary also briefed Grandi along what lines the conversation should proceed. The ambassador, a shrewd and charming Italian, realized that he was being used as a pawn but was delighted to play along, since Eden's resignation

17

would remove one of Fascist Italy's most powerful opponents in the British Cabinet. On February 18 the meeting duly took place and went exactly as Chamberlain had planned it. What he wanted from the Italian ambassador was an assurance that his own "friendly" relations with Mussolini and the Fascist administration in Rome would secure better results than were being obtained by Eden, who had made it plain that he wanted a gesture from the Duce—the withdrawal of Italian volunteers from Spain, for instance—before consenting to negotiate with him.

Grandi willingly complied. The aim of the meeting was to demonstrate, without subtlety, that Neville Chamberlain was determined to become his own Foreign Secretary, that when he took an active role he made friends and influenced the policies of his opponents, and that Eden had better become accustomed to a subsidiary role. It was a shrewd move on the part of the Prime Minister; he may not have known the nature of the dictators, but at least he understood the character of his Foreign Secretary. Eden retired from the meeting both angry and humiliated. He deeply resented the way in which Chamberlain was beginning to by-pass him and make foreign policy decisions without consulting him first, and he was particularly insulted that this should have been rubbed in during an interview with a foreign envoy.

Grandi reported to his Foreign Minister, Count Galeazzo Ciano: "Chamberlain, in fact, in addressing his questions directly to me, expected from me—this was obvious—nothing less than those details and definite answers which were useful to him as ammunition against Eden. This I at once realized and naturally tried to supply Chamberlain with all the ammunition which I considered might be useful to him to this end. There is no doubt that in this connection the contacts previously established between myself and Chamberlain through his confidential agent proved to be very valuable."

There was another meeting between Grandi and Sir Joseph Ball, who had a message for him from the Prime Minister. "Purely as a matter of history," the Italian ambassador reported to Ciano on February 19, "I inform your Excellency that yesterday evening, after the Downing Street meeting, Chamberlain secretly sent his agent to me (we had made an appointment in an ordinary London taxi) to say that he sent me cordial greetings, that he appreciated my statements, which had been very useful to him, and that he was confident that everything would go very well that day."

It did. At the next day's Cabinet meeting, Anthony Eden resigned as Foreign Secretary. It might have been better for him had he stayed on and fought for his job. Certainly it would have been better for the country; as William Strang, a Foreign Office official who worked closely with him, later stated: "It can fairly be said of Neville Chamberlain that he was not well versed in foreign affairs, that he had no touch for a diplomatic situation, that he did not fully realize what it was he was doing, and that his naïve confidence in his own judgment and powers of persuasion and achievement was misplaced." But in order to restore his power in the Cabinet, Eden would have had to rally other members to him, and he could only have done that by attacking the Prime Minister and forcing his hand; Chamberlain would then have had to be prepared to reveal just how determined he was to plot and intrigue in order to rid himself of a popular, and therefore dangerous, colleague. Unfortunately, it was not Eden's nature to be a leader of revolts, inside the Cabinet or out, and so he resigned.

The other members of the Cabinet were fooled completely by Chamberlain's attitude; they believed he was reluctant to see his Foreign Secretary go, and it was not until years later that they learned the truth.

"The P.M. was in fact deliberately playing a part," wrote Alfred Duff Cooper, the First Lord of the Admiralty, "throughout the Cabinet discussions. While allowing his colleagues to suppose that he was as anxious as any of them to dissuade the Foreign Secretary from resigning, he had, in reality, determined to get rid of him and had secretly informed the Italian ambassador that he hoped to succeed in doing so. Had I known this at the time, not only would I have resigned with Eden, but I should have found it difficult to sit in Cabinet with N.C. again."

19

II

Prophets
of Armageddon

Anthony Eden was replaced by Edward, Lord Halifax, former Viceroy of India, tall, amiable, honest, willing, and whose main qualification for the job was exactly what Chamberlain and Sir Horace Wilson were looking for: he had an infinite capacity for being trodden on without complaint. William Strang, who worked under him at this period, later lumped him with certain other British statesmen as "all English country gentlemen, all good public-school men, all good churchmen. They seldom visited Europe, or knew what Europeans were like. None of them could have the slightest conception of the enormity of Hitler. Their whole upbringing conspired against understanding that such people could exist, and that the Nazi state was a lunatic state . . . Although Edward was very clever, the world was an innocent world to him. To live in it in Hitler's epoch with the ideas his father had planted in him was extremely difficult. He was so bound by tradition that he never wavered in the principles he was taught when he was young. No new view of the world or violent changes dinted his orthodoxy."

Neville Chamberlain could not have asked for a better servant.

The question of the fear which palpitated in the hearts of the British and French ruling classes when they considered the menace of Nazi Germany must be emphasized again. It should be said at once that Neville Chamberlain was not afraid of either Germany or Adolf Hitler; from his point of view, there was no necessity for it. By the right kind of negotiations, an arrangement could be made with Hitler which would eliminate any possibility of misunderstandings that might lead to war. It was simply a matter of taking a practical view of the situation and eliminating the points of contention. But when Neville Chamberlain and Sir Horace Wilson took a cold, practical look at the European situation in the summer of 1938, they were aware that there were solid obstacles in the way of an Anglo-German rapprochement, and that the very fear which the threat of Adolf Hitler induced in the "ruling classes" in Britain and France might well be used as a weapon to dissipate them.

The principal obstacle was Czechoslovakia. This Middle European democracy, with its capital in Prague and its frontiers abutting Germany in the northwest and southwest, Poland in the north and east, and Austria, Hungary and Rumania to the south, had been created by the Versailles Treaty after World War I from part of the remnants of the Austro-Hungarian Empire. The bulk of its population, Czechs and Slovaks, numbered close to ten million people, but within its borders there were also just under two and a half million so-called Sudeten Germans* and over a million assorted Poles, Magyars and Ruthenians. After the German occupation of Austria it had quickly become apparent that in pursuing the policy of "bringing our German brothers back to the Reich," Hitler would turn his attention to the Sudetenland and demand its incorporation in the new Germany. However, Czechoslovakia had a mutual-assistance pact of long standing with France, and a more recent one with Russia. (But there was a hitch; Russia would only intervene on Czechoslovakia's behalf after France had come to her aid first.) Besides, Great Britain was an ally of France, and had an obligation to join the French should they be involved in war.

To Neville Chamberlain and his advisers, the situation presented by all these contingencies seemed dangerous, foolhardy, irritating—impossible. In the words of Sir Horace Wilson, why should a country like Czechoslovakia create such embarrassment for the great powers? "It was not a real country at all. It was created out of the necessities

---

* In fact, though German propaganda called them "our brothers," they had never been part of Germany but had always lived inside the Austro-Hungarian Empire.

of Versailles. It didn't really mean a thing." This is the judgment of ignorance but it aptly exemplifies the viewpoint of the Chamberlain administration, and of its determination to ignore the fact of Czechoslovakia's existence. To Adolf Hitler, who was well aware that it was a democratic, anti-Nazi and extremely well equipped country, with up-to-date guns, armor and planes, as well as strong fortifications along the German border, Czechoslovakia was "the aircraft carrier of the enemy" which would always threaten his rear should he ever attack Britain and France in the West.

Hitler's dislike of the Czechs had turned into hatred during the so-called "May crisis" in 1938, when poor intelligence or mischief-making—it cannot now be determined which—led the jittery Czechs to believe that they were about to be invaded. The Czech army was mobilized. Sir Nevile Henderson, the British ambassador in Berlin, visited the German Foreign Minister, Joachim von Ribbentrop, to express his concern and was told by the furious Ribbentrop that the crisis was "all nonsense." It wasn't quite all nonsense; it was simply that Germany had no intention of attacking at that time; her plans for Czechoslovakia had been made for the future. The scare died down, but unfortunately the press headlines did not. Western newspapers hailed the non-event as a victory for Czech resolution and British firmness; Germany had "backed down," they said. This so infuriated Hitler that at a high-level conference on May 28 he transformed a tentative plan for the invasion of Czechoslovakia into a firm resolution. "It is my unalterable decision to smash Czechoslovakia by military force in the near future," he directed.

Neville Chamberlain took the "May crisis" seriously but believed it was a quarrel in a faraway country between people of whom he knew little, and he deprecated all the fuss that was being made over Czechoslovakia in democratic countries over the alleged German threat to attack her. His antipathy toward the Czechs as a people ("Not out of the top drawer—or even the middle," he once said to Sir Horace Wilson) and its leaders as individuals increased during the summer of 1938. Word reached the Czech President, Eduard Beneš, through his minister in London, Jan Masaryk, that the Chamberlain government was scheming to sell out the Czechs to Germany. The two men talked frequently on the telephone and seemed to be supremely confident that because they were talking in Czech, no one listening in would understand what they said. They indulged in some heavy abuse of Chamberlain, Wilson and Henderson, calling them everything from "cretins" to "Nazi bootlickers."* This kind of language may have been understandable, but in the circumstances it was injudicious. The phone was tapped by Field Marshal Hermann Göring's counterespionage service and the transcripts were solicitously sent to London, where Theo Kordt, first secretary at the German embassy, was instructed to pass them on to Sir Horace Wilson for his attention.

An objective, professional expert on foreign affairs might have been able to overlook such verbal extravagances, but Chamberlain was not that kind of man; he never forgave an insult. An urgent message to the Foreign Office demanded to know why the Czech telephone conversations had not been monitored by Britain's own services. It turned out that they had, but that the Foreign Office had thought it prudent not to mention the fact. The department was sharply rebuked by Sir Horace Wilson and told not to be so reticent in the future; the radio stations of the British Broadcasting Corporation were instructed to take a sharper tone toward the Czechs; and a press secretary in the Foreign Office who was reputed to be skeptical of the Chamberlain-Wilson policy was shifted from his job and posted to Athens.

Meanwhile, the French guarantee of Czechoslovakia's integrity remained firm, and if Hitler attacked Czechoslovakia in order to add the Sudeten territory to the Reich, France would be duty-bound to fight and Britain would be dragged in. It was, as Chamberlain remarked to Sir Horace Wilson, a ridiculous situation which must at all costs be avoided. But how?

It was here that fear came to the aid of the British Prime Minister, and four men, one Frenchman and three Americans, ranged themselves fortuitously on his side. In August the French embassy in Berlin received a message from Paris saying that the Commander in Chief of the French Air Force, General Joseph Vuillemin, had been invited to Germany to inspect the Luftwaffe. It was a reciprocal visit

* Typical conversation: MASARYK: "The wicked old ——— is longing to lick Adolf's backside. His tongue is hanging out." BENES: "Stuff it back again! Bring him to his senses." MASARYK: "The old beast hasn't any senses left, except to smell out the Nazi ashheap and hang around it." BENEŠ: "Then have a talk with Horace Wilson. Ask him to warn the Prime Minister that England is in danger too if we do not all stand firm. Can't he be made to understand this?" MASARYK: "How can you talk to Wilson? He is nothing but a jackal."

for one which had been paid to France by Göring's second-in-command, General Erhard Milch, some months earlier.

The idea that Vuillemin was coming caused some consternation among the French in Berlin. Particularly alarmed were General de Geffrier, the air attaché, and his young assistant, Captain Paul Stehlin. They knew quite well what the Germans had ready for the visiting French air chief: a carefully worked out display of German air might which would put the fear of God in him. It did.

The trouble with General Vuillemin was that although he was a fine airman and a person of honesty and integrity, he had neither the character nor the stability to hold a supreme command. More important still, he suffered from a psychological block about bombers and bombing. He had risen from the ranks in the French army in World War I to command one of the first bomber squadrons, which he led across the western front on daring and brilliantly successful raids on occupied Alsace and Lorraine, and on the vast German arsenals in the Ruhr. But on one raid a string of bombs dropped by his squadron—from his own plane, he always believed—missed their target and hit a vast tent in which a circus was playing. The audience consisted mostly of children. Vuillemin was attacked as a child-murderer by the propagandists of Imperial Germany, and his friends believe that, conscience-stricken, he accepted the charge as an accurate one; certainly thereafter he seems to have begun to think of the bombing plane as a monstrous weapon. A worthy and civilized sentiment, but hardly helpful in his job as commander in chief of an air force.

What Vuillemin was shown by the Nazi Luftwaffe during his week's tour of Germany must have been at first alarming and then mountingly horrifying. It began with tours of the Messerschmidt and Heinkel factories, where fighters, fighter-bombers and bombers were coming off the line, and culminated in a visit to the Luftwaffe's Tactical Experimental Center at Barth, on the Baltic, where for three hours high-altitude bombers and dive bombers shattered a series of buildings and moving objects with impressive exactitude. Each bomb burst must have scarred Vuillemin's nervous system and conscience.

Just before the French general's return to France, the Commander in Chief of the Luftwaffe gave him a reception at his sumptuous hunting lodge, Karinhall, some thirty-five miles north of Berlin. At one point Field Marshal Göring fixed Vuillemin with his blue, button eyes and said, *"Monsieur le Général,* what will you do if we are forced to start a war against Czechoslovakia?"

Vuillemin hesitated. His ambassador, André François-Poncet, and Captain Stehlin were with him and were watching him closely. Then he said firmly, "France will remain true to her word."

Göring looked surprised, François-Poncet looked relieved, and Stehlin thought that there was no heart at all behind the words. Nor was there. In the car on the way back to the French embassy, Vuillemin told his ambassador and Stehlin that after what he had seen he was convinced that in the event of war against the Luftwaffe, the French air force would be wiped out in fifteen days. Back in France, he continued to cry woe to all who would listen, and one who did so, just before departing for Munich, was Premier Edouard Daladier.

"General Vuillemin's visit could not have happened at a more unfortunate moment," said Stehlin later. "The Germans set out to make a great impression by opening the window wide on the size and quality of their aerial rearmament. They succeeded, and [Vuillemin's] opinions had more effect than they deserved on the decisions of our government."

It was in this atmosphere that Colonel Charles Lindbergh descended on the scene and reinforced the fear. No doubt with the best intentions, the famous flier had been anxious for some years to convince the Western democracies that the German air force was an invincible weapon of destruction even at a time when—as is now definitely known—it was not. As early as 1936, when he visited Germany, the Luftwaffe had put on a display for him of the kind which would terrify Vuillemin, but Lindbergh was impressed. He was living at the time in a house in Kent which he had rented from his friend Harold Nicolson, the English writer and diplomat, as a haven from the persecutions of the American press. Lindbergh had just returned from Berlin. Nicolson wrote in his diary on September 8, 1936, that Lindbergh obviously was disturbed by what he had seen; he thought that they possessed the most powerful air force in the world and could do terrible damage to any other country. He acknowledged that they were a great threat but doubted that they would be to Britain. In his opinion there would be, sometime in the future, a complete separation between Fascism and Communism, and he believed that if Great Britain supported the "decadent" French and the Red Russians against Germany, this would mean the end of European civilization.

Two years later, on May 22, 1938, Nicolson saw Charles and Anne Lindbergh again, in New York, and found Lindbergh most pessimistic. He considered Britain's defenses inadequate against the overwhelming superiority of the German air force—at least ten times more powerful than that of Russia, France and Great Britain put together. He saw no other way out but for Britain to concede the inevitable and enter into an alliance with Germany. Nicolson thought Lindbergh's views biased and "all tied up with his hatred of degeneracy and his hatred of democracy as represented by the free press and the American public."*

Lindbergh was in Paris in September 1938 after yet another visit to Germany, as well as to Russia and Czechoslovakia, whose air forces he also claimed to have inspected. Doubts have since been expressed that either of the two latter countries would have allowed him to "inspect" a branch of its armed forces. It does not seem likely that Soviet Russia, secretive about its military strength even among friends, would have opened its airfields and hangars to one it knew to be a bitter anti-Communist and pro-Nazi. And while saluting Lindbergh as a hero of the air, Czechoslovakia could hardly have considered him a friend of the country, for he made no secret of his contempt for the "degenerate" French and their "little Balkan allies." But most statesmen hung on Lindbergh's words and opinions, and the moment he arrived in Paris the U.S. ambassador made haste to arrange a dinner party for him so that he could impart his latest report of the gloomy situation to the highest authorities.

The American ambassador to France in 1938 was William C. Bullitt, a man of hearty, forthright, democratic opinions and a warm friend of the French, but gripped, like most men in important positions in France at the moment, by pessimism. He had taken a nine years' lease of a lovely old château at Chantilly, but he obviously did not believe he was going to be there for long. A few months before

* Because of Lindbergh's objections, the British publisher of Nicolson's diary has refused permission to quote the relevant extracts, but they can be found in *Diaries and Letters, 1930–1939* (Atheneum, 1966), pp. 272, 343.

Lindbergh's arrival he had told Secretary of the Interior Harold L. Ickes that he thought a war was coming "that will probably last for twenty years, a war that will be fought to a stalemate, but during the progress of which Paris and other great cities of Europe will be destroyed . . . He is most pessimistic and since my return I find that he has been writing to the President in tones as hopeless as those in which he spoke to us."

What profit Bullitt saw in conveying his pessimism to the French and thus exacerbating the depression which was already there is a mystery; as a diplomat representing the United States, he could hardly have wished to frighten the French into breaking their treaty and abandoning their small and doughty Czechoslovak ally. On the other hand, he could scarcely have believed that Lindbergh would have any words of comfort to give his listeners.

Nonetheless, the American ambassador held his shattering dinner party at Chantilly on September 9, 1938, and the chief French guest was Minister for Air Guy La Chambre. The French air force was singularly unfortunate at this period in having as its leaders men who believed that they were defeated before they started, and La Chambre was one of the most egregious of them. He was a supporter of Foreign Minister Georges Bonnet, an appeaser, and he had friends who were in contact with Otto Abetz, an emissary sent by Germany to make useful friends and contacts for his country in Paris.* La Chambre came to the dinner armed with the bad tidings of General Vuillemin. The position was absolutely desperate, he said; the Germans had such a lead that the French could not possibly catch up with them for years, if at all. The Reich was producing 500 to 800 planes per month, whereas France was making only 45 to 50, and England only 70. (These were, in fact, much exaggerated figures; German production was going through a crisis at the time and Göring was worried about the strength of his forces.) When La Chambre asked for Lindbergh's views, the American refused to give any figures of planes being produced in any of the countries he had visited, but he confirmed La Chambre's fear that Germany possessed overwhelming air superiority, and voiced his conviction that the German air arm was stronger than all the other European countries' put together. When questioned about the air strength of the Soviet Union and

* After the fall of France, Otto Abetz became German ambassador in Paris.

28

Czechoslovakia, he shrugged his shoulders meaningfully.* La Chambre hastened away to report to Premier Daladier and Foreign Minister Bonnet, and soon there was more panic in the Paris salons.

Bullitt reported the substance of this conversation to Washington, and a transcript of it subsequently reached the U.S. ambassador in London, Joseph P. Kennedy. It so happened that during the seven months since his appointment as American envoy to Britain, Kennedy had stayed in close touch with the British Prime Minister. They had met in earlier years when Chamberlain was Chancellor of the Exchequer and Kennedy a millionaire businessman with financial contacts in Washington, and they had quickly established a rapport. Both of them were the kind of "practical men" Sir Horace Wilson so much admired—meaning that they did not allow themselves to be swayed by sentiment. They both looked at the European situation and agreed that for practical men there was only one solution: to make an accommodation with the rampant German Reich; anyone trying to get in the way of such an obviously efficient solution must be either circumvented or defeated.

Ambassador Kennedy had already made plain his views on the relations between Germany and Czechoslovakia, and had assured the German ambassador in London, Herbert von Dirksen, that he would do his utmost to keep the United States out of any European war. This was no more than his duty, but then he wrote a speech which he was scheduled to make at Aberdeen, Scotland, on September 2. Kennedy had previously discussed the address with Neville Chamberlain (they now consulted regularly), and it included the sentence: "I can't for the life of me understand why anyone should want to go to war to save the Czechs." The State Department saw a draft of the speech and ordered the ambassador to tone it down; he refused. President Roosevelt was consulted, and remarked to Secretary of the Treasury Henry Morgenthau, Jr., "The young man needs his wrists slapped rather hard." Presidential orders were cabled for him to drop the sentence, and he reluctantly did so.

While still smoldering under presidential rebuke a week later, Kennedy heard about Lindbergh's foray in Paris and made up his

---

* It has since been established that the Soviet Union had a sizable air force at the time, and that the Czech air force—as the Germans discovered when they took it over—was one of the most modern and up-to-date in the world.

mind. He did not fail to consult Neville Chamberlain, who at once gave his permission. Having scared the living daylights out of the French government, Colonel Lindbergh was invited to come to London and scare them out of the British too.

While Colonel Lindbergh was vaunting the insuperable might of the German air force, the leaders of the Luftwaffe itself were, on the contrary, worrying about its strength and capability for the two-front war it might face if Britain and France came to the aid of Czechoslovakia. They were complaining about the quality of their planes, and they were well aware that they could not possibly go into action against their main enemy, Britain, unless they had airfields in Holland and Belgium. Those would have to be captured for them by the German army. At the same time the German army was in a panic of its own, for it too was unequipped for a two-front war. Certainly it was not prepared to attack both Czechoslovakia—whose efficient armed forces it much admired—and the Low Countries on behalf of the Luftwaffe simultaneously. Instead it was desperately playing for time.

All through the summer of 1938 certain German army leaders sent messengers to London to explain their thinking and to plead with the British to resist Hitler in his scheme to conquer Czechoslovakia, and to let them know that they were planning a coup d'état. The first envoy of major importance was a Prussian army officer of the old school ("We must send the English a real gentleman" was how one of the leaders put it) named Ewald von Kleist-Schmenzin. He made his journey at the behest of the former Army Chief of Staff, General Ludwig Beck (who resigned in the summer of 1938 as a protest against Hitler's plans), and several other general officers and highly placed civilians. Kleist-Schmenzin was already suspected by the Gestapo of being anti-Nazi, and he would certainly never have been allowed to leave the country openly; however, he was provided with a false passport by another member of the conspiracy, Admiral Wilhelm Canaris, chief of the Abwehr,* and smuggled aboard a London-bound plane.

* Military intelligence and counterespionage of the Armed Forces High Command (*Oberkommando der Wehrmacht,* or OKW). The full title of this department was *Auslandsnachrichten und Abwehr.*

30

It is typical of the attitude of the British envoy in Berlin at this time that when he heard of Kleist-Schmenzin's hazardous journey, Sir Nevile Henderson cabled London and warned that "it would be unwise to receive him in official circles." An admirer of the Nazis, Henderson was afraid that Kleist-Schmenzin might interfere with plans for appeasing Hitler. As a result he never got to Downing Street, as the conspirators had hoped, but he did see Sir Robert Vansittart at the Foreign Office, and afterward Winston Churchill in his home at Chartwell. He told them both that powerful elements on the German General Staff were so opposed to the Führer's plans for attacking Czechoslovakia that they were preparing to remove him at the right moment.

A British mission of experts from the Foreign Office, headed by Lord Runciman, was in Czechoslovakia at this time. The group had been assigned the task by Neville Chamberlain of bringing the Czechs and the Sudetens together—the idea being that they should meet under Runciman's auspices to talk out their mutual problems, iron out their ethnic and political antipathies, and find a means of living together. But long before Runciman discovered it for himself, the failure of the mission was a foregone conclusion; for one thing, Konrad Henlein, the Sudeten leader, had already been secretly instructed by Hitler to avoid a solution by confronting the Czechs with unacceptable demands. As those correspondents who chased the Runciman mission around Czechoslovakia well remember, the Foreign Office experts soon gave up any hope of achieving a meeting of minds, having discovered from what few meetings did take place that the dialogue between the two sides fell on deaf ears. While the members of the Runciman mission prepared their reports they spent much of their time as guests of eager landowners in the Sudetenland, and since most of these landowners were Sudeten, the reports were not without their anti-Czech bias.

Thus, the Runciman mission was hardly likely to change a menacing situation. In London, all Kleist-Schmenzin asked, on behalf of his sponsors, was that Britain announce her firm determination to stand by France, while at the same time seeing that France kept her pledge to stand by Czechoslovakia. Details of both conversations were sent to the Prime Minister, whose reactions, however, were less favorable than Winston Churchill's. Churchill provided Kleist-

31

Schmenzin with a letter to take back to his sponsors emphasizing that when the crisis came, Britain would indeed stand firm.*

At first Chamberlain did nothing except remark airily to Lord Halifax that the situation reminded him "of the Jacobites at the Court of France in King William's time . . . we must discount a good deal of what he [Kleist-Schmenzin] says." Then he had a sudden and quite unexpected qualm and sent a note to Halifax saying that he thought perhaps they ought to do something. As a result Sir Nevile Henderson was summoned from Berlin, informed of the nature of Kleist-Schmenzin's message and instructed to take two steps: first, to issue a warning to Hitler that Britain would stand firm; and second, to explore the possibilities of Anglo-German conversations. The second order appealed to Henderson much more than the first, and after expressing great skepticism over the possibility of an army conspiracy against Hitler, he pleaded with Chamberlain not to make him give a warning to the German Chancellor. Evidently it had been only a momentary whim, for Chamberlain amiably agreed to withdraw his first instruction. Instead, Henderson should see Hitler to find out whether friendly Anglo-German talks could not be started. This was hardly what the conspirators had in mind.

There were other envoys, and each brought further details of the army plot against Hitler. One of them was Dr. Erich Kordt; he acted as liaison officer between the conspirators at considerable risk, for his official position was *chef de cabinet* to Foreign Minister Joachim von Ribbentrop, who was a fanatical Nazi, a hater of England and a firm supporter of Hitler's war plans. Erich Kordt's brother, Theo, was also one of the chief conspirators, and perhaps he lived the strangest double life of them all, for he was first secretary at the German embassy in London. In his official capacity he was a regular visitor to the Foreign Office in Whitehall, where he faithfully delivered the verbal and written instructions of his Nazi masters, but privately he was also seeing Vansittart at his home in Kensington, keeping him up to date about the conspiracy. On September 5, 1938, he brought information of such importance that Vansittart asked him to talk to Sir Horace Wilson. Even that apparently imperturbable man was

---

* It was a well-meant letter but an unfortunate one. In the first place, Britain did not stand firm. In the second, during the purge of 1944 the letter was found in Kleist-Schmenzin's desk after the attempt on Hitler's life, and used as evidence to condemn him to death.

32

momentarily warmed by Theo Kordt's news,* and he arranged to have the German smuggled into No. 11 Downing Street by the back entrance and taken to see Lord Halifax.

Kordt reported that General Franz Halder, who had succeeded General Beck as Army Chief of Staff, had agreed to join the conspiracy, and that the Commander in Chief of the Army, General Walther von Brauchitsch, was aware of the plot and though unwilling to play a part in it, had promised not to betray it.† Kordt revealed that Hitler would probably mobilize the German armed forces about September 16 and planned to march into Czechoslovakia on October 1. The conspirators were prepared to strike on the day that mobilization was announced. General Erwin von Witzleben, commander of the Berlin army corps area (*Wehrkreis*), was an essential part of the plot; his troops would be used to surround Hitler's headquarters in the Reich Chancellery and arrest Hitler himself when the time came. The chief of police in Berlin, Count Wolf von Helldorff, and his deputy, Count Fritz von der Schulenburg, would maintain order in the city; General Walter von Brockdorff-Ahlefeldt, commander of the Potsdam infantry division, would surround the capital, and battle Heinrich Himmler's SS troops if they tried to intervene; and General Erich Hoepner, commander of the Thuringia *Wehrkreis,* would bring up reinforcements if necessary. Plans had also been made to bring Hitler to trial.

What part had Britain to play in all this? All Theo Kordt asked was that Britain and France make it clear to the world—and particularly to the German people, who were growing increasingly apprehensive over the possibility of war—that they would honor their pledges and come to the aid of Czechoslovakia in case of attack.

Lord Halifax listened noncommittally to this startling recital and saw Kordt to the door without making any other comment than that it had been most interesting. Kordt could hardly have guessed why Halifax was so reserved, for he was told nothing about Chamberlain's

---

* It had been passed on to Erich Kordt by the conspirators. Since he was being too closely watched by Ribbentrop at the time, he had his cousin, Simone Simonis, memorize the message, travel to London and repeat it to Theo.

† Indeed, Brauchitsch was as worried as most other senior German army officers over Hitler's plans. At a meeting on September 3 with Hitler and General Wilhelm Keitel, Chief of the Armed Forces High Command, he had, much to Hitler's fury, pointed out the dangers of an attack on Czechoslovakia, and urged that if there was the slightest risk of British and French intervention, the operation should be abandoned.

private overtures for negotiations with Hitler. With the exception of Halifax and two other members of his Cabinet, Sir John Simon and Sir Samuel Hoare—and, of course, Sir Horace Wilson—the British Prime Minister was taking no one into his confidence and had told Halifax to be equally discreet; he did not want his plans sabotaged by those who might be unsympathetic to his views.

This time it was Lord Halifax, normally quite content to walk in the shadow of his Prime Minister and Sir Horace, who had sudden spasms of uneasiness. Despite his unemotional response, he had been impressed by Kordt's message; despite his wish for a quiet life and no arguments, he was beginning to wonder whether Chamberlain's appeasement of Hitler was a wise thing. He had spent sleepless nights worrying about the Czechs, and his matutinal emotional hangovers were not eased by a message which reached him a few days later by a roundabout route from Berlin. It seemed that Professor Carl F. Burckhardt, the Swiss savant who was High Commissioner of the League of Nations in Danzig, the Free City on the Baltic, had passed through Berlin recently and had had a long talk with Baron Ernst von Weizsäcker, now Undersecretary of State for Foreign Affairs and second-in-command to Ribbentrop.

Baron von Weizsäcker was yet another sympathizer with the conspirators and an opponent of war against Czechoslovakia, and he had emphasized to Burckhardt the need for the Western allies to make their position plain. In fact, he urged them to issue a warning to Hitler before he made his projected policy speech at the *Parteitag,* the annual Nazi party rally, which had opened in Nuremberg on September 5, the same day that Kordt had delivered his report in London. Burckhardt took Weizsäcker's message so seriously that he at once got in his car and drove straight to Switzerland, pausing only for gas and a snack on the way. (It demonstrates his opinion of Sir Nevile Henderson that he did not consider it worthwhile to report his conversation to the British embassy in Berlin.) Once in Geneva, he went immediately to the British ambassador and asked him to transmit the purport of Weizsäcker's message.

In view of Theo Kordt's information and this additional reinforcement of it, Lord Halifax thought that for once he would be justified in making a move independently of his Prime Minister. He sent a message of urgent priority to Sir Nevile Henderson instructing him to seek an interview with Hitler and warn him of the grave

34

consequences should he commence hostilities against Czechoslovakia.

When Henderson received this message he was in the sleeping car of a train parked in the railway station at Nuremberg, where the party rally was in progress. The ambassador was already experiencing symptoms of the cancer which would eventually kill him, and he found his quarters claustrophobically uncomfortable. He had omitted to bring his secretary with him, his cipher books, or even paper to write on. He had always been in awe of Adolf Hitler, from whom he constantly sought praise and was only too apt to receive insults, and the prospect of approaching the great leader with a warning at this climactic moment in the Nazi year when the party leaders were inclined to froth at the mouth with Germanic exaltation, filled him with panic. He tore pages from the detective novels which he had been reading during his sleepless nights and scribbled a message on them, beseeching London to let him off the hook. Alfred Duff Cooper, an M.P. and the First Lord of the Admiralty, wrote in his diary on September 12 that "there were a series of messages from Henderson which seemed to me almost hysterical, imploring the government not to insist upon his carrying out these instructions, which he was sure would have the opposite effect to that desired. And the Government had given way."

The government had given way because Neville Chamberlain had made up his mind. Enough of this nonsense about Czechoslovakia; enough of French insistence that France must fulfill her treaty obligations to Czechoslovakia, for then Britain would inevitably be involved in war with Germany. On the other hand, it was increasingly obvious that France was panicking at the prospect of war. People like Colonel Lindbergh and General Vuillemin had done their work only too well, and Premier Edouard Daladier, his Cabinet and the French General Staff cringed before the prospect of a Paris flattened and in flames from German bombing. In Britain too the virus had spread. The climate could not be more propitious for what Neville Chamberlain had in mind.

Such was the situation on September 13, 1938, when the tragic little battle of Eger took place in the Sudetenland of Czechoslovakia, and the conspirators were ready to move the moment Adolf Hitler announced mobilization of the German army on, as they thought, September 16. But on September 14 the British Prime Minister an-

35

nounced in the House of Commons that he was leaving the following day for Germany to see Adolf Hitler at Berchtesgaden. Premier Daladier, who had not been informed beforehand, immediately telephoned to ask whether he should come too and was curtly told to stay where he was; the situation was in British hands now.

The conspirators in Germany hoped that Neville Chamberlain had taken note of their warnings and was flying to Berchtesgaden to present Hitler with an ultimatum. For the moment, they called off their plans. In any case, the plot could only work if the Führer was in Berlin rather than at his well-guarded stronghold in Bavaria.

∎

Except for his three confidants—Sir John Simon, Chancellor of the Exchequer; Sir Samuel Hoare, the Home Secretary; and Halifax—the Prime Minister had told no one in the Cabinet of his projected visit until it was set. But Sir Horace Wilson, who had initially suggested this method of approach, knew of it, as did Sir Nevile Henderson, who had arranged it in Berlin. It is a measure of Halifax's weakness as Foreign Secretary that he not only did not ask to accompany Chamberlain on his journey—he, at least, had been to Germany once before—but that he did not protest when the Prime Minister chose Sir Horace Wilson to go with him. Otherwise, the party was a tiny one: William Strang, who was an expert on Central European affairs, a Scotland Yard detective and Miss Kirkpatrick, a civil service secretary. When they took off for Munich on the morning of September 15, it was Sir Horace Wilson's first airplane flight and for Chamberlain only his second, but the new experience did not worry them; Wilson and Strang were too busy reading congratulatory telegrams and godspeed messages to the Prime Minister as the plane lifted over Kent's hop fields and made for Germany.

Certainly neither Chamberlain nor his aides had any idea of what they had let themselves in for. Harold Nicolson has described them as flying off into the blue with "the bright faithfulness of two curates entering a pub for the first time; they did not observe the difference between a social gathering and a roughhouse; nor did they realise that the tough guys assembled did not either speak or understand their language. They imagined that they were as decent

36

and as honourable as themselves." In fact, it was Sir Horace Wilson who suddenly had qualms and wondered what they might have blundered into. "We should have travelled with about fifty secretaries and an imposing array of aides and bodyguards," he said later. "Instead we had this tiny delegation, and for a great power we looked puny. We didn't know any better. If we had, perhaps I should be an earl today."

The plane landed at Munich, where Ribbentrop and Henderson were awaiting them. There was a long journey by train to Berchtesgaden, where they were given twenty minutes to freshen up in their hotel before they started their ride up the mountain to Hitler's residence, the Berghof. Neville Chamberlain was in a car with Ribbentrop; Wilson, Strang and Henderson traveled in another car behind. All the way up, the winding mountain road was lined on either side with black-uniformed, jackbooted SS troops with arms at the salute. "I remember thinking to myself," recalled Sir Horace, "as we climbed the mountain past all those guards, 'I wonder if we'll come out of this alive. I wonder if we will ever get down again.' " It is doubtful that these fears were troubling Neville Chamberlain; apparently he had no trepidations.

"My Lord Hitler was waiting for us on the steps of the Berghof," said Sir Horace Wilson, "I remember I wasn't at all impressed with his uniform. He looked just like a draper's assistant. He greeted Neville Chamberlain and we all went inside for tea. The weather had changed by this time and it had begun to rain. We were taken into this large room with a great picture window which was supposed to look down on Salzburg, but all it looked down on at that moment was rain and mist. We all seated ourselves around a large table. Hitler sat next to N.C., with Schmidt, the translator, on N.C.'s right, and then Göring, Keitel, then me and Strang and Nevile Henderson. I was sitting right opposite Hitler, and I was glad of that. It gave me the opportunity of having a good look at him. When I was a negotiator in the Ministry of Labour, I always liked to be sitting in a position where I could take a good look at my adversary so that I could size him up and see what sort of a chap he was. I looked at Hitler. I didn't like his eyes, I didn't like his mouth; in fact, there wasn't very much I did like about him."

On the other hand, despite the remarks he was to make about Hitler later, Chamberlain seemed to be quite impressed by him—

37

although their meeting began with some of the most banal small talk in the history of high-level negotiations.

CHAMBERLAIN: I have often heard of this room, but it is much larger than I expected.
HITLER: It is you who have big rooms in England.
CHAMBERLAIN: You must come and see them sometime.
HITLER: I should be received with demonstrations of disapproval.
CHAMBERLAIN: Well, perhaps it would be wise to choose the moment.

After some more of this, the Prime Minister and the Führer thoughtfully sipped their tea (very weak and too much milk in it, according to Sir Horace Wilson). A slight rise in Chamberlain's eyebrows became noticeable as his eye caught a painting of a Junoesque blond nude on the wall beside him; his own tastes were prim and he was a firm believer in the proper use of fig leaves. Presently the two statesmen rose and went upstairs to the Führer's study, accompanied only by the interpreter, Dr. Paul Schmidt. It was to be a tête-à-tête between the two men, since Chamberlain had been warned that Foreign Minister Ribbentrop might make trouble if allowed to take part in the proceedings; Chamberlain dispensed with Wilson's presence and that of an English interpreter in order to keep Ribbentrop out. But if the Nazi Foreign Minister's personal presence was barred, his influence was not. Hitler sat down in his study beside a table on which were two glasses and a bottle of mineral water—and a teletyped message. It was Konrad Henlein's report of the battle of Eger.

Hitler and Chamberlain talked for three hours that afternoon. Chamberlain was calm, polite, detached, speaking the crisp language of the practical man. Hitler was more emotional, his voice breaking each time he mentioned the hated Czechs or their President, Eduard Beneš.

CHAMBERLAIN: This business of the Sudeten Germans isn't really our affair, you know. We are only interested in it because of Great Britain's interest in the maintenance of peace.
HITLER: How can you talk about peace when peace in Czechoslovakia has already ceased to exist? Let me make it clear once more that I am determined to solve this problem one way or the other. It can no longer be tolerated that a minor country like Czechia should treat the great two-thousand-year-old Reich like an inferior.
CHAMBERLAIN: But look here, I am a practical man. How can it be arranged in a practical manner that the Sudeten Germans can be brought

38

back into the Reich? They don't live in one single, solid, concentrated area of Czechoslovakia. They are spread out. Even if one conceded to Germany those areas where there are eighty percent Sudetens, there would always remain a large proportion of vaguely German inhabitants in the other regions. Why worry about a new frontier? Why not a resettlement?

This was possibly the most intelligent—and startling remark made by Chamberlain during the whole conversation, and it evidently jolted the German Reich Chancellor. The last thing he wanted back in Germany was two and a half million Sudetens *without* the strategic areas they occupied inside Czechoslovakia. He quickly changed the subject. "Obviously the exchange of views of this kind can do no good, they are too theoretical, events happen so quickly." He began to work himself up into a new fury. "Don't you realize that whole districts in the Sudetenland have been evacuated by the people? Ten thousand refugees are already on German soil! The cost of dead and missing is appalling [*ungeheuerlich*]!* I can't bear it any longer. I said in my speech at Nuremberg that I could not allow it to go on, and you would, my dear Prime Minister, be making a mistake if you believed, like some of your newspapers, that I was voicing empty phrases. This persecution of German nationals must stop, and I am determined to put an end to it."

There was silence for a moment or two as Chamberlain stared calmly into Hitler's blazing eyes. Then he coughed deprecatingly. "Well, now. What about a general appeal to both these parties in Czechoslovakia to calm down? Coming from both of us, it might produce the atmosphere in which talks between them could begin on a peaceful basis. Clearly, if your information is correct, conditions in the Sudetenland certainly must be untenable. But I have come across these situations before, and I have often found that when the events were subjected to closer scrutiny it often turned out that things weren't as bad as they seemed."

Adolf Hitler stared at the British Prime Minister in rage and astonishment. It was one of the special peculiarities of the Führer that he implicitly believed what he read in the German newspapers and heard over the German radio. He would summon his press chief, Dr. Otto Dietrich, and Propaganda Minister Joseph Goebbels and meticulously work out with them how a campaign of slander, vilifica-

* In fact, the refugees numbered hundreds rather than thousands, and the number of Sudetens killed in skirmishes with the Czechs totaled twenty-seven.

tion and abuse against the target of his hatred—in this case the Czechs—should be constructed; occasionally he even edited the false reports to give them extra sensationalism and sanguinary details. Nevertheless, when he subsequently read them in print or heard them over the radio, he was horrified and appalled at the treatment defenseless Germans were subjected to by their enemies. There were no lies he believed but his own. Now, at the hint of skepticism—which had even been diluted in Schmidt's interpretation—in Chamberlain's remarks, he swung around, picked up Henlein's report on the Eger battle and read it out in all its gory detail. Fooled by the agonized sincerity in Hitler's voice, the British Prime Minister was visibly impressed.

"In these circumstances, how can I make an appeal to the Sudeten Germans?" Hitler continued. "You cannot ask me to allow the victims of the Czechs even to meet them, much less share a conference table with them. The nervous tension of our nationals on both sides of the border is fast becoming untenable. From this side, you can hear the sound of Czech gunfire against the defenseless Sudetens. I can no longer allow the German people to stand by and watch and listen while old German towns like Eger are attacked by the Czechs. It has become unbearable." He climbed to his feet and began beating his fist on his other hand. "Mr. Prime Minister, bear this in mind. In 1918, Germany was a very much defeated nation. But she never failed to take the hero's way throughout her two-thousand-year history, and she did not fail to do so in the last war; nor will she now. She will choose the hero's way." His voice rose. "I tell you that the Czechs are inhuman horrors [*Grausen*] and cowards at heart. It surely cannot be wrong to go to the aid of our brothers when they are being treated with such brutality by these worthless people. Just imagine how you would feel in your heart and in your head if these things were being done to your people."

"All right," Chamberlain conceded, "point taken. But if you feel this way and so violently, why did you allow me to come and see you? If you are bent on a violent course, what is the use of talking of a peaceful approach?"

"There is only one way to attain the atmosphere for a peaceful approach: the Czech police must draw back and the Czech army must be confined to their barracks."

Hitler must have looked closely at Chamberlain while he said this, well aware, as Chamberlain was not, that the German army was mobilizing and closing in on the Czech frontiers. The British Prime Minister nodded his head as if he felt that this was not an unreasonable request. It was then that the exchange came between the two leaders which was to settle the fate of Czechoslovakia once and for all—and the question of peace or war in Europe too.

"As to the general situation," Hitler continued, "let me get it clear in my mind. Does England really want to settle the question of the Sudetenland? Would England, for instance, be willing to agree to a separation of this territory and a consequent change in the character of the present state of Czechoslovakia, or not? If England is willing to agree to such a separation and prepared to announce it to the world as the fundamental basis for ending the affair, the conditions will quiet down. But what is England's attitude? It is necessary to know." He paused, turned to Chamberlain and said slowly, "Are the English agreeable to the separation of the Sudetenland from Czechoslovakia on the grounds of self-determination? This isn't just a German idea. Self-determination for this area was first discussed as long ago as 1919. If you wish further talks, Mr. Prime Minister, they could proceed, but only if you first make it quite clear whether you recognize the Sudeten Germans' right to self-determination."

It was the key passage of the whole talk, but no one in the West had publicly admitted this possibility so far.* Until this moment the Sudeten Nazi leaders had agitated for the incorporation of their people and territories in the German Reich, and this of course was what Hitler had always wanted. He didn't want Sudeten Germans; he wanted the Sudeten territories, which the Czechs had fortified and made into a defensive wall against the German *Drang nach Osten*.

In view of the fact that Czechoslovakia was one of the principal allies of France and a friend at Germany's rear in the event of war, it seems inconceivable that a Western ally of France could envision with anything but nightmarish fears the idea of allowing the well-

* Though the *Times* of London, in an editorial published September 7, 1938, had expressed the opinion that it might be better for everyone, including the Czechs, if the Sudetenland were conceded to the German Reich. The British government denied that this was their view, though it cannot have been entirely coincidental that Geoffrey Dawson, the appeasement-minded editor of the *Times,* saw Chamberlain and Sir Horace Wilson just before the appearance of the editorial. The *New Statesman* and *La République* in Paris had expressed similar views, though theirs were less authoritative.

fortified Sudetenland to secede and join a potential enemy. But even at this menacing stage, Neville Chamberlain did not consider Nazi Germany a potential enemy. To him the Czechs were unimportant people "not out of the top drawer." That they were the staunch allies of France mattered even less, since he did not think much of the French either. Now he cleared his throat and made his declaration.

"Without consultation, I cannot of course give a categoric declaration on behalf of the English government. I must naturally consult France and Lord Runciman and the British Cabinet. But I can give you my own personal opinion. After hearing what you have said, and sympathizing with your motives, and after having seen the situation as a result in a much clearer light, I can only say that I am ready to discover whether my personal view is also shared by my ministers at home. Personally I can say here and now that I recognize the principle of the separation of the Sudetenland from Czechoslovakia on the basis of self-determination."

It was said. Though other days and other crises would intervene, it was done. Through its Prime Minister, the British government had declared itself willing to accept the amputation of the Sudetenland from Czechoslovakia and its incorporation with the Reich. True, Chamberlain had pointed out that he must reinforce his own personal conviction with that of his Cabinet and the French, but Hitler was well aware of the Prime Minister's influence over the Cabinet, and sufficiently well informed of the panic in French governmental circles to know that his bloodless battle was won.

Too easily won, he was to decide later, as he watched the foolish old Englishman drive happily down the mountain to his hotel.

III

The Antipathetic Alliance

It was downhill all the way from that moment onward. There were some shabby deeds performed by the British and French governments in the two weeks that followed, and though it is customary for historians to blame the Foreign Minister of France, Georges Bonnet, for the most underhanded of these activities, he had a worthy companion in Neville Chamberlain. Not that the British Prime Minister had to exercise more than a modicum of chicanery to make his Cabinet agree to what had, only a week or two back, seemed outrageous and impossible—the dismemberment of Czechoslovakia and the handing over of the Sudetenland to Germany.

"The P.M. then told us the story of his visit to Berchtesgaden," wrote Duff Cooper of the Cabinet meeting on September 17, which was held shortly after Chamberlain's return to London. "He recounted his experiences with some satisfaction. Although he said that at first sight Hitler struck him as 'the commonest little dog' he had ever seen, without one sign of distinction, he was obviously pleased at the reports he had subsequently received of the impression he had made. He told us with obvious satisfaction how Hitler had said to someone that he, Chamberlain, was 'a man.' But the bare facts of the interview were frightful. None of the schemes which had been so

43

carefully worked out, and which the P.M. had intended to put forward, had been so much as mentioned."

The Cabinet was put in the right mood for concessions. They too had been enduring the kind of pressure which Bonnet had so successfully exerted on the French. Chamberlain had called for a report from his air experts on defense possibilities in the event of war. Between them, Chamberlain and his Air Minister, Sir Kingsley Wood, carefully edited the report to give the blackest possible slant to the facts presented.* Sir Horace Wilson let it be widely known in government circles that there wasn't enough hose pipe in the London fire brigades to put out peacetime fires, let alone those from bombing raids. Ambassador Kennedy was being kept fully informed by Neville Chamberlain and made no secret of his complete approval of such subterfuge. In this he differed from Franklin Roosevelt. Harold L. Ickes wrote in his diary after a Cabinet meeting at the White House on September 18, 1938: "The President thinks that Chamberlain is for peace at any price. Britain and France, in the President's graphic language, 'will wash the blood from their Judas Iscariot hands.' "

Peace at any price. But though the French were panicking, there were still some elements in Daladier's Cabinet and in the French press who were steadfastly maintaining that for her own sake France should fulfill her treaty obligations to Czechoslovakia. Those elements had to be quashed quickly if public opinion was not to be roused. The most active worker for appeasement was Georges Bonnet, flitting here and there on his sinister errands. He was now closely in touch with Otto Abetz, Hitler's well-heeled Nazi propagandist in France; he was conniving with extreme-right-wing groups; and he was also seeing a good deal of Sir Eric Phipps, the British ambassador in Paris, who was hardly the most brilliant or courageous envoy in

* Captain B. H. Liddell Hart, the military correspondent for the *Times* of London, had had his reports suppressed by that paper when he suggested that in the event of war, Czechoslovakia would prove a most useful ally and had a fine air force and efficient army. He was a member of an anti-appeasement committee led by Winston Churchill which opposed Chamberlain's policies. Of one of their meetings at this period he wrote: "We heard that Sir Kingsley Wood . . . had been telling Ministers and Opposition leaders that in the event of war Germany could spare 1,500 bombers to attack Britain and that we must reckon on half a million casualties in three weeks. I questioned this assumption as I knew that the Air Staff estimate of the strength of the whole German bomber force was under 1,500 machines, and that the Air Staff calculation was that only one third of them could be used against this country."

44

the history of British diplomacy. Bonnet made no secret in his talks with Phipps of his determination to make France break her word and throw the Czechs overboard. Hence, when Daladier and Bonnet arrived in London on September 18 to get firsthand details of the Berchtesgaden meeting (they had also been invited so that the Prime Minister would be able to find out where the French stood), it did not take Chamberlain long to persuade them to accept the principle of self-determination for the Sudeten people. True, while agreeing to the idea of a cession of Sudeten territory to Germany, Daladier demanded that Britain in return guarantee the truncated remainder of Czechoslovakia. This was the last thing the Prime Minister had in mind; he wanted Germany to have a free hand toward the east—anywhere, in fact, except in the direction of England. But since time was short and he wanted to return to Germany for another talk with Hitler, he agreed. If France could contemplate breaking guarantees to Czechoslovakia now, why couldn't England later? The Anglo-French statesmen then ironed out a proposal to the Czechs which opened by stating: "We are both convinced that, after recent events, the point has now been reached where the further maintenance within the boundaries of the Czechoslovak State of the districts mainly inhabited by the Sudeten-Deutsch cannot in fact continue any longer . . . and the safety of Czechoslovakia's vital interests cannot effectively be assured unless these areas are now transferred to the Reich."

Neville Chamberlain preened himself. Glibly explaining to his cowed Cabinet the next day that there hadn't been time to consult them about the statement, he overrode the objections of the few* who pointed out that such concessions would fatally weaken Czechoslovakia, and sent his proposals off to Prague. No, he assured his critics in the Cabinet, he would put no undue pressure on President Beneš to accept them; all he wanted was a speedy reply, since he had promised to meet Hitler again—at Bad Godesberg, this time—two days hence. In Paris, Georges Bonnet was giving a similarly smooth promise to members of the French Cabinet that the Czechs would not be pressured into accepting.

* Among them were Duff Cooper; Oliver Stanley, President of the Board of Trade; and Leslie Hore-Belisha, Secretary for War.

45

But within minutes of the end of the French Cabinet meeting, Bonnet was on the telephone to Prague instructing the French minister, De Lacroix, to urge the Czechs to accept. When the Czechs, thunderstruck at the Anglo-French betrayal, delayed their reply to the proposals, Chamberlain developed a slow-burning rage that became stronger as each hour passed. His temper was not improved when the ever-thoughtful Germans sent him some new intercepts of conversations between Beneš in Prague and Masaryk in London in which his ancestry and character were described in choicest Czech argot. Finally he decided that he could wait no longer; the moment had come to start applying pressure. When he heard about it, Bonnet was all in favor. On instructions from their governments, Lacroix and Sir Basil Newton, the British minister, saw President Beneš at two o'clock on the morning of September 21 and presented what has since been called "the Dawn *Démarche*." It was more of an ultimatum, for it specified:

1. That what has been proposed by England and France is the only means of averting war and the invasion of Czechoslovakia;
2. Should the Czech reply in the negative, she would bear responsibility for the war;
3. This would destroy Franco-British solidarity, since England would not march;
4. If under these circumstances the war starts, France will not take part, i.e., she will not fulfil her Treaty obligations.*

The Czech President crumbled visibly before the eyes of the two envoys as they read him the terms; being decent men, they found it difficult to carry through their miserable duty without a sign of their own emotions. They knew the man's condition; he had not slept for days, and he was prey to the fears and irresolutions of a man of liberal faith who has trusted the good will and promises of others instead of his own strong right arm. But they got the answer their governments needed. Beneš accepted the ultimatum; the Czechs would agree to the dismemberment of their country.

Whether it would have been wiser for the Czech President to

---

* There have been assertions, particularly by Georges Bonnet, that the Czechs themselves asked for this ultimatum in order to demonstrate to their people that they had no alternative but to give way. I can find no evidence of this in the documents now available at the Czech archives in Prague. M. de Lacroix has maintained that his own reports dealing with this incident (now in the French archives) have been mutilated and tampered with.

stand firm and fight is one of the ifs of history which no one will ever be able to decide. Certainly, as it turned out, it would have been better for the Czechs to resist their enemies and allies in 1938 than to suffer the humiliations which followed in 1939. In the hours which preceded the Anglo-French "Dawn *Démarche*," Beneš had tried to establish whether the Soviet government would come to his aid in the event of a German attack. He summoned the Soviet minister and asked him "whether the Soviet Union would act if France acted, and whether she would act in accordance with Articles 16 and 17 of the League of Nations Covenant," and was told flatly that the Soviet Union would so act. But curiously enough, Beneš then let the Soviet envoy go. It was not until just before his meeting with Newton and Lacroix that he asked Klement Gottwald, the Czech Communist leader, whether Russia would come independently to Czechoslovakia's aid if she were attacked—that is, even if France did not. Quite understandably, Gottwald replied that Beneš must ask this question of the Russians themselves.

This he never did. It confirms the suspicion, which Beneš half admitted during his years in exile, that he refrained from asking for Russian help not because he thought it would be refused but because he feared that it might be granted—and that Czechoslovakia would be drawn into the Russian orbit once and for all. Rather than that, he preferred to lose the Sudetenland to Germany. Had he not been in such an exhausted state, he might have thought it out more realistically.

But from the point of view of Britain and France, there can be no doubt that it would have been far better for them to have faced Germany with Czechoslovakia as their ally in 1938 than to have gone to war without her in 1939. The Czechs were ready. They bitterly resented the acceptance by Beneš of the Anglo-French plan, and their attitude forced the resignation of his Cabinet, with General Jan Syrový succeeding Milan Hodža as Premier. It was a time for weeping in Prague.

■

Not so in England. Everything went as Chamberlain had hoped and planned. All that needed to be done now was to visit Adolf Hitler once more in Germany and bring him the good news that the Balkans were open to him. The time had come for a far-reaching Anglo-German understanding for the future.

The second meeting between the German Reich Chancellor and the British Prime Minister took place at Godesberg, in the Rhineland, from September 22 to 24, 1938. Chamberlain had brought the same staff with him, plus a legal expert from the Foreign Office who could pass judgment on any agreements made at the meetings.

It should be emphasized that though Europe was fraught with anxiety, though even the German people were desperately worried over the prospect of war, Neville Chamberlain apparently was full of confidence as he made ready for his second encounter with the Führer. This time the Germans seemed to have gone out of their way to make the British welcome. At Berchtesgaden the arrangements had been hurried; at Godesberg there was a guard of honor, a band playing "God Save the King," and a dozen different lotions, hair oils, toothpastes, scents and assorted unguents in each delegate's room at the spectacular Hotel Petersberg overlooking the Rhine. Photographs of Chamberlain arriving for the first meeting show him as serene as a newly elected beauty queen as he was ferried across the river to the hotel where Hitler was to meet him. All should now go smoothly; was he not bringing news that Britain and France had consented to the dismemberment of Czechoslovakia on Germany's behalf—and that Czechoslovakia had agreed to the amputation?

In the next few hours Chamberlain was to get his first real taste of the nature of Adolf Hitler. It began when the Prime Minister told him that all was arranged, that the Sudetenland was his. Did he mean, asked Hitler, that the Allies had agreed to turn over the Sudeten German areas to Germany? With Czech consent? That's right, replied Chamberlain, waiting for expressions of gratitude and thanks.

Hitler shook his head. He was sorry, but it wasn't enough.

Chamberlain stared at him in surprise and dismay. Had he spent all this time wearing down the English, French and Czechs on behalf of the Germans, only to get a reply like this? He could hardly believe his ears.

In fact, Hitler, having taken the Prime Minister's measure, had soon regretted the amiability of his initial encounter with this extraordinary old man. The contempt which he was to make very plain later had already begun to rise in him then; now he had only to look at

48

Chamberlain to realize that he need never have had any doubts. At one time he had said that if Britain opposed him in his ambitions to occupy Czechoslovakia and territories beyond, he would hesitate and probably call them off. But at their first meeting Chamberlain's attitude and actions had confirmed the Führer's passionate conviction that no matter what his generals said, the British would never oppose him. They had lost their muscle and will; he could do whatever he wanted and they would not fight. Why should he be content with an Anglo-French plan for the cession of the Sudetenland; why not make his own? To this end he had prodded Poland and Hungary to demand the return of their "ethnic territories." It would help bring about the collapse of Czechoslovakia as a state and enable the whole of it to come under the control of Germany. For though Hitler had always publicly stated that he wanted only Germans and "German lands" back in the Reich, Czechoslovakia *in toto* was what he really coveted.

In any event, Hitler now told the Prime Minister, the problem had to be settled once and for all before October 1. And the concessions Chamberlain had brought were, he repeated, "no longer enough."

In the next seven days, the world went through paroxysms of fear as the prospect of war seemed to draw near. While Chamberlain was still at Godesberg, the Czech army was allowed by the French and British to mobilize. The British navy called its reserves back to the fleet and got its ships ready for action.* The French army began to summon its troops to their action stations on the Maginot Line. The German army was already assembling for an attack on Czechoslovakia.

It was, in fact, all a great bluff. Neither Britain nor France had any intention of going to war on behalf of Czechoslovakia—or on behalf of themselves at this moment, as it turned out. Adolf Hitler knew this and told his Party leaders not to worry; he was convinced that Chamberlain would not stand up to him. As for his generals, who knew the weakness of the German armed forces, he railed at them for cowardice and lack of trust in his judgment and intuition. True, he had a moment of anxiety when it was rumored that the

* The Russian fleet also mobilized, a fact conveniently forgotten by most British historians.

British fleet was being mobilized. Hitler had always had a healthy fear of the British navy, remembering how it had starved Germany into surrender in 1918. But his information from France and Britain was good; his intelligence services were excellent at this time in assessing the mental processes of the Anglo-French leaders. If worst came to worst, he could always back down—but he was convinced that he need not.

So for days the world wallowed in a crisis that actually was without foundation, but Hitler's personal and virulent attack on President Beneš in a speech at the Sportpalast on September 26 did not help assuage these fears. After a tirade of abuse against Beneš (and some appeasing words about Chamberlain), Hitler ended his discourse before an hysterically cheering audience with the words: "But I must also declare before the German people that so far as the Sudeten German problem is concerned, my patience is now at an end. I made an offer to Herr Beneš which was no more than the realization of what he had already promised. He now has peace or war in his hands. Either he will accept this offer and at length give the Germans their freedom, or we will get this freedom for ourselves." Menacing words, deliberately calculated to scare the wits out of the democracies.

President Roosevelt sent messages of appeal to all the European leaders in which he mentioned the word "peace" so many times that some people began to get the impression that he too was a secret appeaser.* The Pope issued pleas for talks and accommodations.

Right from the start, there had been rumblings of revolt in the British Cabinet. Several of its members felt that this was the moment to stand firm. Having by this time swallowed and digested Hitler's humiliations and excused them, Chamberlain was irritated by the murmurings of conscience and uneasiness in the Cabinet room, but felt it necessary to soothe them. Yes, he said to his more obstreperous ministers, perhaps it would be wiser to make Hitler aware of the firmness of Britain's attitude against any further concessions, but first let us find out what our French friends have to say, so Daladier and Bonnet were asked to come to London the next day.

The Prime Minister had little doubt that the panic into which the French had now worked themselves would soon subvert the fighting cocks in his Cabinet, for he had just received an extraordinary dis-

---

* He proposed, on September 27, a conference of "nations directly interested in the present controversy" in a neutral country in Europe.

patch from Ambassador Phipps in Paris. Dated September 24, 1938, it read: "Unless German aggression were so brutal, bloody and prolonged (through gallantry of Czech resistance) as to infuriate French public opinion to the extent of making it lose its reason, war would now be most unpopular in France. I think therefore that HMG [His Majesty's Government] should realise extreme danger of even appearing to encourage small, but noisy and corrupt war group here. All that is best in France is against war, almost at any price (hence the really deep and pathetic gratitude to our P.M.) ..."

Chamberlain had no intention of encouraging any war group, "corrupt" or not, British, French or Czech. He was confident, moreover, that the French Premier and his Foreign Minister would be his strongest allies in emphasizing their weaknesses and the impossibility of war. He was right about Bonnet. On the eve of their departure for London on Sunday, September 25, Bonnet saw U.S. Ambassador William Bullitt, who reported to Washington that the French Foreign Minister "said that it was his conviction that the British Government would not go to war on behalf of Czechoslovakia and (since he personally desires to avoid war at all costs) he was much more cheerful than yesterday as he felt that his position would be supported by the British Government."

On the other hand, the French Premier appeared to have undergone a change of mood and was beginning to mutter under his breath phrases like "the sanctity of treaties" and "the honor of France." He had only belatedly seen the demands which Hitler had made at Godesberg in place of the Anglo-French proposals; even Chamberlain himself had called them a *Diktat,* for they demanded the evacuation by the Czechs of the Sudetenland by October 1, with nothing at all—whether furniture, livestock or arms—to be removed by the retreating Czechs. Daladier described the demands as "cruel" and "insufferable," and by the time he reached London he was in a belligerent mood.

"The Anglo-French meetings held in London on September 25 and 26, to consider the results of the Godesberg talks," wrote William Strang, "were among the most painful which it has ever been my misfortune to attend."

Chamberlain had refrained from answering back when Adolf Hitler ranted at him at Godesberg, preferring to swallow the insults, but now he regurgitated them over the unsuspecting head of Edouard

51

Daladier. The British Prime Minister had been prepared to treat the French with cool superiority and get an agreement out of them as swiftly and as painlessly as possible, but the first signs of opposition from Daladier brought out all his antipathy and contempt for the French. He suffered from gout; the wine he drank at dinner had provoked a painful attack, and this may have been responsible both for the high flush in his cheeks and his barely controlled anger as he icily asked Daladier what he would do should Germany now march into Czechoslovakia.*

DALADIER: Herr Hitler will then have brought about a situation in which aggression will have been provoked by him.

CHAMBERLAIN: What then?

DALADIER: Each of us will do what is incumbent upon him.

CHAMBERLAIN: Are we to understand from that that France will declare war on Germany?

DALADIER: Surely that is clear. France will fulfill her obligations. I have already asked a million Frenchmen to go to the frontier.

CHAMBERLAIN: But do the French General Staff have a plan? If so, what is it?

DALADIER: It is not possible for France to send help directly to Czechoslovakia by land, but she can help by drawing the German army toward the French frontier and the Maginot Line.

Sir John Simon, Chancellor of the Exchequer, now took up the questioning. In nonpolitical life he was a lawyer who was well known for his ruthless cross-examinations of witnesses in court, a cold man of whom someone once wrote:

* It has been suggested to the author that the British members of the Anglo-French confrontation described in the subsequent paragraphs were quite right to be concerned about French military planning. So they were. It is true that the French armed forces appear to have made no real plans to go to the aid of Czechoslovakia and that the military-political co-ordinating committee had not met since March 1938. (Ironically, this was the month when the British Joint Chiefs of Staff had met and pointed out that Britain was in no condition to go to war that year; they were equally pessimistic about the future and just as slack in their planning.)

But the point about the Anglo-French meeting is not the directness of the questions leveled at the French but the sour air of hostility shown toward them by Chamberlain and Simon. Lord Strang remembers it with acute embarrassment and sorrow, and Daladier himself with anguish. At least the French Premier recognized the moral nature of the dilemma the two delegations were facing and was willing to speak about it. One cannot help but suspect that the attitude of Chamberlain and his latter-day apologists stems from unworthier motives. Daladier has since maintained that given firm British support at the meeting, he would have stood firm against Hitler, even to the extent of going to war, though he believes that Hitler would then have either backed down or been overthrown by the German conspirators.

52

Sir John Simon
Is not like Timon.
Timon hated mankind.
Simon doesn't mind.

With Sir Samuel Hoare, the Home Secretary, he was one of the staunchest supporters of Chamberlain's appeasement policy.

SIMON: When the French troops have been called up to do their duty, is that duty just to man the Maginot Line and remain there without a declaration of war, or is it the intention of the French government to declare war and take active measures with their land forces?

DALADIER: That depends.

SIMON: Will the French air force be used over German territory?

Daladier was now beginning to look annoyed, not so much at the questions as at the evident unfriendliness of their intention and the tones in which they were delivered. He flushed angrily when Simon said at one point, "I will repeat my question, as it seems not to have been understood," and retorted, "Obviously, I would consider it ridiculous to mobilize the French land forces, only to leave them under arms doing nothing in their fortifications. It would be equally ridiculous to do nothing in the air. I believe that in spite of Hitler's recent declarations, the German system of fortifications is much less solid than Hitler has indicated. It will be several months before the Siegfried Line is really strong.* I therefore believe that after our troops have concentrated, an offensive should be attempted against Germany on land. As far as the air is concerned, it will be possible to attack certain important German military and industrial centers, which can easily be reached by our planes in spite of certain legends which have been spread abroad."

There was a heavy silence. Chamberlain in particular looked disconcerted. This was far from what he had been expecting from the French. He was even more dismayed when Daladier, now thoroughly angry, changed his tack and touched on the morality of the situation; this was most distasteful to Chamberlain, Simon and Hoare, all High Churchmen and therefore not particularly comfortable when their motives now were questioned.

"But I am more interested for the moment in the moral issue than in strategy," Daladier continued. "Like a barbarian, I have been

* His information, which came from the Deuxième Bureau, French military intelligence, was quite correct.

53

ready to cut up this country [Czechoslovakia] without even consulting her and handing over three-and-a-half million of her population to Hitler. That has not been an agreeable task for me. It has been hard, perhaps even a little dishonorable. But I have felt that this was better than to begin again what we saw twenty years ago. Now the situation changes. The Anglo-French proposals are bad enough, but where are we to stop? I cannot agree to the Godesberg demands as they stand."

Simon interjected to ask what France would do if the Godesberg demands were rejected. Daladier said they could begin new discussions on the basis of the Anglo-French plan.

Chamberlain was barely able to control himself by this time. "I am sure Herr Hitler will not accept this," he said. "The Germans might be in Prague within a few days.* The British government must know what attitude the French will take in that case. I have had some disturbing reports"—here he shuffled some papers on the table before him—"about the state of the French air force and the capacity of French industry to supply it. Can France defend herself against air attack and make an effective reply? The French press certainly doesn't give the impression that France is ready for war. It will be a poor consolation if, in trying to help Czechoslovakia, France herself collapses."

Daladier was thoroughly nettled by this time, his chin jutting, his words spilling out. "What about the British government, then? Is it really prepared to give way? Is it really ready to accept the Hitler demands of Godesberg and apply the necessary pressure in Prague? The sentiment of France and the French people should not be inferred from what is said in French newspapers." He paused, glanced belligerently at Chamberlain, and then went on, "I can say that France is perfectly capable of mobilizing its air force and attacking Germany. The Russians must not be forgotten, either. Russia can hold her own with Germany too."† Here he ignored the restraining hand of Georges

---

* It was always tacitly assumed by the British and even by some French that the German army would easily destroy the Czech defense forces. This opinion was never shared by the German army itself.

† Would the Russians in fact have come to Czechoslovakia's aid if she had decided to fight and if France had fulfilled her treaty obligations to Prague? The Soviet minister in Prague had told Beneš that she would. In his assessment of potential opponents if he attacked Czechoslovakia, Hitler himself presumed that they would consist of France, Russia and Britain. There is no doubt about two actions which Russia took at the time of the crisis: she mobilized her fleet and she sent her

Bonnet, who by this time was thoroughly alarmed at the unexpected fervor of his Premier. While the frozen faces of the British ministers were turned to him in obvious dismay, Daladier asked, staring straight at Chamberlain, "Finally, let me put three questions to you. Do the British accept the Godesberg plan? Will they press Prague to accept it? Do you think that France should do nothing?"

Neville Chamberlain decided that it would not be wise to answer any of the questions. He contented himself with saying that it was up to the Czechs to decide whether they should accept Hitler's Godesberg proposals, and that it was up to the French themselves to decide what they would do on the basis of the decision of their Czech ally. But the British must know quickly.

There was a scraping of chairs. The two allies gazed into one another's eyes with unconcealed antipathy and retired for the night.

Late that evening Neville Chamberlain, Sir John Simon and Sir Horace Wilson gathered at No. 10 Downing Street to discuss strategy. Their plans had been considerably upset by Daladier's sudden attack of scruples, and they belatedly realized that their well-planned campaign not only to avoid war but to reach a long-lasting rapport with Germany was in peril. Their mutual distaste for Daladier had barely been concealed as they parted for the night, and now it was frankly discussed in the Prime Minister's study. Somehow, the French Premier must be worn down.

As shown by the relevant documents, and as Chamberlain had always suspected, the English had an ally in the French camp. In the early hours of the morning of September 26, Georges Bonnet telephoned Paris and through Sir Eric Phipps suggested a way out. All the British government had to do was assure Daladier of its determination to stand up to Hitler and consent to a new move. "The Premier is not insisting on his point of view," said Bonnet. "All he asks is a gesture to show the people that he is doing his best."*

After talking to Phipps, Chamberlain realized that this was just

---

aircraft across Rumania to wait on Slovak airfields. These are hardly the actions of a nation which has no intention of intervening. Of course, the Russians have always maintained since that they were prepared to act in concert with France and Britain, and the use of Czech documents by Western apologists for Chamberlain to prove otherwise have no stronger validity than this contention. Documents now available in Prague demonstrate equally well Russia's determination to honor her agreement.

* This was a favorite gambit of Bonnet's. It will be recalled that it was he who suggested that the Czechs needed pressure on them from Britain and France in order to appear "forced" into capitulation.

the guideline he had been seeking. When the meeting resumed later the same morning (at which General Maurice Gamelin, the French Army Chief of Staff, joined Chamberlain and Daladier), the British had altered their attitude. The Prime Minister went out of his way to be friendly. He quite understood the French Premier's qualms and could assure him that Britain too was determined to resist Hitler's blackmail. They would brace themselves and stand firm; more than that, they would make their position clear.

With this, the British Prime Minister cleared his throat and announced that it was his intention to send an envoy to Germany to see Herr Hitler and break the news at once to him of the new determination of the Allies. He would send along a message to the Reich Chancellor urging him to allow the transfer of the Sudetenland territory and its people to be carried out, and the situation be settled, without bloodshed or undue distress to both sides, by an international body of impartial men composed of Germans, Czechs and English.

"And what if Hitler refuses?" Daladier asked.

"Then we will have to present him with an ultimatum too. Our envoy will say that if worst comes to worst, France and Britain will both fight for Czechoslovakia together."

Incredulous, Daladier stared at him. Were the British really changing their minds and policies and beliefs, and siding with the French against the Germans? He said, "I am much relieved at your news. Whom are you sending as your envoy?"

Without blinking an eyelid, Neville Chamberlain replied, "My good friend and adviser, Sir Horace Wilson."

Earlier that morning of September 26, Neville Chamberlain had called Sir Horace Wilson into his office at No. 10 Downing Street and said, "Here. You are to take this to Hitler."

It was a letter signed by the Prime Minister and addressed to the Chancellor of the German Reich saying that Wilson was his personal envoy, enjoyed his complete confidence and had powers to negotiate with the Führer. There was a second letter, from the Czech government, which announced that after full consideration it had rejected Hitler's Godesberg proposals. There was also a short memo which had been drawn up by Sir John Simon after a meeting of the British

56

Cabinet, a message which pointed out that after careful thought the British government could not bring itself to advise the Czechs to accept the Godesberg *Diktat*—and that the Czechs had therefore rejected it. The implication was that if Germany launched an attack upon Czechoslovakia, France might well march, and if France marched, then it was inevitable that Britain should come to the aid of her ally. Wilson and Chamberlain both regarded this memo as an "ultimatum" to the Germans, and the Prime Minister counseled his assistant very carefully as to the circumstances under which it should be presented: *only if Hitler "refused to see reason."*

Wilson remembers thinking at the time that "it seemed a bit much that I had been chosen for this mission. I had been working all summer desperately trying to secure peace, and now I was being chosen as the man who would hand Hitler an ultimatum threatening war. It was a terrible responsibility, and I was very well aware of it. After all, who was I? A mere nobody whose name hardly anyone had heard of; yet here I was going to negotiate with a formidable dictator."

Wilson boarded the special plane waiting for him at Croydon; the only other passenger was a secretary from the Foreign Office, in case he should wish to dictate notes. He sat alone as the plane took off and spent most of the journey memorizing the "ultimatum" so that when the time came he could deliver it "while looking Hitler in the eyes." He was met at Tempelhof Airport by Sir Nevile Henderson, who drove him to the British embassy for tea and told him he had made an appointment with Hitler at the Reich Chancellery for five o'clock.

At four-forty that Monday afternoon Wilson, Henderson and Sir Ivone Kirkpatrick, first secretary at the embassy, who spoke German fluently, left the embassy, which was at the corner of the Wilhelmstrasse and the Unter den Linden, to walk down the Wilhelmstrasse to the Reich Chancellery at the other end. It was a lovely autumn afternoon. Wilson noticed that everywhere he looked there were people in uniform, brownshirts and SS men, and every so often along the streets would come more men in uniform, usually led by a German band, "one of those German bands I remember used to go puffing and blowing through the streets in England when I was a boy." Kirkpatrick told him that these were Nazi delegates from all over Germany who had come to Berlin especially to hear Hitler make an important speech that evening at the Sportpalast, the city's biggest arena. Wilson was very impressed; the atmosphere seemed full of martial menace.*

As he was taken into Hitler's study, Sir Horace Wilson felt that this was going to be a negotiation of the kind he had been conducting all his life, though possibly more difficult than usual. He still thought of the Nazi leader as a particularly obstreperous trade union leader trying to make a hard bargain, and he had no doubt that he could handle him.

"Like all dictators," he recalled, "he had this habit of putting himself at the end of a long room so that you had to walk the whole way across before meeting him, with him staring straight at you. Quite an ordeal. Hitler was sitting on a settee with quite a lot of other people in the room,† and I sat down next to him, so that our knees were nearly touching—as close to him as I ever got—with the others around me. I first of all handed over my note from the Prime Minister, and Schmidt [the official German interpreter] read it out, and since it proclaimed my status, Hitler smiled and seemed quite pleased."

It was the smile on the face of a tiger, and the last one Sir Horace Wilson was to see, for Schmidt now read the second letter which Wilson had brought, the one from the Czechs saying that they could not accede to the Godesberg demands. Before he had finished the first two sentences, Hitler bounded to his feet, and turning around, roared at the astonished British negotiator, "So! That settles it! Now I will really smash the Czechs!"

He turned back and started to march toward the door, waving his arms angrily above his head. "Well, you know how it is with dictators," recalled Wilson. "When one of them stands up, all their lackeys stand up too. Ribbentrop and the others had snapped to their feet as Hitler began to stamp and rave. But I stayed where I was. Nevile Henderson started to get up but I pressed him down. I

---

* It is an ironic fact, and an indication of the British government's lack of touch, that the atmosphere in Berlin was anything but militant at this time and that Hitler was well aware of it. On his instructions, an armored brigade with marching troops in full war kit and tanks moved down the Wilhelmstrasse on the very next day. Hitler came to the window of his study to watch them, but soon went back inside again, angry and dismayed. Far from cheering this martial display, the crowds on the sidewalks watched it in tense and uneasy silence.

† They were Ribbentrop; Colonel Rudolf Schmundt, Hitler's military aide and personal adjutant, who was present at most of his important meetings; Weizsäcker; and a number of secretaries.

58

thought to myself, 'I am an Englishman. This Hitler is being rude. In the circumstances, I am going to stay where I am. I will not stand up.' It worked. Hitler reached the door on his way to make a dramatic exit, but he was suddenly aware of the fact that I was still sitting. He stopped, turned, and then came back and sat down again."

But if Sir Horace had not been intimidated then, he soon was, for Hitler had now worked himself up into one of those furies which his intimates knew so well; he could bring them on with the facility of a great actress, and they looked and sounded remarkably genuine. A "very violent hour" followed. Both Wilson and Henderson hastened to assure him that they had not accepted the Czech rejection as the last word, and that they still hoped to move them in the direction of a settlement. They referred Hitler to the passage in the first letter Wilson had presented, in which the Prime Minister asked for a meeting to be arranged between Czech and German representatives and said that he was "willing to arrange for the representation of the British Government."

Hitler went into a paroxysm of vituperation at this, pouring scorn on Chamberlain and Wilson. His frequent taste for gutter language emerged. "What do I care about British representation?" he cried. "The old Scheisshund must be mad if he thinks he can influence me in that way."

Wilson looked shocked. "If Herr Hitler is referring to the Prime Minister," he said primly, "I can assure you that he is not mad, only interested in peace."

Hitler looked over Wilson's head. "The observations of his ass-lickers* do not interest me. All that interests me are my people in Czechia who are being murdered and tortured by that foul sodomite, Beneš. I will not stand it any longer. It is more than a good German can bear! Do you hear me, you stupid pig!"

The Führer stopped suddenly, perhaps fearing that he had gone too far, and said, "Very well, it is agreed. We will have a meeting with the Czechs, but only on condition that they accept the [Godesberg] memorandum and the October first date [for evacuating the Sudetenland]." Then he began to rant again. "Whether by negotiation or force, the territory will be free on the first of October. Take your pick.

* In his official report to the Cabinet, dictated to his female secretary from the Foreign Office, Sir Horace remarked, "The epithets applied to Mr. Chamberlain and Sir Horace Wilson could not be repeated in a drawing room."

But I must know for certain within the next day or two whether the Czechs accept, or we might well have to sweep the Czechs out *before* October first. Yes, indeed. On reflection, I will give them two days. I must have an affirmative reply within two days; that is, by Wednesday."

"Midnight, Wednesday?" Henderson asked.

"No, by two P.M.!"

There are many words one can use to describe Hitler's tantrum, and one of them is certainly "unreasonable." He was not only in a frenetic rage, spouting hate and abuse with every sentence; he was also unrelenting about the Czechs and was obviously not going to give way, no matter what the proposition. Sir Horace Wilson was mindful of his instructions and of the words he had so painstakingly memorized on the plane from London, to be presented only if Hitler "refused to see reason."

"Obviously he was not seeing reason!" Wilson has recalled. "But I suddenly remembered all those German bands and Brown Shirt delegates in the streets of Berlin. I remembered the vital speech he was going to make that night at the Sportpalast. I thought to myself, 'If I say what I'm supposed to say now, it might just send him over the edge—and then we're really in for it.' And I made up my mind."

So Sir Horace Wilson did not deliver what he and Chamberlain called the "ultimatum" that evening. "I have been blamed for that. When I got back to London some members of the Cabinet were furious,"* Sir Horace recalled. "But I couldn't forget the way he talked. Hitler was still raging. At one point he said to me, 'If you want to know what I think about the Czechs, come along to my speech at the Sportpalast tonight.' I thanked him and said I couldn't come, but that I certainly would listen to it on the wireless."

Hence, Adolf Hitler was allowed to go to the Sportpalast and hurl an ultimatum at the Czechs without knowing that the British and French had declared that they were prepared to act in concert

---

* Duff Cooper commented: "Then Horace Wilson told us of his mission to Germany. He had not delivered the important part of his message, namely that England and France would fight, at his first interview with Hitler, so that Hitler had not heard of it before his speech. When he delivered it on the following day it was so tied up with additional clauses that it had lost half its force." Duff Cooper does not explain what he means by "additional clauses," but the context suggests that he thought Wilson's praise of Hitler's speech spoiled the effect of his message.

60

in the event of a German attack on Czechoslovakia. If the document had been handed to Hitler before the speech it would certainly have given him a considerable jolt, even if it had failed to divert him from his plans. Next morning was too late. The message had lost its impact, as even Sir Horace Wilson himself realized. "He was calmer then," he recalled, "but still in a bad temper. I congratulated him on the ovation he had received, but he brushed it aside. Then I delivered my ultimatum, but he hardly seemed to notice it now."

It was a gross error of judgment on Wilson's part. Delivered at the right time, the message might have given Hitler pause and saved the Western allies from the humiliations to come at Munich.

■

Neville Chamberlain's announcement of the forthcoming Four Power meeting at Munich to solve the Sudeten problem was made during his speech in the House of Commons on September 28, 1938, and it has since been interpreted as one of the great dramatic moments of the decade. By this time even Chamberlain's opponents were beginning to wonder whether appeasement was not a better way out than bombs raining on London and the possible disintegration of the Empire. Chamberlain, Wilson and their supporters had a strong argument for giving way to the German demands, an argument not based solely on the horrid prospect of annihilating raids by the Luftwaffe. The Prime Minister could point out that the members of the British Commonwealth (who were holding an unofficial conference at that moment in Sydney, Australia) were by no means solidly behind the government's preoccupations about Eastern Europe. Led by the Canadian High Commissioner, Vincent Massey, a persuasive supporter of appeasement, the Empire governments conveyed their "deep concern," and Massey himself strongly hoped that Chamberlain would compromise. The Australians made it plain that they did not wish to be involved, and the South Africans were openly hostile to any attempt to make war on Germany. Duff Cooper and other activists snorted that these doubts and divisions would immediately be composed once Britain took a firm stand, but others were not so sure. They were inclined to believe Chamberlain when he hinted that they were facing the breakup of the Empire simply

61

for the sake of an academic argument about a small Central European country.

Nor were the doubters encouraged by the attitude of the United States. It was all very well for Franklin Roosevelt to encourage them to be firm, but they suspected—quite rightly—that America would stand aloof should a war actually begin. "If a European war should take place between Liberal and Totalitarian countries," declared Herbert Hoover, "the only hope for survival of democracy is for us to stay out of it." True, Chamberlain had been as half-hearted in trying to secure American support against Hitler as he had been in seeking Russian aid; he was antipathetic toward the first and distrustful of the second.

These considerations did not so much affect the public, whose indignation against Hitler was high, as it did the members of the so-called Establishment upon whose influence Chamberlain must rely to back him in his appeasement policies. They were riddled with fears and doubts; they discounted any prospect of American support; they were haunted by the specter of a broken Empire and a Europe laid prey to Communism. But mostly they were afraid. The prophets of Armageddon had done their work only too well.

As an example, one of the most assiduous workers for "understanding" with Germany, Thomas L. Jones, an intimate of most Tory leaders, had decided in the summer of 1938 that Hitler must be resisted. He was jolted back into appeasement again by sheer terror at the spectacle conjured up for him by Colonel Lindbergh. On September 29 he wrote in his diary that since he spoke to Lindbergh on Monday he had come to side with those working for peace at any cost, because of the picture Lindbergh had painted and because of his conviction that the democracies would be defeated.

In this atmosphere of high-minded terror—for Hitler's deadline had expired at 2 P.M. that day—the House of Commons assembled on the afternoon of September 28 to hear Neville Chamberlain report on his efforts to get Hitler to see reason. He described Wilson's visit to Berlin, spoke of the message he had sent to the Führer, and revealed that he had asked Mussolini to use his influence with Hitler to prevent the disaster threatening Europe.

No better description of the moment has been given than that written at the time by Sir Harold Nicolson, a Member of Parliament and a stern opponent of Chamberlain's policies: "September 28,

1938. I walked down to the House at 2:15 P.M., passing through Trafalgar Square and Whitehall. The pigeons are clustering around the fountains and there is a group of children feeding them. My companion says to me, 'Those children should be evacuated at once, and so should the pigeons.' As we get near the House of Commons, there is a large, shuffling, shambling crowd and people putting fresh flowers at the base of the Cenotaph. The crowd is very silent and anxious. They stare at us with numb and inquisitive eyes . . ."

In the House of Commons: "Mr. Chamberlain rose slowly in his place and spread the manuscript of his speech on the box in front of him. The House was hushed in silent expectancy . . . Mr. Chamberlain began with a chronological statement of events. He spoke in calm and measured tones and the House heard him in dead silence . . . The chronological method which he adopted increased the dramatic tension of the occasion . . . He began to tell us of his final appeal to Herr Hitler and Signor Mussolini. I glanced at the clock. It was twelve minutes after four. The P.M. had been speaking for exactly an hour. I noticed that a sheet of F.O. [Foreign Office] paper was being rapidly passed along the Government bench. Sir John Simon interrupted the P.M. and there was a momentary hush. He adjusted his pince-nez and read the document that had been handed to him. His whole face, his whole body, seemed to change. He raised his face so that the light from the ceiling fell full upon it. All the lines of anxiety and weariness seemed suddenly to have been smoothed out; he appeared ten years younger and triumphant. 'Herr Hitler,' he said, 'has just agreed to postpone his mobilisation for twenty-four hours and to meet me in conference with Signor Mussolini and M. Daladier at Munich.' That I think was one of the most dramatic moments which I have ever witnessed. For a second the House was hushed in absolute silence. And then the whole House rose to pay tribute to his achievement." At the side of this entry, Nicolson scribbled: "I remain seated. Liddall (a Tory M.P.) behind me hisses out, 'Stand up, you brute!' "

Winston Churchill ostentatiously stumped out of the Chamber in disgust.* From the Distinguished Strangers' Gallery, Kennedy

---

* His contempt for Chamberlain's actions is well summed up by a remark he made at this time: "The government had to choose between shame and war. They chose shame and they will get war."

beamed his warm approval; like several other Chamberlain intimates, he had received strong hints from the Prime Minister that this was going to happen, and had confidently been reporting for some days that there definitely would be no war. Far from being the fortuitous event which it seemed to the spectators in the House of Commons, there now seems little doubt that Chamberlain knew before he began to speak that a conference at Munich would take place, and that he would be able to announce it in the course of his speech. On the evening of September 27, when Sir Horace Wilson "crawled back" (his own words) from his interviews with Hitler to confess to the Cabinet that he had failed them, the Prime Minister had defended him from the angry reproaches of some of the ministers. Afterward he took Wilson to one side. "You must not worry," he said. "I think you were quite right in what you did." A little later he called Wilson to his office. "I have been thinking things over. I think in the circumstances that it would be a good thing if we have a meeting—Hitler, Mussolini, myself and Daladier. I have taken the necessary action."

Chamberlain had asked for the help of his "good friend" Benito Mussolini, and at seven in the morning on September 28 negotiations were afoot in Berlin through the Italian ambassador, Signor Bernardo Attolico. By lunchtime all was arranged, and an hour later the news was on the way from Rome to London that Hitler had agreed to the meeting.

There is no doubt that Neville Chamberlain was a master of timing.

With the announcement of the Munich Conference, a wave of relief swept through the West. Unlike Chamberlain and Wilson, who had never really believed in it, most of the world had been fearful of the imminence of war. Prayers for peace were still being said in churches; urgent appeals were still going out from President Roosevelt and the Vatican. Some people were disturbed over the prospect of what might happen at Munich, whether a final demand by Hitler or a last-minute stand by Chamberlain and Daladier might not plunge them back into crisis and fear.

They need not have worried. On September 29, while Edouard Daladier was flying to Munich as head of the French delegation,

Georges Bonnet was seeing U.S. Ambassador Bullitt. The Foreign Minister was in a cheerful mood and made no secret of the reason. Bullitt reported to Washington that according to Bonnet, "France positively would not march in support of Czechoslovakia . . . [Beneš] can't refuse. Simply in order to maintain the domination of 7 million Czechs over 3½ million Germans, we will not let Beneš drive 40 million Frenchmen to their deaths, and he knows it."

News that the surgeons at Munich would soon be operating on the body of Czechoslovakia had spread among that country's neighbors; sniffing blood, they had begun to close in. Troops had been mobilized in Hungary and Poland, and ultimatums were being written for dispatch to Prague.

Bullitt reported: "To my amazement, when I referred to the Polish ambassador's statement that the closing of the Czech frontier had placed Czechoslovakia in a bottle in which she would be asphyxiated, since neither Germany, Poland nor Hungary would open the frontiers again until Czechoslovakia agreed to the demands of all three countries, Bonnet replied: 'That would perhaps be the best solution. It would not entail war.' "

In London, Minister Jan Masaryk was called to the Foreign Office to be told of the forthcoming meeting. "But this is a conference to discuss the fate of my country," he said. "Are we not being invited to take part?"

He was told firmly that it was a conference of "the Great Powers only."

"Then I take it," he said, "that the Soviet Union is also being invited. After all, Russia has a treaty with my country too."

With some embarrassment, Lord Halifax replied that there had been no time to invite the Russians, and added that in any case insistence on their presence might have turned Hitler against the whole idea. He did not add that the decision to exclude Russia had been a deliberate one on the part of Neville Chamberlain, at the suggestion of Sir Horace Wilson.*

* "It would only have complicated things," said Wilson to the author. "You couldn't trust the Russians, anyway. They've always been tricky. I remember a cartoon from *Punch* in the eighties entitled 'He Who Sups with the Devil,' and it was about working with Russia. They would have gone to Geneva and made fighting speeches, but I don't think anything more." In fact, throughout the Czech crisis the Russians insisted that they would fulfill their obligations and act in concert with Britain and France.

Masaryk stared up at the pale face of the Foreign Secretary and quietly said, "If you are sacrificing my nation to preserve the peace of the world, I will be the first to applaud you. But if not, God help your souls."

The meeting at Munich between Adolf Hitler, Benito Mussolini, Edouard Daladier and Neville Chamberlain began on the morning of September 29, 1938, and did not end until the agreement was signed at two-thirty the following morning. But in fact it was all over in the first hour, when the four statesmen agreed that Czechoslovakia should be dismembered; what took place afterward was only a haggling over details. Adolf Hitler had brought a huge delegation with him, including Foreign Minister Joachim von Ribbentrop and Field Marshal Hermann Göring, in a shining white uniform and medals jingling from his massive chest. Mussolini had brought his Foreign Minister and son-in-law, Count Ciano. Daladier had with him the shrewd and cynical Chief Secretary of the French Foreign Ministry, Alexis Léger, who had few illusions about the significance of this conference. As usual, Neville Chamberlain had Sir Horace Wilson at his side.

While the great men talked and the world waited for their decisions, so did the Czechs. In an anteroom of the Führerhaus, where the meeting took place, sat two emissaries of Prague waiting to hear their fate. For hours on end no one came near Dr. Voytech Mastny, the Czech minister in Berlin, and Dr. Hubert Masarik, of the Czech Foreign Ministry. At last, almost as an afterthought and at least twelve hours after the meeting had begun, Sir Horace Wilson entered the room.

"It is almost over," he said, smiling happily. "You will be glad to know that we have reached agreement on practically everything."

Dr. Mastny asked grimly, "And what is to be our fate?"

"It is not as bad as it might have been. Herr Hitler has made several concessions." Sir Horace produced a map and spread it on a table in front of the two Czechs, who winced as they looked at it. In appropriately red ink, great chunks of territory had been carved out of Czechoslovakia.* As they looked more closely, Mastny exclaimed

---

* One of the concessions Hitler had made was to move up the deadline for the evacuation from October 1 to October 10.

in anger and amazement, "But this is outrageous! It is cruel and it is criminally stupid. Not only are you giving away our land, but you are sacrificing our defenses. Look, this is our defensive line—and here— and here—and here," stabbing the map with his finger. "All given to the Nazis."

The smile faded from Wilson's face. "I am sorry," he said. "It is no use arguing. I have no time to listen. I must go back to my master."

He hurried away, leaving the Czechs fuming and desperate. Presently another member of the British party arrived, Frank Ashton-Gwatkin, an estimable member of the foreign service but in the circumstances hardly a welcome visitor. He had been a member of the Runciman mission which Chamberlain had sent to Czechoslovakia in the summer, and had allowed himself to be completely fooled by Konrad Henlein, the Sudeten Nazi leader; he described him as "a sincere and honest man" in a report to the Foreign Office at the very moment when, on instructions from Hitler, Henlein was being particularly mendacious. Now Ashton-Gwatkin bounced in to confirm Wilson's earlier message that agreement had been all but reached. "You must be prepared for much harder conditions than perhaps you anticipated," he added.

"But not only we will suffer, but so also will France and Britain if this is allowed to go through," said Hubert Masarik. "You are giving away our flesh and blood, but you are also giving away your own security. Can't we be heard?"

"We should at least be given credit for our sincerity," retorted Ashton-Gwatkin crisply. "It is not very easy having to negotiate with Herr Hitler. Do you accept or not? If you do not, you will have to settle your affairs with the Germans alone, quite alone. Perhaps the French will equivocate a little, but you can believe me when I say that they share our views. They are not interested in Czechoslovakia now."

"Then God help them!" Mastny exclaimed.

So it was over. Hitler had got what he wanted. So had Neville Chamberlain and Sir Horace Wilson. So had Georges Bonnet. At the news that agreement had been reached at Munich, an ecstasy of relief convulsed the people in England, France, America, Italy, even in Germany. War had been averted! The German people, who had been desperately afraid of the consequences if Hitler attacked, cheered Chamberlain and Daladier out of sheer relief—and also hailed the shrewdness of their Führer. The German generals who had been planning revolt threw away their plans and—a little resentfully —saluted this man who could win wars without battles. Even as percipient a statesman as President Roosevelt felt that Munich had cleared the clouds from the international sky, and committed himself to sending a telegram of congratulation to Neville Chamberlain, which Kennedy hurriedly took around to No. 10 Downing Street. But if Kennedy approved of Chamberlain's tactics, he at least realized what their cost might be in the future. "I went over to Ten Downing Street the day I received the cable," he said later, "but instead of handing the cable to Chamberlain, as is customary, I read it to him. I had a feeling that cable would haunt Roosevelt someday, so I kept it."

Only in Czechoslovakia and in the hearts of prophetic men was there pain when they heard of the crime which had been committed. Perhaps some of that pain had even touched a few delegates at Munich when the moment came for the two Czech representatives to be told officially what had been done. Edouard Daladier, filled with a mounting feeling of guilt ("I felt like Judas," he was to say later), wanted to take the coward's way out; he told his delegation that he could not face the Czech emissaries, who were still waiting in the anteroom. Alexis Léger sternly told him that he must steel himself and gave him a large brandy.

Neville Chamberlain felt no such qualms. Earlier he had airily suggested that Daladier fly to Czechoslovakia and convey the news personally to President Beneš of what had been done, and he could not understand why fires blazed in the tired eyes of the Frenchman as he curtly refused the task. (Daladier now confesses that he was nearer to murder that day than ever before in his lifetime.) While the French Premier fortified himself with still another drink, Chamberlain briskly led his delegation back into the conference hall, from which Hitler and Mussolini had triumphantly departed a few moments before.

The Czech emissaries were brought in. "We were taken into the hall where the conference had been held," wrote Masarik later. "There were present Mr. Chamberlain, M. Daladier, Sir Horace Wilson, M. Léger . . . Mr. Ashton-Gwatkin, Dr. Mastny and myself. The atmosphere was oppressive: the sentence was about to be passed.

68

The French, obviously nervous, seemed anxious to preserve French prestige before the court. In a long introductory speech Mr. Chamberlain referred to the agreement and gave the text to Dr. Mastny."

While Mastny, who by now knew the substance of the contents, read through it, Chamberlain remarked that the agreement was perhaps unpalatable but that it had avoided war—and added that in any case it had already been agreed to by the powers. Both Mastny and Masarik noticed that Chamberlain was now yawning frequently and seemed to hear little of what they were saying.

"I asked MM. Daladier and Léger," wrote Masarik, "whether they expected a declaration or answer of our government to the agreement. M. Daladier was noticeably nervous. M. Léger replied that the four statesmen had not much time. He added hurriedly and with superficial casualness that no answer was required from us as they regarded the plan as accepted, that our government had that very day sent its representative to Berlin to sit in on the commission,* and finally that the Czechoslovak officer who was to be sent would have to be in Berlin on Saturday in order to fix the details of the evacuation of the first zone. The atmosphere, he said, was beginning to become dangerous for the whole world. He spoke harshly enough to us. This was a Frenchman . . ."

While the words were being spoken, Mastny had begun to weep openly. When Masarik looked at him, tears came into his eyes too. "They don't know what they are doing," he whispered to his compatriot, "to us or to themselves."

Sir Horace Wilson looked at his master, who was beginning to yawn again. "Come, gentlemen," he said. "It is very late. I am sure we all must be very tired."

There was an awkward silence, and then Chamberlain turned and started for the door, Daladier following.

As they strolled down the street about three o'clock in the morning on their way back to the Vier Jahreszeiten Hotel, Alexis Léger discussed the events of the past day with another French delegate, Captain Paul Stehlin, the assistant air attaché in Berlin.

Stehlin knew as well as Léger the tragedy implicit in the agree-

---

* An International Commission had been agreed upon by the Four Powers to oversee the transfer of people and territory.

ment. He had served in Prague, and he knew and liked the Czechs and admired their esprit, the caliber of their weapons and soldiers, the strength of their defenses, above all their value as allies of France. But though downcast at losing all this, he was still a victim of the euphoria of the moment. Realizing the consequences for France and for Europe of this bloodless defeat, he still believed that it had all been for the best—that at this juncture France could not have fought and won. Though its implications were plain, Munich had its brighter side; for the moment, it had avoided the war which he, like every Frenchman, feared.

"*Mais enfin,*" he said to Léger, "*l'agrément, c'est un soulagement.*" (Anyway, this agreement is a relief.)

Léger was silent for a moment. Then he said, "*Ah oui, un soulagement! Comme quand on a merdé dans sa culotte.*" (Oh yes, a relief! Like crapping in your pants.)

History seems to have proved that it was a good analogy.

70

TWO

The Road to Prague

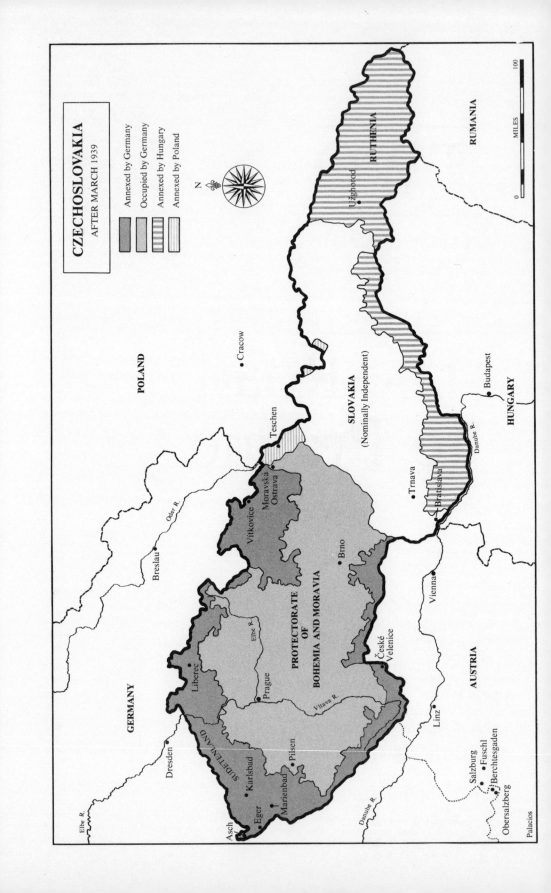

CZECHOSLOVAKIA
AFTER MARCH 1939

Annexed by Germany
Occupied by Germany
Annexed by Hungary
Annexed by Poland

N

MILES

0   100

GERMANY

Elbe R.

Dresden

Asch
Eger
Marienbad
Karlsbad
SUDETENLAND
Pilsen

Liberec
Elbe R.
Prague

PROTECTORATE
OF
BOHEMIA AND MORAVIA

Vltava R.

České
Velenice

Vítkovice
Moravská
Ostrava
Brno

Teschen

Breslau

Oder R.

POLAND

Cracow

SLOVAKIA
(Nominally Independent)

Trnava

Bratislava

RUTHENIA

Užhorod

RUMANIA

Danube R.

HUNGARY

Budapest

Vienna

AUSTRIA

Linz

Danube R.

Salzburg
Fuschl
Berchtesgaden

Obersalzberg

Palacios

IV

"How Long Will This Burlesque Last?"

It was October 3, 1938. For forty-eight hours the German army had been moving into the Sudeten regions of Czechoslovakia, and there had been nothing but chaos and confusion all the way. The armed forces of Adolf Hitler's Greater Germany,* which had so impressed Colonel Lindbergh and the statesmen of Britain and France, had marched into Czechoslovakia on the heels of the Munich Agreement looking rather like a man answering a knock at the front door while still zipping up his trousers. One wonders what would really have happened if the Germans had had to fight their way in.

One general, Walter von Reichenau, was heard to remark that a Czech peasant with a blunderbuss could have held up the army. Reichenau was one of the few members of the General Staff who was an ardent Nazi and a staunch admirer and supporter of Adolf Hitler. It was so unthinkable that he would ever question, much less oppose, the Führer's policies that none of his fellow generals had considered approaching him when they planned their coup d'état in the weeks before the Munich meeting. He would have contemptuously rejected the necessity had they done so, for unlike his colleagues, he never for one moment feared the intervention of the Western allies over the invasion of the Czechoslovak Republic. Like Hitler himself, he be-

* *Grossdeutschland,* so called since the annexation of Austria.

75

lieved implicitly that the democracies were weak and decadent, and he was convinced that under no circumstances would they go to war unless and until they were directly attacked—a contingency which was unlikely to arise until they had first been deprived of such outer defenses as Czechoslovakia.

But even Reichenau had had no conception of how disorganized and unprepared for a campaign were the German forces which crossed the Czech border on October 1. There were disasters almost every mile of the way. Communications broke down; armored columns were immobilized for hours on end because of the dilatoriness of the repair staff and the bad positioning of supply points. *Fali Grün* (Plan Green), as the Czech operation was called, had been meticulously worked out for more than a year and rehearsed over and over again in the summer of 1938; yet none of the lessons seemed to have been learned. As commander of Army Group 4, charged with the occupation of Bohemia from Asch down to the Austrian border, Reichenau had been infuriated by the incompetence of his column commanders. The two miracles which had saved him from complete humiliation were the unquestioning compliance of the Czech army and the blinkered eyes of Adolf Hitler during his visit to the area.

Once President Beneš had accepted the terms of the Munich Agreement and the dismemberment of his country, the order had gone out from Prague to the Czech army and air force confining them to their barracks and grounding their planes. To the amazement of the German High Command, which had expected *some* opposition, even if disorganized, the Czech commanders and their troops had obeyed to the letter. The fortifications which ran through the Sudetenland along the German border were superbly built and sited, using the steep heights of the Bohemian escarpment to bring natural defenses to the aid of concrete bunkers and heavy guns. The Czech army gunners and infantrymen filed out of them docilely and locked themselves in their barracks. Behind them, the air force pilots retired to their messes and peach brandy, and proceeded to get quietly drunk, leaving their planes undisturbed and unsabotaged on the airfields. An army of 750,000 men had been mobilized by the Czechs and an air force of 1,360 planes was waiting to do battle with the Luftwaffe, and until the news came of the Munich Agreement they were ready to preserve the sovereignty of their country. Now, forty-eight hours

76

later, they waited passively for the Germans, who gave thanks for their amazing subservience.

Adolf Hitler crossed the frontier at Wildenau and drove in triumph through the crowds of cheering Sudetens. He failed to notice the empty tanks squatting just off the road and the trucks grounded by lack of fuel. Inspecting a group of Czech bunkers in the hills above Karlsbad, he slapped Reichenau on the back, elated at the thought that they had been captured intact. "Let's see what they're made of," he said. "Put some shells into them."

A tank and a mobile gun were brought up to within three hundred yards of one of the bunkers and ordered to start shelling. It took five direct hits before a major penetration was made. Hitler looked thoughtful, then cheered and began to laugh. "What does it matter how strong the concrete is," he said, "so long as the will is weak!"

They drove back down to Karlsbad along a road already packed with Czech refugees making their way eastward out of the Sudetenland and into Czechoslovakia proper. Hitler frowned when he noticed some of the German troops handing out cups of hot soup and hunks of bread to the refugees. "Why do they waste good German bread on those pigs?" he asked Reichenau.

He did not seem to realize that it was Czech bread, confiscated by the Germans; nor that the Czechs were leaving their homes, where their families had lived for generations, with only the clothes they were wearing. By the terms of the Munich Agreement, they were forbidden to take along their furniture, household goods or even the family horses or cows on their trek eastward. Checkpoints on the way into Pilsen were manned by SS *Kommandos** who searched thoroughly and made sure that nothing larger than a watch or a piece of jewelry got through. The Sudeten Germans trying to escape to Prague fared even worse; for many of them the route was westward to the concentration camps at Dachau and Osnabrück.

On October 3 General von Reichenau took over the Park Hotel in Karlsbad as his headquarters and proceeded to drink the hotel

---

* The *Einsatzkommandos,* one of Himmler's innovations, were used here for the first time. Culled from the *Sicherheitsdienst* (or SS Security Service, under the notorious Reinhard Heydrich), these cold-blooded killers were to follow on the heels of the German army in the campaigns against Poland and the West, and later in Russia, spreading fear and terror among the civilian populations by their ruthless "cleaning-up" actions.

dry of its stock of champagne. Sitting in the vast lounge of the hotel, he shouted drunkenly to a companion, "What a shambles! If our enemies only knew what a mess we have made of it! Beneš was a fool not to fight!"

The man on the opposite side of the table was Major Hans Grosscurth of the Abwehr. With his two chiefs, Admiral Canaris and Colonel Hans Oster, he had been touring the Sudetenland since the first troops crossed the frontier. Like Reichenau, he too had been appalled at what he had seen during his journey, though for different reasons. It was not the disorganization that shocked him, but the behavior of Himmler's armed units which had operated as part of the 4th Division.

"The SS Standarte [regiment] Germania has murdered, pillaged and evicted in a bestial fashion [*viehischer Weise*]," he wrote in his report. "I saw one unfortunate girl who had been raped nine times by a gang of these rascals [*Lausbuben*], while her father had been murdered and her mother locked in a closet and left to scream. Admittedly, the girl was Czech and these troops believe all they have read in our newspapers about Czech atrocities against our brothers [*Sudeten Volksgenossen*]. But that does not excuse them for having set fire to the farm where the girl and her family had been living. It is most wasteful, for the farm will be taken over by a Sudeten and now there is nowhere to live."

Nor had the Einsatzkommandos or the Gestapo agents who swarmed in behind them shown much more concern for the rights and dignities of the Sudetens themselves. Earlier that day Grosscurth had visited the wife of Konrad Henlein, the Sudeten leader, and found her nervous and apprehensive about her husband's future. "They are trying to push him out," she said. "He has as many enemies among the Gestapo as he has among the Czechs."

Grosscurth thought that she was exaggerating, but when he drove over to Eger to consult with Karl Hermann Frank, Henlein's deputy, he too hinted at a sinister campaign against the Sudeten leader, and angrily charged the Gestapo with making mass arrests of Sudetens "so that Reich Germans can move in and take over our jobs." He added, "I tell you, we are coming to the conclusion that the fight to get our freedom from the Czechs will be nothing like as bitter as the fight to keep our jobs and our lands from the Reich Germans."

Grosscurth wrote in his diary: "I went on to Marienbad, where we talked to the commanding general [Raschick] and Lieutenant Colonel Köhler of the G. Kdos XIII [one of the specially trained Abwehr units]. They were very angry because the Gestapo had already begun arresting many of the members of the Sudeten German party. We had already heard from Frank in Eger that difficulties were being experienced. Frank had found two men in the SD who had been spreading hate against Henlein. We also spoke at H.Q. to Gauleiter Frank,* a former Austrian General Staff Officer, who also complained in the strongest possible terms against the Gestapo arrests. Frank spoke of the 'rascals' of the Gestapo who destroy everything . . . He said that a new clique was being built up that was anti-Henlein and that an infamous power struggle was beginning. These things must be told to the Army Group commander [Reichenau] and his chief of staff in Karlsbad."

So now Grosscurth was at the Park Hotel in Karlsbad to make his report to Reichenau. But as he stared at the bleary-eyed general opposite him, he decided that it was no moment to plead the cause of the Czechs or Sudetens. Having damned the army dunderheads who had made such a mess of the occupation arrangements, Reichenau had now passed on to his two favorite subjects, Adolf Hitler and himself.

"Just think," he said, "with Czechoslovakia at our mercy and not a shot fired! No wonder I find inspiration in my Führer! He has no fear, even when the stakes he is playing for may involve him in war with the West if he loses. I tell you, Grosscurth, if the Führer were a poker player he would win a hundred thousand marks every evening." He gulped some more champagne and laughed. "But he is playing for more than that. Oh, yes. This is only the first stage. I can let you in on a secret. Within a very short time, the Führer is going to solve the whole Czech business. Not just the Sudetenland—the whole lot. Not only that. Just wait, you'll find that he will be active and at work in other places as well."

Reichenau gazed at the Abwehr officer and nodded solemnly. Grosscurth ventured the opinion that so far the Führer's policy had only involved the return of German nationals (*Volksgenossen*) to

* District leader and Sudeten member of the Czech Senate.

79

the Reich. The rest of Czechoslovakia was something else again; its integrity had been guaranteed at Munich, and this time the Western democracies might react sharply to an act of aggression.

"They don't have the guts!" said Reichenau. "Shall I tell you what the Führer thinks of Chamberlain and Daladier? Chamberlain is an old man and the Führer can put him in his pocket any time he wants to. As for Daladier, he is nothing more than a master baker."* The general shook his head. "I can tell you, I'm an optimist. I hate war. But there won't be any, take it from me."

Still drinking and talking, the general now began to boast of how highly Hitler thought of him, of how soon he was going to be promoted, and what he intended to do to the General Staff once he had the power. Finally Grosscurth took his leave and wandered out into the main street of Karlsbad. A German army band was playing on the stand in front of the ornate bathhouse. Where Kaiser Wilhelm, King Edward VII and the gouty aristocrats of Europe used to stroll, Nazi Brown Shirts and SS men in their black uniforms now stood around self-consciously sipping the warm waters of the spa through the spouts of porcelain jugs. Several of them had brought their wives or girl friends, who prattled excitedly about the shopping sprees they had been on since their arrival. All the clothes, cosmetics, cooking fats and wines which had long since disappeared from Germany were available here in abundance, and at bargain prices. Like locusts, the Reich Germans were devouring the stocks—realizing, unlike the Sudetens, that there would be no more after this. Grosscurth thought cynically that even when they were in uniform it was easy to tell the Sudetens from the Reich Germans; the Sudetens were the ones with disenchanted expressions on their faces.

■

In Hradčany Castle in Prague, President Beneš was in his study overlooking the Vltava (Moldau) River. The evening sky was cloudy on this fourth day of October and there was a hint of rain in the air. It was symptomatic of the subdued gloom of the time that the power system of the city seemed suddenly to have developed a malaise, and

* Grosscurth later reported this description of Daladier by Hitler to one of his staff. "There speaks a master painter about a master baker," he added wryly.

80

the lights in the room and on the Charles Bridge, spanning the river from old city to new, had gone dim.

In a few minutes General Jan Syrový, the former Commander in Chief of the Armed Forces, who had taken over the premiership just before the Munich crisis, and the new Foreign Minister, František Chvalkovský, would arrive with their aides for a meeting which Beneš had set for eight-fifteen. Eduard Beneš did not look forward to it, for it would put the stamp of finality on the tragedy which had been played out in the past five weeks.

To those who had known Beneš in his heyday, he now presented a haunted figure of desolation. Once he had been the gay, witty, debonair leader of what had been the most advanced and enlightened democracy in Central Europe; now he was the despairing President of a nation which had been butchered, its virility and independence gone. It was typical of the character of Eduard Beneš that even now he did not rail or rage against those whom he might have blamed, just as in his telephone conversations with his London minister it was always Jan Masaryk who bitterly cursed Hitler, Chamberlain and Daladier. Beneš was much more inclined to inveigh against himself— possibly with some justice. Pinned to his desk was an aphorism which he had once cut out of an American magazine because it had both amused and impressed him. It read: "If you are in need of a helping hand, never forget that there is one at the end of your arm."

Had Beneš been wrong in refusing to allow Czechoslovakia's arm to be raised in her own defense? Were his Communist critics in Prague right when they said that "the trouble with Beneš was that no matter what happened to Czechoslovakia, he knew that he was safe." The quip circulating around the city was: "He keeps telling us that he has a plan, but what he really has is an *aeroplan,* waiting at the air-field to take him to safety."

In the days before the meeting at Munich, there had been several occasions when Beneš was fully prepared to fight, come what may. He was confident that he would have the majority of his people behind him and that his army and air force would fulfill their tasks not only with bravery but with skilled efficiency.* He also had a promise from

* The Germans claimed afterward that if Czechoslovakia had decided to fight, they had a plan to blitz their airfields and destroy their planes before advancing. But the Czechs also had a plan for attacks on eastern Germany with exactly the same purpose.

the Russians—and an indication that the promise would be kept. By the second week of September, the Soviet army had moved 30 infantry and 10 cavalry divisions, 1 tank corps, 3 tank brigades and 12 air brigades to her frontier with Poland toward Czechoslovakia. Over 328,000 reservists had been called up, and an additional 30 infantry and 10 cavalry divisions were in a state of readiness. All through the summer of 1938, the Russians had been building an airfield at Vinnitsa in the Ukraine, close to the Rumanian frontier. At the beginning of September twenty Russian bombers took off from this airfield, flew across Rumanian territory and landed at the Užhgorod airfield in Czechoslovakia. They were the first batch of a total of sixty bombers which the Russians had promised Zdenek Fierlinger, head of the Czech diplomatic mission in Moscow, and which they would deliver to the Czech air force for use against the Germans in the event of war. With the planes came a commitment from Maxim Litvinov, Commissar for Foreign Affairs, and his deputy, Vladimir Potemkin, that Russian aid would be forthcoming should Czechoslovakia be involved in war with Germany, and that neither planes nor pilots would be stinted.* At the same time Litvinov informed Beneš that the Soviet ambassador in Warsaw had talked to Colonel Józef Beck, the Polish Foreign Minister. He had heard that the Poles, eager to be in on the kill if and when Germany attacked, were planning to move troops to the northern borderlands of Czechoslovakia, in the Teschen area, where there was a Polish minority. The Russians curtly informed the Poles that any aggression against the Czechs would be viewed with the utmost gravity by Moscow, and that appropriate action would be taken.

The Russians could not have made it plainer to their Czechoslovakian ally that they would be by her side. Beneš had seen the Soviet minister in Prague, Alexandrovsky, on September 19 and asked him two questions: 1) Would Russia fulfill her treaty obligations even if France failed to fulfill hers? and 2) How would Russia

---

* This and other Soviet offers of aid and support were always viewed with contempt by Chamberlain and Bonnet, on the grounds that Rumania—which separated Czechoslovakia from the U.S.S.R.—would never allow troops to cross or planes to fly over its territory. They never asked the Rumanians to clarify the position. But as early as September 15 Rumania had withdrawn its objection. In fact, one Soviet plane which force-landed in Rumania on its way to Czechoslovakia was repaired and sent on its way.

fulfill her treaty obligations if France reneged after Czechoslovakia had become involved in a war with Germany? Alexandrovsky had consulted Moscow and got a definite yes to the first question, and a rigmarole about the League of Nations in reply to the second. Beneš asked for further clarification, and Alexandrovsky thereupon consulted Moscow again. On September 21 he told Beneš: *Should it come to a war, with Germany as the aggressor, this would be sufficient for the Czechoslovak government to make a formal complaint at Geneva and so inform the Soviet Union, which would thereupon fulfill its obligations.*

Then why had Beneš decided not to fight? Did he not trust the Russians? He never indicated later that they would not have fulfilled their pledge. It is doubtful whether even he could explain, except to excuse himself on the grounds of exhaustion, despair, fear of Communist domination, the fact that he was a liberal of Western mentality, and that the betrayal by his French ally and so-called British friends had numbed him into accepting defeat. Set against that appalling desertion, the Russian offer of aid and support made no impact on his mind; Beneš deliberately never even tried to find out if it was unconditional.* The final blow, which had virtually destroyed all of Beneš' remaining pride and confidence, was the Polish betrayal. Czechoslovakia had a treaty of friendship with Poland, and Beneš had always made it clear to the Poles that he was willing to make an amicable adjustment of the territories around Teschen. But that was not what the Poles wanted. Foreign Minister Beck was a man of few scruples who wanted to present his people with both a crisis and a victory. Neither of these would make headlines if the Czechs took the wind out of his sails by giving in, so he ignored all the friendly gestures made by Beneš. He took the risk—the Poles always seemed ready to take risks where the Russians were concerned—of ignoring Soviet Russia's warning, and sent Czechoslovakia an ultimatum on September 30 demanding that it get out of the Teschen area within twelve hours.†

* Russian spokesmen have always maintained that it was; that they were waiting for Beneš to resist and to ask for their help.
† Beneš was to write bitterly later that the Polish ultimatum "is almost identical with the ultimatum which Hitler sent to Beck himself a year later with respect to the solution of the question of Danzig. This is certainly characteristic. Perhaps the chief difference lay in the fact that the ultimatum of the Polish government to Czechoslovakia was limited to twelve hours." The Germans gave the Poles two days.

Beneš gave way once more, as he had given way to the British and the French and the Germans. He was done; there was no more fight in him. "The reply sent to me by the Poles," he wrote afterward of Warsaw's rejection of his plea for talks, "provided me with the last and decisive reason for the fact that *in spite of the insistence of Moscow, I did not provoke war with Germany in 1938*. But it was clear to me already in September 1938 that Poland would pay a terrible price for what she had done . . ."

Now the Poles were moving into Teschen, "like the ghouls who in former centuries crawled about the battlefield to kill and rob the dead and wounded."* Beneš realized that he had better leave the country which he had done so much to create and which somehow, enlightened spirit though he was, he had so abysmally failed to rally when the crisis came. It was ironic that his departure should subject him to yet one more humiliation. He had been determined to resign the moment the Munich Agreement was announced, but as the first German troops marched into Czechoslovakia the following day, October 1, Field Marshal Göring summoned the Czech minister in Berlin to see him. Adolf Hitler, he told Dr. Mastny, could not bear the thought that Eduard Beneš still remained President of the Czech republic. He must go, and go quickly; if he did not, the German government would act with the utmost savagery in implementing the terms of the Munich Agreement. Thus, even the old man's resignation would now seem to be yet another capitulation to the Nazis.

There was a knock on the door and a secretary entered to announce that the ministers had arrived. Eduard Beneš took his place at the head of the conference table. General Syrový, dabbing at a troublesome tear duct leaking moisture below the black patch covering his blind eye, took his place on the right and Foreign Minister Chvalkovský the seat on the left. The electric lights were jumping very fitfully now.

"Gentlemen," said Eduard Beneš, "these are trying times and cruel ones, and I know that you have much to occupy your minds. But I can at least lift one burden from your shoulders. You will be relieved to know that as of this moment I, Eduard Beneš, am no longer President of the Republic of Czechoslovakia . . ."

* François-Poncet, French ambassador to Germany.

. . .

Down below in the Old City, the great bell called Sigismund began to toll from the tower of St. Vitus' Cathedral, calling the people of Prague to evening service. Ever since the announcement of Munich, the churches throughout the land had been packed with citizens praying for their country, for themselves and for their children. There were few tears to be seen on their faces; once the realization of the partition of their country had sunk in, they had reacted with fear and anger.

That morning in St. Vitus', the Primate of the Ancient Kingdom of Bohemia had read a prayer from the pulpit: "The land of Saint Wenceslas has just been invaded by foreign armies, and our thousand-year-old frontier has been violated. This sacrifice has been imposed on the nation of Saint Wenceslas by our ally, France, and our friend, Britain. As Primate of the Ancient Kingdom of Bohemia, I pray to God Almighty that the peace efforts prompting this terrible sacrifice will be crowned with success. Should they not, I pray to the Almighty to forgive all those who impose this injustice upon the people of Czechoslovakia."

The congregation dutifully said "Amen," but that was hardly the measure of their feelings.

■

At the Foreign Ministry on the Wilhelmstrasse in Berlin, members of the so-called International Commission were in session. By the terms of the Munich Agreement the evacuation of the Czech army and civilian population in the Sudetenland had to "be completed by the 10 October, without any existing installations having been destroyed," so the question of settling the new frontiers of the Second Czech Republic was urgent.

The International Commission comprised the Undersecretary of State for Foreign Affairs, Baron Ernst von Weizsäcker, the ambassadors André François-Poncet, Bernardo Attolico and Sir Nevile Henderson, and the Czech minister, Dr. Vojtech Mastny, together with their staffs and military advisers. All disputes over frontier adjustments were to be discussed and decided by mutual agreement.

It hardly worked out that way. From the start, the Germans made

85

it clear that they were not going to stand any nonsense from the other delegates, and that they were determined to grab every inch of territory, every industrial area, every railway line and every fortification which came remotely near the Sudetenland.*

After the first formal meeting of the commission, Baron von Weizsäcker turned the direction of the German delegation over to Colonel Walter Warlimont of the Armed Forces High Command (OKW), who gave short shrift to the diplomats. Sir Nevile Henderson, who had worked so hard to bring about Munich and who had never made a secret—at least to the Germans—of his loathing of the Czechs, smiled at the Nazis with the expression of a good dog which now expects to be thrown a bone. His attitude seemed to be, "Well now, we've got what we wanted and have put those irritating Czechs in their places, so can't we afford to be a bit magnanimous and sometimes give them the benefit of the doubt?"

Not for the first time, the British ambassador was misjudging the men with whom he was dealing. The High Command had no intention of showing magnanimity; they wanted their pound of flesh and more. When Warlimont indicated on a map the demand for a whole industrial area largely inhabited by Czechs, Henderson coughed deprecatingly and said, "But that's a bit much, surely. Couldn't we possibly spare that?"

Warlimont replied, "You might possibly spare it for them, Excellency, but then, it is not in your power to do so. The High Command of the Wehrmacht has already decided that the region is part of the Sudetenland, and it will be annexed accordingly."

Henderson looked like a cur that has just been kicked. Afterward his colleagues were to say that whenever anyone mentioned the International Commission, he flushed.

Mastny was treated with such contempt that he lapsed into gloomy silence. His military adviser, General Husarek, tried a different tactic and took François-Poncet urgently to one side. "Don't you realize," he asked, "that not only are the Germans taking over our fortifications, but are also getting the guns inside them? Those guns were made by Skoda and they are the best in the world. Where do you

---

* The only concession they made was to order Sudeten irregulars out of part of the old Bohemian town of Pilsen. Not even the Germans could claim this as being Sudeten.

think they will go if you allow the Germans to have them? To man the Siegfried Line against France, that's where!"

François-Poncet said he would immediately make a call to Paris and ask for power to intervene. He spoke to Foreign Minister Georges Bonnet, who listened to him and then said curtly, "Forget it. Don't argue with them. It's all over. Let the Germans have anything they want."

François-Poncet returned, shaking his head in despair. "At least I did consult my government," he said afterward. "Nevile Henderson didn't bother to ask anyone. He simply nodded his head and agreed to everything."

Ironically enough, it was only the Italian ambassador who continued to side with the Czechs and fight the Germans when their claims went too far. But it was no use. Like their President after Munich, the Czechs suddenly seemed to lose heart, as if they realized the hopelessness of their position, and soon they began turning more and more toward their enemies, the Germans, rather than their old allies, the British and French.

Captain Paul Stehlin, who was a member of the French military delegation, sensed the feelings of the Czechs at the second meeting of the commission. Walking into the conference room at the first session, "I was filled with an intense emotion as I looked at the officers of the Czech delegation. The decorations which they wore on the chests of their uniforms demonstrated how many of them had once fought for France: there were Légion d'honneur, Médaille militaire, Croix de guerre medals among them. But when the officers appeared at the second session, there were blank spaces where they had been—to show how they felt about the way we had abandoned them.

"The German delegation did not lose any time in making it brutally clear to us that the Sudetenland was going to be occupied strictly according to the orders of the Wehrmacht. The directives which the three other delegations received played into their hands. They were vague, imprecise; they always counseled conciliation, which in other words meant 'Don't argue.' In any case, even when we did ask for guidance, it always arrived so late that the Germans were able to take advantage of us. Three times in the course of our meetings we saw Colonel Warlimont get up, leave the room followed by his colleagues and then come back a few minutes later and begin his

statement with 'The High Command of the Wehrmacht has decided . . .' The arrogance and intentions of Hitler appeared—clap!
just like that. The period of euphoria which had emerged for a brief
time at Munich was of short duration. The atmosphere started getting
heavy and threatening again."

At Munich, Britain and France had signed a rider to the agreement which stated: "His Majesty's Government in the United Kingdom and the French Government have entered into the above Agreement on the basis that they stand by the offer, contained in paragraph
6 of the Anglo-French proposals of the 19 September, relating to an
international guarantee of the new boundaries of the Czechoslovak
State against unprovoked aggression . . ."

It was obvious what the Czechs thought about that. "From the
second day," said Stehlin, "in addition to unhooking their French
decorations, the Czech delegation showed every sign of ignoring the
French, British and Italian delegations, and of talking directly to the
Germans. 'Look,' said the British military attaché, 'it's as if they were
allies of the Germans already.' "

In the circumstances, it is difficult to understand how he could
have expected otherwise.

In Paris, joy was still in the air. *Le Petit Parisien,* a right-wing journal
with a wide circulation (and a regular subsidy from the Germans),
opened a visitors' book in which all who approved of the Munich
Agreement were invited to inscribe their names. They collected a million signatures. *Paris-Soir* began a subscription to buy Neville Chamberlain a house in the Dordogne, where he could fish in peace and
comfort and reflect on how grateful the French people were to him
for having saved the peace. The fund reached 500,000 francs in three
days.* Edouard Daladier, who was so frightened on coming home
from Munich that he made the plane circle twice when he saw the
crowd surrounding the airfield, had received not only a kiss on both
cheeks from Bonnet but a hero's welcome all the way into Paris.
However, he was not deluded by this popular euphoria, and did not

* The house was neither built nor bought. I have been unable to discover what
happened to the subscriptions.

forget for one moment that the document he had signed at Munich was not only dishonorable, not only a defeat, but above all dangerous for France. Later he was to confess that he needed solace during the days that followed, and got very little from the people around him. The only event he approved of was the decision of the senior Roman Catholic dignitary in Paris, Cardinal Verdier, who was approached by zealous members of the government and asked to order the bells of Notre Dame to be rung in celebration of the peace. They were firmly told that the bells would not be rung even in despair, but would remain silent in mourning for what had been done.

Daladier's feeling of guilt would have provoked only contempt in Neville Chamberlain, had anyone drawn his attention to it. Not only was the Prime Minister also a popular hero for what he had achieved at Munich, but he was confident that it was an acclamation truly deserved. He had capped his coup by bringing back to England, along with the Munich Agreement, a document which deserves to enter the history books as one of the most mischievously false declarations, both in content and in promise, ever to have been foisted upon a gullible public.

In the morning hours after Munich, as the German army made ready to march into its bloodlessly conquered territories in the Sudetenland, as the Czech refugees began to flee eastward, as the Sudeten German Social Democrats began to wonder how long it would be before the Gestapo caught up with them, as the armies of Poland and Hungary began to close in on Czechoslovakia's flanks, Neville Chamberlain had driven to Adolf Hitler's apartment in Munich. It was a rendezvous he had personally requested, having buttonholed the Reich Chancellor the previous night just before Hitler marched out of the Führerhaus with Mussolini to celebrate the signing of the agreement.

William Strang, who was a member of Chamberlain's delegation, had gone to bed at three o'clock in the morning, but was awakened by a phone call from the Prime Minister at seven.

"I have an appointment with Herr Hitler after breakfast," Chamberlain said. "I want some sort of statement I can persuade him to sign—about future Anglo-German relations—the sort of thing he will approve of. You know the form. Will you draw me up a draft?"

Strang got out of bed, and while dressing and breakfasting "composed three paragraphs," which he then took along to Chamberlain's suite for him to read. Chamberlain looked it over, rewrote the second paragraph and made some other minor changes. "This should do it," he said. "I think Herr Hitler will be pleased."

He asked Strang about the noise outside the window and was told that there was a crowd in the streets below come to applaud him for "what he had done to save the peace." Strang suggested that he go out on the balcony and acknowledge the cheers of the multitude. Chamberlain immediately did so, and came back much enlivened. "Indeed they like me," he said.

Strang asked the Prime Minister whether the French knew that he was going to see Hitler, and whether they shouldn't see the statement which had been concocted. Chamberlain looked annoyed and curtly said that it was none of their business. This was to be a strictly Anglo-German occasion.

Half an hour later Chamberlain was with Adolf Hitler, and in another hour he emerged triumphantly from the Führer's apartment and was driven to the plane waiting to take him back to England. As in the case of Daladier's return to Paris, a hysterically happy crowd awaited him in London. Excited by the cheering, he pulled out a piece of paper. "It is peace in our time," he said, waving it before them. Then, like an awestruck fan who cannot quite believe that he has had the good luck to capture an elusive celebrity's signature, he said, "See, here is a paper that bears his name."

The document held aloft by Chamberlain was a promise that Britain and Germany would never go to war against each other, and it reinforced—at least the Prime Minister believed it did—Adolf Hitler's claim that his last territorial ambition in Europe had now been fulfilled, that Germany was now satisfied, that there would be no more trouble.

There were those in England who were skeptical. One of them was Alfred Duff Cooper, who resigned his seat in the Cabinet as First Lord of the Admiralty. Winston Churchill arose to make a ponderous speech in the House of Commons spelling out the defeat which Britain had suffered at Munich, and was greeted by catcalls from other members. With a contemptuous smirk, Chamberlain himself remarked that anyone who criticized Britain for having agreed to Munich was "fouling his own nest." A Member who suggested that a loan to the Czech government was a new version of "thirty pieces of silver" was knocked down by a passionate pro-appeaser.

Still there were skeptics. One of them was sufficiently bold to suggest to Chamberlain that perhaps Adolf Hitler was deceiving him, that the Führer had made promises before and then broken them.

"You see, my dear fellow," said the British Prime Minister, "this time it is different; this time he has made his promises to me."

But if Neville Chamberlain had no doubts, the British people were soon by no means so happy. The first feelings of relief were giving way to uneasiness and guilt, especially when they began to read reports in their newspapers from the Sudetenland and Czecho-Slovakia.* They had been assured by their government that the partition would be implemented in civilized fashion and that the Nazis would take no more from the Czechs than that territory whose population was overwhelmingly German. But now they read of ruthless annexations of vast areas for purely strategic or economic reasons, without any ethnic justification. By October 10, 1938, Czechoslovakia had not only lost her President but most of her only railway system, 70 percent of her iron and steel resources, 76 percent of her railway carriage works, 80 percent of her textiles, 80 percent of her cement works, 90 percent of her porcelain and glass works, 40 percent of her timber and 70 percent of her electrical power supplies. Pathetic stories were beginning to filter back of evicted Czech refugees streaming out of the Sudetenland, the homeland where their families had lived for generations.

But there were other refugees too, and for them the future was even more horrible. Until the very last there was a sizable proportion of German-speaking inhabitants in the Sudetenland (their numbers were estimated at half a million) who had refused to join the Nazi party and who opposed the return of the territory to Germany. Konrad Henlein had vowed to "make them suffer until they turn black." Right on the heels of the German troops crossing the frontier the Gestapo, with the Reichsführer-SS Himmler and his vicious assistant, Heydrich, directed the hunt for Social Democrats and Communists. But thousands of them, warned in time, escaped to

* Since Munich, the name was officially spelled with a hyphen, to give "equal importance" to the country's two main ethnic groups.

91

Czechoslovakia proper and took refuge in Pilsen, Brno and Prague. This infuriated the Gestapo chiefs and they sent angry telegrams to Berlin demanding action in Prague. The German minister there, Ernst Eisenlohr, a decent and civilized man, was ordered by Berlin to demand the return of the refugees from General Syrový. Not willing to resist anything now, the embittered Syrový gave in, and an agreement was drawn up and signed on October 15. Significantly, it was backdated to October 1. "It will save us having to feed them," Syrový said coldly.

When the news of this shabby deal became known, there was an outcry both inside Czechoslovakia and out. British social workers, including teams of young women, had already arrived at the refugee camps and were hard at work there. The British people had started a fund for the refugees and raised £318,000 by mid-October. But when Werner Jaksch, the Social Democratic leader, flew to London to plead for something more valuable than money—visas to enable his people to leave before they were delivered up to the Gestapo and the concentration camps—he found officialdom adamant. He pleaded with Lord Runciman, who had been Chamberlain's emissary in Czechoslovakia that summer, to intercede for his people with the Prime Minister. "You cannot allow this cruel campaign to succeed," he said. "It is just revenge on the part of the Sudeten Nazis because we would not join them. Why, the pact Syrový has signed with Berlin has even been backdated to Munich so that everyone of us will be caught in the net."

Lord Runciman looked uncomfortable. "I believe the Lord Mayor [of London] is opening a fund for you, and if so you will certainly find my name among the contributors."

"But it is visas, visas, visas that we need!" cried Jaksch.

Visas were just what they were not going to get. Chamberlain would rather have a few thousand Sudetens turned over to the Gestapo than offend his new German friends. Having established what he firmly believed to be a "close rapport" with Adolf Hitler, he did not wish to irritate him.

Meanwhile the Lord Mayor of London, Sir Harry Twyford, flew to Prague to personally deliver funds for the refugees. After several days and some urgent requests, he was eventually received by General Syrový.

John Wheeler-Bennett, who went to Hradčany Castle with the

Lord Mayor for the interview, wrote afterward: "[Syrový] was a changed man from the one who had been prepared to fight, if necessary alone. Now he was adamant about the refugees whose return—all those who were registered on October 1—Germany was demanding. They were now being rounded up by the Czech police."

Sir Harry Twyford pleaded with the Czech leader to let at least those refugees be spared who had entered Czechoslovakia before the signing of the pact on October 15. Syrový "glared balefully through his one eye, and his black patch quivered." He replied, "Not fifteen days, not fifteen minutes! The Germans have asked for them and back they go!"

This was delivered in a high, emotional falsetto. Syrový then rose and began pacing the room, as if to calm himself. Speaking more quietly, he added, "In this affair, messieurs, we have been willing to fight on the side of the angels. Now we shall hunt with the wolves."

In the Sudetenland itself, while waiting for their victims, Himmler and Heydrich were superintending the opening of a new training school for SS recruits in a castle at Hirschberg. Both of them sensed that the time was coming when they would need more personnel to keep pace with the Führer's plans to have the Gestapo rule the new and expanding territories of Greater Germany and to carry out the raids on spies, Social Democrats, Reds, Jews and other elements hostile to the Reich, and to have the SS man the new concentration camps that would be opened as a result.

Inside the castle at Hirschberg as they arrived, the new candidates were drawn up to greet the two men, hands stiffly lifted in the Nazi salute, "Heil Hitler!" on their lips. All of them had been filtered through the rigid screening tests to which aspirants for the SS were subjected, and had answered meticulous questionnaires demanding details of their ancestry as far back as the fourth generation. A succession of inspectors had ordered them to strip and then examined them. (A circumcised male was subjected to particularly intensive scrutiny.) The length of their ear lobes was measured, the color of their eyes and hair noted, and—because Heydrich had a theory about this—the inspectors sniffed under their arms to determine whether the odor they exuded was of a "Nordic" or "Semitic" character.

Now, dressed again, they awaited a final review from their

masters. Himmler left it to Heydrich to decide whether a candidate had the right Nordic physical characteristics to be a member of this elite corps. It was a chore that the Reichsführer's deputy particularly enjoyed. He was a tall, slim, handsome, artistic-looking man with a face that rather resembled a bird: thin cheeks, lofty brow, beak-like long nose and delicate nostrils. As one of his chief assistants, Walter Schellenberg, once said, he had "an incredibly acute perception of the moral, human, professional and political weaknesses of others . . . His unusual intellect was matched by the ever-watchful instincts of a predatory animal, always alert to danger and ready to act swiftly and ruthlessly." He also had what Schellenberg called an "ungovernable sexual appetite." To this he would surrender himself without inhibition or caution, and the calculated control which characterized him in everything else deserted him completely. But in the end he always regained sufficient mastery over himself to prevent serious repercussions.

Heydrich passed down the line of earnest recruits, their blue eyes ablaze with ideological fervor, the young men in their lederhosen, the girls in gray skirts and green leather jackets, fair hair falling to their shoulders. It was the beginning of an intensive period of recruitment by the SS.

■

Adolf Hitler had long since decided that the Munich Agreement was far from being the victory which all other nations had conceded him. True, it had demonstrated the weakness and decadence of the Western powers—but that he had always suspected. What it had not done was give him the complete control of Czechoslovakia which he would have won in the summer of 1938 had not Britain and France got in his way. "That fellow has cheated me of my entry into Prague," he said when he returned to Berlin. He was talking about Neville Chamberlain.

On October 9, while the Prime Minister was still happily talking in London of "a new era of peace and good European relations," Adolf Hitler went to Saarbrücken to make a speech. It was a peculiarity of his that even when he despised the British most he never failed to be irritated, even infuriated, when they attacked him, and in the

94

past days the criticism in the British press and the speeches in the House of Commons had wounded him, particularly one by Winston Churchill.

"It would be a good thing if people in Great Britain would gradually drop certain airs which they have inherited from the Versailles period," Hitler declared in his address. "We cannot any longer tolerate the tutelage of governesses. Inquiries of the fate of Germans within the frontiers of the Reich—or of others belonging to the Reich—are not to be endured. We will not stand them. We would like to give these gentlemen the advice that they should keep their noses in their own affairs and leave us alone."

Sir Horace Wilson took the transcript of the speech into the Prime Minister's room, saying, "Master, I'm afraid you are not going to like this."

Chamberlain read it through and said, "It's that damn Winston! Headlines, that's all he's interested in." Then he cheered up. "But whatever he says, he can't really challenge us. We are on a firm wicket. Hitler has promised me, and I believe him. We have made Europe safe."

It was just about the time that Chamberlain was talking in this fashion to Wilson that the Führer decided to make another visit to the Sudetenland, this time a tour of the fortifications which the Czechs had built between Austria and their own territory in the frontier country north of Linz. Major Grosscurth, who was by now attached to the entourage of Konrad Henlein, was asked to bring the Sudeten party leader to Linz without delay. "We went by way of Obersalzberg to Linz," he wrote in his diary on October 16, "where I found in the hotel the drunken Obergruppenführer [SS Lieutenant General] Bruckner and the likewise drunken adjutant, Schmundt. No quarters for us, only for Henlein."

The next morning Henlein joined Hitler and General Wilhelm Ritter von Leeb, the local commander, at the head of a motorcade and traveled north to the old Czechoslovakian frontier at České Velenice. They drove on toward Bohemia and eventually stopped "at a small village inn where about twenty of us sat around a table and a sort of lunch was served us. Near to the Führer was Von Leeb, General von Schobert, Konrad Henlein, Seyss-Inquart [Nazi gov-

95

ernor of Austria], and several officers and SS officers." Schmundt had brought fruit juice, cereal and Viennese cream cakes for the Führer, who was a strict vegetarian and teetotaler, but the others ate ham, sausages and baked potatoes, and sipped steins of beer with showy abstemiousness. On this occasion Hitler was in a curious mental state; his moods ranged from black rage, as when he cursed Chamberlain for having "cheated" him, to soaring exhilaration when he drew fervid pictures for his listeners of the future victories he would secure for them.

"Right from the beginning of the meal," Grosscurth recalled, "the Führer began to make a long statement about the political situation and the possibilities for the future. The door to the room was open and the chauffeurs and the villagers were hanging around the door and hearing everything. They stared at him, fascinated, as he got wilder and wilder in his talk. I had a most disagreeable impression of the whole scene. It was very dangerous."

Hitler did not go into any details of his plans but confined himself to wild threats against "the enemies of National Socialism and the Third Reich." Chief among them, of course, was England. "The English," he said, "it is always the English who are criticizing me. Weak, decadent, led by degenerate aristocrats with no chins, or by old fools like Chamberlain. Yet they dare to stand in my way. I will not allow it! I will attack them and I will destroy them! The French too! Latin curs and lickspittles! You can buy any politician in France, no matter what his politics. Jew-ridden scum! They will be stamped and squashed if they dare to get in my way!"

Surprisingly, Hitler then went on to attack the Hungarians, who were nominally the friends of Germany and certainly the allies of Fascist Italy. But as a native-born Austrian, Hitler had inherited many Austrians' antipathy for their Magyar neighbors, and his innate prejudice had been exacerbated by the Hungarians' reluctance to move quickly enough against Czechoslovakia during the crisis. At a conference with Admiral Miklós von Horthy, the Hungarian Regent, earlier in the year Hitler had told him of his plans and added, "If you want to eat the meal you must first help to cook it." But the Hungarians were quite rightly afraid that their ramshackle army would suffer heavily should the Czech forces react to their incursions, and they held back until they were sure their neighbors were helpless.

96

"Cowards, swine, Slav weaklings!" Hitler cried, and went on to tell his numbed listeners what he would now be doing to Hungarians if only they were not under the protection of "my good friend" Mussolini.

"The Poles, now," he went on, "they are Slavs too, but a very different people. I admire the Poles. They are like the Yugoslavs—they are a great people. They are not afraid. I can be friends with the Poles, and I will let my good friend Lipski [the Polish ambassador in Berlin] know that he can count on me."

Grosscurth whispered to his companion, Major Günther Blumentritt, "That means no war against Poland *this* year."

Abruptly, Hitler sprang to his feet and led the way back to the car. The cavalcade was off again, this time to the estate of the Prince von Schwarzenberg. It had been arranged for the party to climb a tall tower on the grounds of the estate from which there was a celebrated view of the wooded hills of Bohemia, but by the time the cars drew up at the spot, a mist had come down. Hitler's mood had suddenly changed, and he was silent; he glanced up at the tower, shivered and turned back to his car.

A day or two later, however, the Führer's liveliness returned and words spilled out of him. He had moved north into Moravia, to the old Czech fortifications which ran along the Bohemian escarpment from the German frontier to the Polish. This time a special train had brought some fifty members of the Armed Forces High Command from Berlin. The party included General Keitel, General von Brauchitsch and General Ernst Udet of the Luftwaffe, and they spent the morning touring the old Czech fortifications. They were much impressed with their strength and positioning, and Keitel made copious notes, for he was particularly interested at this time in the construction of the West Wall [Siegfried Line] along the Reich's frontier with France. Afterward the party gathered for lunch, once more in a small village inn, and once again Adolf Hitler was soon in full spate, regardless of the open door and the listening attendants.

Colonel Warlimont had acted as guide for his fellow officers through the fortifications. Now he was quite taken aback as the Führer began to reel off his plans. "As was usual with him during meals, he took over the whole of the conversation himself," Warlimont said. "He was very excited. His voice was raised, and if I hadn't known otherwise, I would have said he was drunk or drugged. He paid absolutely no attention at all to the outsiders who were all listening with their mouths open."

On this occasion Hitler discussed his plans for Czechoslovakia. He had been tricked at Munich, he said; there had been a conspiracy to appeal to his better nature, his sentimentality, and it had succeeded. He had let himself be persuaded that it was better to do things gradually. In a sudden spurt of rage he added that the German people had been accomplices of the insidious forces of the West in wrongly evoking and encouraging his "weak, humanitarian side," and he had given way because he suddenly realized that the German people were not prepared for the blood and sacrifice that the new Germany needed.

"But now I see things clearly," he said. "It was stupid of me to allow myself to be persuaded. It was a moment of weakness. There was Chamberlain's pleading, there were the fears of the German people, there were the doubts of my generals. I gave way. But no longer. I return to my original plan. I am determined to have the whole of Czechoslovakia inside the German Reich. And soon."

Warlimont noted that by this time not only the servants and the villagers were transfixed; so were the generals, particularly the area commander, General Gerd von Rundstedt, whose doubts about the preparedness of the German armed forces had not been eased by Munich. As he now tentatively suggested, "That was a bloodless victory, my Führer. But surely the occupation of Prague would be a different story!"

This was an excuse for Hitler to launch into a tirade against his generals and their lack of know-how and experience. He had been shocked, he said, "by the inefficiencies and maladroitness of the army during its occupation of the Sudetenland" (it had not taken long for informers to apprise him of the chaos of the first forty-eight hours). Though Germany had not had to fight—which was something for which *he* should be thanked, rather than the High Command—it had still been a costly operation, and the Reichsbank would have to empty its coffers to pay for it. The bankers were even impudently trying to threaten that they could not provide that sort of money again. Though such threats could be dealt with, they had a point.

"It is my opinion," the Reich Chancellor said, "that for the next stage in Czechoslovakia a mobilization, and all the time and money

98

it involves, will not be necessary. We don't need the army to take over Bohemia and Moravia. It will be done—all the preparatory work will be done—by political means." He swung around to Keitel and Rundstedt. "All that you need to do is trust in your Führer and have your army ready to move. Rely upon me. There will be no war over this. I know my adversaries by now. They will not fight over this. All I ask of you is that you have the armed forces ready to march. No mobilization. No unnecessary expense. The Czechs may squeal, but we will have our hands on their throats before they can shout. And anyway, who will come to help them?"

Presently Grosscurth and Warlimont slipped out of the inn and strolled in the fitful afternoon sunshine, and soon General von Rundstedt followed them. Grosscurth watched him as he paced up and down, face blank, hands behind his back, unmindful of the puddles in the potholed village street. Rundstedt was one of the senior general officers, and from Abwehr sources Grosscurth knew how strongly opposed he was to Adolf Hitler's grandiose plans. Only a week or two before, as the German army rolled into the Sudetenland, the general had said to Grosscurth's chief, Admiral Canaris, "It will all end so badly. Canaris, how long will this burlesque [*Narrentheater*] last?"

Canaris did not answer him because, knowing the nature of Nazism and the caliber of the leadership in the West, he would have been forced to say, "Longer than you think."

■

In the United States, the appeasement of Nazi Germany at Munich had received a bad press, and Franklin D. Roosevelt reacted strongly to the newspaper comments. He made it known, but not too publicly, that he despised Chamberlain for his evident sympathy with National Socialism and his obvious "spellbound admiration" for Adolf Hitler, and that he felt nothing but sorrowful contempt for the French. Admittedly there was another section of American opinion which welcomed the Munich Agreement as the only solution to an obscure and difficult geographical problem. On the whole, the isolationists were sympathetic to the dilemmas facing the Western democracies in Europe, but not to the extent of doing anything about them; for

99

instance, one of the leaders of the group, Senator Gerald P. Nye, loudly and peremptorily demanded that the U.S. government "stay out of" the quarrels in which "insincere" nations like Britain were involving themselves.

Roosevelt's initial impulse had been to welcome the agreement, but his euphoria faded quickly as the implications sank in. To some thoughtful Americans, though not as many as the wishful thinkers imagined, Munich was in part a defeat for the United States as well as for Britain, and an ominous warning of what crises might face an unprepared overcomplacent nation in the near future. Roosevelt realized this, but he also realized that it would not be politic to say so too loudly, for it would only alarm the American people and play into the hands of the isolationists. Shortly after Munich he began to harden his line toward the dictators, but only gradually.

On October 7, 1938, the President called a meeting of his Cabinet at the White House, and afterward Secretary Harold Ickes wrote in his diary: "I have it from the President that he expects some such move as the following in the near future: Germany will be wanting colonies, and in the process of satisfying its appetite, it is suspected that England will offer her Trinidad and prevail upon France to offer her Martinique. This would give Germany strong outposts on our Eastern coast as well as the coasts of Central and South America. Then this country will be urged to agree to these transfers 'in the interests of world peace.' "

Ickes added sharply: "The President had made up his mind that if any such thing as this happens, the U.S. Fleet will forthwith be sent to take both these islands."

FDR's "suspicion" about colonies for Germany was based on American intelligence reports; no mention of Trinidad and Martinique can be found in either German or British documents but it is a fact that Neville Chamberlain was thinking about reinforcing his "rapport" with Hitler by giving him some colonies as sweeteners.

But if the political line against Germany was hardening in Washington, such was not the case in the U.S. embassy in London. On October 19 Ambassador Kennedy was accorded a singular honor by the British and invited to speak at the Trafalgar Day dinner of the Navy League. He dutifully informed the State Department that in his speech he would express his pleasure over the peaceful conclusion of the Four Power conference, and the department offered no objec-

100

tions. Why should they? Had not Roosevelt himself telegraphed his congratulations to Chamberlain? But they neither referred the matter to the White House, nor checked the content of Kennedy's speech.

The ambassador himself realized that this was an important occasion for him and that he must weigh every word. He knew that by this time he was a controversial figure both in his own country and in Britain. His enemies in Roosevelt's Cabinet—and the President, too, for that matter—felt that he had been "taken in hand by Lady Astor and the Cliveden set" and become too pro-British; many of the English, on the other hand, considered that he was a strong influence behind Chamberlain's pro-appeasement policies. But Kennedy's opinions were too strong to be disguised, and in one section of the address he declared: "It has long been a theory of mine that it is unproductive for both the democracies and the dictator countries to widen the division now existing between them by emphasizing their differences, which are now self-apparent. Instead of hammering away at what are regarded as irreconcilables they could advantageously bend their energies toward solving their common problems by an attempt to re-establish good relations on a world basis. It is true that the democratic and dictator countries have important and fundamental divergencies of outlook, which in certain areas go deeper than politics. But there is simply no sense, common or otherwise, in letting these differences grow into unrelenting antagonisms. After all, we have to live together in the same world whether we like it or not."

This was an accurate reflection of the policy of the British government and might almost have been written by Chamberlain himself. With the exception of the *Times* of London and other supporters of appeasement, the address got a bad reception in London and an even worse one in the United States. The President reacted to the criticism by rapping the State Department for having let the speech go through, and the Department in turn began looking for excuses or scapegoats. Jay Pierrepoint Moffat, head of the Division of European Affairs, wrote: "The Secretary [Cordell Hull] is very upset. . . . He thinks we should have definitely called Kennedy off in advance, despite his claim that he was advancing 'a pet theory of my own.' The Secretary asked Sumner [Welles] why he did not see the danger of the speech. Sumner replied that he had been thinking of Mexico and had assumed that the Secretary himself had given attention to the matter and had initialed blind. The Secretary then said that I had not appeared un-

101

The Road to Prague

duly perturbed when I discussed the matter with him. This is not strictly accurate as I told him that there would undoubtedly be repercussions but that I thought the phrase 'a pet theory of my own' would keep the Department and the Secretary out of range of editorial attacks. The truth of the matter is that the Secretary dislikes calling down Kennedy and Bullitt, as they have a way of appealing to the White House over his head." But a "goat" was needed, Moffat went on, "and I shall have to be the goat."

It was time, Roosevelt decided, to rap the fingers of his appeasement-minded ambassador again. When the President went on the radio for a "fireside chat" a week after the Trafalgar Day speech, he took a hard line which was accepted as a direct rebuke to Kennedy: "There can be no peace if the reign of law is to be replaced by a recurrent sanctification of sheer force. There can be no peace if national policy adopts as a deliberate instrument the threat of war . . ."

Kennedy considered the speech "a stab in the back," and he did not desist in his encouragement of Chamberlain's policy of appeasement.

■

On October 18 Adolf Hitler's private trimotored Junker plane, *Horst Wessel,* took off from Tempelhof Airport in Berlin. Inside were two Frenchmen, one of whom was planning to carry out an appeasement mission of his own. André François-Poncet, who had been named envoy to Italy, was flying to see Hitler at Berchtesgaden to say goodbye, and he had asked Captain Paul Stehlin to accompany him.

François-Poncet was embittered by the treatment which had been meted out to Czechoslovakia. The defeat at Munich, however, had persuaded him that there was now no way out for France but to come to some accommodation with the Führer. He had lost his taste for the alliance with Britain; having watched the behavior of Chamberlain and Wilson at Munich he had, in fact, lost his taste for the British, and he had been particularly incensed by Chamberlain's tête-à-tête with Hitler after the conference, and the signed piece of paper which it produced. If only to spite the British, he was determined to arrange that France get a piece of paper of her own.

The Führer's plane landed at Berchtesgaden at three o'clock in

102

the afternoon and the two Frenchmen were received by an SS colonel who led them to Hitler's own Mercedes. They began the journey up the mountain of Obersalzberg, where they expected the Führer to receive them, but to their surprise they passed it and continued up a series of hairpin curves until their ears were popping. Suddenly they stopped before a vast double door of gleaming bronze which swung open at the same moment, so that they could see beyond into a brilliantly lit room.

The SS officer led them inside and asked them to be seated in armchairs which were spread around the salon. As they did so, there was a low hum and they suddenly realized that they were in a huge elevator. When it stopped, a door opened and there was Ribbentrop holding out his hand; he led them into a room toward a huge picture window through which there was a spectacular view of the Alps. Hitler, waiting to greet them, "pale, face drawn, but amiable and courteous," was honoring the Frenchmen by receiving them in his special retreat, the "eagle's nest."

It was five o'clock in the evening, and tea was served. While they sipped it, Hitler began a bitter attack on the British and on Chamberlain, which appeared to embarrass François-Poncet. The Führer hastily remarked that he had no criticisms at all to make of the French, that he considered Daladier to be a great statesman, and that he desired nothing but friendship and co-operation with France. At this he took the ambassador by the arm and led him into an adjoining room, where they talked alone for half an hour. When they emerged, both were smiling and François-Poncet had a glint of triumph in his eyes.

"Did you notice how Hitler went out of his way to be agreeable?" he said to Stehlin as they drove down the mountain. "During our talk, in spite of the seriousness of the subjects we went over, he never once got worked up. He proved that he can be moderate and wise. He talked a lot about Europe, of European civilization, of his deep, profound and reasoned feelings about Europe."

In his official report to Georges Bonnet, François-Poncet wrote: "The same man who can be so debonair, so sensible to the beauties of nature and who can discuss over a cup of tea reasonable ideas about European politics, is at the same time capable of frenzied rages, of the most savage exaltations and the most far-fetched ambitions." But he went on to add that he believed that France could make an accommodation with the Führer and that he had laid the groundwork for it.

Georges Bonnet was delighted and began making immediate arrangements for preliminary talks, which would lead to a Franco-German agreement. France would get her signed piece of paper from Hitler too.

But not yet. A young man named Herschel Grynszpan intervened.

V

"Don't You See? . . . It's the German Insurance Companies That Will Have to Pay!"

It was difficult to guess that there was a concentration camp at Buchenwald. Most of the roads leading to it from the villages of Thuringia had no signs, and when the camp guards of the Death's-Head units (SS Totenkopfverbände) and their female colleagues came into town for weekend leave, they said nothing about their duties except that they were "in training."

Indeed they were. 1938 and 1939 were the years of expansion, and they were bracing themselves to meet the challenges to come. Since 1933, when Adolf Hitler came to power, the rounding up of political prisoners had gathered momentum, and such "detention centers" as Dachau, Osnabrück and Belsen had been built quickly to take care of the influx. Gone were the days when the enemies of National Socialism were rounded up and flung into bunkers in the cities, where they were beaten by the bullies of the Brown Shirt army; this made too much noise and started too many stories. In a 1935 decree Heinrich Himmler had put the whole business on a practical, organized basis, by reserving for the Gestapo and the SS the right to arrest, interrogate and incarcerate any citizen, and they were now running the detention camps with flawless efficiency. The hard core of their prisoners were members of the left-wing parties and the trade unions who had been arrested in 1933; to these had been added

Jews, gypsies and any "enemies of the state" who had run afoul of the Party organizations in the intervening years and who were too poor to bribe their way out of imprisonment. The Anschluss with Austria had brought a new wave of political detainees, including the Austrian Chancellor, Kurt von Schuschnigg, and now the Liberals and Social Democrats of the Sudetenland were beginning to flow in.

But Heinrich Himmler, the Reichsführer-SS in charge of all police forces and the security of the Reich, knew that he must brace himself to cope with the challenges to come: many more prisoners must be dealt with in the spirit of racialism and the German Reich; more camps had to be opened; more SS guards had to be recruited to handle them. He feared that his beloved Führer was weakening in his attitude toward the enemies of the state and was showing signs of being in favor of ameliorating conditions in the concentration camps. Himmler was so disturbed at this latter possibility that he had written Hitler a letter to point out the disastrous consequences which might follow:

YOUR EXCELLENCY:

About two months ago, you spoke to me to the effect that according to your opinion too many people in the concentration camps were being shot while trying to escape. Although I personally did not share your viewpoint, because, in the cases which have occurred so far, the shots have always been fired at a distance of 30, 40, 50 or 80 meters, I have ordered SS General [Gruppenführer] Eicke to impress upon the Death's-Head organizations once more that shots shall be fired in extreme emergency only.

The result was shocking to me!

The day before yesterday I was in Camp Buchenwald and was shown the body of a brave twenty-four-year-old SS man whose skull had been smashed with a shovel by two criminals. The two criminals then escaped.

I have again looked over the inmates of the camp, and I am deeply distressed at the thought that now, through too much clemency, which always prevails when official regulations are relaxed concerning shooting in escape attempts, one of my best men had to lose his life.

I have to inform you that I have canceled my order to fire only in extreme emergency, and that the old regulation to the effect that shots will be fired according to official regulations—calling three times, or, in case of actual attack, without warning—has become effective again.

106

Two other criminals, who obviously knew about the planned escape attempt, were shot, after the SS man had been slain, when they were trying to escape and challenged from 50 to 60 meters. I have ordered all means of pursuit to be utilized to capture the real murderers.

I shall ask the Führer, after the regular court has sentenced them to death, not to allow them to be executed in the precincts of a regular court, but in Camp Buchenwald in front of the formation of 3,000 inmates, preferably by hanging from the gallows.

Heil Hitler!
Himmler

The SS chief did not have to worry; he soon heard that the Führer was prepared to back him. In the time between the writing of his memorandum and its reception by Hitler, one of the two escaped inmates had been captured. Himmler's chief adjutant, SS General (Gruppenführer) Karl Wolff, sent a note to the commander of Buchenwald saying:

"The Führer and Reich Chancellor approved yesterday the report of the Reichsführer-SS suggesting that the murderer of SS Corporal Kallweit be hanged at Buchenwald. The Reichsführer-SS requests that criminal proceedings be instituted as quickly as possible against the murderer, Emil Bargatzy, and that he be informed of the execution of the death penalty."

Bargatzy, a former Socialist and trade union leader, was hanged two days later. But by a macabre coincidence, his companion was not arrested until November 9, and on that day the boom in the concentration camp business which Heinrich Himmler had so confidently expected received just the kind of incentive that the Gestapo and the SS needed.

At nine o'clock on November 7, 1938, a young third secretary named Ernst vom Rath was opening the day's mail in the German embassy in the Rue de Lille, Paris. Vom Rath, the scion of an old Prussian line of aristocrats, had entered the German foreign service under distinguished auspices; his sponsors were Baron Ernst von Weizsäcker and Dr. Erich Kordt. Vom Rath shared their antipathy to the regime in Germany, but being a young man of no great courage, he kept his mouth shut except in the presence of his closest friends.

107

Weizsäcker and Kordt envisaged for him a steady, worthy and un-distinguished career. He would be a good foreign service official, they felt, but few people outside the department would ever know his name.

Nor would they have, were it not for the fact that as Vom Rath was slitting envelopes in his office that morning, a visitor entered the embassy lobby. He was under five feet tall, and was wearing a khaki raincoat, and to the guard at the information desk he looked like "a schoolboy, a worried one." He said in German, "I would like to see a person of importance who is *au courant* with German secrets, because I have some very important information to give him."

The guard hesitated and then told the youth to follow him up to the first floor. It was too early in the day for any senior member of the embassy to be at his desk, but in the office opposite the staircase he saw Vom Rath busy with the morning mail. He showed the visitor in and left them together. Vom Rath told the young man to be seated in the chair opposite him and then asked why he had come. There was silence for some seconds, and then the visitor reached into his raincoat pocket and pulled out a revolver. Without saying a word, he pointed it at Vom Rath and fired it carefully five times.

At the first shot the third secretary rose to his feet and began to shout for help. The sound changed to a scream and then to a strangled groan as a second shot hit him in the throat. The other three shots missed their mark, and Vom Rath, eyes wide open, was lying on the floor, bleeding but still conscious, gurgling "*Warum, warum?*" (Why, why?) when the guard burst into the room.

As the police were alerted and an ambulance summoned, the youth made no attempt to escape. He sat calmly in the chair, staring at the bleeding figure on the floor and, the guard recalled, "looking very sad." Eventually he was taken by the police to the station in the Rue de Bourgogne, where he refused to identify himself. All he would say at first was, "I am sorry he isn't dead. I wanted to revenge my co-religionists."

When he was searched, however, the police found the young man's passport. His name was Herschel Grynszpan, he was a Polish Jew and he was seventeen years old. Inside his passport was a letter which had been mailed in Germany on August 31, 1938; it read in part: "Tonight it was announced that Polish Jews were being expelled from the cities. At 9 o'clock the police arrived at our house and took our passports and took us to the police station. There we met many other Jews. They are going to expel us from Germany and make us go back to Poland. What shall we do there, son? And what will they do to us? Thank God you are safe in France . . ."

The letter was from Herschel Grynszpan's father, and as a police officer read the words aloud, the boy began to weep. Slowly, between sobs, his story came out. His parents had lived for twenty years in Hanover, where the father worked as a tailor and the mother as a seamstress. They had suffered the same humiliations as the other Jews around them after the Nazis came to power, but their Polish passports had saved them from violence, eviction and the concentration camp. They asked nothing more for themselves than to be allowed to go on working, but they sought salvation for their son. They had sent him to study at a yeshiva, and there, young Grynszpan said, "I tried to learn why I was a Jew." In a sudden spurt of anger he added, "It is not a crime to be a Jew. I am not a dog. I have a right to live. The Jewish people have a right to some part of the earth. Wherever I have been, I have been treated like an animal."

In July 1938 the Nazis had begun to encourage sporadic demonstrations against the Jews, and life became more difficult for the Grynszpans in Hanover. Father and mother talked over the problem while their son, home for summer vacation, slept in the room above them. Finally they made up their minds, and the next morning Herschel's father told him what he must do: "I have a brother who lives and works in Paris. He's not doing too well, but he is your uncle and he will look after you. You must go to him. You must stay in France until all this blows over."

"And when will that be?" Herschel remembered asking them, and got the reply, "Not in our lifetime, son, but maybe in yours."

So they had seen him off, a pathetic waif of a boy, on the train, and that was the beginning not of a new life but of new unhappiness. He arrived in France at the beginning of August and was admitted as a temporary visitor by the reluctant border guards. France had been getting too many refugees from Austria and Germany lately, and anti-Semitism, never far below the surface among the French bourgeoisie, was beginning to show itself in isolated acts of racial prejudice. Herschel's uncle took him in but made it plain that he would

109

need to find a job as soon as possible, and for this he must have a work permit. He applied for one on August 11; it was not only refused but he was given a week to leave France. He was well aware what this meant—back to Germany, for no other country would take him in.

Instead, Herschel went into hiding in his uncle's house. It was while he was there, brooding in a back attic, that letters began to arrive from his father telling how his parents had been chased from their home after twenty years; how two thousand Polish Jews had been herded to the frontier and told by the SS guards to go back where they belonged; how the Poles had refused to allow them in; and how they were now living in tents, huts and caravans in no man's land, with little food and no clothes and the Polish winter drawing nearer.

It was then that Herschel Grynszpan emerged from his hiding place for the first time since August. He knew his uncle had a revolver, because he had seen it once; it was an unsavory neighborhood and one of the petty crooks of the *quartier* had left it in his uncle's keeping just before being hauled off to jail.

The boy put the weapon in his pocket and set off on the long walk across the city to the Rue de Lille and the German embassy. He didn't quite know what he was going to do until he found himself sitting opposite Ernst vom Rath. He had never seen him before in his life, but suddenly "I had to make my feelings clear."

That evening, as Herschel Grynszpan sat in his cell at Fresnes Prison near Paris awaiting trial, the beer was foaming in the steins in the Bürgerbräukeller in Munich. The Bavarian capital was beginning its annual celebration, and the city was full of visitors. All day Brown Shirts, Hitler Youth and German Maidens (Bund Deutscher Mädel) had been arriving in the city, and as darkness fell they happily faced a long and frothy night. The young people gathered in the Marienplatz before the medieval Rathaus (the Town Hall), linked hands and danced away the evening chill, cheering and shouting "Heil Hitler!" Saloons and cafés all over the city were jammed with the faithful, matching each other's drinking capacity. From the loudspeakers, hung from lampposts, came the plangent, martial strains of the Nazi hymn, the "Horst Wessel Song."

Herschel Grynszpan could not have chosen a day for his act of

110

desperation more calculated to arouse the fury of the National Socialists, for November 8 was the eve of the anniversary of the Beer Hall *Putsch*. On November 9, 1923, Adolf Hitler had led three thousand storm troopers on a march from the Bürgerbräukeller in the southeast outskirts of Munich to the center of the city after exhorting them to overthrow the government of the day. Shots were exchanged between the army and the SA. The lines broke and sixteen Nazi storm troopers were killed. Hitler and his accomplices were arrested and tried for treason. Hitler was convicted and sentenced to five years in the fortress prison of Landsberg but was released after nine months, just long enough to enable him to complete the writing of his magnum opus, *Mein Kampf,* which soon became the bible of the National Socialist movement.

Adolf Hitler's followers considered him a martyr after the Beer Hall *Putsch,* and he was duly grateful. Each year since he came to power in 1933 he had celebrated with his Old Guard in the Beer Hall. This time he drove there from Bayreuth, where he had been staying with his old friend Winifred Wagner, the English daughter-in-law of the great composer, who was one of the Führer's most passionate admirers. He was in an emotional mood by the time he reached the Beer Hall, and his fervor was quickened when Joseph Goebbels handed him a message from Ribbentrop informing him of the attack on Vom Rath. Hitler's eyes flamed. "The Jewish pig!" he cried. "Who gave him the orders? Who paid him? This is something they will regret!"

Also present at dinner that night was Hitler's old army comrade, Captain Fritz Wiedemann, who had been the Führer's company commander on the western front during the war, and his friend and confidant until he openly showed his disenchantment with the Nazi policy of aggression. Now he was on his way out—in a few weeks he would be "banished" to San Francisco as consul general—but he still had sufficient influence to counsel moderation. "It's a time of political peace and reconciliation," he said. "Why stir up any more mud?"

But though he realized the wisdom of his subordinate's counsel, Hitler was incensed. What did it matter that Vom Rath was not a member of the Party? The shooting was not against an individual but against the German Reich—*by a Jew*. As such it must be punished. Scarlet pictures of the Jewish menace to the world flashed before his

111

eyes, and he was filled with hatred, rancor and bile. Joseph Goebbels had moved into the hall, where he hopped on his special boot from group to group,* clinking steins with the Old Guard, swapping dirty stories and teasing the perspiring comrades about the hangovers they would be suffering in the morning. Now Hitler called him back, and they conferred.

The guests at the wooden tables that night were the old faithful of the party, most of them veterans from the brawls of the early days, the street-corner fights with Communists, the raids on Liberals and Democrats, the burnings and the back-street killings. They were fatter and sleeker and well-to-do now. Most of them had been promoted to *Gauleiter* or *Kreisleiter*,† and prosperity and self-confidence shone from their red faces.

Hitler gave this audience the pep talk they expected, warning them that even after fifteen years the German Reich was not safe, that goals were not attained, that dangers were ever present, that battles were still to be fought. It was no time to relax; enemies were menacing from every side—overt ones like the hypocritical powers in the West and the insidious criminals of Moscow. But there were other, more dangerous and secret enemies hiding in their midst, who were already established inside the citadel and were waiting only for a turned back or closed eyes in order to strike.

The Führer particularized no more than that before launching into his peroration about the destiny of Greater Germany. Then he departed, leaving the Gauleiters to their beer, and to the rumors that were beginning to circulate among them.

In a reek of beer and cigar smoke and a hubbub of songs, shouts, slogans and regurgitations, Joseph Goebbels now rose to his feet and hammered a stein on a wooden table for attention. He had a slip of paper in his hand.

"Members of the Old Guard," he said. "We meet here tonight to celebrate one more year of the development of our party and our

* Did Goebbels have a clubfoot or was one leg shorter than the other? Goebbels himself insisted on the latter, as a result of which his enemies adapted an old German saying, "Liars have short legs," to "The Liar has a short leg" (*der Lügner hat ein kurzes Bein*).

† Since 1933, Germany was divided into thirty-two Gaue, or administrative regions, each governed by a Party *Gauleiter*. Each *Gau* was subdivided into *Kreise*, or districts, and headed by a *Kreisleiter*. Progressively smaller divisions were called *Ortsgruppe* (local group), *Zelle* (cell) and *Block*, each headed by a party leader.

WIDE WORLD PHOTOS

Full of confidence, Neville Chamberlain is shown at Heston Airport
on September 15, 1938, departing for Berchtesgaden and his first encounter with
Adolf Hitler. *On the left:* Sir Horace Wilson, the Prime Minister's adviser
and close confidant. It was Mr. Chamberlain's first airplane trip.

WIDE WORLD PHOTOS

The Berghof, Hitler's retreat at Berchtesgaden, in the Bavarian Alps.
He is shown here on the terrace with Eva Braun, from whose photo
collection this was taken.

RADIO TIMES HULTON PICTURE LIBRARY

In August 1938, Chamberlain had sent Lord Runciman to Prague to mediate in
the disputes stirred up by the Nazi leader in the Sudetenland,
Konrad Henlein. *Left:* Viscountess Runciman.

RADIO TIMES HULTON PICTURE LIBRARY

AP PHOTO

After Chamberlain's second meeting with Hitler, at Bad Godesberg, the French leaders came to London for talks. *From left to right:* French Foreign Minister Georges Bonnet, Premier Edouard Daladier and General Gamelin, the military commander in chief.

Sir Horace Wilson arrives in Berlin on September 26 with a personal message from Chamberlain to Hitler. With him is Sir Nevile Henderson, British ambassador in Berlin.

Sir Robert Vansittart, former Permanent Undersecretary for Foreign Affairs.

RADIO TIMES HULTON PICTURE LIBRARY

RADIO TIMES HULTON PICTURE LIBRARY

Henlein with an appreciative Führer.

RADIO TIMES HULTON PICTURE LIBRARY

On September 28 in the jam-packed Sportpalast, Hitler made one of his most vituperative speeches, against the Czechs in general and President Eduard Beneš in particular.

RADIO TIMES HULTON PICTURE LIBRARY

Czech President Eduard Beneš.

WIDE WORLD PHOTOS

Jan Masaryk, Czech minister in London.

RADIO TIMES HULTON PICTURE LIBRARY

Chamberlain being escorted by Joachim von Ribbentrop, the German Foreign Minister *(right),* on his arrival in Munich on September 29.

KEYSTONE PRESS AGENCY LTD.

The British Prime Minister is cordially greeted by Hitler.

AP PHOTO

The signators of the Munich Pact (which did not include any Czech
representative) are pleased with the way they settled the Sudeten crisis.
From left to right: Field Marshal Göring; Hitler; interpreter Paul Schmidt;
Count Ciano, the Italian Foreign Minister; Mussolini; Daladier; Chamberlain;
and André François-Poncet, the French ambassador in Berlin.

WIDE WORLD PHOTOS

A confident Neville Chamberlain waving the signed agreement on his return to England . . .

RADIO TIMES HULTON PICTURE LIBRARY

. . . but on arrival in Paris, Premier Daladier, shown here with Bonnet and other members of his Cabinet, is less happy.

Hitler's triumphal return
to Berlin after Munich . . .

RADIO TIMES HULTON PICTURE LIBRARY

. . . and his welcome to
Karlsbad, in the Sudetenland,
a week later.

RADIO TIMES HULTON
PICTURE LIBRARY

people. As our beloved Führer said, we are on the march and we have already scored our successes. But we still have enemies, and they lurk in wait for us—to strike us down and grind us in the muck when we are off our guard." He paused and then waved the piece of paper. "I have news for you here tonight to demonstrate what happens to a good German when he relaxes his vigil for one moment . . . Ernst vom Rath was a good German, a loyal servant of the Reich,* working for the good of our people in the German embassy in Paris. Shall I tell you what happened to him? He was shot down! In the course of his duty, he went, unarmed and unsuspecting, to speak to a visitor at the embassy, and had two bullets pumped into him. His life is now in danger."

Another pause, and then the small, lean, brown face darkened to chestnut, the fist slammed down on the table. "Do I need to tell you the race of the dirty swine who did this foul deed? A Jew! A creeping, cunning, unscrupulous Jew! Tonight he lies in jail in Paris, claiming that he acted on his own, that he had no instigators of this awful deed behind him. But we know better, don't we?"

The Old Guard had been sobered for a moment by this news, but now they had their opportunity for release. There came shouts of "Yes, we know! Dirty Jews! Down with the Jews! Kill the Jews!"

Goebbels banged his stein for silence, and the growling and shouting slowly subsided. "Comrades, we cannot allow this attack by international Jewry to go unchallenged. It must be repudiated. Our people must be told, and their answer must be ruthless, forthright, salutary! I ask you to listen to me, and together we must plan what is to be our answer to Jewish murder and the threat of international Jewry to our glorious German Reich."

Someone cried, "Tell us what to do!"

So Joseph Goebbels proceeded to tell them.

At 11:55 P.M. on November 9, Gestapo headquarters in the Prinz Albrechtstrasse in Berlin began to feed an urgent message into the teletype machines which connected them with every police headquarters in the Reich:

---

* Ironically, Vom Rath had been under surveillance by the Gestapo for some time, ever since they become aware of his antipathy toward Nazi policy.

113

Berlin NUE 243 404
November 9—23:55 se.

TO ALL STATE POLICE BUREAUS—
Chiefs or Deputy Chiefs—Confidential

1) Demonstrations against the Jews and particularly their synagogues will take place very shortly throughout all Germany.
These demonstrations will not be interfered with, but measures will be taken in co-operation with the regular police
[Ordnungspolizei] to prevent looting and similar excesses.
2) Important archives which may be found in synagogues are to
be safeguarded immediately.
3) Preparations will be made for the arrest of some 20,000–
30,000 Jews in Germany (about 5,000 in Austria). Primarily
well-to-do Jews will be chosen. Further instructions will be
issued in the course of the night.
4) The most severe measures will be applied against Jews found
in possession of weapons during the demonstrations. Reserve
SS and regular SS troops may be drawn upon for all phases of
the operation. The State Police, however, will take appropriate
measures to see that they remain in control of the actions.
Looting, theft, etc., must be prevented at all costs. Communications with the Security Service [Sicherheitsdienst] commands
(main and sub divisions) will immediately be established for
the purpose of safeguarding exempted property.
5) Supplementary instructions for the State Police, Cologne:
There is especially important material in the Cologne Synagogue.* The speediest measures will be taken in co-operation
with the Security Service to safeguard this material immediately.

Gestapo H.Q.
Müller

This message was followed by a teletyped instruction which was
sent out at 1:20 A.M. on November 10.

Flash Munich 47 767
10 Nov 38 0120—Chu

TO ALL STATE POLICE HEADQUARTERS AND BRANCH OFFICES,
ALL SECRET SERVICE COMMANDS IN THE MAIN AND
SUB DIVISIONS [Ober- und Unterabschnitten]

Flash, urgent, immediate delivery
For urgent and immediate delivery to the chief or his deputy

SUBJECT: Measures to be taken against Jews tonight.

* An ancient scroll.

114

As a result of the attempt on the life of Embassy Secretary vom Rath in Paris, anti-Jewish demonstrations are to be expected throughout the Reich tonight—November 9–10. The following instructions will be observed in dealing with these demonstrations:

1) The State Police chiefs or their deputies will, immediately upon receipt of this TWX, communicate by telephone with the Gauleiter or Kreisleiter and arrange a conference on the execution of the planned actions. This conference, which the appropriate inspector or chief of the regular police will also attend, will notify the Political Division that the regular police have received from the Reichsführer-SS and Chief of the German Police the following orders to which the measures of the Political Division will be suitably adapted:

a) Only such measures will be taken as do not endanger German lives or property (e.g., synagogues may be set afire only if there is no danger of spreading flames to neighboring buildings).

b) Jewish shops and homes may be destroyed but not looted. The police are instructed to ensure the observance of this order and to arrest looters.

c) Special precautions will be taken in business streets in order to protect, without fail, non-Jewish shops.

d) Foreigners, even if Jewish, should not be molested.

2) Provided that the instructions listed under Para. 1) are observed, the demonstrations should not be interfered with but merely supervised in order to keep them within the limits defined.

3) Immediately upon receipt of this TWX, police will confiscate the archives of all synagogues and offices of the Jewish communal organizations so that they will not be destroyed in the course of the actions. Attention should be paid to historically valuable documents and materials rather than to such items as recent tax lists, etc. This archival material will be delivered to the appropriate Security Service [SD] office.

4) The State Police will direct the measures taken by the Gestapo in connection with the anti-Jewish actions, except where the inspectors of the Gestapo give their own orders. Criminal Police [*Kriminalpolizei*] officers and members of the Security Service, reserve SS and regular SS troops may be called upon for the execution of these measures.

5) As soon as conditions after tonight's actions permit, the officers assigned this duty will proceed to arrest as many Jews in all districts as the available jail space will hold. Well-to-do Jews will be singled out for arrest and primarily only healthy male adults of not-too-advanced age rounded up. Immediately

upon completion of the arrests, the appropriate concentration camp will be notified in order to provide for the speediest transfer of Jews to the camp. Special care must be taken that no one arrested in these circumstances is mistreated.

6) The contents of this order will be transmitted to the appropriate inspectors and chiefs of the regular police and the Security Service main and sub divisions, with the supplementary note that these police measures have been ordered by the Reichsführer-SS and Chief of the German Police. The chief of the regular police [Obergruppenführer Kurt Daluege] has issued corresponding orders to the regular police and the fire-fighting police. Closest co-operation for the execution of these measures will be ensured between the Gestapo and the regular police.

Receipt of this TWX will be acknowledged through TWX to Gestapo HQ, attention SS Colonel [Standartenführer] Müller, by the State Police chief or his deputy.

Heydrich
SS Major General [Gruppenführer]

On the night of November 9–10, 1938, the pogrom began.

The demonstrations had been planned by Goebbels, Himmler and Heydrich as a controlled demonstration of German hatred for the "Jewish enemy in our midst." For some time each of them had felt that the German people needed some kind of release from recent tensions—their anxieties over the threat of war just before Munich, for example—and what better safety valve than to let them riot against Jews? The Jews were beginning to get uppity again and were in need of a lesson. What could be a more fitting celebration of the fifteenth anniversary of the Beer Hall *Putsch* than some synagogue fires, a little horseplay with rabbis and Orthodox Jews, and some arrests of the richer Semites? But on the morning of November 10 Ernst vom Rath died of his wounds, and Goebbels could not resist ordering his radio and press to whip things up.

In the next twenty-four hours the orderly and disciplined German people demonstrated how they could behave when given the right kind of provocation and encouragement. At the last moment Heydrich had ordered his SS men to change into civilian clothes, and in most of the towns and cities it was they who incited the mobs and encouraged them to beat, burn, and loot. In Berlin they swarmed

116

down the Unter den Linden and the Kurfürstendamm, where the big stores were situated, smashing plate-glass windows, hauling out furs and jewels and silver. In Berlin-Dahlem, a fashionable suburb, they battered their way into the mansions where many of the richer Jews still lived, dragged off the able-bodied males, stripped and taunted the old men, and in some cases dragged the daughters into bedrooms. When they left, furniture had been smashed, priceless vases flung to the floor, paintings ripped, and in at least fifteen instances, women molested.

At No. 2 Brückenhalle in Berlin was a fine house full of antiques and art treasures, owned by Herr Franz Rinkel, a Jew who had rented part of his house to Raymond H. Geist, a consul at the U.S. embassy. Unfortunately Geist was away when a mob burst into the house, locked Rinkel's family in the room upstairs and began to beat him. Presently two men in uniform made their way into the melee and pushed the crowd out of the room. Soon the bleeding Rinkel was alone with the two SS men and a man behind them, whom he recognized as a Nazi lawyer named Dr. Lilienthal. Rinkel had had dealings with this man before; Lilienthal wanted his house, had offered to buy it for half its value and had been curtly refused.

Now the lawyer pulled out a paper. "Think of your womenfolk," he said. "Think of your own life if that mob comes back. But you will come to no harm if you sign this paper."

It was a bill of sale for Rinkel's house; Lilienthal was offering one fiftieth of the price he had suggested earlier. Rinkel signed, then was taken by the SS men to the local jail, and thence with a number of other Jewish prisoners to the Sachsenhausen concentration camp. It was not until a week later that his American tenant was able to trace and rescue him.

In Sachsenhausen with Rinkel was Eugene Garbaty, owner of one of Germany's largest cigar factories. Before Geist could use his influence to get him out as well, Garbaty had sold his factory for one million marks, one tenth of its value, and his country house near Dresden had been confiscated. To obtain an exit visa to leave Germany he bribed Count von Helldorff, the chief of police in Berlin, with half a million marks and paid the other half million in fines.*

Glass was smashed all over Germany. The synagogues were on

* Garbaty is now a U.S. citizen.

fire, and in the Jewish neighborhoods blood was beginning to run. All instructions against looting and violence had been forgotten by now, and the SS and Brown Shirts had begun helping themselves to booty, women and the joys of beating up Jews. Cells in the local jails had been filled, emptied and filled again and again, and trucks packed with rich Jews were rolling off to the concentration camps.

On November 12 the State Police in Berlin sent out a flash:

TO ALL STATE POLICE HEADQUARTERS AND BRANCH OFFICES

The Buchenwald concentration camp is filled to capacity with current deliveries. Therefore, further transfers to Buchenwald are to be canceled, with the exception of transports already under way. To prevent errors, this H.Q. will be informed well in advance of transfers to the Dachau and Sachsenhausen camps.

Heinrich Himmler had been quite right when he predicted that his resources were inadequate. There just weren't enough concentration camps to go around.

The morning after the *Kristallnacht,* Berlin awoke to the sour stink of smoke and the crunch of broken glass. The binge was over and now the hangover had to be endured. Small knots of people watched firemen putting out the last fires in the big department stores, but most citizens hurried by with faces averted, as if ashamed. Except for police wagons hooting through the streets, little traffic was to be seen. A few foreigners wandered around, their expressions stunned as they took in the evidence of the night's holocaust. Could this really be the work of these solid, disciplined people?

In the Reich Chancellery on the Wilhelmstrasse, Herman Göring had just been admitted into Hitler's study, and it was soon evident that he was angry.

Göring was not only chief of the German air force; since 1936 he had also been in charge of the Four-Year Plan, whose purpose was to put the Reich on a solid economic basis for waging war. In the course of the night he had learned that Propaganda Minister Joseph Goebbels was responsible for having incited the riots against the Jews. "But it's impossible," he said to the Führer. "How can I have things like this happening just now? I am reaching the peak of the effort for the Four-Year Plan. I am concentrating everything to see that not a

118

grain is wasted. I have appealed to the nation to save every old tooth-paste tube for me, every rusty nail, every bit of scrap material so that it can be collected and used. And what happens? Goebbels interferes and destroys my plans."

"You must understand that Goebbels was provoked," Hitler replied. "He can't keep calm when these Jews emerge from their hiding places and attack us."

"But for one Jew, why mobilize a nation?"

They parted, and before they met again late the same afternoon, Goebbels had been to see the Führer. They had regaled each other with reports of the damage and discomfiture the Jews had suffered, and when Göring returned he found to his annoyance that "Hitler had somewhat changed his mind. Just what Goebbels had told him and to just what extent he referred to the excitement of the mob, to the urgently needed settlements [of German-Jewish relationships?] I don't know.* At any rate, the Führer's views were not the same as on the occasion of my first complaint. While we were conferring, Goebbels, who was in the building, joined us and began his usual talk: That such things could not be tolerated! That this was the second or third murder of a National Socialist committed abroad by a Jew! It was on this occasion that he first made the suggestion that a fine should be imposed on the Jews."

Göring told the Führer that to avoid all unnecessary emotion and waste of property, a meeting should be held of the National Socialist leadership to settle the fate of the Jews once and for all, and Hitler agreed.

"Thereupon," said Göring, "I called the meeting of November twelfth with those departments which had jurisdiction over such matters as the Jews, property, citizens' rights, and such. Unfortunately, the Führer demanded that Goebbels be a member of the committee, and that caused complications."

The committee to discuss the pogrom of November 9–10 and its effect on the German economy met at the Haus der Flieger, the German Air Ministry, at 10 A.M. on November 12. Göring was chairman, and Heydrich and Daluege represented the SS. Dr. Ernst Woer-

* Apparently Goebbels had rekindled Hitler's eagerness to see the Jews suffer even more.

mann was there for the Foreign Ministry, Goebbels and a number of his subordinates for the Propaganda Ministry, and Dr. Walther Funk for the Reichsbank. From the start it was a fight for hard facts against racial hatreds and obsessions.

It has been suggested by latter-day apologists that unlike the other Nazi leaders, Hermann Göring was not anti-Semitic and that some of his best friends were Jews. There is no evidence for this; apparently he shared all the Nazi fantasies and antipathies about Jews. It was only for practical and selfish reasons that he strongly condemned the November pogrom.

The Field Marshal banged his gavel and brought the meeting to order. "Gentlemen, today's meeting is of a decisive nature. I have received a letter, written on the Führer's orders by [Martin] Bormann, requesting that the Jewish question be now, once and for all, co-ordinated and solved one way or another. Yesterday on the telephone the Führer reiterated that he wished me to take co-ordinating action in this matter. Since the problem is mainly an economic one, it is from the economic point of view that it will have to be tackled. Naturally, a number of measures will have to be taken which fall into the sphere of the Ministry of Justice and the Ministry of the Interior, but it is here that we must make the practical decisions."

Göring then informed his listeners that the Party had already taken steps to further Aryanize (a Nazi euphemism for "expropriate") the German economy, and that the Jews should be "taken out of it and put in the debit ledger." He was referring to plans to squeeze the last of the financial resources out of the Jews by means of a gigantic fine.

"But to our discredit, we have made all sorts of petty plans and we have been too slow in carrying them out. We then had a demonstration, right here in Berlin, in which we told the people what would have to be done. But again nothing happened. Now we have had this affair in Paris, more demonstrations, and this time I insist that something must be done." Göring's face flushed and he said angrily, "Because, gentlemen, I have had enough of these demonstrations. They don't harm the Jews! They harm me—because I am the chief authority for co-ordinating the German economy!"

He banged on the table. "Don't you see? If today a Jewish shop is destroyed, if goods are thrown into the streets and set on fire, it isn't

120

the Jews who suffer the damage. It is the insurance companies that will pay! German insurance companies! Furthermore, the goods that are destroyed are consumer goods, belonging to the people! If, in the future, demonstrations should take place which we may consider necessary, I beg you to see to it that they be so directed as not to hurt us, us, us. Because it's insane to clear out and burn a Jewish warehouse and then have a German insurance company make good the loss. And the goods which I need desperately, whole bales of clothing and such, are being burned, and I need them everywhere. I may as well burn the raw materials before they arrive. Of course the people don't understand that, so we must now urgently make laws to show that something is being done."

"Why not simply exempt the insurance companies from having to pay?" Goebbels suggested.

"I am going to issue a decree," Göring said, "and I am of course going to ask the support of all government agents in channeling the claims in such a way that the insurance companies will not suffer. But we have to be careful. It may be, as I am told, that these insurance companies have reinsured in foreign countries. If that's the case, foreign bills of exchange would be available, and I would not like to lose those."

Göring then mentioned that he had asked the German insurance companies to send a representative to the meeting to explain their situation in detail, and at that moment a Herr Hilgard was ushered into the room.

In talking about the looted shops, Göring asked, "Are they insured against damages caused by public disturbances?"

Hilgard replied, "May I give you an example? The most striking instance is the case of Margraf, on the Unter den Linden. The jewelry store of Margraf is insured with us through a so-called comprehensive policy. This covers practically any damage that may occur. The damage was reported to us as amounting to one million, seven hundred thousand marks, because the store was completely stripped."

Göring turned to the SS representatives. "Daluege and Heydrich, you'll have to get me that jewelry. Stage raids on a tremendous scale!"

DALUEGE: The order has already been given. People are being searched and places raided all the time. According to my reports, a hundred and fifty people were arrested yesterday afternoon.

GÖRING: Otherwise they'll hide them. If somebody comes into a store with jewels and claims he has bought them, confiscate them at once. He's stolen them or traded them, all right.

HEYDRICH: We've also got to remember that looting was going on all over the Reich, contrary to what we supposed. More than eight hundred cases. But we already have several people in custody who were plundering, and we are trying to get the loot back.

GÖRING: And the jewels?

HEYDRICH: That's difficult to say. Much of it was thrown into the street and picked up there. The same thing happened with the furriers, for example in the Friedrichstrasse, District C. There the crowds were naturally rushing to pick up the minks, skunks, etc. Even children began filling their pockets, just for fun.

HILGARD: These damages are not covered by the policy, I believe. But may I say a word in general about our liabilities? We would like to make it a point, Herr Field Marshal, that we not be hindered in fulfilling the obligations which our contracts call for.

GÖRING: I forbid it! This is important to me.

HILGARD: If I may, I'd like to give the reasons for this request. It simply has to do with the fact that we deal quite extensively with foreign countries. We have a very sound basis for our business transactions abroad, and to maintain a favorable balance of foreign exchange in Germany, we have to make sure that confidence in the German insurance companies is not ruined. If we now refuse to honor clear-cut obligations imposed upon us through lawful contracts, it would be a black spot on the shield of honor of German insurance.

GÖRING: It wouldn't be the minute I issued a decree! A law sanctioned by the state.

HILGARD: I was leading up to that.

HEYDRICH: Why not this: the insurance may be granted, but as soon as it is paid, it will be confiscated. That way we will have saved face.

HILGARD: I'm inclined to agree with what General Heydrich has just said. First of all, use the mechanism of the insurance companies to check on the damage, to regulate it and even pay it, but give the insurance company a chance to—

GÖRING: Just a minute. *You'll* have to pay in any case, because it's the Germans who suffered the damage. But there'll be a lawful decree forbidding you to make any direct payment to Jews. You will also have to make payment for the damage the Jews suffered, but not to the Jews but to the Ministry of Finance.

HILGARD: Aha!

GÖRING (sharply): What the Minister of Finance does with the money is his business!

SCHMER (a member of the Finance Ministry): Your Excellency, I should like to make a proposal. A certain rate should be fixed, say, fifteen percent or perhaps a little higher, of all registered Jewish wealth. I under-

122

stand that one billion marks is to be levied as a fine on the Jews,* so that all Jews should pay equally, and from the money raised in this way the insurance companies could be refunded.

GÖRING: No, I wouldn't dream of refunding the insurance companies. The companies are liable. No, the money belongs to the State. You will fulfill your obligations, you may count on that!

DALUEGE: One more question ought to be cleared up. Most of the goods were not the property of the Jewish store owner but were kept on the books of the firms which had delivered them. Then there are the goods delivered by other firms and not paid for, which are definitely not Jewish but Aryan, those delivered on consignment.

HILGARD: We'll have to pay for them too. Also, there is the question of the glass that was destroyed in the shopwindows. Most of it came from Holland and Belgium and will have to be replaced from there.

GÖRING: With our foreign-currency reserves! [Bitterly, turning to Heydrich] I wish you had killed two hundred Jews instead of destroying so many valuables!

HEYDRICH: Well, there were thirty-five killed. And there will be more!

After the insurance official had been shown out, the committee went on to discuss the general question of Jewry. To Dr. Fritz Doerr, the stenographer who was making the transcript, the keynote was the cynical amusement with which the Nazi officials referred to the plight of the Jews. The riots of two nights before might have been a fiesta, to judge by the remarks made about it. Every time reference was made to the billion-mark fine, there were bursts of laughter.

Only Joseph Goebbels, an archbaiter of Jews and Christian churchmen, rarely smiled, and then only from satisfaction at some major disaster suffered by his ethnic enemies. One of the occasions was when Heydrich read out a list of the damage suffered by the Jewish community during the riots: 101 synagogues destroyed by fire, 76 synagogues demolished by cranes and bulldozers, 7,500 stores and shops wrecked and ruined.

GOEBBELS: I am of the opinion that this is our chance to dissolve the synagogues once and for all. All those not intact shall be razed—by the Jews. The Jews themselves shall pay for it. We must make them suffer!

GÖRING: A billion marks will make every Jew suffer!

GOEBBELS: More than that! I consider it necessary to issue a decree forbidding the Jews to enter German theaters, movie houses and circuses.

---

* As punishment for having "provoked" the German people into demonstrating against them, Hitler had decided that Goebbels' suggestion should be adopted and the Jewish community fined by this amount.

I am already issuing the decree by the authority of the law of the Chamber of Culture [Reich Kulturkammer]. Considering the present situation in the theaters, I believe we can afford that—our theaters are crowded; we have hardly any room. Then there is the question of travel. Do you realize that today in Germany it is still possible for a Jew to share a sleeping compartment with a German? Therefore we need a decree from the Reich Minister for Communications stating that separate compartments shall be set aside for Jews. If all compartments are filled, Jews shall not be able to claim a seat; they will be given a place only after all Germans are seated. They will not be allowed to mix with Germans, and if there is no more room they must stand in the corridor.

GÖRING: In that case, I think it more sensible to give them separate compartments.

GOEBBELS: Not if the train is overcrowded!

GÖRING: Just a minute. There'll only be one Jewish coach. If that is filled, other Jews will have to stay at home!

GOEBBELS: But suppose there weren't many Jews going on the express train to, say, Munich; suppose there were two Jews on the train and the other compartments were crowded. These two Jews would then have a compartment all to themselves. Therefore the Jews should be allowed to get seats only after all Germans have theirs.

GÖRING: I'd like to give the Jews one coach or one compartment. And should a case such as you mention arise and the train is overcrowded, believe me, we won't need a law! We'll kick him out and he'll have to sit all alone in the toilet all the way!

GOEBBELS: I don't agree. I don't believe in this. There ought to be a law! There ought to be a law banning Jews from beaches and resorts. Last summer . . .

After adjourning for lunch, they returned to tackle this thorny problem again.

GÖRING: As the Führer says, we will have to talk over this question of foreign Jews in Germany with the countries who also do something against their own Jews. Poland, for instance. That every dirty Polish Jew has a legal position here in Germany and we have to stand for it—that ought to stop. The Führer was not very happy about the agreement he made with the Poles.* He thinks we should take a few chances and say, 'All right, we are not going to do that; let's talk over what we can accept together. You are doing something against your own Jews in Poland. You dislike them, too. But the minute a Yid [*Itzig*] has left Poland and arrives here, we have to treat him like a Pole.' I'd like to have that altered, disregarded.

* The ten-year German-Polish treaty of friendship of 1934 required each country to give equal treatment to citizens of the other.

124

They reverted to the question of more punitive measures: how to force Jews into ghettos, whether to forbid them to drive cars, or in the case of Jewish girls, wear provocative dresses.

GÖRING: So we are agreed, gentlemen. I shall close the meeting with these words: German Jewry shall, as punishment for their abominable crimes, etc., etc., have to make a contribution of one billion marks. [He stood up.] That should work. The pigs won't commit another murder. I will tell you this, gentlemen: from now on, I would not like to be a Jew in Germany!

"Oh, what tedious people these Germans can be!" said Neville Chamberlain when he read the reports of the anti-Jewish riots and the measures which followed. "Just when we were beginning to make a little progress!"

Had he faced facts, the British Prime Minister would have realized that the progress made was very little indeed. To everyone but the really dedicated appeasers, it was obvious that Anglo-German relations were almost as bad as they had been a year before. Hitler took every opportunity to pour scorn on the English and their leaders. Among the British people themselves, a realization of what had really happened at Munich was beginning to sink in, and the euphoria of the early autumn was fast fading away. When they heard the news of the racial riots from Germany, they were appalled—and repelled by the thought that such people should be offered the hand of friendship.

Unfortunately the "practical" men who were running Britain at the time did not entirely share the revulsion of their citizens. It would be unjust to charge them with being impervious to the crimes being committed in Germany; many public officials denounced such persecution. But it would also be wrong to ignore the fact that a latent antipathy to Jews permeated the upper stratum of British public life. "I loathe anti-Semitism, but I do dislike the Jews," Harold Nicolson, one of the keenest opponents of Munich, was to write later. In the Cabinet itself, Sir John Simon issued a public statement pointing out that he was of Welsh extraction in spite of his Biblical name. The only Jewish member of the Cabinet, Leslie Hore-Belisha, complained bitterly to his friends that he was "one apart" and that his racial background was principally responsible for his cool relations with

125

the Prime Minister. Lord Camrose, proprietor of the *Daily Telegraph* and a powerful supporter of Chamberlain, successfully sued Sir Oswald Mosley's British Union of Fascists, now more pro-Nazi than pro-Fascist, for having called him a Jew. And Dean Inge, of St. Paul's Cathedral, one of the most influential ecclesiastics in the kingdom, wrote an article charging that Jews were "using their not inconsiderable influence in the Press and Parliament to embroil us with Germany."

In this atmosphere, it is not surprising that the appeasers were annoyed at the Jews for having got in the way when the Nazis struck. Nevertheless, Sir Horace Wilson suggested that the Prime Minister should make some public gesture to show his abhorrence of Nazi anti-Semitism, and together they searched for an appropriate method. Eventually they decided that a recent letter from Germany would do: Neville Chamberlain had been asked to accept the presidency of the Deutsche Shakespeare Genossenschaft (the German Shakespeare Society). The Prime Minister declined the offer, but typically, he explained his refusal in the letter to the Genossenschaft as "lack of time," and then had it privately whispered around that he had really done it "because they have banned Jewish members."

Meanwhile, despite all rebuffs Chamberlain pressed ahead. There is an old German saying: *Willst Du nicht mein Bruder sein, schlag' ich Dir den Schädel ein* (Be my brother, or I'll bash your head in). The Prime Minister seemed to be saying to Germany: "I'm determined to be your brother, even if you do keep bashing my head in."

In France as well, the news from Germany was a most unwelcome interruption in the arrangements for collaboration with Germany. In the Foreign Ministry at the Quai d'Orsay, Georges Bonnet had been so busily pressing ahead with the plan for a Franco-German rapprochement, which Ambassador François-Poncet had initiated on his farewell visit to Hitler, that he scarcely noticed the headlines in the newspapers. What alarmed him at first was the fact that the incident which had supposedly initiated the pogrom had occurred on French soil; he sent his profound apologies at once to Berlin, promised to take immediate measures against the "murderer, Grynszpan," and earnestly hoped that it would not impair relations between the two countries. When the memorial service for Secretary

126

vom Rath was held in Paris, Bonnet not only attended but persuaded the President of the Republic, Albert Lebrun, to do so as well. The German Foreign Ministry was represented by Baron Ernst von Weizsäcker; Bonnet was relieved to hear from him that France "would not be blamed for this dastardly crime" and that the negotiations could continue.

Therefore the Foreign Minister was taken aback when he attended a Cabinet meeting in Paris on November 23 and proudly presented a copy of the Franco-German declaration, which, he announced, would be signed by himself and Herr Joachim von Ribbentrop on December 6 in Paris.

"Several ministers regretted the untimeliness of this declaration, in view of Germany's isolation after the anti-Semitic demonstrations," wrote the Minister of Education, Jean Zay. "Daladier pointed out that the negotiations had begun well before that and regretted that it had not been made public earlier. Ribbentrop's arrival in Paris in the next few days was generally opposed, and the Premier certainly seemed to be of this opinion. Bonnet urged his point. I observed that it was easy to see that it was very much in Germany's interest to have herself rehabilitated by France. But were we no longer free? We were bound to cause the most lamentable effect in England and America. There would be deep feeling among the French people. The journey should be postponed.

"Bonnet said that Germany's interests were not concerned, and that she was consenting to the agreement solely to please us. Campinchi was afraid of demonstrations if Ribbentrop were to come to Paris. Monzie suggested Strasbourg.

"I asked whether the agreement could not be signed by the ambassador. Mandel called for postponement of the journey. So did Reynaud. As Daladier pointed out in the end, we were all in agreement on the text. As for the journey, it was agreed that Bonnet should receive the ambassador and tell him frankly that it could only be considered in a calmer atmosphere."

The calmer atmosphere took only a few days to achieve, and Ribbentrop arrived in Paris as scheduled, on December 6. He had asked for a reception "at least equal to that shown when the King and Queen of England came to Paris."* Since France was still a democ-

---

* The royal pair had visited Paris earlier in the year and been acclaimed.

racy, this sort of acclamation proved impossible to arrange, but at least there were no hostile demonstrations. Ribbentrop drove through Parisian streets which were almost completely deserted, but from the point of view of Foreign Minister Georges Bonnet the main object had been achieved. Later that day, on behalf of their two countries, he and Ribbentrop signed the declaration, which said:

1. The French government and the German government fully share the conviction that peaceful and neighborly relations between France and Germany constitute one of the prime elements in the consolidation of the European situation and the maintenance of general peace. The two governments will therefore use all their endeavors to ensure that the relations between their countries develop in this direction.

2. The two governments observe that there is no question of a territorial nature still unsettled between their countries, and they solemnly recognize as definitive the frontier between their two countries as it stands at present.

3. The two governments are determined, subject to their special relations with third powers, to remain in contact on all questions concerning their two countries and to consult one another should the subsequent developments of these questions run the risk of leading to international difficulties.

Of course the declaration was worthless. While Neville Chamberlain had seriously believed that he had received an honest pledge from Hitler when he signed the Anglo-German declaration at Munich, Georges Bonnet was not so stupid; he regarded his piece of paper merely as a political sop for use domestically to quiet his critics.

As for the Germans, they were willing to sign anything that might keep the French calm and off guard. On returning to Berlin, Ribbentrop referred contemptuously to the "ridiculous French, sapped by liberals, Bolsheviks and Jews."

VI

Hitler
over Bohemia

The Kabarett der Komiker was a small night club which operated in a back room of a building on the Kurfürstendamm in the fashionable West End of Berlin, and any foreigner who visited it in 1939 was astonished at what he saw and heard. Not that the entertainment offered was prurient; when the Nazis came to power in 1933, one of their first acts had been to close down the homosexual and lesbian joints and the sadomasochistic striptease dives for which Berlin was famous. After-dark entertainment was now confined to high-kicking legs and an occasional glimpse of a bosom.

The Kabarett der Komiker had survived the Nazi purge because it relied on verbal rather than visual effects to make its impact. The entertainment was divided between sentimental singers, an occasional dancer, some slightly risqué sketches, and the services of what the Germans call a *Conferencier,* a sort of master of ceremonies who tells jokes and sometimes sings between acts. The only difference between Werner Finck and his counterparts in other countries was that his jokes were almost all political, and that every time he voiced them he gambled with his life and liberty.

Werner Finck* was an anti-Nazi who made no secret of his con-

* An indestructible who is still appearing at the Kabarett der Komiker on the Kurfürstendamm today.

129

tempt for Adolf Hitler and the men who were running Germany. He did something no one else in the Reich had the courage to do publicly: he made fun of them. Bouncing onto the Kabarett der Komiker's minuscule stage in his floppy suit, outsize bow tie and sloppy hat, he would lift his hand in a majestic Hitler salute. Then, after a pause, without a muscle moving in his face he would say, "That's how high my dog can jump."

Finck always knew the latest gossip about the Nazi leaders. When Field Marshal Göring's wife, Emmy, announced that she was pregnant, Finck sidled onto the stage and said in a whisper to his audience, "Psst! D'you know what she's going to call the baby if it's a boy? No? I'll tell you! Hamlet. Yes, Hamlet! Why Hamlet? Well, obviously!" And then, hand on his chin, he began pacing back and forth across the stage, reciting, "*Sein oder nicht sein, das ist die Frage!*"*

And each time he concluded his act for the evening, Finck would march to the wings, turn, give the Nazi salute and shout in a strident voice, "Heil . . . er . . . er . . . Now, what *is* that fellow's name?"

No one knows why the Komiker was allowed to stay in business. Between 1936 and 1939 it was temporarily shut four times by Joseph Goebbels, and on five occasions Werner Finck was jailed for "insulting behavior toward the state." But each time the cabaret reopened and Werner Finck returned, his repertoire as bitingly contemptuous as ever.

On January 25, 1939, Captain Paul Stehlin, the assistant air attaché at the French embassy, was sitting at a corner table with General Karl Bodenschatz, Göring's chief aide and the fourth most powerful man in the German air force. As the Frenchman turned to his companion he was relieved to see that Bodenschatz was laughing at Finck's mordant comments on the Nazi leaders. "So long as he doesn't mock the Luftwaffe!" said Bodenschatz.

Handsome, gregarious and popular in Berlin, Paul Stehlin had been born in Alsace-Lorraine and brought up there while it was under German occupation during World War I. He spoke perfect German and was—though the Germans did not know it—a member of the Deuxième Bureau. Since his arrival in Berlin two years before, he had made considerable progress in establishing contacts with the German

---

* Which in German means either "To be or not to be, that is the question" or "His or not his, that is the question."

air force, though he was the first to admit that luck had had a good deal to do with it. There had been an evening a year before when the French ambassador learned at the last moment that one of his guests was ill and could not come to dinner. Stehlin was called in to fill the vacant place and found himself sitting next to a Frau Olga Riegele. Gradually it dawned on him that she was Hermann Göring's sister. He was a good-looking and charming young man, and he obviously appealed to Olga Riegele. Twenty-four hours later he was called in by the ambassador, who told him with a certain hauteur that apparently he had made an impression: he had been invited to dinner the following evening at Frau Riegele's. Stehlin modestly assumed that like other eligible bachelors in diplomatic circles in Berlin, he was once more being called in to fill a vacant place at the dinner table. Not at all; Frau Riegele had quite obviously upset the balance of her table to include him.

At the end of the evening Stehlin was asked to stay behind when the other guests had left, and with a sinking heart he feared that the time had come for him to pay for his supper. He was quite ready to do so, he gloomily decided, since it would all be in the line of duty and for France; he only wished that Frau Riegele were a little younger and slimmer. But instead of being led to the boudoir, he was ushered into the study, where he was presently joined by General Bodenschatz and Hermann Göring himself, both back from an air force dinner and in a talkative mood. What they told him that evening—about Germany's plans for building the West Wall—formed part of an important dispatch which the French ambassador cabled to Paris the next day, and Stehlin's association with the leaders of the Luftwaffe progressed from that night on.

Bodenschatz was one of the few high officers of the Luftwaffe—or of any other branch of the armed forces or Nazi party—who would have dared to patronize the Kabarett der Komiker. Most of the audience was composed of well-to-do Germans deliberately demonstrating their independence of the party, with a sprinkling of foreign diplomats and foreign correspondents, plus the inevitable Gestapo agents. Although Bodenschatz was a loyal admirer of his chief, Hermann Göring, and reflected his views on both air force and political affairs, he was often quite vocal in his criticism of National Socialist policies and Adolf Hitler. The Komiker and its irreverent *Conferencier* seemed to give him relief when he felt particularly frustrated. In any case, it was a good place to meet his young French friend. Who would guess that amid the chatter in the tiny room they were talking secrets? Especially since every so often a couple of pretty girls from the show would join them for a drink.

Bodenschatz was not a spy; he was not that kind of a German. Everything he said to Stehlin was deliberately thought out—almost certainly with Göring—to make the maximum impression on the young Frenchman and to make sure that he relayed the items to his superiors. Stehlin was (and remains) convinced that Hitler himself would have been furious had he known what information was being passed on.

On this evening in January, Bodenschatz seemed to be in a particularly good mood. Stehlin, however, sensed that no earth-shattering revelations would be forthcoming on this occasion. He guessed that Göring's passion of the moment was to widen the estrangement, initiated at Munich, between the French and their English ally. The current policy was to woo the French, sneer at the English and suggest that between them, France and Germany could ensure peace because they had nothing to fear from each other.

"I hope you will let your ambassador know," Bodenschatz said, "that Germany would very much like an entente with France. The fact that we have developed our fortifications in the West is definite proof of our peaceful intentions. You don't build defensive walls if you are going to attack . . . I can tell you that the Führer has the greatest confidence in Daladier. His attitude at Munich and his firmness with the Italians* have made a very strong impression. He has gained the respect of all Germans."

Then Bodenschatz leaned close to the Frenchman and added, "I can tell you this. For Hitler the caliber of the person who heads a foreign state is a much more important factor than its military apparatus. Chamberlain, for instance—the Führer would never have followed the same policy of intimidation against England if she were led by a Lloyd George instead of by Chamberlain."

Here they were interrupted by another appearance of Werner Finck and by the show girls who joined them at their table. For the next half-hour they drank and laughed and flirted.

When they were alone, Bodenschatz began to talk about Göring.

* Daladier had replied tartly to Italian propaganda claims to Nice, Corsica and Tunisia.

In spite of rumors which had been circulating, he could assure Stehlin that Göring was and would remain Hitler's heir, and that dispositions had already been made to this effect.* "It's a good thing," the general said. "He is a man of peace, and a civilized man. He was the first to disapprove of the violence against the Jews. Why, he actually tried to get Goebbels thrown out of the government for inciting the riots."

Bodenschatz then talked about the German air force. It was reorganized and rejuvenated, he said, adding hastily, "to deter our enemies, not to frighten our friends." General Udet was being put in charge of German aerial rearmament. The size of the Luftwaffe should be tripled by 1941, and "If it weren't for the shortage of raw materials, we would already be three times as big."

The general switched back to peace talk again, and to the need of Franco-German understanding. A twinkle came into his eye. "Speaking of Franco-German co-operation," he said, "do you know who else is very interested in it? The American—the transatlantic flier—Colonel Lindbergh. I can't tell you any more about it now. But you'll see; you'll be getting a call from Paris very soon."

Suddenly he turned away his head, and Stehlin saw that he was laughing.

It was dawn before the German general and the French captain parted, but Stehlin wrote out a full report of his conversation before he went to sleep. He was not fooled by what he had been told; he knew that one of the aims of such talks was to divide the Allies and to encourage the appeasers. But since the propaganda was often larded with useful information, and since Bodenschatz was good company, he welcomed the contacts and reported without comment whatever he was told.

The next morning Stehlin took his report to François-Poncet's successor, Ambassador Robert Coulondre, and waited while he read it. As the envoy came to the end, the assistant air attaché saw his eyebrows lift in surprise.

"Now, where could he have got that information?" Coulondre asked. "About getting a call from Paris, I mean." He pushed a teletype across his desk. "Here—this is for you."

It was a message from the French Air Ministry recalling Stehlin immediately for consultations.

* The official announcement of Göring's role as Hitler's successor was not made until September 1, 1939.

. . .

Twenty-four hours later Stehlin arrived in Paris by the night train from Berlin and went straight to the Deuxième Bureau to report to his chiefs. The intelligence men were completely mystified and had no explanation for his sudden recall. But when he reported to the Air Ministry, Stehlin was told that he had an appointment with Minister Guy La Chambre that very afternoon. He spent the next few hours worrying about this. Once previously, in the weeks before Munich, he had transmitted news of German plans as related to him by Frau Riegele and General Bodenschatz, and had ventured to draw certain conclusions from them. He had been sharply informed that General Gamelin, the Army Chief of Staff, had read the report and demanded to know why a junior officer was allowed to express opinions, especially when they did not coincide with those of senior and more experienced officers. He was told emphatically not to do it again. Had he transgressed? Was he about to be sacked by the minister himself? He prayed not, for he liked his job and was fascinated by Berlin.

To Stehlin's relief, Guy La Chambre appeared friendly when he entered the office, and he even congratulated him on his work. Then he settled back in his chair and said, "Charles Lindbergh has just made a long visit to Germany." Stehlin nodded; he had met him at a cocktail party at the U.S. embassy and was well aware of Lindbergh's obsession with Nazi strength and the decadence of the democracies. "He returned to Paris afterward and I talked to him. What he told me, particularly about plane production in Germany, corresponds by and large to what you have told us in your reports. According to Lindbergh, the German aircraft industry is superior to any in the rest of the world, both in quality and output. France and Great Britain will have to make a considerable effort if they wish to catch up. It's the same in the United States, he says; since the end of the war, aviation there has been divided between the Navy and Army and has been neglected."

Stehlin listened intently, wondering where all this was leading to.

"Lindbergh thinks that Germany doesn't want war, despite what has happened in Austria and Czechoslovakia," La Chambre went on. "He believes that the readjustments which Germany wants from Poland with regard to Danzig and the Polish Corridor can be ar-

134

ranged peacefully by negotiations. At the same time, he believes it would be suicide for France, as well as for Great Britain, to let themselves be dragged into a war against Germany now that its air force is so strong and well trained. Great Britain would immediately be neutralized by aerial bombardment, and France would be invaded and beaten by the combined action of tanks and planes."

Here the minister paused, and Stehlin thought to himself, "Here it comes."

La Chambre said, "Lindbergh thinks that after the happy business of the Franco-German accord of last December, it is to be hoped, and it is certainly possible, to develop this good agreement into something more—into a technical co-operation between the two air arms. The Germans have an excellent engine, much more powerful than any other—the Daimler-Benz 601. We have an excellent prototype, the Dewoitine 520. The combination of the two would be a remarkable technical achievement, and at the same time it would be politically sound with a view to maintaining co-operation between France and Germany. This is Lindbergh's proposition, Captain: together, Germany and France should build and manufacture the same aircraft."

The minister didn't ask Stehlin what he thought about the idea, which was just as well, for the young Frenchman couldn't have answered. He was "both stunned and paralyzed." The idea that at this moment in history anyone could conceive of such a project left him incapable of comment.

As if he sensed Stehlin's stupefaction, the minister shuffled his papers for a few minutes, and then said, "Now I'll tell you what has developed about this matter. Field Marshal Göring is *au courant* with the proposition, but for the moment he prefers to claim ignorance. It is through General Udet that the affair is being handled. He is treating it in a private capacity, and I would emphasize that it is very private *indeed*. You know him well, I believe." Stehlin nodded. "You will go to see him—but at his home, not his office. To begin with, at least, the negotiations should be carried on in the greatest secrecy. You mustn't talk to anyone about it—not anyone, neither to your ambassador nor to your chief, General Geffrier."

This time Stehlin could not prevent himself from blurting out, "But *Monsieur le Ministre,* I couldn't possibly keep this affair secret from my ambassador or my chief."

135

La Chambre said testily, "All right, then, just tell General Geffrier."

Stehlin replied, "But in that case it is General Geffrier who will refuse to keep anything of such a serious nature from the ambassador."

Now La Chambre looked annoyed, and Stehlin remembered thinking that the minister was probably beginning to regret having talked to him at all. However, he said, "All right, you can talk to the ambassador and the air attaché, but be sure to stress the extreme secrecy of this matter." He fiddled again with his papers, and then added, "By the way, when you talk to General Udet there is a code word which you should use. It's 'Fieseler Storch.' "*

Stehlin drove straight from the Air Ministry to the airport, flew back to Berlin and at once reported this strange story to General Geffrier. "I refuse to believe it!" the air attaché said immediately. "They couldn't be so mad as to think of such a thing!"

The French ambassador was more receptive. As a politician, he could see possibilities in the project, he said, and encouraged Stehlin to start negotiations at once.

A few days later Stehlin arrived at General Udet's apartment in Berlin and was shown into the study, where he found the general with three colleagues from the Luftwaffe. A couple of bottles of brandy were on the table and it was obvious that all of them had been drinking for some time. Udet greeted the Frenchman with bearlike claps of friendship on the back and poured him a large cognac. Stehlin hastily drained it; this was clearly not the moment to demonstrate abstemiousness.

After a few minutes of badinage and joshing—a well-known Berlin beauty had a passion for Stehlin, and it was becoming known— the young assistant air attaché ventured to explain that he had come to talk about "Fieseler Storch."

General Udet chose to misunderstand him. Yes, he said, the Fieseler Storch was being built and it would prove to be a most useful aircraft. Germany had already built scores, and would build many more. How many was France interested in purchasing?

Stehlin made his stupefaction obvious. "I'm not talking about aircraft," he said. "I'm talking about the project *Fieseler Storch*."

* Fieseler Storch was actually the name of a short-takeoff reconnaissance and communications plane which the Germans were then developing.

136

Udet filled his own glass again and drained it, then recharged those of his guests and urged them to have more. He was very drunk. Finally he said, "All right, I know. You're interested in the Daimler-Benz engine. Well, everything I've said about the Fieseler Storch sums it up. What are you going to do?"

Then he began to laugh, and his friends joined in. Stehlin laughed too; it was the only thing to do. He was beginning to realize that the Germans had been bluffing. They were amazed that Colonel Lindbergh had fallen for the idea, and they must have been even more surprised that it had been taken seriously by the French. They must have been impressed, too—not so much by Lindbergh's naïveté as by France's pathetic eagerness to achieve any kind of rapprochement with the Reich. Nothing further ever came of the scheme, of course.

Early in February, news of the ill-conceived Franco-German project reached the ears of the *Conferencier* at the Kabarett der Komiker. "Have you heard about the new Franco-German bird they have hatched in the aviary at Frankfurt?" Werner Finck asked his audience one night. "It's the result of a mating between a German eagle and a Strasbourg goose. The first thing it did when it was hatched was try to give a German salute with its right foot, and it fell flat on its face in the mud, squawking loudly. 'What's that you're saying?' asked the keeper, helping it up. 'Heil Hitler!' replied the bird, between mouthfuls of mud. 'It may have been "Heil Hitler" to you,' said the keeper, 'but it sounded much more like '*Merde*' to me!'"

Once again Bodenschatz joined Stehlin in the laughter.

In spite of the almost pathetic eagerness with which he was now urging loans and trade agreements on the scornful Führer, Neville Chamberlain was not making much progress in his appeasement of Adolf Hitler. Repeatedly rebuffed, but occasionally nagged by doubt, he searched for a panacea to remedy the situation and restore his stature with the British people. He was aware that not only the "Churchill-Eden-Jewish" clique, as Sir Horace Wilson called the anti-appeasers, was beginning to murmur against his policies now; and though he had no intention of changing his program, it would

137

have been helpful if just once in a while Hitler had thrown him a scrap of encouragement instead of showing irritation with him—some people might even have called it contempt—each time he spoke in public.

In Chamberlain's opinion, Munich had settled the fate of Czechoslovakia and Eastern Europe; henceforth they were to be regarded as in the German orbit. Though he took care to let no one outside his immediate circle—certainly neither Parliament nor the public—know of this startling surrender of British interests in Europe, he confided his views to Ambassador Joseph P. Kennedy through his official spokesman, Lord Halifax. The previous October, while taking tea with Kennedy, the Foreign Minister had expatiated on Chamberlain's post-Munich outlook. Halifax said he thought that there was no point in fighting unless Hitler directly interfered with Britain or the dominions. It was a question of Britain building up her air strength so that she could no longer be threatened. Kennedy also reported Halifax as saying that "Reasonably soon Hitler will make a start for Danzig, with Polish concurrence, and then for Memel, with Lithuanian acquiescence, and even if he decided to go into Rumania it is Halifax's idea that England should mind her own business. He contends again that Britain would never have got into the Czechoslovakian situation if it had not been for France." Apparently the thought that Britain, together with France, had agreed at Munich to guarantee the frontiers of this rump state filled the Prime Minister with distaste, and he was determined that no power on earth would make him implement it in the event of a new crisis. On this general point, Chamberlain and Hitler were singularly of one mind, though for different reasons. Hitler's aim was total disintegration of the Czechoslovak Republic, and internal events seemed to be playing into his hands.

In the weeks following Munich, Slovakia and Ruthenia made increasingly strong demands for autonomy in what was now a federal state. Tiso had taken over the Slovak People's party—right-wing, with Fascist leanings—after its founder, Monsignor Andrej Hlinka, died in August 1938, and three months later, autonomy was granted to Slovakia and Ruthenia. Emil Hácha was made President of the government in Prague, and Jozef Tiso became Premier.

Now then, how to make the Führer more amenable? Chamberlain

thought of trying his friend Mussolini. He had great influence on Hitler; perhaps he could steer him into more peaceful waters. So on November 27 a telegram went off to Lord Perth, the British ambassador in Rome, asking him to arrange a meeting between Mussolini and the Prime Minister.

H.M. Ambassador to Italy, the Earl of Perth, Hereditary Thane of Lennox and Hereditary Steward of Menteith and Strathearn, Privy Councillor, Grand Commander of the Order of St. Michael and St. George, and Knight Commander of the Bath, thought Mussolini was wonderful, and not simply because he had made the trains run on time. He strongly opposed his own government's policy of resisting any of Italy's projects, from the conquest of Abyssinia to support of Franco in Spain, and he hoped that his love for the Italians was returned. He was so naïve that he did not realize—although he had had several warnings—that the Italians had broken the British diplomatic code by infiltrating an agent into his embassy, and that all his messages to London and all reports sent him by the Foreign Office were in the hands of Mussolini and Foreign Minister Ciano within a few hours. Indeed, Lord Perth had even had his own dispatches quoted back to him by Ciano without guessing that someone must have passed them on.

One of the situations which made a visit to Italy difficult for Neville Chamberlain was that he would be meeting "on friendly terms" a dictator whose planes were deliberately bombing British ships in the Mediterranean at this very time. By an accord made between Italy and Britain nearly a year before, Mussolini had agreed to withdraw the Italian troops who were helping General Franco to take over Spain; at the same time, it was implied but not stated that the "unknown" planes and submarines which were sinking the British ships that supplied the Loyalist forces would be called off.

Perth made tentative approaches to Count Ciano, promising to ratify the Anglo-Italian agreement, provided that, first, Mussolini would call off his planes, and second, he would keep the matter secret for the time being. Ciano immediately informed the Italian press of the ambassador's approach, blandly told Perth that he had "no control over Italian planes in the service of General Franco," and then awaited the next move. He was delighted a few hours later to be brought a decoded transcript of Perth's dispatch to London saying that the Italian government had refused to order the cessation of attacks on British ships, but did "this matter since the crews of these ships nearly always had been Greek"?

It was in this atmosphere of scarcely veiled contempt that Neville Chamberlain and Lord Halifax were received in Rome in January 1939, when they came to ask the help of Mussolini in dealing with Hitler. The Italians, never willing to miss a pageant, entertained their guests lavishly. There was a grand banquet in the Palazzo Venezia at which Benito Mussolini wore the sash and insignia of the Grand Commander of the Order of the Bath. Lord Halifax sat next to Edda Ciano, Mussolini's daughter who was married to the Foreign Minister, and recalled the time when she had dined with him and his wife in India when he was Viceroy.* He came to the conclusion that she was not the nice, respectable girl he had known in those days but had acquired "certain sophistications." (Apparently in the course of their conversation she asked Halifax whether Mrs. Chamberlain had a lover, and which member of the entourage had been chosen—a suggestion that filled the puritanical Englishman with indignation.)

Except for propaganda purposes, there was no reason at all why Chamberlain should have made his visit to Rome. He had nothing to gain from talking to the Italian dictator, unless reassurance, delivered tongue in cheek, was the anodyne he was seeking. This Mussolini gave him without hesitation.

As they had their final talk in Rome on January 12, Chamberlain ventured to ask the opinion of the Duce on a matter of some delicacy. He had hoped that after the Munich settlement, which the Duce had done so much to bring about, it would be possible to put relations between England and Germany on a better footing.

Mussolini replied that this was Italy's hope too—all Europe's hope. Chamberlain said he regretted that it had not been possible. He found it hard to fathom the motives of the Führer, who had rejected every overture. The attitude of Germany had given rise to a good deal of anxiety and doubt. The Prime Minister hesitated, and then spoke of recent rumors from Eastern Europe. Some people thought that the massing of German troops might mean a move toward the Ukraine

---

* "Though I did not remind her of the report," he wrote later, "of her having kicked a young subaltern in the stomach who tried to kiss her at some moonlight entertainment at Humayum's tomb."

140

or Poland, or against Poland and Russia combined. There was another pause, which perhaps was meant to imply that such moves would not be unfavorably received by Chamberlain and his government, and then he added that there were also rumors that Hitler might be planning a sudden attack against the West.

Mussolini looked at the Englishman with the wry expression of a benevolent uncle coping with an unsuccessful nephew on the verge of being evicted by the bailiffs, and then told him to put this out of his mind. An attack on the West was out of the question. Nor did he believe the Führer was thinking of attacking the Ukraine and setting up an independent unit there. There was no reason to worry; Hitler was too busy digesting his new and expanded Reich.

Chamberlain shook his head. He still thought it was an uneasy situation. "I wish you would talk to him," he said, and Mussolini agreed to do so.

Chamberlain departed, well satisfied with his visit, convinced that Mussolini was now on his side. But as soon as he was out the door, the Italian dictator commented, "Oh, these tired sons of the decadent British! [They] will lose their empire!" And Count Ciano wrote in his diary: "They [Chamberlain and Halifax] would be ready for any sacrifice if they could see the future clearly. This somber preoccupation of theirs has convinced me more and more of the necessity for the Triple Alliance [military treaty between Italy, Germany, and Japan]. With such an instrument in our hands, we could get whatever we want . . . I have telephoned Ribbentrop that the [British] visit was a fiasco."

It was at about this time that Ambassador William Bullitt in Paris was reporting to Washington that the French had recovered their nerve after the humiliations of Munich, and were ready to stand up to their adversaries again—particularly the Italians. Had not Premier Daladier responded to Italian cries for Nice, Corsica and Tunisia by a firm rejection?

"France is now becoming quite spunky," reported Harold L. Ickes after a Cabinet meeting at the White House on January 29, 1939. "It has announced through its Chamber of Deputies and its Government that it will fight rather than lose an acre of its Empire. Bill

141

Bullitt thinks that France will fight if Italy starts to slice pieces from off her. But will England support France, or has Chamberlain already sold the British Empire down the river?"

In fact, France was already selling herself down the river. On February 4, within five days of Ickes' comment, a secret emissary from France arrived in Rome to see Count Ciano. He was Paul Baudouin, president of the French-controlled Bank of Indochina, and he brought credentials from both Premier Daladier and Foreign Minister Georges Bonnet.

The German ambassador to Italy, Hans Georg von Mackensen, reported to his Foreign Minister the same day:

"Count Ciano saw me early today to ask to give you, in the greatest secrecy, the following information:

"Herr Baudouin . . . with the secret backing of Daladier and Bonnet . . . told him that [the French] were ready to start talks with the Italians over Franco-Italian questions with the aim of reaching a friendly solution to these questions. It went without saying that for these talks a full discussion would be held of Italian wishes about recognized territory.

"In connection with such a program of talks Herr Baudouin had the following suggestions:

"1. a. Djibouti [in French Somaliland, East Africa, and the only port connecting the Red Sea with the Italian-held kingdom of Abyssinia]. A harbor. Arrangement of a wide Free Zone (half the harbor?) . . . Co-operative work in developing the harbor.

"b. Railway, Djibouti–Addis Ababa: that part running through French Somaliland to remain French, that in Abyssinia to be turned over to Italy, with the French ready to provide the necessary capital to keep it going. Co-operative enterprise to build a new station in the Free Zone.

"2. Suez Canal. Since much of the capital is English and Egyptian, and not France's alone, joint action would be necessary [to give membership to Italy], but France is ready for a solution in the interest of the states using the Canal, and the necessary alterations to the Board of Control. Further, France is willing to see an adjustment of the tariff. Ciano here remarked that he drew Baudouin's attention to the need to find a solution which would also meet our—German —wishes in this area.

"3. Tunis. Return of the rights of Italians in Tunis. Baudouin

142

didn't precisely outline French views, but Ciano said the Italians must have absolutely full rights returned to them.

"Ciano agreed that the negotiations would be official but would be handled with great secrecy and discretion. Baudouin said that if there was any leak, it would be denied . . ."

The German Foreign Minister realized that once started, official negotiations might well lead to a Franco-Italian rapprochement, which was the last thing Germany desired at the moment. At this time Hitler and Ribbentrop were working hard to draw Italy once and for all into the German camp by persuading Mussolini to sign a military pact of mutual assistance. Agreement with the French could sabotage it. Therefore Ribbentrop immediately leaked the news of Baudouin's approach and the aims of Daladier and Bonnet, and had the satisfaction of watching the two French politicians angrily denying everything in the face of the outcry from the French and British public.

■

In Adolf Hitler's mind there had never been any doubt that Czechoslovakia would eventually come completely under the control of the German Reich; it was merely a question of how and when. In the months following his easy victory at Munich he had come to believe that Chamberlain and Daladier, with the misguided connivance of Mussolini, had tricked rather than appeased him, and that a more forthright and determined attitude would have given him the whole of Bohemia and Moravia instead of merely the Sudetenland. Long after the event, he continued to complain that Chamberlain was "that fellow [who] cheated me of my entry into Prague," and the more he saw of the supine attitudes of the Western democracies, the more he regretted not having been tougher.

But the Führer was shrewd enough to see that with patience he would get all he wanted, and without having to fight for it. Was that, however, really what he had in mind? Would the fact that the new Czechoslovakia was practically pleading to be regarded as an obedient satellite of the Reich satisfy his needs? For Hitler had needs, as far as the Czechs were concerned: a need to see himself in control of their destinies, since he suspected that as non-Germans they despised him; a need to demonstrate to the world that though they proclaimed

143

themselves so-called democrats and liberals, they would do his bidding at the crack of a whip. In his attitude toward the peoples of Central and Eastern Europe, Adolf Hitler remained an Austrian and was as arrogant a racialist as Emperor Franz Josef of the Austro-Hungarian Empire had been.

The new government in Prague never made any bones about its willingness to be considered a puppet state, and each time its Foreign Minister, Chvalkovský, was summoned to Berlin, he bent his small head in submission and pleaded to be helped and understood by the overlords of Greater Germany. He attacked the English and French; he sneered at the United States; he presented statistics to prove that the Jews and Communists were being driven out of Czech life. When pressed, he would admit that the change from freedom and democracy to wholehearted dependence on the Reich was perhaps not as swift as it might be, and that there were some Czechs who were not completely co-operative, but he added, "I hope that the Führer will have a good word for the Czechs sometimes. That could do wonders."

And yet if the remainder of Czechoslovakia fell into Germany's hands, just like that, what would be the triumph? Eduard Beneš had once defied Germany from the heights of Hradčany Castle in Prague; Hitler had seen pictures of him in the palace, which dominated the swift-flowing Vltava River. It was a building and a site that appealed to his sense of the dramatic. It was here that German kings had once ruled, waged wars, received vassals and settled the destiny of Central and Eastern Europe. But how could he ever usurp the seat once occupied by the hated Beneš if a subservient Czech state simply went on doing what the Germans told it to do?

But by March the Czechs provided him with the excuse he was seeking to turn a servile satellite into a dependency needing his "protection."

Some months earlier, in November 1938, the Germans and Italians had presided over a congress in Vienna to settle the eastern frontier of Czechoslovakia. Hungary in particular was seeking large tracts of territory which would extend far beyond those areas of Slovakia and Ruthenia where the majority of the population was Magyar. Encouraged by the Italians, with whom they had a long-standing alliance, they even went so far as to threaten to occupy the city of Bratislava, the ancient capital of Slovakia. Since Bratislava (or Pressburg, as the Germans called it) was just across the Danube from Austria and not many miles from Vienna itself, this was too much for Adolf Hitler. In any case, like most Austrians, he was fundamentally anti-Hungarian and was contemptuous of their cowardice during the Munich crisis. Why should they eat the meal they had refused to help to cook? Hence he ordered Ribbentrop to resist the Hungarian demands and to support the Slovak delegates in their pleas for the retention of their capital and territory—and so it was decided, to the ill-concealed disappointment of the Hungarians and Italians.

In approving the frontier in favor of the Slovaks, Hitler had only one idea in mind: to bring about the final disintegration of the Czechoslovak state. Ribbentrop had made it clear to the Slovak leaders, headed by Monsignor Jozef Tiso,* that they were being saved from the Hungarians in order to become independent and to break off their relations with the Czechs under President Emil Hácha in Prague. In the weeks that followed, however, not only did the Slovaks show no signs of breaking away; the Czechs made it clear that they would not be allowed to do so by moving troops into the area, especially into Bratislava, and threatening to use force against any Slovakian coup d'état.

On the evening of March 9, 1939, a message reached President Hácha as he was having supper with his daughter in Hradčany Castle. His Foreign Minister wanted to see him urgently.

The tiny gnome who now represented the external relations of Czechoslovakia was perspiring visibly when he came into the President's study, and it was obvious that he was extremely nervous. From Chvalkovský's hand a piece of paper fluttered, and he stammered several times before he could begin speaking. He had important news, he said. A message had just come through from Bratislava, and he feared that they were in for trouble unless they moved swiftly. The paper came from a most reliable source in the city, Klinevsky, the chief of police and head of intelligence in Slovakia.

Hácha reminded the Foreign Minister that he could not see well in such poor light and asked him to read it.

Chvalkovský did so. "I have to report that from the most reliable sources of information inside the Cabinet itself, a coup d'état is being

---

* Political priests were an old tradition in this part of Europe. The Roman Catholic Premier's principal political opponent, Karol Sidor, was also of the priesthood.

prepared by Tiso and Durčansky [Minister of Communications in the Slovak federal government]. They have already been in contact with Seyss-Inquart and Bürckel in Vienna [Seyss-Inquart was the Nazi governor of Austria, and Josef Bürckel Gauleiter of the district abutting the Slovakian frontier], who have agreed to co-operate. Arms are being smuggled into Bratislava by the Nazis and will be given to the Hlinka Guard [the Slovak fascist group] and the German minority under Kerminski, their leader. They will conduct demonstrations and threaten a rising if Tiso does not declare Slovakia's independence of Prague. Tiso will bow to the demands of the people, and will sever his connection with the central government on March tenth."

There was a long silence, broken only by the crackle of paper as Chvalkovský folded the message. Finally the Foreign Minister coughed. What should be done?

The old man shook himself as if he had been asleep; he was old and tired and frightened.

There was only one thing to be done, he answered, if the state was to be saved from disintegration: act at once. The rebellion must be put down. The orders must be sent through at once to the army. Tiso and Durčansky must be arrested. A new Cabinet should be formed at once—under Karol Sidor, of course. At least he was reliable.

There was silence again. Chvalkovský waited, but the old man was sunk in gloom. After a few minutes he slowly tiptoed out of the room and motioned to Hácha's devoted daughter, Mrs. Milada Radlova, waiting outside, to tend to him.

Later that night in Bratislava, Czech army officers called on Monsignor Tiso in his office in the old rathskeller overlooking the bridge across the Danube leading to Austria, and politely informed him that he was under arrest.

Tiso seemed astonished. "What is the reason?" he asked.

They told him that they did not know the precise reason but believed it was to prevent the coup d'état he was planning.

"What coup d'état?" Tiso asked. "I know nothing about it. I am loyal to Prague."

The priest was taken to a monastery some fifty miles from the city, where a cell had been prepared for him and a guard stationed at the gates.* Then the army officers set off to find Durčansky. But warned of the orders for his arrest, more aware of what was going on than Monsignor Tiso, Durčansky had already crossed the Danube.

Meanwhile Klinevsky, the Bratislava chief of police and Prague's "reliable" intelligence chief in Slovakia, was on the telephone with Bürckel to report that all had gone well: the Prague government had swallowed the bait. For it was in connivance with Durčansky and the Germans that Klinevsky had drawn up the report for Hácha of Monsignor Tiso's planned coup d'état. It was completely false.

The trap had been set for Prague. Now all that was needed was the order to spring it.

■

The city boosters of San Remo, the large Italian resort just over the French border from Menton, have always maintained that its winter climate is warmer, sweeter and calmer than its more famous neighbors. They call it the City of Flowers, and to prove it they decorate every space with masses of the carnations and other opulent blooms cultivated in the surrounding countryside.

Field Marshal Hermann Göring had traveled south to this city at the end of January with his buxom, jolly wife Emmy and their baby daughter for a rest after his labors with the rearmament of the Luftwaffe and the rigors of the Four-Year Plan. It had seemed a good time to leave; the Führer appeared to be in a good mood and no longer bemoaning his being cheated of a victor's ride into Prague. As far as Göring could see, the crisis with the democracies, and the war which even he regarded as inevitable, would not come now until 1941–1942, and by that time he hoped to have both the air force and the economy in shape to meet it. In the meantime he was on holiday, and enjoying himself, for he felt particularly at home among the Italians. He was sure that of all the Nazi leaders his personality was perhaps the only one which the Italians found simpatico. When he took his morning walk along the sea front with Emmy, baby and nurse in tow, the young men cheered, policemen stopped the traffic, and the girls blushed with pleasure at his open admiration of their qualities. With the tourists too he was popular, and when he was

* Twenty-four hours later the monks let Tiso out and he made his way back to Bratislava.

gambling at the Casino in the evening, an English general or milady usually came over to congratulate him about Munich. Rumor had it that although Mussolini had stage-managed the Munich Conference, it was Göring who several times had saved it from collapse or from sabotage by Ribbentrop.

But in the fifth week of the Field Marshal's stay at San Remo his complacency was shattered by a letter from Hitler, brought by an emissary from the German embassy in Rome. By the time Hermann Göring had read it through, his good humor had disappeared.

No copy of the letter exists, but as Göring recalled it afterward, the import was that the Führer felt he had made a mistake in not occupying Prague the previous September. Why had he not done it? The democracies would never have dared to interfere. Instead, he had allowed himself to be satisfied with the Sudetenland, and look what had happened since. In Prague they still allowed Jews to work on newspapers and to attack the Reich. The Czechs professed to have ended their pact with the Bolsheviks and to have made Communism illegal, but everyone knew that they were still in touch with Moscow and with Beneš, and that the Bolsheviks had merely gone underground . . . The Slovaks were a disappointment. They showed no spirit and let themselves remain tied to Prague's apron strings . . . In any case, though the Czech ministers groveled, the people still showed signs of not knowing who their masters were . . . The Führer could not let these developments go on indefinitely . . . He had come to the conclusion that there was only one solution to the problem: he would have to occupy the remainder of Bohemia and Moravia.

Göring was alarmed by the letter. While the courier stood by, he canceled his arrangements for the evening and sat down to compose a reply which was to be delivered to Hitler as quickly as possible. He pointed out that to occupy Prague at this time would only create turbulence in the atmosphere just at the moment when the skies were clearing for Germany . . . It would mean a serious loss of prestige for the British Prime Minister, and the Field Marshal doubted that he would survive it. And what would happen if he did not? Then Winston Churchill would come to power, and the Führer knew only too well Churchill's malevolent attitude to Germany . . . Secondly, the move would not be understood in Germany or abroad, for only a short time before, Hitler had said that things were settled to his general satisfaction . . . Thirdly, though he understood the Führer's

148

concern over the danger from the Czechs, surely the occupation and control of the land and people could be achieved, admittedly more slowly, but in a way which would avoid exciting either the Czechs or other nations. Since the incorporation of Austria and the Sudetenland, the economic penetration of the rest of Czechia must be a matter of time. That is to say, he hoped that by strong economic ties a customs union could be formed which would serve the economic interests of both countries. If this took place, then a sovereign Czechoslovakia would be so politically bound to Germany and German interests that there would never be any danger from her again.

The courier set off with the letter, and Hermann Göring tried to get back into his holiday spirit. It was no use; the mood had been broken. For the next few days he hung around, fretting, waiting for an answer from the Führer. It did not come. Instead, at about the time when Monsignor Tiso was escaping from his monastery in Slovakia, Adolf Hitler told Colonel Schmundt to send a telegram to Göring. All it said was: "Return at once."

General Wilhelm Keitel, Chief of the Armed Forces High Command, had been waiting for orders since the end of February. He knew the signs; German newspapers had begun to fill with all the old stories. The savage Czechs were on the rampage again, but this time they were not only persecuting innocent German minorities; they were also bullying and brutalizing the Slovaks. Not a day passed without the *Völkischer Beobachter,* the official Nazi newspaper, reporting that a pregnant Slovak mother had been cold-bloodedly kicked in the stomach by a Czech soldier, or a Slovak student had been insulted by a Czech professor.

"The Führer repeatedly announced that he had put up with as much as he could stand and did not intend to stand impotently by," Keitel wrote later. "I gathered that the so-called 'cleaning up' of rump Czechoslovakia was drawing near. Although when I asked the Führer he would neither admit his ultimate intentions nor give me any kind of date, I took the necessary steps to see that the War Office was assured of being able to unleash a swift and sudden invasion should the need arise."

In early March, Hitler had called a meeting of his two senior generals, Keitel and Brauchitsch, the Commander in Chief of the

Army, and told them flatly that he had resolved upon military intervention in Czechoslovakia. He called it a "pacification operation" and said that it would not require any military conscription over and above that provided for in the orders still in force from the crisis of the previous autumn. But even now he did not give his generals a date.

"I put my own money on 'the Ides of March,' " wrote Keitel. "Apart from 1937, it had always been the date since 1933 that Adolf Hitler had chosen to act on. Was it always coincidence or superstition? I am inclined to believe the latter . . . Sure enough, on March 12 the advance orders went out to the army and air force to stand by for a possible invasion of Czechoslovakia at six o'clock on the morning of March 15; no forces were to approach within six miles of the frontier before then. None of us soldiers learned what circumstances were to be invoked for the unleashing of such an attack."

When he heard the news, Keitel went to his office in the Bendlerstrasse and at once sent out a top-secret memorandum to his senior generals telling them to be ready. Within thirty minutes a copy had been received by Admiral Canaris, and was also being scanned by his assistant, Colonel Oster.

Word was quickly passed to General Halder, the Army Chief of Staff, to Count Helldorff, the Berlin police chief, to General von Witzleben and all the other senior officers who had been involved in the stillborn *Putsch* against Hitler in September 1938. Had their moment come again? Surely this time the British and French would not let Hitler get away with it. Had they not guaranteed the frontiers and integrity of the new Czechoslovakia? Had not Hitler promised that the Sudetenland was his last territorial claim in Europe, and that he would never try to incorporate non-Germans in the Reich?

To activists like Oster and Canaris, this seemed to be the opportunity for resuscitating the conspiracy and for ridding Germany of Hitler once and for all. But General Halder was more skeptical. The behavior of the British at Munich had shocked and dispirited him, and he had lost faith in the determination of the democracies to fight even for themselves, let alone Czechoslovakia. Hence, his reply to the conspirators was that he would join them and take part in a coup—but only if the Western democracies intervened once Hitler had crossed the Czech frontier.

150

If the democracies were informed of Hitler's intentions in advance, would they take the necessary steps?

Canaris handed over the Keitel memorandum to Oster, who did not need to be told what to do. He already had several contacts with the British Secret Service.

On March 11 the head of the British Secret Service telephoned from his office in Whitehall and asked for an immediate appointment with Sir Alexander Cadogan, Permanent Undersecretary at the Foreign Office. The two men met, and Sir Alexander was handed a decoded message from Germany which read:

THE GERMAN ARMY WILL INVADE BOHEMIA AND MORAVIA AT SIX A.M. ON MARCH 15. IRREGULAR FORCES WILL CROSS THE FRONTIER SOME HOURS AHEAD OF THIS BUT THESE WILL BE FOR DIVERSIONARY PURPOSES AND ARE NOT TO BE CONFUSED WITH THE MAIN OPERATION. AN ULTIMATUM OF SHORT DURA-TION WILL BE HANDED TO THE CZECH AUTHORITIES AND TO THE CHIEF OF THE CZECH ARMED FORCES ORDERING THEM TO LAY DOWN THEIR ARMS, GROUND THEIR AIRCRAFT AND RETURN TO BARRACKS, BUT THIS WILL NOT BE DELIVERED UNTIL THE LAST POSSIBLE MOMENT. THE MAIN ELEMENT OF THE OPERATION IS SURPRISE.

In view of the stupefaction and indignation which the British Prime Minister was subsequently to display over the events of the next few days, the history of what happened to this message is worth noting. In the first place Sir Alexander Cadogan, who must have been told by his intelligence chief the source of the message, seemed to show surprisingly little alarm. To be sure, he wrote in his diary that "it made my hair stand on end," and he did say that he would show it to the Foreign Secretary and the Prime Minister at once. But thereafter he allowed Halifax to depart for various engagements around the country. As for Chamberlain, apparently it did not occur to him to summon the Cabinet for a briefing or to call in his service chiefs and discuss the situation with them.

In the meantime Captain Stehlin, responding to hints from Frau Olga Riegele, had been out in his private plane over the area between the Czech frontier and Dresden. He reported back to Paris that heavy troop movements were in progress toward Bohemia. What Paris

151

thought of the reports he never found out. There was no reaction at all to his message.

In a private apartment on the outskirts of Bratislava, a group of frightened men were holding a meeting early on Sunday morning, March 12.

Karol Sidor, Premier of the Slovak government, had held his first Cabinet meeting the evening before in the rathskeller in the center of the city, close to the Danube, and quickly learned something of the situation which he and his people were facing. At ten o'clock, halfway through the discussion, the doors were suddenly flung open and into the room marched Seyss-Inquart, Gauleiter Bürckel and five men whose uniforms and insignia identified them as generals in the German army. They had driven across the Danube from Austria and, as Seyss-Inquart explained to the mortified Slovaks, they hadn't much time to spare, for there was a great deal to do back in Vienna. Events were on the march.

All he had come to say, Seyss-Inquart went on, was that the Slovak government should not delay in proclaiming its independence. The Führer was not uninterested in the fate of Slovakia, but that fate was not likely to be a happy one if there was any more procrastination in Bratislava. His friends were—indicating the generals—witness to the fact that the German army was not far away.

Then he stalked out, the generals following, though Gauleiter Bürckel stayed behind to whisper to Sidor, "The Führer has decided to settle the fate of the Czechs once and for all. For God's sake, don't waste any more time in proclaiming independence—otherwise I can't tell you what will happen to you!"

The Slovakian Premier promised to keep the warning in mind, but stated firmly that neither he nor his colleagues could make a decision without first consulting Prague. He spent the rest of the night talking to Chvalkovský on the telephone, getting nowhere. Then, having decided that the rathskeller was too near the Danube and Austria, he asked his Cabinet to come to his own apartment at eight o'clock in the morning. He was about to put the issue to them when Klinevsky, the chief of police, rushed in. "You'll have to get out!" he said. "I have information that the Hlinka Guard knows you are meeting here and may attack you at any moment."

152

Sidor said that if so, they could not carry on government business in Bratislava. They were too near the Germans and their *francs-tireurs*. They should move the seat of government to Trnava, a small town twenty miles farther from the border.

Klinevsky told him that this was impossible; German troops had taken up positions on all routes leading from the city, and they would never get through.

Where, then, could they meet in safety? Sidor asked plaintively. Klinevsky suggested going to the *Slovak* offices. *Slovak* was the chief newspaper of Monsignor Tiso. Since he was such a bitter opponent of Premier Sidor, no one would guess that they would hold a Cabinet meeting there.

They finally agreed on this, but when the panicky members of the Cabinet filed into the editor's office, whom should they find sitting there but Monsignor Tiso himself, fresh from his monastery-prison. Without any formality he told his visitors that Gauleiter Bürckel had just delivered a telegram to him from Adolf Hitler summoning him to Berlin at once.

Sidor said firmly that Tiso must refuse to go, since it was no longer his responsibility. Tiso replied that he could not refuse—for Slovakia's sake. Bürckel had told him that if he did not comply with the Führer's request, two German divisions would occupy Bratislava; they were just across the river now. Furthermore, the Hungarians would be given carte blanche; Hitler had already promised them Ruthenia. If Tiso did not go to Berlin, Hitler would let them take eastern Slovakia as well.

Klinevsky agreed that the priest should go. Hitler might hate the Czechs, but he was Slovakia's friend. There was everything to gain by his going.

Tiso added that what he had most to gain was time. There was no train to Vienna before Monday morning, the next day. He could not possibly be back before Tuesday evening to deliver whatever decision the Führer decided to make. This gave the others time to consult Prague, and time for Prague to consult Warsaw—for Poland would certainly not be uninterested in their fate—and the situation might well be different by the time he returned.

Different it was, but not quite in the way Tiso had hoped, for the Germans had shrewdly anticipated his thinking. When the Monsignor's train arrived in Vienna just before noon on Monday morning,

March 13, two Gestapo officers were waiting for him. They saluted him and politely invited him into a waiting car. Forty minutes later he was in a plane on his way to Berlin, and his former deputy, Durčansky, was in the seat beside him. At six-forty that evening they were led into the Reich Chancellery to meet the Führer.

Outside, Berliners were buying the evening newspapers and staring at the flaring red headlines. "GERMAN BLOOD FLOWS AGAIN IN CZECHIA" read the one on the front page of the *Völkischer Beobachter*. It was just like old times.

Inside the German legation in Prague, the minister was reading a secret telegram which had just been delivered to him from Berlin:

> WITH REFERENCE TO TELEPHONIC INSTRUCTIONS GIVEN BY KORDT TODAY, IN CASE YOU SHOULD GET ANY WRITTEN COMMUNICATION FROM PRESIDENT HÁCHA, PLEASE DO NOT MAKE ANY WRITTEN OR VERBAL COMMENTS OR TAKE ANY OTHER ACTION BUT PASS THEM ON HERE BY CIPHER TELEGRAM. MOREOVER I MUST ASK YOU AND THE OTHER MEMBERS OF THE LEGATION TO MAKE A POINT OF NOT BEING AVAILABLE IF THE CZECH GOVERNMENT WANTS TO COMMUNICATE WITH YOU DURING THE NEXT FEW DAYS.

The message was signed by Joachim von Ribbentrop, the German Foreign Minister.

Up the hill, in Hradčany Castle, President Hácha asked once more whether there had been any reply to his calls to Bratislava.

Foreign Minister Chvalkovský shook his head. The lines must be cut; they could get no answer at all. When Hácha suggested that they perhaps should consult the Germans and ask for their advice, Chvalkovský replied drily that the way events seemed to be leading them, any consultation would have to be by written message. The German embassy also did not seem to be answering that evening.

■

Sir Horace Wilson remembers how happy Neville Chamberlain was all that week. "Very cheerful. Extremely optimistic," he recalls.

154

On Thursday the Prime Minister had given a small party for Lobby correspondents in his room in the House of Commons* and waxed so benign on the prospects ahead for Europe that the reporter from the *Daily Telegraph* wrote the next morning, attributing his remarks to "Cabinet circles," that "unofficial and semi-official contacts have recently shown, it is thought, a point of view much nearer to the truth than official statements. The visit of Mr. Oliver Stanley, the President of the Board of Trade, to Berlin this month will lead to another step in the settlement of outstanding differences in Europe."

Some days before, Chamberlain had been consulted by his Home Secretary, Sir Samuel Hoare, about a speech he was due to make to his constituents in Chelsea. Should he be wary or hopeful, gloomy or optimistic?

"Cheerful," said Chamberlain. "There is every reason for it."

When Hoare stepped onto the platform at Chelsea Town Hall, in King's Road, he pulled out all stops. "Suppose," he said, "that political confidence can be restored in Europe . . . Suppose that the peoples of Europe will be able to free themselves from the nightmare that haunts them, and from an expenditure on armaments that beggars them. Could we not then devote the inventions and discoveries of our time to the creation of a Golden Age? . . . Five men in Europe,† if they worked with a singleness of purpose and a unity of action, might in an incredibly short space of time transform the whole history of the world . . ."

On the following day, March 11, the editors of *Punch* (not only a humorous magazine but also an organ of the Establishment and a strong supporter of Chamberlain), met at their weekly conference in Bouverie Street to plan next week's edition. Bernard Partridge, the staff artist, had already roughed out his cartoon and laid it on the wooden table before the editors. It showed the Specter of War disappearing through John Bull's window, and the caption jibed at the scaremongers. The cartoon was approved by the editors for publication in their issue of March 15.

Intelligence reports were now coming into Whitehall from Prague, Warsaw, Bratislava and Berlin forecasting that the German

* Like their White House counterparts, Lobby correspondents are often given confidential information by ministers and M.P.'s for background or for publication without direct attribution.

† He was referring to Hitler, Chamberlain, Mussolini, Daladier and Stalin.

army would march into Czechoslovakia on March 15, and each of these were sent by Cadogan to Halifax and by Halifax to Neville Chamberlain.

Early in the morning of March 14, Erich Kordt telephoned from the Foreign Ministry in Berlin to his brother Theo in London. "Aunt Theodora leaves Berlin tomorrow," he said. This simple code meant that the German army would march into Czechoslovakia the following day. "Will you tell Cousin Anthea?" he added. Cousin Anthea was not only a real relative of the brothers; it was also the code name for Britain.

"Anthea already knows," replied Theo Kordt. "But somehow she can't seem to keep the date in her head. She keeps saying it isn't important."

"I am disappointed in Slovakia," said Adolf Hitler. "The way your people have been behaving lately, they might almost be Czechs."

He was addressing Monsignor Tiso and Durčansky in the Reich Chancellery on the evening of March 13. Across the room, facing them and seated beside the Führer, were Joachim von Ribbentrop, General Wilhelm Keitel and an assortment of Foreign Ministry officials. The two Slovaks bowed their heads and listened politely; they had a feeling that they were not expected to say a word.

For half an hour Adolf Hitler had been ranting about the sins of Prague, which had become a "hotbed of unrest" since the détente at Munich. He had no longer any patience with them; their future must be settled once and for all. But Slovakia—he had expected better things of their country. In the past year he had been forced to face a difficult decision—whether or not to permit the Hungarians to occupy Slovakia, as they had repeatedly requested. At first he had thought that this was what the Slovaks themselves wished. Their country was far away; he had more important things on his mind. It was only when the Munich crisis arose that he was dissuaded, for then it was put to him that Slovakia wished to conduct her own affairs . . . But what happened? He had sent Wilhelm Keppler as his envoy to Slovakia, and to him Sidor had declared that he was a soldier of Prague and would oppose separation from the Czech union. If Hitler had known this earlier, he would not have antagonized his friends the Hungarians, and would have let events take their course.

156

The Führer had begun pacing up and down the room, and now he suddenly swung around on Tiso. He had let the Slovaks come to Berlin in order to get the question settled quickly. He had no interests east of the Carpathians; he didn't care what happened there. But he demanded to know what the people of Slovakia really wanted. There were signs of internal instability, and that he would not tolerate. He had let them come to Berlin so that they could hear his decision. It was not a question of days but of hours. He had said that if Slovakia wanted her independence, he would support this endeavor and even guarantee it. He would stand by his word, but only so long as Slovakia made it quite clear that this was what she wanted. If they hesitated or if they refused to dissolve their connection with Prague, he would leave Slovakia to the mercy of events.

Hitler then turned to his Foreign Minister and asked him if he had anything to add.

Ribbentrop said that he only wanted to emphasize what the Führer had just said—that it was a matter of hours and not days. Thereupon he handed a message to the Führer which, he said, he had just received. Hitler read it aloud; it reported Hungarian troop concentrations along the Slovakian border. There, he said, they could see that events were moving fast and that he was no longer responsible for them.* Slovakia must decide, and decide quickly.

Now at last the Slovaks were allowed to speak. Monsignor Tiso swallowed hard and said how grateful he was to the Führer for the words he had spoken. For some time he had been longing to learn how the Führer felt toward his country and people. Now he knew, and he wanted to assure the Führer that he could rely on Slovakia. He wished to apologize for saying that the impression made by the Führer's words had been so deep that he was unable at this moment to clearly express his opinion or to make a decision. Might he withdraw with his friend—pointing to Durčansky—and think over the whole question? But he assured the Führer that they would show him that they were worthy of his care and interest in their country.

---

* The Hungarians were, in fact, moving because they had been given permission by Hitler to occupy Carpathian Ruthenia, Slovakia's neighbor to the east. Just before the meeting with Tiso, Hungary's Regent, Admiral von Horthy, had telegraphed his thanks and gratitude to Hitler. "The dispositions have already been made," he wrote. "On Thursday, March 16, a frontier incident will take place, which will be followed by the big blow on Saturday. I shall never forget this proof of friendship, and your Excellency may rely on my unshakable gratitude at all times."

Hitler nodded. "All right, but don't waste any time. You can settle the details with my staff." He indicated that they were dismissed, and they quickly left the room.

At eight o'clock on Tuesday morning, March 14, deputies of the Slovak Diet, apprised by Tiso that they were threatened by Hungarian troops on one side and German on the other, voted to break with Prague and declare their independence. It was, of course, a sham, and Hitler demonstrated it by announcing that he would "protect" the new state.

The Führer was satisfied. Slovakia was taken care of. Ruthenia could be left to the Hungarians. Of the former sovereign state of Czechoslovakia, only Bohemia and Moravia now remained to be dealt with.

President Hácha received the news in Hradčany Castle just before noon, by way of an army field telephone. The commander of the Czech troops in Bratislava was urgently requesting instructions.

"Tell him to do nothing—nothing whatsoever," said the President to General Syrový, who was now his Minister for War. Then, turning to Chvalkovský, he said, "I think the time has come for us to consult our friends"—he hesitated slightly over the word—"in Germany. You had better ask the legation if the Führer can receive us, and as soon as possible. Tell them that we urgently need his advice."

He was to get much more than advice.

■

Snow was falling and melting into sludge in the gutters of the Wilhelmstrasse in Berlin at midday on March 14, as General Keitel hurried into the Reich Chancellery. He had an appointment with Hitler to discuss arrangements for the attack on Bohemia and Moravia the following morning, and the weather reports worried him. Snow was falling thickly east of Dresden, and the ground frost which was forecast meant ice on the roads; it was no weather for an invasion, even one which did not promise too much resistance.

158

But if Keitel was fretting, Adolf Hitler's mood was positively sunny. He was almost smiling as he listened to the general's recital of the preparations which had been made, and Keitel noticed that the hand on the stomach and the attacks of wind which were symptoms of the Führer's nerves during times of crisis were not in evidence today. Toward the end of his report he realized why, for Hitler broke in to tell him that President Hácha had requested a meeting and that he was expected in Berlin that evening.

Keitel was relieved, and immediately asked permission to return to his office in the Bendlerstrasse to warn the General Staff.

Of what? asked the Führer.

Of the fact that in view of the President's visit, the invasion was to be postponed for the time being. Hitler replied that Keitel misunderstood the situation completely. He was letting the old man come to see him, but he had no intention of postponing the invasion. He would march into Czechia at six o'clock the next morning, whatever the outcome of the talks. Civilized behavior, he implied, could be forgotten when dealing with creatures like the Czechs.

As the special train from Prague sped across the whitening hills of Bohemia, President Hácha slept for the first time in days. His daughter Milada had tucked a rug around him to keep out the draft, and as his mouth fell open and he began to snore she smiled at him fondly. Like her father, she had no qualms about what would happen when they got to Berlin. After all, had not the Four Powers, Germany included, guaranteed the integrity of the Czechoslovakian state? Surely it could be in nobody's interest to allow it to fall to pieces. Adolf Hitler would know what to do to bring all this unrest and chaos under control.

The train stopped briefly at Pilsen, the last Czech city before the new frontier with Germany, and Chvalkovský stepped out and asked for news from a liaison officer on the platform. "We have heard nothing," the officer said. "There seems to be something wrong with the telephone." Although Chvalkovský did not say so to President Hácha, he guessed that the lines had been cut. Indeed they had—all but one, as Chvalkovský later discovered.

What Chvalkovský could *not* guess was that while they rode eastward toward Germany and darkness began to fall over Bohemia,

159

Nazi troops were filtering across the Czech border. Zero hour for the invasion proper was still twelve hours away, but in Moravská Ostrava, on the Polish border in the north, a crack squad from the Leibstandarte Adolf Hitler* was moving toward the small Czech town of Vítkovice. Vítkovice had one of the most modern steel mills in Europe, and the Germans wanted to make sure of acquiring it intact. So the troops were on their way ahead of time, just in case the Poles, faced with a disintegrating Czechoslovakia, were tempted to make a grab for this plum.

General Keitel arrived at the Reich Chancellery at nine o'clock that evening and reported to Adolf Hitler. He had been summoned to pick up the orders for the invasion, and then pass them on to the General Staff and the Air Force High Command. To his astonishment he found himself in the middle of a party. The Führer and his guests had just risen from dinner; Göring was there, just back from San Remo, as well as Ribbentrop, Frau Goebbels, Himmler and about a dozen uniformed courtiers and young women. Hitler led his guests into the drawing room, which had been equipped as a movie theater, and patted a place beside him for Keitel to sit. The lights were turned off, and while the general squirmed with impatience, the title of the film they were going to see—a mediocre German romance called *Ein hoffnungsloser Fall* (*A Hopeless Case*)—appeared on the screen.

Hitler whispered to Keitel, "Don't worry. The old man is not due until ten o'clock. I shall let him rest and recuperate for two hours, and then receive him at midnight."

Keitel squirmed anew. "Considering the circumstances, I felt properly out of place in this milieu," he wrote afterward; "within eight or ten hours the first shots would be being exchanged, and I was gravely disturbed."

It did not seem to have occurred to Hácha that by going to Berlin he was walking into a trap. It is true that he was an old man and that once having accepted the facts of Munich and the political domination of Germany over Central Europe, he thought that since Czecho-

* Elite SS regiment, which had originally been formed for the sole purpose of protecting the Führer's life.

slovakia was no longer a danger to Germany, it was not now a target of Hitler's ambitions. Was his country not in the National Socialist German orbit already? Did she not do exactly what she was told? In any case, had not Adolf Hitler declared to the great statesmen of Europe that he did not want the Czechs in Germany, and had he not joined in a guarantee of the independence of the country with Britain, France and Italy?

All this may have convinced the unwary old man that there was nothing to fear. But his astuter advisers should surely have warned him; they could have spelled out for him the ominous moves of the past few days, reminded him of Adolf Hitler's hatred for the Czechs and counseled him to stay home. But no one told him. "I had no suspicion of what they were going to do to me," he said afterward.

He was a foolish old man. Only thirteen months earlier the Austrian Chancellor, Schuschnigg, had gone to see Hitler to ask for advice and help, Hácha might have remembered what had happened to him and to Austria, or at least Chvalkovský might have reminded him that Austria was now a part of Germany and that Chancellor Schuschnigg was cleaning latrines in a German concentration camp.

"Look," said President Hácha to his daughter, "they are doing us proud."

It was eleven o'clock on the night of March 14. Because of the weather the special train had arrived an hour late, but the German government was evidently determined to observe all the amenities. The Czechoslovak flag flew beside the swastika from the flagpoles, and an SS guard of honor (ironically enough, from the same regiment which was at that moment operating inside Czechoslovakia) was drawn up on the platform of the Anhalter Station. Accompanied by Cabinet Minister Dr. Otto Meissner, Chief of the Presidential Chancellery, Dr. and Mrs. Voytech Mastny, Chvalkovský and the commanding SS general, the old man solemnly marched with his daughter along the serried rows, and peering through the frigid gloom, tried to pretend that he was inspecting the burnished troops drawn up before him. A high wind was blowing and scurries of snow whipped through the drafty station.

Eventually it must have occurred even to the Germans that the proceedings were a farce. A huge bouquet of flowers intended for Hácha's daughter, to be presented by a buxom German maiden, was waved away and the old man and his party were whisked off to the

161

Adlon Hotel. There, while the old man retired to the bedroom, the flowers and a box of chocolate were duly presented to Mrs. Radlova. It seemed a good augury to her, as it did to her father when she popped a candy into his mouth just before midnight, as he prepared to leave for the Reich Chancellery.

"In the Reich Chancellery, to which I was accompanied by Minister Meissner and Chvalkovský," Hácha reported later to his government, "I was met in the courtyard by a guard of honor and then immediately by the Reich Chancellor, Adolf Hitler, who came to meet me and to whom I said how much I appreciated this personal meeting with the most powerful statesman of our time. The Reich Chancellor then invited me to be seated at his right hand among a circle of the foremost personalities of the Reich, among whom were General Field Marshal Göring, Minister von Ribbentrop, General Keitel and also Meissner."

The journey, the cold, the fatigue and worry had all had their effect upon the old man; by now his voice was almost gone and he spoke in a croak. His accent was peculiar, and this, combined with his hoarseness, made him sound like a wounded frog. The Nazi hierarchy present had some difficulty in keeping their faces straight as they listened to him, and at one point Hitler whispered to Keitel that "the old gentleman sounds like a drunken sot."

Of course, Hácha still had no inkling that his country was going to be invaded by Germany in a few hours' time. He had come to ask not for mercy but for help against the forces of disintegration in his own state. He began with a long, humble and groveling dissertation of his career in the Austrian civil service. Hitler interrupted him and said that as the hour was late, they should discuss the political reasons why Hácha had asked to be received by him. He signaled to all the others to withdraw save Chvalkovský, Ribbentrop and the interpreter, Dr. Walter Hewel. But twice Keitel returned. The first time it was to report that the Leibstandarte Adolf Hitler had successfully and without opposition occupied Vítkovice and its steel works in Moravská Ostrava. This news was given to the Führer in writing, and of course Hitler, nodding satisfaction, did not communicate it to the Czechs. The second occasion was to warn Hitler of the lateness of the

162

hour; "the army was asking for a final decision on whether they were to march or not," Keitel wrote later. But he was dismissed abruptly by the Führer with the muttered reply that it was now only two o'clock in the morning, that the troops were not due to march until six, and that the order would be issued before four o'clock.

By this time Hácha was beginning to realize that the lifeguard whom he had come to summon to the rescue of Czechoslovakia was showing signs of turning into a shark, and he launched into an appeal for his country.

"Now I come to the thought which moves me most." His voice was not much more than a throaty whisper. "I have already given my opinion of the Slovaks in seizing their independence. I am not shedding tears over them. But the fate of my own people, the Czechs: I believe that you, your Excellency, are one of the few people who will understand me if I say that Czechoslovakia has the right to a national life. The geographical location of Czechoslovakia requires her to have the best possible relations with Germany. This is and will be the basis of her existence as an independent nation, and it is one approved by the great majority of the Czech people. Czechoslovakia is being reproached for still harboring many adherents of the Beneš system, but there really aren't all that many now. It is only the journalists who are giving them publicity, and the government will soon silence them for good . . ." His voice trailed away, and then he added pathetically, "That is all I have to say, really . . . I'm an old man . . ."

Hitler had been listening to the Czechoslovak President with obvious signs of impatience. Now he began to speak, and Ribbentrop and Hewel prepared themselves for the inevitable monologue. It went on for a long time, for the Führer, now that the opportunity was there, had a great deal of venom to dispense. All his rancor against the Czechs welled up as he contemplated the two little men standing humbly in front of him (for he had risen from his seat, and they had automatically jumped to their feet too). He went back as far as 1936 to list examples of Czech hostility to Germany; his grating voice rising as his passion spilled over, he came down the years, incident by incident, to indict the country for daring to stand up to him.

As the hatred gushed forth, the two Czechs kept glancing stealthily at each other, and Hácha furtively wiped away tears with a trem-

163

bling finger. Every so often Chvalkovský, who had an arthritic knee, would surreptitiously raise his leg and bend it slightly to ease the ache.*

Now Hitler reached his peroration. "If Czechia had drawn closer to Germany after Munich," he said, "I would have felt an obligation to protect her in times of unrest. I no longer have that obligation . . . I have always made it clear that I would ruthlessly smash her if the old, pro-Beneš tendencies were not revised. Chvalkovský understood this and asked me to have patience. I understood his point of view, but then the months went by without change. This new regime failed to eliminate the old one psychologically. I knew this from what appeared in your press, from word of mouth, from the dismissal of German civil servants, and many other things indicative of the general attitude . . . The consequences were plain to see—in a few years, Czechia would be back where it was six months ago [before Munich]. Why didn't Czechia immediately reduce her army to a reasonable size? It was a tremendous burden for such a small state, and it only made sense if it was there to back a foreign policy. And that is meaningless, because Czechia doesn't have a foreign policy! No foreign policy! No mission, except to face the facts of her situation! No future unless she does so!"

His voice dropped as he turned toward the two Czechs, as if remembering suddenly that they were there. Unfortunately, he said, the Czech people had refused to understand the facts of their situation. "Thus it was that the die was cast last Sunday. I sent for the Hungarian minister and I told him that I am washing my hands of this country. And now we face the new situation. I have given the order to the soldiers of the German army. At six o'clock this morning they will march into Czechia and incorporate it in the German Reich."

He paused to let the news sink into the minds of the two men standing before him. Then he continued, quietly now, "I want to give Czechia the fullest autonomy and a life of her own to a much larger extent than she was ever allowed during Austrian rule. But Germany's attitude toward Czechia will be determined by her behavior

* Dr. Paul Schmidt, Hitler's official interpreter, says that at this point the visitors "sat as if turned to stone. Only their eyes showed they were alive." But Dr. Schmidt was not at this meeting. The above account comes from the remarks later made by Dr. Hewel to his Foreign Ministry colleagues, and by Dr. Josef Klement, a member of Hácha's staff who afterward talked about the meeting with him.

164

tomorrow and the day after tomorrow, and it depends on the attitude of the Czech people and the Czech army toward the German troops." His voice took on a new tone of grievance. "I no longer trust your government. I believe in your honesty, Herr President, and your straightforwardness, Herr Minister, but I have fears that your government cannot assert itself over the people."

Hácha was now weeping openly and Chvalkovský was looking at the map-covered table.

"All I can say is, they had better! The German army has already crossed the frontier today, and one barracks where resistance was offered was ruthlessly destroyed. Another barracks gave in at the deployment of heavy artillery. At six this morning the German army will invade from all sides and the German air force will occupy Czech airfields. There are two possibilities, Herr President. The first is that there will be resistance and the invasion of the German troops will lead to a battle. In that case, this resistance will be broken up by all and every means of physical force. The other possibility is that the invasion of the German troops occurs in a bearable form. In that case, I will be generous and give Czechia a generous life of her own, her autonomy, a certain national liberty . . . But if fighting breaks out today or tomorrow, the pressure will result in counterpressure. The annihilation will begin and it will no longer be possible for me to alleviate the lot of the Czech people. Within two days the Czech army will be wiped out . . . The world will look on and not move a muscle."

It was now nearly three o'clock. Hácha looked for a chair and sank into it. "You have made the situation quite clear, your Excellency," he said. "In any case, resistance is quite useless. But how am I to go about it? How can I tell the Czech army not to resist, with only four hours left before the invasion?"

As if at a signal, Göring and Keitel had come back into the room. Keitel said, "You could telephone Prague and have the orders issued to the army at once."

"But that is not possible," Chvalkovský exclaimed. "All the lines to Prague have been cut."

"All the civilian lines," said Keitel. "But there is one line open. You can speak to Prague at once."*

* A German army intelligence group, aided by Sudeten Germans operating on both sides of the Czech frontier, had protected the line expressly for this purpose.

165

"If you will go with these gentlemen," Hitler said, indicating Göring and Ribbentrop, "they will be able to help you make arrangements."

As the Führer signaled for Keitel to remain, the other four sidled out of the room, Göring's hand helpfully holding up the tottering figure of the Czech President as they passed through the door.

But the hand which supported President Hácha as he went through the door was being brandished before him in fury a few minutes later. Despite Adolf Hitler's lackadaisical manner, the time when the German forces were due to move was dangerously near, and no one was more apprehensive about the operation than Göring. He was even more nervous than General Keitel, for though bad weather would make the advance hazardous for the troops, at least they could move. The Luftwaffe could not. All evening he had been receiving reports from his three assistants, Generals Milch, Udet and Bodenschatz, telling him that the air force was grounded.* The situation was extremely risky. What if the Czechs decided to resist? Their army was tough and well directed, and in this weather they would have all the advantages.

At this point President Hácha began to recover his nerve, and this sudden access of resistance could not have been more dismaying for the Reich ministers. Göring, who was against the whole operation anyway, grew agitated when Hácha suddenly began to speak rapidly in Czech to Chvalkovský. He was telling his Foreign Minister that it was really too much, that he realized Czechoslovakia was helpless in face of this ultimatum but that he could not bring himself to give in.

"What is it?" asked Göring nervously.

"It is several things. But principally, for the moment, it is this." Chvalkovský indicated a draft agreement which Ribbentrop had unceremoniously thrust under the old man's nose. With Chvalkovský's help, the President had fingered and muttered his way through it. It was a proclamation to be signed by Adolf Hitler, Ribbentrop, Hácha and Chvalkovský, announcing the acquisition of Czechoslovakia by Germany, with Czechoslovakian consent.

* It was still grounded twenty-four hours later, and had to cancel a projected victory flight over Prague.

166

RIBBENTROP: What's wrong with it? Hasn't he already agreed that there is no use resisting?

HÁCHA: You don't understand, Herr Minister. It says here that I should sign this proclamation in my own name and in the name of my government. [With a sudden straightening of his shoulders] That I could never do. It is not fitting. According to the Constitution of the Czecho-slovak state, I am not empowered to make a statement in the name of the government.

RIBBENTROP: All right. Simply sign for yourself.

GÖRING: No. It must be legal. He must sign for the government as well as for himself.

RIBBENTROP: But it is nearly three o'clock! We haven't much time.

GÖRING: Leave it to me.

The Field Marshal advanced upon President Hácha and said in a wheedling voice, "Excellency, why don't you sign? It's only a formality. It will save so much trouble."

Neither he nor Ribbentrop seemed to acknowledge the fact that the old man had already conceded defeat and that this was only a spasm of geriatric stubbornness—a last, desperate clutch at the letter of Czechoslovakian law by a sick and frightened man. With typical Teutonic respect for form they insisted on the letter of the law, when all they needed to do was lead Hácha to the telephone and tell him to speak to Prague.

"Excellency, please sign," Göring prodded him. "I hate to say it, but my job is not the easiest one. Prague, your capital—I should be terribly sorry if I were compelled to destroy this beautiful city. But I would have to do it, to make the English and French understand that my air force can do all it claims to do. Because they still don't want to believe that this is so, and I should like an opportunity of giving them proof."*

It took some time for the significance of Göring's statement to sink in. Hácha had no means of knowing that the Luftwaffe was grounded and that Keitel was concerned about the obstacles facing his troops. All he could think of was the prospect of Prague being bombed.

* "*Ich habe ein schweres Amt. Es würde mir ungemein leid tun, wenn ich diese schöne Stadt vernichten müsste. Aber ich müsste es tun, damit die Engländer und Franzosen wissen dass meine Luftwaffe eine hundertprozentige Arbeit zu leisten vermag. Denn sie wollen es noch immer nicht glauben und ich möchte den Beweis hierüber bringen.*"

167

"Sign," said Ribbentrop.

Almost by reflex action Hácha continued to resist. Like a lady in a Victorian melodrama, he even pretended to faint. Ribbentrop did not turn a hair; he was prepared for everything. In scuttled Adolf Hitler's personal physician, Dr. Theodor Morell, who felt the old man's pulse, which was fluttering weakly, and prescribed a stimulant. Hácha protested; his aim seemed to be to gain time. But at the sight of Göring and Ribbentrop glowering over him, the Field Marshal shouting "Think of Prague!," he allowed himself to be given an injection of dextrose and vitamins.

After coffee and a ham sandwich, the old man nodded his head. "Bring me the telephone," he said. Later he wrote: "I telephoned Army General Syrový about the situation and gave him precise orders to direct all garrisons not to resist the German troops. Afterward I informed the Premier by telephone, and a short while later I received his reply to the effect that the government, which had meanwhile assembled, takes heed of my procedure and agrees with it."

Hácha was led in to see Adolf Hitler once more, and then signed the document which proclaimed the Protectorate of Bohemia and Moravia:

Berlin, March 15, 1939

At their request, the Führer today received the Czechoslovak President, Dr. Hácha, and the Czechoslovak Foreign Minister, Dr. Chvalkovský, in Berlin in the presence of Foreign Minister von Ribbentrop. At the meeting the serious situation created by events in recent weeks in the present Czechoslovak territory was examined with complete frankness.

The conviction was unanimously expressed on both sides that the aim of all efforts must be the safeguarding of calm, order and peace in this part of Central Europe. The Czechoslovak President declared that in order to serve this object, and to achieve ultimate pacification, he confidently placed the fate of the Czech people in the hands of the Führer of the German Reich. The Führer accepted this declaration and expressed his intention of taking the Czech people under the protection of the German Reich and of guaranteeing them an autonomous development of their ethnic life as suited to their character.

At last the old man was led off and taken back to the Adlon Hotel, where his daughter was waiting for him. Adolf Hitler came out into the hall, great gusts of laughter braying from his throat, his

168

hands outstretched to grasp and shake those of anyone in his path.

General Keitel approached the Führer and asked him to issue forthwith an order for the invasion to the General Staff, "but with a clear instruction not to open fire, in similar vein to the instructions issued to the Czech army . . . This order was passed to the [German] army at three o'clock, which left three clear hours for its distribution." He added, "It was a great weight off the minds of us soldiers; Brauchitsch and I admitted to each other how relieved we were at this outcome."

In the Anhalter Station, on the chill morning of March 15, President Hácha could not understand why the train which was to take him back to Prague was so late in starting. Nor why, once it got on its way, it stopped and dawdled at so many small stations.

For Adolf Hitler's special train, there were no such delays. It delivered him as fast as it could carry him through Dresden to the Czechoslovak border, where the party switched to automobiles.

"From the frontier onward, we drove in a long convoy of motor-cars along the broad road to Prague," wrote General Keitel. "Very shortly we came across the marching columns of our army. It was cold and wintry, there were snow drifts and black ice, and the mobile columns with their trucks and guns had to overcome the most formidable obstacles to their progress, particularly whenever our convoy wanted to overtake them."

It was dusk when the motorcade reached the outskirts of Prague. Here they paused, and Hitler got out to look at the valley of the Vltava with the misted shapes of Prague below him. The first German units had already driven into the city, and the news came back that there had been no resistance at all and that the few people in the streets had simply stood and stared in a state of shock.

The convoy started off again and soon was making its way swiftly through the darkening streets across the river to the diplomatic quarter, and then through the narrow streets of the Old City to the majestic cliffs of Hradčany Castle. A guard of Leibstandarte Adolf Hitler was waiting at the entrance. There were no Czechs in sight, and the city was freezingly cold and still. Even Hitler, staring down into the gloom, shivered a little. But not for long. After he had retired to wash and change, Ribbentrop led him to the magnificent banquet

169

hall of the old castle. Candles were burning, and lights glowed on the paintings, sculptures and armor of ancient German kings. From the window, Hitler could look down and see the glow of lights among the statues of the saints on the Charles Bridge. On the table in the banquet hall was an impressive cold buffet of Prague ham, pâtés, cold meats, game, cheese, fruit and beer.

Turning from the window, the Führer beat his fists on his chest, as if he were a victorious gorilla in the jungle. Suddenly, in a gesture quite out of character, he picked up a small stein of Pilsner, and putting it to his lips, drained it dry. He grimaced, and then laughed. It was the only time anyone had ever seen him take an alcoholic drink. But it measured his mood. This was the great moment of his career; now he was not only Führer of the German Reich and Austria, but of Bohemia and Moravia too. "Czechoslovakia has ceased to exist!" he cried exultantly.

Would anyone dare to stop him now? Was anything beyond his grasp?

President Hácha's train arrived in Prague at eleven o'clock that evening, six hours after the Germans had established themselves. He was driven at once to Hradčany Castle, but began to protest when his chauffeur skirted the main entrance and took him to the servants' quarter in the back.

"Don't worry, Father," said his daughter. "Just let us get home."

It was not until Hácha was tucked in bed that Chvalkovský came to tell him that the main part of the castle was now in German hands, and that henceforth he and the Czechs must use the servants' entrance in their own land.

170

THREE

Warsaw or Moscow?

VII

The Führer
Is Sick

There were two Britains in Britain in 1939, and in most ways the twain did not meet. Universal suffrage had given every man and woman over twenty-one the vote, but what had they got out of it? The previous government of the people, the Labour administration under Ramsay MacDonald, had been dismissed, sabotaged or betrayed—the appropriate verb depended upon one's political conviction—after the financial crisis of 1931. Since then the Tories had ruled the land, and unemployment was the order of the day. As Chancellor of the Exchequer, Neville Chamberlain had insisted on a balanced budget and a tight economy; as Prime Minister, he had never lost sight of the fact that a controlled budget and a reserve of unemployed kept the economy healthy and the trade unions under control, and it did not seem to bother him that there were still over one million unemployed in Britain in 1939.

To someone like Neville Chamberlain, who came from a prosperous family, or Sir Horace Wilson, whose civil service job was permanent, with a pension at the end, the gulf separating them from the unemployed was unbridgeable: their minds were incapable of spanning the chasm. The jobless were those who had fallen by the wayside through laziness, inefficiency and fecklessness; their state was one which they should bear silently and with fortitude, and they should be thankful that the government was giving them a dole to keep them from starving. In the weeks preceding the occupation of Prague whole factories had closed down and there had been demonstrations by the unemployed to protest the tightening of benefits, the inability of the government to find them work and the refusal to allot extra "winter relief" for the purchase of fuel.*

To most of the ruling class these were not cries of pain and distress, but the dangerous growls of the proletariat tugging at their chains. When groups of unemployed descended upon London and organized a series of demonstrations, there were calls for "stern action" by the police from alarmed Members of Parliament. It was bad enough when forty unemployed men lay down in Oxford Circus and held up traffic, and snorts of indignation came from patrician nostrils when others marched into the Ritz Hotel in their cloth caps and mufflers, held out their money and demanded to be served,† but upper-class hackles really began to rise when a coffin with the words "He Did Not Get Winter Relief" on the side was delivered to No. 10 Downing Street.

Most members of the Establishment had no doubt that the unrest was all part of a threatening Red revolution among the masses, especially since some of the demonstrators had been joined by anti-Franco veterans from the Spanish Civil War. Lady Winterton, wife of one of Chamberlain's ministers, spoke for many Tories when she said, "It is a pity that men who come home unemployed and make a nuisance of themselves with coffins and by chaining themselves to railings were not shot in Spain."

Even those who opposed Chamberlain's appeasement policy seemed to live the cushioned life of clubs, parliamentary smoking rooms and country weekends which kept them removed from what the British people were thinking, and even such an intelligent observer as Harold Nicolson, a member of a determinedly anti-Chamberlain group, thought he had caught the authentic voice of England when he wrote: "[The Duke of] Devonshire told me a curious story tonight which illustrates vividly the attitude of the

* For an admirable study of this period, see Malcolm Muggeridge's *The Thirties*.
† The outraged servants of the Ritz found an easy way of discouraging the intruders. The men had entered the grill room by mistake, and it was haughtily pointed out that tea was never, never served there. No one told them where the tea lounge was, and eventually they left.

176

British public. On saying goodnight to his chauffeur, he remarked, 'Well, Gibson, and what do you think about Hitler?' 'Well, your Grace,' the man answered, 'it seems to me that he should know by now that he is none too popular in this district.' "

In the circumstances, it is hardly surprising that Neville Chamberlain and Sir Horace Wilson were more alarmed by Red scares at home than by Hitlerian lawlessness in the remote reaches of the Continent. "The wealthy class in England," Franklin D. Roosevelt had told Lord Lothian a few weeks before, "is so afraid of Communism, which has constituted no threat at all to England, that they have thrown themselves into the arms of Nazism, and now they don't know which way to turn."

It was a good description of the Chamberlain-Wilson attitude—except for the final phrase. The government certainly did know which way to turn—into a closer embrace with Nazi Germany than before.

It was therefore with some surprise, but not with much alarm, that Chamberlain learned that a number of his ministers were outraged at the German occupation of Prague. He had called his Cabinet together at last, but only after Czechoslovakia had ceased to exist, and read a draft of the statement he proposed to make to the House of Commons that afternoon, March 15. He was taken aback when Lord Halifax coldly remarked that surely the statement, which only expressed Chamberlain's disappointment and dismay, did not go far enough. Halifax had been appalled at the German action, and for once he spoke out. It was a brutal breach of faith, he said, and negated all that had been achieved at Munich. The time had come to demonstrate to Adolf Hitler that this sort of behavior could not be tolerated.

Chamberlain raised his eyebrows as if to say, "Surely you are taking all this far too seriously, Edward," hurriedly brought the meeting to a close and retired to his room to discuss his speech further with Sir Horace Wilson. When he rose in the House of Commons later that afternoon, it quickly became apparent that he had no inkling whatsoever of the mood of either the Members of the House or the people in the country, to whom the news of the German coup had been a heavy blow. He was sad, he said, that Czechoslovakia had "become disintegrated," but it would be very wrong to exchange angry words about Germany and Herr Hitler. He went on loftily, "I

177

have so often heard charges of breach of faith bandied about that I do not want to associate myself with any charges of that character."

There was a gasp of surprise. Then a voice shouted, "What about our guarantee to Czechoslovakia?"

"His Majesty's Government have endeavored to come to an agreement with the other governments represented at Munich on the scope and terms of such a guarantee," Chamberlain replied, "but up to the present we have been unable to reach any such agreement. In our opinion the situation has radically altered since the Slovak Diet declared the independence of Slovakia. The effect of this declaration put an end by internal disruption to the State whose frontiers we had proposed to guarantee, and accordingly the condition of affairs . . . which was always regarded by us as being of a transitory nature, has now ceased to exist, and His Majesty's Government cannot accordingly hold themselves bound any longer by this obligation."

So much for the guarantee which Chamberlain had so reluctantly given at Munich, and which he had never had any intention of implementing.* Now he turned to what seemed to him much more important than the fate of the Czechs.

"I bitterly regret what has now occurred." The Prime Minister paused and surveyed the House, then lifted his voice: "But do not let us on that account be deflected from our course. The aim of the Government is now, as it always has been, to substitute the method of discussion for the method of force in the settlement of differences . . . This is no time for the abandonment of well-tried and well-thought-out ideas." And then he uttered what even his most fervent supporter had hoped not to hear: "We will continue to pursue our policy of appeasement."

Lord Halifax had been listening to the speech in the Peers' Gallery of the House of Commons, and reporters afterward described the expression on his face as "a study in aristocratic distaste." He came down to the Lobby of the House as soon as the talk was over and mixed with the Members to find out their reactions. He was swiftly

---

* Later in the debate his Chancellor of the Exchequer, Sir John Simon, found an even flimsier excuse for abandoning the guarantee. He quoted Goebbels' remark that Czechoslovakia had ceased to exist, and blandly asked how you could guarantee a nonexistent country.

joined by Captain Margesson, the Government Chief Whip,* who was in something of a panic.

"The House isn't with him," Margesson said. "Can't understand what's got into them. They didn't seem to like the statement. Thought it ought to be stronger. Stand up to Hitler, show the Nazis they can't get away with it, all that rot." Suddenly, looking at the Foreign Secretary, he became aware that his indignation was not being sympathetically received by Halifax. "Don't tell me you believe that rot too, Edward? My dear fellow, not really! For God's sake don't spread it abroad, we'll have a party rebellion on our hands." He paused and then said, "Do you think these chaps are right? Should we binge up the Old Man a bit?"†

In the next twenty-four hours the managers of the Tory party were quite sure that this was what was needed. From all over the country, messages were coming in demanding that the government show its anger at the Nazi action in Czechoslovakia, and its determination to stand up to any further examples of Nazi aggression. All the pro-appeasers, who had so fervently welcomed the Munich Agreement and had so vehemently attacked Chamberlain's critics, now excelled one another in proposing vengeance for the assault on their *amour-propre*. One of the most enthusiastic supporters of the Chamberlain group, Lord Nuffield, the automobile magnate, declared angrily, "If it weren't for Neville Chamberlain's feelings, I would advocate the starting of war against Germany tomorrow." A ground swell of criticism against appeasement had begun to develop from the first news about Prague, and it grew with every hour.

The day after the occupation of Prague, March 16, the German ambassador to Britain, Herbert von Dirksen, called on Lord Halifax at the Foreign Office. Dirksen, a German career diplomatist who had toadied to the Nazis but had as little luck in winning their approval as his opposite number, Nevile Henderson, blandly remarked that he had come to report good news. The German decision to turn Bohemia and Moravia into a protectorate had re-established peace and order in Central Europe, and he hoped that the British government appreciated the contributions to general understanding which his country had made by its actions of the past twenty-four hours.

* Whose job it is to keep party members in line and make sure that they vote with the government on vital issues.
† Old-fashioned Tory slang, via Eton, for "stiffen his back."

Halifax was a weak man and a poor Foreign Secretary. He wanted a quiet life, and he never liked to say things to strangers which might upset them. But unlike Chamberlain, he had been deeply offended by the rape of Czechoslovakia. Words of honor were involved; pledges had been broken. He was a lofty man of some six feet five inches. His voice was an astringent, deprecative tenor which tended to a stammer on those rare occasions when he became emotional. He began to stammer now.

"I can well understand Herr H-H-H-Hitler's taste for b-b-b-bloodless vice," he said, "but one of t-t-t-these d-d-days he may find himself up against something which will n-n-n-not be bloodless. Recent events will certainly have made opinion in many parts of the world feel that this sort of thing is a g-g-g-good deal more probable than they had previously hoped, and they will make their plans accordingly. The German government must have weighed all these c-c-consequences, and the c-c-conclusion that everyone in this country and far outside it would draw must be that you have n-n-no desire to establish good relations with this country, that y-y-you are prepared to disregard world opinion, and are s-s-seeking to establish a position in which you can b-b-by f-f-force d-d-d-dominate Europe, and if p-p-possible the world."

Dirksen was impressed. At once he cabled Berlin: "The difference of opinion between Chamberlain and Halifax, which has already shown itself occasionally, is becoming more and more evident, the latter advocating a stronger attitude." A few hours later he reported that "the more extreme group within the Cabinet, represented by Lord Halifax, who is entirely under the influence of the Foreign Office, has gained the upper hand."

It was not the Foreign Office, however, but the mutterings of revolt among normally subservient Tory M.P.'s which were worrying Chamberlain and Horace Wilson now. "The feeling in the lobbies," wrote Harold Nicolson in his diary on March 17, "is that Chamberlain will either have to go or completely reverse his policy. Unless in his speech tonight he admits that he was wrong, they feel that resignation is the only alternative. All the tadpoles are beginning to swim into the other camp . . . The idea is that Halifax should become Prime Minister, and Eden, Leader of the House."

The speech to which Nicolson was referring was to be made in the Guildhall in Birmingham, as much a stronghold of Chamberlain

180

power and influence as Boston was to a Kennedy, and the original draft the Prime Minister had prepared with Sir Horace Wilson was to be a hymn to sentiment and hope. He would be seventy years old the following day, and he proposed to speak of his devotion to the cause of European peace, and his determination to see it established before he was another year older. There was to be only one passage, more-in-sorrow-than-in-anger and turn-the-other-cheek in character, referring to the Nazi occupation of Prague. But Wilson had his spies in the parliamentary lobbies, and the whispers of revolt against his master quickly reached him. His devotion to Chamberlain was profound, and he was determined to safeguard him against any attempts to replace him as Prime Minister—especially since the antipathy between Anthony Eden and Wilson was still strong, and a return of the former Foreign Secretary to power would almost certainly mean his own departure from the limelight of Downing Street to the dim corridors of the Board of Trade.

"Master," Wilson said now, "we must tear up your speech and write another." It should be one that faced up to the facts of the situation and demonstrated that the government realized that an outrage had been committed, that in the beginning the Prime Minister was too shocked by it all to react strongly enough, but that he was now firm in his resolve to say "No further."

Chamberlain's speech to his fellow citizens in Birmingham on March 17 followed this line. He apologized for the absence of forthrightness in his previous reaction, but the news from Prague had been only "partial, much of it . . . unofficial" and there had been no time "to digest it, much less to form a considered opinion upon it." Hence, his address in Parliament had "a very restrained and cautious exposition . . . and perhaps naturally, that somewhat cool and objective statement gave rise to a misapprehension . . . that . . . my colleagues and I did not feel strongly on the subject." Then he took a deep breath. "I hope to correct that mistake tonight," he said.

The remarkable thing was that even now Chamberlain still felt it necessary to launch into a long justification of his Munich policy. There was an emotional passage as he thanked all those who had congratulated him for having saved the peace last September. (Cynics murmured that he was reminding some well-known politicians that they were implicated and vulnerable too.) He crisply maintained that had it not been for him, Czechoslovakia would have been attacked

181

and destroyed then, and that even if Britain and France had fought on her behalf and won, "never could we have reconstructed Czechoslovakia as she was framed by the Versailles Treaty." He reminded his listeners of how Hitler had promised him that the Sudetenland was his last territorial demand in Europe, and that he did not want any non-Germans in the Reich. But now "Herr Hitler has taken the law into his own hands. Before even the Czech Premier was received and confronted with demands which he had no power to resist, the German troops were on the move."

The Prime Minister paused now and on his face appeared the expression of a man whose heart was grieved. At Munich he had barely concealed his contempt for the Czechs; now he said emotionally, "Who can fail to feel his heart go out in sympathy to the proud and brave people who have so suddenly been subjected to this invasion, whose liberties are curtailed, whose national independence is gone?"

Suddenly Czechoslovakia seemed close to his heart and his interests. England would now turn, he said, to her partners in the Commonwealth and to her ally, France. Then he added, "Others, too, knowing that we are not disinterested in what goes on in Southeast Europe, will wish to have our counsel and advice."

It sounded as if at long last Neville Chamberlain had decided to stand up to Hitler—or was he just playing to the mutinous backbenchers of his party?

In Paris, Foreign Minister Georges Bonnet strode up and down his office at the Quai d'Orsay, his face contorted in an expression of indignation. "It is monstrous!" he cried. "We must show the world what we think of barbarians who act in this fashion. The strongest possible protest must be made to the Wilhelmstrasse."

His Chief Secretary, Alexis Léger, watched him cynically. He was used to Georges Bonnet and knew that the heat he was engendering was only to camouflage indecisiveness. Bonnet had known several days earlier, just as the British Prime Minister had, that Germany was planning to occupy Prague; his agents in Germany had given him the exact hour and date. They had been ignored, as they had been by Chamberlain, because acknowledging the information might have meant having to take action. It was much easier to send an outraged note afterward than to take a stand before. In any case, there is some reason to believe that Georges Bonnet had all but connived with Germany's plans.*

The stiff protest which the French ambassador to Germany, Robert Coulondre, presented to Baron von Weizsäcker at the Foreign Ministry was couched in the same terms as those which the British envoy, Nevile Henderson, had been instructed to deliver.† But though the British protest was accepted, Coulondre found himself involved in a considerable verbal fracas. The note dictated by Bonnet stated that the action of the German government had confronted France with "a flagrant violation of the letter and spirit of the agreements signed at Munich . . . The circumstances in which the agreement of March 15 has been imposed on the leaders of the Czechoslovak Republic do not, in the eyes of the government of the French Republic, legalize the situation registered in that agreement. The French ambassador has the honor to inform his Excellency the Minister of Foreign Affairs of the Reich that the government of the French Republic cannot, under these conditions, recognize the legality of the situation created in Czechoslovakia by the action of the German Reich."

Weizsäcker began the interview with Coulondre by coolly asking to be acquainted in general terms with the contents of the French note, and when assured that it was a vehement protest, he refused to receive it.

WEIZSÄCKER: May I suggest that you refer the note back to your Foreign Minister and ask him to reconsider? In the circumstances, I do not see how he can protest against what has happened.

COULONDRE: I insist that I be allowed to present this note from my government. I have never heard of any kind of diplomatic usage which would prevent me from doing so. I have a duty to my country to make her attitude to these lamentable events known, especially since a solemn act, signed by the two governments, is in question.

WEIZSÄCKER: But how can it be in question, *Monsieur l'Ambassadeur?* As long ago as last December, Monsieur Bonnet agreed with the Reich Minister for Foreign Affairs that Czechoslovakia would never again be a matter of dispute.

COULONDRE: I deny this. There is nothing in the declaration of

* It will never be definitely known whether Bonnet had, in fact, consented to German hegemony in Central and Eastern Europe. German documents say he did; the French documents have disappeared.

† Ribbentrop refused to see either envoy.

December 6, however widely interpreted, which implies the eventual suppression of Czechoslovakia. On the contrary, it specifically calls for consultation in such an event.

WEIZSÄCKER: But the Czechs consented.

COULONDRE: Under duress.

Weizsäcker eventually agreed to receive the protest as if it had been "mailed" to him. Coulondre left for Paris, as did Henderson for London, recalled "for consultations." Such empty gestures by England and France meant nothing under the circumstances.

Anyway, what did it matter? Czechoslovakia was gone: its army, its air force, its productive Skoda armament works, its coal mines, its industrial know-how, its *presence* as an antagonist to Nazi designs in Europe—all gone.

■

The order went out from the Postmaster General in Washington to the U.S. embassy in Paris to start hiring postal clerks. A rush of mail was to be expected because all correspondence addressed to Czechoslovakia from the United States was to be diverted to the Paris embassy, where it would stay until forwarding instructions were delivered.* In the meantime, radio and press appeals were requesting everyone who had written to the stricken republic to indicate at once whether they wished their mail to go through or be returned.

There was no doubt about the abhorrence with which the American public received the news of the annexation of Czechoslovakia. Prayers were read in churches and cynical words were said about the hypocrisy of the British and French. It was announced that the United States government would refuse to acknowledge the annexation and would continue to maintain diplomatic relations with the Czechoslovak government-in-exile. So far no such government had been set up, but Eduard Beneš was in London and was in close touch with Winston Churchill.

President Roosevelt called a meeting of his Cabinet at the White House on March 18, and announced that he was declaring a state of emergency in order to block the transfer of Czech assets in America

---

* This only concerned mail on American ships, of course. By the terms of the International Postal Convention, the United States could not hold up mail carried on German or other national ships. There was no air mail at that time.

into German accounts. He also declared that he was going to have all German property in the United States seized, as a gesture of reprisal. The President was asked whether this included German transatlantic liners, one of which, the *Europa,* was in New York harbor at the moment, and his answer was "Yes, why not?"

Admiral William Leahy was at the Cabinet meeting representing the Navy Department, and Roosevelt asked him, "What would you do if I gave you orders to seize the *Europa* while she is sailing out of New York harbor?"

"Carry out orders, Mr. President."

"What if the *Europa* refuses to heave to under your orders?"

"I'd sink her."

"You mean . . ."

"Well, not at once. I would first fire once or twice above the water line, and then I would gradually go lower until the *Europa* surrendered."

The *Europa* was allowed to sail unmolested by the U.S. Navy, but all Czech assets remained blocked, and control was instituted over certain German assets, an action which provoked a new spate of Nazi press charges that the Americans were "gangsters" and "Jew-driven thieves."

Britain had blocked Czechoslovakia's assets too, and though the holdings in Britain and the Commonwealth were considerable, there was remarkably little reaction to the move by the Nazis. The peculiar silence moved a London financial writer named Paul Einzig to ask himself why, and his subsequent investigations uncovered a remarkable story—one which demonstrated that though the Chamberlain government was now presenting a refurbished image to the public and to Parliament, the philosophy of appeasement still lay just beneath the surface.

When the first German columns rolled into Prague on March 15, a car and a troop carrier broke away as soon as they had crossed the Vltava, sped into the New City and stopped before the entrance of the Czech National Bank. German soldiers jumped from the carrier, swiftly took up positions outside and began setting up a machine-gun post; others ran around the corner to the rear entrance of the bank. From the car descended Herr Karl-Edrich Müller, a director of the

German Reichsbank. He hammered heavily on the iron door of the bank until a frightened porter opened it. "Take me to your manager," he said in German.

Bewildered, the porter gaped at him, and Müller, thrusting him aside, walked into the entrance hall. The lights were on, and most of the staff, who had been called in as soon as news of the crisis was known, was present.

Müller barked out his request to one of them, and a few minutes later was sitting opposite Joseph Malik, the general manager of the bank. After handing over his note of authorization, Müller said, "I would like to be taken to your vault. I have come to collect your deposits of gold. They will be transferred to the Reichsbank in Berlin at once."

Malik answered, "As you wish." He seemed ready to co-operate in every way possible and led the German banker out of his office and down the stairs into the vault, where he signaled an aide to throw it open.

The room was stocked with documents of the investments of the Czech National Bank, of the records of its depositors, and in the corner, its gold deposits.

"Is this all there is?" Müller asked, and Malik replied, "That is all."

In containers were piles of old English and French sovereigns, gold rings, pendants, brooches, bracelets and trinkets—the 18-carat bric-a-brac of a nation's heart.

"There you see the sacrifices of our people," Malik said. "Last September we appealed to them for financial aid if war came and we found ourselves fighting the Germans. The people gave what they could—their wedding rings, their heirlooms, their small savings. Here it is. Take it. Hand it over personally to Herr Hitler!"

"You misunderstand me, sir. I'm a bank official, not a politician. I have no personal or political involvement in this; I am merely obeying instructions." Müller cleared his throat nervously. "But where is the gold? I understand there is six million pound sterling of it under the control of the Czech bank. I am instructed to ask you to produce it at once."

"Ah yes, the Czech gold. I understand that Field Marshal Göring is badly in need of it for his Four-Year Plan. What is the phrase in English, Herr Müller? It will come just in time to *bail him out*."

"Never mind, where is it?"

"In London, Herr Müller, where I hope neither you nor Göring ever get your hands on it."*

"Herr Malik, I must ask you to sign at once an authorization to the Bank of England releasing these holdings to the government of the Reich. Here is the—." He looked around, but Malik had disappeared.

The frightened face of a clerk appeared around the door. "Herr Malik asks to be excused," he said. "You know, of course, that his grandmother is very ill. He has had an urgent call. Could you wait, perhaps until tomorrow?"

For four days Malik used every stratagem he knew to avoid signing the authorization. In the meantime he contacted the British and French legations to warn them of what was happening and to plead that they ask their governments not to release the gold.† Finally, in March 19, coldly threatened with the arrest of himself and his staff by the Gestapo, he took the document proffered him and signed. The paper was then rushed to the Bank for International Settlements in Basel for immediate action.

Paul Reynaud, the new Finance Minister in the French government, had been informed of what was afoot. It seemed utter madness to him that Germany should gain not only Czechoslovakia but also her gold to buy the raw materials she needed from the world market to make herself even stronger. He called upon the two Frenchmen connected with the bank, Roger Auboin, the general manager, and Fournier, a director, to resist the transfer, and in the meantime sent an urgent message to London asking for a similar refusal by the British government.

It was too late. Mr. Montagu Norman, the president of the Bank of England, and Sir Otto Niemeyer, the two British directors of the Bank for International Settlements, had already consulted Sir John Simon, the Chancellor of the Exchequer, and had been told not to hinder the Germans. When Dr. Beyen, the Dutch head of the Bank for International Settlements, got in touch with his directors he pointed out that the decision to transfer the gold to Germany could

---

* In November 1938, after Munich, the Czechs had astutely moved their £6,000,000 in gold into the vaults of the Bank of England as part of their deposit with the Bank for International Settlements.

† France held no Czech gold, but she did have a say about its disposal.

easily be delayed by tabling the question for a subsequent meeting. The French were in favor of this, but neither Norman nor Niemeyer would support them.

Einzig, who had been busy ferreting out these unsavory facts, wrote: "According to competent legal opinion, the surrender of the gold by the Bank for International Settlements was entirely unjustified. It is the banking practice in Switzerland, as in most countries, that if a banker has reason to believe that the instructions he has received were given under duress, it is his right and duty to refuse to comply . . . Anyone acquainted with the conditions prevailing in Prague after the German occupation, when Czechs were being rounded up by the Gestapo by the thousand, must have been aware that the surrender of the gold could only possibly have been agreed upon under extreme pressure."

When the next board meeting of the Bank of International Settlements was held in April 1939, Fournier told Sir Otto Niemeyer, the chairman of the board, that he wished to place the question of the gold on the agenda. Niemeyer asked him not to bother: 80 percent of the gold had already been transferred to Germany; what did the other 20 percent matter?

All this would have taken place under circumstances of complete secrecy had not Einzig ferreted out the facts and persuaded Members of Parliament to keep badgering the government for information about it. As Winston Churchill said in a subsequent debate, "Here we are going about urging people to enlist, urging them to accept new forms of military compulsion; here we are paying taxes on a gigantic scale in order to protect ourselves. If at the same time our mechanism of government is so butter-fingered that this six million pounds of gold can be transferred to the Nazi government of Germany, which only wishes to use it, and is only using it, as it does all its foreign exchange, for the purpose of increasing its armaments . . . it stultifies altogether the efforts our people are making in every class and in every party to secure national defense and rally the whole forces of the country."

■

"No one must come near the Führer! No messages! Everybody keep away!" cried Colonel Schmundt.

188

Adolf Hitler was sick. He had been sick ever since the pocket battleship *Deutschland* left Swinemünde harbor thirty-six hours before and sailed into the Baltic at the head of a German naval cruiser squadron.

It was March 21, 1939, and the latest Nazi conquest was about to take place. Now that Czechoslovakia had crumbled, the next step was a piece of tidying up which would provide a convenient tidbit of victory for the German people without stirring too much resentment among the Western democracies. At least they couldn't regard *this* as a brutal infringement of other nations' territory, or the incorporation of non-Germans into the Reich.

Memel was an ancient German city on the Baltic, inhabited almost completely by Germans, which had been snatched from the Reich by the Treaty of Versailles and given to Lithuania. In the chapter on Eastern and Central Europe which Adolf Hitler was now rewriting, Memel was but a comma, but its annexation—or rather, its reincorporation into the Reich—was a convenient and symbolic snap of the fingers in the face of world reaction to the occupation of Czechoslovakia. Memel was an opportunity for Hitler to show, with little risk, that he was unrepentant. For who, when it came to the moment of decision, would choose to obstruct him in reclaiming this German city now under the control of a small country which had few scruples and few friends in the world? Therefore the Führer had sworn to regain the city for the Reich, and to witness the annexation personally. Thanks to a brisk recruiting campaign, Memel's citizens were strongly pro-Nazi, and they were prepared to hail him as their liberator.

But how was he to reach them? Memel was on the Baltic coast, and the only approach overland was through East Prussia via the Polish Corridor—which, of course, was not yet part of the Reich. In the circumstances, it would hardly have been tactful, or even practical, to ask permission to take his entourage through Polish territory to the seat of his latest conquest. The only alternative was to go by sea.

So far as researches can discover, it was the first time in his life that Adolf Hitler had ever ventured on the water in anything stronger than a summer zephyr. He was leery of water, in any case; he did not even swim. He was an Austrian, with that inlander's suspicion of any expanse of water that tasted of salt, stretched beyond the horizon and developed waves higher than those lapping the barges on the Danube in Vienna. The previous summer, when he had sailed from the Baltic to the North Sea with Regent Horthy of Hungary and anchored for a party off Helgoland, he had told Schmundt that he had much enjoyed the outing. Since the Führer had always had an eye for a pretty girl, political discussions had been interspersed with entertainments for which starlets and models in Berlin had been imported, and Hitler had subsequently congratulated his staff on their arrangements.

On this occasion, however, the girls were missing and it was stormy March, not July. As he stood on the flag deck of the *Deutschland* with Admiral Erich Raeder, the Commander in Chief of the German Navy, the winds from the north swept down upon the eastbound ships and the rolling commenced almost at once. For three hours Hitler stood on the bridge ashen-faced, watching the waves sweep the decks, and refused to be persuaded to go down to his cabin. Then the alarm hooter bansheed through the ship, the accompanying destroyers wheeled like whipped horses and sped away into the drifting spray, and the *Deutschland* herself abruptly altered course.

"Just evasive action," Admiral Raeder assured the Führer. In fact, a Polish torpedo boat, alerted by watchers on the shore, had raced out to investigate this menacing squadron cruising so close to their territorial waters. Before it had completed its full circle of the German ships, Adolf Hitler had had enough. He retired to his cabin, and for the next twenty-four hours he retched and raved with fury. His stomach, which had always been the weakest organ of his body, belching and rumbling whenever he was nervous, was now completely out of control, and each mouthful of bile was a humiliation. But what made his misery complete and brought his temper to the boiling point was the fact that things had gone wrong with the occupation of Memel. It had all looked so easy when he put to sea in the *Deutschland*. He had left specific instructions with Ribbentrop about what should be done.

On March 19 the Lithuanian Foreign Minister, Juozas Urbsys, had arrived in Berlin on his way back to Kaunas, the Lithuanian capital, from a visit to Rome. He paid a courtesy visit to the Nazi Foreign Minister and almost immediately must have wished he had done nothing of the kind, for as soon as he sat down Ribbentrop told him that the German government demanded the immediate cession of the Memelland to the Reich. He had no doubt that Urbsys and his

190

government would agree to this, for it had right and justice behind it; Memel was German and belonged to the Reich. But should the Lithuanian Foreign Minister have any idea of resisting the rightful demand of the German government, or should he attempt to ask other countries for help in frustrating Germany, Ribbentrop could assure him that the matter would no longer be dealt with in a diplomatic but in a military sense.

Like Hácha and Chvalkovský a week earlier, Urbsys played for time. He would have to return to Kaunas to consult his government, he said.

Ribbentrop pointed to the instrument on his desk. As he had said to Hácha, he now said to the Lithuanian, "There is the telephone. A line to Kaunas is open. Speak to them from here."

But Urbsys was younger and tougher than Hácha. He shook his head; no, he must return to Kaunas to consult.

Since his Führer was at sea by now and waiting for news, Ribbentrop frowned with anger and impatience, but finally agreed. Urbsys could return to his country, but he must be back in Berlin as soon as possible—within three days, no more. And he had better remember that if he asked anyone else for help, Germany would be forced to take action. It was a domestic affair.

Urbsys returned to the Lithuanian legation in Berlin furious at the way he had been treated. How dare they humiliate him; how dare they try to treat him like a decrepit and frightened old man? He sat down to dictate a note to his Premier setting down in detail the course of his interview with Ribbentrop and the ultimatum which had been delivered to him. He ordered a copy to be sent to the British, French and Polish embassies in Berlin. It is typical of the situation prevailing in the diplomatic corps at the time that Urbsys decided at the last moment to send his communication, which was a thinly disguised plea for help, not to the ambassadors but to their military attachés. He was so wary of the pro-Nazi tendencies of Nevile Henderson and, as he believed, of Józef Lipski, the Polish envoy, that he felt they might not forward his communication to their governments should they receive it direct. Ironically enough, he did not send a copy to the Soviet embassy, where reaction would certainly have been lively, and perhaps positive; Lithuania was far too afraid of the Soviet Union for that.

191

Then Urbsys took the train back to Kaunas and waited for signs of help from Britain, France or Poland. He waited in vain.

So, vomiting his way through the Baltic, did Adolf Hitler. As the hours passed, messages began to pour into the Foreign Ministry in Berlin from Schmundt, demanding to know when the agreement would be signed so the Führer could get back to dry land.

On March 22 a German aircraft arrived in Kaunas and took off shortly afterward to bring Foreign Minister Urbsys back to Berlin. So far he had received nothing but expressions of sympathy from the British, French and Poles. He was met at Tempelhof Airport in Berlin with the same ceremonies as had been arranged for President Hácha, and then led to a waiting limousine. The ministerial suite at the Adlon Hotel had been prepared for him, he was told. "The same suite as President Hácha's?" said Urbsys, smiling grimly. "I am sorry. I do not wear dead men's clothes."

Instead he went to the Lithuanian legation, from which he emerged two hours later for the meeting with Ribbentrop at which all would be settled. It was evident that everyone was nervous. The German Foreign Minister was not present—it was murmured that he was busy, as in fact he was, dealing with the stream of cables from the *Deutschland*—and Baron von Weizsäcker presided at the meeting. The wrangle that ensued in the next two hours became increasingly acerbic. Still playing for time, still hoping that someone would rescue him, Urbsys argued against the agreement which the Germans had presented for his signature, and offered them equal rights in Memel instead of the outright sovereignty they were demanding. From this position he refused to budge. Weizsäcker kept looking nervously at the clock while messengers slipped in and out of the conference room.

It was twelve-fifteen in the morning when one of the messengers came through the door and gave Weizsäcker a slip of paper. The Undersecretary of State coughed, interrupted a German lawyer reading out yet another paragraph of emendation, and said, "Herr Urbsys, will you follow me, please?"

He led the Lithuanian into the next room, which was the Foreign Minister's study, and then withdrew. In the light of the desk lamp, Ribbentrop sat before a pile of cables, his face yellow and distraught with worry and frustrated rage. He picked up a paper and shook it

192

in Urbsys' face. "We have no more time!" he said. "The delay is intolerable. Either you sign at once, or—" He waved the paper again. "The German navy is at sea. It will shoot its way into Memel harbor!"

About forty-five minutes later Foreign Minister Urbsys walked before the waiting cameras and spotlights, with the full authority of his government, and formally signed the document ceding Memel to the Reich. At once the news was flashed to the *Deutschland* at sea, and Colonel Schmundt risked disturbing the groaning Führer to tell him.

Early in the morning, after a breakfast of vegetable soup, Hitler emerged on deck looking very subdued. Faintly through the haze he could see land. He said to Raeder, "Where are we now?"

"Just off Zoppot, my Führer. See, over to the east is Danzig, and beyond that, East Prussia. Our own East Prussia."

Hitler pointed to the haze. "And that?"

"Gdynia, and beyond that the Polish Corridor."

"The Corridor which separates Germany from Germany!" To Schmundt Hitler said, "If the Corridor were German, as it should be, there would be no need for Germans to go by sea to Memel or East Prussia."

"No, my Führer, no need," said Schmundt.

"It is intolerable!" cried the Führer, and went below to be sick again. As he disappeared, Schmundt had a premonition. Any foreign territory which forced Adolf Hitler to go the long way around, and to be seasick in the bargain, did not have much of a future.

It was a very pale Führer who rode through Memel at the head of his troops on March 23, and the cheers of the crowds did little to stir him. His mind seemed to be elsewhere. Perhaps he was thinking about Poland, Danzig and the Corridor.

VIII

The Panic Pact

The ifs of history are tantalizing. For instance, if a certain Virgil Tilea hadn't had a large and stimulating lunch on March 16, 1939, Britain and France might not have been at war with Germany on September 3.

Tilea was the Rumanian minister in London, an engaging man whose character, like that of so many Rumanians, was full of fire, temperament and easily aroused emotions. Whoever gave him lunch that day* had questioned him closely about the trade negotiations taking place at that moment in Bucharest between the Rumanian government and Helmuth Wohltat, the Nazi counselor for the Foreign Ministry Trade Section. Then his host proceeded to read Tilea certain reports which were filtering back from Rumania implying that these were not simply discussions over economic exchanges but thinly disguised German plans for taking over the country. It was all part of a well-engineered plot, the Englishman suggested. First Bucharest would sign away her oil and crops to Germany, and then the Germans and Hungarians, whom the Rumanians particularly feared and loathed, would move in and take over the unsuspecting country. If so, would it not be Tilea's vital duty to alert the British government of this dreadful danger and persuade them to help at once?

* It has been hinted that it was a high Foreign Office personality who opposed Chamberlain's appeasement policy.

195

Tilea's first instinct was to return immediately to his legation and telephone Bucharest to find out more about this imminent invasion of his beloved country. His host suavely dissuaded him; did he not know that all lines to Bucharest were tapped by the Germans? Did he wish to force the Nazis into imminent action and compromise his colleagues? Would it not be better . . . ?

The Rumanian minister agreed. He drained his wine, dashed from the table and raced down Pall Mall, an exalted Joan of Arc, to the rescue of his country. An hour later he was closeted at the Foreign Office with Sir Orme Sargent, pouring into his receptive ears—for Sargent was a strong anti-appeaser—his fears that "he had good reason to believe" that Rumania was next on the list, and that within a few months the Germans "would reduce Hungary to vassalage and then proceed to disintegrate Rumania."

Finishing this torrent, Tilea gazed fiercely at the Briton behind the desk and asked, "How far can we count on Britain in this event?"

Sargent said that he would have to make inquiries and would be in touch. The Rumanian hurried off into the dusk to toss and turn about the fate of his country. But he did not telephone Bucharest to inquire, even in the most indirect manner, how the trade negotiations with Wohltat were going, and the next day he was back at the Foreign Office, this time demanding to see Lord Halifax himself.

At this moment in Britain, anger against Hitler for his action in Czechoslovakia was at its height; there were demands in the press for "firm attitudes" to the "Nazi brutes" who were terrorizing Europe, and even those newspapers which had obediently followed the Chamberlain line were now demanding that "something be done." Halifax's usually unflappable calm in the face of unpleasant events had cracked, and he had spent the morning "binging up" Chamberlain and informing the Russian and American ambassadors that "Britain is now going to take a firm line." Thus, Tilea could not have entered the Foreign Secretary's office at a more propitious moment. As the Rumanian proceeded to relate the "alarming news" from Bucharest, Halifax stood with his hands behind his back, staring like an elongated Napoleon across the asphalt of the Horse Guards Parade to where a troop of cavalry was maneuvering, and it was as if the sound of rallying trumpets were in his ears.

Tilea reported that during the last few days the Rumanian government had received a request from the German government to grant them a monopoly on Rumanian exports, and to adopt certain restrictive measures on Rumanian industrial production for the sake of German interests. If these conditions were accepted, Germany would guarantee Rumania's frontiers. This seemed to his government very much like an ultimatum.

The minister did not state which member of his government had made this observation. He went on to say that in his government's opinion, it was of the utmost importance that His Majesty's Government consider with all urgency whether they could give a precise indication of the action they would take in the event of Rumania being the victim of German aggression. If it were possible to construct a solid block of Great Britain and France, Tilea thought the situation could be saved. He paused and then added, "It is a matter of days."

While the Rumanian waited in heavy silence, Halifax studied him for some moments. He asked none of the searching or skeptical questions which would almost certainly have come to his lips a year before, had this been the Czech minister; instead he showed plainly that he was greatly alarmed. As he rose to show Tilea to the door, he assured him that he would pass on the Rumanian's alarming information "with all urgency" to the Prime Minister.

On the strength of such encounters are the policies of nations decided and the course of history changed. In fact, as became apparent the following day and as a study of the documents has since proved, no ultimatum at all was being presented by Germany to the Rumanian government. Adolf Hitler did not need one; he could get all he wanted out of Rumania in oil and other supplies by barter agreements. The discussions in Bucharest were exactly what the Germans said they were: trade negotiations. It is true that the purpose of these was the domination of the Rumanian economy, but Chamberlain had always regarded this as inevitable. Grigore Gafencu, the Rumanian Foreign Minister, sent an urgent message to London on March 18 assuring Lord Halifax that Tilea had "misrepresented the situation," that the Bucharest negotiations were "on completely normal lines, as between equals," and that he had given his envoy in London "a tremendous head washing." Georges Bonnet, who saw him three days later, wrote that "when I questioned Tilea myself on this subject, he seemed to be extremely embarrassed."

197

But by the time Gafencu's message arrived, it was too late; the wheels of history had begun to turn.* Halifax had spoken to Chamberlain, who was on his way to Birmingham to make his "fighting" speech, and had been given a green light to take action. The British public was demanding urgent measures. So was Washington, where Roosevelt had already instructed Ambassador Kennedy to press Britain to support Rumania—or risk losing all American sympathy and moral support.† Now here was an opportunity to show everyone that Britain was flexing her muscles and preparing to raise her strong right arm against Hitler at last—not necessarily to make war, but at least to cry "Enough!"

At ten o'clock on the evening of March 17, eighteen hours before Gafencu's clarification reached him, Halifax sent out warning messages to the British envoys in Warsaw, Athens, Belgrade and Ankara retailing Tilea's alarmist message and asking them to contact the Polish, Greek, Yugoslav and Turkish governments respectively to find out what the attitude of these countries would be if Tilea's dire prophecies came true and Germany took over Rumania. It was in this way that the French were alerted; Georges Bonnet received an urgent cable at the Quai d'Orsay from his ambassador to Turkey, René Massigli, giving the contents of the British envoy's message to the Turkish government. The French Foreign Minister immediately got in touch with London, for the French public was showing restiveness too, and he wished to cover himself. Like Halifax, Bonnet instructed his envoys to ask the governments in question for their

---

* According to the Rumanian historian V. Mosiuc, the instructions on which Tilea spontaneously acted and his own record of the conversations held have no reference to a German ultimatum. As is pointed out, however, by D. C. Watt, Reader in International History in the University of London, "he was, however, instructed to do his utmost to secure a positive British policy in Southeast Europe, and he did tell the British that his government had reason to fear that they might be the next victim of German aggression." Watt remarks that "it is difficult to find any trace of an ultimatum in the German records of [Wohltat's] conversations" and concludes: ". . . that he [Tilea] succeeded in duping the whole British Government; and that the episode, as here and elsewhere recorded, throws into stark relief the occasional lapses into total panic of which the Foreign Office, at first sight so Olympian, and its still more Olympian political head, Lord Halifax, were capable."

† It was the beginning of a period, Kennedy said afterward, when Chamberlain was to complain that "America and world Jews" were forcing Britain into war. The President kept telephoning Kennedy, telling him to put some iron up Chamberlain's backside, and Kennedy kept replying that "putting iron up his backside did no good unless Britain had some iron with which to fight, and they did not."

reactions should Rumania be attacked. In more or less polite terms, all replied to the same effect. They had been disillusioned by the weakness of Britain and France at Munich and over the occupation of Prague; now their answer was: You tell us what you will do, and then we'll tell you what we will do.

■

On March 18 President Albert Lebrun of France, accompanied by Georges Bonnet, arrived in London for a state visit and was met at Victoria Station by King George VI. There were several days of pomp and ceremony, of gold-plate dinners at Buckingham Palace and Windsor, turtle soup at the Guildhall, and processions through streets decked with flags and packed with waving crowds shouting "*Vive la France!*" Apparently the bitterness of the past few months had been forgotten, and the spirit of the Entente Cordiale seemed to reign once more.

By this time Neville Chamberlain and his Foreign Secretary had been told that Tilea's warning of German designs on Rumania was a false alarm. However, this did not seem to matter any longer. Tilea was not even discredited as a source of information or advice; on the contrary, Halifax continued to consult him. He had stimulated the British government into taking action, and that was enough.

The Prime Minister was in a mood of some exaltation; the warm reception his speech at Birmingham had been given by the public and press appeared to have gone to his head. He said to his Minister for War, Leslie Hore-Belisha, "I'm the man with the umbrella. When I speak seriously, the nations take all the more notice." And after the dinner given by the King at Buckingham Palace, he told Bonnet, "Hitler has violated the agreements he signed. He wants to dominate Europe. We will not permit him to do so."

The remark had come a little late in the day, but Chamberlain did not seem to notice; he had paid his lip service to the Czechs, and now there were other things on his mind. How to give aid to Rumania, for instance, in view of the "threat" to her independence; there was no way for Britain or France to approach the country by land, and only through the Dardanelles into the Black Sea by water.

Halifax decided that what was needed was another ally, who

could be presented to the Germans as part of a stern front against future Nazi aggression. Tilea suggested Poland, which had a common border with Rumania and certainly did not wish to see further German expansion in Eastern Europe, particularly along her own frontier. This seemed to Halifax a splendid idea. He consulted Chamberlain, who agreed; indeed, he was, if anything, even more enthusiastic than his Foreign Secretary. For would not the inclusion of Poland in the front against Germany do the trick? Was she not on friendly terms with the Reich? Did they not have the same anti-Jewish attitude, and therefore a close understanding of each other's ideas? Yes, with Poland tied to Britain by a treaty, Hitler would be bound to listen.

Since there was a good deal of agitation in Parliament and among the Churchill group of anti-appeasers at this time for some sort of approach to Soviet Russia, on the advice of Sir Horace Wilson the Prime Minister proposed a brilliant idea. Ever since Prague, the Soviet Foreign Commissar, Maxim Litvinov, had been repeating the suggestion he had made before Munich: Britain, France and the Soviet Union, together with other interested countries, should consult and co-ordinate their actions to resist Nazi aggression. Litvinov had been brushed off so far. Now Chamberlain suggested to the Russians that they join with Britain, France and Poland in a joint declaration guaranteeing Rumania's autonomy. Litvinov consulted Moscow and returned with the message that the Soviet Union would agree if Poland also signed.

Poland would not sign, for she was anti-Russian to the point of phobia.* When the British and French approached Colonel Józef Beck, the Polish Foreign Minister, and enthusiastically put before him the suggestion of a Four Power declaration, he replied in sum, "It must be a Three Power declaration. It is either Russia or Poland. You will have to choose."†

Looking back, it seems incredible that Neville Chamberlain chose Poland.

He chose Poland because he believed that of the two countries, Poland's armed forces were far superior to those of the Soviet Union.

---

* For good reason; she had suffered badly under Czarist rule. But she had also wiped the slate at least partly clean in 1918, when she had acquired and incorporated large slices of Russia while the civil war was raging.
† See Bonnet's *De Munich à la guerre*.

He chose Poland because he believed she was in no danger from Germany, and through her friendly influence would therefore act as a brake on the expansionist ambitions of Adolf Hitler.

He was disastrously wrong.

In 1939 the government of Poland was known as "the government of the Colonels." There were three of them: President Ignacy Mościcki, who had once held that rank in the Polish army; Marshal Edward Smigly-Rydz, Commander in Chief of the Polish Armed Forces, who had of course once been a colonel; and the smoothest and most influential of the trio, Colonel Józef Beck, who had been all sorts of things.

Everyone who ever met or had dealings with Józef Beck had a story to tell about him. The dossier on him in the files of the Deuxième Bureau in Paris is almost as long as the Polish Corridor. It dates from the time when, as assistant military attaché in Paris, he purloined a secret document off the desk of a French general; goes on to recount how he accepted bribes from the Germans to pass French military secrets to the Reich, for which he was expelled from France; details his ruthless behavior at the time of Munich; his deliberate suppression of appeals from the Czechs, and the manipulation of certain other approaches, all designed to nullify the Polish-Czech pact of friendship still existing in 1938.*

Józef Beck was an alcoholic, but that was the least of his vices. In 1938 and 1939 he was drinking particularly hard because he had cancer and found alcohol an anodyne for the pain from which he suffered almost constantly. A few months before, he had entertained a group of official Britons led by Alfred Duff Cooper, the First Lord of the Admiralty, and his beautiful wife, Diana. Together with a party of guests, they had poured ashore at Gdynia from the Admiralty yacht *Enchantress*.

"It was high jinks last night and no heelers," wrote Diana Cooper in her diary, "and tziganes and bonnets high over the windmills of Gdynia. We trooped out to dine with Colonel Beck at a Government House suite of rooms. Scrumptious fare of bortsch and crayfish and vodka. I sat next to Beck. There must be more to the Colonel than I

* Thus enabling Poland to cross the Czech frontier and seize tracts of the Teschen territory.

can see, for I saw nothing but an Ancient Pistol, and a weak tipsy Pistol at that. He repeated himself with the persistence of a cuckoo and waved his tail with peacock vanity. Still, he is a colourful freak and enjoys everything in life, I should think. He has told me so often that he is 'the only Colonel Beck' that I'm beginning to think that he protests too much. The ribbons he wears, he says, are equivalent to Victoria Crosses. He has fought fifteen wars, and he says that Hitler has power and charm and flair, but he is 'not a Colonel Beck,' that the man in the street is his friend *parce que je ne suis pas méchant,*' and that if the man in the street smiles at you it shows the splendid kind of man you are.

"Duff went back after dinner to write all these things home, but we went on to be stifled and delighted in a little night club. The Poles danced like reeds in the breeze, and the Colonel pinched all our thighs and tangled our toes and became less articulate in his sketchy French, and repetitions followed more quickly as the champagne slopped over . . . [Next morning] We've had an all-Beck day. The fellow is so intense and concentrated a bore that we took him on in shifts. The demon alcohol must be the trouble. I don't believe that he was once sober . . ."

The encounter with the British minister and his gay passengers did as much to disenchant Beck as it bored Diana Cooper. He had never had a high opinion of the English—he admired French culture and sophistication and German drive—but he had hoped that stead-fast British devotion to principle and justice would hold the balance in Europe. Quite wrongly, he saw national weakness in the levity of Duff Cooper and his party; in fact, these drink-and-be-merry people represented a surprisingly solid opposition to appeasement policies, and they were ready at all times to down their glasses and fight.* But British character was not something Colonel Beck understood. To him, they were a frivolous and gullible people. Poland was in a difficult position; how could she exploit the situation to her own advantage?

In 1939 Poland was one of the shabbiest and most pathetic nations in Europe. It had been re-created by the Treaty of Versailles out of territories which had once been ruled by Russia, Austria, and

---

* As mentioned earlier, Duff Cooper had resigned as a matter of principle after Munich but he remained a Member of Parliament.

Prussia, and most recently by Germany. However, the Poles were indeed a people, and a proud one. Crushed by the Czar, the Emperor and the Kaiser, they had kept their culture and their hope of independence alight, and in 1918 freedom had finally come to them again. But the realm which was their due was much less than that which they claimed. They exploited the weakness of defeated Germany to push their territories in the west as far as the banks of the Oder River in one small segment, encompassing thousands of Germans in their annexations; to the east they penetrated even farther into the Ukraine and Byelorussia to seize great tracts of land which had never been Polish but seemed to the rulers in Warsaw strategically and economically well worth having—especially since the embattled Russians were too embroiled to prevent their appropriation.

Curiously enough, though they had lost much more, the Russians complained far less than Germany—publicly at least—about the boundaries of Poland in 1939. Nevertheless, the three "colonels" suspected that if they made a mutual-assistance pact with the Soviet Union, and if Russian soldiers ever had to march westward into Poland to help them, they would never get them out again. Their relations with their huge Communist neighbor were therefore polite, but extremely wary and suspicious. To buttress themselves against the possibility that the Soviets might someday ask for or retake by force the territories they had lost, the Poles needed a powerful neighbor who would come to their aid should they be threatened. In 1934 they had signed a pact of friendship with Nazi Germany, and up until the Munich crisis, and even a few weeks beyond, relations with Adolf Hitler had been amicable. He continually said he liked and admired the Poles, particularly since they also hated the Jews.

After the Sudetenland had been absorbed, however, Hitler turned toward Poland with a glint in his eyes. The Poles had two assets he needed, and he hoped he could get them by friendship rather than by force. The first was Danzig, which was situated on the Baltic near the Vistula River. This splendid old Hanseatic city and port between Germany proper and East Prussia had been made into a free city by the League of Nations after World War I, and its nominal head was the High Commissioner of the League of Nations. However, the population of Danzig was almost completely German, and it had rallied to the Nazis soon after Hitler took power in 1933. The internal affairs of the Free City (i.e., the city of Danzig and its surrounding territory) were governed by a senate, which was controlled by the National Socialists, but by the terms of the League statutes the Poles were in charge of the customs posts of the Free City and pocketed the dues thus obtained, and they controlled external affairs as well. Adolf Hitler wanted all this changed. Danzig must be returned to the Reich.

There was also the matter of the so-called Polish Corridor. This strip of land, varying in breadth from fifty to one hundred miles, was Poland's only connection with the sea, with Danzig and with the neighboring Polish port of Gdynia. It had a mixed population of Poles and Germans who in normal times lived on terms of uneasy tolerance. Hitler could have accepted the fact that Germans were living there under Polish rule; such conditions only became important when they suited his political strategy. What he found unendurable was the fact that the Polish Corridor cut Germany in two, separating Germany proper from East Prussia and forcing Germans to cross Polish territory in sealed trains or to go by sea should they wish to travel from Berlin to, say, Königsberg, the East Prussian capital.

The proposals which Adolf Hitler made to Colonel Józef Beck, first after the Munich Agreement, and again early in 1939, were in his opinion the mild requests of one friend to another. He asked that Danzig be returned to the Reich, in which case he would immediately give the Poles free rights in the port and access to and from the city. He also asked for permission to build an autobahn, a six-lane highway, and a railway line from Germany to East Prussia across the Corridor—the road, the railway and a narrow strip of territory on either side to be German territory.

Beck flatly refused. He would be willing to allow a road to be built across the Corridor, but it would be on Polish territory and under Polish control. As for Danzig, a change in its status was impossible.

Hitler was taken aback, and Ribbentrop was furious. But they still wore smiles, though somewhat fixed ones, as they pressed Beck and his government to reconsider the generosity of the offer. They also sweetened their terms; if Beck would only give way, the treaty of friendship of 1934 could be turned into a straightforward alliance,

204

and Poland would be invited to join the Anti-Comintern Pact.* It is an extraordinary example of Beck's arrogance and self-confidence that he flatly turned down this gesture as well. It was a fatal error. Sandwiched between two great powers like Russia and Germany, Poland could only be secure when she was in alliance with one or the other; she was simply not strong enough to remain independent.

This, however, Beck and his fellow "colonels," as well as most of the Polish people, refused to believe. Not only were they a great people but a great power—greater than Russia, the equal of Germany, France and Britain. They were convinced that come what may, they could meet the challenge. They firmly believed that their army (which was ill equipped and spearheaded by cavalry divisions "addicted to Balaclava-like charges," as Liddell Hart described them), together with the air force (which was minuscule), could take on the Red Army or the Wehrmacht and rub their noses in the mud.

In the first weeks of 1939, as it became evident that the Poles were adamant and that Beck really meant what he said, Hitler's conciliatory attitude soured into resentment and then into slow-burning fury. More pressure was exerted, and it was suggested that Germany might have to take Danzig back by force. This bit of saber rattling was only answered in kind; "Any attempt to incorporate the Free City into the Reich," wrote Beck, "would inevitably lead to conflict."

The trouble was that when the Poles saber-rattled it was actually sabers they were rattling.

Only when Hitler marched into Czechoslovakia and turned Slovakia into a puppet state did Beck show any signs of alarm, for he realized that with this move his country had been outflanked. If the Germans now wished to move against Poland, the armies could attack from three directions: East Prussia, whose frontier was only a hundred miles from Warsaw; Germany proper; and Slovakia in the south. This did not persuade Beck to alter his policy toward Germany, but he did instruct his ambassador in Berlin, Lipski, to protest.

* Germany and Japan had signed this treaty in November 1936; Italy joined a year later. Ostensibly a bulwark against Communist expansion, it was in reality a mutual-security pact against any future Russian moves.

205

Ribbentrop reacted sharply; all his amicability was gone now. The Führer was becoming increasingly amazed at Poland's attitude, he said. He was tired of waiting for a definite reply to the request for a road and railway through the Corridor, and he wanted an affirmative answer about Danzig. These were the prerequisites for the continuation of Polish-German friendship. Poland must understand that she could not have it both ways and take a middle course between Russia and Germany. Their only chance of survival was a reasonable relationship with Germany and the Führer. He also told Lipski to inform Beck that his presence was needed in Berlin soon; Hitler wanted to see him. He hinted broadly that when the Colonel came—"and the talk should not be delayed too long"—he had better bring concessions with him.

This exchange took place on March 21, the same day that Beck was approached by the British and French and asked to join a Four Power guarantee of Rumania. The wily Beck saw that the moment had come but that only by appearing cool could he bring off his coup. At once he told both the British and French that not only did he not wish to be associated with the Russians, but if Poland and the Soviet Union joined forces it would infuriate and antagonize Hitler.

Beck was quite sure that Chamberlain and Bonnet would choose Poland in preference to Russia. Bonnet was as strongly anti-Communist as himself, and Chamberlain's feelings about the Soviets can be gathered by a quote from a letter he wrote to his sister at about this time: "I must confess to the most profound distrust of Russia. I have no belief whatever in her ability to maintain an effective offensive, even if she wanted to. I distrust her motives."

Chamberlain also agreed with his Foreign Secretary's estimate of the potential power of the Russian army. In a conversation with Ambassador Kennedy, Halifax stoutly maintained that Poland was of more value to the democracies than Russia because his information showed Russia's air force "to be weak, old and short-ranged," the army "poor" and its industrial background "frightful." Assuming that the Russians wanted to be of help, the most that could be expected from them was "some ammunition to Poland in the event of trouble." Kennedy was no lover of Russia himself, but after this he expressed his opinion that the British government was "punch-drunk."

Therefore Beck was not surprised when Neville Chamberlain allowed Russia to fade out of the picture, but now he began to play

206

hard to get. He did not let a whisper of the growing Polish-German tension reach the ears of the British and French, for he was sure that Chamberlain would be frightened off if he knew that Poland was now being threatened by Hitler. Beck resisted each British blandishment with cool confidence; his attitude was that Poland was independent and could take care of herself. This tactic worked so well that all Chamberlain could think about was how to *force* Poland into joining with Britain and France.

As the rumors started to circulate in political quarters in London of Chamberlain's ardent wooing of Colonel Beck, others began to think he was punch-drunk too. Even the General Staff was alarmed. "I also received a note from Lord Beaverbrook," wrote Captain B. H. Liddell Hart, the military correspondent of the *Times* of London and an adviser to the Minister for War. "The guarantee to Poland had been given against the advice of the General Staff, who declared that they were not capable, with the resources we had, of fulfilling the commitments we had thereby undertaken. Hore-Belisha had asked the Prime Minister that he might circulate to the Cabinet the paper expressing the General Staff point of view, but the Prime Minister refused, saying that this would be 'tantamount to a criticism of his policy.' "

What the General Staff and its Minister for War did not understand was that Chamberlain did not care whether the British armed forces could really help Poland in a crisis; nor did he seem to worry over the fact that his own military attaché in Warsaw, backed by the British ambassador there, warned him that the Polish army was all boast-and-wind and not capable of withstanding modern warfare. To Chamberlain, this was not important; Poland was simply an excuse to make a gesture. He believed the assurances of Colonel Beck and of his own envoys—singularly ill informed, as usual—that Polish-German relations were normal. (In fact, to encourage him in this state of mind, Beck leaked a hint to a British intelligence agent that he was preparing to make "large concessions" to Germany over Danzig, which was certainly not the case.) In the Prime Minister's eyes, no danger attached in achieving a closer relationship with Poland. But *how,* since Beck was so cavalier in refusing all overtures?

It was then that the Foreign Secretary fell into the trap which Colonel Beck had so neatly set for the British. Incredibly, Halifax suggested that Britain simply ignore all of Poland's objections and *insist* on giving the country a guarantee of the integrity of her frontiers. In turn Poland would then agree to guarantee Rumania, and all would be well. Typically, Chamberlain agreed that this was a good solution.

The British ambassador in Warsaw, Sir Howard Kennard, hurried over to Beck's private apartment in Warsaw—the Colonel was ill at the time—and presented him with the British plan. It was exactly what Beck wanted; still, he hesitated, only reluctantly accepted it, and made no promise at all of a quid pro quo in the form of a guarantee for Rumania. Instead, he insisted that the agreement be a secret one—not even the French were to be told—lest the Germans or the Russians be "concerned" about it.

When this news was cabled back to London, Chamberlain and Horace Wilson were dismayed. They had counted on an announcement of the guarantee to Poland not only to quell the revolt in the ranks of the Tory party, but to persuade the British people and the United States that they were now standing up to the threat of aggression. Secret agreements were of no use at all in rehabilitating his image and that of his cohorts. "It seemed quite unjust that having decided to revolutionize his attitude, he should be prevented from demonstrating its drive and its object," said Sir Horace Wilson.

The search began for a way of publicizing what had occurred. At this moment, an unwitting newspaperman played into the hands of the British government. Ian Colvin was the Berlin correspondent of the liberal London daily, *News Chronicle,* and had a considerable rapport with German critics of Hitler's political and military policies. Several times he had acted as liaison between anti-Nazi groups in Germany and the British government. His information was always first-rate; unfortunately, it was sometimes a little previous, and in March 1939 he made a mistake.

As did his informants. At about this time, Adolf Hitler had so lost patience with the Poles that he resolved to crush them if he could not get what he wanted any other way. But when he harangued his generals about the probability that one day he would have to take over Poland, he added the words "Not yet."*

Ian Colvin and his sources did not hear about those two words, and so he sent a scarifying dispatch to his newspaper toward the end

---

* During his tour of Czechoslovakia after March 15. Instructions for the attack on Poland were not drawn up until April 3, *after* the British guarantee to Poland.

208

of March forecasting an imminent invasion of Poland by the German army, and then hurried to London to tell his friends in the Foreign Office why he believed this to be so.* To his surprise, Colvin found himself taken first to see Halifax, and then the Prime Minister. He recounted in detail the reasons why he believed that a German attack on Poland was imminent, and was listened to with respectful attention. He could not have guessed that no one in the room believed a word he was saying—quite rightly, as it happened; he was months in advance of the facts—nor could he have known that he was playing into Chamberlain's hands.

Here was the excuse the Prime Minister was seeking. Using Colvin's "inside" information and his well-publicized stories as a pretext, he instructed Halifax and his two Foreign Office aides, Sir Alexander Cadogan and Undersecretary of State Richard Austen Butler, to draft an immediate declaration of support for Poland. The draft was finished at 1 A.M. on March 30, and sent to the Prime Minister. He rewrote it before allowing it to be cabled to Warsaw, and sent a revised version the following day.

Beck accepted it, as he was to say afterward, "between two flicks of the ash off a cigarette." The same evening in the House of Commons, weary, yellow-faced but triumphant, Chamberlain rose to announce that the Poles were now under British protection and that if "any action were taken which clearly threatened their independence, His Majesty's Government and the French Government would at once lend them all support in their power." He had not even waited for French permission before making the statement. True, the French already had an arrangement with Poland (just as they had had an arrangement with Czechoslovakia), but the last thing they wanted was to be reminded of it.

The House cheered. The nation approved; it seriously believed what it was reading in the newspapers, and thought that Poland was in imminent danger.

A few days later Beck was in London, where by a mixture of blandishment and downright lies he ran rings around the self-confident Chamberlain and his mild-mannered Foreign Secretary. When pressed to give the guarantee of Rumania which had started the

---

* Some historians appear to believe that Colvin had been expelled by the Nazis when he came to London on this occasion. This was not so; he returned to his post immediately afterward.

whole business, he side-stepped any question of doing so with a bull-fighter's skill. Why not wait, he said, until the Danubian question had cleared up a little?

Chamberlain was exasperated. The heart of the matter was the protection of Rumania, and to get it Britain was making this grand gesture—just how grand he did not realize—but still, not even in gratitude would Beck reciprocate.

To scare the Pole into a concession, Chamberlain conjured up the picture of Rumania under Nazi occupation. In this event Poland would have a long frontier with Germany, he pointed out.

The Prime Minister should have looked at his atlas before he spoke. Beck, who knew his geography, grinned and shook his head. The additional border would be quite short, he said. It was mountainous too, and could be held with a small force.

They moved on to a discussion of Polish-German relations. Beck looked Chamberlain straight in the eye and said that there was no strain between them at all. Take Danzig, for instance, the Colonel said; Germany had never contested Polish rights in Danzig; in fact, she recently confirmed them.

Of course this was an unblushing lie. Only the week before, Ribbentrop had threatened the Poles if they did not agree to the Free City's return to the Reich. But Beck airily remarked that Germany would never risk a conflict with Poland over "local matters," and that the Danzig question was "not in itself a grave one." He added that he didn't propose to trouble the British over Danzig in any case; it wasn't important enough. This problem should be left to the Poles; they would handle it themselves.

As the talks continued, Chamberlain and Halifax became more and more irritated, and Beck increasingly stubborn. Russia? Any association between Poland and Russia would push Germany into war with Poland, Beck stated. If Britain and Russia wanted to get together, well and good, but Poland would keep clear.

A mutual agreement by a number of states acting together? This was what he had in mind, Chamberlain reminded the Pole, whereas what they seemed to be getting was a bilateral Anglo-Polish agreement.

Beck nodded. This was just what Poland wanted—no more, no less. It was against Polish tradition to express definite opinions about third countries without directly consulting them. It was a bilateral agreement or nothing.

The Colonel could speak with confidence. He knew that Chamberlain was in a corner and that the British people were demanding action from him. Having already publicly declared Britain's agreement to protect Poland, he could not now renege on it. The Prime Minister looked at Beck in despair, and then agreed.

When Colonel Beck left London for Warsaw on April 4, Britain's "temporary unilateral assurance to Poland" had been altered to read "permanent and reciprocal agreement."* He was smiling triumphantly as he waved good-bye—and with good reason, for the agreement changed British policy and history by allowing the Poles to decide if and when an act of aggression had been committed by Germany.

"Never before in our history," wrote Duff Cooper, "have we left in the hands of one of the smaller powers the decision whether or not Great Britain goes to war."

"Britain's frontier is no longer on the Rhine but on the Vistula, hundreds of miles to the East," Daladier remarked with some astonishment.

"The British must be mad," said Gafencu, the Rumanian Foreign Minister. "Poland is the least moral country in Europe."

Captain Liddell-Hart has written: "What is clear is that the unqualified terms of the guarantee placed Britain's destiny in the hands of Colonel Beck, a man of very unstable judgment. The Polish Guarantee was the surest way to produce an explosion and a world war. It incited Hitler to demonstrate the futility of such a guarantee to a country out of reach of the West, while making the stiff-necked Poles even less inclined to consider any concession to him, and at the same time making it impossible for him to draw back without losing 'face.' "

It is difficult to find any virtue in the Anglo-Polish agreement at all. It not only infuriated the Germans (who had already prepared *Fall Weiss,* the plan to attack Poland in case it became necessary), it also alienated the Russians (who knew that Chamberlain had chosen Poland as the worthier ally). It did not even achieve its primary

* Which, though still to be formally signed, made clear to the world (and particularly to Hitler) the nature of Britain's guarantee of Poland's security.

objective of persuading Poland to join in a guarantee of Rumania; that guarantee was never given.

Two weeks after Beck returned to Poland, Chamberlain learned that the Pole had lied to him and that he had been tricked. The Poles and the Germans *were* on the verge of war. With sudden panic he realized that he might actually have to fight for Poland one of these days, which had never been his intention. But by then, of course, it was too late. Another step had been taken along the road to war.

IX

Hitler Briefs
His Generals

The sun was shining over Berlin on April 28, 1939, and warm spring winds were thawing out chilled bones in Europe, if not apprehensions. It was six weeks since the occupation of Prague, and five since the annexation of Memel. Not to be outdone by his more powerful partner in the Axis, Mussolini had decided on a little conquest of his own after Hitler went into Prague, and chose Albania as his target. At the time this country was already in the Italian orbit and showed no desire to be otherwise; in fact, its Ruritanian monarch, King Zog, had heard rumors of Italian designs on his country and wrote to Mussolini and Count Ciano offering to submit to even more control from Rome. But the Duce would not be placated. Hitler's actions in Czechoslovakia and Memel had been carried out without giving him advance warning; only when they were over did the Prince of Hesse, Hitler's special envoy to Italy, arrive with a message of amity from the Führer. "Every time he takes a new country he sends me a letter!" the Duce fumed.

Now he was going to acquire a new country himself, and he wasn't going to tell Hitler. On Good Friday, April 7, he sent his warships into Durazzo harbor and took over Albania without a fight. Zog fled into exile and a crowing Mussolini rushed to the palace to tell King Victor Emmanuel that he had a new title: he was not only King of

213

Italy and Emperor of Ethiopia but would soon be crowned King of Albania as well. He was furious when he discovered that Victor Emmanuel, a monarch minuscule in size but large in sagacity, had retired to the country in disgust.

The outrage was general in the non-Fascist world, except in government circles in Britain, where Neville Chamberlain's reaction was mild. He was determined not to let this "lapse" by Mussolini interfere with Anglo-Italian relations, he said, conveniently ignoring that the Duce had assured him during his last visit to Rome that he would indulge in no more Mediterranean adventures. However, Sir Horace Wilson pointed out to his master that there was a certain amount of indignation in the country against Mussolini, and perhaps some sort of gesture was called for.

The Prime Minister agreed, and finally had an inspiration. A new British ambassador, Sir Percy Loraine, had just been appointed to succeed Lord Perth in Rome. When Sir Percy presented his credentials they would be made out to Victor Emmanuel III, King of Italy and Emperor of Ethiopia, but *not* King of Albania. Surely this would make Britain's feelings clear.*

Franklin D. Roosevelt's reaction was a little more forthright, but unfortunate nonetheless. On April 15 he addressed an appeal to Adolf Hitler and Benito Mussolini in which he listed some thirty countries in Europe, the Near and Middle East, and asked the two dictators to pledge themselves not to invade them. He suggested ten years as "a minimum period of assured nonaggression" or even twenty years, "if we dare to look that far ahead." If Hitler and Mussolini agreed to this, Roosevelt would transmit their assurances to the governments concerned, who would no doubt make them reciprocal. The President also declared his readiness to take part in discussions on international trade which would enable every nation in the world "to buy or sell on equal terms in the world markets."

Harold Ickes congratulated FDR on his messages and described them as "not only a brilliant move on the President's part, it was an act of striking statesmanship as I see it. Apparently he has put both Hitler and Mussolini in a hole . . ."

On the contrary, this well-meant but ham-handed act had played

---

* In fact, even this mild protest was muted. Sir Percy's credentials had been signed on March 28, before the expropriation of Albania, so that the absence of the new title was hardly a rebuke.

into Hitler's hands, and he immediately announced that he would reply to it in his speech to the Reichstag on April 28. In the meanwhile, he handed the President's message to Baron von Weizsäcker at the Foreign Ministry and asked him to write a reply that he could use in his speech.

In the spring sunshine of April 28, Hitler arrived with his cortege of SS guards at the Kroll Opera House,* and marched inside to a packed gathering of excited Reichstag deputies in Brown Shirt uniform. The galleries were filled with diplomats, for they had been told that this was to be an important occasion.

It was. Adolf Hitler was angry. The Anglo-Polish pact had infuriated him, as any realistic observer could have predicted, for it meant that Britain was bolstering the arrogant refusal of the Poles to negotiate over Danzig and the Corridor. Until Chamberlain's gesture to Colonel Beck, the Führer had been convinced that it was merely a matter of time before the Poles would realize the vulnerability of their position and consent to compromise. He had been certain that there would be no war over Danzig and the Corridor, but now Britain had fanned the Polish fires by offering them direct military aid should they be threatened, and of course this could only increase the defiance of the already pouter-chested Polish militarists. As for Roosevelt's message!

As a speaker, Adolf Hitler wielded a peculiar kind of magic. There were some people who, like the pure virgins faced by the sorcerers of old, were impervious to his words, but others, though they hated the passion in his voice, the verbal infelicities and grammatical errors and obvious tricks, were impressed in spite of themselves by his ability to catch, hold and shake his audience. He was an orator of considerable emotional skill, and his feel for a situation was uncanny.

On April 28 the Führer seemed to realize that this was not the occasion for one of his ranting, bowel-moving appeals to hatred and violence, but the opportunity to voice the calm, more-in-sorrow-than-in-anger words of a statesman who has tried to be conciliatory, who has been misunderstood and who has now been reluctantly forced to face the facts that there are enemies beyond the battlements who must either be driven away or annihilated.

---

* The meeting place of the Reichstag since that building had been burned in 1933.

215

First Hitler saluted his own actions in Czechoslovakia as a service to the peaceful settlement of European problems, and then went on to deplore the way in which his moves had been received in England. For England's reaction had not been to thank him for pacifying Europe, not to reciprocate the regard Germany had always had for the English people, but to decide that war was inevitable. The old game of encircling Germany had begun again. Britain had found allies who would help her in that scheme—Poland, for instance.

"Poland!" said the Führer. "All I wanted to do with Poland was reach a settlement with her. Poles and Germans have to live side by side, whether they like it or not. Do I want to prevent Poland from having access to the sea? Indeed I do not! But we Germans have legitimate demands too: access to our own East Prussia and the return of the German city of Danzig to the Reich."

He paused and sighed. "I tried to solve that problem. I made an unprecedented offer to Poland—and I repeat the terms—of an alliance between our two countries, and in return only the grant of road and rail facilities through the Corridor and the return of the Free City to the country to whom it and its people belong. What happened? The Poles not only rejected the offer, but worse. They have begun to lend themselves—as the Czechs did last year—to the lying campaign against Germany. The international warmongers have drawn them into their camp."

With that—louder now, very firm of voice—Hitler denounced the Anglo-German naval agreement of 1935 and the German-Polish friendship treaty of 1934. Next, he congratulated Mussolini for "so gallantly" overcoming "the threat" from Albania, and then he dealt with the message from President Roosevelt.

What followed was a masterly example of the Hitlerian destruction of an opponent by oratory. He had not taken offense, he said, at the President's request that he guarantee the integrity and security of all the thirty—or was it eighty?—states he had mentioned, even though he knew that had he made similar inquiries about America's activities in Central and South America, he would have been referred to the Monroe Doctrine. Instead, he had approached all the states mentioned and asked them whether they felt threatened by Germany.

"Not all of them have been able to reply," he said, amid the laughter of the Reichstag deputies. "In Syria and Palestine, for ex-

216

ample, the views of the inhabitants cannot be ascertained, due to the occupation of the French and the British [pause] not German [pause] troops." He was silent for a moment, and then said, "The German government is still willing to give assurances against aggression to any of the states referred to by President Roosevelt, but only so long as they come forward and ask for those assurances themselves."*

At this point Hitler addressed himself directly to America, and most pointedly to the isolationists who opposed Roosevelt's preoccupation with Europe: "Mr. Roosevelt! I fully understand that the vastness of your nation and the immense wealth of your country allow you to feel responsible for the history of the whole world and for the history of all nations. I, sir, am placed in a much smaller and more modest sphere. I once took over a state which was faced by complete ruin, thanks to its trust in the promises of the rest of the world and to the appalling misgoverning of previous democratic governments . . . Since then, Mr. Roosevelt, I have only been able to fulfill one simple task. I cannot feel responsible for the fate of the world, since this world never took much interest in the pitiful state of my own people. I have been called by Providence to do nothing more, and nothing less, than look after my people alone. And I have done it. I have lived day and night for the single task of awakening the power of my people, deserted by the rest of the world . . . I have conquered chaos here in Germany, re-established order, increased production . . . found useful work for seven million unemployed . . ."

Everyone in that audience was listening spellbound now.

"Not only have I united the German people politically, but I have also rearmed them. I have begun, page by page, to destroy the [Versailles] Treaty, which in its four hundred and forty-eight articles contains the vilest oppression which nations have ever had to endure. I have brought back to the Reich provinces stolen from us in 1918. I have led back to their native country millions of Germans who were torn away from us and were in misery. I have re-established the historic unity of German living space [*Lebensraum*]. And, Mr. Roosevelt, I have tried to do this without spilling blood and without bringing to my people, and consequently to others, the misery of war."

* In fact, nineteen of the countries mentioned in Roosevelt's message were overrun by Germany in the course of World War II.

Then Hitler turned toward the Diplomats' Gallery, where Alexander Kirk, the U.S. chargé d'affaires, was sitting with members of his staff. "Twenty-one years ago I was an unknown worker and soldier of the people, and today, Mr. Roosevelt, this is what I have achieved by my own vitality . . . Yours, Mr. Roosevelt, is a much easier task. You became President of the United States in 1933 when I became Chancellor of the Reich. From the very start you stepped to the head of one of the largest and wealthiest nations in the world . . . everything was yours . . . unlimited resources. You are only one-third greater than the Reich in population, yet you possess fifteen times as much living space. So you have time. Conditions are such with you that you have time to bother about universal problems . . . But my world is much smaller, although for me it is more precious than all else, for it is limited to my people. I believe that this is the way in which I can be of service to that with which we are all concerned— the justice, the well-being, progress and peace of the whole human community."

Hitler sat down to a roar of hysterical approval from his deputies, and even some of the foreign observers could scarcely forbear to cheer. No matter how insincere, it was a masterly speech. As they filed out into the Unter den Linden, the diplomats did not need to be told that Adolf Hitler's words had changed something, though they were not yet sure exactly what.

■

Maxim Litvinov, the People's Commissar for Foreign Affairs in the government of the U.S.S.R., who had spent much time in Geneva in the past year, was back in Moscow for the May Day celebration in Red Square. Though he was invited to the rostrum with the party hierarchy to review the parade, he noticed that whenever he looked in the direction of Josef Stalin, the Russian dictator turned away ostentatiously.

"I have a feeling, Ivy," he said unhappily as they made their way home.

"And I have heard rumors from the wives," said his wife.

"They are changing their policy. I knew it would happen," Litvinov said gloomily.

218

"Damn that fool Chamberlain!" said his wife in English.*

When Litvinov arrived at the Ministry of Foreign Affairs the next day, May 2, Vyacheslav Molotov came out of the Commissar's office and announced that he had taken over; Litvinov was sacked, and the announcement would be made officially the following day. With unusual geniality, for he was not a friendly man, Molotov told his predecessor that he was not being blamed by the Politburo but that they felt it was time for a change, and that he would be given a job worthy of his talents.

Litvinov was relieved. As chairman of the Council of the People's Commissars, Molotov was a member of the Politburo and his word was gospel; these were still dangerous days in Moscow, even though the worst of the purges were over, and sacked commissars had a habit of disappearing forever.

In truth, Litvinov could not be blamed for the wrecked condition of Soviet foreign policy toward Western Europe, for he had done his best. The blame lay in No. 10 Downing Street and the Quai d'Orsay, where stubbornness, suspicion and stupidity had hindered him at every turn. The previous September, before Munich, he had offered Russia's help to Britain and France if they would stand up to Hitler on Czechoslovakia; he had not only been rebuffed, but though the Soviets had an alliance with the Czechs, they were not even invited to the Munich conference table.† After the occupation of Prague, Russia had expressed its readiness to join in a guarantee of Rumania, and had been snubbed by Britain in favor of Poland. Then, on April 17, had come the final insult. On that day Litvinov had made an offer to Britain and France which was as much of a turning point as Chamberlain's guarantee to the Poles.

Litvinov was a Jew, but it was not simply because of his race that he hated Nazi Germany; to him it was an evil regime which must be wiped out if there was to be peace and justice in the world, and though he found Chamberlain's politics distasteful and despised the

---

* Ivy Litvinov was the daughter of the British historian Sir Sidney Low. She later repeated this conversation to friends in London.

† Afterward the French ambassador in Moscow saw Vladimir Potemkin at the Ministry of Foreign Affairs and was coldly received. "I simply state the fact . . . ," he said, "that the Western powers deliberately excluded the U.S.S.R. from the negotiations." Then emotion overcame him. "My poor friend, what have you done? For us I see no other way out than a fourth partition of Poland."

219

corrupt statesmen of France, he felt that an alliance with the countries they represented was the only salvation for his own. It was through his personal pleading that Stalin and the Politburo had allowed him to make a last try. He asked Britain and France to join with the U.S.S.R. in a guarantee of mutual assistance in the event of aggression by another nation in Europe and against "the Eastern European States situated between the Baltic and the Black Sea bordering on the U.S.S.R."* It was an offer which, Winston Churchill was to say afterward, should have been accepted at once. Any statesman with his eyes open could see the way things were going. In a speech on March 10 Stalin had given the world a clear warning that Russia was becoming disenchanted with the idea of pleading for an alliance with the West.

Joseph E. Davies, the former U.S. ambassador in Moscow, and one of the few foreigners who had spoken at length with Stalin, saw the smoke signals at once. In his diary for March 11 he wrote: "The Moscow radio yesterday and the press reports today carry Stalin's speech on the foreign policy of the Soviet Union . . . It is a most significant statement. It bears the earmarks of a definite warning to the British and French governments that the Soviets are getting tired of 'nonrealistic' opposition to the aggressors. Stalin said in effect: 1) We want peace and friendly relations with all countries and desire also to strengthen our trades ties where possible; 2) We seek neighborly relations, particularly with border countries; 3) We support peoples who have become victims of aggression in their fight to preserve their own independence; 4) We fear no aggressor and we are ready to deal a 'double counterblow' in case of attack from either East or West. He then went on to say that the nonaggression states, and particularly England and France, were and are 'retreating and retreating' and 'making one concession after another' to the dictators. They had, he said, completely repudiated the policy of 'collective security' and the plan of a united front for protection against 'the bandits.' Even more significant, he charged that these two countries in their own interests were inciting Germany to attack the U.S.S.R.; that their purpose in this was selfish, to enable them, after the combatants had exhausted themselves, to intervene 'in the interests of peace' and dictate the conditions of peace solely on the basis of their own interest."

* Though Litvinov had made several approaches to Britain and France since Munich, this was the first time a definite proposal was put on paper.

Davies added, significantly: "Knowing Russia as I do, I feel that this is very discouraging and really ominous for the negotiations which are going forward now between the British Foreign Office and the Soviet Union in connection with the guarantees to Poland and Rumania in the event of a German attack. It is certainly the most significant danger signal that I have yet seen. It will be a disaster if the democracies do not use the strengths which exist here against Hitlerite aggression."

At this time Davies was ambassador to Belgium, an excellent post for enabling him to hear all the gossip. Moreover, he still kept his lines open to Moscow and soon found out about the suggestions which Litvinov was making to Britain and France for a pact of mutual protection. As the days passed by and the British and French procrastinated, meanwhile negotiating with the Poles, Davies grew increasingly worried. Eventually he telephoned Winston Churchill and was promptly invited to fly over to spend the weekend of April 1 at Chartwell, Churchill's home in Kent. There they drank much brandy and talked long into the night. The two men stimulated each other; though they differed on details and national standpoints, they agreed on fundamentals—one of which was the urgent necessity to get some sort of agreement with Russia, and to hell with the Poles! They were well-seasoned statesmen who knew the villainies of which Russia under Stalin was capable, but of the need for Moscow's signature on a pact they were in no doubt whatsoever. *Never mind the details, just get the signature,* was Churchill's attitude, and Davies heartily concurred.

The American came away on Monday morning enlivened and encouraged, particularly since Churchill had given him some information about the progress in British rearmament and a forecast that by midyear "this damnable blackmail menace from the air will no longer exist, because we will be prepared."* But later that day Davies lunched with Joseph P. Kennedy at the American embassy, and at once found himself back in the atmosphere of appeasement. "Took the opportunity of going into the Russian situation at length with Kennedy," he wrote, "and suggested that he could tell Chamberlain

---

* It was at about this time that Sir Horace Wilson received a report from Lord Crewe, a director of the Bank of England who had been put in charge of Royal Air Force rearmament, and handed it to Chamberlain. Wilson added, "If you want to stand up to Hitler now, you can do so."

221

from me that if they are not careful they would drive Stalin into Hitler's arms. Britain and France had snubbed Russia, their then ally, by excluding the Soviets from Munich; that the Soviets did not trust them anyway and feared that Britain and France were trying to use Russia as a catspaw and would leave them to fight Hitler alone. That Stalin wanted peace for Russia above all else; that he might decide to take Hitler as his best bet for his security, at least for the time being."

Davies didn't make a dent on Kennedy's opinions. As a Catholic, the ambassador felt an instinctive antipathy to Russia; his attitude was reinforced by the erroneous briefing of the Soviet Union's fighting capacity which had been fed him by Lindbergh. He also shared Chamberlain's view that Russia had no choice but to stay on the side of the democracies; to him it seemed out of the question that the Bolsheviks and Nazis might find common ground.

Kennedy told Davies that "he recognized the value of Russia in the military situation; but, as a matter of fact, Russia would have to fight for Poland or Rumania anyway, and regardless of whether there was a formal agreement with France and Britain or not, because it was vital to Russia's self-interest."

Davies replied, according to his diary, "A wrong theory. It is first things first in Russia. The Soviets are desperately trying to keep out of war, unless they can feel assured, through specific, realistic plans and obvious preponderance of strength, that they, in combination with France and England, can beat Hitler in the event of war, or scare him off hostilities by serving notice on Hitler that he will have to fight all three."

Davies added further that he had reliable information that Hitler was desperately trying to wean Stalin away from Britain and France, "because it is vital to his military success that he closes his Eastern door before he makes his attack on the Western front." But he failed to convince Kennedy, and he made no impact on Chamberlain. "Somehow or other," he commented, "it seems impossible to make an impression on this London atmosphere." His temporary euphoria from the encounter with Churchill evaporated, he returned gloomily to Brussels to cable Roosevelt: "It is my firm conviction that the deciding element in Hitler's determination as to whether there will be peace or war this summer in Europe will be whether Britain and France will make a definite agreement with the Soviet Union which

222

will assure to them the military support of Russia in the event of a German attack on Poland."

Litvinov's offer of April 17 was the opportunity for which Britain should have been waiting. Even Bonnet saw the advantages and pleaded with London to accept. Days passed. Chamberlain appeared to be in no hurry, but the Soviets were. These were two weeks of procrastination from London, two weeks during which Litvinov fretted and hoped. He told his wife that this was the democracies' last chance and hinted the same thing during an interview—his last— with the British ambassador to Russia, Sir William Seeds. But the statesmen in control in England took little notice of their experienced advisers and listened only to those who agreed with their own narrow outlook.* "Stick to the Poles—you can't trust the Russians," said Sir Horace Wilson to Neville Chamberlain.

While the English temporized, the Politburo was meeting. On May 3 Litvinov was dismissed officially and Molotov took his place. Henceforth, the Western allies would have to deal with the cold-blooded, ruthless Soviet bureaucrat whom Lord Halifax once described as having "a face of smiling granite." Halifax was lucky to have seen him smile; most diplomats saw only the granite.

No one in the British Cabinet seemed to realize that if they wanted a pact with Russia now, they would really have to work for it.

There were plenty of people who railed against the folly of Chamberlain's and Halifax's blind faith in Poland's strength and their bourgeois hatred of the Soviets. John W. Owens, editor of the Baltimore *Sun,* had been touring Europe and talking to Litvinov and Davies, as well as British, French and Italian statesmen. On May 10 he sent a sharply worded dispatch to his paper that summed up the situation: "Consummate the alliance, say the Russians, and Mussolini would be negotiating in London and Paris within twenty-four hours. There would be peace. Fail to consummate the alliance, or water it down, or even parley too long—again stating the policy when Litvinov was in office—and there will be war this year . . . Are the Russians al-

---

* At this time Sir Robert Vansittart, the Foreign Office adviser, was continually sending messages to Chamberlain urging him to negotiate seriously with Moscow. After a while he suspected that his papers were never read. He arranged them out of order, and they came back undisturbed. Later he tried the same trick with dispatches from British envoys abroad. They too were obviously unread.

truistic? They say not. Any major war, they reason, will retard their development. And no one knows where Hitler will strike . . . They claim they are not so vulnerable as Britain and France, but still they are vulnerable. Hence they serve themselves when proposing an alliance that, in their opinion, will bring Hitler to a halt."

The old lion of British politics, David Lloyd George, rose in the House of Commons on May 19 to complain of the Cabinet's slowness. "We do not quite know where we are," he said. "All this business about Russia is proof of that. We do not know quite what we want. There is a great desire to do without Russia. Russia offered to come in months ago. For months we have been staring this powerful gift horse in the mouth."

WING COMMANDER JAMES (a Chamberlain supporter): And seen its false teeth!

LLOYD GEORGE: We are frightened of its teeth. That means you cannot make up your mind. But other people can . . . There has been a campaign of detraction of the Russian army, Russian resources, Russian capacity and Russian leadership—a regular campaign of detraction. A good deal of it has been in public but most of it has been in private. We shall never forget the Lindbergh episode . . . [The truth is] they have the most powerful air force in the world, they have an extraordinarily powerful tank force. And they are offering to place all this at our disposal provided they are treated on equal terms. Why is not that done? . . . Why do we not make up our mind and make it up without any loss of time, that we should come to the same terms with the Russians as we do with the French? . . . The chances against the war would go up.

NEVILLE CHAMBERLAIN: I think the right honorable gentleman painted a somewhat overgloomy picture.

WINSTON CHURCHILL: You are up to your neck already! The question is how to make the system effective, and effective in time.

"Russians, Russians, no one seems to talk about anything else!" said Neville Chamberlain afterward. He and Sir Horace Wilson both agreed that they were "a tricky lot" and really not worth bothering about.

On the other hand . . . On Chamberlain's desk was a copy of a Gallup poll taken a few days before in which 92 percent of the Britons canvassed had voted in favor of an alliance with Russia. Neville Chamberlain was never one to ignore the voice of the electorate; if

224

that was what the voters wanted, he would go on negotiating with
Moscow.

But not too urgently—that would only make Stalin increase his
price.

■

On the morning of May 2 the telephone rang in Captain Paul Stehlin's house in West Berlin. General Bodenschatz was on the line. "Can
you come and see me at once?" he asked. "Before you go to the
embassy? I'll be in my office."

When Stehlin entered Bodenschatz's office a half-hour later, he
noted that the German was tense and edgy. As soon as Stehlin was
seated, Bodenschatz asked him abruptly whether he had read the
speech delivered a day or two before by Colonel Beck, the Polish
Foreign Minister. The Frenchman nodded. Colonel Beck had firmly
rejected German claims that the Anglo-Polish agréement presented
any threat to Germany, and saw no reason why it should have caused
Hitler to cancel the German-Polish nonaggression pact of 1934.

"An adroit speech, well founded, ably argued from a juridical
point of view," said Bodenschatz. "But those are just the kind of
arguments for which the Führer has the greatest contempt. We can't
subscribe to them, for they contain a flagrant contradiction. Beck
knows perfectly well what Germany's position is; the Führer has told
him about it often enough. What we want to see settled is the question
of Danzig and the incorporation of East Prussia with the Reich. This
could have been arranged without too much trouble had it not been
for the interference of this Anglo-Polish agreement. Now—"

"Now you will have to go to war to get them," Stehlin answered.
"Is that what you mean? To judge by the tone of your newspapers,
isn't war imminent?"

Bodenschatz shook his head. "No. As things stand at the moment, so far as Germany and Britain are concerned, we simply don't
have the advantage; we aren't as strong as you are. Britain and
France, particularly France, have decided to stand up for Poland;
that is the fact of the situation which troubles us. There will be no
war for the moment."

By this time Stehlin had lost his bearings; he did not understand

225

why Bodenschatz had called him in. It was obvious to the assistant air attaché that his friends in the Luftwaffe were using him as a pipe line to the French government, but what was the meaning of this rigmarole, except that the Nazis were angry at the Poles? He said, "What are you trying to tell me, General?"

"That Hitler won't move until he has all the aces in his hand."

"Certainly he is smart; I didn't expect him to do anything else. But what aces?"

"You don't think they are there in the pack? You're not very observant, Paul. They've been there all the time. You know what the fear in Germany is, don't you—that we should once more have to fight on two fronts. We can't possibly resist an invasion of the barbarians from the east and their friends from the west—if, of course, they attack together."

Bodenschatz paused, then came over to Stehlin and looked him in the face. "But why should we risk such a thing? There is another way out. Why should we have operations on two fronts? So long as Britain and France refuse to recognize the equitable requests we have made to Poland, there is only one alternative."

"Such as?"

"An entente between the Third Reich and the Soviet Union would be essential."

"I don't believe it," Stehlin replied. "Germany has always said that Bolshevism is the enemy."

"But didn't you notice that there was not one hostile mention of the Russians in the Führer's latest speech? Are you out of touch? Didn't you hear that certain negotiations are in progress—that the Russian ambassador and his military attaché have been called back to Moscow? Before they left, Ribbentrop talked to them and so did General von Brauchitsch. My friend, there are surprises in store for you; one of these days you'll find out that things are happening in the East."

"But how can you reconcile this with the Führer's own statement that he will never come to an agreement with Soviet Russia?" Stehlin asked.

"Don't bandy words with me. We're talking soldier to soldier, and Hitler is a soldier. Once he has decided to carry out a plan, he doesn't worry about ideological or legalistic considerations. Germany and Soviet Russia? Look, you're a well-read man. You know that a very

226

Catholic kind of France did not hesitate once to make a pact with the Turks against the Christians of Vienna. Anyway, what's the great difference between Soviet Russia and Germany, really? Aren't they almost identical economically speaking, even though we have retained some private enterprise?"

"I still don't understand what the Führer has in mind," Stehlin said.

"The situation will be something like this," Bodenschatz said. "The Poles think they can be insolent and arrogant toward us, relying on the backing of France and Britain, and believing that in the event of war they will get material aid from Russia. They're fooling themselves! Just as the Führer didn't think of solving the Austrian and Czech problems without first securing the agreement of Italy, so he does not now contemplate solving the difficulties with Poland without first securing the consent of Russia."

"I find it hard to believe," Stehlin said.

"So did we all, until we remembered German history." A pause, and then the general added, "Don't ever, my dear Paul, underestimate Adolf Hitler. He is not, as journalists so often claim, a man who makes his decisions irrationally and in a fit of temper. He waited until 1933 for the most favorable opportunity to take power in Germany. In foreign policy, everything he has done is the result of long reflections, of possibilities studied in the minutest detail; he is a genius at understanding and overcoming the fallibilities and frailties of those in the enemy camp."

Bodenschatz rose from his desk and again walked over to the Frenchman. "No matter how they try to wriggle out of it, the hour will come for the Poles. They will have to accept our reasonable claims, or fight. I think we can arrange it so that you will have no reason—or at least no inclination—to intervene. Poland's hour will come. When we nearly went to war over the Sudetenland, the Führer took the risk of being unpopular with the German people. That will not be the case with the Poles; a war against them will be very popular."

It was not Bodenschatz's final remark that sent the assistant air attaché rushing back to the French embassy, but his broad hints of a coming German-Russian entente. Could it be true? Why had he been told about it? Especially at a moment when the British and French were still, no matter how half-heartedly, trying to bring the Soviet

227

Union over to the side of the democracies.* Stehlin asked to see his ambassador immediately, and recounted what he had been told. Coulondre asked him to set it down in writing and told him to come back for lunch.

That evening Stehlin's report was sent to Paris for the urgent attention of Foreign Minister Georges Bonnet. Coulondre considered the dispatch of such significance that after an hour or two of reflection he called Stehlin in to see him and said, "There have been rumors in Berlin of a German approach to the Soviet, and I have reported them previously. But yours is the first news from a primary source. I think it's important enough to make sure that our friends in France believe it. I have sent a message to Paris—you are to go there at once and report personally to the Foreign Minister."

Stehlin left for Paris the following morning, went directly to the Quai d'Orsay and wrote a note for Georges Bonnet's secretary explaining why he had come. He was told to telephone the following morning, which he did. He called again an hour later, and then all through the day. Since he could not understand why there should be any difficulty getting an appointment, he kept telephoning. Did he not have important news? Hitler was plotting to sabotage British and French negotiations with Stalin and make a Russo-German pact of his own. "I waited and waited and waited," said Stehlin. "The replies I got from the Foreign Minister's office were quite amazing—evasive, embarrassed, even discourteous."

Stehlin cooled his heels for six days, then returned to the airport and flew back to Berlin. Two weeks later he got a letter from a friend in the Foreign Ministry, via the diplomatic pouch. The friend had been absent during Stehlin's visit to Paris. Now he wrote a warning. If Stehlin wished to stay on in Berlin, he had better confine his reports to aviation in the future and write nothing more about political matters. No one believed them, anyway.

On the other hand, the United States believed the signs it was getting. It so happened that America had a prime source of information about

* To this day Stehlin has not quite decided why he was given the news of an imminent German-Russian pact. He is still in close touch with General Bodenschatz, who has never given him a satisfactory explanation. Perhaps the most plausible is that the general's beloved chief, Göring, who was vehemently anti-Russian and had a soft spot for the Poles, hoped to sabotage Hitler's plans for an alliance with Russia.

the political moves of the German government toward Russia at this time, for their intelligence came direct from the German embassy in Moscow. One of its officials, a covert but determined anti-Nazi,* had struck up a firm friendship with Consul Charles "Chip" Bohlen,† at the U.S. embassy, and regularly passed on to him the contents of the cables between Berlin and Moscow.

Toward the end of April, Bohlen's informant had met him at a diplomatic gathering, pulled him into a corner and told him that he had some intriguing news. The German ambassador, Count Friedrich Werner von der Schulenburg had just arrived back from Persia, where he had gone to represent Germany at the royal wedding in Teheran. But he did not come straight back; Hitler had summoned him to Berchtesgaden first. Schulenburg had always urged Germany to make a pact with Russia; it was his life's ambition to see it materialize, thus securing Germany's rear in the event of war in the West. The German secretary had just read Schulenburg's report, which stated that the Führer had given permission to start negotiations. The entente would begin with a trade pact, and a political arrangement would follow.

Bohlen made his report to Ambassador Laurence Steinhardt that evening and it was cabled to Washington the following day. Shortly after this, Secretary of State Cordell Hull saw the British ambassador and asked him to pass on the information to London.

Hence, both Britain and France were warned in good time of what was afoot. But what happened? Bohlen discovered afterward that this report of German-Russian moves, like a later one, apparently was never read by high officials in the Foreign Office, and he now suspects that it was deliberately suppressed—or at least not passed on—by a Soviet agent in the department.‡

■

Propaganda Minister Joseph Goebbels seemed to be in a happy mood as he came out of the dining room of the Adlon Hotel on the night of Sunday, May 21. He had dined well, there was a pretty blond starlet

* He is now a high official in the West German government, and I have been asked not to mention his name.
† Later ambassador in Moscow and Paris, and now in the State Department in Washington.
‡ The Foreign Office received other warnings too. One of them had a comment in the margin: "Highly improbable."

229

on his arm, and he was looking forward to the rest of the evening. There would be some pleasant dalliance with his attractive companion in his private apartment just around the corner, and then he would rejoin his wife at the Reich Chancellery, where every night the ministers, adjutants and hangers-on of the regime gathered to listen to the Führer, a dedicated night owl, talk himself hoarse into the small hours. Goebbels was lucky in that Adolf Hitler found his wife a congenial listener and liked to have her around; this excused his own absence, kept him up to date on the Führer's thoughts, and made certain that Frau Goebbels could not check on his own activities. He knew that she suspected what he was up to—practically everybody in Berlin gossiped about his affairs with any young actress who needed a part—but it was just as well that she was otherwise engaged when his assignations took place.

Goebbels and his blonde were crossing the Adlon lounge when she drew his attention to a couple in the far corner. An auburn-haired Viennese actress who had recently arrived to make a film at the UFA studios was sitting with Joachim von Ribbentrop, one of Goebbels' bitterest enemies among the influential men around Hitler. The Propaganda Minister flushed with annoyance and limped swiftly over to the table, where he kissed the lady's hand in proprietary fashion, and then gave a stiff greeting to Ribbentrop.

"I thought," Goebbels said to the Viennese actress, "that you had an early appointment at the studio tomorrow morning. Wasn't that the reason why you were going to bed so early tonight?"

"Ah," Ribbentrop interrupted, "but that was before she knew that an old friend had arrived in Berlin."

"What old friend?"

"A very old friend!" said Ribbentrop. "And one, I think, that the Führer is very anxious that she keep. Surely you remember that Count Ciano has just arrived from Rome? We have the big ceremony tomorrow, you know. In the meantime, our Italian comrade is giving a quiet little supper in his rooms upstairs. Just a few friends. When I told the Führer that one of the Count's oldest and closest"—he emphasized the words deliberately—"friends was here in Berlin, he urged me to let him know." He turned to the girl and patted her creamy shoulder. "Where were you last together, *gnädiges Fräulein*? Capri, was it, or on the Lido? No matter—you will be able to catch up on old times later."

The actress looked up at Goebbels half fearfully, half defiantly, evidently wondering what this encounter was going to do to her German film career. Ribbentrop watched them both, a smooth smile on his yellow face, and then said, "Come, *gnädiges Fräulein,* we mustn't keep our Italian friend waiting. I hear that he is a little nervous about tomorrow's ceremonials."

They rose and passed through the lounge toward the elevator, leaving Goebbels staring after them. The starlet slipped her hand under his arm, but he shook it off petulantly. Apparently his appetite for blondes had suddenly disappeared.

Count Galeazzo Ciano was indeed in a nervous condition, and Ribbentrop had shrewdly divined that only the attentions of an attractive woman would be likely to assuage the doubts consuming him.

For just as Colonel Beck of Poland had tricked Neville Chamberlain and Lord Halifax into accepting an Anglo-Polish agreement on his terms, so Germany was about to dupe Benito Mussolini and Ciano. The following day Ribbentrop and Ciano would sign an alliance to be known as the Pact of Steel. It was the fruit of several weeks of consultations, which had begun in April, between Göring, Ribbentrop, the Duce and Ciano, along with staff talks between the military chiefs of the two countries. Already angered by Hitler's cavalier treatment of him over the occupation of Prague, but vaguely worried by Britain's negotiations for a pact with Turkey, Mussolini had resisted for a time; he feared, quite rightly, that Hitler was trying to drag him into war, and he knew that neither his armed forces nor his people were ready.

To Hitler, however, the time had come to force Italy to sign on the dotted line. A pact was needed to demonstrate to the democracies that the totalitarian states were united and determined; it was all part of his plan to face Britain and France with a combined front and terrorize them into backing down. He was in a hurry because he had plans for other alliances, and this one must be settled before he proceeded.

That Ribbentrop secured Italy's consent must be acknowledged as one of his cleverest coups—though not, as it turned out, his most brilliant. He knew that Italy was reluctant to sign any paper binding her irrevocably with Nazi Germany. The Italians had broken the

231

British diplomatic code and were passing Chamberlain's secrets to Berlin, but they did not know that the Germans had broken the Italian code and were reading everything that was sent by their ambassador in Berlin to the Foreign Ministry in Rome. Attolico kept pleading for caution, warning his superiors of Hitler's "unsteadiness" and the dangerous waters into which he was sailing.

But the Italians were no match for Ribbentrop's guile. When they met in Milan early in May, he soothed Ciano by deprecating any suggestion that Germany was planning to go to war. He agreed with Mussolini that like Italy, Germany did not want to engage in any hostilities with the West before 1942 or 1943. There was no danger to the Pact of Steel; it would merely demonstrate the defiance of the dictatorships in face of the hostility of the democracies. The Foreign Minister succeeded so well in quieting Ciano's qualms that the Italian telephoned his father-in-law to tell him that all went well, and that like themselves, Germany was convinced of the necessity of peace for not less than four or five years. He added that Ribbentrop had convinced him that Britain and France would "lose interest" in Poland after a month or two, and that meanwhile Germany would let the question "mature."

This so comforted the Duce that he made the same kind of error that Chamberlain had committed with Beck, and immediately announced to the Italian public and the world that the terms of an Italo-German pact had been agreed upon.* This was just what Ribbentrop had been waiting for; at once he produced a draft of the treaty. Having read it through, Ciano declared, "I've never seen a pact like this; it's real dynamite." Indeed it was, for it created automatic liability for each signer to enter war should the other be involved in hostilities. "If it should happen, against the wishes and hopes of the contracting parties," said a vital clause, "that one of them becomes involved in warlike complications with another power or with other powers, the other contracting party will come to its aid as an ally and will supply it with all its military forces on land, on sea and in the air."

This was putting Italy in Germany's hands, just as Britain had been sweet-talked into Poland's. The Reich's actions or interpretation of events now controlled Italy's destiny for peace or war. It was left

---

* What undoubtedly encouraged him to do so was an announcement in the House of Commons about the Anglo-Turkish negotiations regarding a guarantee, and this was an opportunity for a riposte.

to Hitler to decide just what a "warlike complication" was, and Mussolini and Ciano joined Chamberlain and Halifax as political dupes.*

On May 22 the arc lights at the Reich Chancellery were lit, the cameras were set up, and the pact was ceremoniously signed by Ribbentrop and Ciano. Hitler, Göring, Grand Admiral Raeder and General von Brauchitsch were there to witness the document and embrace "our good Fascist Italian brother." That night Signor Attolico gave a dinner at the Italian embassy, and after the toasts and speeches were over, Ciano went across to Ribbentrop and ceremonially draped around his neck the Collar of the Annunziata, the highest Italian decoration, and announced, "This makes you a cousin of our dear King and Emperor, Vittorio Emanuele!"

Hermann Göring, the peacock of the Reich who collected decorations as magpies do trinkets, looked across the table at the red sash and sparkling diamonds with tears in his eyes. "That should have come to me!" he said. "It was I who created the German-Italian alliance!"

Attolico leaned over and soothed him by promising that he would put a word in the right quarter, and the Field Marshal would be made a cousin too.

Adolf Hitler went to his private apartments immediately after witnessing the signature of the Pact of Steel and called in his close advisers, including Keitel. The next day his military leaders discovered why; he called them to a conference and lectured them for three hours on the future policy which he had chosen for Germany.

The conference of May 23, 1939, has since been described as a council of war. It was—but for some future war, not one which Hitler was contemplating that year. Up until now historians have had to base their accounts of this meeting on notes which were scribbled down at the time by the Führer's adjutant, Colonel Schmundt. The written and mental shorthand which Schmundt used omits one salient

---

* Though Mussolini was quicker to realize this than Chamberlain. On May 30 he sent a message to Hitler conveying his "thoughts" (they were really second thoughts) about the pact. In it he stressed the need for the Axis to wait before taking aggressive action. "I have given reasons why Italy needs a preparatory period which may extend to the end of 1942," he wrote. "The reasons are as follows: the two European Axis powers need a peacetime of at least three years. Only after 1943 can a war have the greatest prospects of success . . ."

fact which he and all the others present at the meeting* knew: *that this was not a plan for a campaign in 1939, but for a war which Germany would fight three or four years hence,* in 1942 or 1943, or possibly even later. Viewed in that light, the contradictions of Hitler's lecture suddenly make sense, for when he discussed Poland and Danzig he was talking about what would be achieved in 1939, but when discussing Britain he was thinking of a mighty clash with his greatest enemy some years in the future.

There was a glass of lemon barley water in the Führer's hand from which he sipped as the officers filed into his study, and for a few moments, as he greeted them, he continued to drink from it, a sign that his stomach was upset and his nerves frayed. But there were no signs of nerves when he started to speak. He began with a quick recapitulation of recent Germany history—the Nazi version—and of how the ideological problems of the Reich had been solved. Now came the economic problems, and this was where the real trouble arose.

"The equilibrium of the Great Powers is disturbed when Germany's demands for the necessities of life begin to make themselves felt, and Germany herself re-emerges as a great power. All our demands are regarded as 'encroachments.' It isn't a threat of simple force which frightens the English, but the dangers to her economic hold on the world as well. But she cannot evade them, nor can any German evade the inevitable corollary: that to achieve our economic aims is impossible without the invasion of foreign states and attacks upon foreign property holdings. For living space in proportion to the magnitude of the state is the basis of all power. One may refuse for a time to face the problem, but finally it is solved one way or the other."

The Führer summarized the first part of his lecture: "The choice is between advancement or decline. In fifteen or twenty years we shall be compelled to find a solution. No German statesman can evade the question longer than that."

Then he turned to the immediate problem of disposing of Poland: "Poland is no 'supplementary enemy.' Poland will always be on the

* Attending the conference were Field Marshal Göring, Grand Admiral Raeder, Generals von Brauchitsch, Keitel, Milch, Halder and Bodenschatz, Admiral Schniewind and Lieutenant Commander Albrecht, Colonels Warlimont and Jeschonnek, Captains Engel and von Below.

234

side of our adversaries. In spite of friendship treaties, Poland has always secretly intended to exploit every opportunity to harm us. Danzig is not the subject of the dispute at all. It is a question of expanding our living space in the East and of securing our food supplies; of solving the Baltic problem. The ground is fertile but neglected, and systematic German exploitation will enormously increase the surplus."

To crush Poland and take it over was the only possibility for Germany and German-controlled Europe. "If fate brings us into conflict with the West, the possession of extensive areas in the East will bring great advantages. We shall be able to rely on record harvests, as much in time of war as in peace. The population of the occupied non-German areas will perform no military service and will be available as a source of labor.

"There is therefore no question of sparing Poland and we are left with the decision *to attack Poland at the first opportunity*.* We cannot expect a repetition of the Czech affair. There will be war. Our task is to isolate Poland. The success of the isolation must be decisive. Therefore I, your Führer, must reserve the right to give the final order to attack." (One can picture the tone of his voice and the nature of his expression as he said this to his generals, whom he had several times castigated as cowards and bunglers.) "There must be no simultaneous conflict with the Western powers. If it is not certain that a German-Polish conflict will not lead to war in the West, then the fight must be primarily against England."

But Hitler doubted this, and though he was to be proved wrong, he had good reason to believe so at this time. "Fundamentally, therefore, the situation is this: conflict with Poland, beginning with an attack on Poland, will only be successful if the Western powers keep out of it." He added, "The isolation of Poland is a matter of skillful politics," but he did not tell his audience that this skill was being exercised at that moment in both London and Moscow.

Adolf Hitler had much more to tell his audience at the May 23 conference. Most of it dealt with the long-term strategy which must be adopted for the eventual clash with England. Read as a program for an immediate campaign against the West, it sounds like the nonsensical ravings of an unco-ordinated mind—and some historians

---

* The italics are in Schmundt's notes, from which this account is taken in part.

have so interpreted it. In actual fact, Hitler spent most of his briefing dealing with the future, after the petty irritations of Poland and Danzig had been dispensed with. He talked about the power of the German navy and air force to cow British opposition—but always in the future: "The aim will be to force England to her knees. A weapon will only be of decisive importance in winning battles so long as the enemy does not possess it. This applies to gas, to submarines, and to the navy and air force. It would be true, for instance, of the air force so long as England has no countermeasures." He exhorted his admirals and generals to think of the future. "However great the increases in the armaments of our adversaries, they must at some time come to the end of their resources, and ours will be greater!"

Then he dismissed them; they must go away and study the facts he had given them. He concluded: "We shall not be forced into a war, but we will not be able to avoid one. But secrecy is the decisive requirement for our success. Our objective"—he did not say which one—"must be kept secret even from Italy or Japan." It must also be kept secret from the bulk of the General Staff. Thereupon Hitler appointed a planning committee to study the problem of future strategy, a panel composed of "men with great imaginative power and the best technical knowledge, as well as officers of sober and skeptical judgment."

General Milch said gloomily to General Bodenschatz as they left the meeting, "That would seem to let us out."

"What do you mean?"

"He asked for men of sober judgment!" answered Milch. "I haven't been sober since he occupied Prague. Come on, let's go get a drink."

But General Milch had to postpone his drink with Bodenschatz that morning because as he was about to leave the Reich Chancellery, Colonel Schmundt came hurrying after him. "The Führer wishes to see you," he said.

Back in Hitler's study, Milch found himself facing a man who was now nervous, almost distraught, a startling contrast to the controlled and superbly confident lecturer to whom his generals had just been listening.

236

"I caught sight of your face during the conference," Hitler said. "You expressed certain doubts."

"Not in your conduct of the nation, my Führer. I'm on your side. All of us at the Luftwaffe are with you and behind you. But your conference this morning disturbed me. I'm worried."

"About what?"

"About bombs. I gathered from the program you outlined today that the question of bombs is now urgent. We have enough to take care of our immediate needs, but there are no reserves. The situation is very dangerous. It must be understood that in the event of a major war—rather than a campaign against Poland—the bomber fleets of the Luftwaffe are simply not ready for it. You have talked about taking annihilating action against England. We do not have the planes, the crews or, in particular, the bombs. I must ask you again, my Führer, to authorize me to start manufacturing them."

"And how much steel would be necessary? I've talked with Göring. We can't spare it. You must wait."

"But how can we wait, my Führer? You talked today of a major war against the West. It will take weeks, even months, to make a sufficient quantity of bombs to destroy them. A quick decision is mandatory. We must have bombs."

"Don't worry. There will be plenty of time for that later."

Milch said afterward, "From this I came to the conclusion that Hitler's words on the twenty-third of May were not meant as seriously as they sounded to me. Hitler was not thinking of war—not in the West. He had other ideas."

Not that the Führer was willing to allow any opportunity slip to put the Poles in the wrong, especially if in so doing he could demonstrate to the British and French what hotheads their allies were and how dangerous it was to allow them to wander around with guns in such a powder keg as Danzig. On the same weekend during which he prepared the speech to his military leaders, the Poles played into his hands.

The situation in Danzig was a complicated one. The Polish customs service controlled the port of Danzig and also maintained posts along every route leading out of the Free City. The Germans there did not mind the customs posts along the frontier with Poland, but they were infuriated and severely inconvenienced by those along the frontier leading from Danzig into German East Prussia. In these places the Poles were particularly tough in controlling traffic into the Free City, and it was through here that the Germans were now smuggling in most of their arms in preparation for a rising and a coup d'état that would drive out all Polish officials, unseat Carl Burckhardt, the High Commissioner, and make the territory part of the Greater German Reich.

On the weekend of May 20, 1939, the Danzig Nazis were planning a particularly large infiltration of arms, and they were determined that the Poles should neither stop them nor see what they were bringing in. On the night of the infiltration, a detachment of Danzig Brown Shirts surrounded the customs post at Kalthof, on the East Prussian border, and after the Poles had gone to sleep they burst in on them. Still in their night attire, the customs men were piled into trucks and driven off into the field some miles away, where they were released. Then their customs house was set afire while the arms convoys sped over the border and made for the weapon caches inside Danzig.

The next day, when the distraught and frightened customs men told their story to the Polish commissioner, Chodacki, in Danzig, he telephoned Arthur Greiser, the Nazi leader of the Danzig Senate, and told him that he was sending his deputy to inspect the damage at Kalthof immediately. He demanded from Greiser a "strong police detachment" to protect the deputy commissioner while he was investigating, and the Nazi promised that the police would be waiting for him.

They were not. Instead, a large crowd of Danzigers had collected near the burned-out customs house. They were silent when the Polish deputy descended from his car and went into the smoking ruins, but the moment he had disappeared from view they began to boo and shout Nazi slogans. A crowd of young storm troopers advanced upon the deputy's car, with the evident intention of setting fire to that too. The Polish chauffeur panicked; taking one look at the advancing Nazis, he pulled out his revolver and fired. A young Brown Shirt fell to the ground, and that evening he died in the hospital.

This was just what Hitler needed, and he summoned Propaganda Minister Goebbels and Dr. Otto Dietrich, his press chief, and told them to start a campaign. The Danzig Senate met in special session and sent a savagely worded note to the Polish commissioner demanding the recall of the deputy commissioner, the payment of compensation and a public apology. There was a vast funeral procession for the dead Brown Shirt, led by Gauleiter Albert Forster, the Nazi leader in Danzig, and Hitler himself sent a wreath. The old familiar headlines about "atrocities" began to spread across the front pages of the Nazi press both in Danzig and in Germany.

In Berlin, Nevile Henderson read these stories nervously. He had never liked either the Polish agreement or the Poles, and now he sent a gloomy note to London about Britain's reckless allies. Adolf Hitler could not have agreed with him more.

■

"There is a theory that the appeasers (Simon, Hoare and Horace Wilson) have regained their influence," wrote Harold Nicolson in his diary at the beginning of April 1939, in a reference to Chamberlain's policy toward the Germans. A month later he added: "Bower told me that he heard the following dialogue on the part of two Tories on the bench [in the House of Commons] behind him: 'I suppose we *shall* be able to get out of this beastly guarantee business.' 'Oh, of course! Thank God we have Neville!' "

In fact, on the day of this entry, May 4, Neville Chamberlain had not yet made up his mind to sabotage the Anglo-Polish guarantee, but a week or two later Sir Horace Wilson was strenuously pursuing this objective. The appeasers were definitely in control again.

After only a short pause to swallow the shame and humiliation of Prague, the propitiation of Germany had resumed, and it continued throughout the spring and summer of 1939. Mysterious envoys from Britain—always carefully announced as "unofficial" or "just businessmen"—traveled back and forth between Britain and Germany to propose loans or trade agreements, always with the tempting phrase that from such golden beginnings political agreements might follow. One of the messengers of appeasement was a friend of both Chamberlain's and Wilson's called Henry Drummond-Wolff, who hastily explained to his Nazi hosts that the Wolff part of his name was strictly Aryan. He was pushing a theory of the Prime Minister's advisers that Germany might be more amenable if Britain abandoned her own "most-favored-nation" privileges in the Balkans in favor of the Reich. "Internationally," he said placatingly, "the right of the most-favored-nation treatment must form the basis of economic relations, but in the particular national interest, exceptions must be admitted. Internationally minded Jewry is the greatest opponent of any relaxation of the right to most-favored-nation treatment."

These approaches were lightly dismissed by the Germans, who were after more tangible evidences of British co-operation than trade agreements. But there seemed not much doubt that if the Nazis held out for bigger bribes, they would come in time. The German ambassador, Dirksen, cabled Berlin from London early in July: "Within the Cabinet, and in a small but influential group of politicians, efforts are being made to replace the negative policy of an encirclement front by a constructive policy toward Germany . . . Chamberlain's personality gives a certain guarantee that British policy will not be delivered into the hands of unscrupulous adventurers."

By this time Chamberlain's supporters were urging appeasement again. How could they get out of the Anglo-Polish agreement? Why had they ever allowed themselves to initial it?

Their words were echoed with drunken emotion by a young man at the French embassy in Berlin toward the end of May, a few days after the Führer conference.

"Why? Why did you sign it if you didn't mean it?" he asked belligerently.

"We didn't. Nor have the British—not yet, anyway," said Ambassador Coulondre. "It is a guarantee against certain eventualities."

"Don't confuse me with words," said the young man. "I know what you're planning. You can't fool me! I've read all the documents."

Aware that guests in the vicinity, among whom were several German agents, had their ears cocked, the ambassador gestured to one of his aides and they maneuvered the young man into an anteroom. "Keep him talking," said Coulondre to the aide, and then to the young man, "Let me get you another drink. I'll return in a moment."

The young man was Dr. Karl Boehmer, and every newspaper

240

VERLAG KURT DESCH

. . . and Admiral Wilhelm Canaris,
chief of the Abwehr.

WIDE WORLD PHOTOS

Two of the conspirators: Dr. Theo Kordt, counselor
at the German embassy in London . . .

AP PHOTO

General Wilhelm Keitel (shown here with
his field marshal's baton, after
his promotion in 1940).

MICHAEL JOSEPH LTD.

General Heinz Guderian, one of the great
panzer leaders of World War II, whose tanks
annihilated the Polish cavalry.

Field Marshal Hermann Göring chatting with French Air Minister Joseph Vuillemin (in dark uniform) on occasion of the latter's visit to Germany. *In background* (with mustache), Ambassador François-Poncet; *second from right,* General Karl Bodenschatz; *far right,* Captain Paul Stehlin.

WIENER LIBRARY

Herschel Grynszpan after his arrest on November 7, 1938.

RADIO TIMES HULTON PICTURE LIBRARY

Prime Minister Chamberlain held discussions with the Duce in Rome in January 1939.
Center: Mussolini's son-in-law, Foreign Minister Galeazzo Ciano.

KEYSTONE PRESS AGENCY LTD.

Chamberlain and his Foreign Secretary, Lord Halifax, leaving the Palazzo Venezia.

Emil Hácha, who had become
President following Beneš'
resignation after Munich,
with his Minister for War,
General Jan Syrový.

KEYSTONE PRESS AGENCY LTD.

German troops crossing the Charles Bridge in Prague on March 15, 1939.

German troops parading before Czech representatives of the Protectorate government on the square in the Old City on March 15.

RADIO TIMES HULTON
PICTURE LIBRARY

The Polish Foreign Minister, Colonel Józef Beck, arriving at Victoria Station in early April for the talks with Chamberlain which led to the fateful British guarantee of Polish sovereignty against any aggressor.

Alfred Duff Cooper with his wife, Diana.

WIDE WORLD PHOTOS

WIDE WORLD PHOTOS

At an altitude of 5,274 feet, above Berchtesgaden, was Hitler's hideaway, the "eagle's nest." The road, the tunnels leading to the "nest," the elevators and the house itself took three thousand laborers and three years to complete. Hitler was presented with the structure on his fiftieth birthday, April 20, 1939.

WIDE WORLD PHOTOS

SA and SS men assembled at the village of Oliva, in the Free City of Danzig, to hear Gauleiter Albert Forster boast that Danzig would return "home to the Reich."

WIDE WORLD PHOTOS

Goose-stepping German police were a frequent sight in Danzig.

WIDE WORLD PHOTOS

Russian Foreign Commissar Maxim
Litvinov was replaced by
Vyacheslav Molotov in May 1939.

RADIO TIMES HULTON PICTURE LIBRARY

William Strang, Foreign Office representative, on
his way to Moscow in June 1939, with orders from
Chamberlain to bring about a rapprochement.

RADIO TIMES HULTON PICTURE LIBRARY

Mr. Strang's mission having failed, an Anglo-French military delegation sailed to Leningrad in early August, for discussions with Marshal K. E. Voroshilov in Moscow.
Left to right: Admiral Sir Reginald Plunkett-Ernle-Erle-Drax, General Joseph Doumenc, Air Marshal Sir C. Stuart-Burnett and Major General T. G. G. Heywood.

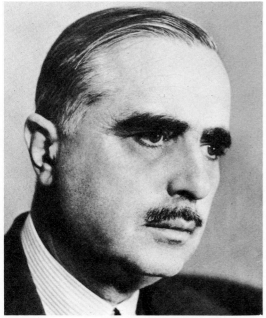

WIDE WORLD PHOTOS

Carl J. Burckhardt, the Swiss High Commissioner of the League of Nations in Danzig.

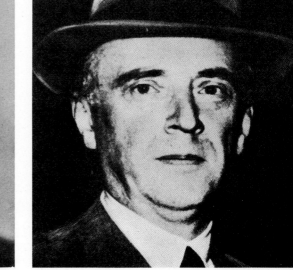

WERNER BROCKDORFF

Birger Dahlerus, the Swedish businessman who tried to save the peace.

RADIO TIMES HULTON PICTURE LIBRARY

German Foreign Minister Joachim von Ribbentrop at Tempelhof Airport,
Berlin, just before his departure for Moscow on August 22, 1939.

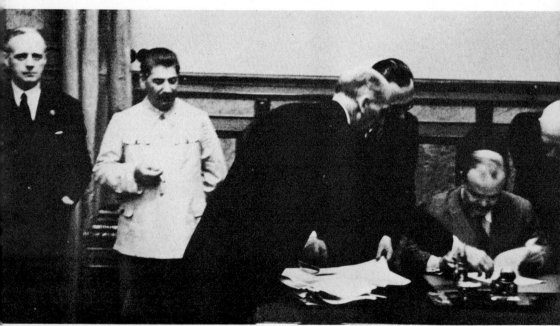

WIDE WORLD PHOTOS

The signing of the German-Russian nonaggression pact on August 23, 1939.
Left to right: Ribbentrop; Josef Stalin; Dr. Friedrich Gaus, German
Foreign Ministry legal expert; Gustav Hilger, counselor at the German
embassy in Moscow; and the German ambassador in Moscow,
Count Friedrich von der Schulenburg.

correspondent in Germany in 1939 will remember him, some with regret. Boehmer was chief of the Foreign Press Department in the Ministry of Propaganda, and unlike his immediate superior, Dr. Dietrich, he was fond of newspapermen, foreigners and parties. When he had had a few drinks, his conviviality spilled over into confidential revelations about what his department was planning and the way his chiefs were thinking. At first correspondents in Berlin had received these morsels with some skepticism; they felt sure that Boehmer was being used to "plant" startling but inaccurate stories in order to get them into difficulties. But soon it became apparent that Boehmer's predictions were almost always correct. He was a prime source—as long as he was primed.*

Karl Boehmer had a great deal to tell Robert Coulondre that night late in May, and as a result the French ambassador was able to send a very important dispatch to Paris. Although he did not learn from Boehmer that Adolf Hitler had been briefing his High Command, he was able to inform the Quai d'Orsay that the Führer had been holding consultations with Keitel and Brauchitsch about his plans for the immediate future. Boehmer revealed that Dr. Dietrich had received a report of the meeting which stated that "German diplomatic representatives abroad have been instructed to spread the report that France and England would not go to war over Danzig." But according to Boehmer, the Führer had also said he had to take care of all eventualities, and he asked his generals whether, in the event that Danzig did drag the West into war, Germany would be victorious. Keitel and Brauchitsch replied that this depended on whether Russia stayed out of the conflict.

Then Hitler had asked whether Germany would win if Russia did keep out. Keitel answered "Definitely," Brauchitsch "Probably." But when the Führer wanted to know what they thought would happen if Russia came in on the side of the Western democracies, Keitel replied that he found it difficult to be optimistic of the outcome, and Brauchitsch stated flatly that Germany would lose the war.

Coulondre had no doubt about the way Adolf Hitler was thinking. "If Poland stands firm," he telegraphed Paris, "Hitler's decision will depend on whether the Anglo-Russian pact is signed. It is be-

* Subsequently he was jailed by Hitler for drinking and talking too much.

241

lieved he will risk a war if he need not fight Russia, but if he knows that he will also have her against him, he will draw back rather than expose his country, party and himself."

Coulondre urged his government to press ahead with negotiations in Moscow for an agreement with Russia, and advised Daladier to persuade the British to do likewise. The French Premier had aroused himself from the torpor which had overtaken him after Munich and Prague and was beginning to act like a chief of state again. He needed little persuasion to press for an agreement with Moscow; he had been certain from the start that a guarantee of Poland by France and Britain would do little to deter Adolf Hitler. "Hitler's fear is that of having to wage war on two fronts," he said. "But when he says two fronts, he means two real fronts. Poland is not a real front. She is no menace to Germany. The only enemy Hitler fears in the East is Russia, and Russia we must have on our side if we are to be safe." Promptly he conveyed Coulondre's information to the British ambassador in Paris, and pressed him to galvanize his government in their talks with Moscow.

Anthony Eden had been mouse-trapped into resigning from the government in 1938 by Chamberlain and Sir Horace Wilson, but his influence among the public and governments abroad was still considerable. Hitler and Mussolini considered him an unswerving enemy of themselves and their policies, but Stalin also knew him and admired his acumen. They had first met in March 1935, and had got on well. Curiously enough, Stalin found that the handsome, aristocratic and high-strung Briton, whom he had expected to crush and bully, was as firm as a rock when it came to defending British interests; whereas Eden had discovered that the brutal Stalin could be pleasantly pliable and co-operative once he trusted the man with whom he was negotiating.

Though he was no longer in the government, it seemed natural to Eden that his advice on how to deal with the Russians might be useful. Early in May he telephoned Lord Halifax, his successor at the Foreign Office, and was asked over for lunch. Shortly before, Eden had made a speech in the House of Commons which expressed the eagerness of the anti-appeasement group for an agreement with Russia as soon as possible. The government had let it be known that one of the snags to a pact was that Russia was asking for joint guarantees of *other* countries' independence—Poland and Rumania, for example—which those countries did not want because they feared the Russians' coming to their aid as much as they dreaded a German attack.

Eden's solution for this was "a tripartite alliance between [Britain], France and Russia based on complete reciprocity; that is to say, that if Russia were attacked, we and France would go to her help, and if we or France were attacked, Russia would come to our aid. Then, if any other nations of Europe were victims of aggression and called for help, we should make it clear that we would be prepared, all three of us, to give that help and to the fullest extent of our resources."

This plan might not have disposed of Poland's objections, but it would have opened a dialogue with them; at the same time it would demonstrate to the Soviet Union the democracies' understanding of its fear that there was a conspiracy to goad Germany into attacking Russia and then abandoning her to face the onslaught alone.

It was with this in mind that Anthony Eden lunched with Halifax. It was a civilized repast. They spoke the same language and appreciated the same food and wines, but regarding Soviet Russia they were far apart.

"Why don't you go to Moscow, Edward, and lead a delegation?" Eden asked the Foreign Secretary.

An invisible shudder passed down the aristocratic Halifax's long frame. He was a High Churchman of great piety and conventional in his beliefs, and the idea of dealing with the godless Russians, in particular with the ruthless Josef Stalin and his humorless cohorts, filled him with distaste. "I should be no good whatsoever," he said. "They are not my kind of people. Absolutely no rapport with them whatsoever."

Eden pointed out that Neville Chamberlain had flown three times to Germany to talk to Hitler and prevent war over Czechoslovakia. No one was suggesting that he now fly to Moscow; that might really turn the Soviets against Britain once and for all. (There was no smile from Halifax.) But the stature of the leader of the delegation should demonstrate to the Russians that there was no prejudice against them, and that someone of real authority had been sent to get serious negotiations under way. "If it were agreeable to the govern-

243

ment," Eden said now, "I would be willing to go myself. It would have to be understood, of course, that I was completely in the picture and knew exactly what I had to do."

Halifax pondered the proposition, and even, as Eden has recalled, seemed to like it. The Foreign Secretary said he would certainly mention the idea to the Prime Minister, "and I thought it his intention to recommend it."

But Eden had not forgotten that Chamberlain and Sir Horace Wilson were his bitter enemies. It was unlikely that something which might be good for the country, which might even help to prevent a war, would appeal to them if it meant that a hated opponent would get all the credit. "I soon heard," he said, "without surprise, that Chamberlain would not agree." Halifax did assure him, however, that "a good man" would be sent to strengthen the British negotiating team. Speculation was rife. If not Eden or Halifax, then possibly some well-known military man, or even a member of the Cabinet?

The nation waited. Were the British serious at last? Moscow and Berlin watched and marked time.

On June 7, 1939, it was announced that Mr. William Strang of the Foreign Office was on his way to Moscow. The fact that of his last four journeys out of England, three had been to accompany Neville Chamberlain on his visits of appeasement and capitulation to Hitler can hardly have convinced the men in the Kremlin that serious bargaining was about to begin at last.

Strang arrived in Moscow with his assistant, Frank Roberts, on the morning of June 14 and went straight to the British embassy where he was to stay with the ambassador, Sir William Seeds. It was Seeds who had been carrying on the negotiations—or rather, keeping the talks barely alive—with the Soviet government ever since Halifax had repulsed Litvinov's offer of a tripartite pact in April. Seeds was in no condition to put up a good fight with the hard men of the Kremlin, particularly the craglike Molotov, for he was a sick man, and though he tried his best, he could not conceal the fact that his instructions from London were to stall rather than to make decisions. He was obviously relieved to see Strang and hoped that he came with more solid backing.

So did the newly arrived French ambassador, Paul-Emile Nag-

244

giar, who had been dispatched from Paris with instructions to get an agreement out of Moscow and to prod the British into doing likewise. When Strang came down from his room overlooking the Moskva River and the Kremlin, he found that Seeds had called in his French colleague, who "at once asked me pointblank whether our Government really wanted to come to an agreement with the Soviet Union or were they merely going through the motions?"

Strang reassured him. "Though we might be somewhat more cautious in our attitude than the French Government, we certainly want to build up a peace front in Eastern Europe."

"But with Soviet Russia?"

"With the help of Soviet Russia, provided we can do so in prudence and honour."

Exactly what he meant by that not even Strang could say twenty-eight years afterward.

Around the time of Strang's arrival in Moscow, Baron von Weizsäcker and one of his assistants, Dr. Friedrich Gaus, who was the German Foreign Ministry's legal expert on treaties, were on their way to Freienwalde and a rendezvous with Joachim von Ribbentrop. The German Foreign Minister had summoned them urgently from Berlin for a consultation at his estate at Sonnenburg.* Dressed in plus fours tailored for him in Savile Row, he was waiting for them on the terrace as they drove up. He led the two of them into the library, and as they sipped afternoon tea he said, "It may or may not come as a surprise to you, but the Führer has decided to establish more tolerable relations between Germany and the U.S.S.R. We are not quite sure whether the soil is fertile at the moment, so we propose to scatter a few seeds in order to find out whether they will sprout. Nothing important, you understand, just a few seeds. Have you any suggestions?"

There was silence for some time, and then Gaus mentioned the

---

* Ribbentrop had done well in real estate during the past twelve months. He had acquired a hunting lodge in the Sudetenland from an evicted Czech after the Munich Agreement, and the house and grounds at Sonnenburg from a Jew who had fled Germany. He also had his own house in Berlin. His favorite residence, however, was Fuschl, near Salzburg, a lovely house which had been signed over to him by a Jew who apparently believed he was buying his freedom with it. Not so; he died in the concentration camp at Dachau.

fact that Czechoslovakia was still a contentious problem between the Reich and Moscow, since Russia had not yet been allowed to establish consular relations in the Protectorate. Would it not be a good idea to dispatch a sympathetic pro-Nazi Czech to Moscow to inquire, under the guise of re-establishing consular relations, whether the Russians would be willing to discuss other matters with Germany?

Ribbentrop considered this a good idea. "We could send Syrový," he said. "He has very good relations with the Soviet Union and has lately shown signs of wanting to co-operate with us."* He put down his cup. "All right, gentlemen. To business. Before dinner let me have the draft of a message that we can send to Schulenburg [the German ambassador in Moscow], and I will submit it to the Führer."

Ribbentrop left the two Foreign Ministry officials in the study, and they started to work. In the evening a secretary teletyped the text of the draft to Adolf Hitler in Berchtesgaden.

It was not until next afternoon that the reply came. "He doesn't like it," Ribbentrop said. "The proposals are too explicit. They show our hand."

The Foreign Minister seemed depressed. He made it plain that he at least was eager for a change in Soviet-German relations, and that this hesitation by the Führer disappointed him.

On June 15 Sir William Seeds, Ambassador Naggiar and William Strang went to the Kremlin for Strang's first meeting with Molotov. The face of granite was smiling.

"The two ambassadors were surprised to find Molotov so genial in manner," Strang cabled home. "On previous occasions his attitude has been both stiff and hostile."

What was the reason for the change? A more pliant attitude toward the Western democracies? Hardly. "Though this made the interviews more pleasant," continued Strang, "it did not add to their practical results."

Perhaps the explanation lay in the fact that Count von der Schulenburg had also seen Molotov that day. There is no record of

---

* General Syrový, the former Commander in Chief of the Czech Armed Forces, had held several ministerial posts after Munich. He was arrested and imprisoned by his fellow countrymen after the war and died shortly after his release. He had become embittered by the betrayal of his country by the West in 1938.

what was said at this meeting, but it is known that the German ambassador had just received a telegram from Ribbentrop. After hesitating, Adolf Hitler had decided that there was treasure to be mined
in Moscow after all. "Contrary to the tactics hitherto planned,"
Ribbentrop cabled Schulenburg, "we have now decided after all to
make a certain degree of contact with the Soviet Union."

It was not yet the beginning of the end, but it was a confirmation
of the trend.

X

The Conspirators
Are Worried

There was a spy at the Foreign Ministry. His name was, ironically enough, Martin Luther, and he was a close friend of Ribbentrop's. He had no experience of foreign affairs and his reputation both in the party and in the business world from which he came was unsavory. He was a mean-minded nonentity who had tricked his way up the ladder of National Socialism and helped himself from the till along the way; only the intervention of the Foreign Minister had saved him from prosecution for embezzling party funds. Earlier, he had twice gone bankrupt after floating small companies in Berlin and Munich.

Nevertheless, Ribbentrop recruited Luther into the Foreign Ministry with the senior rank of counsellor and in 1938 made him head of the Deutschland Department.* The Foreign Minister let it be known that this was his first move in the process of "National Socializing this place. I want dedicated Nazis in here, pursuing a Nazi foreign policy, instead of all you honorary members of the party."

This was said pointedly to his assistant, Erich Kordt, who hardly troubled to conceal his contempt for preening party officials.

---

* This section was Himmler's and Heydrich's link with the Foreign Ministry. In 1943 it became Adolf Eichmann's Protocol Section for the Office of Jewish Emigration (euphemism for "extermination").

249

"Introduce fanatic amateurs into this office, and you will lose the service of your professionals," Kordt replied. "That is one way to turn the foreign policy of this country into the laughing stock of Europe."

Ribbentrop's yellow face flushed. "Sometimes you are too impertinent to be tolerated, Kordt. Be careful you don't go too far."

Kordt knew that he was safe so long as Ribbentrop and the party believed him to be a harmless skeptic, but his life would have been worth nothing had they known that he was an active member of a conspiratorial group, and that twice in the past twelve months he had taken part in a plot to overthrow Adolf Hitler. Now he realized that he would have to be doubly careful. It was no longer possible to discuss anything but official matters in the office, for Martin Luther had all rooms and telephones bugged. Already he had trapped some junior members of the ministry into making rash statements, which he had duly reported, and when the senior officials were out of their offices, not a drawer or safe or scrap of paper could be concealed from his prying eyes.

Erich Kordt managed to get a warning about Luther to his brother Theo in the London embassy and frequently telephoned and wrote him, and he also informed Admiral Canaris, a fellow enemy of Hitler.

Canaris did not need a reminder to exercise caution. Until the beginning of spring the conspirators had met frequently at his house in the Dianastrasse, on the south side of Berlin, but lately he had changed the rendezvous to the open air. Though he was chief of Military Intelligence, even he did not feel safe from the snooping of Himmler and his assistant, Heydrich. "Heydrich has been far too friendly lately," he said. "He keeps asking me and my wife over to his house for dinner. He must be suspicious of me."

So now the group met each morning in the Tiergarten, close to the Abwehr office on the Tirpitzufer, where they would ride together: Canaris, gray-haired, ruddy-faced, a good horseman despite his short legs; Colonel Hans Oster, his chief assistant, not quite in control of his restive pony; General Halder, the Army Chief of Staff, majestic on a placid mount; and Kordt, a born equestrian, who rode as if he and his horse were one.

The work of the anti-Nazi conspirators, which had begun in 1938 and came to its bloody conclusion in 1944, has never been given full credit. For various political reasons, its validity and force were questioned and dismissed both by the Nuremberg Tribunal and by historians after the war. It was a time when the very word "German" raised the hackles of the rest of the world, conjuring up visions of humiliated Jews, concentration camps, reprisals and mass slaughter. To acknowledge the existence of a conspiracy in this atmosphere was like suggesting that there were saints working in hell.

In fact, the conspirators were anything but saintly. Their aims were much lower than heaven; they only hoped to save Germany. They believed that Adolf Hitler was driving their country to perdition by policies and excesses which would eventually force Britain into war and thus bring about Germany's defeat. They were sure that each belligerent move which challenged Britain's strength and influence in Europe—the occupation of the Sudetenland, the annexation of Czechoslovakia, the capture of Memel—would further goad her into militant opposition. They also believed that the war which would inevitably follow would plunge Britain and Germany alike into Bolshevism, and so they conspired to prevent it. Before the Munich Agreement they had planned a coup d'état; if Hitler went to war against Britain and France over the Sudetenland, then they would rise and sabotage his plans. It is certainly not a reflection on their determination that Neville Chamberlain suddenly accepted Hitler's demands. The conspirators could hardly have been expected to rouse the Germans to revolt just at the moment when the Führer had been handed everything he had asked for, without a shot being fired.

One might have thought that the anti-Nazi opposition would collapse from that moment on. In fact, it did not; nor, surprisingly enough, did it lose its faith in England. Though intelligence chiefs like Canaris and professional diplomats like Kordt, who had access to information about the sorry state of the British government, might have been expected to abandon any hope of a determined British opposition to Hitler, they continued to hope for her co-operation in their fight against National Socialism. How could it be otherwise? Was it not obvious that to stop Hitler was a matter of life or death for the British Empire? Its reluctance to do so was understandable, but in the end, act they must from sheer self-preservation.

So the conspirators argued, and they were quite right. The only trouble was that neither Neville Chamberlain nor Sir Horace Wilson shared their views.

251

. . .

"Neville Chamberlain is a *Dummkopf!*" said Admiral Canaris on one of the morning rides.

He had just read the news of the British guarantee to Poland. How could it possibly solve anything? "Does he think he is dangling a threat before the Führer?" he went on. "That Hitler will now turn around and say, 'All right, *Kamerad,* this is it. I give in! You've got me in a corner. I can't possibly fight on two fronts!' "

The admiral reined in his horse and turned to Kordt, snorting, "Poland isn't a second front! That isn't what the Germans fear! I have all the information that anyone could need about the Poles, and I pass it on to the OKH [Army High Command]. Poland is no threat to Germany! We can go through her like a knife through butter. What stupid dolts they are in London! If they wish to encircle Germany—and I think that's the only way to stop Hitler now—they don't want to do it with daisy chains. They need bands of steel. They don't sell anything but daisy chains in Warsaw."

General Halder joined them at the end of the bridle path and cantered with them toward the stables. He said, "I think our friend should go to London again. The British appear to think that the agreement with Poland will solve everything. It will not."

"Only the British seem to be ignorant of that fact," Canaris answered. "Dolts! Fools!"

"I have been thinking, and so have some of our friends," Halder said. "It's hard to swallow a pact between the British and the Russians, for that would certainly encircle Germany. On the other hand, it's the only thing that will stop Hitler now. He has talked to Keitel and Brauchitsch. They tell him he has a clear way ahead so long as the British and the Russians don't get together. He will certainly not move if the Russians come in against us." He nodded at Kordt. "You should get that across to the British. I don't like to think of Germany crushed between the West and the Bolsheviks, but it's the only way, I think."

"Can you get away?" Canaris asked Kordt.

"I will talk to Weizsäcker," Kordt answered.

Erich Kordt flew to England on June 15, with permission from Baron von Weizsäcker, to visit his brother Theo on "family business."

It was a journey which so far has not received adequate recognition, for aside from the personal risk for Kordt, he also brought messages of great import, and he returned to Berlin with information which was to have a crucial influence on the course of anti-Hitler opposition in Germany.

Theo met Erich at Croydon Airport and they drove back to 8 Cadogan Gardens, Kensington, Theo's official residence close to the Germany embassy. Later they strolled from Belgrave Square into Kensington Gardens and along the paths beside the Round Pond, where children played with their boats under the eyes of staid English nannies, and talked, talked, talked about the German problem. That evening they left the embassy and walked through the quiet streets of Kensington to Cornwall Gardens. Here, in one of the old Edwardian houses, their Welsh friend Dr. Philip Conwell-Evans lived. The Kordt brothers had known Conwell-Evans for many years, both in Germany and Britain, and to them he represented the best type of Britisher: a typical public-school type, gay, witty, debonair, superficially shallow but deeply sensitive beneath the surface, and much concerned about the future. The fact that he was an ardent member of the Anglo-German Fellowship, an association which contained some aristocratic screwballs and some shameful anti-Semites,* did not deceive the Kordts into thinking that Conwell-Evans was either pro-Hitler or pro-German. They suspected, in fact, that he was a British undercover agent—as indeed he was—but from their point of view, this was an advantage. Through him they could make sure that what they had to say reached the right places. Unfortunately, the only thing the Welshman could not do was make sure that the "right places" listened.

Conwell-Evans had acted as a go-between for Theo Kordt in his unofficial contacts with the British government on several occasions in the past. He had turned up at Nuremberg during the annual Nazi party rallies and passed on information from Erich Kordt about Hitler's thoughts and intentions which it would have been dangerous to entrust to someone like Sir Nevile Henderson. He had never let the

---

* As well as Communist spies. Kim Philby, one of NKVD's (the Soviet Security Service, which was recently renamed MVD) most important agents in the British foreign service, had become a prominent member of the Fellowship to "cover" his Communist activities.

brothers down;* twice through his good offices Erich Kordt had seen and talked to Sir Robert Vansittart, and once to Sir Horace Wilson and Lord Halifax. This time Erich had asked to see Vansittart again, for though the brothers knew that Vansittart was in eclipse, they considered him the most reliable channel of communication with the British, since even Downing Street would not dare ignore what he had to report—or so they thought.

Now, as the housekeeper opened the door, Conwell-Evans immediately appeared and said, "Van has just phoned through. He will be here any minute."

Before he had finished mixing them a drink, the doorbell rang and Sir Robert Vansittart was ushered in. As usual, he had arrived by taxicab, bringing with him a Special Branch detective from Scotland Yard; the cab and the officer now waited on the opposite side of the road. The Chief Diplomatic Adviser to the British government greeted the brothers with great friendliness, but Erich got the feeling that for once this urbane, cultivated, worldly Briton was extremely nervous, almost as if he could hear whisperings behind the door. For a while they made what Erich afterward called a *"tour d'horizon"* of the political events of the last few months, and then, using a passing mention of Poland as his pretext, the younger Kordt launched into the message he had brought from Germany.

Erich said that he would stress once more that he came not to present his own personal viewpoint on the way things were going, but as spokesman for a group of influential men in Germany, among whom were generals—Beck† and Halder, among others—an admiral, high state officials and statesmen—Schacht, for instance—all of them opposed to Hitler's policy in Germany because they were convinced that it would lead to war, and all of them eager to join forces with Britain in frustrating the Führer's plans. To that end, Erich went on, they had urged Britain since before Munich to demonstrate to Hitler without any equivocation that if he continued his aggressions in Europe, she would resist him to the point of war.

"Well, it may be a little late in the day, but have we not done that at last with our guarantee of Poland?" asked Vansittart.

---

* Nor, until after the war, did he ever do so. Then, when the Kordts asked him to testify at the Nuremberg trial of Ernst von Weizsäcker (at which they would be witnesses), he refused to appear or even swear out an affidavit.

† Though Beck had resigned the year before, he was still in close touch with the others.

"But in giving Warsaw that guarantee, you have allowed her carte blanche to define aggression. The initiative has been taken out of your hands. There are reckless elements in Poland. My group has been worried ever since you guaranteed the Poles that some incident might be provoked by them—just the sort of incident which might give Hitler the excuse to attack them."

"I think you are worrying too much," Vansittart replied. "We have the Poles well in hand; our influence in Warsaw is strong. I can assure you that they have their reckless elements under control."

This did not satisfy Kordt, and he quickly made it plain that when he and his friends in Germany talked of a firm stand by the British, the last thing they were thinking about was a guarantee to Poland. "I have to say on behalf of my group that we have viewed with sorrow this very policy of guarantee which the British government has begun since last April. The guarantees Britain has given in East and Southeast Europe [to Poland, Rumania, Greece and Turkey] will, we are sure, do more to provoke Hitler than to frighten him."

"Why?"

"Because it offers him the excuse to claim that an encirclement of Germany is afoot—and that is one which, rightly or wrongly, always frightens the German people."

Vansittart grunted complacently, indicating that this did not particularly trouble him; after all, a frightened Germany rather than an arrogantly belligerent one was what he wanted. It took some time for Erich Kordt to make his point that it was the German people who were beginning to be frightened of encirclement, rather than Adolf Hitler—at least so long as the encirclement was confined to countries like Poland, whom he knew he could smash at will. "What he *is* frightened of is Soviet Russia," Kordt added.

Vansittart immediately looked wary.

"My friends have no doubt whatsoever about the peaceful outlook of the British government and of their lack of aggressive intentions," Kordt continued. "Otherwise they would have been alarmed at the approaches which have been made recently by Britain to the Soviet Union. After giving the matter some thought, and not without a certain hesitation, they approve these approaches."

Vansittart raised his eyebrows theatrically, as if to say, "How very big of them!"

The German went on nonetheless, "But what does alarm them is

255

the fact that having started these negotiations, the British have not yet achieved any result." He paused now, for he was reaching the main point of what he had risked his neck to come to England to tell the British government. It was important that he be completely understood.

"You realize, of course, that it would be logical for Hitler to try to make trouble over your negotiations? You should not forget that through your negotiations with Russia, you have made the Soviet Union respectable [*hoffähig*] again. Not all the slanderous talk and insults which have been exchanged between the German and the Russian governments will prevent Hitler from sitting down with them at a table if it suits him. He will not scruple to make a compromise with Stalin."

Now Kordt took a deep breath and said, "We have most reliable information that Hitler has not just played with these thoughts. He has already taken steps to get together with the Soviet Union for talks, and nothing your side has done so far has eliminated them. I warn you, and my friends warn you, that if you do not bring your heterogeneous coalition* together now, Adolf Hitler will unite with Josef Stalin. And then there will be war." He paused and then added in English, "I have it from the horse's mouth."

Vansittart seemed about to interrupt, but before he could do so, Kordt continued, "This is the situation. To sum up, what Hitler has said is: 'If Chamberlain makes a pact with Stalin, this autumn I will not do anything—except call my congress at Nuremberg "the *Parteitag* of Peace." But if Chamberlain fails, I will move in and smash the Poles, because the West will not be able to make contact with them and my rear will be safe.' "

Theo Kordt broke in now to emphasize that no good German— and he and his friends considered themselves good Germans—could feel complacent at the thought of his country being encircled by the West and the Soviet Union. Nonetheless, a British-Soviet pact was, in their opinion, the only way to halt Hitler's war plans, and the more quickly this was achieved the better for the world.

Vansittart had obviously not taken kindly to Erich Kordt's criticisms of the guarantee to Poland—not unnaturally, for he was a firm believer in it and considered the Poles strong and potent allies.

* Meaning the combined forces of Britain, France and the Soviet Union, diverse though their ideologies were.

256

But now, as the brothers continued to urge a swift agreement with Russia, he suddenly said, "You need not worry. This time Hitler will not be given the chance to cheat us [*übertölpeln*]. This time he will not find us asleep." Then he added the words which Erich Kordt carried back in triumph to Germany to his co-conspirators: "Put your minds at ease. I can assure you that we are definitely concluding the agreement with the Soviet Union."

It was a downright lie; the negotiations were going badly. To this day Erich Kordt cannot understand why Vansittart so deliberately deceived him. At the time he believed him, and on his return he told Canaris and Halder not to worry, that the British government had the agreement in their briefcases.

Whereupon the conspirators relaxed. No matter how Hitler huffed and puffed from now on, there would be no war this year, for he would never dare to risk it on two fronts.

Winston Churchill was better informed and therefore more realistic. He too was in touch with Vansittart, and the Chief Diplomatic Adviser to the Foreign Office did not lie to his friend as he had to the Kordts. Churchill knew that the Russian negotiations were going badly, and he writhed at the ineptitude, stubbornness and prejudice of Chamberlain. On the night before the Kordt brothers had their fateful talk with Vansittart, however, gloom was abruptly displaced by sheer anger and pure patriotism. That evening Churchill was the guest of honor at a small dinner party given by Kenneth Clark, the director of the National Gallery, at which the other guests were Harold Nicolson, M.P., Mr. and Mrs. Julian Huxley and Mr. and Mrs. Walter Lippmann. Lippmann was depressed, and when asked why, he explained that he had been talking to Ambassador Kennedy, who had not only informed him that war was inevitable but that Britain would be licked.

Across the table, his head hunched into his shoulders, cigar in one hand, a stiff whiskey and soda in the other, Churchill roused himself and began to growl like a lion. "It may be true, it may well be true," he said, "that this country will at the outset of this coming and to my mind inevitable war be exposed to dire peril and fierce ordeals. It may be true that steel and fire will rain down upon us day and night scattering death and destruction far and wide. It may be true that our

257

sea communications will be imperilled and our food supplies placed in jeopardy. Yet these trials and disasters, I ask you to believe me, Mr. Lippmann, will but serve to steel the resolution of the British people and to enhance our will for victory. No, the Ambassador should not have spoken so, Mr. Lippmann; he should not have said that dreadful word. Yet supposing, as I do not for one moment suppose, that Mr. Kennedy were correct in his tragic utterance, then I for one would willingly lay down my life in combat, rather than, in fear of defeat, surrender to the menaces of these most sinister men. It will then be for you, for the Americans, to preserve and to maintain the great heritage of the English-speaking peoples. It will be for you to think imperially, which means always of something higher and more vast than one's own national interests. Nor should I die happy in the great struggle which I see before me, were I not convinced that if we in this dear, dear island succumb to the ferocity and might of our enemies, over there in your distant and immune continent the torch of liberty will burn untarnished and, I trust and hope, undismayed."

Churchill returned to his whiskey and his cigar, and the company began to talk about the giant panda which had just arrived at the London zoo. They knew that Winston was never more serious than when talking in his purplest prose.

■

Earlier in the year, in April, Colonel Beck had lied to Neville Chamberlain in order to secure the guarantee from Britain. Then the British and French proceeded to lie to the Poles.

On May 14 the Polish Minister for War, General Thaddeus Kasprzycki, arrived in Paris with a delegation to begin talks with the French General Staff. They had come at their own suggestion rather than at the invitation of the French, to whom the prospect of military discussions with the Poles was unpalatable in the extreme: obviously the Poles would immediately ask what their ally would do in the event of an attack by Germany, i.e., when and how the French would counterattack, and in what strength.

Indeed, this was exactly what the Poles did ask. General Vuillemin, the French Air Minister, swallowed hard, avoided the eyes of the Army Chief of Staff, General Gamelin, and then stated that

Poland could rest assured that within hours of a German attack, the French would be in the air to relieve the pressure on their fighting allies. General Kasprzycki then turned to Gamelin. What about the French army? Naturally it would direct its attacks against the German defenses opposite the Maginot Line to take advantage of the weakness there while Hitler concentrated on the East, but when and in what force? Gamelin replied smoothly that the land forces would be just as prepared to help as the air force.

Colonel Joseph Jacklicz, a member of the Polish General Staff, asked, "Yes, but how soon?"

"It could not be earlier than the seventeenth day," answered Gamelin. "Before that we will make diversionary attacks, but not until the seventeenth day can we promise a massive move against the Siegfried Line, with probably some thirty-five to thirty-eight divisions."

"It is not soon enough," Kasprzycki said. "But at least it is something."

Gamelin then proceeded to sign an agreement with the Poles which contained the sentence: "As soon as the German effort begins to concentrate against Poland, France will release an offensive action against Germany with her main forces (beginning on the fifteenth day after the first day of general mobilization in France).*

This was downright deception; neither General Gamelin nor the French General Staff had any intention of opening a second front on behalf of the Poles, and had already conveyed this fact to the British during the Anglo-French military staff talks which had been going on in London. The British concurred. In fact, Air Vice Marshal John Slessor, R.A.F., reported to Air Marshal Sir Cyril Newall, Chief of the Air Staff: "The two-front war might well be a far less formidable affair for Germany than it might appear at first sight—particularly if the Germans stood entirely on the defensive in the West till they had settled with Poland. In that event the initiative in the West would be left entirely with the Allies and, without, I hope, being unduly pessimistic, it is very difficult to see what we could do that would be any use." Slessor "therefore suggested to the C.A.S. that [Colonel] Beck should be warned that as far as we were concerned,

---

* "*Dès que l'effort principal allemand s'accentuerait sur la Pologne, la France declencherait une action offensive contre l'Allemagne avec le gros de ses forces (à partir du quinzième jour après le jour initial de la mobilisation générale française).*"

the Poles would have to rely entirely on their own resources to defend their own territory."

Newall passed the suggestion on to the Cabinet, but no warning was ever conveyed to the Poles. General Sir Edmund Ironside, Chief of the Imperial General Staff, arrived in Warsaw some weeks later and watched maneuvers of the Polish army and air force. He was profoundly depressed as wave after wave of cavalry galloped gallantly across the turf, followed by a few tin-can tanks of questionable reliability, while overhead Polish airmen performed aerobatics in out-of-date planes. Nevertheless, when with the British chargé d'affaires he called on Marshal Smigly-Rydz and Colonel Beck the next day, he "started by giving the Marshal an assurance that Poland could absolutely rely on Great Britain."

It is ironic that after years of lies and deception toward other states, the "colonels" could not recognize the poison when it was served them. They swallowed it, and it was fatal. They believed that if and when Germany attacked them, their Western allies would be battling with them as soon as possible. They shaped their policy accordingly, and as a result they lost their country and millions of Polish lives.

To the appeasers, the situation was not tidy at all. With the blithe self-confidence of a town dweller in a jungle, too bemused by the rich colors of the orchids to notice that a panther is poising to spring from a tree overhead, Neville Chamberlain was planning a general election for November, with the slogan "Safeguarding World Peace with Chamberlain." But before the Prime Minister could go to the country and begin his campaign for re-election, there were some tiresome odds and ends to be cleared up, not least the guarantee which Britain had given in Eastern Europe. To Wilson, as to his master at No. 10 Downing Street, it seemed that the precipitate promise made in April to stand side by side with Poland against Germany was now nothing but an embarrassment. It had encouraged Polish intransigency, especially over the subject of Danzig, which after all was a German city. Chamberlain and Wilson were inclined to agree with Nevile Henderson, who made it plain both in his reports to London and in his conversations with Nazi officials that "heaven knows what Poland is going to cost us" unless they could be persuaded to

260

boast "a little less" about their bravery and ponder "a little more" the realities of their geographical situation.

The solution, as Wilson saw it, was either to persuade the Poles to make concessions—an all-but-impossible task, since every suggestion made to Warsaw that they be more "liberal" in their attitude to the Free City's future status was leaked by the Poles to the anti-appeasement forces in London;* or to achieve harmony through a new measure of Anglo-German co-operation that would make it possible for the British to stop worrying about the Poles. For despite the negotiations in Moscow, it was of a rapprochement with Germany that Neville Chamberlain and his servant still dreamed. But how to get things going?

Henderson suggested that the Prime Minister write a letter to Adolf Hitler, and even sent over a draft of how it might read: "It is quite clear that confidence and tranquillity can only be restored in Europe by means of Anglo-German cooperation. To this end His Majesty's Government . . . will be ready . . . to discuss with the German Goverment all such problems as limitations of armaments, trade barriers, raw materials, *Lebensraum,* and eventually colonies, provided you, Herr Reichskanzler, are willing on your part definitely to reassure me of your pacific intentions."

By this time Neville Chamberlain was too wary to fall into *that* trap. One word to the British public that he had been writing friendly notes to the Führer and he would be engulfed by a wave of public indignation. Instead he searched for a more clandestine modus vivendi, and Sir Horace Wilson found it for him.

It so happened that in the early summer of 1939 the ubiquitous Herr Helmuth Wohltat, representing the Trade Section of the German Foreign Ministry, came to London as his country's representative at the International Whaling Conference. It was an appropriate moment to harpoon him and suggest that he engage his mind on the preservation of the human species in addition to the sperm whale, and he was directed to the Board of Trade, where Robert Hudson was waiting to talk to him. What followed in the next few weeks was a good indication of the path which the British Cabinet was pursuing in its efforts to reach any sort of agreement with Germany.

Robert Hudson, Secretary of the Department of Overseas Trade,

---

* "We could not say boo to Beneš last year till we were on the abyss of war. And we can't say boo to Beck this year," complained Nevile Henderson later from Berlin.

was an opponent of appeasement, but one of those who apparently valued office above his beliefs. He would rather keep silent than resign—or rather, he spent a considerable part of his hours outside his office and the Houses of Parliament inveighing against the weakness of his Cabinet colleagues, and the rest of the time voting with them in favor of Chamberlain's policies. It must have pained him to have to deal with Herr Wohltat and to suggest that all that separated Britain and Germany was a large loan which Britain would offer and Germany would swallow, but that is what he had been told to do, and that is what he did. While Wohltat was digesting this unexpected mouthful of honey, he received a message asking him to come to see Horace Wilson—not at his office at No. 10 Downing Street, however, but at his home in Kensington. When he arrived, Sir Horace stressed that the rendezvous had been approved by the Prime Minister because the fact that the British were negotiating with the Germans must under no circumstances reach either the press or the French government. "You have Mr. Chamberlain's political future in your hands," said Sir Horace. "If this leaks out, there will be a great scandal and Mr. Chamberlain will be forced to resign."

Wilson made no apology for the fact that in talking to Wohltat in such circumstances, he and Chamberlain were deliberately deceiving their French allies. Not only that; they were deceiving their own Foreign Office too, as well as the British Cabinet and Parliament, though Chamberlain had long since ceased to worry about *them*.

What followed is a good example of the way in which Chamberlain and his cohorts worked, and why so few of their maneuvers will be detailed in the official records when the British government eventually releases them. Of his subsequent talks with Wohltat, and later with Ambassador von Dirksen, Sir Horace sent certain reports to the Foreign Office "to keep them in touch." But even Sir Horace today admits that those reports were "perhaps somewhat inadequate," and anyone delving into the German reports—which are extremely circumstantial—of the same conversations would agree that the British accounts were divested of much of their detail and validity.

At one of the meetings at his home, for instance, Sir Horace suggested to Wohltat that there was still an opportunity for Anglo-German co-operation despite all the brouhaha in the press, and that all that was needed was an effort to create conditions "that would make that co-operation feasible." He reported this part of the conversation to the Foreign Office, but what did not get into their files was what followed.

Sir Horace's secretary brought in a memorandum which had been written by him and Chamberlain, without consultation with the Foreign Office or the Cabinet. It made Wohltat sit bolt upright, and Dirksen later sent an urgent message to Ribbentrop about it. The only reason why it did not make Adolf Hitler burst his sides laughing was because he had never expected anything else; he had anticipated just this move in his conversations with his generals.

What Sir Horace Wilson proposed were secret negotiations with Germany in which only the two countries should be involved;* neither France nor Italy was to be informed of them, and it did not occur to him even to mention the Russians or the Poles.

What intrigued Herr Wohltat about the memorandum was not so much the general proposals made to Germany for the preservation of peace in Europe, but the readiness of Britain to abandon the attitudes which she had adopted since the spring of the year. For instance: "1) A joint German-British declaration that forcible aggression will not be employed by either country as an instrument of international policy. ('Joint Anglo-German declaration not to use aggression.') This should not take the form of a nonaggression pact between the two countries but of a general declaration of a political principle whereby both countries renounced the use of forcible aggression as an instrument of policy. Here Sir Horace takes the view that such a declaration would make Britain's guarantee to Poland and Rumania superfluous, since, as a result of such a declaration, Germany would not attack these states and they could not therefore feel that their national existence was threatened by Germany.

"2) Mutual declaration of noninterference ('noninterference') by Germany in respect of the British Commonwealth . . . and East and Southeast Europe. Sir Horace [said] that Britain was only interested in keeping her share of European trade.

"*Note.* By the declaration of principle in respect of 1) and 2), the British apparently wish to establish a new platform for dealing with the questions between Germany and Poland. The Danzig question after a broad German-British agreement would play a minor part for Britain. . . ."

* Sir Horace even suggested they might be held in a neutral country—Switzerland, for instance.

But the British government still felt that above all else, money was the most likely oil with which to lubricate Anglo-German relations. It was a solution that came naturally to them, since this self-same lubricant is what Chamberlain and Wilson had been using most of their lives to grease the wheels of trade—Chamberlain as Chancellor of the Exchequer, Sir Horace Wilson as a negotiator with recalcitrant union leaders at the Board of Trade. A tax incentive by the one and the offer of a wage hike by the other had never failed to work with the British proletariat, so why should it not work with Hitler?

Hence, in between Wilson's tête-à-têtes with Wohltat and Dirksen, Hudson was told to jingle money in front of the Germans. The details remain one of the intriguing, half-solved puzzles of this period. How much did Hudson offer the Germans? Was it £500,000,000 or £1,000,000,000? And how, considering the great secrecy which had been emphasized by both Chamberlain and Wilson, did the story leak to the newspapers? For suddenly the London *Daily Express* carried an item by its political correspondent hinting at the loan negotiations, and followed it with an interview in which Robert Hudson himself admitted that such discussions were afoot. But who let it out?

As far as the press leak was concerned, the tip-off came from French sources. French intelligence had learned of the negotiations going on in London behind their backs and had reported to Daladier and Bonnet, both of whom were incensed at such squalid maneuvers by a pledged ally. Their tempers were not soothed when they also learned that the Tory go-between, Sir Joseph Ball, had been sent by Chamberlain to Wohltat to tell him of his plans for a general election in the fall, and citing this as a reason for starting Anglo-German conversations as urgently as possible. Therefore, realizing that the British public and Parliament would share their anger at these back-room deals, the French decided to leak them to the British press.

Until now the intriguing puzzle has been the identity of the Englishman who told the French in the first place. For, on Chamberlain's instructions, neither the Cabinet nor the Foreign Office was given any details of what was going on; they believed that the Wilson-Hudson-Wohltat meetings were merely informal trade talks. But Sir Horace Wilson himself has no doubt about the identity of the culprit, and a note of irritation still comes into his voice when he speaks about him. "It was Hudson himself, surely, who let it out," he has said.

264

The Secretary of Overseas Trade, who had been disciplined before for voicing opposition to the Prime Minister's policies, evidently paid lip servce to them, but that did not stop him from sabotaging them at the same time.

Not that he needed to, in this case. Despite Wohltat's evident eagerness, for the moment Adolf Hitler was not interested in a loan, but in territory—in Danzig and in Poland. Still, when Ribbentrop read Wohltat's reports of his talks with Wilson, especially those sections of the Chamberlain-Wilson memorandum hinting at a growing antipathy to the Polish guarantee, he telephoned London for more details and then brought his own special envoy in London, Fritz Hesse, back to Berlin to report to the Führer. Hesse's account of Chamberlain's thinking, combined with two later reports from Dirksen convinced Hitler that his instincts were right once again. "It is necessary to state as a general preliminary remark," wrote Dirksen, "that Great Britain has not pledged herself 100 percent to support Poland in *any* conflict. This would be contrary to the British disposition always to leave a loophole." Later, after a further long talk with Sir Horace Wilson, Dirksen wrote that "Wilson affirmed that the conclusion of an Anglo-German entente would practically render Britain's guarantee policy nugatory . . . and . . . would enable Britain to extricate herself from her predicament in regard to Poland."

There is an ironic footnote to Chamberlain's offer of a £ 1,000,-000,000 (or £ 500,000,000) loan to Nazi Germany. At almost the same time there was a Polish delegation in London seeking a loan to bolster their armaments program. The Poles asked for £ 50,000,000 from their allies, but were told by the British that this was far too much; instead they were offered £ 8,500,000, and even this never reached them.

265

XI

"You Must Think We Are Nitwits and Nincompoops!"

At ten o'clock in the morning of June 17, 1939, a large Rolls-Royce flying the Union Jack and the Tricolor of France rolled across Red Square and swept into the courtyard of the Kremlin. The Moscow weather, which can be the vilest in Europe, was cool and pleasant that Saturday morning, and a faint breeze drove a light froth of clouds through the blue sky above the onion-shaped towers of the Communist citadel. As Red Army soldiers snapped to attention, three men descended from the car and started up the steps of the Commissariat for Foreign Affairs. Two of them, William Strang and Sir William Seeds, were clad in the conventional Whitehall uniform of black coat, striped trousers and black Homburg; the other, Paul-Emile Naggiar, wore a dark-gray lightweight suit. Down the steps to greet them came the slight figure of Vladimir Potemkin, the Deputy Commissar for Foreign Affairs. Since Litvinov's dismissal he was known to be the most pro-Western official in the Commissariat, and usually there was a smile on his face when he greeted Strang and the two ambassadors. But he was not smiling this morning, and his face was pale and drawn.

"From the way our friend looks," muttered Naggiar, "I have a feeling that this is going to be a difficult morning."

"I think not," replied Sir William Seeds, a perennial optimist.

"He's probably worrying about his own skin, poor fellow." There were rumors that since Litvinov's departure, Potemkin's own position had become precarious.

After shaking hands, the Deputy Commissar led them down the long corridor to the room where Molotov awaited them. Strang's heart sank once again as he entered. The two ambassadors appeared to have accustomed themselves to the setting, but though Strang was to come to this room several times more, he never got used to it. Rarely would he negotiate under conditions that were physically and psychologically so difficult.

The face of smiling granite, but with no smile this morning, stared at them from behind his large desk on a dais. They took their seats below him in a semicircle, rather like schoolchildren; unlike schoolchildren, however, they had no desks and had to rest their papers on their knees and make notes as best they could. There was a table just behind them around which they could have conferred comfortably, but neither the Russians nor the ambassadors suggested using it, and Strang did not feel that he could do so. Just beyond the table was a door, and it was always open, a fact which Strang found "faintly disturbing, as though there was someone listening."

Molotov leaned over and fiddled with something behind his desk. Strang presumed that it was a recorder, for neither he nor Potemkin ever took notes and there was no one else in the room.

"Good morning, gentlemen," said Molotov in English. Then he continued in Russian, "You will remember that on the second of June the government of the U.S.S.R. handed to you, as representatives of Great Britain and France, a draft treaty which, it was suggested, should be signed by all three governments. I need not remind you of its details.* The special delegate from the British government brought me the reply of your governments, and it was a rejection." He paused while Potemkin translated this into French. The Deputy Commissar did not use the same tone of faintly veiled contempt that had been present in Molotov's voice as he spoke the phrase "special delegate from the British government."

It was the term "a rejection" which moved Strang to intervene.

---

* Its vital sentence was: "France, England and the U.S.S.R. undertake to render to each other immediately all effective assistance should one of these States become involved with a European power as a result of . . . aggression by that power against Belgium, Greece, Turkey, Rumania, Poland, Latvia, Estonia and Finland, all of whom England, France and the U.S.S.R. have agreed to defend against aggression."

268

He certainly had not brought "a rejection" from London, he said; he did have "observations to the effect that before signing such a pact there must be a clear threat of force [by Germany], and there must also be abandonment of independence by the threatened State . . . We cannot agree to any text that would give the impression to the world at large that we were interfering in the internal affairs of another State."* But, he said, this was by no means a rejection; he had even brought suggestions for improving the draft treaty.

"It was a rejection," said Molotov flatly. "As to the proposals which the British delegate brought with him, I said at the time that they seemed most disappointing to me, but that I would think about them. I have now thought about them."

The Foreign Minister's face flushed with anger as his pale-blue eyes swept the three foreigners, and he raised his voice in impassioned Russian. Then, abruptly, he halted and nodded to Potemkin to translate, watching the faces of the others as he did so.

Potemkin hesitated, stammered and then said, "The People's Commissar for Foreign Affairs says of the British government's new proposals—I will give his exact words: 'If you think that the Soviet government is likely to accept these proposals, then you must think we are nitwits and nincompoops!' "

Potemkin was speaking in French, but the last three words he used were in English.

Molotov went on to assure his listeners that the Soviets were not "nitwits and nincompoops." They had asked Britain and France to guarantee the Baltic States. The result? They made conditions. But guarantees of the Baltic States were indispensable, and the Allies' refusal to offer them would place the Soviet government in a humiliating position. He leaned down for a moment and twiddled with whatever it was behind his desk. Then he went on to state flatly that unless the governments of Britain and France were prepared to do regarding Latvia, Estonia and Finland what they were asking the Soviet government to do regarding their own five client states . . .

He paused to allow for translation, leaving his ultimatum hanging in midair. Was this a threat to break off the talks?

---

* Strang had not given the real reason for British hesitation. Signing such a draft would have given the Soviet Union, as well as France and Britain, the right to decide when Germany was an aggressor. The British had given such a right to Poland, but in Chamberlain's eyes Russia was something altogether different.

. . . then it would be better to drop the whole idea of giving guarantees to other states, and to confine the treaty to a straight agreement of mutual assistance, to come into force only in case of direct attack by an aggressor on the territory of Great Britain, France or the U.S.S.R.

Whereupon Molotov rose to his feet abruptly. "That's all, gentlemen," he said crisply, and walked quickly through the door into the other room.

The Frenchmen and the two Englishmen looked at one another. He had let them off the hook; at least he hadn't broken off the negotiations. But as they drove out into Red Square again, Strang was gloomy. He knew what the two ambassadors didn't know: Neville Chamberlain didn't want a straight treaty with the Soviet Union. If he had to have an ally in Eastern Europe he preferred Poland, for he still believed that between it and Russia, Poland was by far the stronger of the two.

The following day, Sunday, June 18, was Brown Shirt Day in Danzig, as well as the last day of the Nazi-sponsored Cultural Congress. All week, to attend the second and in anticipation of the first, special night trains had been rolling across the Polish Corridor from East Prussia and Germany proper,* bringing "tourists" by the hundreds; hundreds more of them poured off the Kraft durch Freude (Strength through Joy) liners which had entered the harbor from Hamburg and Bremen. That the bulk of the tourists looked surprisingly young and uneasy in civilian clothes was not surprising, and few of them bothered to conceal the fact that they were German soldiers "on leave." What they did not mention was that quite a few of them would not be going back to Germany. They strolled around the exhibits of Nazi-approved art, nodding approval at the heroic thighs, broad buttocks and bursting breasts of the sculptures, eyes lighting up at the paintings of the victorious battles on the Spanish front. They sat in the beer gardens, where adoring local maidens urged them to try Danziger Goldwasser or some of the other sweet liqueurs which were the Free City's specialty. But by noon, all of them had made their way to the arena on the outskirts of the city. It was there that Danzig's

* A Polish transit visa was needed by Germans traveling across the Corridor by day, but not if they used the sealed, nonstop trains which crossed by night.

Brown Shirts would march, and it was there that Dr. Joseph Goebbels would accept the salute.

Goebbels had already spoken the previous afternoon, whipping up fervor against the "decadence" of Western art and the "obscene influence" of Jewish artists, but since his discourse had been addressed to an audience of writers, painters and sculptors, however blinkered, he had been restrained. Now, before the common herd of the Nazi party, he let himself go in a shrieking denunciation of the Poles, British and Jews. Few people noted the fact that like all senior National Socialist officials after Hitler's address of April 29, he made no mention of that hitherto standard target of Nazi hatred, Soviet Bolshevism.

"We are not gathered here today, citizens of Danzig, to decide whether this great city should return to the Reich, but *when* it should return. Soon, comrades, soon! There is not much time to waste. Just like the Jewish whores who try to sneak into our beds and rob us of our manhood—but our robust German maidens can outwit them by both taking and giving, can't they? [cries of *Yes, yes!*]—so do the Poles and the British scheme to steal our land and our people. All we ask for is what rightly belongs to us. Danzig is German. It must return to Germany. It is our understandable, clear, definite and sacred wish! But our enemies seek not only to stop us from this—they are arrogantly planning worse than this. Old and ignorant men in London and braggart bullies in Warsaw have made up their minds; they will not only refuse to give what belongs to us, but they will snatch what does not belong to them. Already the Polish wind-and-piss characters in Warsaw talk about claiming East Prussia and German Silesia. Already they claim that for their protection the Polish frontier should be on the Oder. And don't fool yourselves, if we let them they will go further than that. They will claim that their frontier should be on the Elbe—or possibly even on the Rhine. And why not, pray? It would be convenient for them! They could then rub arses with their new friends, the British, whose frontier also is now on the Rhine."

Goebbels paused, and then cried, "If we let them! But will we let them? [*No!*] You're right, we will not let them! We will drive them out of Danzig! And should they continue to threaten us, these poxy pygmies and their arrogant friends, we will drive them out of other places too!"

271

All the way back into the city, banners had been strung across the road. OUT WITH SPIES AND AGENTS, said one. WE WANT TO GO HOME TO THE REICH, said a second. WE LOVE OUR FÜHRER, said a third. A fourth had been put up just opposite a Polish administration office. HITLER HAS GIVEN US GREATER GERMANY, it said. The Poles grinned at it; it did not seem to worry them.

From Berlin, Ambassador Robert Coulondre described Goebbels' speech as marking "a date and an epoch in the development of the German problem," but it did not prevent him from departing a few days later for his annual holiday in the south of France. His assistant air attaché, Paul Stehlin, decided, on the other hand, to cancel his vacation and stay on in Berlin; he had a feeling he would be needed. It was he who had supplied most of the information in Coulondre's final dispatch before he departed, which said in part: "Here in Germany all the measures preparatory to war are being taken. The General Staff is acting as if it should be ready by a fixed date, which apparently falls sometime in August, after the harvest has been gathered, the fortifications [in the West] have been finished and large numbers of reservists assembled in the camps."

Stehlin knew that there would be two million Germans under arms in the Reich by August 15.

But would the situation lead to war? William C. Bullitt, the U.S. ambassador to France, thought it would, and he was almost as pessimistic about its outcome as Ambassador Kennedy. He had arrived in Washington to have a dislocated shoulder attended, in the wake of the visit of King George VI and Queen Elizabeth, and the first thing he wanted to know was: "Did they put reefs in George's sheets at the White House?"

He roared with laughter when told that they had. Earlier in the year Bullitt had received a letter from Eleanor Roosevelt saying that the King and Queen of England were coming over in the summer for a state visit, and since they had recently been on a similar visit to France, could he find out if they had any particular quirks about their accommodations? Bullitt had turned the whole matter over to his chauffeur-valet, Offie, who had gone to work in his usual inde-

272

fatigable manner, and his report had been duly sent back to the White House. It was only later, when Bullitt read it in detail, that he realized the thoroughness of Offie's research. The habits of the various ladies-in-waiting were duly described, as were the specific requirements of the servants and various needs in the royal bedroom, including a good old-fashioned pot under the bed and on it Irish linen sheets, each one reefed at the bottom so the royal feet could not stick out.

Over dinner with his friends the Ickes', Bullitt served them his usual excellent champagne, caviar, splendid claret and good food, but he depressed them with his war talk. He felt that the crisis would come soon, perhaps even in mid-July, when the Germans would move troops up to the Polish border to threaten the country just as they had Czechoslovakia earlier in the year. Chamberlain, he said, would decide what would happen in these circumstances, and he had no idea what was in Chamberlain's mind.

And if it came to war? Well, Bullitt said, France and England were in a much better position to defend themselves than they had been after Munich. Even France now had some planes. But could they win a war against Germany? He didn't think so.

In Warsaw, Colonel Beck did not think it would come to war at all. He addressed a meeting of the Polish Cabinet on July 5 and urged his fellow ministers not to be too alarmed by recent events in Danzig. They were just trying to scare Poland, he said. They might try to step up their terrorism in the next week or two, but it was nothing to worry about. His advice was to take economic reprisals rather than use force against these *agents provocateurs* and their hired louts. Hamper their trade, hit the good German burghers in their pockets by closing the customs against their fish, wheat and butter—that would bring them to heel. There would be no war; he could assure the Cabinet of that. He had it from someone who knew.

Beck's information came, in fact, from Benito Mussolini. The Italian dictator was still under the impression that Hitler and Ribbentrop meant it when they said that Germany would not go to war before 1942 or 1943, and he had passed on the good news to his friend Józef Beck.

When the Cabinet meeting was over and Beck returned to his office, he found the Minister for Economic Affairs, Kwiatkowski,

273

waiting to see him. He had been reading a situation report from Polish intelligence, Kwiatkowski said, and it had alarmed him, for it stated that Germany was secretly mobilizing for a campaign in the East before the end of the summer.

Nonsense, retorted Beck. Anyway, what concern was it of the minister's?

Kwiatkowski said he had long-term plans to make about Polish foreign trade. What should they ship abroad? Armaments, for instance? Should they not retain all their armaments in case of trouble? And what about their industrial program? He waved a sheaf of papers. He had plans for many new factories in the central industrial area, but they would be directly in the line of a German advance. What should he do about them?

"Build them!" Beck answered. "Continue to trade!" It was all Hitler's bluff; he was trying to frighten Poland into concessions. He would not go to war.

In fact, at that moment Adolf Hitler himself was not sure whether he would go to war or not. Paul Stehlin had met General Karl Bodenschatz at the Kabarett der Komiker toward the end of June, and for a time they exchanged small talk about the stage and theater, flirted with the girls and drank. Bodenschatz seemed distraught. He had just come from Karinhall, Field Marshal Göring's estate outside Berlin, where he had spent several hours talking with his chief. Göring had been seeing a good deal of Hitler in the past few days, but now the Führer had departed for Berchtesgaden.

"The Führer is in a bad mood," Bodenschatz said. "He has these periods of doubt, you know. He's in the midst of one now. Doubts about Germany, about its leaders, even about himself."

The general paused when a comedian came on the tiny stage, but this evening Werner Finck was absent, and his substitute was vulgar and lacked bite. He turned back to the Frenchman. "It's a mistake to think that Adolf Hitler wants war," Bodenschatz continued. "He fears war. He doesn't want it. At this moment he is worried about being drawn into war—and it's against his wishes because his popularity, his prestige, his mystique, his own legend are based on the opposite—on the successes he has won without resorting to arms."

He hesitated, took a gulp of his beer and sighed. "On the one

274

hand, Hitler dreams of being a great captain, a Caesar, a Frederick the Great, a Napoleon. He has the works of Clausewitz at his bedside and reads them avidly. But on the other hand, he sees a crisis coming with his generals. He keeps telling them that if he keeps on with his policy, it will succeed without Germany having to go to war. But they don't trust him . . . He's very disturbed. Very angry, too. He shouts at people. He never goes to bed at all."

Joachim von Ribbentrop had also gone south, to his estate at Fuschl, to be near to the Führer. They communicated with each other and with Berlin by telephone and teletype.

This was a period of crisis for Ribbentrop too. He had taken Hitler's rebuff over German-Soviet relations badly, but he had not given up. He still believed that for Germany the key to the whole European situation lay in Moscow. He refused to believe that Britain had any intention of honoring its guarantee of Poland, and that no war with the West would result if Germany annexed Danzig or advanced on the Polish Corridor. But a Russo-German pact, eliminating the threat to Germany's rear—for he did not consider Poland any threat, either—would make Britain's nonintervention absolutely certain. That the Führer's hesitations could eventually be overcome he had no doubt; for Russia and Germany to come to an entente was by no means the far-fetched idea that so many people in the West evidently considered it, and sooner or later Hitler would accept it. In fact, the so-called incompatibles had much in common; in particular, they shared a desire to recover territory which had been taken from them by Poland. If the bribe were large enough, Stalin too would see the advantages of an accommodation with Germany.

But would both the leaders realize it in time? And could the rival suitors be eliminated? It was this which worried Ribbentrop most. His contacts in London (no doubt fooled by Vansittart, as Kordt had been) reported that the Anglo-French negotiations in Moscow were going well and would almost certainly result in an agreement. The receipt of this news plunged him into profound depression, and his wife complained to his secretary that "he never goes to sleep and won't let me sleep either, but paces the room all night."

However, that was in mid-June. On June 29 Ribbentrop received

275

a report which changed his mood entirely. It was from his ambassador in Moscow, Count von der Schulenburg, and it contained an extract from an article by Andrei Zhdanov in the official party organ, *Pravda*. The preamble to the article pointed out that the writer's opinions were purely personal, but of course this fooled no one. Zhdanov was a member of the Politburo, as well as president of the Foreign Affairs Committee of the U.S.S.R., and was regularly consulted by Stalin. In the Soviet fashion, the headline over the article was long and unwieldy, but its meaning was clear: BRITISH AND FRENCH GOVERNMENTS DO NOT DESIRE A TREATY ON THE BASIS OF EQUALITY FOR THE SOVIET UNION.

Under it Zhdanov wrote, in part: "It seems to me that the British and French governments are not looking for a real agreement acceptable to the U.S.S.R., but only for talks about an agreement in order to demonstrate before the public opinion of their own countries the alleged unyielding attitude of the U.S.S.R. and thus facilitate the conclusion of an agreement with the aggressors. The next few days will show whether this is so or not."

Ribbentrop called in his secretary and began to dictate a message to Moscow. So the British had been bluffing, and a pact with the Soviets was not certain after all! There was still time to seduce the Bolsheviks to Germany's side.

The purport of Ribbentrop's message to Schulenburg was that at all costs he should keep talking to the Russians. Even if Hitler had some doubts about a German-Russian agreement on occasion, Ribbentrop never had any. For the moment the only dialogue between Moscow and Berlin was about a trade agreement, and even that had slowed to a desultory pace since Hitler's rebuff. Until the Führer's mood changed, the talks had to be kept moving.

Three days later Ribbentrop had additional proof that the British would never fight for Danzig. The telephone rang and on the line, switched through from Berlin, was Albert Forster, Gauleiter of Danzig. He had some intriguing news, he said; Gerald Shepherd, the British consul general in Danzig, had been dismissed. He was leaving for London almost at once, and a replacement was on the way.

Ribbentrop inquired haughtily how this could possibly be of interest to him. He was not interested in what happened in the lower rungs of the British diplomatic service.

But did the Reich Minister realize the significance of this move?

276

Forster asked. They had their spies in the British consulate and had always known that Shepherd was against them—a pro-Pole if ever there was one. He had been spying on German plans and movements and had been sending provocative messages back to London. But no longer; Henderson in Berlin had intervened.

Actually, Forster had got his facts slightly garbled. True, Gerald Shepherd had been abruptly recalled to London—not through the interference of Nevile Henderson, however, to whom consular officials were a lesser breed, but on the direct instructions of Lord Halifax. Shepherd had made the mistake of going beyond his responsibilities in Danzig. As consul general he was, unlike the head of an embassy, instructed to report facts only and eschew observations. He had indeed fed facts to London continuously all through the spring and summer, reporting the build-up of Nazi strength inside the Free City and of evidence on every side of a determination by the Germans to take over. But in a dispatch which he sent to the Foreign Office on July 1 he dared to express an opinion. He was fighting mad at the time because of certain slurs on Britain which he and his staff had been hearing during recent days, and he duly reported that Germans in Danzig were contemptuously remarking that "Britain and France will leave Poland in the lurch by not fighting on account of Danzig."

This was a legitimate report to make, but Shepherd went beyond it and urged the British government to reject these insulting suggestions by confronting the Nazis. He further expressed the opinion that if Danzig fell to Germany it would almost certainly be followed by the "absorption of most, if not all, of the remainder of Poland." This must not be allowed, he said, and he ended his dispatch by exhorting his government to stand up firmly to their obligations.

From Halifax's point of view, this dispatch could not have come at a worse time. Bonnet had telephoned him to inform him that the French public and Cabinet were growing restive about rumors of German designs on Danzig. The French Foreign Minister had therefore been instructed to send a peremptory note to the German government pointing out that an attack on Danzig would produce inevitable Polish reactions, and this would automatically bring the Franco-Polish military agreement into play and oblige France to give immediate assistance to her ally. Would Halifax, Bonnet asked, call in the German ambassador and give him a similar warning?

277

No, replied Halifax, he certainly would not. He made it plain that as far as the British Cabinet was concerned, Danzig was a boring embarrassment. If France wanted to make a fuss about it, well and good, but Britain would not.

The dispatch from Gerald Shepherd, which arrived within an hour of this exchange, therefore provoked an immediate, angry reaction from the Foreign Secretary. How dare a mere consul general venture to express an opinion? Bring the man home at once!

So Gerald Shepherd was recalled. But just so that no one would notice, the Foreign Office went through the lists very carefully for his replacement and found exactly the one they were looking for. Gerald Shepherd packed his bags and came home in disgrace for having dared to tell the truth as he saw it, and the new consul general, name of Francis Shepherd, slipped into his place in Danzig.

Though the British tried to keep it secret, Ribbentrop learned all this within a few days of the call from Gauleiter Forster, and it gave him great pleasure to pass on the facts to Adolf Hitler.

In the meantime the French had gone ahead—alone—with their protest about Danzig. Bonnet's note had arrived in Berlin on July 1, and reached Ribbentrop the following morning. It referred to the Franco-German agreement of the previous December for the peaceful resolution of all problems, particularly in Eastern Europe, and continued: "I consider it my duty clearly to state that any action, whatever its form, which by trying to change the status quo in Danzig provoked Poland's armed resistance, would bring the Franco-Polish agreement into operation and oblige France to give immediate help to Poland."

Had this note come at a moment when Ribbentrop still believed in close Anglo-French co-operation and the eventual conclusion of an Anglo-French-Russian pact, he might have replied with caution. But conditions had changed by the time he answered it. His agents had reported to him the facts about Shepherd's departure, and they indicated that Britain didn't want to be bothered about fighting for Danzig. Despite British and French propaganda, the reports from Moscow hinted that the negotiations with the Russians were going badly. Evidently the British and French were at odds again; otherwise, why had no similar protest about Danzig come from London?

It was time to abandon caution and let Bonnet and the French Cabinet know just how little Germany really cared about them. Ribbentrop dictated a blistering reply to Bonnet's message in which he denied that France any longer had any right to concern itself in the affairs of Eastern Europe. "Germany's relations with her Eastern neighbors," he wrote "whatever form they take, in no way affect French interests . . . It is only for your personal information that I wish to tell you what follows concerning the view taken by Germany of the Polish question. The Polish government has replied to the historic and unique offer of the Führer for settling the Danzig question and definitely consolidating German-Polish relations with a threat of war which can merely be described as bizarre. It is impossible to say at present whether the Polish government will give up this peculiar attitude and recover its senses. But while it persists in its unreasonable attitude, I can only say that any violation of Danzig soil by Poland, or any Polish provocation incompatible with the prestige of the German Reich, would make Germans march immediately and annihilate the Polish army."

Frau Ribbentrop reported that her husband was sleeping again, and so was she.

■

Hermann Göring gave a party on July 6, 1939. Joseph Goebbels, who had not been invited, was furious because the guests, in addition to those from the air force, were drawn from the film and theater worlds of Berlin and Vienna—Goebbels' favorite milieu. Most of them had dressed for the occasion; the high officers of the Luftwaffe were in white uniform and gleaming white patent-leather boots, their shoulders covered with gold lace. The stars and starlets of Germany's show business wandered across the lawns in sleeveless dresses of gold and silver and silk, for they knew that here at least the puritanical bent of National Socialism was not enforced, and they could even flaunt their figures in foreign fashions.

The setting deserved the effort most of the women had made. Göring's principal country estate was Karinhall, a short distance from Berlin, amid the lakes and rolling countryside of Prussia. It was here, near the small town of Eberswalde in the Schorfheide, that Göring had bought a hunting lodge in 1933. His first wife, Karin, a gentle

279

Swede of great beauty, had died in 1931, and so great was his love that her loss drove him to the drug habit which had racked him since the war. From this purgatory he recovered, but the death of Karin remained an ache, and in the Prussian woods he found surcease. He had bought what at first was to be a humble memorial to her: a small, thatch-roofed Nordic blockhouse which he used as a weekend hide-out and a base for hunting trips to the woods. But that was in the early days of National Socialism. Since then he had grown in power, and Karinhall had grown and changed in character. True, the memory of Karin herself was still preserved. The ashes of his beloved were deposited in a small temple flanked by Greek pillars on the grounds; when one entered, it illuminated itself and at the far end a full-breasted bust of Karin turned on a table under a spotlight.

Elsewhere, like almost everything else in Germany, the estate had swollen to heroic size; the grounds spread for miles around and were stocked with deer, pheasant and capercaillie for the sport of the diplomats whom Göring invited for weekends. The forest glades were filled with bronze statues of animals and hunters. The log cabin had been transformed into an enormous two-story house, still thatched in German style, but with a great central hall and wings of bedrooms leading off. The walls were covered with old masters—Rubenses, Rembrandts and an El Greco—all of them the "gifts" of Jewish citizens who had found it necessary to leave the Reich in a hurry after the *Kristallnacht* pogrom the previous November and had been duly grateful to the Field Marshal for his help. There was a hundred-seat cinema and an elaborate model railway, and always the tang of roasting meat in the air in preparation for a feast. The servants wore tight breeches and hunting jackets, and the morning air was rent by the sound of hunting horns. The host himself was usually clad in breeches, a silk shirt with flowing sleeves, and a jerkin of yellow elk skin; in this costume he resembled an aging tenor out of *Der Freischütz*.

On July 6, however, Göring was dressed in his uniform of Generalfeldmarschall of the Luftwaffe, all white silk and gold, with splashes of red across his breast. Staring through the window of his study toward the lawn and the lake, where his first guests were beginning to arrive, he looked worried.

He *was* worried. That morning he had received a report from his staff in Berlin on the state of the economy, of the Luftwaffe and of

280

the raw materials available to the Reich in the event of war in 1939, and in each instance the situation was disquieting. There was no doubt that Germany was ready for a war against Poland; she would not need to mobilize more than a small part of her men, weapons or resources. But what if there was a general war? Then, even though Poland was an insignificant enemy, Germany's capabilities for fighting on two fronts were quite inadequate.

More than all the other ministers of the National Socialist hierarchy, Hermann Göring considered a war with the West unnecessary. Though he professed to share the confidence of Hitler and Ribbentrop that Britain and France would never dare to fight, he had an ingrained fear that they just might be foolish enough to do so, and this would be disastrous for Germany as well as for Western Europe. Global war, he believed, would inevitably follow; if so, Germany would eventually be defeated and the land reduced to Bolshevism. Why have a war, anyway? He was convinced that deft handling of the democracies could secure the fruits Germany wished to pick in the East without provoking England or France. But not by the threats and terrorism with which Hitler had succeeded so far; the time had come to change tactics and use blandishments instead of bludgeons. It was all a matter of skill, patience and the kind of bonhomie which the Field Marshal exuded in his meetings with foreign statesmen—a chubby charm which, he believed, oiled the lamps of peace and kept them burning. Indeed, he was in the process of oiling a new lamp at the moment.

As Göring watched the arrival of his elegant guests, a Luftwaffe Mercedes drew up in the courtyard and out stepped a squat figure in a business suit. A few moments later he was being shown into Göring's study, where the Field Marshal greeted him warmly. "Welcome to Karinhall, Dahlerus," he said and handed him a glass of champagne, which his guest did not touch. "Now tell me," Göring went on eagerly, "what have you learned from the Englishmen?"

"They tell me that if you attack Poland, they will stand by their guarantee," the visitor said.

"Nonsense," said Göring, but his tone was nervous when he added, "They're just bluffing."

"I don't think they are bluffing," the visitor said. "If you attack Poland, there will be war."

Outside, on the lawn, an orchestra had struck up and the sound of a Lehár waltz drifted through the windows. There was a tap on the door and an adjutant poked his head inside. "The guests are here and are waiting for you, Herr Field Marshal," he said.

"They must go on waiting," replied Göring. "Go away! Can't you see that I'm busy?" He turned back to his visitor.

Birger Dahlerus was a Swede, but he was more than that: he was a phenomenon. Only a man of great egotism or great faith would have believed that he could single-handedly stop a war between Britain and Germany, and Dahlerus was too simple, too honest and too humble to be an egotist. In the summer of 1939, stopping the war was the task to which he dedicated himself, and his intervention in the affairs of the British and German governments in the ensuing weeks was to prove one of the most bizarre episodes of the period.

Dahlerus was a successful businessman who had spent many of his formative years working in Britain, particularly in the North, and he had come to admire the solid honesty and sense of purpose of the British workingman. A frequent visitor to England, he counted some of the most important men in the government and in the financial world as his close friends. He had a touching faith in the British; from the moment that Britain gave her guarantee to Poland, he believed steadfastly that it would be kept. An Englishman's word was his bond, and there was no question of its being broken.

Dahlerus also considered Göring his friend. Many years before, the Field Marshal had done him a favor. Mrs. Dahlerus was German, and there had been some complication over a property arrangement before the marriage which Göring had straightened out. A few years later Dahlerus found a job in Stockholm for Göring's Swedish step-son, Tomas von Kantzow. Thereafter, each time he came to Berlin the Swede would see the Field Marshal at least once, and they had come to trust each other.

On Midsummer Eve 1939, as he was crossing to London by sea from Gothenburg, Dahlerus had a sudden inspiration. Why not use his powerful connections in London and his friendship with Göring to bring the two sides together? To his shipboard companion, Björn Prytz, he said that he was sure it was all a misunderstanding. The threat of war could be dissipated if only someone could get them talking.

282

"You mean another Munich?" said Prytz.

No, not this time, replied Dahlerus. It was the British this time who had given their word. Last time it was the French, and they had broken their pledge. One expected it of the French, but not of the British. This would be no Munich; rather, it would be an occasion for the British to point out that Hitler could no longer gain by force the changes he desired in Europe. There must be a peaceful settlement, and the changes must be justified by right and not by greed. Dahlerus declared that he was sure it would work. The British would tell Göring, and Göring would tell Hitler. Then they could talk.

By the time he arrived in London, Dahlerus was inspired by his idea and his enthusiasm was catching. A group of powerful businessmen and financiers, all staunch supporters of the Tory party, broke up their weekend—a fact which much impressed him—and gave him a Sunday dinner at the Constitutional Club in London to hear what he had to say.* Before Dahlerus left London to fly to Germany, they had been in contact with Chamberlain and Halifax, who also thought the idea had merit. It seemed much more promising than the Wohltat-Wilson-Hudson conversations, and much less risky to the government if there was a leak, since no members of the Cabinet or the House of Commons would be involved.

Dahlerus flew to Germany at once and telephoned his friend Hermann Göring. He was promptly invited to Karinhall, where he proposed that Göring meet the English businessmen and exchange points of view. But where? Dahlerus suggested a place in southern Sweden; he had a friend there who would lend him his castle.

The plan appealed to the Field Marshal, for he had always loved his first wife's country, and he promised to let Dahlerus know.

On July 8 Göring called Dahlerus back to Karinhall and said, "I have talked to the Führer about your proposed meeting with the Englishmen in Sweden. He has agreed in principle—on one condition. The fact that we are meeting to discuss the European situation must be kept absolutely secret."

It was soon obvious to both men that there could be no secret negotiations of any kind if the chubby figure of Hermann Göring were seen arriving in Sweden; recognition would be inevitable. So a

---

* The Britons present at the dinner were Bryan S. Mountain, Sir Robert Renwick, the Hon. Charles McLaren, S. W. Rossen, A. Holden, Sir Holberry Mensforth and Charles F. Spencer, their chairman.

house which Mrs. Dahlerus owned near the town of Bredstedt in Schleswig-Holstein, close to the Danish border, was chosen instead.

The Swede, who from this moment on began to bounce all over Europe like a ping-pong ball, caught the next plane to London and was taken to see Lord Halifax. The Foreign Secretary was now beginning to show some enthusiasm for the proposed talks with Göring; perhaps he realized that the conversations with Wohltat were getting nowhere. "An open discussion, free of all restraint, between leading Englishmen and members of the German government could be of great use at this moment," he said. "But I must explain that the British government does not want to be directly involved and will not send any of its members to the conference." Then he added, "On the other hand, we will be interested to receive a detailed account of the results from the Englishmen who take part in the talks. If they prove to be of a positive nature, this meeting ought to pave the way for a future conference between authorised delegates. It could take place in Holland or in Sweden."

Back to Berlin went Dahlerus to confer with Göring once more. The first Anglo-German meeting in Schleswig-Holstein was finally fixed for Monday, August 7.

By that time Europe had moved much closer to war, and Dahlerus was in the thick of it.

■

William Strang's room in the British embassy in Moscow overlooked the towers of the Kremlin, and every time he gazed down he got a feeling in his bones. He was well aware of the rumors which had been circulating for some time—in London, in Berlin, in Paris and in Moscow itself—about the possibility of the Soviet government turning away from the Western democracies and seeking arrangements with Germany. After a month in Moscow, he still found it hard to believe that such an about-face would take place; he chided himself for being naïve, but he hoped that there was enough idealism inside the walls of the Kremlin to realize that supporting the Western democracies, no matter how venal they had shown themselves to be, was preferable to betraying the spirit of the Revolution by an alliance with the greedy tyrants in Berlin. But . . .

William Strang was an honest man and a shrewd one, but his

choice as the leader for Britain in the Moscow talks had been disastrous, and he knew it. The trouble was that he had no standing. International diplomacy is rather like the old days of Hollywood: it was not so much what the film was about as who the stars were. Similarly, to Moscow the quality of a diplomat's brains and his expertise were not as important as the position he held in his government. William Strang knew this well, and though he had been given special powers by his government when he went to Moscow to negotiate for a pact, they were not plenipotentiary powers. He had no authority to decide for himself on the spot; all he could do was state that he thought his government would agree on a point, and then consult London.

Under this system, days would pass while Chamberlain, Halifax and Sir Horace Wilson mulled over a decision in London, shook their heads, counseled caution, and then instructed Strang to try another tack. (They would also consult the French before replying to Strang, but this was only a waste of time; though they were intent on obtaining an agreement with Russia at all costs, by this time the French had become so subservient to the British that their views hardly ever prevailed. It was the slough of despond for Franco-British relationships; rarely have two allies had so little in common— or wanted to have.)

In those days, when officials of the British Foreign Office in their posts abroad were dispirited they wrote not to the Foreign Secretary but to the head of the permanent staff of the Foreign Office, Sir Orme Sargent, a permanent official, a man of sympathy and understanding, and—though he did not let it obtrude—an opponent of Chamberlain's appeasement policy. Sir Orme shared many of Strang's opinions and knew only too well what a task he had undertaken with no prestige to back his words, no authority from London to make decisions, and no faith in the Communists with whom he was dealing, since they were likely to betray him at any moment. On July 20 Strang spread notepaper before him and began to write a letter to Sir Orme Sargent:

"Molotov does not become any easier to deal with as the weeks pass. He has, it is true, now made himself familiar with the details of our problem; and you will have noticed that the drafts he produces, which either are his own or prepared by his experts, are ingeniously constructed, though they are, I am told, couched in inelegant Russian.

285

But it is difficult to get to grips with him. He seems to be bored with detailed discussions, and the admirable argumentative material with which you supply us makes little impression upon him . . . Indeed, we have sometimes felt that the difficulties which have arisen between us might perhaps be based on some colossal misunderstanding. And yet we have usually come to the conclusion in the end that this is not so, and that Molotov has seen clearly the extent of the difference between the respective positions of the two sides.

"On the whole, the negotiations have been a humiliating experience. Time after time we have taken up a position and a week later we have abandoned it; and we have had the feeling that Molotov was convinced from the beginning that we should be forced to abandon it. This was I think inevitable. It was not the Russians who took the initiative in starting negotiations. Our need for an agreement is more immediate than theirs. Unlike them, we have assumed obligations which we may be obliged to fulfil any day [the guarantee to the Poles]; and some of the obligations which we have undertaken are of benefit to the Soviet Union since they protect a good part of their Western frontier. Having committed ourselves to these obligations, we have no other policy than to build up the Peace Front. The Russians have in the last resort two alternative policies, namely the policy of isolation, and the policy of accommodation with Germany. We are being urged by our Press and our public to conclude an agreement quickly; and the Russians have good reason to assume that we shall not dare to face a final breakdown of the negotiations. This is the strength of their negotiating position, and this makes it certain that if we want an agreement with them, we shall have to pay their price or something very near it . . ."

But what was the price now? The political side of the talks was still a wrangle, and Molotov made no secret of his deep suspicions of the motives of the democracies.

"Their distrust and suspicion of us have not diminished during the negotiations," Strang continued, "nor, I think, has their respect for us increased. The fact that we have raised difficulty after difficulty on points which seemed to them unessential has created an impression that we may not be seriously seeking an agreement; while the fact that we have yielded in the end would tend to remind them that we are still the same Powers who have (as they see it) capitulated in the past to

286

Japan, Italy and Germany and that we are likely to do so again."

Strang made no secret of his own feelings: "We should perhaps have been wiser to pay the Soviet price for this agreement at an earlier stage, since we are not in a good position to bargain and since, as the international situation deteriorates, the Soviet price is likely to rise. We could probably have got a better agreement by closing quickly with the substance of the Soviet draft of 2 June than we shall get today."

The price had indeed begun to rise, for Molotov was not only insisting that the British and French guarantee the Baltic States against "direct" and "indirect" aggression; he was also demanding military talks while political negotiations were still in progress.

Strang sympathized with the Soviet viewpoint on the Batlic States, even if Chamberlain and Halifax did not. "If we wish to understand how they feel about the Baltic States," he wrote, "we have only to imagine what our own attitude would be to the establishment of German influence over Holland or Belgium. This, you will remember, was very much in our minds last February when we reached an understanding with the French about common action in the event of German action against Holland."

But to start military conversations with the Russians before the conclusion of a political agreement was something else again. Strang commented that "it is indeed extraordinary that we should be expected to talk military secrets with the Soviet Government before we are sure that they will be our allies." Nevertheless, he advised the British and French governments to agree to Molotov's suggestion and to send a military delegation at once.

After some discussion back in London, Neville Chamberlain reluctantly agreed to do so. On July 31 he announced that a French-British delegation would be leaving for staff military talks in Moscow in the course of the next few days.

It was news that confirmed reports Adolf Hitler already had, and it galvanized him, as Molotov had expected it would.

About the same time that Strang was writing his letter in Moscow, an official of the Soviet embassy was on his way to keep an appointment with Dr. Julius Schnurre, the Commissioner for Trade at the Foreign

287

Ministry in Berlin. He had news that was destined to break the Russo-German deadlock brought about by Hitler's last-minute doubts.

For the moment the Soviet government were not anxious to show their hand in the great poker game which was now beginning, and their reluctance was undoubtedly due to the fact that they were still not sure whether the cards they held would win. Were the Germans dallying with them? Were they talking with the U.S.S.R. not to secure a hard agreement but simply to sabotage the Anglo-French-Russian conversations? From the Kremlin, Stalin and his Politburo looked westward suspiciously; they knew they could trust neither side. They feared that at any moment the procrastinating representatives of the democracies and the tempting talkers in Berlin would reveal themselves as tricksters, and turn to each other once again as they had at Munich, leaving the Russians more isolated than ever. It was a time for caution.

Nevertheless, the Kremlin had been impressed and somewhat alarmed at breaks which had occurred in the Russian-German contacts. Was Hitler abandoning his contacts with Moscow, or was he simply playing hard to get? It was time, Stalin decided, for him to take the initiative, if only to put pressure on the British and French. But to begin with it would be an initiative at a low level.

Therefore it was Babarin, the Soviet trade representative in Berlin, who turned up at Julius Schnurre's office in the Foreign Ministry on July 18. "I have a message from the Commissariat for Foreign Affairs," he said, "which I hope will give the government of the German Reich as much pleasure as it does me. Discussions have been held, and I have been instructed to inform you that the government of the U.S.S.R. is strongly desirous of extending and urgently building up economic relations between the two countries."

Babarin then proceeded to read aloud a long memorandum, at the conclusion of which he said, "The differences between our two countries on the subject of trade exchanges are slight. If they can be ironed out, I inform you that I am empowered to sign a trade agreement with the German government here in Berlin."

Schnurre did not bother to conceal his pleasure, nor did Ribbentrop when he heard about it. The Russians were biting again. He sent for Weizsäcker and told him to cable Ambassador von der

288

Schulenburg in Moscow to tell him that the trade negotiations were on again:

> WE WILL ACT HERE IN A MARKEDLY FORTHCOMING MANNER, SINCE A CONCLUSION, AND THIS AT THE EARLIEST POSSIBLE MOMENT, IS DESIRED HERE FOR GENERAL REASONS . . . YOU ARE THEREFORE EMPOWERED TO PICK UP THE THREADS AGAIN THERE, WITHOUT IN ANY WAY PRESSING THE MATTER.

Germany was in the game again, though not yet quite sure how she was going to play her cards.

XII

Slow Boat to Leningrad

Frau Riegele, Field Marshal Göring's sister, telephoned Paul Stehlin at the French embassy on July 24 and asked him to a party. "You must come," she said. "It may be our last chance to see each other for some time."

"It will be very difficult," Stehlin said. "The ambassador is on vacation, and I've been very busy."

"It's not just that I would like to see you, Paul. There are other reasons. Please find the time."

Stehlin found the time.

The party proved to be a bore. The rooms were full of half-drunk Nazi officials and air force officers. After an hour the whiskey ran out, and he drank schnapps until Frau Riegele pulled him into another room where a bottle of Vat 69 was produced. "I must go," he said. It had been a wasted evening.

"Don't," said Olga Riegele. "Stay just half an hour more."

She kept looking at the door, and at eleven o'clock, just when Stehlin thought that he could stand it no longer, General Bodenschatz and Field Marshal Göring arrived. They mingled with the guests for a while, listening to the conversation, and then Frau Riegele led them away. Presently she came back and beckoned to Stehlin.

Göring and Bodenschatz were in the study. A magnum of champagne and a bottle of whiskey were open, and they motioned Stehlin to help himself. Then Göring turned to him and said, "Your ambassador—he's not in Berlin. Where is he—in Paris?"

"He's on vacation in the Midi," Stehlin replied.

"There can't be too many here when things begin to happen," Göring went on. "When will he return?"

"Around the fifteenth of August."

Göring looked worried. "That's very late. Do you think you will see him before that date?"

"No, but I could write to him."

"It is more important that the head of your government be alerted to the turn events may take." Göring paused, sipped some champagne and then said, "France should not take risks over Poland; it would be contrary to her interests. Nothing is going to happen immediately, but in two or three weeks we are going to find ourselves in a crisis much more serious than last year's."

"I will go to Paris and let my government know," Stehlin replied. "But first a request."

"All you have to do is ask. We are always ready to help you."

"The plane of the French air attaché in Prague has been grounded there since the fifteenth of March and we have not been able to get it out. Will you release it? I could go there and fly it back to Paris."

Göring turned to Bodenschatz. "See to it, Karl." Then he said to Stehlin, "Anything so that you get to Paris and tell your government what is going on."

Two days later Paul Stehlin flew to Prague in a small liaison plane lent him by the Luftwaffe. He drove into the city for lunch and was sorry he had done so. A swastika was flying from Hradčany Castle, German soldiers in uniform were snapping pictures of their girl friends on the Charles Bridge, and the Old City sat sadly under the weight of the Nazi occupation. The next day he flew back to Tempelhof Airport in Berlin in the French embassy plane, picked up an assistant, and continued on to France, not neglecting to fly low over the German fortifications—after all, he had Luftwaffe permission—while his companion photographed the West Wall as meticulously as possible.

The following day Stehlin reported in to his chiefs at the Deuxième Bureau, but found most of them on vacation. From there

292

he proceeded to the Ministry for Air. General Vuillemin saw him that afternoon, but reluctantly. By this time Paris was beginning to be wary of Paul Stehlin. He was a harbinger of bad news, and whenever he appeared he sent shivers down the spines of his superiors.

Stehlin reported his conversation with Göring and then declared, "I am convinced that the Germans will attack Poland within the next four weeks."

Vuillemin was incredulous. "Surely you must be misinformed. The government has quite the opposite information. As we understand the situation, things are improving and there will be no attack. But in any case, we have already taken measures to face any eventuality."

"But it isn't just a question of taking precautions," Stehlin answered. "What we need to know at the embassy in Berlin is exactly what we will do *if* the Germans move. Where will we attack? What objectives will we bomb? Don't you see that if Hitler is convinced through our preparations that there is no doubt of a French offensive in the West, then there is a chance that he will hesitate and consider a solution other than war? But if the Germans know as much about us as we know about ourselves, then I haven't the slightest doubt what will happen."

"Don't push it too far, Captain Stehlin!"

"I was posted to Berlin to gather information, and I think I have no other function than to report as best I can to the quarters where decisions are made."

Vuillemin looked impatient and irritated, and Stehlin realized that only their friendship prevented the general from showing his anger.

"I expect you want to tell all this to the minister," Vuillemin said. "Don't. He's too nervous already."

"But, *mon général,* it's my duty to tell this to the minister and also to the Premier himself," Stehlin retorted angrily. "If I keep my mouth shut, I would be negating everything I have been doing for the past four years."

Vuillemin sighed. "All right. Go and see the minister. But keep this in mind: our fighters are good but our bombers don't exist. The Luftwaffe can strike back with a much superior force. Our bombers won't have a chance against their fighters and ack-ack. The government knows this. I'm not much happier now than I was at Munich.

293

Nothing that you can tell the minister will alter things very much."

"All the same, I must tell him."

"Then tell him! Tell the Premier too!"

That same afternoon Stehlin saw the Minister for Air and repeated his story. Guy La Chambre made a few desultory notes and
looked disinterested. He advised against any interview between the
young air attaché and Daladier, but promised to pass on the information to him. Stehlin is convinced that he never did.

When Stehlin returned to Berlin, the city was blacked out and search-
lights pricked the sky searching for planes droning overhead. The
summer maneuvers of the Luftwaffe had begun. This time, contrary
to similar occasions in the past, the foreign air attachés were not invited.

Many people have suspected that throughout 1938 and 1939 Adolf
Hitler had a spy well placed in British government circles who kept
him informed of what Neville Chamberlain, Lord Halifax and Sir
Horace Wilson were thinking, but no one has ever been able to prove
this. It *is* known that Nevile Henderson's cables from the Berlin
embassy to London were deciphered by the Germans, but that cannot
have helped them much, for they already knew the trend of his thinking; and of course the Italians had broken the code used by the British
embassy in Rome and were turning over to the Germans some—but
not all—incoming and outgoing messages. But it was not from these
sources that Hitler so uncannily anticipated and interpreted the way
Chamberlain's mind worked in crisis, nor was it from the intelligence
reports supplied by Canaris of the Abwehr, which Hitler never read.
Did the Führer receive information from some quite unsuspected
source close to the Cabinet and the Foreign Office, or was he clair-
voyant? We will probably never know, since a meticulous examination of all the German documents has failed to uncover any clue,
and if members of the British Secret Service have any information,
they are not talking.

However, one thing is certain: on July 24, 1939, someone informed Hitler that the British and French governments had agreed

294

to send a military delegation to Moscow. The official announcement was not made by the Prime Minister in Parliament until July 31, but on July 28 Count Johannes von Welczeck, the German ambassador in Paris, reported "from an unusually well-informed source" that the military talks were about to begin, and even named the French delegates. But already on July 25, three days earlier, Ribbentrop had telephoned from Fuschl and instructed Julius Schnurre to begin working on the Russians, explaining that the Führer now knew that the British and French "were getting desperate and were starting military talks in Moscow."

These instructions by-passed Weizsäcker in the Foreign Ministry, but both the baron and Erich Kordt were soon informed of the move, for Schnurre confided in them. He was beginning to grow alarmed, he told the Undersecretary, at the turn the German-Russian negotiations were taking: he had thought they were concerned solely with maintaining good trade relations, but now he feared that they were being used by Germany as a means of making war possible for Hitler. It seems hard to believe that Schnurre could have been so naïve as not to see this earlier, but it was the line he took with his friends at the ministry.

In any case, Schnurre's fears did not prevent him from carrying out Ribbentrop's instructions to the letter. He telephoned the Russian chargé d'affaires, Georgi Astakhov, and invited him and Babarin to dinner at Ewest, a small but luxurious Berlin restaurant, on July 26. The three men ate and drank well. The ostensible reason for the meal was economic discussions, but Astakhov altered tack by saying, more in pain than in anger, that Moscow had never understood why Germany had been such a bitter enemy of the Soviet Union, and that a political rapprochement between the two countries was in the best interests of them both.

Schnurre warmly agreed, and added that German policy in the East had changed. "On our part there could be no question of menacing the Soviet Union," he later wrote. "Our aims were in an entirely different direction . . . I could imagine a far-reaching arrangement of mutual interests, with due consideration for vital Russian interests."

This was the crux of his message, and Schnurre had made it plain by his tone that his country wished Russia to take particular note of this point. "But this possibility would be barred," his memo continued, "the moment the Soviet Union aligned itself with Britain against Germany. The time for an understanding between Germany and the Soviet Union was now ripe, but it would no longer be so after the conclusion of a pact with London."

The three men had begun eating at nine o'clock, and it was now after midnight. They sent for more coffee and brandy.

"What could Britain offer Russia?" Schnurre's report went on. "At best, participation in a European war and the hostility of Germany. What could we offer against this? Neutrality and keeping out of a possible European conflict. Also, if Moscow wished, a German-Russian understanding on mutual interests . . ."

He left dangling in the air what those mutual interests might be, and continued: "Controversial problems between us, in my opinion, did not exist anywhere along the line from the Baltic to the Black Sea and to the Far East.* Despite all the differences in our outlook, there was surely one thing common to the ideologies of Germany, Italy and the Soviet Union alike: we opposed the capitalist democracies in the West."

The party broke up at twelve-thirty with smiles and backslapping, and a promise by Astakhov that he would report to Moscow at once.

Then Hitler and Ribbentrop waited for a reaction from the Kremlin. Three days passed, on each of which Ribbentrop called Weizsäcker anxiously to ask whether there had been a report from Moscow. There was none.

On July 29, unable to bear the suspense any longer, the Foreign Minister instructed his deputy to send the following message to Count von der Schulenburg in Moscow: "It would be important for us to know whether the remarks made to Astakhov and Babarin have met with any response in Moscow. If you see an opportunity of arranging a further conversation with Molotov, please sound him out along the same lines. If this results in Molotov's abandoning the reserve he has so far maintained, you could go a step further."

Ribbentrop then inserted the first of the German bribes: "This

---

* This reference to the Far East was significant and the Russians must have realized it. For Germany's fellow member of the Anti-Comintern Pact in the Far East was Japan, even then clashing with Russia in Asia. A small war was being waged at the time between the Manchukuo government (sponsored by Japan) and Outer Mongolia (Russian-backed) over frontiers. Schnurre's reference could only mean Germany's neutrality in the area.

applies in particular to the Polish problem. We would be prepared, however the Polish problem may develop . . . to safeguard all Soviet interests and to come to an understanding with the government in Moscow . . ."

This was sent to Schulenburg by special courier, but just as it was delivered, the Foreign Minister told Weizsäcker to send another urgent message to make sure that Molotov was apprised at once of German eagerness:

> WITH REFERENCE TO OUR DISPATCH OF JULY 29 ARRIVING IN MOSCOW BY COURIER TODAY: PLEASE REPORT BY TELEGRAM THE DATE AND TIME OF YOUR NEXT INTERVIEW WITH MOLOTOV AS SOON AS IT IS FIXED. WE ARE ANXIOUS FOR AN EARLY INTERVIEW.

At last Adolf Hitler had given Ribbentrop permission to pursue a German-Soviet political agreement with no further hesitations. He had become convinced that a pact was urgent; at any moment, the Anglo-French military delegation might arrive in Moscow and draw the Russians irrevocably into the democratic camp. Any qualms he might still have had about offending Japan, his Anti-Comintern partner in the Far East, were abandoned in face of this threat to the Reich.

■

All through July, Sir Nevile Henderson had been tapping his heels in the anterooms of the Foreign Ministry in Berlin wondering why no one listened to him. In fact, they had no need to, for he made it obvious to everyone he met that he was in complete accord with the German attitude toward Danzig and that he considered the Poles a bunch of upstarts. It was an odd standpoint for an ambassador whose country had undertaken to support the Poles in the event of war, but it might have been understandable had such evident sympathy with the German point of view given Henderson an entrée to the hierarchy of the National Socialist party. In fact, most of them despised him; in a country where bootlicking was a political necessity, they relieved their own humiliations by sneering at such foreigners who slobbered at the feet of the Führer.

For some time the Foreign Office had been urging Henderson to

297

have a "heart-to-heart talk" with Hitler and to put to him "point-blank" the "hard facts" of the situation. They had given a guarantee to Poland, and if Germany attacked, Britain would have to come to her aid. "Tell him just that," urged Sir Orme Sargent.

But how, when every attempt Henderson made to see the Reich Chancellor resulted in a snub? Not even Ribbentrop would talk to him any more.

At last Henderson had an idea. It was the end of July, and the Bayreuth Festival was about to begin. Adolf Hitler never failed to attend. Was not Wagner the composer *d'honneur* of the Nazi Revolution, and did not the Führer so cherish Wagner's daughter-in-law Winifred, an Englishwoman, that he always stayed with her during the festival? Then Henderson would go to Bayreuth himself, hope to catch Hitler's attention and "give him a talking to." "Though absolutely unmusical, I like Wagner," the ambassador pointed out. In his youth he had even learned all the leitmotifs of *The Ring*.

What Henderson did not know was that for most of the festival Adolf Hitler would be away. General Keitel took him on an inspection tour of the West Wall. "[It] was made as much for propaganda purposes as for inspecting actual construction progress . . ." wrote Keitel later. He did not include what subsequently went into the reports of the engineers: that the fortifications of the line were behind schedule and severely vulnerable, and that Hitler was aware of it. "The whole landscape is open to attack," he said at one point of his tour, "and we have no power to stop it." And then he added, "Except bluff! In some cases, bluff is more powerful than concrete!"

The Führer left western Germany on July 29 and went to stay overnight with Winifred Wagner. Like a converted Roman Catholic, she had become rather more Nazi than some of the party members,* and she always fed Hitler a strong brew of anti-British tea which he sipped avidly.

On the day before Hitler's return Winifred took pity on Henderson; she invited him for lunch and promised to do her best to bring them together. But she warned him that the Führer was in a curious mood. He had never really forgiven Chamberlain for having stiffened the opposition of the Poles. Without the British guarantee, there would have been no problem about Danzig; he knew this and it

---

* A fact which had caused her daughter, Friedelind, to leave Germany and take refuge in the West after Munich.

angered him. Moreover, Hitler was emotionally involved at the moment. It was this question of Unity Mitford. She was being foolish; she had heard rumors about another woman and was acting stupidly. It disturbed him; he had no time for females when they made a fuss.*

Nor did Hitler have time for the British envoy, as it turned out. Henderson spent the afternoon and evening of July 31 at a performance of *Die Walküre,* and in the long intermission he wandered in the woods behind the theater, listening to the good German burghers babbling in the distance, and hoping to be called to the presence. But all he caught was a glimpse of the Führer marching in for the last act; the Reich Chancellor did not even wave to him. Henderson returned to Berlin feeling rather like one of the Nibelungen.

■

For all the bets and raises between Moscow and Berlin, and the more hesitant calls from London and Paris, the game was not yet decided. Now it was Germany which was raising the ante; and at once the almost automatic reaction in Moscow was to hedge.

On July 30 *Izvestia,* the official government newspaper, observed the twenty-fifth anniversary of Russia's involvement in the World War with an editorial on its application to the present day. The U.S.S.R. had always stood "for the establishment of a genuine peace front capable of halting the further development of Fascist aggression, a peace front erected on a basis of full reciprocity, full equality, and honest, sincere and resolute repudiation of the fatal policy of 'nonintervention.' "

Was this a sign to the democracies that the game was still open? Neutral observers in Moscow were so certain of it that Harold Denny cabled to the *New York Times:* "The tone of the Soviet press . . . is so definitely pro-French and pro-British and so anti-German that neutral diplomats believe Moscow will sign the pact if that last gap—

* It was at about this time that Adolf Hitler had begun to let it be known beyond his intimate circle—at least to his party lieutenants—that Eva Braun was a permanent member of his household. Unity Mitford, a fervent Nazi and sister-in-law of the British fascist leader, Sir Oswald Mosley, had been in love with him for some time. Her infatuation had flattered Hitler, particularly since she had aristocratic parents, and he had put great faith in her views about British decadence. Now, however, he began to have doubts about her judgment and mental stability.

the definition of indirect aggression—can be bridged by a formula fully satisfying Moscow's strict demands."

But for the moment neither the British or French nor the Russians were trying to bridge the gap. The negotiating team of Strang, Seeds and Naggiar sensed that the pact was slipping away from them, but they lacked the stature, drive and authority to restore the situation. Because of the short-sightedness of the Foreign Office in London, the instructions they were given, and which Strang faithfully followed, had brought the talks to a stalemate—and all because of trivialities and debating points.

By the end of July, Molotov had made Russia's position plain. He was ready to conclude a pact of mutual assistance in the event of German aggression, to comprise all nations which had been guaranteed by the democracies. But he wanted the treaty to include a definition of two kinds of aggression, *direct* and *indirect*. What was "indirect aggression"? This was where the sterile arguments foundered. Russia declared that any Baltic state which turned Nazi or allied itself with Germany would be a victim of "indirect aggression";* this the Western allies would not accept because they thought it far too drastic.

The trouble was that the Anglo-French negotiators in Moscow and their myopic masterminds in London and Paris had got their priorities wrong. It was *they* who were asking for the alliance with Russia, *they* who needed it, *they* who must toe Russia's line. In the end, what did the interpretation of "indirect aggression" matter? The situation was there; if Russia wished to occupy a Baltic state because of "indirect aggression" by Germany according to the Russian interpretation, she could do so at any time and there was nothing France or Britain could do about it. So why argue?

But argue they did, with Molotov sourly lecturing Strang on his imprecision, staring down contemptuously at the three foreign capitalists from his desk on the dais until they reached stalemate. Both sides were now waiting for something to turn up—and that something was called the Anglo-French military mission. The face of smiling granite made the position clear: he was tired of theories and possi-

---

* Russia had made it clear that the nonaggression pacts Latvia and Estonia had signed with Germany (in June) did not constitute "indirect aggression"—not, that is, at the moment.

bilities and semantics; now he wanted facts. "If war comes with Germany, I wish to know exactly how many divisions each party will put into the field, and where they will be located," he declared.

Only the military mission could tell him that. Or could it?

William Strang had written to London about the military mission: "If we do start military conversations, and if it should be agreed that they are to take place in Moscow, it is desirable that we should send at least one officer of high rank to give them a start. The Russians will expect to be treated in the same kind of way as the French and not less well than the Poles. [General] Ironside's visit to Warsaw has been prominently reported in the Press here, and the Soviet Government would be offended if we did not send someone of the same rank here."

Strang might have added that it was also vitally important that the military mission arrive as quickly as possible.

But though he continued to protest publicly that he was pressing for a pact with the Russians, Neville Chamberlain was now stalling; he was in no hurry at all to make an agreement in Moscow. At this moment Europe was a miasma of ugly rumors and tensions, and one could almost hear the trouble simmering in Danzig and the Polish Corridor.

In such circumstances, and though he was perhaps skeptical about the chances of the military mission achieving anything, Chamberlain could at least have dressed up the delegation to make it look important and impress the Russians. In fact, he did just the opposite.

As the leader of their delegation the French chose General Joseph Edouard Doumenc, who, though sixty years old, was the nation's youngest general of the army, an expert on tactics and motorization, and a keen supporter of fresh ideas. He knew his job, recognized the need for a pact with Russia and was determined to get it. On July 31 he saw Daladier. The French Premier told him to return with an agreement at all costs, and the general promised that he would.

Doumenc was convinced that between them the British and the French could still do it—but this was before he heard who was to head the British delegation. Admiral Sir Reginald Plunkett-Ernle-Erle-Drax was a sailor of great charm who had fought with bravery and distinction in the World War, but he was not even on the Naval Staff, and no one outside naval circles had ever heard of him before. One of the members of the French delegation, Captain André Beaufre, caught his caliber accurately enough in a polite sketch of him which he wrote later: "The Senior British officer was . . . tall, mild in expression, courteous and cold; he looked like a version of Admiral Rodney minus the wig. His speech, slow and hesitant, like that of all English people from good families, was held up even further by constant coughing due to a weak throat. Not very quick on the uptake because of his scrupulous mind, he possessed utter intellectual honesty and the will to negotiate with the Soviets in all frankness, but was baffled by the difficulties and complexity of the task which had been thrust upon him. Nevertheless, his personality was perfectly adapted to what was expected of him; Admiral Drax represented in the highest degree the traditions of England, and in putting him at the head of the Mission, his Government ensured that, in so delicate an operation with their Russian opposite numbers, the British delegation would always instinctively react with the same reflexes which had made the greatness of the British Empire."

The Russians would have phrased it somewhat differently, though the substance of their comment was probably the same.

On August 2 Sir William Seeds read out the names of Drax, Air Marshal Sir Charles Burnett and Major General T. G. G. Heywood to the Soviet Commissar, who made no comment at all but looked frigidly over the heads of the diplomats. Strang himself felt a chill as he looked up at those opaque blue eyes. He thought that Molotov had swallowed the last insult from the West; the contempt on his face was so obvious that it made Strang feel sheepish and want to look away.

The Soviet Commissar launched into another discussion about "indirect aggression" and then abruptly brought up a statement which had been made in the House of Commons a few days before by Undersecretary of State R. A. Butler, the Foreign Office spokesman, which seemed to imply that Russia was looking for an excuse to take over the Baltic States. Butler had not suggested anything of the kind—though it was certainly in his and his colleagues' mind—but the Russians had inferred it. "It is a gross misrepresentation of what we have in mind," said Molotov. He wagged his finger at Strang. "You appear to be deliberately misunderstanding us. Do you not trust the Soviet Union? Do you not think we are interested in security too? It is a grave mistake. In time, you will realize how great a mistake it is to distrust the government of the U.S.S.R." Then, as usual, he rose abruptly and walked through the open door into the next room. It was the last the negotiators saw of him. Strang left the following day for London to report, and never came back. Nor did Molotov.

But perhaps all was not lost. The Anglo-French military mission was on its way—on a slow boat from Tilbury, Essex.

"The natural wish would be to go by air," reported the *Times* of London on August 2. "But as the British and French missions are each taking at least twenty advisers, to travel by air would mean chartering a small armada."*

So the British government had chartered a liner instead. Not a fast liner, however, but an old packhorse of the British merchant marine named the *City of Exeter*. Its maximum speed was eleven knots, which meant that the voyage from Tilbury to Leningrad would take longer than a transatlantic crossing. The French delegation traveled by rail and sea to London and thence proceeded to Tilbury, and on August 5 the *Exeter* pulled out into the Thames and headed its bows for the North Sea, the Skagerrak, the Kattegat, the Baltic and Leningrad.

In Moscow, the Anglo-French negotiators waited and fretted while Molotov was holding conversations with the German ambassador.

Would the posse arrive in time? At this point the British and French public regarded the dispatch of the military delegation in terms of an old-fashioned Western. Democracy was in danger, but out on the North Sea the rescuers were on their way—though slowly, and un-ruffled as well. "On board the *City of Exeter*," reported Captain Beaufre, "life was very agreeable, punctuated by copious repasts of curry served by Indian stewards in turbans." There was shuffle-

---

* Inaccurate. Even in 1939 it was possible to get thirty or even more people on an aircraft.

303

board on deck, tea-dancing in the lounge and a deck tennis tournament between the two delegations which was won by Admiral Plunkett-Ernle-Erle-Drax.

But there was work too. Each day the delegations met in what was normally the children's playroom to discuss the tactics they would adopt once they were face to face with the Russians. It was here that the French got a shock. Were the English really seeking an agreement—or a stalemate? The British instructions had been forwarded to the French in a memorandum an inch thick, "which examined every facet of the problem without producing any ideas as to directive," wrote Beaufre. "It was recommended that we should proceed only with the utmost prudence, never pass over any information [to the Russians], bear in mind constantly that German-Soviet collusion was possible, and above all to spin out the negotiations as long as we could.

"It appears that the British had no illusions as to the outcome of the conversations which they were about to open, and that they were above all anxious to gain time."

What the British did not realize, of course, was that the Germans already knew exactly what they were thinking. On July 28, days before the military delegations had even boarded their slow boat, Ambassador von Welczeck cabled Ribbentrop from Paris: "If at this moment Great Britain and France prepared to enter into military conversations before reaching political understanding and further pursuing the idea of military conversations with particular ardor, it is due to the following consideration: a) Great Britain and France desirous at any costs of avoiding any adjournment or rupture of negotiations because they believe that so long as these negotiations continue, Germany will make no move toward Danzig . . ."

Three days later Ambassador von Dirksen cabled from London: ". . . The Wehrmacht attachés are agreed in observing a surprising skepticism in British military circles about the forthcoming talks with the Soviet armed forces."

Ribbentrop had taken steps accordingly. While the *City of Exeter* was still taking on supplies, he followed up his previous urgent messages to Count von der Schulenburg with an equally eager missive: "Yesterday I had a lengthy conversation with Astakhov . . . I expressed the *German* wish for remolding German-Russian relations and stated that from the Baltic to the Black Sea there was no problem which could not be solved to our mutual satisfaction. In response to Astakhov's desire for more concrete conversations on topical questions . . . I declared myself ready for such conversations if the Soviet government would inform me through Astakhov that they also desired to place German-Russian relations on a new and definitive basis."

The pilotfish, such as Astakhov and Schnurre, were moving out of the game, and the sharks were taking over.

On August 9, 1939, the *City of Exeter* trundled through the pearly waters of the Gulf of Finland into the port of Leningrad. It was eleven o'clock at night when the ship entered the harbor, but the sky was still pale pink and the glow of it fell on the formal uniforms of the British and French delegates, who had decided to dress for dinner on their last night at sea. They leaned against the railing and looked down on the shabby civilians and ill-kempt soldiers on the dock while the Indian crew warped in the ship. "It would be difficult," wrote Beaufre, "to find a neater picture to sum up the difference between the two worlds which were now to confront one another."

The Anglo-French delegation stayed on board that night and then entrained for Moscow, where they arrived the following afternoon. On the evening of the eleventh, a reception was given for them by Marshal Klementy E. Voroshilov, the head of the Soviet military delegation, at his headquarters in the old Czarist palace called the Spiridonovka.* They entered a great gothic room modeled on Westminster Hall in London, with an oak ceiling and a huge fireplace, and were seated at a vast horseshoe table at which all the silverware, glasses and linen bore the arms of the Czar. The British were in dress uniform with all medals flying, as were the Russians. Only the French felt out of place; no one had warned them, and they wore plain khaki. The peacock of the occasion was Voroshilov's aide, Marshal Budyenny, in a white-flannel dress uniform and high white boots.

The two delegations dined long and well. For three hours they toasted their three countries, and then moved into a large white apartment called the Music Room, this one copied from Versailles. The cigar smoke drifted up to the ceiling and the brandy flowed. A little

---

* Spiridonovka was also known as the Frunze House, after Voroshilov's predecessor, Marshal Frunze.

old man with a gray beard and ancient dinner jacket appeared, a sort of Czarist gnome, and proceeded to announce the entertainers: singers, violinists, acrobats and conjurers.

Late that night the delegates staggered back to their hotel, full of too much food and wine and vodka, thinking that perhaps everything would turn out all right. The Russians were obviously being cordial; evidently the posse had arrived in time.

The next morning they awoke to the hangovers.

FOUR

Moment
of Truth

XIII

The Walrus

When he returned to his house in West Berlin on August 1, Paul Stehlin found a message to call Frau Riegele. That evening he drove over to see her. She was distrait and preoccupied, and the halls and corridors of her house were piled with half-filled suitcases. "I wanted you to know," she said, "that I shall be leaving next week for Bavaria."

"But I thought you were spending your vacation in the north?"

"No. Not any more. Hermann thinks it better that I go to our place in Bavaria. I shall be out of the way there if—" Olga did not finish the sentence but went on, "Hermann is very nervous. He doesn't like the way things are going."

Indeed, Göring did not. He was Hitler's heir presumptive, but only at the end of July had he heard definite details of the way the negotiations were going with Russia, and they infuriated him. He hated the Reds and believed that it would be fatal for Germany to make a pact with them. He was even more disturbed by the fact that the negotiations with Moscow were being handled by his worst enemy, Joachim von Ribbentrop, who would gain all the kudos should an agreement be reached. Added to which, he did not want war; he suspected that Ribbentrop did, and that only by a peaceful arrangement with England could it be averted.

311

The Field Marshal appreciated the paradoxes of the situation. Ribbentrop would welcome war, but insisted that Britain and France would never fight; he himself wanted peace but was convinced that the Western allies would go to war if they were pushed too far. It was essential to persuade Britain, who he realized was the dominant partner in the West, to sit down and talk, and to keep the discussions going until an arrangement could be made. After all, what were the differences between Germany and Britain—Danzig? The Polish Corridor? Henderson had already made it plain that these were not corners of a foreign field for which the English were willing to fight and die. It was only a question of getting a dialogue going.

Which is where Birger Dahlerus came in. By this time he was known to the Foreign Office in London by the code name "the Walrus." The Walrus had been busy in the last week of July flitting between London, Berlin, Stockholm and Schleswig-Holstein, preparing for the meeting which was scheduled for August 7. Göring was taking the meeting seriously, for he believed that there was now no other way to maintain contact with the British government. Henderson was too hysterical, and Chamberlain and his advisers were too vulnerable to risk personal involvement.

In the meantime, six British businessmen who had been approved by the Foreign Office were briefed by Halifax as to exactly what they should say when they met the Germans. The line they were to take was that this time Germany should not underestimate the British; they had given a guarantee to Poland, and they would fulfill their pledge. But they were also to stress a willingness on the part of the government to talk and listen.

It was on this frail reed that Göring was relying to convince Hitler that neither war nor a German-Soviet pact was necessary. Unfortunately, the events of August 4 intervened.

For some time it had been obvious to any objective observer that the Nazis in the Free City of Danzig were in the process of taking over. There was, in fact, little attempt to hide any of the preparations being made on the outskirts of the territory. Workmen on the riverbanks and roads freely admitted the military nature of their labor. A member of the General Staff in Berlin, General Eberhardt of the

1st Corps, had arrived with his aides, and masquerading as a visiting businessman, was organizing the Danzig Home Army (*Heimwehr*). A clumsy floating landing stage, drawn by a tug, still carried the daily bus across the river Vistula from East Prussia into Danzig, but downstream at Rothebude a pontoon bridge had been built and was ready to swing into place.

"All approaches to hills and dismantled fort, which constituted a popular public promenade on western fringe of city, have been closed with barbed wire and '*Verboten*' notices," cabled the British consul general to the Foreign Office. "The walls surrounding the ship-yards bear placards 'Comrades, keep your mouths shut or you will regret the consequences.' "

The dockyards, particularly the large German yard owned by the Schichau shipbuilding company, were the main bases now for the reception of smuggled arms, especially tanks and heavy guns. The method of delivery was simple, reported Major Cartillieri of the Abwehr. Ships were loaded with arms in Stettin, in Germany proper, with papers made out for shipment to Königsberg, in East Prussia, on the opposite side of the Polish Corridor. "Engine trouble develops in the vicinity of Danzig and forces the steamers to make port in Danzig and to moor at the Schichau shipyard. At night busy activity starts in the yard, because only at night can the precious cargo be unloaded. In this way the equipment comes through 'night work' to Danzig and is smuggled away, from horseshoe nails to 15-cm. guns, from barbed wire and posts to armed reconnaissance cars."

Cartillieri further reported: "Poland asks questions and Poland clamors in all her newspapers. Poland threatens to pulverize Danzig. Poland moves additional troops and tanks to Danzig border. Highest state of alarm in Polish army, and over and over, repeated reports of imminent Polish surprise attack on Danzig—that is the gist of the intelligence at the moment when the Eberhardt Heimwehr is being formed. Add to this the fact that the mobilized Polish soldier in the forests along the Danzig border is getting impatient because he cannot understand the purpose of remaining inactive while his family leads a wretched life at home. For it is not only the active troops who are in readiness but already several classes of recruits have been con-scripted."

Why don't the Poles attack? Cartillieri asked rhetorically, and

313

then answered his own question: "Poland does not march because England does not permit it. Time and time again we hear this report from reliable agent sources."

It was true that by this time Lord Halifax was urging the Poles not to let themselves be provoked. But for once they did not need to be told; Colonel Beck was behaving very coolly. Precautions had been taken, and bridges leading into Poland from Danzig had been mined. There was a spit of land in a commanding position at the mouth of the Vistula called Westerplatte, which was only two miles away from the great Lutheran cathedral and the Hanseatic houses of central Danzig. Westerplatte had always been extraterritorially Polish and had formerly held a garrison of eighty-two men, but now it was being secretly reinforced with men and guns. Arms had also been smuggled into the Polish post office, the commissioner's office and the railway station.

But Beck had no intention of attacking Danzig, for he still believed that commercial reprisals would bring the burghers of Danzig to heel. Toward the end of July he threatened to ban imports of Danzig margarine and herring into Poland if the harassment of the customs posts and frontier guards continued. Greiser, the president of the Danzig Senate, sent a sharp note to the Polish commissioner, Chodacki, threatening countermeasures and refusing to recognize the Polish border guards. On August 1 Beck's sanctions were imposed. For the next three days Greiser swallowed his anger, but on August 4 he picked up his telephone and began to bark out orders.

That afternoon an SS sergeant and a score of Nazi police drove up to each of the four customs houses on the East Prussian border. To the inspectors at each post a Polish-speaking Nazi delivered a curt ultimatum: the customs personnel must be reduced by two-thirds, and the frontier guards must be removed. If they were not gone by 7 P.M. on August 6—in just forty-eight hours—the Nazi police would return and throw them out by force.

The police returned to their cars and the Polish inspectors rushed to their telephones.

The news reached Warsaw on the evening of August 4. Józef Beck went at once to see Marshal Smigly-Rydz. A firm reply was in order, he believed. He was sure that the Nazis were bluffing, and that it would be fatal not to call their hand.

Smigly-Rydz agreed, but thought it would be wise to inform

314

London and Paris, just in case. On Beck's instructions, Chodacki sent a note to Greiser the same evening which was as tough as the Poles could make it. The situation could not be tolerated; immediate action must be taken. Poland demanded a note from the Senate president to the effect that he cancel the order by August 5 at 6 P.M. At the same time, all Polish customs officers and frontier guards were ordered into uniform, and the Nazis were informed that any action against them would be regarded "as an act of violence against Polish state officials in discharge of their official duties" and that reprisals would follow.

When Dr. Carl Burckhardt, the High Commissioner in Danzig, heard about the note, he dashed across the road at once to the Senate Building, where he found Greiser halfway through a bottle of schnapps, staring at the document. It was one o'clock in the morning, and the Nazi was in a belligerent mood, but the Commissioner sensed that he was frightened too. He had taken the action against the customs posts without first consulting Berlin, and now he wondered if he had gone too far.

That was a foolish and unnecessary crisis, Burckhardt told him. It should never have been allowed to happen. Why was such an order given? Greiser explained that it was a misunderstanding. They had gone beyond his orders; he never meant an ultimatum to be given.

Then Greiser must make that clear at once to the Poles, Burckhardt said, and reply at once to that effect.

Greiser banged his fist on the note. And apologize to those swine after they dared write to the Germans like that? Never! They had insulted the Germans. Their noses should be rubbed in their own shit.

Did Greiser have authority from Berlin for taking this attitude? Burckhardt asked. Greiser said that nobody could make him write an apology to such scum.

Then telephone, Burckhardt advised.

Greiser picked up the telephone and called the Polish commissioner's office. There followed a long and complicated conversation in which Greiser explained that his orders had been misinterpreted by "irresponsible elements" and that there had been no intention of creating violence at the frontier posts. Chodacki frigidly demanded that the Nazi put the words in writing. Greiser hesitated and then said that he could not do this; all sorts of technicalities were involved. Anxious not to exacerbate the situation, Chodacki replied that he would not press for a written reply but would ask his government in Warsaw to treat Greiser's explanation as "a *note verbale*."

Beck was overjoyed when he heard the news; the bluff had been called. But the Nazis were not going to get off the hook that easily. "A verbal explanation is not acceptable," he told Chodacki. "I want a written note—or else."

He got it, for by this time Berlin had been consulted. Knowing that Germany was not ready for a crisis and absorbed in his pursuit of a Russo-German Pact, Ribbentrop had no time for gnat bites; he brushed the whole affair aside with instructions to Greiser to write an apology.

There the affair might have ended, had it not been for the fact that Danzig at the time was full of correspondents from all over the world who promptly reported the fact that the Nazi-controlled Danzig Senate had retreated before an ultimatum from the Poles. From there the commentators took over; National Socialism and Adolf Hitler had suffered a defeat, they said. Germany's bluff had been called, and they had ignominiously crawled before a threat of force.

"What did I tell you!" exclaimed Józef Beck. "Stand up to the Nazis! Don't give an inch! They'll back down every time."

Rarely had he made a more dangerous mistake.

In Cracow on August 6 there was a parade of veterans of Pilsudski's armies, the men who had wrested Poland back from the Russians twenty-five years before. It was a day of feverish celebration, and the keyed-up crowd cheered Marshal Smigly-Rydz to the skies as he declared, "No one is going to infringe Poland's rights and interests. Anyone who attempts to do so will be repelled by force. No one is going to take Danzig from us. She has been united with Poland for centuries and she will stay united!"

The next day the Cracow *Czas,* usually a temperate newspaper, wrote: "Let the Nazis try to effect a *fait accompli* in Danzig, and Polish guns will speak!"

At Berchtesgaden, Adolf Hitler flung to the floor the press clippings which Dr. Otto Dietrich had handed him. He was livid. He would stand it no longer, he said. This time the Poles had gone too far! From now on, they would regret it. He swung around toward Dietrich. He wanted stories in the newspapers, he commanded—every day more and more. Stories about atrocities committed by the Poles against the German people, stories about corruption in Warsaw and what incompetent pigs their rulers were. He wanted his Germans to know the Polish people as they really were: a bastard race, not fit to have a country of their own.

It was dangerous to humiliate Adolf Hitler. He reacted like a madman—but a cunning one.

■

In the circumstances, the meeting under the aegis of Birger Dahlerus between Hermann Göring and his British guests was not off to a propitious start. On August 6, at the height of the Danzig scare, Dahlerus was driving the British businessmen from Hamburg to Bredstedt in a convoy of cars flying Swedish flags, and at Berchtesgaden the Führer was screaming imprecations at Gauleiter Albert Forster. How dare he allow Germany to be humiliated? the Führer shouted. Forster had made it appear as if Germany had crawled to the Poles. Never, never, never! The Gauleiter must return to Danzig and let the world know that Germany would not be stopped. More— he should let it be known that the Reich would take Poland too, because the Poles were not fit to rule their own country!

The following morning was bright and sunny in Schleswig-Holstein. Dahlerus had slept in a nearby hotel in order to give his guests more room, but he was back in his house at eight o'clock to make sure that they all enjoyed a real English breakfast. He also went out to the garden to hoist the Swedish flag. They were in Germany, but so far as he was concerned this was now "Swedish, and therefore neutral, territory." Then he drove to the station at Bredstedt.

The British had come in secret, each delegate traveling separately to Hamburg in order to avoid the inquisitiveness of the press, but the Field Marshal did Dahlerus proud. He arrived by special train, and included in his entourage were Paul Körner, head of Göring's Four-Year Plan; General Bodenschatz; and Dr. Schrötter to act as interpreter. As the two friends drove back toward the house where the British were waiting, the Field Marshal remarked that he had only one object in mind: Anglo-German conversations on a high level.

317

At lunch Dahlerus made a speech of welcome; Göring replied with a toast to the English people, and followed this by asking the delegates to rise and drink a toast to peace. They all solemnly did so, and then the Field Marshal proceeded to defend German policy. "You want decency and order in Europe and the world. But it is the fault of the British government that there is none. Why do you not have the strength to make it clear exactly how you stand? In 1936 there was the crisis with Italy over Abyssinia. The German government of Adolf Hitler was ready to help you there. We offered to support sanctions against Italy, and had we been at your side, they would have been effective. All we asked in return was that the Reich should have a free hand in her affairs with Austria. But what happened? Germany was turned down. Abyssinia was conquered by the Italians. Austria became German anyway."

The leader of the British party was Charles Spencer. He had been well briefed, and he replied, "That is all over now. So are the hesitations of the British government. We have definitely decided that we will not stomach any further aggressions in Europe."

"But are you ready to talk?" Göring asked. "And are you willing to admit that the situation in Europe is different now? Germany is a great power and must be reckoned with as such, and don't forget that her policy is constantly changing. It must have been noticed even in England that lately Germany has abstained from all criticism of the Soviet Union."

Spencer said, "We are agreed that there should be talks."

Göring shook hands all around, expressed cordial feelings toward England and departed for his special train, which was to take him by the causeway to the island of Sylt for the night. There Dahlerus telephoned him the next morning to say that the Englishmen had spent the night discussing the situation. They were now strongly in favor of a conference, but they felt that it should be a Four Power rather than a Two Power conference, with Italy and France invited. Göring replied that Bodenschatz had already left for Berchtesgaden to report on the meeting to the Führer, but that he would get in touch with him there.

The Englishmen assembled their notes, motored back to Hamburg and then flew to London, while Dahlerus set off for Berlin. In the next three days, like the beaver he was, he toiled strenuously at building the dam which he was convinced could halt the rush to war.

318

He spent hours on the telephone talking to Spencer in London and to Göring at the Haus der Flieger and at Karinhall. The Field Marshal was no less active. The meeting had convinced him once and for all that this time the British were not bluffing, and that if Germany marched into Poland the Western allies would fulfill their pledges to Warsaw. But if he could get them around a table at the kind of Four Power conference which they had suggested, Germany would obtain everything she wanted anyway.

All this the Field Marshal put to the Führer. Adolf Hitler listened sourly; Ribbentrop, he interjected, insisted that the British and French would never stand by Poland whatever happened, and he was inclined to believe him. The decadence of the democracies would be beyond belief were it not for the evidence of it confronting them on every side.

But Göring insisted that the Englishmen whom Dahlerus had introduced him to were well briefed and sincere. He believed them, and in any case, what was the harm in talking, especially if Mussolini were present to help once again? The Field Marshal evidently relished the thought of another Munich, especially if he could play an even more prominent part in it this time.

At last Hitler agreed. If the British wished to talk, fine—as long as Germany got what it wanted from Poland.

Göring rushed to the telephone to inform Dahlerus that in principle the Führer had accepted the idea of a Four Power conference in Sweden. There was no talk of secrecy this time. Dahlerus immediately informed Spencer in London and then sped to Stockholm to see Per Albin Hansson, the Swedish Premier, to ask him to act as host to the conferees. The Walrus was happy and his hopes were high.

But as the days passed and no reply came from London, Dahlerus' spirits sagged. Finally he tried to telephone Spencer in London and was told he was on vacation in Aix-les-Bains. When he reached him there and asked what was happening, the Englishman was hesitant. At last he said, "It is very difficult to get a decision, you see. All the important people are away on holiday."

In London, Parliament had adjourned on August 3, despite the protests of scores of members, particularly Winston Churchill. Pressed to summon M.P.'s back from their holidays in the event of an emergency, Neville Chamberlain had given an evasive reply, and then departed for grouse shooting in Scotland.

319

■

"Emile* is going through a crisis. The courtiers cringe every time he comes out of his room," reported Admiral Canaris to Erich Kordt in the second week of August. "It seems he can't make up his mind."

Adolf Hitler's mood was an ugly one. At one moment he would roar with rage and hurl imprecations at the Poles; at the next he would sit in grim silence, hands on his stomach, brooding like a gray bird.

On August 8 the Führer had received Count István Csáky, the Hungarian Foreign Minister, and shouted at him, "We will not only smash the Polish army but we will smash the Polish state too!"

He began to rave about Polish bestiality toward the German minority in Poland. "I have not yet permitted publication of the fact that Germans have been castrated by the Poles†—it would cause too much of an uproar. As it is, the German people already find the attitude of the Poles impossible." He waved his fist in Csáky's face. "Do you have any idea what the mood of the German army is at this moment? The Poles deride them in their newspapers; Beck mocks them. I'm glad about this. It means that the German army can hardly wait to get their hands on the Poles and would be terribly disappointed if they yielded to reason."

On August 11 Hitler talked to Dr. Carl Burckhardt, who had been brought south from Danzig in Hitler's own plane. There were rumors that Burckhardt was pro-Nazi, but it would be more accurate to say that he had an antipathy toward the Poles. Like some United Nations commissioners of a later date, he found the going difficult but did his best to resist the bullying from both sides. There was little to choose between their methods, but possibly because he was a bourgeois German-speaking Swiss and understood the nuances of the language, he may have been more sympathetic to the Germans in Danzig than to the excitable Slavs.

Burckhardt spent two and a half hours with Hitler and reported later that he found him "nervous, pathetic, almost shaken at times."

* "Emile" was the Abwehr chief's nickname for Hitler.
† Hitler had a curious obsession about castration, and always demanded "castration stories" in the Nazi press when a propaganda campaign reached its height. The explanation may lie in his own equivocal sexual status: though no one knows for sure, it has been rumored that he was impotent.

320

The Führer left no doubt in the mind of the Swiss professor that he had been mortally insulted by the crowing from the West and from Warsaw over recent events in Danzig. Beck had dared to boast that he had won a war of nerves at the expense of the German government, said Hitler, and the foreign press declared that the Reich had lost the war of nerves! They were even saying in Warsaw that the only reason why the German bluff had not been called the year before was that then it was the Czechs who were involved, but that this time it was the Poles with whom he had to deal—and that this made all the difference. Smacking his hand in his fist, as he always did at these moments, Hitler cried, "They will see! They will see!" From this moment on, if the Poles tried anything, *anything,* he would fall on them like a bolt of lightning, and they could not conceive what kind of blows they would receive.

Burckhardt pointed out that this surely would mean a general conflict, which was not, he hoped, what the Führer had in mind.

Hitler declared that he had no intention of waging war like Kaiser Wilhelm, who had always been too finicky and scrupulous about the way he employed his forces in the World War. But he, the Führer, would fight to the last, and without mercy. Why should he be concerned? Italy and Japan were ready to fight beside Germany. In the West he could count on sixty divisions* to contain the Allies while he annihilated the Poles. That would take three weeks . . .

Burckhardt asked why it was necessary to go to such extremes. Surely the Führer realized that the democracies were ready to settle all these matters by negotiation?

Why did they go on inciting the Poles if they wished to negotiate? asked Hitler. Why did they give them guarantees? What could be better for Poland than the offer he had given them last March? Instead, the democracies encouraged them to be arrogant. What was their excuse for it? He laughed. The Poles were insane, and so were those who encouraged them. Now, if it were the Czechs, then he could understand. Since they took over Czechia the Germans had come to understand why those people had been so intransigent. Their army was in excellent condition, their equipment modern and well maintained, and the General Staff knew what it was doing. He laughed again. The Poles! He knew exactly what their army consisted of. He

---

* In actual fact, German forces in the West were very much weaker than this: twenty divisions at the most.

had their plans! He had known them for months! The plans were inferior and their technical equipment inadequate. The Polish army already had the mark of death stamped on its countenance.* Arrogance, sheer arrogance—that was all that motivated the Poles.

At this point Hitler's mood suddenly changed. From the nervously incensed opponent of the Poles, he became the apostle of Western solidarity against the menace from the East. A reasonable solution was still possible, he told Burckhardt. These things could be arranged. He would refrain from interfering with the Poles provided that they were sensible, left Danzig and his people there alone, and let the Germans in Poland live in peace. His eyes blazing at Burckhardt, Hitler added that everything he was planning was fundamentally aimed at Russia. If the West were so stupid and so blind as to attack Germany, he would be forced to join with Russia in order to annihilate the West. Then, with the power he had gained from this, he would attack Russia in turn and bring the Ukraine into the German orbit.

It was a startling statement, but Burckhardt did not seem to appreciate its significance. After leaving Berchtesgaden, he immediately proceeded to his home in Basel, where he summoned the British and French ministers and gave them a summary of his conversation with the Führer.

Historians have since wondered why Hitler's remarks about Russia were not included in the dispatches which the envoys subsequently sent to their governments. Did Chamberlain and Daladier suppress them?

Not in this case. The explanation is simple: Burckhardt thought Hitler's remarks were so far-fetched that he did not consider them worthy of mention to the foreign envoys. A German-Russian pact was simply too absurd to contemplate.†

* It was not the first time Hitler used this phrase; he had said it three days before to Count Csáky.

† Some historians have other theories, even suggesting that Burckhardt invented the passage about Russia for his memoirs. This seems most unlikely. My own talks with Burckhardt convince me that though he may at times have been more pro-German than his position as High Commissioner warranted, he was an honest man and a conscientious historian—most unlikely to distort history for the sake of effect.

322

XIV

Stalin Makes Up His Mind

On the morning of August 12, 1939, the first session of the Anglo-French-Russian military talks opened in the Spiridonovka Palace in Moscow. To the satisfaction of everyone save Admiral Plunkett-Ernle-Erle-Drax, the atmosphere was completely different from the frigid formality of the political meetings with Molotov. The delegates arranged themselves around a huge table in no particular order of precedence, and as time passed, more and more secretaries were brought into the room in order to get everything down in French, English and Russian.

To the dismay of Drax's aide-de-camp, who was anxious about the admiral's weak throat, everyone followed Marshal Voroshilov's example and smoked almost continuously. At first Drax coughed quietly with a patient smile, but he was soon registering obvious annoyance as a Frenchman or Russian blew smoke in his direction.

To the English the opening of the conference was inauspicious, for Marshal Voroshilov immediately rose and solemnly read out the credentials of the Soviet mission, which gave them "the power to sign military agreements for the maintenance of peace and against aggression." Turning first to General Doumenc and then to Admiral Drax, he asked them to indicate what powers were vested in them for the purpose of the negotiations.

323

Doumenc looked nonplused for a moment but improvised quickly. He presented his orders, signed by Daladier; happily, they contained a phrase saying that he had "authority to negotiate on all military questions." Though he certainly had no power to sign anything, the phrase seemed to satisfy the Russians.

Voroshilov then turned to the English admiral, who began to cough more than ever, obviously very ill at ease. He had to admit that he had no written instructions. On the other hand, he added, it must be obvious to the Soviet mission that his government would hardly send a mission if it was not given the power to act. But no, he had nothing on paper.

Voroshilov, who was not one of the world's most flexible or intelligent soldiers ("He would have made a good sergeant major in anyone else's army," one military attaché commented), looked shocked and angry. After conferring with General Boris M. Shaposhnikov, his Army Chief of Staff, he rose and said that he regretted that the Soviet mission had been placed in such a position that it was negotiating with delegations which had no powers.

Doumenc answered that perhaps he should explain that so far as their two countries were concerned, military missions did not negotiate treaties; they merely recommended certain points of agreement to their governments. But he could rest assured that they would press on and work hard . . .

Voroshilov conferred again, and then reluctantly agreed to continue the conversations. But almost at once he shocked the Western delegate again by demanding that they reveal in detail their plan of action for the common defense of the three countries against aggression. "We have a complete outline, down to detailed figures," he pointed out. "Have the French and British missions plans and propositions for the defense of our country? We have some proposals to make on this subject; but we hope that the military authorities and the governments of France and Great Britain have a plan, because we have some delicate matters to discuss and because hitherto political negotiations have not gone well, precisely because of the absence of any positive thinking. We need to know from the start the plans which have been made by Great Britain and France with Poland and Turkey, etc. . . ."

Admiral Drax began to cough again, not simply because of the cigarette smoke. This was just the kind of question he was hoping would not be asked, and one he had instructions to avoid answering. Of course, it was also a question which exposed the simmering suspicions existing between the West and the Russians. "This comedy of laying military secrets on the table," Captain Beaufre was to write later, "considerably worried both France and Great Britain. It was felt again and again that the Soviet had organized the conference in order to obtain, on the eve of war, an idea of our plans, and then, naturally, to pass them on to Germany."

In fact, the Russians had decided no such thing—not yet. Though they were tempted, Stalin and the Politburo of the Supreme Soviet of the U.S.S.R. still had not made a decision.*

The Politburo had met in the Kremlin on August 11, the previous day, with a report from Marshal Voroshilov before them. The report made a scathing attack on the vagueness and incompetence of the Allied delegates, particularly the British, and asked for guidance.

To Josef Stalin, it was not so much a question of giving guidance to his military mission as of taking the right road himself. The problem was pressing. Should he ally himself with the Western powers in what might prove to be a war against Germany? Or should he make a pact with Germany which would keep Russia neutral, though it would also provoke an attack by Germany on Poland and might subsequently involve Britain and France?

Practically speaking, there was no doubt what the Soviet Union should do, as Stalin saw it. From an association with Germany, Russia could hardly lose—with certain provisos. For what would be the immediate result of a Russo-German agreement? First, German troops would take Danzig and the Polish Corridor; then they would probably move into Poland itself and occupy the whole country. Stalin had no illusions about the extent of Hitler's ambitions. However, this would bring the German armies to the frontiers of the Soviet Union—and this he did not want at all.

Molotov told Stalin that there was no need to worry about this. He had talked to Ambassador von der Schulenburg, who had not yet made specific suggestions, but had said that the Germans were ready to make a deal: there would be a buffer state between Germany and the U.S.S.R.

* The Politburo is the supreme policy-making organ of the Communist party.

325

Stalin wished to know whether the Germans could be pinned down on this question. Would it be a good idea to open conversations of a political nature with them?

Molotov thought it would. There would be no arguments; the Germans were in a great hurry.

Then, as if to stifle some inner qualms, Stalin pointed out how much better it was to avoid involvement with the Western democracies. They were weak and uncertain, they could not be trusted, and anyway, he didn't believe they would fight.

Molotov said he had evidence that the democracies were already negotiating with the Germans for another Munich. There had been conversations with Wohltat in London, and now secret talks were going on in Denmark (an obvious reference to the discussions initiated by Dahlerus on the Danish border). They had no intention of keeping their guarantees with Poland; they would come around.

But if they did not? asked Stalin.

That was for the Politburo to decide, replied Molotov.*

However, the Politburo had made no decision on this problem on August 11; instead, it was resolved to keep the two alternatives open. Both Germany and the Western allies now needed the help of the Soviet Union, and it was a nice position to be in. For years they had been insulted and humiliated by both sides; now they would play hard to get. From Stalin's point of view, there was plenty of time.

However, Adolf Hitler had decided that there was no time at all, not any more. By August 12 he apparently had made up his mind, and he made the position clear to Hermann Göring: if the British and French decided that they would like to talk, or the Poles decided that they would be reasonable over Danzig and the Corridor, well and good. In the meantime, he was convinced that this was the moment of Germany's destiny. He would move east, and damn the consequences. (To be sure, he believed that the consequences were not really likely to be serious, for Britain and France would not dare stand up to him.)

This was the beginning of a period of elation for Adolf Hitler. Only twenty-four hours before, he had convinced Carl Burckhardt

* I have been asked not to specify the source of this information, which reached Ambassador Steinhardt through German channels.

326

that he was "nervous, pathetic, almost shaken at times," but when Count Ciano saw him on August 12 he was bursting with self-confidence and serenely determined to follow a course of action which had obviously been decided already.

The Italian Foreign Minister had come from Rome in a mood of fraught anxiety which was shared by his father-in-law, Benito Mussolini. For too long they had gone on believing what they had been told at the time of the signing of the Pact of Steel: that there was plenty of time, that eventually there would be war with the democracies, but that the confrontations would not come until the public, the economy and the military were prepared—in other words, not until 1942 or 1943.

Ambassador Attolico in Berlin had warned his government several times that it was living in a fool's paradise. His messages had become urgent toward the end of July: German troops were mobilizing; the whole city was filled with rumors; Poland was to be attacked. At length, Mussolini was sufficiently impressed to suggest to Hitler that they meet and discuss the situation, but he was brushed off.

Not that the Italians really believed that Hitler had made up his mind. Surely he would have consulted Italy first—a naïveté in view of the fact that he had not done so in the case of Czechoslovakia and Memel. However, eventually it was decided that Ciano should go north to see Ribbentrop and the Führer to find out what was going on, and that Signor Attolico and Count Massimo Magistrati of the Berlin embassy should join him there.

"The Duce is more than ever convinced of the necessity of delaying the conflict," Ciano wrote in his diary of August 10; "he himself has worked out the outline of a report concerning the meeting at Salzburg which ends with an allusion to international negotiations . . . Before letting me go, he recommends that I shall frankly inform the Germans that we must avoid a conflict with Poland, since it will be impossible to localize it, and a general war would be disastrous for everybody."

In point of fact, Galeazzo Ciano was incapable of frankly informing anyone of anything, except to tell a pretty girl that she was beautiful. He arrived at Ribbentrop's house in Fuschl on August 11 and spent the next ten hours in a conversation which chilled his marrow, for he was left in no doubt by Ribbentrop that an attack on Poland was imminent. Afterward he was to record the most telling exchange from their conversation, when he asked the German

Foreign Minister (they spoke English), "Well, Ribbentrop, what do you want, the Corridor or Danzig?"

"Not that any more," replied Ribbentrop. "We want war."

It was a reply deliberately meant to impress. The two men came from the same milieu, shared a lack of moral fiber and scruples, and despised each other. Since Ribbentrop was working for the stronger side, he felt no need to be polite to his opposite number. What did it matter? They drove to the White Horse Inn at St. Wolfgang for lunch, and so strong was their mutual antipathy that they found barely a word to say to each other. Ciano was terrified of what Germany was planning. At one moment, he ventured to suggest that the Reich was being rash in presuming that Britain and France would not intervene.

Ribbentrop looked at him contemptuously. "Perhaps you would like to make a wager on it?"

Ciano agreed. But what would be the stakes? It was eventually decided that Ciano would bet an Italian painting against a set of German armor that the Western allies would fulfill their obligations.* They continued to glower at each other throughout the rest of the meal. "*Siamo alle botte!*" (We are almost come to blows!) the Italian whispered at one point to Magistrati. He kept trying to glean precise details from his host about Germany's plans, but was waved away with the imperious remark, "All decisions are still locked in the impenetrable bosom of the Führer."

Ciano was scared. That evening he ordered an Italian guard to stand by his plane at the Salzburg airfield; so conscious was he of Ribbentrop's hostility that he feared sabotage. Later, when he, Attolico and Magistrati wanted to talk over their impressions, they went into Ciano's bathroom and turned on the taps; under the cover of this noise they discussed their relations with their German ally.

But if the Italian Foreign Minister was frightened on August 11, he was shattered on August 12 and 13. When the three Italian diplomats were shown into the Führer's study at Berchtesgaden, they found not only Ribbentrop and Schmidt, the interpreter, but an arrogant young man whom Ciano knew only too well. His name was Eugen Dollmann, and he was a Gestapo agent attached to the German embassy in Rome, where he specialized in assembling dos-

---

* Ribbentrop lost but never paid up, as Ciano bitterly reflected while waiting in the Verona prison in 1943 for his execution by the Fascists.

siers on the private lives of the Fascist ministers. Ciano was uncomfortably aware of what must have been recorded and conveyed to the Führer about him. Nor was he allowed to have his two companions bolster him during the interview; Hitler greeted them all with great friendliness but at once stated that what he had to say was for Ciano's ears alone. He rang a bell; a hulky man in SS uniform who came into the study was introduced as Martin Bormann and was told to take Attolico and Magistrati away and "entertain them."

After they withdrew, Hitler turned to the maps spread across his desk and on the walls. These were marked with German fortifications, the French and British defenses, Polish troop concentrations and the flying times between Germany and Warsaw, Paris and London. There followed a lecture on the military dispositions of the opposing powers. Ciano, who had never been much of a military man, listened to this with a certain detachment at first, but then he began to realize with growing horror that Adolf Hitler was not talking about a war in the distant future but one which might break out at any moment. The time to attack was now, the Führer began to make clear.

The quality of the Polish army varied greatly, he said. Besides several crack divisions, there were a number of inferior units. Poland was very weak in antiaircraft and antitank defense. At present France and England could not supply her. If, however, Poland was supplied economically by the West for a considerable time, she could acquire these weapons and Germany's superiority would be reduced . . . He left it to Ciano to draw the logical conclusion that therefore speedy action was necessary.

Ciano remarked that he was quite surprised to hear of the seriousness of the situation. Neither in the Milan talks, he said, nor during his visit to Berlin had any indication been given that the situation with regard to Poland was so grave. On the contrary, Herr von Ribbentrop had said that in his opinion the question of Danzig would be settled in due course. On the basis of this state of affairs the Duce had decided, true to his conviction that a conflict with the Western democracies was unavoidable all the same, to make his preparations for this eventuality in, say, two or three years. Ciano paused, and then added that if an immediate conflict was unavoidable, Italy would of course be on Germany's side. However, for various reasons Italy would strongly welcome a postponement of the general conflict, for she

329

believed that a conflict with Poland would not be restricted to that country alone; it would grow into a general European war.

Hitler replied loftily, "Opinions differ on that point. Personally, I am firmly convinced that the Western democracies will shy away in the end from precipitating a general war."

"I only hope you are right," answered Ciano. "I don't believe it."

Then, like a timid schoolboy trying to weasel out of a raid on an apple orchard by telling his fellows that he would love to go but his grandmother is ill, his father has told him to mow the lawn, and anyway, he has sprained his ankle, Ciano launched into a torrent of statistics to prove that Italy couldn't possibly engage in a war at this moment. By the time he finished, he had so successfully managed to convey the impression that his country was flat on its back that Ribbentrop burst out, "We don't need you!"

Nettled, Ciano answered, "Time will show."

The Italian now produced a draft communiqué which he had drawn up with Mussolini; this was written in poor and misspelled English and was brushed aside by Hitler. Ciano then suggested a conference, but this too was dismissed.

Once more the Führer terrified the Italian by talking of war. "There is no time to be lost in the solution of the Polish problem. The further we get into the fall, the harder military operations in Eastern Europe will be. The air force can hardly be employed at all after the middle of September in these regions because of the weather conditions. Motorized units will be unusable because of the condition of the roads—they turn to mud when the rains start in the fall. From September to May, Poland is one big swamp and absolutely unsuitable for any military operations. And there is the danger! Poland can simply take over Danzig in October—that is probably what she intends to do—and Germany won't be able to do anything about it. We cannot shell and destroy Danzig. It is too precious to us."

Ciano then ventured a question the answer to which he didn't really want to hear: "By what time, then, will the question of Danzig have to be settled, in your opinion?"

"One way or another, by the end of August."

Hitler then began to rail against Colonel Beck for having rejected his proposals earlier in the year. It was all due to the intervention of England, whose treaty had made the Poles arrogant and cocksure. "Poland's aims now can be read in her newspapers. They want to

330

occupy all of East Prussia, they want to advance on Berlin, and so on. It is unbearable that a great power should tolerate such a hostile neighbor only one hundred and fifty kilometers from her capital. So I have made up my mind. I will make use of the opportunity provided by the next [Polish] provocation, such as sending an ultimatum, brutally mistreating Germans, trying to starve out Danzig, or something similar, to attack Poland within forty-eight hours and solve the problem this way."

Here, as if to make sure that Ciano had the date imprinted on his mind, Hitler again stated that the matter would have to be settled "at the latest by the end of August. The decisive part of the military operations against Poland can be executed within two weeks, but the final liquidation will require another two to four weeks, and that brings us to the end of September or the beginning of October . . . The end of August must be set as the time limit."

The Italian Foreign Minister thanked the Führer for his candor, promised to convey his friendly wishes to Benito Mussolini, and fled back to Rome, his knees knocking.* "I return to Rome," he wrote in his diary on August 13, "completely disgusted with the Germans, with their Führer, with their way of doing things. They have betrayed us and lied to us. Now they are dragging us into an adventure which we do not want and which might compromise our regime and Italy too."

One of the first things Ciano did on reaching Rome was to contact the channel of communication which he had sporadically kept open with an intelligence department of the Foreign Office in London. To this source he leaked a digest of his conversations with Hitler, so that twenty-four hours later Vansittart was able to send the gist of it to Lord Halifax.

Thus the British also knew that the end of August was the deadline set by Adolf Hitler.

During the course of the conversation between Hitler and Ciano on August 12, a messenger had appeared with two telegrams. From the conversation between Ribbentrop and the Führer it soon became

---

* The conference had taken two days, and Ciano was to say later that only the bad news of the second made the first day's irritations bearable.

apparent that one was from Tokyo, the other from Moscow. Ribbentrop passed them over to Hitler, who read them through and then, with hardly an apology to Ciano, left the room with Ribbentrop. Shortly afterward they reappeared.

"It's a telegram from Moscow," Ribbentrop began, and Hitler went on, "The Russian government has agreed to the opening of political negotiations, and has asked for a minister to be sent."

They waited for Ciano to comment, but he said nothing. In truth, he didn't feel any comment was necessary; he was convinced that he was being bluffed, that this was all part of a Nazi scheme to galvanize the Italians and bring them in willingly on Germany's side in the disasters to come. As a result, like Burckhardt, he did not mention Hitler's plans for a pact with Russia in his communication to London.

There has been some confusion about this telegram. No copy of it has been found in the German archives,* and historians have therefore presumed that it never existed. On the other hand, what has been known until now is only that the Politburo of the Supreme Soviet met on August 11, but not that it gave a clear inference of the direction in which Stalin's mind was veering. There can be no doubt that German intelligence in the Soviet Union was very well informed. This is indicated by the fact that there was an anti-Nazi spy in the German embassy who kept the United States *au courant;* time and time again he revealed secrets of Kremlin thinking which were shrouded from other intelligence services.†

There certainly would have been sufficient time for the Germans to receive a report of the Politburo meeting by August 12, and to convey to the Führer its implicit agreement to open political conversations, but not time to more than hint at a Russian-German agreement to Burckhardt on August 11.

■

In the Spiridonovka Palace, the French and British military delegations quailed before the increasing intransigency of the Russians. Though they did not know it, they were reaching the moment of truth in their negotiations with the Soviet military mission. On their an-

---

* It should be pointed out that even now not all of the documents have been read and classified.
† See Notes for Chapter XVI at the end of this book.

swers and attitudes would depend whether there was to be peace or war in Europe.

It was August 14. In Rome Count Ciano had reported to his anxious father-in-law, and they were nervously wondering what to do next. Lord Halifax, the information from Ciano now in his hands, was drafting a telegram to the British ambassador in Warsaw, Sir Howard Kennard, instructing him to press Beck to make it plain to the Germans that "Poland was at all times ready to examine the possibility of negotiations over Danzig." A few hours later Beck made it clear that if "negotiations" meant the surrender of Danzig to Germany, his government would not co-operate. Neville Chamberlain was on holiday in Scotland. Sir Horace Wilson was in Bournemouth, his hometown, gazing over the white cliffs on the Channel, which divided England from the turbulent Continent. Winston Churchill was on his way to France to pay a visit to the Maginot Line defenses, which protected the Republic from Germany.

In the Spiridonovka Palace, General Doumenc had led the discussions so far for both France and Britain, though not without some interference from the Russians. As requested, he had specified what forces the French army would field in the event of conflict, but had skirted the truth so frequently that at one point Voroshilov said sharply, "Your talk is meaningless."

Admiral Plunkett-Ernle-Erle-Drax had little useful to say, and contented himself with assurances of the strength and fortitude of the British navy. Red-faced and furious, Voroshilov finally rose to his feet and said, "I ask once more, what action do the General Staffs of France and Great Britain consider the U.S.S.R. should take on land in the event of aggression against France, Poland, etc. . . . Let us not cloud the issue, we are now talking solely of land forces. I will put to you questions which will perhaps clarify my point of view—General and Admiral . . ."

Here came the vital questions, the answers to which the whole Politbureau of the Supreme Soviet was awaiting: "Will Poland accept the entry of Soviet troops in the Vilna Corridor* in order to make contact with the enemy; likewise, will Poland give our troops access to Galicia; likewise, will they allow them passage to get to Rumania? For our delegation these questions are cardinal to our negotiations."

* A narrow strip of Polish territory separating Soviet Russia from German East Prussia.

But these were the very questions which the British and French delegations had mutually agreed not to discuss, for both they and their governments knew that Poland would never allow Russian troops to enter her territory lest they subsequently refuse to leave. There was justification for this attitude; not twenty years earlier, Russian troops had been at the gates of Warsaw, and for a long time before that, Poles had felt the whips of Russian masters. As Marshal Pilsudski, the great Polish hero, had once put it, "With the Germans we risk the loss of our liberty, but with the Russians we lose our souls."

Moreover, though they masked it by an attitude of fervent anti-Communism, Poland had a guilt complex about Russia. When Russia was torn and weak from the birth pangs of the Revolution, the Poles had stolen large tracts of her territory. They knew that Russia wanted them back, if only as a buffer against the threat of Germany.

As Doumenc searched for an answer which would satisfy Voroshilov, he must have cursed the Poles for the absurdly gallant, feckless people that they were. Did they not realize the helplessness of their position? Could they not see that they *needed* Russia, perhaps even more at this moment than the Western democracies did? Otherwise their fate was certain. Why were they such fools, and why did they persist in tilting at windmills? If they wouldn't accept aid from the Reds, why not make a settlement with the Nazis?

While Doumenc was hesitating, Admiral Drax intervened; coughing delicately, he expressed the hope that Russia's intentions toward Poland would be understood in Warsaw. Voroshilov openly sneered. A few moments before, he had offered the West all the aid of which Russia was capable. (The following day General Shaposhnikov put this at 120 infantry divisions, 16 cavalry divisions and 5,000 fighter planes.) In return he expected a quid pro quo, part of which was access to Germany through Poland.

Doumenc tried to bring the discussion "for a moment" back to the question of "where the Russian forces will be disposed."

The Red marshal bluntly swept his temporizations aside. "I want a straight answer," Voroshilov said. "I am not talking about troop concentrations. I want to know the view of the French and British General Staffs in the event of aggression against Poland and Rumania. Is it that Soviet troops may enter Poland in order to make contact with the enemy in East Prussia? The passage of Soviet troops through Poland and Rumania is a first condition; after that is agreed, everything else can be discussed. Otherwise, if the Soviet troops are denied the ability to move, it is difficult to see how a fundamental agreement can be arrived at."

"I have already expressed the hope and belief that Poland and Rumania will ask for help when it is needed," Drax answered.

Voroshilov said wryly, "I doubt if it will turn out like that. They might ask for aid from the U.S.S.R., or they might not, or they might ask for it too late—and in the last situation the U.S.S.R. could do nothing which would be of any help to the Allies. A conference of three great powers and their representatives at this level has got to make up its mind on this. If Rumania and Poland do not ask for aid, or ask for it too late, their forces will be destroyed. These troops should be used as an additional Allied asset; it is in the interest neither of England nor of France nor of the U.S.S.R. that they should be destroyed." He paused to let his words sink in, and then added, "I insist that we must from the start discuss the principle of Soviet troops passing through Poland and Rumania; this is essential." With that he sat down.

There was a silence, and then General Doumenc suggested a recess. The delegates trooped into the garden, where Admiral Drax gratefully gulped the tobacco-free air. "I think our mission is finished," he said.

Drax was not entirely serious, but neither was he very worried; he had never had much hope of securing a pact with Russia, anyway. To a great extent his views reflected those of Neville Chamberlain and Sir Horace Wilson, and he saw the negotiations more as a sop to public opinion at home than as a serious search for an alliance whose efficacy he doubted and whose political morality he found slightly repellent.

General Doumenc, on the other hand, was downcast by the frank exchanges of August 14, but was still determined that they should not sabotage an agreement. He saw the crucial need of an alliance with the Soviet Union if, as he believed, the Western allies were going to be involved in war with Germany, and he had no faith in the strength of the Polish army.

335

That evening Doumenc persuaded Drax to agree to a telegram which he sent off immediately to his government in Paris, with a copy to London. It read:

THE THREE DELEGATIONS HAD TWO SESSIONS ON 13 AUGUST AND ONE LONG ONE ON 14TH.

SOVIET DELEGATION EXPRESSED DESIRE TO BRING MATTERS TO A HEAD AND ASKS THAT GENERAL PRINCIPLE ACCEPTED BY ALL BE PUT ASIDE IN FAVOR OF CONCRETE QUESTIONS . . . SOVIET DELEGATION TODAY PUT AS CONDITION FOR ACHIEVING MILITARY PACT ASSURANCE THAT SOVIET ARMY, IN EVENT AGGRESSION AGAINST POLAND AND RUMANIA, WILL HAVE RIGHT OF ENTRY INTO VILNA CORRIDOR, GALICIA AND RUMANIAN TERRITORY. DESPITE THIS, WORK CONTINUES. OUR AMBASSADOR BELIEVES, AND I CONCUR, QUICKEST SOLUTION TO SEND GENERAL VALIN ON MISSION TO WARSAW SPECIALLY ACCREDITED BY YOU TO POLISH GENERAL STAFF. WE MUST ENDEAVOR OBTAIN FROM THEM SECRET AGREEMENT IN PRINCIPLE ALLOWING FRANCO-BRITISH DELEGATIONS TO TREAT MILITARY ASPECT OF THIS QUESTION WITHOUT OFFICIALLY IMPLICATING POLISH GOVERNMENT. BRITISH MISSION IN ENTIRE AGREEMENT. YOUR INSTRUCTIONS REQUESTED MATTER OF URGENCY.

No reply ever came to this telegram. In any case, it did not matter, for on the evening of August 14 the Politburo of the Supreme Soviet met again. They had a full report from Voroshilov of the day's meeting, and the significance of it was plain. The Western democracies were not serious about an agreement; they wanted Soviet Russia's help but without any quid pro quo; above all, they could not be trusted. They preferred Poland to the Soviet Union, and evidently they preferred Nazi Germany to them both.

During the discussion Stalin pointed out that the British were still secretly meeting with the Germans. Simultaneously they were trying to frighten Berlin into a settlement by pretending to negotiate with Russia. It was time the game was halted. Let the democracies take the consequences of their deception; they had asked for them long enough. The U.S.S.R. should begin political negotiations with the Reich, and Stalin indicated that Molotov should let the Germans know.

Motolov said that he would do so at once, but Stalin disagreed. Not at once, he said; they had plenty of time. It was the others who did not have time. If Hitler wished to move against Poland this summer—and they knew that he did—he must do so quickly, before the weather changed. Therefore he was in a hurry for an agreement with the Russians. This was to their advantage. The more desperately Hitler needed them, the longer they must make him wait—while the U.S.S.R. decided what price they would charge him.

Molotov asked about the British negotiations. Wasn't it time to bring them to an end?

By no means, said Stalin. Let the democracies roast a little longer. As long as they went on roasting, the Germans would go on roasting too! It was good politics.

Though a member of the Politburo, Voroshilov was not present at this meeting. For the moment, it was decided not to tell him that henceforth he would be continuing sterile negotiations. So, day after day he went on bludgeoning the Anglo-French mission with brutal home truths and demands for facts instead of hazy prevarications.

337

XV
Hitler
Takes a Hand

Though Josef Stalin was in no hurry for his decision to reach the German government, it was in the possession of Ribbentrop and the Führer by the same evening, August 14.* It could hardly have come at a better moment for the Nazi Foreign Minister. On the basis of earlier reports from Moscow and on the constant reassurances of Ribbentrop, Hitler had called his generals to Berchtesgaden that day, and told them that the political situation was about to reach a military climax. Britain and France would not fight; he was sure of it, he said. In any case, there were no leaders to stimulate them; "The men I got to know at Munich are not the kind to start a new world war."

And if England did come in and France followed, what would happen? "A drive against the West Wall is unlikely," the Führer stated. "A northward swing through Belgium and Holland will not bring speedy victory. None of this will help the Poles. All these factors militate against the English and French entering the war."

At this point Hitler made a statement—so far his generals had heard only rumors—which made them prick up their ears, and which is of interest to espionage aficionados as well: "I can assure you," the

* Washington was alerted at the same time by Ambassador Steinhardt through information supplied by Charles Bohlen.

339

Führer declared, "that Russia is not in the least disposed to pull chestnuts out of the fire on behalf of the British and French." He said no more, except to hint broadly that negotiations were in progress. But his use of the phrase "chestnuts out of the fire" revealed how closely informed he was about the Anglo-French-Russian conversations of the past weeks. It was a phrase which Molotov had used several times, and at one point the repetition irritated William Strang and Sir William Seeds intensely.

But the primary fact to emerge from the August 14 military meeting was that Hitler was now ready to move eastward and that his generals must prepare for the attack. They had rarely seen him so confident. As they filed out of this briefing, which seemed to have had no purpose except to inspire them—an exercise which their leader believed to be vitally necessary, for he despised the "spinelessness" of most of them—they voiced no doubts.

But at least one of them had some. General Georg Thomas, chief of the Economic and Armaments Section of the Armed Forces High Command and a latecomer to the ranks of those who feared the outcome of Hitler's plans, was not worried about an isolated war, but he was no longer convinced that hostilities could be limited to Poland. He knew about the disillusionment of those German officers who had put their hopes in British resistance before Munich and Prague, but now he felt that even Chamberlain had been forced into a corner and that the British would have to fight. In which case . . .

A few days after the meeting with Hitler on August 14, Thomas drew up a memorandum outlining Germany's situation. Its main point was not to deny the probability of a speedy German victory in Poland, but to point out that "a quick war and a quick peace" were a complete illusion. There could be no such thing as an isolated war, no matter what the Führer said; an attack on Poland would touch off a greater war, and then the wealthier nations, with their reserves, raw materials and food supplies, would inevitably prevail.

General Thomas was so sure of his thesis that he asked to see and was received by General Keitel. He began to read his memorandum aloud, but Keitel interrupted him to ask, "You seriously wish me to forward this to the Führer?"

"Yes."

"My dear general, we are interested in facts, not academic theories. You've got things all wrong."

340

"I'm sure I have not," Thomas answered.

"You talk of the danger of a world war. It's a danger which does not exist," Keitel said. "There will be no military reaction in the West. France is too degenerate, Britain too decadent, America too uninterested to fight for Poland."

"My information is that—"

"Your information shows that you have been infected with defeatism and pacifism. You should shake off these doubts. Don't worry. The Führer's greatness, his superior intelligence, will solve all these problems which are worrying you, and solve them to the advantage of Germany."*

Joachim von Ribbentrop began to draft a telegram for Moscow, after a discussion with his chief. Like most of the Foreign Minister's messages, it was long and woolly in content, but there was meat inside for those who studied it, as Molotov and Stalin certainly did.

The cable was sent to Moscow via the Foreign Ministry in Berlin, where it was read by Erich Kordt and Baron von Weizsäcker. They relayed it without comment, but Kordt slipped out later to inform Admiral Canaris of what was afoot, and that evening jotted down in his diary—somewhat dramatically, but not without reason: "The friends of peace are losing the race."

THE CRISIS WHICH HAS BEEN PRODUCED IN POLISH-GERMAN RE-LATIONS BY ENGLISH POLICY [cabled Ribbentrop] AND THE AT-TEMPTS AT AN ALLIANCE WHICH ARE BOUND UP WITH THAT POLICY MAKE A SPEEDY CLARIFICATION OF GERMAN-RUSSIAN RELATIONS NECESSARY. . . . IT WOULD BE FATAL IF, THROUGH MUTUAL IGNORANCE OF VIEWS AND INTENTIONS, THE TWO PEOPLES SHOULD FINALLY DRIFT APART.

AS WE HAVE BEEN INFORMED, THE SOVIET GOVERNMENT ALSO FEELS THE DESIRE FOR A CLARIFICATION OF GERMAN-RUSSIAN RELATIONS. SINCE, HOWEVER, ACCORDING TO PREVIOUS EXPERI-ENCE, THIS CLARIFICATION CAN ONLY BE ACHIEVED SLOWLY THROUGH NORMAL DIPLOMATIC CHANNELS, I AM PREPARED TO MAKE A SHORT VISIT TO MOSCOW IN ORDER, IN THE NAME OF THE FÜHRER, TO SET FORTH THE FÜHRER'S VIEWS TO M. STALIN. IN MY VIEW, ONLY THROUGH A DIRECT DISCUSSION OF THIS KIND

* The text differs in some ways from Thomas' own in "Gedanken und Ereignisse," but see Notes at the end of this book.

CAN A CHANGE BE BROUGHT ABOUT. IT SHOULD NOT BE IMPOSSIBLE THEREBY TO LAY THE FOUNDATIONS FOR A FINAL SETTLEMENT OF GERMAN-RUSSIAN RELATIONS.

There was much more to the message than this. At one point it reiterated the "mutual interest" which the two nations had in stabilizing the situation in Eastern Europe, and, holding out the carrot, it included the name of Poland among those countries where "satisfactory settlements" were necessary.

This was the half-whispered bribe for which the Russians were waiting, and it was accompanied by the flattery which Stalin never seemed able to resist: an alliance with Russia was so vital that, unlike the British, the Germans would send someone really important to see him. Ribbentrop would come himself.

The German Foreign Minister ordered Ambassador von der Schulenburg to deliver this message to Molotov not in written form but to read it to him (a mysterious instruction for which no one has yet been able to offer a satisfactory explanation), and then to repeat it personally to Stalin if possible. On August 15 Schulenburg was able to do the former, but not the latter. Not that it mattered; Molotov was well primed, and after expressing pleasure at the content and tone of Ribbentrop's message, he took command of the interview. First, he made a suggestion that Germany might use her good offices to improve relations between the Soviet Union and Japan.* Then he came to the nub of the conversation: would Germany agree to a joint guarantee of the Baltic States?† Secondly, if Ribbentrop were to come to Moscow and talks were to begin, they must be in concrete terms; the meeting could not consist merely of an exchange of opinions.

It was as much as Adolf Hitler hoped for and far more than Schulenburg had expected. There was only one snag. Mindful of Stalin's instructions, Molotov made it clear that these negotiations could not be hurried. The Russians did not trust anyone at this moment, and they were determined not to be used by either side as a stick with which to intimidate the other. If the Western democracies could use Russia as a threat with which to persuade Germany to

---

* A minor war was reaching its climax at this moment between Russo-Japanese troops and planes along the Siberian-Manchurian border.

† Such a guarantee would inevitably lead to a nonaggression pact between Germany and Russia.

342

negotiate, so could the Germans use her to force a surrender by the West—after which each side might back away again from Moscow. This Stalin had resolved should not happen, for now, having turned against the West, he had not only made up his mind to secure a non-aggression treaty with Germany, but was also determined to see Germany go to war. Not necessarily against Britain and France—that was up to the democracies. But Stalin now wanted an invasion of Poland by Germany that would not only bring Danzig and the Polish Corridor into the Reich but would also return Polish territory along Russia's western frontiers to the Soviet Union.

Thus, though the end of the game was in sight, it must still be kept going for as long as possible to stiffen the price Hitler would be prepared to pay, and to make impossible a peaceful settlement with Poland, from which Russia would gain nothing.

Therefore Molotov repeated to Schulenburg, "Adequate preparation for a discussion of the problems is indispensable."

He was not going to allow Ribbentrop to come to Moscow yet.

Charles Bohlen reported to his ambassador, Laurence Steinhardt, that he had news from his contact at the German embassy: Joachim von Ribbentrop would shortly be coming to Moscow. Unless the Western allies took desperate measures, it looked as if a Russo-German pact was in the bag.

The next day Steinhardt saw Molotov, who was extremely reticent when questioned about negotiations with Germany. The American ambassador was snubbed when he warned Russia of the dangers of tying herself to Germany, and Molotov denied that this was the Soviet Union's intention. Nevertheless, Steinhardt trusted his source to the extent of cabling a summary of the Schulenburg-Molotov conversation to Washington that evening, and suggested that London be immediately informed. On August 17 Sumner Welles relayed it to the British ambassador in Washington, who in turn cabled London and then sent a full transcript of the conversation.

What happened to it? Once more, like an earlier warning, it went astray. Neither Halifax nor Chamberlain ever saw the cable until long after it was too late. Bohlen says that several years later Anthony Eden (now Lord Avon) told him that the cable had been deliberately held up by a Communist spy in the Foreign Office. Asked about this, Lord Avon was unable to recall the conversation, and pointed out that he was no longer in the Foreign Office at the time. But two men who have since been unmasked as Communist spies, Guy Burgess and Donald Maclean, certainly were.

No one at the U.S. embassy in Moscow thought of passing on the news to the unfortunate members of the Franco-British military mission. Perhaps protocol prevented them from doing so officially, but surely someone might have dropped a hint. The mission went on negotiating with Voroshilov, and it was days before they heard the rumors.

■

On August 17 General Bodenschatz telephoned Paul Stehlin and told him that they could not count on seeing each other from now on. "I will be very busy," he said. "It will be impossible for us to get together. I only hope that we will find it possible to meet again soon."

Stehlin did not need any more explicit hint to make him realize that the crisis was coming. In any case, he was fully informed about the build-up of German forces which had quietly been going on for the past forty-eight hours; he had been watching it himself.

Unfortunately, the Gestapo was now watching Stehlin, as well as the French embassy plane. Whenever he got into his car to drive to the embassy or the airport, a Gestapo car was on his tail. It was easy enough to dodge surveillance in the city; he made an arrangement with friends who slightly resembled him to dress in his clothes, take his car while he took theirs, and thus free him to rendezvous with agents in the city. He is still proud of the fact that not one of them was discovered.

But such evasion was impossible in the air. Each time Stehlin took up the embassy plane, the ground staff warned the Gestapo and the Luftwaffe. On two occasions during these tense days he flew with his chief, General Geffrier, but this became too risky as the crisis neared, and his secretary came as passenger instead to make notes of what could be seen below.

They always went eastward on their flights, toward the roads and railways leading to Poland, and soon it became clear to them that though no official announcement had been made, mobilization was

344

in full swing. Every road leading to Poland was jammed with military transport.

Stehlin was a superb pilot. He loved his plane, a Simoun, as he would a favorite horse, and knew just how to handle it. To shadow him, the Gestapo sent up two planes each time he took off, and whenever he came near a garrison town or an airfield they harassed him. Stehlin would pretend not to notice them, even when they came within a few feet during a maneuver; only when General Geffrier was aboard did he make a protest after they landed to the liaison officer of the Luftwaffe, who of course professed to know nothing about it.

But having failed to frighten the Frenchman, the Gestapo took the obvious course and sabotaged him. One morning he received a call from the Air France official who looked after his plane.

"You're not going to like this," the official said.

"They have grounded my plane," Stehlin guessed.

"Worse than that. There was an accident last night—a German aircraft taxied into yours as it was coming into the hangar."

"Badly?"

"Badly enough to make sure it will never fly again—at least not in Germany."

That night Stehlin went to the Kabarett der Komiker in search of a laugh, for he truly loved his plane and mourned her. But Werner Finck was gone—he had been arrested again and was in a concentration camp—and even the show girls seemed afraid to come over to his table.

Ambassador Robert Coulondre, back from his vacation, digested Stehlin's reports of increasingly heavy troop movements with a resigned nod of his head. He had been to see Baron von Weizsäcker at the Foreign Ministry, and received a distinct impression that the sands of time were running out.

"Stupidity sometimes has its merits," Weizsäcker had told him, "and that goes for the Poles too. The stupidity of the Poles shows their friends what harm they have done and can continue to do. Surely this must release them from their obligations. Will France and England really risk their existence for the sake of a mad friend who insists on running amok?"

"We must still stand by our friends," Coulondre replied. "If

345

France were to let Poland be overrun by Germany, where would she be? Her own turn would not be far away. If she gives in on this, she will sink to the level of Belgium or Holland."

Weizsäcker listened as if his mind were miles away, and Coulondre had the feeling that "he wished to tell me something." In his dispatch to Paris, he added: "Without being informed of his master's secret, he knows that important decisions are being taken or discussed."

The French ambassador underestimated Weizsäcker, who knew almost exactly what was going on. Unfortunately, he didn't have the courage to speak. Later he was to give his reasons. If he had spoken, he said—either to Coulondre or to his other favorite foreign envoy, Signor Attolico—they would have reported the statement to their governments. This would have been disastrous, since German intelligence had cracked the French, Italian and British diplomatic codes, and would immediately have discovered that Weizsäcker was betraying state secrets.*

But it did not matter. Through Stehlin's reports and his own intuition, Coulondre was able to warn Paris that the pressure on Poland was shifting from the political to the military phase.

Under the circumstances, it would seem that even the British might now have begun to deduce that perhaps it was time for storm warnings to be hoisted. But not yet, not yet. At the beginning of July the chief of the Secret Service, Sir Stewart Menzies, had reported that he was taking his annual holiday immediately and advised everyone in high places to do likewise. He was ignored. Then Parliament ended its summer session, and on August 4 members of the Cabinet had rushed to the moors or beaches. Chamberlain was in Scotland. Halifax was in Yorkshire but commuted to the Foreign Office. One of the most fervent anti-Nazis, Leslie Hore-Belisha, the Minister for War, even retreated as far as the south of France. It was a splendid summer. "In England, as in 1914," observed Winston Churchill, "the carefree people were enjoying their holidays and playing with their children on the sands."

Churchill himself was regarding a very different scene. On Au-

* Weizsäcker never explained why he didn't tell the ambassadors this and ask them to take appropriate precautions.

gust 14 he had arrived in Paris with his friend General Edward L.
Spears, and thence had proceeded on a tour of the Maginot Line.
Their host was General Joseph Georges, commander of the armies
on the northeastern front. Churchill, who was never happier than
when talking military tactics, was escorted along the whole sector of
the main French defenses from Lauterbourg to the Swiss frontier,
and he was delighted with what he saw and what he was told. "Here
along the Rhine . . . All the temporary bridges across the river had
been removed to one side or the other. The permanent bridges were
heavily guarded and mined. Trusty officers were stationed night and
day to press at a signal the buttons which would blow them up. The
great river, swollen by the melting Alpine snows, streamed along in
sullen, turgid flow. The French outposts crouched in their rifle pits
amid the brushwood. Two or three of us could stroll together to the
water's edge, but nothing like a target, we were told, must be presented. Three hundred yards away on the farther side, here and there
among the bushes, German figures could be seen working rather
leisurely with pick and shovel at their defences. All the riverside
quarter of Strasbourg had already been cleared of civilians. I stood
on its bridge for some time and watched one or two motorcars pass
over it. Prolonged examination of passports and character took
place at either end. Here the German post was little more than a
hundred yards away from the French. There was no intercourse
with them. Yet Europe was at peace. There was no dispute between
France and Germany."

Impressed by the fortifications and by the spirit of the French
soldiers, Churchill was nevertheless dispirited by the automatic acceptance of his hosts that should war come, their action would be
mainly defensive. When he returned to Paris, he gave a lunch for
General Georges, who had brought with him details of French
strength and Deuxième Bureau estimates of German forces facing
the Maginot Line along the West Wall. The Deuxième Bureau had
doubled its estimates of the number of German troops who were
actually ordered to duty in the West; nevertheless, having seen the
French frontier, and matching it against the exaggerated estimate of
its German opponents, Churchill said, "But you are the masters."

General Georges seemed surprised and even slightly annoyed.
He hurriedly pointed out that the French troops would never be
allowed to strike first.

347

Considering this answer, it is hardly surprising that when Churchill returned to England, he asked his old friend Inspector C. R. Thompson, a retired Scotland Yard Special Branch detective, to rejoin him as bodyguard, and to bring his gun along. He also polished up his own pistol. "There were known to be twenty thousand organised German Nazis in England," he wrote, "and it would only have been in accord with their procedure in other friendly countries that the outbreak of war should be preceded by a sharp prelude of sabotage and murder." While he waited for the appeasers like Chamberlain and Halifax to disappear from the scene, no one, he was determined, was going to get rid of him.

■

There was a betting box in Baron von Weizsäcker's office in the Wilhelmstrasse where the staff could make a wager—though not for money—on the chances of peace or war. Until August 16, only one chit repeatedly wagered on war, and Erich Kordt didn't need to look to know that the bet came from the office spy, Martin Luther; the rest, for one reason or another—some because they wished for peace, others because they believed that the West would give way—bet on peace. However, on August 16 everyone else in the office stopped betting—except for Martin Luther, who was now wagering on peace. Like his chief, Joachim von Ribbentrop, and his Führer, he had good reason to think that peace was a clear winner. The Russo-German negotiations were going well; if they were successful, the Western allies would be bound to give way.

Still, even at the end of teletype and telephone lines, Joachim von Ribbentrop was growing increasingly difficult to live with. His nerves were on edge as he waited for news from Moscow. When Schulenburg's report of his interview with Molotov on August 15 was finally telephoned through to him just before seven in the morning on August 16, he had already called for it four times during the night. At once he ordered his car and was driven across the mountain pass to Berchtesgaden, but on arrival he had to pace and fume impatiently for nearly three hours. As usual, Hitler had been up all night declaiming before his court of sycophants, and no one would think of awakening him. Ribbentrop filled the time by going over Schulen-

348

burg's message with Dr. Gaus, the Foreign Ministry expert on treaties, and composing a reply to Molotov's suggestions.

When Hitler finally did appear, he shared his Foreign Minister's joy at the Soviet Commissar's reaction, and together with Gaus the two of them spent a working lunch completing the reply, which was dispatched that afternoon. It was marked "Most Urgent," and Erich Kordt in Berlin was told by Ribbentrop to relay it to Moscow as quickly as possible; now that the Soviets had taken the Nazi bait, there was a desperate need to hook them firmly. Within a week Hitler must make up his mind about two of the main events of the National Socialist year: the annual party rally at Nuremberg and the great military celebration at Tannenberg* in East Prussia. These might have to be canceled, for if he decided on war, the troops would be needed elsewhere; the date he had fixed with his generals when they drew up *Fall Weiss* (the attack on Poland) had always been September 1. There were only fourteen days left to beach the Soviet shark.

Erich Kordt read the Hitler-Ribbentrop reply to Moscow, and with a sinking feeling realized why Martin Luther was betting on peace. Schulenburg was ordered to seek an immediate interview with Molotov to inform him that all his conditions were accepted by the Reich without qualification. The message read, in part:

GERMANY IS PREPARED TO CONCLUDE A NONAGGRESSION PACT WITH THE SOVIET UNION, AND IF THE SOVIET GOVERNMENT SO DESIRES, ONE WHICH SHOULD BE UNDENUNCIABLE FOR A TERM OF TWENTY-FIVE YEARS. FURTHER, GERMANY IS READY TO GUAR-ANTEE THE BALTIC STATES JOINTLY WITH THE SOVIET UNION. FINALLY, GERMANY IS PREPARED TO EXERCISE INFLUENCE FOR AN IMPROVEMENT AND CONSOLIDATION OF RUSSO-JAPANESE RELATIONS.

But there was need for hurry, Schulenburg was instructed.

THE FÜHRER IS OF THE OPINION THAT IN VIEW OF THE PRESENT SITUATION AND OF THE POSSIBILITY ANY DAY OF SERIOUS EVENTS (AT THIS POINT, PLEASE EMPHASIZE TO MOLOTOV THAT GER-

* To commemorate General Paul von Hindenburg's victory over the Russians at the end of August 1914.

MANY IS DETERMINED NOT TO ENDURE POLISH PROVOCATION INDEFINITELY), A BASIC AND RAPID CLARIFICATION OF GERMAN-RUSSIAN RELATIONS AND OF EACH COUNTRY'S ATTITUDE TO THE QUESTIONS OF THE MOMENT IS DESIRABLE.

FOR THESE REASONS I AM PREPARED TO FLY TO MOSCOW ANY TIME AFTER FRIDAY, AUGUST 18, TO DEAL WITH THE ENTIRE COMPLEX OF GERMAN-RUSSIAN RELATIONS, WITH FULL POWERS FROM THE FÜHRER, AND IF THE OCCASION ARISES, TO SIGN THE APPROPRIATE TREATIES.

The Foreign Minister added a goad to his ambassador:

IT WOULD BE OF VERY SPECIAL INTEREST TO US IF MY MOSCOW JOURNEY COULD TAKE PLACE AT THE END OF THIS WEEK OR THE BEGINNING OF NEXT WEEK.

But Molotov was still not to be hurried. What did time matter to Russia? By telephone and teletype, Ribbentrop pursued the exasperated Schulenburg during the next few hours for a reply, but all his ambassador could get from the Soviet was another yellow light instructing him to wait. Now that Molotov saw that the Germans were becoming suppliants at the Soviet table, he could not resist reminding the German ambassador that his country had repeatedly vilified and slandered Russia, and that Hitler had spat insults at her. If, however, the German government now desired a serious improvement in political relations, the Soviet government could only welcome such a change and, for its part, would be prepared to revise its relations with the Reich. However, there were many obstacles to be overcome.

Schulenburg replied that surely these could be settled on the arrival of the Minister of Foreign Affairs, who had been given full authority by the Führer.

Molotov answered that his government was highly gratified at the decision of the Reich government to send Herr von Ribbentrop, since the dispatch of such an eminent politician and statesman emphasized how serious its intentions were. This was in marked contrast to England, which, in the person of Strang, had sent only an official of second-class rank to Moscow. Still, he added, the journey by the German Foreign Minister required thorough preparation. The Soviet government did not welcome the publicity that such a journey would cause; it preferred to do practical work without such disturbances.

Adolf Hitler writhed with frustration when this reply was received at Obersalzberg. It assured him of everything he wanted except speed,

350

and it baited him with its implicit assumption that he must wait for Soviet whims and impulses. He knew that Moscow was holding out for two reasons: time, in order to prevent Germany from betraying Russia by settling with the West, and a bribe that would ensure the Soviets of a large hunk of Poland when it came to divvying up the booty. A new telegram was rushed to Schulenburg under Ribbentrop's signature:

> . . . THE PRESENT UNUSUAL SITUATION MAKES IT NECESSARY, IN THE FÜHRER'S OPINION, TO EMPLOY A DIFFERENT METHOD [than normal diplomatic channels] WHICH WOULD LEAD TO QUICK RESULTS. GERMAN-POLISH RELATIONS ARE BECOMING MORE ACUTE FROM DAY TO DAY. WE HAVE TO TAKE INTO ACCOUNT THAT INCIDENTS MAY OCCUR ANY DAY THAT WOULD MAKE THE OUTBREAK OF OPEN CONFLICT UNAVOIDABLE . . .

But when Ribbentrop reached Moscow, all the problems which troubled the two countries could be settled.

> . . . I SHOULD ALSO BE IN A POSITION TO SIGN A SPECIAL PROTOCOL REGULATING THE INTERESTS OF BOTH PARTIES IN QUESTIONS OF FOREIGN POLICY OF ONE KIND OR ANOTHER. FOR INSTANCE THE SETTLEMENT OF SPHERES OF INTEREST IN THE BALTIC AREA. SUCH A SETTLEMENT WILL, HOWEVER, ONLY BE POSSIBLE IN AN ORAL DISCUSSION.

Again Ribbentrop added a goad to the German envoy:

> PLEASE PRESS FOR A RAPID REALIZATION OF MY JOURNEY AND OPPOSE APPROPRIATELY ANY FRESH RUSSIAN OBJECTIONS. IN THIS CONNECTION YOU MUST KEEP IN MIND THE DECISIVE FACTOR THAT AN EARLY OUTBREAK OF OPEN GERMAN-POLISH CONFLICT IS POSSIBLE AND THAT WE THEREFORE HAVE THE GREATEST INTEREST IN HAVING MY VISIT TO MOSCOW TAKE PLACE IMMEDIATELY.

All these messages were exchanged on August 17 and 18. On the seventeenth, General Doumenc of the French military mission heard the first rumors of a possible rapprochement between the Germans and the Russians, and his reaction to his confreres was: "The Soviets are a peculiar people, and it is unwise to trust them, because they do not trust us. But *au fond,* they believe in the decency of man, and they have fought and died for it in their Revolution. I refuse to believe that they will abandon their principles now, no matter how weak and undecided we appear to be, in order to bind themselves to a despotism like National Socialism. It is up to us to dissuade them. We must take desperate measures if necessary."

That day had been the most trying one of all for the Anglo-French negotiators. At each session Voroshilov had pressed his point that the Soviet army must have free passage through Poland, and each time the French had tried to pretend that when the time came and Poland was attacked, she would ask for Russian help. But the Soviet marshal insisted that he wanted a signed agreement now.

By this time the British were in an awkward position, and the ham-handedness of Admiral Drax had done much to worsen it. Asked by the Russians how many divisions his country could contribute in the event of war, he had instructed his assistant, General Heywood, to give figures which, though puny, were in fact exaggerated: two divisions at once and two more later. Compared with the Soviet Union's three hundred and France's one hundred divisions, this was such a ludicrous figure that Voroshilov at first refused to believe it and asked that it be repeated. It did not occur to Drax—perhaps he did not feel it was important—to point out the resources of the R.A.F. and of the British Empire troops from Australia, New Zealand, South Africa, India and the colonies. Voroshilov was a soldier who had never been outside Russia, who thought in terms of hundreds of divisions, who could not conceive of the far-flung defenses of the British Empire, and who was shocked by the weakness of this so-called great power.

This was not Drax's worst mistake, however. To persuade Russia to ally herself on the side of the West and of Poland, it was necessary to persuade her that the Poles could stand up to the Germans, and that by rallying to their side the Soviets would not be inviting the greatest weight of German vengeance solely on themselves. But evidently Drax could not see this. On the *City of Exeter* he had repeatedly said, "But—ahem—poor old Poland, you know. If she is left to herself, she'll go down in—ahem—two weeks. Hasn't—ahem—got a chance. That's why we need to—ahem—stand up for her."

To which the French had replied that he had better not say anything like that to the Russians. The moment they realized what a weak reed Poland was, they would search for other protection.

But Admiral Drax couldn't help himself; he was that sort of man.

352

Now, to assuage Voroshilov's incredulity, he suddenly leaned toward the marshal and said, "Don't forget that Poland, if she is on her own, may be crushed in two weeks."

It was an obvious appeal by an Englishman to the better nature of a Russian, who of course would never let anyone down. Voroshilov looked across the table as if at a being from another world, and stated, "The Soviet delegate takes notice of the statement by the admiral to the effect that Poland, if left to fight alone, might well be crushed in two weeks. The Soviet delegation has no comment to make on this subject."

As Beaufre, who heard these words, commented later: "There was an impression that he had just received confirmation in a material way of Poland's weakness. Given the conditions under which the struggle in the East was likely to take place, this meant that Russia would never be able to come to the help of Poland in time, and thereafter would find herself facing a victorious German army alone."

Nonetheless, Doumenc was determined to keep trying. In spite of the rumors, he believed that the battle could still be won if only he could persuade the Allied governments to back him all the way, and if only the Poles could be persuaded to make a gesture to the Russians. It was all that was needed: *a gesture*.

That evening, while the diplomatic colony in Moscow buzzed with news of German intrigue, Doumenc decided that somehow he must persuade the Poles to be reasonable. He picked the most junior but most personable and persuasive member of his mission for an urgent task. His brief, a copy of which was sent to Paris, read:

CAPTAIN BEAUFRE WILL PROCEED TO WARSAW TO GIVE GENERAL MUSSE [the French military attaché] ALL USEFUL INFORMATION VERBALLY. I. IT IS OF THE UTMOST IMPORTANCE TO OBTAIN THE AGREEMENT OF THE POLISH GENERAL STAFF TO THE PRINCIPLE OF THIS EVENTUAL PASSAGE THROUGH THEIR TERRITORY. THE RUSSIANS HAVE STRICTLY LIMITED THEIR REQUEST FOR AUTHORIZATION TO THE VILNA CORRIDOR AND GALICIA AND ON THIS POINT WE CAN OBTAIN A FORMAL AGREEMENT FROM THEM. THE STRATEGIC IMPORTANCE OF THIS SUPPORT IS UNDENIABLE. THE IMPORTANCE OF CONCLUDING A MILITARY PACT IS NO LESS SO. 2. IF THIS PRINCIPLE IS ACCEPTED WE MUST OBTAIN AN ASSURANCE THAT COMMUNICATIONS WILL BE ESTABLISHED ACROSS RUSSIAN TERRITORY BETWEEN POLAND AND OURSELVES—WHAT ARE THE TRANSIT STATIONS FROM WHICH THESE COMMUNICATIONS

SHOULD BEGIN IN ORDER BEST TO SERVE THE POLISH REAR AREAS? 3. WE HAVE SAID ABSOLUTELY NOTHING ABOUT THE POLISH ARMY IN ACCORDANCE WITH OUR PROMISE.

Beaufre left Moscow on the evening of August 17, and the hopes of the French delegation went with him. To the Russians it had been announced that he was on his way back to Paris, but when he reached Warsaw the next evening, he was smuggled off the train at a suburban station and taken to the French embassy. He walked straight into a dinner party which lasted until midnight, but after it was over he, Léon Noël, the French envoy, and General Musse retired to the ambassador's study to discuss the problem of persuading the Poles to allow the entry of Russian troops in the event of war.

The conversation profoundly depressed Beaufre, for neither envoy nor military attaché was hopeful of success, nor even anxious to exert pressure. Noël feared that any attempt to strong-arm the Poles would turn them completely against the West and thrust them into the arms of Germany—a most unlikely liaison at this stage, but he professed to believe it. General Musse was simply afraid of the Russians and suspicious of their motives. However, it was agreed that Noël would see Colonel Józef Beck the next day and that General Musse would tackle General Stackiewicz, the Army Chief of Staff.

On August 19, units of the Wehrmacht were moving up to build entrenchments all along the Polish-German frontier, and though no official mobilization had been announced, rumors of the approaching crisis were general in Warsaw. Yet no one seemed to be particularly worried; no special precautions had been taken in the capital. The sun shone; the girls in their light summer dresses looked their provocative best; orchestras played in the open air and the cafés were full of carefree people.

At the Ministry for War, General Stackiewicz acknowledged to Musse and Beaufre that critical times were approaching, but he did not seem unduly worried. He did not exactly repeat Beck's words and describe the German maneuvers as "bluff," but he seemed to think that "matters would adjust themselves" and that Poland would be able to take care of any attack. He was friendly and relaxed until the subject of Russia's request for passage of its troops was brought up; then the charm disappeared. "I understand your point of view personally, but I ask you also to understand ours," he said. "We know the Russians better than you do. They are a dishonest people whose

354

word is not to be relied upon by us or anyone else, and it is quite useless to ask us even to contemplate a proposition of this nature. Obviously I realize the general situation, and it may be that the advent of war may be accelerated, but even this consideration cannot make us alter our point of view."

The other interview was even more disastrous. Beck glared savagely at Nöel as he was shown in. "I know what you have come for!" he said. "They have informed me from Paris what is afoot."

Indeed they had. The previous evening Georges Bonnet had summoned Lukasiewicz, the Polish ambassador in Paris, to the Foreign Ministry and told him bluntly that unless he allowed Russian troops right of access through his country, a Russo-German pact against Poland might be signed. In the past weeks Bonnet had become a fervent supporter of an agreement with Russia, and like Doumenc, he was still hopeful of securing one.

"Beck will never allow Russian troops to occupy the territories which we took over in 1921," said Lukasiewicz. "Would you French allow the Germans into Alsace-Lorraine?"

"Perhaps not. But you forget that to the east and west you have as neighbors two great powers. You are now facing up to a test of strength against Germany, a test which makes it necessary for you to have the help of the Soviets. Only three days ago Hitler told Burckhardt that in three weeks he would smash Poland with his armored forces, whose strength you cannot conceive."

"On the contrary," Lukasiewicz replied, "it is the Poles who will drive straight into Germany during the first few days!"

"I fervently hope so . . . But in the meantime, say yes to the Soviet demand! It is of utmost importance to us. On our negotiations in Moscow depends the question of war."

It was a demand, not a request, and the angry envoy departed saying that he would forward the message but that he knew the answer would be in the negative. Lukasiewicz, who had been born in Russia, hated the Soviets even more than most Poles, and his anger at Bonnet and his loathing of the Communists boiled over into his dispatch.

Now, with the telegram on the desk in front of him, Beck faced the hesitant Noël and sourly declared that all requests about Russian troop movements in Poland would have to be passed on to Marshal Smigly-Rydz. The marshal gave his negative reply that evening, but took time out the following day to listen to a plea from the British, who had now decided to join the French in putting pressure on the Poles. However, the answer remained the same: *Whatever the consequences, not a square inch of Polish territory would ever be occupied by Russian troops.* So that was that. The mission had failed. The blind and arrogant Poles were adamant.

The important strategy now was to keep the Russians from learning of Poland's stubborn refusal, and to get the talks moving again. Before he left Moscow, Beaufre had prearranged with General Doumenc that he would send only one of three words to indicate how his mission had gone: "one" would indicate that he was still talking, "two" that he had succeeded, and "three" that he had failed.

But General Musse had taken no such precautions. Right after the first sessions he rushed to his cipher machine and began to send messages to Paris and to the embassy in Moscow giving the Poles' views, including their strongest anti-Communist statements, and for good measure adding his own suspicious opinions of the Reds. As Beaufre remarked afterward: "To anyone who knows anything about the Russian secret service it must be obvious that any telegram sent in the normal military attaché's code would be immediately deciphered. In almost any embassy in the world the safe is not guarded at night, and a safe unguarded is an open safe."

General Musse's revelation of Poland's outright refusal could not have arrived at a more appropriate moment from Stalin's point of view. The Politburo was meeting on the evening of August 19, and this was the final evidence he needed to convince his associates of the rightness of his decision.

At Berchtesgaden, Adolf Hitler and Ribbentrop were waiting in the Führer's study beside the telephone and teletype. Hitler held his stomach and ate apples, spitting the cores on the floor. Outside, the gang of courtiers and SS men talked in low whispers, aware that drama was in the air but not quite sure what it was all about.

Just after seven o'clock German time, the bell on the teletype tinkled and the machine began to click. Ribbentrop pressed a buzzer on Hitler's desk, and Dr. Gaus slipped into the study. The message read:

356

SECRET—MOST URGENT

THE SOVIET GOVERNMENT AGREES TO THE REICH FOREIGN MIN-
ISTER COMING TO MOSCOW ONE WEEK AFTER THE ANNOUNCE-
MENT OF THE SIGNING OF THE TRADE AGREEMENT. MOLOTOV
STATED THAT IF THE CONCLUSION OF THE TRADE AGREEMENT
IS MADE PUBLIC TOMORROW, THE REICH FOREIGN MINISTER
COULD ARRIVE ON AUGUST 27 OR 28.
MOLOTOV HANDED ME A DRAFT OF A NONAGGRESSION PACT.
A DETAILED ACCOUNT OF THE TWO CONVERSATIONS I HAD WITH
MOLOTOV TODAY, AS WELL AS THE TEXT OF THE SOVIET DRAFT,
FOLLOWS BY TELEGRAM AT ONCE. SCHULENBURG.

Hitler threw his hands up in the air in triumph and laughed, and
Ribbentrop began laughing too. Abruptly the Führer sobered as the
teletype began working again. Turning to it, he read a message from
Schulenburg recounting how he had tried and failed to persuade
Molotov to receive Ribbentrop earlier.

But from Hitler's point of view, the meeting had to be sooner than
August 27 or 28. His deadline for the attack on Poland was September 1; after that the hazards of the weather would intervene. If negotiations did not begin until August 27, all preparations would
have to be suspended; the talks might drag on for days, and the whole
plan would be threatened. Somehow the Russians must be persuaded
to allow Ribbentrop to come sooner. But how?

Adolf Hitler decided to take a personal hand in the negotiations.

XVI

Ribbentrop's Hour of Triumph

On August 19, the same day that the Politburo ratified Josef Stalin's fateful decision, Lord Halifax dispatched a message from the Foreign Office to Neville Chamberlain, on holiday in Scotland. He wrote:

"We have, in the course of the last six months, had so many dates given to us that one is naturally sceptical about any repetition of them, and I do not suppose that we should exclude from our minds the possibility that all this may have its place in the general nerve storm which we have been told was designated to rage during these weeks. On the other hand, the information given seemed to me too circumstantial to ignore and the actual dates given were, so it is alleged, given to the Italian Government, which obviously increases their significance."

Via Vansittart, the Foreign Secretary had received the news leaked by Count Ciano that Germany would move against Poland before the end of August. In his message to the Prime Minister he added, "If the appreciation is a true one, there is no time to lose."

Chamberlain decided to come back to London at once. In Bournemouth, Sir Horace Wilson also decided to return to No. 10 Downing Street, but when the three of them got together to discuss the situation, they seemed to have little idea of what to do.

By this time Lord Halifax had made up his mind that war was

inevitable. He did not like the prospect, and he would do all he could to avoid it—save approve a pact with the Soviet Union, which he thought both abhorrent and useless. But he was filled with forebodings of doom, and though he concealed them from his Prime Minister, he did not hide them from himself. Once, at the time of Munich, he had been troubled with insomnia. He was so perturbed by this phenomenon—apparently he had never been sleepless before—that he had written to Chamberlain and voiced the fears that had come to him in the still small hours. Chamberlain had rebuked him, and so now Halifax did not mention that once again he was sleepless. For what could he or the government do under the circumstances? The whole thing was inevitable.

On the other hand, the instinct of Chamberlain and Wilson was to continue ignoring the fact that their policy, their country and the peace of Europe were in danger of drowning. They were still sure that someone would throw them a lifebelt—Mussolini, for instance. Had not the Duce saved them once before, and could he not do it again? They did not seem to understand that by this time they were clutching at straws.

On Chamberlain's instructions, Halifax picked up the telephone and called the Italians. They knew that neither Mussolini nor Ciano wanted war, and they engaged their aid in halting Hitler. He must be stopped, though not by force! He must be made to see reason—and the Poles too, of course. Mussolini must arrange another conference.

It was at this point that Neville Chamberlain ceased to be the villain of prewar Britain, dragging his nation down by a mixture of arrogance and self-deception, and became a pathetic dupe, aghast at the avalanche of evil consequences about to descend on his head. Now he was ready to try any panacea and seek the aid of any bedfellow to save himself and his country from the results of his folly. Pleas were sent to Mussolini, and the lines to Göring via Dahlerus were kept open.

It was August 20. Since Adolf Hitler had decided that he had better join the Soviet Union rather than fight it, why not signal his adhesion in the most flattering way—by sending his greetings to Josef Stalin himself? With a request, of course.

STALIN, MOSCOW. I SINCERELY WELCOME THE SIGNING OF THE NEW GERMAN-SOVIET TRADE AGREEMENT AS THE FIRST STEP IN

360

CEMENTING GERMAN-SOVIET RELATIONS. THE CONCLUSION OF
A NONAGGRESSION PACT WITH THE SOVIET UNION MEANS TO ME
THE ESTABLISHMENT OF GERMAN POLICY FOR A LONG TIME.
GERMANY THEREBY RESUMES A POLITICAL COURSE WHICH WAS
BENEFICIAL TO BOTH STATES DURING CENTURIES PAST.

I ACCEPT THE DRAFT ON THE NONAGGRESSION PACT WHICH YOUR
FOREIGN MINISTER MOLOTOV HANDED OVER BUT CONSIDER IT
URGENTLY NECESSARY TO CLARIFY THE QUESTIONS CONNECTED
WITH IT AS SOON AS POSSIBLE. THE SUBSTANCE OF THE SUPPLE-
MENTARY PROTOCOL DESIRED BY THE SOVIET UNION CAN, I AM
CONVINCED, BE CLARIFIED IN THE SHORTEST POSSIBLE TIME IF
A RESPONSIBLE GERMAN STATESMAN CAN COME TO MOSCOW
HIMSELF TO NEGOTIATE. OTHERWISE THE GOVERNMENT OF THE
REICH ARE NOT CLEAR AS TO HOW THE SUPPLEMENTARY PRO-
TOCOL COULD BE CLEARED UP AND SETTLED IN A SHORT TIME . . .
IT IS DESIRABLE NOT TO LOSE ANY TIME.

I THEREFORE AGAIN PROPOSE THAT YOU RECEIVE MY FOREIGN
MINISTER ON TUESDAY AUGUST 22 BUT AT THE LATEST AUGUST
23. THE REICH FOREIGN MINISTER HAS THE FULLEST POWERS TO
DRAW UP AND SIGN THE NONAGGRESSION PACT AS WELL AS THE
PROTOCOL. A LONGER STAY BY THE FOREIGN MINISTER IN MOS-
COW THAN ONE OR TWO DAYS IS IMPOSSIBLE IN VIEW OF THE
INTERNATIONAL SITUATION. I SHOULD BE GLAD TO RECEIVE YOUR
EARLIEST ANSWER.

Germany was practically begging, and Moscow appreciated it.
The reference to "protocol" was the bait which Germany was offering
Russia in the event of a pact; when war came, the two countries would
divide the Polish spoils, and protocol would specify how and where.
Moreover, the rest of the message had a "now or never" quality, which
Stalin recognized.

Twenty-four hours passed while Adolf Hitler waited for an
answer. Afterward he was to say that they were the most agonizing
of his life. He stayed up all night at Berchtesgaden, pacing the floor
and haranguing his listeners. At one point, much to the stupefaction
of the courtiers, Eva Braun appeared with a beaker of milk soup
which the Führer began to sip. But as soon as she slipped away he put
it down, belched loudly and began to chew an apple.

In Paris, the Cabinet had been meeting. At last it had made up its
mind that the objections of the Poles must be overridden. On August
21 Daladier himself sent off a telegram to the French delegation:

IMMEDIATE ATTENTION GENERAL DOUMENC.

YOU ARE AUTHORIZED SIGN, IN COMMON INTEREST AND IN AGREE-
MENT WITH AMBASSADOR, BEST POSSIBLE MILITARY AGREEMENT
SUBJECT FINAL APPROVAL FRENCH GOVERNMENT.

In effect, this meant that Doumenc had permission to give the Russians France's agreement to Soviet access to Poland despite the
opposition of Warsaw. It had come at last, but it was too late.
Doumenc hastened to seek out Voroshilov to tell him, but now that
he knew what Stalin was planning, the marshal suddenly became
elusive and it took some time to track him down. When at last
Doumenc did so the following day, the Russian, though he must have
known that it didn't matter now, still subjected the Frenchman to a
grilling.*

VOROSHILOV: I would ask General Doumenc to acquaint me with the
nature of the document which he has received from his government.
I would also like to know if the British mission has received a reply to the
same question.

DOUMENC: I have no document, but I have been informed by my
government that the reply to the cardinal point [access to Poland] is
basically in the affirmative. In other words, my government has authorized
me to sign a military pact which shall stipulate the authorization of the
passage of Soviet troops through all the areas which you have laid down ...

VOROSHILOV: That is the communication from the French government?

DOUMENC: Yes, these are the instructions given me by the French
government.

VOROSHILOV: And the British government?

DOUMENC (who knew very well that the British were not backing the
French on this and that they had no intention of overriding the Poles):
I do not know if Admiral Drax has received similar instructions from his
government; but I know that the admiral has been advised that the
conference can continue.

VOROSHILOV: The British delegation knows about this communication?

Doumenc said yes, and hastily added that he was sure the British
government would send a reply similar to that of the French. In the

* Though there are grounds for believing that he was severely shaken by the
imminent alliance with Germany. "When I saw him just after it," Charles Bohlen
said to the author, "he looked as if he had been dragged through a keyhole."

meantime, France's reply was surely sufficient to warrant the continuation of the conference.

Voroshilov pounced on the Frenchman's slight hesitation, though he had tried to conceal it. "It is possible that the British mission may be agreeable to General Doumenc pursuing these military matters," he said. "Nevertheless it seems to me that the British mission has played and plays, if not a dominant role, at least an equal one in all our conversations. That is why in the absence of any reply from the British government it will obviously be difficult to continue the work of this conference."

Since by now the marshal had received his orders from the Politburo and had no intention to keep the conference going in any case, this was sheer hypocrisy. Nevertheless, the hectoring continued. "There is one other question which interests me," Voroshilov declared. "I must ask you to excuse me, General, but it is a very serious question which I feel I must put to you. You have not in your reply given any indication of the attitude of the Polish and Rumanian governments. Are they aware of exactly what is going on, or does the reply which you have received emanate from the French government without the knowledge of Poland and Rumania?"

By this time Doumenc was sure that the Russians knew exactly what was going on. But such was the caliber of the man that he would not give up. Had he only been in the French government instead of the army, things might have been different.

"I do not know what conversations have taken place between governments," he replied. "I can only repeat what has been said to me by my own government." At which point, like the good tactician, he counterattacked. "I would like to take this opportunity of putting the following question to you: Is it, or is it not, your intention to press on with our conversations with a view to signing a military pact? I have reached that point, and time is passing." He stared across at the Soviet marshal belligerently.

"That time is passing is indisputable, but it is hardly our fault that the representatives of France and Great Britain have spent so long dallying over these questions," Voroshilov answered.

"*D'accord!* It is possible that from the very start we encountered difficulties . . . which did not depend upon ourselves, but I must say once more to you, Marshal, that I too am prepared to work fast—indeed, as fast as possible."

363

For the first time a glint of feeling came into the Russian's eyes. "I do not doubt it," he answered. "In the last few days I have come to know you, and your sincerity and your genuine desire to sign a military agreement as fast as possible are apparent to me."

"Speedily, and with the mutual confidence of soldiers who face a common enemy."

The marshal shook his head. ". . . I cannot agree to any further session around the conference table until all official replies have been received. I do not question that the General has received an affirmative reply from his own government. But the attitudes of Poland, Rumania and Great Britain are still unknown. That is why further talks can lead merely to a lot of chatter which can only be politically damaging." And then he added—and now Doumenc realized that the Russians knew *everything*—"I am quite sure that if the Poles had given their agreement to the passage of Soviet troops, they would wish to take part in our discussions. Indeed, I am convinced that they would demand to be present, for I cannot see their General Staff being willing to remain on the sidelines while questions which concern them so closely are under discussion. For this reason I do not believe they know what is going on."

Doumenc replied, "This may be so, but I do not know and I cannot say."

"Let us wait until everything is clear," the Russian said.

"I can wait with pleasure, but I do not wish to wait to no purpose. I must be frank with you, Marshal. It has already been announced that 'someone' is due to arrive, and such visits do not fill me with pleasure."

"This is quite true, but the responsibility must be laid at the door of Great Britain and France," said Voroshilov. "The question of military collaboration has been under consideration for several years, but nothing has ever come of it. Last year, when Czechoslovakia went down, we expected a signal from France and our troops were ready; but nothing happened. . . ." He shook his head. "Let us wait now until the situation is tidied up . . . The French and British representatives have drawn out the political discussions interminably. For this reason one cannot exclude the possibility that during this time some political development may have taken place." He shrugged his shoulders. "Let us wait. . . ."

They continued to talk, but they both knew that it was all over.

364

. . .

At 10:50 P.M. on August 21, the teletype tinkled at Berchtesgaden, and Adolf Hitler bounded over to see what message it was bringing.

TO THE CHANCELLOR OF THE GERMAN REICH ADOLF HITLER: I THANK YOU FOR THE LETTER. I HOPE THAT THE GERMAN-SOVIET NONAGGRESSION PACT WILL BRING ABOUT A DECIDED TURN FOR THE BETTER IN THE POLITICAL RELATIONS BETWEEN OUR COUNTRIES.
THE PEOPLES OF OUR COUNTRIES NEED PEACEFUL RELATIONS WITH EACH OTHER. THE ASSENT OF THE GERMAN GOVERNMENT TO THE CONCLUSION OF A NONAGGRESSION PACT PROVIDES THE FOUNDATION FOR ELIMINATING THE POLITICAL TENSION BE-TWEEN OUR COUNTRIES.
THE SOVIET GOVERNMENT HAS INSTRUCTED ME TO INFORM YOU THAT THEY AGREE TO HERR VON RIBBENTROP'S ARRIVING IN MOS-COW ON AUGUST 23.

J. STALIN

Once more Hitler's hands went up in the air. "Ho, ho!" he cried. "It's done! We've done it! Now we can spit in everybody's face!" He turned to the radiant Ribbentrop. "Tell Dietrich to announce it at once!"

While subordinates in the Press Department of the Propaganda Ministry were typing out the announcement of the impending Russian-German pact on the night of August 21, there was also a flurry of activity in the Foreign Office in London. It was not because of the negotiations in Moscow, however, but because they were making arrangements to receive a distinguished visitor.

It had always been Hermann Göring's ambition to visit London, and he had been enthusiastically supported in this aim by Nevile Henderson, who often declared it his hope one day to see "the Führer and Hermann Göring ride down the Mall to Buckingham Palace to visit the King." Now it looked as if the Field Marshal was at least going to see something of England, though not its capital. On the morning of August 21 he had telephoned Birger Dahlerus in Stockholm and confessed that he was worried. Events were moving too fast. He did not mention the Russo-German trade agreement, which had been signed in Berlin the previous day, but this, plus the possibilities for even closer association between the two countries, must have been on his mind.

365

Göring asked Dahlerus whether he had heard from his English friends, and the Swede, somewhat aggrieved, answered that Charles Spencer had requested that he come to Paris. Why Paris? Dahlerus had tartly replied that he would gladly go to England, but under no circumstances to France.

Göring answered, "I am going to try something radically different. It's the only way to break the deadlock, I think." He hung up without explaining further.

A few hours later General Karl Bodenschatz was in communication with the British embassy in Berlin, and two hours later Sir Nevile Henderson was happily sending a cipher message to London. Its purport was that Field Marshal Göring believed that the present tension could be alleviated by a personal talk between himself and the Prime Minister. Provided that a meeting between him and Mr. Chamberlain could be guaranteed, and provided secrecy over his visit could be maintained, he was prepared to fly to London and suggested Wednesday, August 23, as the date.

Halifax consulted Neville Chamberlain at once. Racked by doubts and worries now, and increasingly aware that his friend Mussolini was as scared and bewildered as he was, the Prime Minister had no hesitation. In fact, he was flattered that the German leader was prepared to make the journey, and he envisaged the headlines. On second thought, however, he allowed himself to be reminded by Halifax and Sir Horace Wilson that publicity might not be a good idea. Göring did not want it, and in any case the British public was in no mood for further tête-à-têtes with the Nazis; nothing but disaster ever followed them.

The Air Ministry was informed at once and asked to arrange for Göring's reception. It was obvious that the Field Marshal could not come to London; he was far too recognizable. Instead, the Royal Air Force suggested that he should be flown to a little-used airfield just north of Bovingdon, in Herefordshire, from which he would be driven straight to the Prime Minister's official country residence. Sir Horace Wilson was told to arrange for the staff at Chequers to be given leave and replaced by a small squad of secret service and military personnel.

"The telephone is to be disconnected," wrote Halifax. "It looks as if it is going to be a dramatic interlude, and having laid the plans, we await confirmation from Germany."

They went on waiting. They heard nothing more until three days later, August 24, when a message came from Berlin to inform them that the Führer had forbidden Göring's visit, which he no longer considered necessary.

By that time, of course, everyone knew why.

■

Shortly before midnight on August 21 the music on the main German radio service abruptly faded. "Here is a special announcement," the announcer said. "The government of the Greater German Reich and the government of the people's Republics of the Soviet Union have agreed to conclude a mutual nonaggression pact. The Reich Minister for Foreign Affairs, Von Ribbentrop, will arrive in Moscow on Wednesday, August twenty-third, for the conclusion of the negotiations."

The next morning, as the headlines flared across the Berlin newspapers, half about the forthcoming pact, half about the "unbelievable atrocities" being committed by the Poles against their German minority, Erich Kordt cantered onto the bridle path in the Tiergarten, where he found Admiral Canaris waiting for him. Kordt was not looking forward to the encounter, and his apprehensions were well founded.

"So the British had the pact with Russia in the bag, did they, Kordt?" said Canaris. "My dear fellow, how could you let them deceive you! This Emile is more cunning than you think—and much more cunning than your London friends."

As they walked their horses down the path, Canaris said bitterly, "It has started already—the rot, I mean. All around here"—he waved toward the military headquarters in the Bendlerstrasse—"the brass hats* are most impressed with what has happened. They have already begun to learn the words of 'The Internationale' to be ready for Stalin's state visit!"

Ribbentrop had flown from Berchtesgaden to Berlin. Sailing through his office at the Foreign Ministry, he waved an imperious hand at

---

* He used the phrase *Silber- und Goldfasane*. *Silberfasane* were senior staff officers with silver facings on their uniforms. *Goldfasane* were War Ministry senior officers with gold facings.

Martin Luther and a couple of obsequious secretaries who clapped their hands for him as he entered. That evening he and his staff of thirty took off from Tempelhof in two Condor aircraft and flew to Königsberg, where they stayed the night. Just before they landed they saw the lights of a man-of-war beneath them; it was the old German battleship *Schleswig-Holstein,* on its way for a "courtesy visit" to Danzig.

The plane which had brought Ribbentrop to Berlin took Canaris and several high German officers back to Berchtesgaden, where they arrived before noon on August 22. Hermann Göring, General Keitel and General von Brauchitsch were already there; they had been summoned to hear a talk by Adolf Hitler. It was to be a shattering experience.

The great hall at Berchtesgaden was jammed with *Silber- und Goldfasane* of the German armed forces, but there was very little noise. The mood of the admirals and generals was subdued and wary; no one smoked; no one seemed anxious to talk to his neighbor. Presently there was a crash of rifle stocks and the sharp clicking of heels as the guards of the Leibstandarte Adolf Hitler came to the salute, and the Führer himself entered, his slightly crablike way of walking somehow exaggerated this morning. There was no trace of last night's elation, though his eyes were very bright.

"I have called you together," Hitler said, "to give you a picture of the political situation in order that you may have an insight into the individual elements upon which I have based my decision to act, and"—his first jab of contempt toward his generals, whose caution and apprehension he knew so well—"in order to strengthen your confidence. After this we will discuss military details."

The Führer then launched into the exposition of his definitive plans to dominate Europe. "It has been clear to me that a conflict with Poland had to come sooner or later. I made a declaration to that effect this spring, but at that time I thought I would turn first against the West in a few years' time, and only afterward against the East. But the sequence cannot always be fixed. One cannot close one's eyes to a threatening situation. In the beginning I wanted to establish an acceptable relationship with Poland in order to fight first against the West. But this plan, which would have suited me, could not be

368

executed because essential points have now changed. It became obvious that Poland would attack us in the event of a conflict with the West. Poland wants access to the sea. A further development [of Polish hostility] became obvious after our occupation of Memel and it seemed clear to me that under the circumstances a conflict with Poland could break out at a moment when it would be inopportune for us."

So why had he changed his plans? It came down to a question of personalities—the personalities of himself and of Benito Mussolini. There had never been any false modesty about Adolf Hitler, and he showed none now. "Essentially everything depends upon me, upon my existence, upon my political activities. It depends on the fact that no one will ever again have the confidence of the whole German people as I do. There will probably never again be a man with more authority than I have. My existence is therefore a factor of great value. But don't forget that I can be wiped out at any time, by a criminal or an idiot. The second personal factor is the Duce. His existence is also decisive. If something happens to him. Italy's loyalty to the alliance will no longer be certain. The basic attitude of the Italian court is anti-Mussolini. To them the expansion of their empire is a burden. The Duce is the man with the strongest nerves in Italy."*

Hitler also praised Europe's other dictator, General Franco, and then, with contempt in his voice, he turned to the Western democracies. "The other side? A negative picture as far as decisive personalities is concerned. There is no outstanding personality in either England or France. For us it is easy to make a decision. We have nothing to lose; we can only gain. Our economic situation is such that because of the restrictions which bind us we cannot hold out for more than a few years." He gestured to the Field Marshal sitting beside him. "Göring can confirm this. We have no other choice! We must act! Whereas our opponents risk much and can gain little. England's stake in a war is unimaginably great. Yet our enemies have men who are small, below average. No personalities! No masters! No men of action!"

As the hierarchy of the German armed forces listened to the hoarse but abnormally calm voice of their Führer, three or four among them furtively scribbled notes of what he was saying. It was

---

* He was to feel differently a few days later.

understood that this address was to be off the record; not even Hitler's adjutant, Colonel Schmundt, was taking it down. But Canaris did, as did General Halder (in shorthand) and Admiral Hermann Boehm, and probably one other.*

The survey of the difficulties of the Western allies continued. "All these circumstances, fortunate for us, will no longer prevail in two to three years. No one knows how long I shall live. Therefore it is better that we should start the conflict now!"

The audience in the great hall at Berchtesgaden had been silent until now, but at these words there was a sudden stir. General Halder underlined them in his notes, and Admiral Boehm added an exclamation point.

Now the Führer was getting into his stride. There followed, in a voice beginning to rise with indignation, the usual attack on the intransigence of the Poles, on the rejection of the genuine offer he had made them, on Britain's interference and sabotage of a peaceful settlement. Then, as if the fear nagged him, he again referred to the possibility of an attempt on his life, and repeated that no time must be lost.

Would the West interfere with his plans? He thought not. "But I have always accepted a great risk in the conviction that it may succeed. Now we face a great risk again, and we need iron nerves and iron resolution. But for the following special reasons, my ideas [that Britain and France would not interfere] are strengthened. England and France are pledged [to Poland], but neither is in a position for it. There is no actual rearmament in England, only propaganda." At this point he poured his scorn over his generals. "It did much damage to us that many reluctant Germans wrote to Englishmen after our solution of the Czech question. But I carried my point because you lost your nerve, because you capitulated too soon!"

It must have been an awkward moment for the generals who had been plotting against Hitler the previous September to realize that he suspected their activities. Afterward Halder confessed that he winced.

Hitler continued contemptuously, "How is British rearmament proceeding, in fact? The construction program for the navy has not

* See Notes at the end of this book.

370

been fulfilled. . . . Little has been done on land. England will only be able to send a maximum of three divisions to the Continent.* A little has been done for the air force, but it is only a beginning. Antiaircraft defense is in its initial stages. At the moment England has only one hundred and fifty antiaircraft guns. . . . England does not want a conflict to break out for two or three years."

After dismissing Britain's preparedness with a few more statistics, Hitler was even more cavalier in his treatment of the weakness and decadence of France. Between them the two Allies could blockade Germany, but unlike the measure taken in the World War, this would fail because this time Germany would have supplies from the East. They could attack Germany from their positions on the Maginot Line, but this too he brushed off—rather too airily for some members of his audience. Nor would Britain and France violate Belgian, Dutch or Swiss neutrality in order to attack Germany. No, a military offensive on their part was out of the question. "No one is counting on a long war," he said. "If my general here, Von Brauchitsch, had told me that it would take four years to conquer Poland, I would have told him, *It cannot be done*. But it is nonsense to say that England wants to wage a long war. What we will do is hold our position in the West until we have conquered Poland. Then . . ."

He left the sentence hanging in midair, as if to say, "Then we shall see what the Western allies decide to do."

At last Hitler turned to the subject which all of them had been waiting for: an explanation of the negotiations with Russia. "The enemy had another hope: that Russia would become our enemy after the conquest of Poland. The enemy did not count on my great power of resolution. But then, our enemies are little worms! I saw them at Munich! I was convinced that Stalin would never accept the English offer. . . . Russia has no interest in maintaining Poland."

It was Litvinov's dismissal that had given him the clue, he told his audience. "It came to me like a cannonball as a sign of change in Moscow toward the Western powers. I brought about the change toward Russia gradually." He was all triumph and smugness now. "In connection with the commercial treaty, we got into political conversation and the proposal of a nonaggression pact. Then came a

* His information was correct.

371

general proposal from Russia. Then four days ago I personally took a special step. It brought about the Russian answer of yesterday—that she is ready to sign. Personal contact with Stalin has been established. The day after tomorrow Von Ribbentrop will conclude the treaty.

"Now Poland is in the position in which I wanted her! We need not be afraid of a blockade! The East will support us with grain, cattle, coal, lead and zinc! I am only afraid that some *Schweinhund* will now make a proposal for mediation.* The political arm is ready. A beginning has been made for the destruction of England's hegemony. The way is open for the soldier—after I have made the political preparations."

There is a break here in the reports of the meeting, and General Halder cannot remember whether or not there was a brief adjournment at this point. What is known is that at this point Adolf Hitler paused in his lecture and that Hermann Göring immediately rose, thanked him and led a round of applause.†

At any rate, presently Hitler was again lecturing his audience. Now his mood seemed firmer, as if he had become aware of doubts among his audience and felt the need to galvanize them.

"Of course it may turn out differently with regard to England. One cannot predict with certainty. But I believe that there will be trade sanctions rather than a blockade, possibly with a severance of diplomatic relations. It must be met with the most iron determination on our side. We retreat before no one! Everyone will have to make a point of it that we were always going to fight the Western powers, that this is a struggle for life or death, that Germany has always won every war where she has stayed united. It is a question of iron, facing unflinchingly the strain which will be brought to bear on us. A long period of peace would not have done us any good, anyhow. Therefore we must face up to everything with a brave and manly bearing ... It is not machines that fight each other but men! We have the better quality of men. Mental factors are decisive. The opposing camp has

* Some generals who were at the meeting deny having heard this remark. On the other hand, Halder records it, and so does Boehm. It seems most likely that Hitler was expressing his hope that no one would interfere with his military operations in Poland, but from the words that follow he still seems to envision a stalemate with the West.

† One report suggests that the Field Marshal got up on the table and danced with glee. It seems most unlikely; it would have been out of character. Besides, Göring's mood was hardly ecstatic.

372

the weaker people. In 1918 the nation collapsed because the mental prerequisites were not sufficient. It is Frederick the Great who should show us the way, for he secured final success only because of his mental drive."

Then, almost as if wagging a finger at this audience, the Führer whipped himself up to his climax. "Remember that the destruction of Poland is in the foreground of all our plans. The aim is the elimination of living forces, not the achievement of a certain line. Even if the Western powers retaliate and war should break out with them, the destruction of Poland will remain the primary objective. But it must be quick. The season for victory is coming to an end."

Now Hitler turned from strategy to tactics, and briefly touched on a subject which must have puzzled most of his listeners, though Halder, Keitel, Canaris and Himmler's Gestapo knew or suspected what he was talking about. "I shall give a good reason for starting this war which propaganda can exploit—though it does not matter whether it is plausible or not. The victor will not be asked later on by the vanquished whether we told the truth or not. In starting or making war it is not right which matters but victory.*

"As to our conduct of the war: have no pity. Attack and achieve brutally. It is a question of eighty million Germans getting what is their right; it is their security which has to be achieved. It is the strongest who have right on their side, and we must exercise the greatest severity in our actions to make that plain, for we need a quick decision. I believe we will achieve it because I have the greatest faith in the German soldier, for whom the coming days will be the test. They cannot fail. Nothing can fail if"—staring hard at the generals —"the nerves of Germany's leaders stay firm." Here he paused and then added, "The complete destruction of Poland is the aim. I am convinced that the armed forces of the Wehrmacht are ready to do what is required of them. I will probably order the start of operations on Saturday morning."

Whereupon he strode out of the hall, beckoning Göring, Halder, Keitel and Brauchitsch to follow him.

So it was all to begin on Saturday, August 26. This was at least six days earlier than anyone, including the German General Staff, had expected Hitler to strike.

* Hitler was referring to the Gestapo's plans for a fake "incident" which would give him the pretext for invading Poland (see p. 431).

■

August 23 was a fateful day for Europe and the world. Joachim von Ribbentrop had arrived in Moscow, and Molotov was on the airfield to meet him. The band played "Deutschland über alles" (but not the Nazi hymn, the "Horst Wessel Song"*), and the two Foreign Ministers conferred briefly before the motorcade, flying swastika and hammer-and-sickle flags, drove into Moscow. There Ribbentrop went to the German embassy for a snack of caviar, smoked salmon and French champagne before driving to the Kremlin for his first meeting with Stalin at four o'clock.

Friedrich Gaus had drawn up the pact itself, and Ribbentrop submitted it in full expectation that there would be arguments ahead. Not at all; like reformed drunkards who have decided to break the pledge, the Russians were positively eager. The German Foreign Minister and his assistant, Gustav Hilger of their Moscow embassy, emerged after three quarters of an hour smiling broadly. Ribbentrop told Gaus that the "agreement Germany desired was as good as assured"—he only had to settle a small matter with the Führer. There had even been a cozy chat. Stalin confessed to Ribbentrop that Britain "had never told the Soviet government what she really wanted." In reply, Ribbentrop let his spleen against the English run loose. "They always wanted to interfere with relations between Germany and the Soviet Union," he said, a remark which must have made even the Soviet leader blush. "England is weak, though, and wants to let others fight for her claims to world domination—stupid claims." Stalin heartily concurred. England had dominated the world for too long, and it was idiotic that other countries had let themselves be bluffed by her.

Shortly after Ribbentrop left for the Kremlin, Charles Bohlen had slipped into the German embassy, where he was received by his informant on the German staff. He was shown into a cubicle at the back of the man's office and told to keep his pen and paper ready. Upstairs he could hear someone shouting into the telephone to someone obviously a long way off at the end of a very bad line. Over and over he heard the words "Libau! L-I-B-A-U! Windau! W-I-N-D-A-U! Warm-water ports!"

* Though the Russians even did that later.

374

Bohlen did not know then that the man he heard was Erich Kordt's assistant, Brücklemeier, who was trying to learn from Hitler whether the Führer would allow the Latvian ports of Libau and Windau to be included in Russia's sphere of interest under the new agreement. Ribbentrop was finally forced to send a message, which was teletyped to Berchtesgaden.

While they awaited Hitler's reply on the question of the Latvian ports (which was not long in coming and said: "Tell him to agree") the Soviet leader and the German Foreign Minister toasted each other in vodka. After that little matter was settled, the negotiations went smoothly; the Nazi Foreign Minister and his Communist host might have been old friends. Possibly Ribbentrop was a little drunk not only from the vodka but from the thought that he had masterminded this incredible pact. He put his arm on Stalin's shoulder, and that jovial monster quickly responded with a bear hug.

"What about the Anti-Comintern Pact now?" joked Stalin.

"It was never directed against you!" responded Ribbentrop. "Who did it frighten? Not you, but the cowering capitalists in the City of London and the English shopkeepers!"

Encouraged by Stalin's laugh of approval, he went on, "Do you know what they say in Berlin—where they have the monopoly of wit in Germany? They say, 'Just you wait. Josef Stalin will join the Anti-Comintern Pact one of these days.' "

There was a general laugh. Then Stalin looked at the agreement again, and for a moment was sobered. It was the only time that he seemed to have recovered his sense of reality, to have remembered what kind of people he was on the point of making an alliance with. In Gaus's preamble to the treaty, Ribbentrop had inserted several sentences stressing the warm friendship between Germany and Russia and the tenderness of their sentiments for each other. The mustachioed old tyrant prodded the Russian text with his stubby finger and shook his head. "That must go," he said. "The Soviet government cannot suddenly present its public with assurances of friendship from Germany—not after they have had pails of dreck poured over them by the Nazi government for the past six years. That must go!"

It went, but the toasts continued. Stalin raised his glass and proposed a toast to Adolf Hitler. "I know how much the German nation loves its Führer. I should therefore like to drink to his health." The wicked old scoundrel seemed genuinely moved, gazing at the saffron

375

face of the Nazi Foreign Minister as if he were an angel of light. "I believe the Germans desire peace! I will not let them down!"

After this Molotov drank to Ribbentrop's health, and then the two Russian leaders together downed toast after toast to the future of the nonaggression pact and of German-Soviet relations.

"The Reich Foreign Minister in turn," says a report of the occasion, "proposed a toast to Josef Stalin, toasts to the Soviet government and to a favorable development of relations between Germany and the Soviet Union."

Finally, well after midnight, the articles were signed before the cameras and lights of German and Russian photographers.

There was, of course, a secret clause—there usually is on these occasions—and it specified the price Adolf Hitler had to pay. He had what he wanted: an agreement that in the event of war, Russia would remain neutral even if Britain and France fulfilled their obligations to Poland. The secret protocol spelled out the bribe:

> On the occasion of the signing of the nonaggression treaty between Germany and the Soviet Union the undersigned plenipotentiaries discussed in strictly confidential conversations the question of the delimitation of their respective spheres of interest in Eastern Europe.
> 1. In the event of a territorial and political transformation in the territories belonging to the Baltic States (Finland, Estonia, Latvia, Lithuania), the northern frontier of Lithuania shall represent the frontier of the spheres of interest both of Germany and the U.S.S.R.
> 2. In the event of a territorial and political transformation of the territories belonging to the Polish state, the spheres of interest of both Germany and the U.S.S.R. shall be bounded approximately by the line of the rivers Narew, Vistula and San.
> The question whether the interests of both Parties make the maintenance of an independent Polish state appear desirable and how the frontiers of this state should be drawn can be determined only in the course of further political developments. In any case, both governments will resolve this question by means of a friendly understanding.

Thus was the fate of Poland sealed.

. . .

376

Back to the German embassy went Ribbentrop, Schulenburg, Gaus and Hilger, carrying the text of the agreement and its secret clause with them. It was the early hours of August 24 when Ribbentrop returned, but every member of the embassy was waiting to greet him. They stood in a row and applauded him as he marched through the hall to the dining room.

There the Foreign Minister summoned the six senior members of the embassy. "Are these the ones who know about the secret protocol?" Ribbentrop asked.

"Yes," Schulenburg said. "No one else."

"Very well, then. You know that we have pledged the Soviet government that the secret protocol will indeed be kept secret. Not only for their sake—it is important for Germany. It would not do to make it known to the world what we have signed in return for the nonaggression agreement. Is that understood? It must indeed be kept secret."

There was a murmur of assent, but Ribbentrop was not satisfied. He turned to Schulenburg and said, "I suggest that you ask for their word."

With a sudden access of embarrassment, Schulenburg hesitated and then raised his hand in the Nazi salute. "Let us all swear, as loyal members of the Greater German Reich of Adolf Hitler, that we will say nothing whatsoever of the existence of a secret protocol to the agreement which has been signed this night."

Everyone in the room raised their hands and duly swore.*

Down below, in the small room at the back of his informant's office, Charles Bohlen was just completing the copying of the secret protocol. Word for word, it was on its way to Washington four hours later.

While they waited for news of the German-Russian agreement at the British embassy on the evening of August 23, members of the foreign press had come to see the British ambassador at his request. He would make an announcement, they had been told, about the status of the Anglo-French-Russian negotiations.

---

* Later, they and several other members of the embassy staff signed a document pledging secrecy, and this was deposited in the embassy safe.

As the correspondents sat around, impatient, cynical, aware that there was a smell of defeat in the air, John Russell,* the press attaché, entered.

"Come on, John," said one correspondent, "what's it all about? What's the ambassador going to say?"

Russell promptly endeared himself to them all. "I don't know what *he*'s going to tell you," he said, "but it is my opinion that the British government has just been administered a considerable kick up the arse!"

■

In Paris on August 23 the ministers of the French Cabinet and the Chiefs of Staff of the three services† met at six o'clock in emergency session. Georges Bonnet had persuaded Daladier to call the conference. The announcement of the impending Russo-German pact had hit the Foreign Minister like a physical blow, and for a time he had all but collapsed, crying that everything was over, or alternatively railing at the Poles for their arrogance and stupidity. In his mind there could be no question now of France's being involved in war with Germany; Warsaw's stubbornness gave his government every reason, he believed, for backing out of any obligation. He hoped that his colleagues would agree with him.

The ministers and the military gathered in Daladier's study, the evening sun glinting through the windows, the hum of homeward-bound traffic murmuring below them on the Left Bank. As usual in times of emergency, Daladier's peasant face wore a high flush and he seemed nervous, but his voice was firm when he began to speak. "This meeting has been called at the request of the Minister for Foreign Affairs. I do not propose to speak at length myself, but to listen to your views. In the present crisis, I think it is necessary for us to answer three questions. They are: 1. Can France remain inactive while Poland and Rumania (or one of them) are being wiped off the map of Europe? 2. What means has our country at her disposal

* Sir John Russell, son of a famous international policeman and anti-narcotics crusader, Russell Pasha of Egypt, is now British ambassador to Brazil.
† Premier Daladier, Foreign Minister Bonnet, Campinchi (Navy Minister), La Chambre (Air Minister), General Gamelin (Army), Admiral Darlan (Navy), General Vuillemin (Air Force).

for opposing such action? 3. What measures should we take *now?*"

At once Bonnet began to speak. "The Russo-German pact has totally altered the equilibrium of the opposing forces. Poland will now get no help whatsoever from the U.S.S.R. We once thought that the Soviet Union would at least utilize her air force and supply war and other materials. We now must renounce that hope, and accept instead a Russo-German entente against Poland. Rumania will be forced to supply Germany with all she needs, especially oil. Turkey will keep out of the conflict until such time as a Balkan country itself is attacked. On the other hand, England is firmly at the side of France, but she is only at the beginning of her land rearmament. Of the intentions of the Germans we can have no illusions: they are not bluffing and they are resolved to retake Danzig and the Corridor even if it results in a general war."

Those were the facts, the Foreign Minister said drily, and then added swiftly that they might not be the facts if Warsaw had not repeatedly refused France's pleas to allow Russian troops to pass through Poland. "What should our attitude be now? Must we keep faithful to our alliance with Poland? Would it not be better to force Poland to compromise by reconsidering?* We could thus gain time to perfect our matériel and build up our military strength, to improve our diplomatic situation, and thus be in a better position if Germany later on turns against France and attacks her." He turned toward Gamelin. "What is the opinion of the military?"

"The important thing is to persuade Italy to remain neutral," the general answered. Admiral Darlan nodded his head emphatically.

Bonnet said, "We have never in my ministry ceased our efforts to secure Italy's neutrality . . . But to come back to my first question: In spite of Russia's defection, does the alliance with Poland still remain of the first military importance for France? And how long will the Polish forces be able to hold out against Germany?"

Gamelin answered confidently, "The Polish army will offer brave and honorable resistance to the Germans. The cold and the bad weather will quickly arrest all operations, and the battle will still, I believe, be going on in the East in the spring of 1940. That will give time for the French army to be reinforced by British divisions landing on the Continent."

* That is, her unyielding attitude toward Germany.

379

General Gamelin had been overly sanguine in the past, but even he had rarely been so wrong in his prognostications. He appeared to adapt his remarks in accordance with what he thought his listeners wished to hear. A few months before, he had signed a document on behalf of his country promising Poland that the French would launch a major counteroffensive against Germany within fifteen days of an attack on Poland, but now he completely contradicted this. "In the early stages of the conflict we can do little against the Germans. But French mobilization by itself will bring some relief to Poland by tying down some German units on our frontier . . . In the early stages we can bring almost as much help to Poland by mobilizing and concentrating our forces as by entering the war. It is to her interest, in fact, that we declare war as late as possible so that our concentration can be as advanced as possible."

One can imagine the reaction of the Poles if they had heard that.

On the other hand, Gamelin continued to stress—and Darlan vigorously agreed with him—that the French armed forces were in fine order and condition. But after the meeting was over, the general said to Daladier, "You will understand that I did not consider it proper to mention the deficiencies that still exist in our armament and industrial mobilization. You know them as well as I do, and I do not regard Georges Bonnet as trustworthy."

"You did right," the Premier answered. "Had you indicated them, the Germans would have known about them the next day."*

Nevertheless, this discretion was costly. At the meeting Gamelin had stressed that the military was prepared, and it was largely on his confidence and on his abounding faith in the power of the Poles to fight alone all through the winter that the emergency session decided to stand by their pledge to the Poles—for the moment, anyway—while they desperately sought other ways of securing a settlement.

In London on August 23 Neville Chamberlain and Lord Halifax were still waiting, though without much hope now, to hear whether Hermann Göring would be coming to London. In the meantime the

* Afterward Gamelin explained that Daladier was not suggesting that the Foreign Minister was betraying France, "but that he thought Bonnet capable, in his zeal for peace, of talking about these matters in political circles."

newspapers, the public and the Cabinet were demanding a firm response by Britain to the impending signing of the Russo-German pact. The English people had reacted to the alliance of the two dictators not with fear but with anger and belligerence. Far from making them cringe at the thought of war, it aroused militant indignation and a determined "we'll show 'em" attitude.

Hitler was amazed. He found it impossible to swallow the idea that the British public would now demand action from its government rather than submission, and that Neville Chamberlain would face dismissal if he failed to stand up to Hitler rather than knuckle under to him.*

As far as the Cabinet and the general public were concerned, therefore, Neville Chamberlain saw the need to show himself bold and resolute. Mobilization and the evacuation of women and children from London began. The Prime Minister decided that as soon as the news of the pact was announced, he would write Hitler a letter which would demonstrate in no uncertain manner that his government was standing firmly by her obligations to Poland.

"Your Excellency will have already heard of certain measures taken by His Majesty's Government," Chamberlain wrote the dictator. "These steps have, in the opinion of His Majesty's Government, been rendered necessary by the military movements which have been reported from Germany, and by the fact that apparently the announcement of a German-Soviet Agreement is taken in some quarters in Berlin to indicate that intervention by Great Britain on behalf of Poland is no longer a contingency that need be reckoned with. No greater mistake can be made. Whatever may prove to be the nature of the German-Soviet Agreement, it cannot alter Great Britain's obligation to Poland which His Majesty's Government have stated in public repeatedly and plainly and which they are determined to fulfill.

"It has been alleged that, if His Majesty's Government had made their position more clear in 1914, the great catastrophe would have been avoided. Whether or not there is any force in that allegation, His Majesty's Government are resolved that on this occasion there shall be no such tragic misunderstanding.

---

* Indeed, Hitler was so sure that the pact would panic the democracies that on the morning of August 25 he asked Erich Kordt if the British government had fallen. He believed that it would have to be replaced by a "pro-German" administration that would immediately seek an accommodation with Berlin.

381

"If the case should arise, they are resolved and prepared to employ without delay all the forces at their command, and it is impossible to foresee the end of hostilities once engaged. It would be a dangerous illusion to think that, if war once starts, it will come to an early end even if a success on any one of the several fronts on which it will be engaged should have been secured."

Having firmly stated his government's position, Chamberlain proceeded to emphasize that he was still hoping for a peaceful settlement.

"I cannot see that there is anything in the questions arising between Germany and Poland which could not and should not be resolved without the use of force, if only a situation of confidence could be restored to enable discussions to be carried on in an atmosphere different from that which prevails today . . . But I am bound to say that there would be slender hope of bringing such negotiations to a successful issue unless it were understood beforehand that any settlement reached [between Germany and Poland] would, when concluded, be guaranteed by other powers. His Majesty's Government would be ready, if desired, to make such contribution as they could to the effective operation of such guarantees. At this moment I confess I can see no other way to avoid a catastrophe that will involve Europe in war . . ."

It was a strong and clear message. Unfortunately, the British ambassador in Berlin was capable of diluting the most potent brew, and in the next twenty-four hours he succeeded in watering down everything that Chamberlain had written. In so doing he probably convinced Adolf Hitler once and for all that the British were bluffing and would stand aside once he moved his troops into Poland.

By the time Henderson and Baron von Weizsäcker arrived at Berchtesgaden by plane from Berlin, Adolf Hitler had already read Chamberlain's letter. The gist of it, telephoned to the British ambassador the previous evening, had been monitored by Göring's bureau, and the full text had been deciphered by the code-breaking department. A full text had been forwarded by the Foreign Ministry to Ribbentrop, who sneered at it in his conversations with Stalin and scoffed at its "pretensions."*

---

* Apparently everyone was decoding Britain's ciphered telegrams by this time. When Ribbentrop began to read Chamberlain's letter, Stalin waved him aside; he had already read it, he said.

When the nervous British envoy entered the Führer's study he found himself facing what he most dreaded—a Hitlerian rage. As was so often the case, this one was artificially contrived for the occasion; Hitler was actually in a good mood and was still basking pleasantly in the happy news from Moscow. But it was necessary to scare the "worms of Munich," of whom this Englishman was one of the most contemptible examples, and so the Führer indulged himself in the familiar old diatribe. Why had Britain interfered and prevented a peaceful settlement with Poland? How could they support these people—these beasts, these rapists, these brutish torturers of his people? He even provoked himself into revealing his castration complex again, which produced a bitterly humorous exchange.

They were raping his people, defenseless women and helpless girls! the Führer cried. They wanted to emasculate German menfolk in their territory, so that the race would be stifled. It was what the Czechs had done last year to the Germans and what the Poles were doing now—castrating German *Volksgenossen.*

Henderson said mildly that he did not wish to deny that there were persecutions going on, but surely the reports were greatly exaggerated. The Führer had mentioned castration; he happened to know of one case, and the German in question was a sex maniac who had been treated as he deserved.*

Not just one castration case! Six! Hitler cried.

Henderson switched to the Russo-German pact. He had never believed in a Franco-British-Russian pact anyway, he said. The Russians were just tricking the democracies. They wished to deceive Mr. Chamberlain and then profit from the war that would follow. Assuming his loftiest and most contemptuous manner, he added, "Personally, I would sooner have Germany make a pact with those people than England!"

Annoyed, Hitler answered that it would be a long and lasting treaty.

That remained to be seen, said Henderson. The Führer knew as well as he did that the Russians always made trouble.

Henderson was then dismissed to take lunch in Salzburg. Hitler

---

* Henderson seems to have made this up. British and French diplomatic authorities were reporting from Poland at this moment that the German atrocity stories were grossly exaggerated accounts of minor incidents.

had a difficult lunch of his own, with Unity Mitford; it was one of the last times he was to see her. To get rid of Henderson, he made the excuse that he must compose a reply to Chamberlain's letter; in fact, it was already written.

When they reassembled that afternoon, Henderson was handed the text to read. It was a typical Hitlerian diatribe, and said in part:

"Your Excellency informs me in the name of the British government that you will be obliged to render assistance to Poland in any such case of intervention on the part of Germany. I take note of this statement of yours and assure you that it can make no change in the determination of the Reich government to safeguard the interests of the Reich as stated. Your assurance to the effect that in such an event you anticipate a long war is shared by myself. Germany, if attacked by England, will be found prepared and determined. I have already more than once declared before the German people and the world that there can be no doubt concerning the determination of the new German Reich rather to accept, for however long it might be, every sort of misery and tribulation than to sacrifice national interests, let alone its honor."

Tears came to Henderson's eyes as he read this. "I so much regret all this!" he said.

"It is in Mr. Chamberlain's hands," Hitler answered. "He can decide whether there will be war."

"Chamberlain is a friend of Germany! He will go on being a friend!"

"All the more reason to regret that he cannot take a step toward us."

"I can give you proof that he is your friend," Henderson declared. "People clamor, but he has refused to let Churchill into his Cabinet. It is these influences that are responsible. It isn't the Birtish people who are anti-German—it comes from behind, from propaganda, directed by Jews and anti-Nazis!"

"I am fifty years old," Hitler said. "It is better to make war now than when I am fifty-five or sixty." He paused and then looked at the tearful British envoy. "When the next Polish provocation comes, I will take it in hand. The Danzig question will be settled now, one way or another [*so oder so*]! Tell them that!"

384

. . .

While Henderson was flying back to Berlin to make his report, Sir Horace Wilson in London left No. 10 Downing Street and walked to the corner of Whitehall, where he hailed a taxi and was driven to the American embassy.

Joseph P. Kennedy was back in London from his Riviera vacation, bronzed in face and body but severely racked in spirit. His son Jack had just returned from Berlin and brought word from Alexander Kirk, the chargé d'affaires, that he expected war to start within a week. Kennedy prayed that it wouldn't come to that. He was in a highly emotional mood and kept telling everyone who would listen that it was all a matter of gaining time. "Anything that keeps Britain at peace is in the interests of the United States," he said.

The American ambassador had spoken to Chamberlain several times on the telephone since his return, and he knew that Sir Horace Wilson had the full backing of the Prime Minister. There is no record of exactly what was said between the two of them, and neither Sir Horace Wilson nor Mr. Kennedy is able to fill in the details, but half an hour after Sir Horace left the embassy to return to Downing Street, Joseph Kennedy picked up the telephone, called the State Department and reported that the crisis was coming. "The British wanted one thing of us, and one thing only—namely, that we put pressure on the Poles," reported Jay Pierrepoint Moffat of the State Department. "They felt that they could not, given their obligations, but that we could."

President Roosevelt was on a summer cruise aboard the presidential yacht when the news came through of the Russo-German pact, but he had sailed for shore at once and taken a train from New Jersey back to Washington. His reaction to Sir Horace Wilson's plea is summed up in a comment by Moffat: "As we saw it here, it merely meant that they [the British] wanted us to assume the responsibility of a new Munich and to do their dirty work for them."

Kennedy had seen Sir Horace Wilson off with expressions of sympathy. Later that evening he drove over to see Chamberlain and they gloomed together. Afterward the ambassador cabled a report of the Prime Minister's attitude: "He says the futility of it all is the thing that is frightful. After all, they cannot save the Poles. They can merely carry on a war of revenge that will mean the destruction of all Europe."

385

On the same evening Chamberlain drove to Buckingham Palace for a meeting with King George VI, and it is believed that at one point he offered his resignation. It was refused, and he was urged to "carry on."

But carry on with what? The chickens were coming home to roost with a vengeance. The unthinking guarantee to the Poles which Chamberlain had given so readily earlier in the year to show Hitler and the British public that he meant business was now going to drag his country into war.

Unless . . .

FIVE

The Sands
Run Out

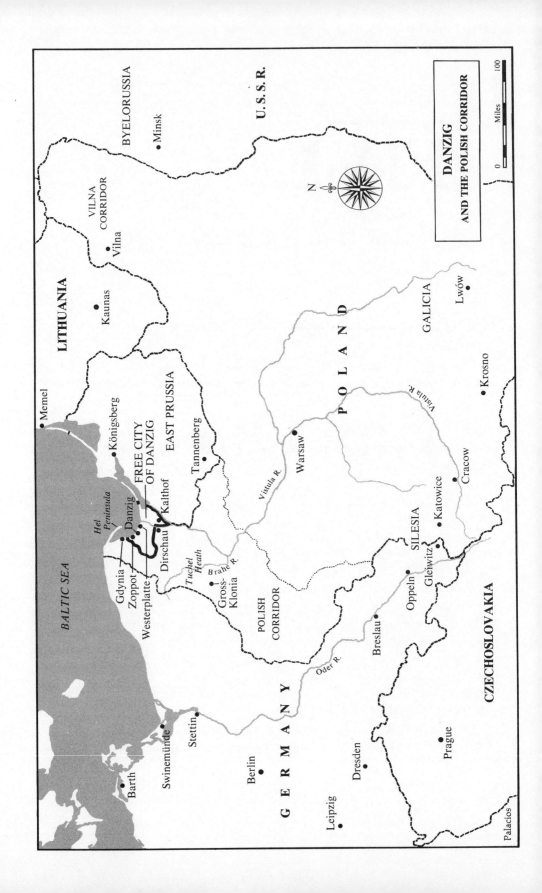

BYELORUSSIA

U.S.S.R.

• Minsk

VILNA
CORRIDOR

Vilna

LITHUANIA

Kaunas

Memel

Königsberg

EAST PRUSSIA

FREE CITY
OF DANZIG

Tannenberg

Hel
Peninsula

Danzig

Kalthof

Dirschau

Gdynia

Zoppot

Westerplatte

Tuchel
Heath

Brahe R.

Gross-
Klonia

BALTIC SEA

POLISH
CORRIDOR

Vistula R.

Warsaw

P O L A N D

GALICIA

Lwów

Krosno

Cracow

Katowice

SILESIA

Gleiwitz

Oppeln

Breslau

Oder R.

G E R M A N Y

Stettin

Swinemünde

Barth

Berlin

Dresden

Leipzig

Prague

CZECHOSLOVAKIA

Palacios

N

DANZIG
AND THE POLISH CORRIDOR

Miles

0   100

XVII

Mussolini Reneges

By this time the whole world cringed at the thought of a European war. Franklin Roosevelt was now back in the White House, from which he penned a message on August 24 to Adolf Hitler and President Mościcki of Poland appealing for negotiations—joint negotiations, however, not the unilateral pressure on Poland which Chamberlain had suggested.

The President's letter said in part: "I therefore urge you with all earnestness—and I am likewise urging the President of the Republic of Poland—that the Government of Germany and Poland agree by common accord to refrain from any positive act of hostility for a reasonably stipulated period, and that they agree, likewise by common accord, to solve the controversies which have arisen between them by one of the three following methods: 1. By direct negotiation. 2. By the submission of these controversies to an impartial arbitration in which they can both have confidence; or 3. That they agree to the solution of these controversies through the procedure of conciliation, selecting as a conciliator or moderator a national of one of the American Republics which are all of them free from any connection with, or participation in, European political affairs."

On the same day, Pope Pius XII broadcast an appeal for peace: "Once again a critical hour has struck for the great human family, an

391

hour of tremendous deliberations, towards which our hearts cannot be indifferent and from which our spiritual authority, which comes to us from God to lead souls in the ways of justice and of peace, must not hold itself aloof. Behold us then with all of you, who in this moment are carrying a burden of so great a responsibility, in order that through our voice you may hear the voice of that Christ from Whom the world received the most exalted example of living . . ."

Adolf Hitler paid no attention to either man; he was too busy with military dispositions. In forty-eight hours his armies would march against Poland. On August 24 he returned from Berchtesgaden to Berlin in order to greet "the new Bismarck," who was returning from Moscow in triumph. Hitler arrived in his private plane, but preceding him, his parasites poured into the Reich Chancellery—"the whole baggage train," thought Erich Kordt, watching them, "paladins, adjutants, orderlies. The anteroom of the Reich Chancellery this day, filled as it was with toadies and lickspittles and arrogant upstarts, reminded me of Belshazzar's Hall." When Ribbentrop arrived, he and the Führer fell upon each other's necks like the victors in a football match.

While still in this euphoric mood, Hitler wrote a long letter to Mussolini to inform him of his plans. Now that the Russo-German pact was signed, there was no more need for hesitation, he told the Duce. The Poles must be destroyed; that was his next objective. Deliberately, he did not give the exact date of the invasion. According to General Keitel, he suspected that his "reliable" servants in the Foreign Ministry would pass the news on to Britain, and he may also have presumed that Count Ciano would do the same. His idea was to panic the West with the information that he was definitely proceeding, without giving them an exact timetable so that they could warn the Poles. From the panic, he hoped, he would get a resurgent eagerness in London and Paris to settle with him—or rather, to allow him to take Poland without interference. To achieve this, he was prepared to use any means to persuade Chamberlain, who would then persuade the French. Therefore, he telephoned Göring and suggested that he send Dahlerus to London with a message for the British that the Germans were really serious in their desire for an Anglo-German understanding.

Göring, still sulking over his canceled visit to England, was slightly mollified. He called Birger Dahlerus, who had just flown in to Berlin, and summoned him to Karinhall. They talked for two hours, and then Göring drove the Swede back to Berlin in his open car. (The crowd cheered Göring when they halted at traffic lights; he was very popular.) Dahlerus agreed to fly to England the following morning. In the meantime, Göring told him that he himself was going to see Lipski, the Polish ambassador, that afternoon. He was a personal friend, Göring said, and he counted on Lipski's influence to secure an understanding with Poland. This ridiculous war could still be stopped.

General Brauchitsch and the staff of the Army High Command had moved to their war headquarters at Zossen, some twenty-odd miles outside Berlin, but in the Reich Chancellery, Hitler and Ribbentrop still held court. The Führer was in a happy mood, moving from clique to clique, talking in a hoarse voice about his plans for Greater Germany, signing papers, taking calls from his generals and admirals and showing no signs of fatigue. It was five in the morning before he went to bed, but before he departed he told Ribbentrop that tomorrow they would get to work on the Englishman.

Ribbentrop grimaced, for he knew that Hitler was referring to Henderson, and the Foreign Minister despised him.

Nevile Henderson had spent the morning in fruitless telephone conversation with Ambassador Lipski, trying to persuade him to ask for a meeting with Hitler "as a sign of good will."

"It will not be taken as a sign of good will but as evidence of weakness," Lipski retorted.

The Englishman hung up, cursing Polish stubbornness—by this time he loathed them even more than the Czechs—and without telling Lipski that he had an appointment with Hitler in a few hours.

The British envoy arrived at the Reich Chancellery at one o'clock on August 25 and was shown into the Führer's study a half-hour later. The ranting mood which Hitler had displayed at Berchtesgaden two days before had given place to a subdued calm, and there was an almost friendly note in his voice as he greeted the Englishman. But what he then began to say was so unreal and transparent that only an envoy of Henderson's caliber could have described it as "sincere"— the word he employed in his subsequent report to Halifax.

He wanted to come to an arrangement with England, the Führer

393

said, of the same decisive character as the one which had just been concluded with Russia. "I am ready to conclude agreements with England which will not only guarantee the existence of the British Empire in all circumstances so far as Germany is concerned, but will also, if necessary, assure the British Empire of German assistance regardless of where such assistance should be necessary."

Only someone as pro-Nazi as Henderson or as naïve as Chamberlain and Halifax could have considered such a suggestion even for a moment. The ambassador was attracted by the offer, though he did make the point that the British government could not consider it unless it also meant a peaceful settlement with Poland. Finally Hitler told him petulantly, "If you think it useless, then don't bother with my offer at all."

But Henderson did not think it useless. He eagerly accepted Hitler's offer of his private plane to fly him to London with detailed proposals. Schmidt handed the envoy a ready-typed copy of these, covered with emendations, as he left the room. And though no peaceful settlement was in sight, the British Cabinet considered the proposals for two whole days.

By the evening of August 25 Birger Dahlerus was already in London, Nevile Henderson was on his way, and there was an air of considerable optimism in Cabinet circles. It is difficult to understand why. In Berlin, telephone and telegraphic communication with the outside world had been cut. Bombers droned overhead on their way eastward, and in the humid summer heat of the German capital, pedestrians looked away from the flaring newspaper headlines about the latest reports of Polish atrocities against the Germans.*

Hermann Göring had packed away his dress uniforms and medals and moved to his private train not far from army field headquarters. In Danzig the Poles had barricaded themselves inside the post office and were listening to the tramp of boots outside. The German battleship *Schleswig-Holstein* had completed her "courtesy visit" to the Free City and slipped out of the harbor, but was now cruising a few

---

* "The ill-treatment, murders, etc., of which Herr Hitler accuses the Poles are sheer calumnies," reported the French ambassador from Warsaw. "The Germans cite no precise facts, no names, no dates, and no protest has been lodged with the Polish government by the German ambassador."

miles out in the Baltic, waiting for the moment to strike. The hour for the attack was twelve hours away, and German divisions were moving up to the line in East Prussia, Slovakia and Germany proper; their guns and those of the navy pointed across the Polish frontier from the four points of the compass.

But when Dahlerus was shown into Halifax's office at six-thirty that evening, he found the Foreign Secretary quite cheerful. Henderson's talk with the Führer earlier in the day had been most promising, Halifax said; it looked as if official negotiations could now get really started and a peaceable settlement achieved.

Much relieved, the Swede left after a brief chat and made his way to the Carlton Hotel, where his English friends were waiting for him. They sat down to dinner in a good mood, for they too had heard the optimistic rumors.

But amid the chatter and the toasts to peace, something nagged at Dahlerus; he felt he must talk to Göring and find out what he thought of the Hitler-Henderson conversations. Going out to the lobby, he tried to place a call to Berlin and discovered that the lines to Germany had been blocked. Anxious now, he telephoned the Foreign Office and asked it to use its influence to get a call through. At ten-twenty he heard the German operator's voice and asked for the Field Marshal, wherever he might be. Minutes later General Bodenschatz was on the other end of the line, explaining that Göring was conferring with other members of the government, but that he would talk to him in a few minutes.

Eventually the Field Marshal's high-pitched voice was heard at the other end, and Göring made it plain at once that Dahlerus had chosen an awkward moment to call. Things were upside down in Berlin; the situation was very serious.

Dahlerus was nonplused. The situation had seemed better when he left. What had happened to change it?

Hadn't he been told yet? Göring asked. Everything had changed because the British had now signed their pact with Poland. Why did they have to do that? Why were they so foolish? The Führer had taken it as a definite challenge—an indication that the British did not want a peaceful settlement after all.

"I can assure you that such is not their intention," Dahlerus answered.

Then the English should hasten to make themselves clear, Göring retorted angrily. He had great expectations from Dahlerus' journey to London, but he must urge his friends to move fast. War could break out at any moment.

In fact, though it was true that the situation had deteriorated on the night of August 25, war could not break out at any moment because Adolf Hitler had forbidden it. The British government had shattered him by a move which he had never expected. At almost exactly the same moment that he was making his magnanimous gesture to Nevile Henderson offering to "guarantee" the British Empire, the Anglo-Polish agreement had been dusted of its cobwebs—it had been on the shelf since April—and put on Lord Halifax's desk. It was a routine move; the underlings of the Foreign Office had taken over. Now that there was no chance of securing a treaty with the Soviet Union, it was suggested, was it not time to turn the Anglo-Polish agreement into a full-dress pact? After all, it had been hanging around for rather a long time.

Halifax agreed, and so did Chamberlain. Obviously they had not the slightest idea of the significance of what they were doing, except that they were determined to demonstrate to the British public and to Hitler that they were "serious." It was a revealing example of the traumatic state which the British government had reached.

Halifax was instructed to call the Polish ambassador, Count Edward Raczyński, who was informed of what the British had in mind. Asking for time to telephone Beck in Poland to get permission, he then returned to say that he was authorized to sign, and did so at 6:35 P.M. on August 25.

The pact bound the two countries to come to each other's aid in the event of attack. It too had its secret clauses, of which two were important. First, the unidentified "European power" against whom the two powers would give each other mutual aid was stated: it was Germany.* Second, the reference to the possibility or threat of aggression against certain "Polish interests" meant Danzig.

Adolf Hitler learned about the signing of this treaty—though not its secret clauses—on the evening of August 25, as his troops were moving toward Poland. At almost the same time a message came from

* This was lucky for Britain. Had not Germany been specified, she might have found herself in a state of war with the Soviet Union in the days to come.

396

Rome. Mussolini was replying to Hitler's letter telling him of his plans, and it was not the slap-on-the-back, we-are-with-you polemic which the Führer had expected.*

In point of fact, Mussolini was in a panic. Despite his bombastic statements, the last thing he wanted was war, and he did not subscribe to Hitler's belief that Britain and France would stand aside in the event of an attack on Poland. As Ciano's diary makes clear, though the Duce writhed with humiliation at having to confess his weakness, he was terrified of being involved in a general conflict, and by August 26 he was determined to keep out. The Duce realized that the Pact of Steel bound him to stand shoulder to shoulder with his Axis partner in the event of hostilities, and the prospect paralyzed him, for he was convinced that within a week of declaring war against the West the whole of northern Italy would be swamped by French troops, and that the Italian fleet would be sunk by the British navy. Bluff was one thing; military facts were another.

Thus, within a few hours on August 26 Hitler learned that the British had signed the Anglo-Polish pact of mutual assistance and that Mussolini had reneged. Not that the Duce put it in such blunt words; he forgave Hitler for not having told him beforehand about the Russo-German pact and expressed his complete understanding about the Polish situation. "As for the *practical* attitude of Italy in case of military action," he went on, "my point of view is as follows: If Germany attacks Poland and the conflict remains localized, Italy will afford Germany every form of political and economic assistance which is requested of her. If Germany attacks Poland, and the latter's allies (that is, Britain and France) open a counterattack against Germany, I inform you that it will be opportune for me not to take the initiative in military operations in view of the present state of Italian war preparations, of which we have repeatedly and in good time informed you, my Führer, and Herr von Ribbentrop.

"Our intervention can, nevertheless, take place at once if Germany delivers to us immediately the military supplies and raw materials to resist the attack which the French and English would predominantly direct against us. At our meetings the war was en-

---

* Earlier in the day the Duce had told Mackensen, the German ambassador in Rome, that he was behind Hitler all the way. But he was speaking purely for effect. Twenty-four hours later he made it clear in black and white how he really felt about going to war.

visaged for 1942, and by that time I would have been ready on land, on sea and in the air, according to the plans which had been concerted."

Hitler immediately ordered his staff to find out exactly what the Italians needed, and whether they could be supplied. A message was rushed to Rome, and the answer would arrive on Hitler's desk the next day telling him that Italy wanted practically everything. But even now he rightly deduced that despite the Pact of Steel, Italy was no longer with him.

It was a crisis. Hitler had gained the neutrality of Russia, only to lose the active partnership of Italy. Britain and France still had not caved in, and the invasion of Poland was only a few hours away. Why had the stupid English not succumbed to his overtures? What had gone wrong? Did he really need to fight the West just in order to have his way with Poland?

Hitler told Colonel Schmundt to summon Keitel immediately, and in a few minutes the general bustled in to the Reich Chancellery, as always obsequious as a valet.

"I need time," Hitler said. "Can the troops be stopped?"

"I would have to look at the timetable."

"Then send for it, man!"

Schmundt was dispatched to get it, and for a moment he and the general pored over it. "Yes, my Führer," Keitel said at last. "I think it can be done—provided that the order goes out at once. There is just time."

"Then give the order. But say that it is preliminary and further orders will follow. The operation is postponed. Further orders follow."

Poised for battle, the German armies ground to a halt along the Polish border. The soldiers were bewildered. General von Brauchitsch rushed back to Berlin to see the Führer and find out what was happening. All Hitler would say was, "I have to reconsider the situation. I need to take an overall view of the situation." Then he added to General Keitel, "I need time to negotiate." Next he picked up the telephone to tell Göring of the cancellation. Hoping that negotiations had come at last, the Field Marshal asked whether the halt was permanent.

"No," Hitler replied. "I will have to see if we can eliminate British intervention."

XVIII

The Indefatigable Swede

August 26, 1939, was a day of rejoicing in the chancelleries of Berlin, where everyone except the most knowledgeable thought that the crisis was over. The signing of the Anglo-Polish pact and the retreat of Italy had done the trick; the West had stood firm, the Axis partnership had crumbled, and Germany was on her own.

The French ambassador, Robert Coulondre, rushed to his desk and composed a message to Daladier which he sent by courier to hail the victory of the steadfast democracies. *"Monsieur le Président,"* he wrote, "the test of force has turned to our advantage. I know from a reliable source that in the past five days Hitler has become hesitant, that there is a wavering inside the party, and that the discontent grows among the people. The attack against Poland was fixed for the night of August 25–26. For reasons still not entirely clear, at the last moment Hitler drew back . . . Certainly we are not at the end and we must use still greater efforts, but as I send you this bulletin, my heart swells with emotion. According to what I told you, Hitler is asking himself how he can get out of the impasse in which he finds himself. If I understand it, he wants Danzig and a corridor through the Corridor. It is necessary to convince him by our firm attitude that he will obtain absolutely nothing by the methods which he has employed up to now. But in achieving this result, it will be necessary to avoid pushing him to an act of desperation."

Coulondre tried to emphasize this point in an analogy that Daladier would understand: "You are a fisherman, I think. *Eh bien,* the fish is wily. It is necessary now to play him with the skill necessary to land him without breaking the line. Because it is vital that these observations should not be bruited about and because I am pressed for time, I am writing direct to you and I will leave it to you to pass it on to MM. Bonnet and Léger . . ."

Coulondre also distrusted the gossips at the Quai d'Orsay. In this case, however, he was quite wrong. His assessment of Hitler's hesitation was wildly off the mark, for by the time Daladier was reading his envoy's letter the next day, Adolf Hitler was giving another date for the attack on Poland—September 1—and he stressed that this was a firm one.

Erich Kordt wrote in his diary on August 27: "I do not share the general optimism. Hitler has already given the new date. The delay is so short that the tension will remain, and this will enable him to exploit the situation. Obviously Hitler surmises that the shock of the Russo-German pact has evoked the courage of despair in the West, but that this will trickle away when they have had time to think. Then they will see clearly that military help to Poland is impossible. Then will come another Munich."

On the same day Ribbentrop ordered a telegram to be sent to the German ambassador in Rome: "According to reliable sources a rumor has been spread in Rome by way of the Italian embassy in Berlin to the effect that a relaxation of the strained conditions has been noted and that conferences are being held. It is his [Ribbentrop's] desire to affirm that exactly the contrary is true and that the situation is gradually coming to a head. 'The armies are on the march.' It would be a good thing if . . . the abovementioned rumor does not become an established fact with the Duce and Ciano."

■

On Saturday, August 26, Birger Dahlerus left the Carlton Hotel in Haymarket in London after an early breakfast and strolled up to Piccadilly, past Simpson's and Fortnum & Mason (where he dropped an order in the box for Peek Frean biscuits, some honey and China tea) and then went on to Green Park, where he watched a small crowd of people feeding the ducks. It seemed a peaceful and untroubled scene.

But in fact England was troubled that weekend. Trains were delayed because partial mobilization was in force. Several of the Englishmen who had interrupted their country weekend to talk to Dahlerus on a Sunday in July used this Saturday to evacuate their families to the country. Their gay mood of the night before had quickly been dissipated by the news he had brought back from his call to Göring.

At eleven o'clock Dahlerus went to see Halifax once more at the Foreign Office. By this time a report of his telephone conversation had been delivered to the Foreign Secretary, and he nodded thoughtfully when the Swede "told him frankly that from my talk with Göring I was obliged to draw the conclusion that the situation was extremely serious. I pointed out that a person in my insignificant position, who was also ignorant of many important factors, naturally could not offer any advice, but I mentioned that I was absolutely convinced that Göring was the only man in Germany who might be able to prevent a war. I therefore suggested that I should deliver a personal letter to Göring from Halifax which would confirm England's genuine desire to reach a peaceful settlement, and expressed my hope that such a gesture might calm agitation in Berlin."

Dahlerus was told to wait while Halifax slipped away to Downing Street to talk to Neville Chamberlain. The Foreign Secretary was back in half an hour to say that yes, the Prime Minister had agreed that it was a useful suggestion, and that he would write the letter at once.

"This letter from the British Foreign Minister, written at a time when the crisis seemed to be at its apex, has not been mentioned in any of the official reports," Dahlerus wrote years later. Nor was it mentioned to the Poles or the French at the time; like the telephone calls and letters which were now passing between Chamberlain and Mussolini asking for the Duce's mediation, such moves were deliberately hidden from Britain's allies.

Later Halifax read the letter to the Swede. "In it he made a frank and friendly assertion of England's definite wish to come to an understanding with Germany. There could be no doubting the writer's good will."

By this time the idea of getting the communication into Göring's hands seemed so important to Chamberlain and Halifax that the Air Minister, Sir Kingsley Wood, ordered the 1:25 P.M. flight from Croydon to Amsterdam delayed until Dahlerus could get aboard. However, since all civilian air traffic between Holland and Germany was now canceled, the Dutch government was asked to let Adolf Hitler's private plane—which had brought Nevile Henderson to London—land at Amsterdam on its way back, pick up Dahlerus and fly him to Berlin.

After the war, when the earnest and honest Swede appeared as a witness at the Nuremberg trials, his role was made to appear that of an unwitting dupe of the Nazis. It was always more than that. "I realized that I was only a pawn in the game," he said later, "but I am convinced that it was an earnest game."

Nor was Dahlerus simply a pawn, for both sides were using him and soon he was to be the only link between them.

It was 7 P.M. on Saturday, August 26, when Dahlerus landed at Tempelhof Airport. Lieutenant Colonel Konrad of Göring's staff was waiting for him with a car, and they raced through strangely quiet city streets and then out on empty roads to Karinhall. But Göring had already left on his train; eventually they caught up with him at a small station called Friedrichswalde, and went aboard just before it moved off again.

The Field Marshal was sweating profusely and was highly nervous. Immediately he wanted to know the state of mind of Chamberlain and his government, and how the British people were reacting, but before Dahlerus could answer fully, Göring interrupted him. "The Führer has canceled the Nuremberg *Parteitag* and the celebrations at Tannenberg. You know what that means." Then, with a rush: "Why don't the British trust us? Why are they suspicious of our good intentions? Eh, Dahlerus?"

"Perhaps because—"

"Terrible things are happening in Poland, terrible!" Göring cried. "Poor Germans murdered, women raped, children beaten. Terrible things . . ."

It was time, Dahlerus decided, to produce his letter. At once the Field Marshal grabbed it and tore it open with trembling fingers. He began to lip-read it, spelling out the English words slowly, for though he could not speak the language he understood it a little. But soon he was exasperated by his slowness and he flung it down before the

402

Swede, saying, "Dahlerus, translate it for me into German. And remember that it is tremendously important that every syllable conveys the exact shade of meaning."

Dahlerus did so, and each sentence seemed to give comfort to the fat figure opposite him. When he had finished, Göring rang the bell and Colonel Konrad entered. "I want the train stopped at the next station," the Field Marshal ordered, "and have a car waiting for me there." To Dahlerus he said, "We are going back to Berlin. The Führer must be told about this letter."

It was midnight by the time the car drew up at the Reich Chancellery in Berlin. Much to Göring's surprise, the building was in darkness, and he was even more amazed when the colonel of the guard, summoned by an SS sentry, informed him that Hitler had gone to bed.

"We will have to have him woken up," Göring said. "He must be told the news." He turned to Dahlerus. "Go back to your hotel, but do not go to bed right away. We may have to wait until morning, or I may need you tonight."

The Field Marshal marched into the Reich Chancellery with the colonel, and the car took Dahlerus to the Esplanade Hotel. Wearily he sat down in the empty lounge and waited. After about a quarter of an hour, two SS colonels approached him. "The Führer is asking for you" (*Der Führer lässt bitten*), one of them said.

Dahlerus was taken to a large open car and driven to the Reich Chancellery. By this time the scene had changed completely; the building was a blaze of light, and officers and men were milling about everywhere. The metal doors were open and the car drove through them into the inner courtyard, where officials awaited him. He was marched down a long gallery to the waiting room outside Hitler's study and left there for ten minutes—enough time for his practical Swedish eye to take in the décor and furnishings: modern German chairs and leather settees, walls hung with "old and famous paintings," fine Khorramshahr carpets, and great bowls, vases and trays of orchids (a specialty of Rothe, the Berlin horticulturist).

The Führer was in one of his favorite poses when the Swede was shown into the study: standing in the middle of the room, legs apart, arms behind his back. Göring stood beside him, beaming at Dahlerus in contrast to Hitler's scowl, as if to say, "See, I woke him up!"

403

"Guten Abend, Excellenz," said Dahlerus.

"Guten Abend, Herr Dahlerus. Bitte . . ." Hitler indicated a couch in a corner of the study and took a chair opposite him, while Göring teetered next to the Swede on the arm rest. Dahlerus cleared his throat and his mind in readiness to deliver his views on the state of British morale and opinion. Instead, to his great astonishment, Hitler launched into a monologue. He made no mention of the letter from Lord Halifax, but began to recapitulate the checkered history of the National Socialist party, year by year, difficulty by difficulty. Then, fixing Dahlerus with a glittering stare, he emphasized with bitter expressions and waves of his hand how contemptuously he had been rejected by the British after each overture he had made. The Swede sat hypnotized like a rabbit before a snake. This demagogic harangue continued for twenty minutes, and Dahlerus was in despair, thinking he would be unable to interpolate a word. Obviously the man was a fanatic. Nevertheless, as Hitler ranted on about the "stupidity" of the British, the "weakness" of the British people, the "effeteness" of their rulers, Dahlerus made an effort to stem the torrent of words. "I regret, *Excellenz,* all you say about the British people. I do not share your view of Britain and her citizens. I know what I am talking about. I once lived as a workingman in England and I know what I am talking about."

"What is that you say?" Hitler asked. "You have worked as a common laborer in England? Tell me about it."

Everything else was forgotten while Dahlerus told about his early days in English factories in the provinces, of workingmen's clubs, of evenings in pubs, of the loyalty and decency and unswerving courage of the British workingman.

"I am glad to hear it," Hitler said. "But the trouble with England is its plutocrats—decadent, effete, Jews or Jew-supporters."

"You may not have the Jews, but you have the decadent plutocrats here in Germany too," Dahlerus answered stoutly. "All countries are the same."

All of this took at least half an hour, and time was slipping away. Almost reluctantly, Hitler finally brought the conversation back to the situation at the moment, and at once he worked himself up into a lather of anger. He mentioned his interview the previous day with Nevile Henderson. He had made him a magnanimous offer—an alliance between Britain and Germany—but could Henderson be trusted to convey its significance to Chamberlain? "Will they understand the situation? This is my last magnanimous offer to England."* His rage continued as he began to expatiate on the "overwhelming superiority" of the German armed forces to those in the West. Göring giggled contentedly as the Führer praised the invincibility of the Luftwaffe, and nodded as his leader described the army's and navy's new weapons.

Dahlerus did his best not to refute Hitler but to calm him down and to remind him of the solid resources of his enemies. "I spoke slowly and quietly," he wrote afterward "to avoid irritating him unnecessarily, since his mental equilibrium was patently unstable. He seemed to ponder what I said, but then got up and, becoming very much excited and nervous, walked up and down saying, as though to himself, that Germany was irresistible and could defeat her adversaries by means of a rapid war." Suddenly he stopped in the middle of the room and stood there, staring. Dahlerus, a man of rational character if ever there was one, knew that he was looking at "a completely abnormal person." Hitler's phrases were staccato, and he was obviously thinking of war. "If there should be war, then I will build U-boats, U-boats, U-boats, U-boats, U-boats . . ." His voice died away like a disk with a stuck needle fading out on the radio. A moment later a spasm shook his body; he lifted his arms high and began to shout at the top of his voice, "I will build airplanes, airplanes, airplanes. I will disintegrate my enemies! War doesn't frighten me! The encirclement of Germany is impossible now; my people admire and follow me faithfully. If there are privations ahead for the German people, then let it be now—I will be the first to starve and set my people a good example. My sufferings will spur them on to superhuman efforts."

Here Dahlerus noted that his eyes were glassy and his voice "unnatural."

"If there should be no butter, I shall be the first to stop eating butter! My German people will loyally and gladly do the same. If the enemy can hold out for several years, I, with my power over the German people, can hold out one year longer. It is because of this that I know that I am superior to all the others."

At this point Hitler began to pace the floor again, as if suddenly

---

* (. . . *Dies ist mein letztes grosszügiges Angebot an England.*)

recollecting where he was. Turning to the Swede, he said, "Herr Dahlerus, you who know England so well, can you give me any reason for my perpetual failure to come to an agreement with her?"

Dahlerus answered hesitantly, "Your Excellency, with my comprehensive knowledge of the English people, their mentality and their attitude toward Germany, I must definitely assure you that I am absolutely convinced that these difficulties are founded on a lack of confidence in you personally and in your government."

Hitler banged his chest with his hand. "Idiots! Have I ever in my life lied to them?"

Dahlerus took this enormous whopper in his stride. "I am just a businessman, your Excellency. In the business world, we always say that an agreement can only be based on mutual confidence. If confidence is lacking—whether justifiably or not—nothing can be done until it is restored."

There was a long silence as Hitler strode back and forth across the large rug in front of his desk, pulling at his chin. Göring still teetered on the arm of the couch.

"Herr Dahlerus," Hitler said at last, "you have heard my side. You must go at once to England and tell it to the British government. I do not think that Henderson understood me. I really want to bring about an understanding."

But what sort of an understanding? Dahlerus asked, and immediately Hitler and Göring got to work. What sort of passage through the Polish Corridor did Hitler want for Germany? An atlas was produced; Göring drew a line on it with Hitler's approval, the page was torn out and Dahlerus put it in his pocket.

What about Danzig? Danzig would be returned to the Reich, but Poland would have a free harbor, a corridor to her port of Gdynia, and territory around it.

What about the integrity of Poland? Germany would guarantee Poland's boundaries.

What about Germany's claim to colonies? The old German colonies would be returned to her, but thereafter she would guarantee the British Empire and pledge herself to defend its borders. "Do you see what that means?" Hitler pointed out. "If Italy and England should ever come into conflict with one another in the Mediterranean or elsewhere, Germany would support England!" He looked over at

406

Göring as he said this and nodded. The Field Marshal nodded back. Suddenly both of them were in high spirits.

Hitler left the room for a moment, and Dahlerus presumed that he had gone to the bathroom. He wished that someone would ask him whether he would like to do the same. In all his peregrinations he was escorted everywhere, fed well and whisked about in private planes, trains or limousines, but no one ever thought about his bladder.

When the Führer returned, he said, "Take the message to the British government!"

Following the Führer out of the room, Göring added, "You know how much depends on you!"

Adjutants were busy arranging for a Luftwaffe plane and trying to obtain permission from the Dutch government to let it fly over their territory, and from the British government to allow it to land. On Sunday morning, August 27, a lovely summer day, Dahlerus again took off in a German plane to fly to London. The pilot invited him into the cockpit, but he declined; he wanted to get some sleep. It would not come, and he sat the whole way looking down at the clouds and sea below him. His was the only plane flying across the frontiers of Western Europe that day. Birger Dahlerus was a truly humble and simple man, and at that moment he felt very much alone.

■

An ominous silence fell over Europe that weekend, broken only by the slitting of envelopes as statesmen opened letters and telegrams asking favors, pleading for concessions and making sly suggestions for evading obligations.

Halifax to Sir Percy Loraine, British ambassador in Rome, August 26: "Please ask Signor Mussolini to suggest to Herr Hitler— but without revealing that the initiative comes directly from us—that if a settlement of the present situation were confined to the return of Danzig and parts of the Corridor to Germany, it does not seem to us impossible, within a reasonable time, to find a solution without war."

Halifax to Sir Howard Kennard, British ambassador to Poland, August 26: "You will of course understand that no indication may be given to the Poles that we are in consultation with Mussolini nor of the kind of procedure for negotiation that we have been turning over in our minds."

Fritz Hesse, Ribbentrop's personal representative in London, to the Foreign Minister, August 26: "My information is that if Germany invades Poland there is no fear of British intervention. Sir Samuel Hoare has the ear of Neville Chamberlain. He is of the opinion that if Poland is attacked, Britain can always fulfill the letter of a declaration of war without going all-out."

Sir Eric Phipps, British ambassador in Paris, to Lord Halifax, August 26: "M. Bonnet told me in strictest confidence that the French government are in touch with Mussolini. I did not reciprocate by revealing that we also are in touch with Mussolini."

Sir Percy Loraine to Lord Halifax after a conversation with André François-Poncet, French ambassador in Rome, August 26: "François-Poncet told me France was thinking of making concessions to Italy to dissuade her from fighting as Germany's ally. French are prepared to make an arrangement over Tunis, possibly the cession of Jibouti and certain Suez directorships. François-Poncet's confidential revelations moved him to ask whether Britain had considered anything of the kind. I had to put on my best pair of skates to avoid answering but I succeeded in preserving a discreet silence except to say that we would always welcome consultations with Italy on subjects of common interest."

Count Ciano to Signor Attolico, Italian ambassador in Berlin, August 26, by telephone: "Please inform the Führer that in order to undertake a twelve-month war now, side by side with Germany, Italy's armed forces require at least 7,000,000 tons of oil, 6,000,000 tons of coal, 2,000,000 tons of steel and 1,000,000 tons of timber, in addition to small quantities of rubber, copper and the rarer metals. In order to protect Italy's industrial quadrilateral Turin-Genoa-Milan-Savona, which is half an hour's flight from Corsica, we need 150 antiaircraft battalions with ammunition."

Attolico sped with this list to the Foreign Ministry, where he presented it to a frigid Ribbentrop. The requirements cited by the Italians were in fact for a long-term period, but when Ribbentrop asked when they were needed, Attolico replied, "Why, at once, before hostilities begin." This was a deliberate deception. But it was believed by the Germans—in fact, it confirmed their intelligence reports—and suited

408

Mussolini's book. He could afterward claim that he was willing but his subordinates were weak.

Adolf Hitler to Benito Mussolini, August 27: "Duce! I have received your communication on your final attitude. I respect the reasons and motives which led you to take the decision. In certain circumstances it can nevertheless work out well. In my opinion, however, the prerequisite is that at least until the outbreak of hostilities, the world should have no idea of the attitude Italy intends to adopt. I therefore cordially request you to support my struggle psychologically with your press or by other means. I would also ask you, Duce, if you possibly can, by demonstrative military measures, at least to compel Britain and France to tie down certain of their forces, or at all events to leave them in uncertainty."

Benito Mussolini to Adolf Hitler, August 27: The enemy will not know before the outbreak of hostilities what the attitude of Italy is."

Premier Edouard Daladier to Adolf Hitler, August 26: "The French ambassador has informed me of your personal communication. [Hitler had assured Ambassador Coulondre that he had no quarrel with France.] You can doubt neither my own feelings toward Germany nor France's peaceful feelings toward your nation. No Frenchman has done more than myself to strengthen between our two nations not only peace but also sincere co-operation in their own interests as well as in those of Europe and the whole world. Unless you credit the French people with a lower sense of honor than I credit that of the German nation, you cannot doubt that France loyally fulfills her obligations toward other powers, such as Poland, which, as I am fully convinced, wants to live in peace with Germany . . . You and I were in the trenches in the last war. You know as I do what horror and condemnation the devastation of that war have left in the conscience of the peoples without any regard for its outcome . . . If French and German blood should be shed again, as it was shed twenty-five years ago, in a still longer and more murderous war, then each of the two nations will fight believing in its own victory. But the most certain victors will be destruction and barbarity."

This letter was presented to Hitler at the Reich Chancellery by Robert Coulondre, who was in a highly emotional mood. "I entreated him before history," he wrote, "and in the name of history, not to dismiss this last chance. For the peace of his conscience I begged him, who has built up an empire without bloodshed, not to shed blood—the blood of soldiers and also of women and children—unless he first made sure that it could not be avoided. I confronted him with the terrible responsibility he would assume toward Western civilization . . . I may have moved him but I failed to deter him. His stand was taken."

Adolf Hitler to Edouard Daladier, August 27: "I understand the qualms you possess. I too have never overlooked the high responsibility which rests on those who are in a position to decide the fate of nations. As an old front-line soldier I have the same feeling about the horrors of war as you do. It is from this conviction and knowledge that I have made honest efforts to eliminate all the grounds of conflict between the two nations . . . Being both old front-line soldiers, perhaps we understand each other more easily on many points. However, I must ask you to understand this too: that it is impossible for a nation with a sense of honor to waive their claim to almost two million people, and to see them maltreated on their own frontier. I have therefore formulated a clear-cut demand. Danzig and the Corridor must revert to Germany. The 'Macedonian' conditions on our eastern frontier must disappear. I can see no other way of inducing Poland, which now believes itself unassailable under the protection of the guarantees, to take steps toward a peaceable solution. I should, however, despair of the honorable future of my people if, under such circumstances, we were not determined to solve the question one way or another. Should fate thereby once more force our two peoples to fight, there would yet be a difference in our motives. I and my people would be fighting to right—and the others to maintain—a wrong which has been inflicted on us . . .

"I am quite aware of the dire consequences which would result from such a conflict. But I believe that Poland would suffer most, for whichever way the war about this question went, the present Polish state would be lost anyhow.

"Not only for you, M. Daladier, but for me too, it is most painful that our two peoples are now to embark on a new bloody war of extermination on these grounds. But as I said before, I cannot see a way for us to induce Poland by rational means to correct a situation which is intolerable for the German people and the German Reich."

This was the last communication between the heads of the French and German governments until the sands of peace had finally run out.

410

. . .

But if Adolf Hitler could not see a way "to induce Poland by rational means," the British government was doing its best to find one for him. They were not alone. Even the Pope had taken a hand now in a more tangible form than an appeal for peace and reason; he instructed the papal nuncio in Warsaw to see Colonel Beck and tell him that His Holiness had been reliably assured that if Poland would cede Danzig to Germany at once, the Reich would consent to negotiations on the question of the Polish Corridor and the German minorities. Beck's sarcastic response to this was to convey the thanks of his government to His Holiness for having given such deep thought to the solution of Poland's problems.

But the most important channel of communication now was between Germany and London, and Birger Dahlerus was the last link. He returned to London from Berlin on Sunday, August 27, and after his friends had spirited him by back streets to the Foreign Office, he was taken to No. 10 Downing Street. Had he been Hitler himself, he could not have asked for a more imposing reception; awaiting him in the Cabinet Room were Neville Chamberlain, Halifax and Sir Alexander Cadogan. They looked grave as he was shown in, and they looked skeptical after he had given them a full account of his conversation with Hitler. The points the Führer had made to him differed considerably from those which he had given to Sir Nevile Henderson.

"Are you absolutely certain that this is an accurate account of what Herr Hitler told you?" Chamberlain asked.

"I assure you that it is."

The Swede had a distinct feeling that by now the Prime Minister was thoroughly suspicious of Hitler. At one point Chamberlain asked suddenly, "What do you think of Herr Hitler? What sort of impression does he make on you?"

Dahlerus hesitated and then said, "I don't think I should like to have him as a partner in my business."

It is a measure of the trust which Chamberlain was beginning to have in Dahlerus, however, that he allowed the Swede to persuade him to make a radical change in the British government's plans. Nevile Henderson was due to fly back that afternoon with the Cabinet's reply to Hitler's offer. Dahlerus suggested that instead the ambassador wait until Monday, while he himself flew back ahead of him with an unofficial reply with which to test German reactions.

411

To Dahlerus' astonishment, Chamberlain then made a remark which seemed to heap the whole burden of the British government on his willing but alien and amateur shoulders. Was Dahlerus willing to take the responsibility for the ambassador's remaining in London until Monday? the Prime Minister asked.

Naturally he couldn't do that, Dahlerus answered, but he could telephone Göring in Berlin and ask him if the German government would agree to the delay.

The Swede was shown into the next room and telephoned the Field Marshal. Half an hour later he called again; this time he was told that Göring had conferred with the Führer and that, provided Dahlerus was returning with a preliminary reply, Germany would be willing to wait for another twenty-four hours for the official British response.

So on that Sunday afternoon in London, while Hitler's armies waited on the Polish frontiers, while air-raid precautions and partial mobilization proceeded in Britain and France, while Mussolini and Ciano fidgeted in Rome, while a Pope and Presidents pleaded, a Swedish businessman sat down with the heads of the British government to work out a reply to the demands of the dictator of the German Reich. It was an extraordinary situation, and only the puny dimensions of the leaders of Britain could have made it possible. To be sure, there was an appearance of firmness in the reply which Dahlerus carried with him, but implicit both in the message and in the method of delivery was the pathetic eagerness of Chamberlain and his supporters to come to some sort of accommodation.

As if to emphasize the furtiveness of the whole affair, the Swede was smuggled out the back door of No. 10 Downing Street. The German plane which was to take him back had been transferred to Scotland, out of the gaze of inquisitive reporters, and it was from there that Dahlerus eventually flew back to Berlin. He arrived at eleven o'clock on the evening of August 27, and was at once rushed to Göring's residence in the Leipzigerstrasse, where he read aloud to the Field Marshal the notes he had taken of the British government's reply.

Göring's response was that it sounded promising but that he must talk to Hitler about it, and so Dahlerus went to the Esplanade Hotel and retired to bed. At one-thirty in the morning the telephone rang. It was Göring, and he sounded happy. "On condition that the note

412

delivered tomorrow by Henderson corresponds with the report you have given us of the attitude of the British government, there is no reason to suppose that we will not be able to reach an agreement."

Apparently a truly tireless man, the Swede climbed out of bed and began to dress. Göring had made certain observations which the British should know about, so Dahlerus called the British embassy at one forty-five.*

Despite the fact that by this time Birger Dahlerus was almost literally acting as plenipotentiary for the British government, he had no authority in writing to do so. All he had been given when he left Downing Street the previous evening was a sheet of Foreign Office notepaper with two names scribbled on it by Sir Alexander Cadogan: those of Sir George Ogilvie Forbes, the chargé d'affaires in Berlin, and Mr. Adrian Holman, the second secretary. At this moment neither of them knew of his existence; no one in London had told them about his role.

Holman answered the telephone and said that Sir George was at home and in bed. It took some time for Dahlerus to persuade the second secretary to give him the private telephone number of the chargé, and even more to convince Forbes that he should get up and come to the embassy at once. Holman suspected a German plant, or that Dahlerus might be a crank. The two diplomats decided to be extremely wary.

Just after two o'clock Forbes and Dahlerus met at the British embassy, and the Swede began to explain himself. He grew increasingly conscious of the fact that the more he spoke, the less he was believed. It was exactly as if he were a visitor from outer space who was trying to persuade earthlings that he had left Venus that morning. The moment he said that he had flown in from London a few hours before, all the Englishman's suspicions rose. How could he have done so? Everyone knew that all air traffic in and out of Germany had shut down. It became increasingly plain that as long as Forbes ("watching me rather sardonically") suspected him of being either a spy or a madman, Dahlerus could make no impact. Not until Holman dashed into the room an hour later, announcing the arrival of a cipher telegram in which the emissary was identified, did Forbes rise

* For instance, Hitler did not want the note Henderson was bringing to be made public until he and his advisers had seen it.

413

to his feet, walk over to the Swede and hold out his hand. It was then that Dahlerus' message from Göring took hold.

It was five-thirty before the Swede left the British embassy. In a Luftwaffe car he drove out to see Göring, who was back on his operational train again. In a "poisonous green dressing gown fastened around his middle with a jeweled buckle," the Field Marshal was in a happy mood when the Swede arrived. "Have you had breakfast?" he asked.

"No. Not yet."

"I don't know how you do it, Dahlerus. When do you get time to eat and sleep?" Without waiting for an answer, he swept the Swede through the train to a conference carriage where his staff was gathered.*

They all gathered around a large table. Dahlerus had been hoping for breakfast; instead he faced a great spread of marked maps over which Göring expatiated upon his plans for Poland in the event of war. Then, seeing the Swede's gloomy face, he hit him on the back. "Don't worry. All will be well. Do the British realize how the Führer is thinking? He has promised to support the British Empire against all the powers who may threaten her—and that includes Italy, Japan *and* Russia. Tell your friend Forbes that!"

Dahlerus obediently telephoned this tidbit to the chargé d'affaires, who promised to pass it on to London.

On August 28 Nevile Henderson returned to Berlin with the official reply of the British government to Hitler's conversation with him three days earlier. Since Dahlerus had already outlined the terms of the reply the day before, the Germans knew exactly what was coming. The Swede had also telephoned from Berlin in the meantime and suggested that a comment be included in the text indicating that "the Poles have been strongly advised to immediately establish contact with the Germans and negotiate." Obediently, Halifax had inserted the paragraph, after first having got the Poles to agree.

Now Henderson took a bath, dressed with care in a dinner jacket and drank a half bottle of champagne while considering how he

---

* Dahlerus recalled that they included Paul Körner, Generals Milch, Udet, Jeschonnek and Bodenschatz, and Colonel Konrad.

414

would tackle the forthcoming encounter. When he departed, his pet dachshund waddled to the door to see him off.

Ribbentrop was with Hitler when the British ambassador was shown into the Führer's study, but the atmosphere was amiable nevertheless. For once Henderson was treated as an equal; the two Germans listened to him carefully while he spoke, and his confidence grew as the interview proceeded. The British note firmly rejected the idea that Germany should "guarantee" or "underwrite" the British Empire, but Hitler did not seem to be irritated by this. Nor did he seem to object to a firm line in the note insisting that if there were to be negotiations with Poland its interests must be safeguarded, and that any settlement should be the subject of an international guarantee.

Henderson had a sense of approaching triumph. Rarely had he felt so at ease in the presence of these strange Nazi supermen. Alas, happiness and ease were dangerous states of mind for him in such company, because as a result he began to elaborate upon his brief, and the elaborations—his favorite theme of Anglo-German misunderstanding and the need for friendship between the two countries— were disastrous.

"Would Britain accept an alliance between the two countries?" Hitler asked.

"Speaking personally, I do not exclude the possibility," Henderson replied.

It was the reaction of a dangerous and incompetent man. When Vansittart heard about it in London, he put his explosive reaction into civilized words when he wrote: "If the Germans were clever enough to allow it to transpire that the question had been put to the British Ambassador and that he had answered it in the terms employed, I think we should have to face a great deal of indignation and suspicion in this country, and above all there would be a loss of confidence and suggestions of perfidy in France, Turkey, Poland, Rumania, Greece and so on. I think Sir Nevile Henderson should receive instructions to avoid this topic altogether. There can be no possible question of anything of this kind within visible time. An alliance means a military alliance if it means anything. And against whom should we be allying ourselves with such a gang as the present regime in Germany? The merest suggestion of it would ruin us in the United States."

415

But in responding as he did, it is no wonder that Henderson's reception was cordial. Just before the meeting, Ribbentrop had shown Hitler a dispatch from Fritz Hesse, saying that Britain would never fight for Poland. Henderson's manner bore out this assertion.

"We will let you have our reply tomorrow," Hitler said to the ambassador.

The next morning, August 29, Dahlerus went to Göring's house in the Leipzigerstrasse and was met by a smiling Bodenschatz. At eleven o'clock Göring arrived. He rushed over and took the Swede's hand in his chubby paws, pressing it affectionately. "God save the Swedes!" he cried. "A wonderful people! Everything goes well! We will have peace! Peace has been assured!"

XIX

Operation "Canned Goods"

It was early in August 1939 that the education inspector came from Breslau to tell Fräulein Lotte Rothemund that the village school where she taught on the outskirts of Oppeln, in Upper Silesia, was being closed until further notice. When the new term began, she and her pupils would be driven each morning to a neighboring school where for the time being they would share a classroom with the children there. Her own school was being requisitioned for work of national importance, the inspector said, but he did not elaborate, and Fräulein Rothemund did not ask questions. Since arriving in Silesia a few weeks before from Duisburg, in the Ruhr, to take up her first teaching job, she had seen too many troop movements, and quite enough requisitioning and maneuvering, not to realize that something was brewing—the solution to the Polish "terror," no doubt, about which the newspapers and radio were so indignantly vociferous.

Still, Fräulein Rothemund and the rest of the small community were intrigued when a big car arrived at the school a few days later, and the rumor spread that the officer who descended from it to inspect the school was none other than Reichsführer-SS Heinrich Himmler. (In fact, it was not Himmler but one of his assistants, SS Lieutenant General [Obergruppenführer]Heinrich Müller, head of the Gestapo.) The big car drove away, but two days later two trucks arrived, one

417

containing a squad of SS men and the other a group of gray-com-plexioned men in strange uniforms. By this time a perimeter had been flung around the school and a guard post set up.

Fräulein Rothemund would have looked the other way, as most people in Germany were doing at this time, had it not been for the fact that she suddenly remembered she had left a number of children's essays in her locker at the school, and that these must be marked and corrected before the fall term began. She made her way to the school but was stopped at the guard post by a soldier who refused to let her through. Though he offered to have someone fetch the essays, she maintained that no one could find them, so eventually a sergeant was called and was finally prevailed upon to let her into the building—as long as she picked up her papers at once and departed immediately.

As she approached her classroom Fräulein Rothemund noticed that the main hall had been turned into a mess for the SS. She was about to enter her room when the sergeant stopped her roughly and told her that she couldn't go in. At that moment the door opened as an SS man came out, and it was then that she saw the other men. They looked pale and ill. Some lay on the floor; others slouched over desks. Fräulein Rothemund at once recognized the Polish uniforms they were wearing, for she had seen pictures of them in the news-papers. But, strangely, the men were speaking German rather than Polish, and even stranger was the fact that they were all manacled. Before she could see any more, however, she was quickly bundled out of the school—without her essays. (The SS sergeant brought them to her the following day.)

It was not until September 1, when Lotte Rothemund listened to the radio, that she realized why the manacled men wearing Polish uniforms had been quartered in her village schoolroom during those waning days of August.*

■

On Tuesday, August 29, Adolf Hitler summoned Nevile Henderson to the Reich Chancellery to receive the official reply to the British

* Fräulein Rothemund mentioned her strange experience to only one person, a childhood friend who was then in the army and by coincidence was camped near Oppeln that August before advancing into Poland. She said nothing until 1945, when she recounted her tale to a British intelligence officer of 21 Army Group at Bad Oeynhausen in Westphalia. By this time she was a nurse in a hospital for wounded German officers.

418

note of the day before. The British ambassador had undergone a radical change of mood since his previous interview with the Führer. His knuckles had been rapped by London for seeming to welcome a German alliance, and he was now suspicious, sullen and looking for traps. This time he did not fortify himself with champagne. A pity; it might have sharpened his wits for the interview which followed.

On the evening of August 29, Adolf Hitler was searching desperately for a way out of trouble. By this time he was acutely aware that there were murmurings and restless stirrings among his generals over his indecision of recent days, and doubts and speculation over his order to postpone the attack on August 26. He had partially restored his authority by giving the new date of September 1 for the invasion of Poland. However, it was a date he would have to abide by, not only for reasons of weather but because his High Command would never stomach another postponement, and this meant that he had little more than forty-eight hours in which to make sure that Britain and France would not interfere when his soldiers attacked—or at least interfered only to the extent of forcing the Poles to capitulate to his demands. For this reason he had decided on a gamble, and chosen Henderson as the horse on whom to place his bet.

When he denounced the German-Polish treaty of friendship six months before, Hitler had sworn that he would never have direct dealings with Poland again. But in the note which he now handed to Henderson in the presence of Ribbentrop, he completely reversed this stand. In part the document read:

"The German government accordingly agrees to accept the British government's offer of their good offices in securing the dispatch to Berlin of a Polish emissary with full powers. They count on the arrival of this emissary on Wednesday, August 30 [the following day], 1939. The German government will immediately draw up proposals for a solution acceptable to themselves and will, if possible, place these at the disposal of the British government before the arrival of the Polish negotiator."

It was a shrewd move on Hitler's part. Until now it has been variously described as "a trap" or "a trick" and not genuinely meant. Those who make this charge base their reasoning on an extract from General Halder's diary which refers to the offer in these words: "Poles directed by English to go to Berlin as required by Germans. Führer wants them to come tomorrow . . . 30.8 [August 30]. Poles in Berlin

419

31.8. Blowup 1.9. Use of force." But until now no one has asked General Halder whether he was in Hitler's confidence when he wrote these words, or whether he had been specifically told by the Führer or Ribbentrop that they would deliberately sabotage any conference which the Poles agreed to attend. The fact is that Halder was *not* in Hitler's confidence and was *not* told either by him or by the Foreign Minister that they were setting a trap. Rather, this was pure speculation on the part of the general, confided to the privacy of his diary.

This does not mean, of course, that Hitler was not gambling to win. He had every reason to believe that he was betting on a sound horse. He was well aware that in influential circles in London not only the appeasers were now worried about the obstinacy of the Poles and anxious for them to negotiate. Two days earlier Captain Liddell Hart, the *Times* military commentator who was read with keen attention by all shades of British public opinion and who was far from being an appeaser, had circulated his views on the situation to several prominent Tories, including Anthony Eden, as well as to the leaders of the Labour and Liberal opposition parties. A copy had been sent to Berlin for Hitler's attention by Fritz Hesse.

"Last March," wrote Liddell Hart, "by our sudden and unconditional guarantee to Poland, we chained our policy to that most romantic and least realistic people in Europe. Subsequently, we allowed them to raise obstacles to Russia's military aid. At the same time our own tone towards Germany developed a perceptibly provocative note—as the military situation deteriorated. At the height of the crisis, we have signed and published a still more specific agreement with Poland which, of its nature, inevitably adds fuel to the flames and makes it more difficult for Hitler to 'save his face' in any peaceful settlement . . . Only a stupid strategist accepts battle when he has been manoeuvred into a bad position; any sensible strategist does his utmost to postpone battle, and manoeuvre afresh with a view to regaining an advantageous position. In the present circumstances it would seem wiser to press the Polish government to *compromise* —as distinct from surrender—with Hitler, pointing out the stark realities of their fate in an immediate war, rather than be drawn into a struggle which, at the best, only promises to end in futility and may lead to irreparable disaster . . ."

Hitler reasoned that if members of the anti-Chamberlain group in Britain were adopting such attitudes, then surely the appeasers

420

themselves would leap at a German offer to negotiate directly with the Poles. But Henderson, far from being overjoyed, listened to the note and its suggestion that a Polish plenipotentiary arrive by August 30, and to the Führer's amazement immediately answered, "That sounds like an ultimatum!"

Ribbentrop bridled at this and Hitler flushed with anger. In the circumstances, what choice did he have except to give the next day as his deadline? The hours were ticking away. D-day was September 1, and if the Poles did not arrive by August 30 there would be no time to negotiate, for he dared not postpone the attack once again.

But Henderson, who had once longed for a pat on the back and a word of praise from the Führer, was now looking for insults and rebuffs. Admiration had turned to hate, and had Hitler now chopped off a finger to show his sincerity, the British ambassador would not have believed him.

Furious at the envoy's skepticism and suspicion (for he had counted on him as a dupe), and since he could hardly explain the real reasons for his haste, Hitler once more used the "atrocities" in Poland as an excuse. They could not be tolerated much longer, he said. "You do not care a row of pins how many Germans are being killed and tortured in Poland!" he cried.

This was the opportunity for which Henderson had been waiting to satisfy his own *amour-propre* and the critics in England who accused him of not "standing up to Hitler." He made a "heated retort" and "proceeded to outshout Hitler . . . at the top of my voice," as he wired Lord Halifax the next day.

Thus, what was perhaps the most important meeting of all between Nevile Henderson and Adolf Hitler—the one which might have made all the difference—ended in a shouting match. As a result Henderson's report to the Foreign Office was couched in such terms that the proposal was interpreted by Chamberlain and Halifax as a belligerent ultimatum rather than the overture Hitler had intended it to be.

At ten o'clock the same evening, Birger Dahlerus was enjoying the first good meal he had eaten for several days when Ogilvie Forbes telephoned and then came over to the Esplanade Hotel to inform him that Henderson's interview with Hitler had gone badly. "We must prepare for the worst," the Englishman said.

421

While they were talking, a page summoned the Swede to the telephone. It was Göring; he too had heard the news, and he asked Dahlerus to join him immediately. He sounded full of wind and fury.

Dahlerus said good-bye to the rest of his meal and climbed into a Luftwaffe car which took him to Göring's home in the Leipzigerstrasse. The Field Marshal was indeed in a towering rage. In one hand he held a glass of whiskey—he did not offer one to Dahlerus—and in the other he waved a copy of the note which the Führer, whom he had just left, had handed to Henderson. Angrily the Field Marshal demanded to know why the British ambassador had refused to accept it. "Even before he has the details, he talks of an ultimatum!" Grabbing a red pencil, he sat down and proceeded to go through the note, heavily underlining the paragraphs he considered to be of special significance. He agreed wholeheartedly with his Führer that the note was worded conciliatorily, and that Henderson's outburst must be regarded as proof that the British did not really want to reach an agreement.

"All the old resentment against England came to the surface," Dahlerus recalled later, "all the points of dispute were revived . . . Now I heard what the Poles were really worth. The explanation of the wording of the note, according to Göring, was that the German government was dubious as to the intentions of the British government.

" 'We know the Poles,' Göring burst out," and then launched into a vituperative harangue against the Polish government and its people, their shameless behavior, their insolence. In the circumstances, it was natural that Germany had taken precautions and marched to the frontier.

"Sixty German divisions are there waiting," the Field Marshal told Dahlerus. "That corresponds to about one million men, but we all hope that nothing will happen, that military action between Poland and Germany will not become necessary. However, in view of the present exceedingly critical situation, we are compelled to insist that a settlement be reached without delay . . . The Poles are mad. Their treatment of their German minority is inexplicable and inhuman. Large-scale organized attacks happen every day. . . . The situation is untenable."

Then Göring began to inveigh against the anti-German propaganda on the Polish radio, and he huffed indignantly at some of the charges. "Today the Polish radio reported that German soldiers who crossed the frontier as deserters were miserably equipped, that their uniforms had been held together with string!" To Göring this seemed to be the greatest insult of all.

The Field Marshal ended by declaring that there was only one reason why Germany did not remedy all her grievances against Poland by force: because she seriously desired a settlement with England. But England and France were mad if they thought they could prevent Germany from intervening in Poland if it were really deemed necessary. As an unexpected afterthought he made a remark which took Dahlerus by surprise: "Italy will be neutral in such a conflict no matter what happens."

After a while the Field Marshal calmed down and began to refer to Henderson's behavior more in sorrow than in anger. He had behaved badly just at a time when the Führer was preparing to make "a great gesture" to Poland; in spite of everything he hoped that Hitler would still make the offer early the next morning. He could not yet give Dahlerus all the details, but he was willing to outline the offer in order to demonstrate the German government's desire to reach an agreement.

With that, Göring tore out a page from an atlas. He shaded over some territory with a green pencil, and then marked in red those areas that could be regarded as purely Polish. Next, he outlined for Dahlerus the plan for the settlement of the Polish question which Adolf Hitler would be prepared to accept. Dahlerus himself summed it up as follows:

"1. Germany would retain—'as mentioned in my early discussions with Hitler'—her claims to Danzig.

"2. In order to achieve a just and lasting solution of the problem of the Corridor, Hitler would probably suggest a plebiscite in the areas involved. This plebiscite would be conducted on approximately the same lines as that in the Saar, and would affect the territories with mixed German-Polish populations. If the plebiscite should give the territory to Poland, Germany would be granted a traffic zone—a corridor through the Corridor—with a broad highway and a four-track railway. This railway would be constructed so as not to interfere with Poland's traffic lines. If, on the other hand, the plebiscite should go in Germany's favor, Poland would be granted similar lines of communication. The agreement would be guaranteed by the five

423

Great Powers (Germany, Britain, France, Italy and the U.S.S.R.)."

It was one o'clock on the morning of August 30 when Göring handed Dahlerus the page from the atlas and the outline. "Take this to London and show it to Chamberlain and Halifax," he said. "This is what we are offering."

Thereupon the Field Marshal once more arranged for a special plane for Dahlerus, and four hours later the Swede again took off for England. At ten-thirty on the morning of August 30 he was talking with the Prime Minister and Halifax at No. 10 Downing Street.

And this is where the mystery begins. For if these were the terms which Hitler was willing to discuss with the Poles, there is no apparent reason why Britain should not have urged Poland to begin talks at once. They were fair terms on which to base discussions, and they were the terms which the British and, in particular, the French had previously thought eminently reasonable.

Yet no effort was made that day by Neville Chamberlain to pass on the details of these terms to Warsaw, or to persuade them to begin conversations. Henderson's hostile encounter and his affronted dispatch seemed to have turned the appeasers—at just the wrong moment—into die-hards. They had decided to dig in their heels. Poor Birger Dahlerus was suddenly treated as if he were the devil's advocate and was coolly advised to return to Berlin, where "any decision reached by the British Government would be passed on to me at the British Embassy . . . Cadogan made it quite clear to me that England would scarcely encourage Poland to conduct negotiations in Berlin."

Why not, if the bases for discussion were as promising as those suggested by Göring?

It is true that by this time Neville Chamberlain was skeptical of the Führer's sincerity, but considering all the circumstances, his lack of initiative at exactly this moment was the height of folly. Did the British wish for a peaceful settlement between Poland and Germany or not? Of course they did,* and so did everyone else. From his intelligence services Chamberlain knew that Hitler was in a difficult position; the pact with Russia had not had the effect upon the de-

* "The Polish Government would make a great mistake if they sought to adopt a position in which discussion of peaceful modifications of the status of Danzig was ruled out," Halifax had cabled to Kennard, the British ambassador to Poland, on August 25.

424

mocracies which he had hoped for, and Mussolini had made it plain he was not entering a war involving the West. Yet German troops were mobilized and waiting on the Polish frontier. The date for their advance had been altered once. In what circumstances could they be called off again? Only if an announcement were made that talks about Danzig and the Corridor were to begin between Germany and Poland. Hence it was surely in the interests of peace for the Prime Minister to find out whether Dahlerus' message meant a serious disposition on the part of the Germans to negotiate.

Nevertheless, it was not until midnight on August 30–31, after many precious hours had ticked away, that Nevile Henderson returned to the Foreign Ministry in Berlin with another note from the British government. The message welcomed Germany's desire for improved relations and still approved of direct negotiations between Berlin and Warsaw, but considered "that it would be impracticable to establish contact so early as today."

But why not? Considering the circumstances, the sooner contact was established the better for everyone.

The Ribbentrop-Henderson encounter which followed has wormed its way into history as the most dramatic and stormiest clash between two diplomats in modern times. No one has bothered to add that it was also a tempest in a teapot. Admittedly, Ribbentrop had not expected the British note to be quite so unbending in its refusal to endorse a speedy meeting between the Germans and the Poles. He became increasingly angry as Henderson coldly read out each succeeding paragraph. For once this was understandable. The Secret Service had already informed the Foreign Office that September 1 was the day when the attack on Poland would begin, and from such information it could have been deduced that Hitler had very little time in which to maneuver.

As it became clear that Hitler's gamble had failed, Ribbentrop grew more and more agitated and kept bounding up from his chair to ask, "Is that all?"

Henderson would reply, "No, it isn't all!" and read on remorselessly.

Soon Ribbentrop interrupted again, and then suddenly their mutual contempt gushed forth as they began to abuse each other.

Finally Henderson gulped down his last insult and after a pause asked, as he had been instructed to do, what proposals the German

425

government now had for a settlement of their dispute with Poland.

"It is too late now, in any case!" Ribbentrop retorted. "We asked for a Polish envoy to arrive on August 30. It is now past midnight and therefore too late." He paused. "However, I am prepared to read them to you." Then, as Henderson reported it later, he "proceeded to read them in German at top speed, or rather gabbled them to me as fast as he could, in a tone of utmost annoyance."

In fact, Dr. Paul Schmidt* was there as interpreter and Henderson could have appealed to him to translate. But obviously the British envoy was acting like many another diplomat and was relying on obtaining a transcript of the conversation afterward.

Henderson later wrote: "Of the sixteen articles, I was able to gather the gist of six or seven, but it would have been quite impossible to guarantee even the accuracy of these without a careful study of the text itself. When he had finished I accordingly asked him to let me see it. Ribbentrop categorically refused, threw the document with a contemptuous gesture on the table and said that it was now out of date since no Polish emissary had arrived by midnight."

It has since been suggested that the terms which Ribbentrop "gabbled" at Henderson were a deliberate hoax. Everyone has admitted that they were reasonable terms, and they could have formed the basis for negotiations which might well have saved the world from World War II—at least in 1939. But, most historians claim, they were given to Nevile Henderson in such a form and at such a late hour that it was impossible for Britain to do anything about them.

This is simply not true. Birger Dahlerus had already relayed the broad outlines of Hitler's proposals to Chamberlain and Halifax at ten-thirty on the morning of August 30. At that point there was plenty of time for Britain to urge Warsaw to send an envoy.

Moreover, at six o'clock that same evening, Baron von Weizsäcker had cabled Theo Kordt the complete script of the sixteen articles of the proposed Polish settlement, but instructed him to hold them "for the time being." Theo Kordt did not do so; instead he sent over the full transcript to the Foreign Office for their perusal, so convinced was he that they would pave the way for a general settlement.† Thus, the Foreign Office had the complete text by seven-thirty that

---

* Schmidt afterward denied that Ribbentrop "gabbled."
† See Notes at the end of this book.

evening. Even then there was still time to convey the sixteen points of Hitler's offer and to urge the Poles to send an envoy to Berlin.

The British leaders did not do so—at least, not until too late. They knew on the evening of August 29 that Adolf Hitler had performed an about-face and would agree to receive a Polish negotiator, which was exactly what the British and French wished him to do. By the next morning they had a strong indication that Hitler was willing to discuss reasonable terms, but *quickly,* for obvious reasons.

Suddenly, however, as if clutched by a death wish, Chamberlain and his group of appeasers were in no hurry at all. It was as if they had given up all hope. "He says the futility of it all is the thing that is frightful," Ambassador Kennedy had reported in describing Chamberlain's mood to the State Department on August 23. "After all, they cannot save the Poles . . ."

The Prime Minister did not even try to do this until too late. It was not until the early hours of August 31 that he instructed his ambassador in Warsaw to inform Colonel Beck that the Germans were willing to see a Polish envoy and start negotiations, provided that he arrived before midnight on August 30—some hours past— and even then the Poles were not told what Hitler was offering.

What Beck would have replied if the proposal had been conveyed to him in time can only be conjectured; probably he would have been just as obstinate. As it was, he said, "They can invite me to Berlin, but I will not go. I have no intention of being treated like President Hácha."

There, you see, the British leaders were able to say to themselves, *it would have done no good anyway, even if we had approached the Poles in time.*

Suddenly Nevile Henderson had recovered his zest for peace. His mood had changed again. To be sure, Joachim von Ribbentrop had insulted him and had "gabbled" the terms of Hitler's offer to Poland, but at least the terms had sounded promising. Perhaps it was not too late after all; perhaps he could still save the situation single-handedly.

At two o'clock on the morning of August 31, Henderson persuaded the Polish ambassador to come over to the British embassy. The two of them met in the Englishman's study overlooking the Wil-

427

helmstrasse, and the British envoy solemnly read out the sixteen points of Germany's proposal to Poland.* "They are not unreasonable," he pointed out.

Ambassador Lipski made no comment.

"Please take my advice and act urgently on it," Henderson said. "Ring up your Minister for Foreign Affairs and tell him you have heard from me that detailed proposals have been individually elaborated. Suggest that you would like to call on Herr Ribbentrop with a view to communicating them to the Polish government. Do this tonight, I urge you!"

"Not tonight," Lipski said. "It is too late!"

"Tell your government that Marshal Smigly-Rydz should meet Field Marshal Göring at once. They would get on well together. Something could be arranged."

"I will put the suggestion to Warsaw—but not tonight," the Pole answered.

Lipski departed in a daze, as if already asleep. In the morning he was unavailable when Henderson telephoned him once before breakfast and once during midmorning, and when eventually he was reached he refused to come to the British embassy. He was "too busy," he said. Indeed he was; he was packing.

Henderson, who had an appointment at the Foreign Ministry with Weizsäcker, decided to send Dahlerus and Ogilvie Forbes to see the Pole and emphasize to him again the details of Hitler's offer. The sleepless Swede, who must have been wondering what would be asked of him next, reluctantly consented to undertake the mission and was driven across Berlin in Forbes's open two-seater car.

Though no one knew it then, it was the last morning of peace. "The gravity of the situation struck as we crossed the threshold of the Polish embassy," Dahlerus later wrote. "The hall was crowded with packing cases, and the staff and servants were preparing for departure. Lipski received us in his office, which had already been cleared of most of its furniture."

By this time the Polish envoy was on the verge of the nervous breakdown he subsequently suffered. His face was green-white and

---

* By this time, to make sure that the British knew the exact terms of the offer, Göring had dictated the details to Dahlerus, who had in turn given them to Ogilvie Forbes, who had handed them over to Henderson.

he continually tore up pieces of paper and twisted them into little balls.

Forbes jotted down the main points of Hitler's sixteen-point proposal and handed them over to the Pole, who took the paper with trembling fingers. "He gazed at it for a minute and then said he was incapable of reading it," recalled Dahlerus. "I then offered to dictate the note to his secretary. She was summoned and given instructions, and I went with her into the next room, where she took down my dictation directly onto her typewriter." The Swede then returned and handed over the paper, which Lipski held without looking at it; he nodded vaguely as the Swede and the Englishman took their departure.

On the way back to the British embassy, Ogilvie Forbes said to Dahlerus, "Do you know what Lipski said while you were out of the room? He had *no interest* whatsoever in notes or any other kind of proposals from the Germans. He said he has a very clear understanding of the situation in Germany after five years as ambassador. He said he knows Göring intimately and all the other leading Nazis, and he is sure of one thing: in the event of war, there will be uprisings and rebellion in Germany, and the Polish army will march in triumph into Berlin."

Nevertheless, at one o'clock that afternoon, August 31, Lipski did call the Foreign Ministry and asked for an interview with Ribbentrop. He had been requested to do so, he said, by his government.

This the Germans already knew; they had instantly decoded the telegram sent to Lipski from Warsaw. A direct result of the British approach to Beck about negotiations in Berlin which had been sent to Warsaw only hours earlier, it read:

REQUEST A MEETING AND STATE AS FOLLOWS:
LAST NIGHT THE POLISH GOVERNMENT RECEIVED FROM THE BRITISH GOVERNMENT A REPORT OF AN EXCHANGE OF VIEWS BETWEEN THE GERMAN AND BRITISH GOVERNMENTS REGARDING THE POSSIBILITY OF AN AGREEMENT BEING REACHED BETWEEN THE GERMAN AND POLISH GOVERNMENTS. THE POLISH GOVERNMENT WILL CONSIDER THE BRITISH GOVERNMENT'S PROPOSAL AND WILL MAKE A FORMAL REPLY TO THE BRITISH GOVERNMENT WITHIN A FEW HOURS.

But it was the last paragraph of the telegram which galvanized the Germans, and Adolf Hitler in particular:

THE FOLLOWING SPECIAL AND SECRET MESSAGE IS ADDRESSED TO
THE AMBASSADOR:
DO NOT UNDER ANY CIRCUMSTANCES ENTER INTO ANY FACTUAL
DISCUSSIONS; IF THE GERMAN GOVERNMENT MAKES ANY VERBAL
OR WRITTEN PROPOSALS, YOU ARE TO REPLY THAT YOU HAVE
NO AUTHORITY WHATEVER TO RECEIVE OR DISCUSS SUCH PRO-
POSALS AND THAT YOU ARE ONLY IN A POSITION TO DELIVER THE
ABOVE MESSAGE FROM YOUR GOVERNMENT AND THAT YOU MUST
AWAIT FURTHER INSTRUCTIONS.*

That was enough for the Führer; he now knew that the Poles would
never negotiate according to his timetable, and that what he wanted
from them he could only get by force. Hence, at 12:40 P.M. on
August 31 he gave the order. *Fall Weiss,* the invasion of Poland,
would begin on schedule at dawn the following morning, September 1.

In the short time that was left, Hitler still hoped to neutralize the
British and French.

■

SS Major (Sturmbannführer) Alfred Helmut Naujocks had been
waiting for final instructions ever since August 16 at his post at
Gleiwitz in Silesia, about forty miles southeast of Oppeln, and he
was beginning to wonder whether the operation to which he had been
assigned would ever take place.

In 1939 Alfred Naujocks was twenty-seven years old. He had
been in the SS since he was eighteen, and a member of the Sicherheitsdienst since he was twenty-one. He was already a veteran of
several of the choicest campaigns masterminded by Heydrich, the
chief of the SD: smuggling arms into Austria and the Sudetenland in
1938, burning synagogues, with some enjoyable Jew-baiting on the
side in the fall of the previous year, and countless raids on suspected
opponents of the regime that satisfied his taste for violence. This was
the only assignment which had turned out to be a bore.

On August 10 Naujocks had been called into Heydrich's office at
Gestapo headquarters in the Prinz Albrechtstrasse and told that there
was a job for him. He must have guessed that it would not be long
before Germany took final action against the Poles, said his chief;

* The Polish government deleted this last paragraph of the message from the
Polish White Book.

430

indeed, the Führer was on the point of making his decision now. Undoubtedly the Poles would be too cunning to give Germany a valid excuse for attacking them; they would continue to commit barbarities against the German minority of Polish nationality but would avoid molesting German nationals or German property. Therefore it was necessary to manufacture the outright provocation which they refused to give.

On a large map of Prussia and the Polish frontier, Heydrich pointed to a circle on the map around the town of Gleiwitz, some ten miles inside German territory. It had a little radio station, a booster station for the Deutsche Rundfunk in Breslau. Its very smallness made it useful for Gestapo purposes, and it would be Naujocks' job to capture it.

Naujocks asked the obvious question: If it was already a German station, why must it be captured?

Simple, said Heydrich. Because Naujocks and the five men with him would not be Germans for the purpose of this operation, but Poles. A Polish-speaking German would be attached to the unit. Once they had taken possession of the station, he would broadcast a message in Polish announcing that the Polish army had crossed the frontier, that the station had been captured, and urging the Poles in Gleiwitz—there were about one hundred and fifty living and working there—to rise and attack the Germans.

And what would happen to the raiders? asked Naujocks.

Nothing, answered Heydrich. As soon as the broadcast had been made, they would withdraw.

Naujocks was skeptical. In Polish uniforms? They would be sitting ducks!

They would not be in Polish uniforms, Heydrich answered, but in civilian clothes. However, when they retreated, they would leave behind evidence that would definitely prove Polish provocation— evidence that could be shown to the German and foreign press.

What sort of evidence? Naujocks asked.

That he would find out later, Heydrich replied. In the meantime he was to choose the men he wanted to take with him. He should plan to be in Gleiwitz by August 16, and thereafter was to do nothing except reconnoiter the ground and wait for the code word signaling the moment when he was to capture the radio station.

And what was the code word?

431

Heydrich smiled. "Operation *Konserven*,"* he said. "You will learn later why we have called it that."

So Alfred Naujocks had been waiting obediently in Gleiwitz for two weeks, and by now he was bored, bored, bored.

In the head teacher's room in the school at Oppeln a field telephone rang just after one o'clock on the afternoon of August 31. The call was for Obergruppenführer Heinrich Müller, second-in-command to Heydrich, and was from his chief, who informed him that Operation *Konserven* was now scheduled for eight o'clock that night. The message should be passed on at once to Naujocks at Gleiwitz. Was everything prepared?

After assuring Heydrich that all was ready, Müller called for an orderly and asked whether the prisoners had eaten their midday meal. He was told that they had been given soup and bread, but he ordered an extra ration for them—a glass of beer for each man and a portion of canned meat (perhaps the choice of the latter was not co-incidental). Finally Müller asked that Dr. Strassburger, the SS doctor attached to the unit, report to him immediately.

Lotte Rothemund had been quite right when she deduced that the manacled men in Polish uniforms she had seen inside the school-house at Oppeln were not Poles at all, but Germans.

There were thirteen of them. Until August 15 they had been in-mates of the concentration camp at Oranienburg. At one time each of them had been condemned to death for murder by the courts, and then reprieved. Now, though they did not know it, they were about to be victims of a different kind of death sentence. All they had learned from their guards was that they would shortly be taking part in an "exercise" which, if successful, might win them clemency. An ill-fed bunch of men who were only too glad to have escaped the conditions at the camp, they did not speculate too much on the nature of the "exercise."

At four o'clock on the afternoon of August 31 the first of the prisoners was taken from Fräulein Rothemund's classroom into the

* Operation "Canned Goods."

432

main hall of the schoolhouse. He had been unmanacled, and he was marched up to a table behind which a man in glasses, his small figure clothed in a white surgical coat, stood with a syringe in his hand. This was SS Captain (Hauptsturmführer) Dr. Strassburger.

"Off with your coat! Roll up your sleeve!" ordered an SS guard.

The prisoner could leave his coat half on, the doctor said. His right arm was all that was needed.

The prisoner did as he was told. The needle plunged in, and as the sleeve of the Polish military jacket was rolled down again, the guard shouted "Dismissed!"

The prisoner turned to go, took two steps and then fell forward in a crumpled heap on the floor.

Strassburger turned to Heinrich Müller, who was watching from a corner of the room. The victim would be unconscious for five hours, the doctor said, which should give the SS all the time they needed.

He was a humane person, Müller declared. It was better that these men did not know what was going to happen to them. Whereupon he told the guards to pick the man up, pack him in the truck and send in the next prisoner.

In the address to his generals on August 22 Adolf Hitler had said, "I shall give a good reason for starting this war which propaganda can exploit—though it does not matter whether it is plausible or not. The victor will not be asked later on by the vanquished whether we told the truth or not. In starting or making war it is not right which matters but victory."

At eight o'clock on the night of August 31 the Führer was provided by the Gestapo with his "good reason for starting this war." At that hour Alfred Naujocks and his companions took over the German radio station at Gleiwitz and broadcast in Polish for ten minutes. Then they retreated, but before doing so they strafed the walls and windows of the station with machine guns, and when they departed they left behind the body of a man in Polish uniform—one of the thirteen prisoners. (It had been decided that this would lend more credibility to reports of the "attack.") "He was still alive, but he was completely unconscious," Naujocks said later. "I tried to open his eyes, but I could not tell from his eyes if he was still alive, only by his breathing."

433

The man did not last long. The drug was fatal after five hours, but long before that the wound in his neck where he had been shot finished him off.

Some miles away, in a wood near Hohenspitzen, another phase of Operation *Konserven* took place. SS men were propping the bodies of twelve drugged men in Polish uniforms against the trees as Heinrich Müller and four of his aides (Kriminalinspektor Scheffler, Kriminalinspektor Hein, Kriminalrat Lange and Kriminalassistent Paul Schulz) looked on. Much to the amusement of the others, Dr. Strassburger had asked to be excused.

When the men were suitably arranged, the SS guards drew back some distance and Müller and his assistants took their place beside them. After the Gestapo chief made sure that each body was facing Germany, he gave the order to fire.

Thus, with Germans massacring Germans, the excuse was given for the invasion of Poland.*

Only one hour before the Gleiwitz incident, at seven o'clock on August 31, the Italian ambassador, Bernardo Attolico—who had always been the most astute of the Berlin envoys, and also the one most determined to keep his country out of war—arrived at the Reich Chancellery for an interview with Hitler. He had received instructions from Foreign Minister Ciano in Rome to try "at all costs" to persuade the Führer to accept mediation over Danzig and the Polish Corridor. He did not have much hope; his sources in the German capital were good, and he knew how things were going.

The Italian found Adolf Hitler in a curious mood. He listened to the message which Attolico read out offering Mussolini's good offices, and waved his hand impatiently. He seemed uncertain, almost in a coma, Attolico said afterward, as if he was no longer listening to those who came to talk to him but only to inner voices. Ribbentrop, who was present, stood by with a look of contempt on his face,

---

* All of Himmler's men who participated in Operation *Konserven* save Naujocks subsequently received the Iron Cross. Naujocks was excepted because Heydrich had not been able to get the "pirate" broadcast from Gleiwitz on his radio. (Naujocks did get one later that year, for hijacking a British Secret Service agent from Holland.) Both Naujocks and Müller are wanted for war crimes, but are still at large.

especially when Hitler in a half-dreamy voice asked that his best wishes be conveyed to the Duce and "the valiant Italian people." However, when Attolico pressed the subject of mediation again, he said abruptly, "Too late!"

"Am I to understand that everything is at an end?" Attolico asked.

Hitler nodded his head. He did not look around as Attolico left the room.

The Italian ambassador hurried back to the embassy. Quickly he telephoned Ciano and reported his interview with Hitler. It could mean only one thing: war was unavoidable.

At once there was even greater panic in Rome. Several days before, in return for accepting Italy's passive role in the conflict, Hitler had asked for a quid pro quo: Italy should pretend to the Allies that she was standing faithfully by her pledge in the Pact of Steel. By troop movements and belligerent statements, Italy was to demonstrate that if Germany went to war she would be by her side. But now the danger of this position occurred to Mussolini and Ciano. What if the Allies believed their bluff? Might they not overrun the Italian defenses in the Alps, attack the Italian fleet in the Mediterranean and bomb the towns in the Po Valley?

It was no time, the Italian leaders decided, for such hazardous tricks. If they couldn't afford to go to war, they couldn't afford to make faces either—not now, anyway.

Ciano reached for the telephone and called the British ambassador, Sir Percy Loraine. When they met, Ciano confessed that under no circumstances would Italy join in a war against the British or French. He added that the Duce was aware of his indiscretion and approved of it.

Sir Percy Loraine thanked the Italian for his frankness. "He was moved," Ciano wrote in his diary. "He is on the verge of tears. He takes my two hands in his and says: 'I have known this for fifteen days.' "

This was quite true. It had been an open secret in Rome for some time that Italy had no intention of going to war, and it was for this reason that both the British and French had continually sought Italy's mediation. But the fact that the Italians were now admitting the truth could mean only one thing: the Germans had taken the fateful step and war was imminent.

435

Loraine cabled this fact to Halifax; the message reached the Foreign Office that night at eleven o'clock British summer time.

∎

Five and three quarters of an hour later, at 4:45 A.M. Central European time, September 1, the old German battleship *Schleswig-Holstein* swung into Danzig harbor and opened up with its big guns on the Polish garrison in Westerplatte.

Inside the city itself, a reviewing stand decorated with swastika flags had been erected opposite the High Commissioner's residence.* From behind the stand, Nazi Heimwehr troops directed a burst of fire into the offices of the Polish commissioner until, after half an hour, Chodacki and his staff came out with their hands up.

Only at the Polish post office, where the employees had barricaded themselves, was there any real opposition. It took twelve hours of sporadic firing and some heavy shells from a German field gun before the Poles eventually decided to give up.

By late afternoon Danzig was German. It had proclaimed itself so the day before, but only now was the city completely in the hands of the Nazis. The "Horst Wessel Song" poured out of the loudspeakers on the lampposts and there was rejoicing in the streets. Boys and girls in Heimwehr uniforms had their first taste of a potent local specialty, a stein of beer mixed with a slug of Danziger Goldwasser.

Out in the harbor, the Poles entrenched in Westerplatte held their position. Soon not only naval guns but dive bombers would be brought in to subdue them.

H-hour was 4:45 A.M. all along the Polish frontier and in the air above it.

By synchronized watches, the armored divisions of the XIX Army Corps rolled across the frontier at precisely that time, their commanding general leading the way through the thick morning ground mist in a half-track of the 3rd Panzer Brigade. For the first phase of the invasion, he had ordered that there be no firing until targets could be seen, but this did not prevent a near-disaster. The jittery gunners of the 3rd Panzer Division thought they heard sounds

---

* Dr. Burckhardt had hurriedly left for Geneva two days before.

436

of the enemy approaching and began firing wildly into the mist. Their first shell landed fifty yards ahead of the general's vehicle; the second, fifty yards behind it. "By God," he cried, "the next one will get us!" To his driver: "Start weaving, man, start weaving!"

The driver promptly spilled the armored vehicle into a ditch, ripping off its half-track, and the general ran back through the mist toward the German guns, screaming imprecations at his trigger-happy artillerymen.

Half an hour later the general was off again in a second armored vehicle, and twenty minutes later he and his tanks were in contact with the first line of Polish defenses. His orders were to cross the river Brahe and make with all speed for the Vistula, in order to cut off the Polish army stationed inside the Corridor and trap them inside an armored German vice. He was an admirable choice for the task ahead, and not only because he was a brilliant general; he also knew this country. By eight o'clock that morning he was fighting hard on the outskirts of the small Polish town of Gross-Klonia. The town and its castle had once belonged to his great-grandfather, his grandfather was buried there, his father had been born there, and he had spent his early childhood there.

The commanding general's name was Heinz Guderian, and he was to become the greatest German tank commander of the war.

The bridge over the lower Vistula at Dirschau, on the outskirts of the Free City of Danzig territory, was of vital importance to the Germans, and the Poles knew it. With the bridge secured, the Wehrmacht could sweep into the Free City and into the Corridor at will. Therefore all approaches to it had been mined for weeks, and a small garrison of select Polish troops stood guard. Their captain was confident that he could hold the approaches against all comers until the bridge was blown, no matter from what direction the attack came.

It had not occurred to the captain, however, that the attack might come from the air. Just before six o'clock on the morning of September 1, he heard the sound of several planes flying low and circling above him in the mist. His first thought was that they were Polish, but he realized quickly that they sounded too modern for that. But if they were German, what were they doing overhead? Surely the Nazis wouldn't bomb a bridge they needed so badly.

437

Suddenly one of his soldiers dashed into the hut, and almost at the same time he heard the sound of small-arms fire from the fields beyond the river. "Captain," the soldier cried, "they're dropping down on us! Paratroopers! They've come to get the bridge."

The officer reached for the button that would sound the general alarm, and as the siren began to whine he dashed through the mist for the bridge itself.

The Poles were lucky; the paratroopers had been dropped well away from the bridge. The defending troops held the perimeter for over an hour before the Germans broke through at seven-thirty. Through the swirling wreaths of fog, the captain saw the first four men in field-gray uniform racing across the span, firing as they came. Beyond was the vague figure of a Polish soldier sprawled beside his hut. This meant the electric firing apparatus had been captured.

The captain had five yards to go before he reached the spot just under the span, on the riverbank, where the emergency plunger was hidden. He had almost covered the distance and was scrambling toward the water when the Nazi paratroopers saw him and opened fire. A shot ripped into his right shoulder and spun him around, but it flung him so hard down the bank that he almost fell on the plunger. With his left arm he pressed down, and in an instant he, the Nazi paratroopers and the Dirschau bridge all went up in a roar of smoke, flame, mud and water.

The Luftwaffe began their attacks with bombing raids led by Dornier 17's (called "Flying Pencils") on the Polish air force bases at Katowice and Cracow. In the first hour they killed two hundred and fifty soldiers, destroyed seventeen aircraft and wiped out all the defenses. Then the Dorniers flew off and the dive bombers took over, strafing the fields into unusable rubble.

Shortly afterward the bombers turned their attention to Gdynia, Lwów, Krosno and Warsaw. By nightfall of September 1 the Polish air force was all but useless.

The Poles were amazed at the uncanny accuracy of the German bombers despite the bad visibility. They did not know that the Russians were helping. At the request of the High Command, the German embassy in Moscow had asked the Russians to keep their

438

radio station at Minsk on the air as long as possible, and to identify it as often as possible.

Stalin was glad to oblige his new allies. The Minsk radio station lengthened its transmission service by two hours at the beginning and end of the day on September 1, enabling the navigators in the Nazi bombers to take a pinpoint on it to guide them to their targets.

Thus the war began. But what kind of war was it?

SIX

World War II

XX

Common Action —
or Another Conference?

Just before they swarmed across the frontiers into Poland from Germany, East Prussia and Slovakia on September 1, 1939, a proclamation from the Führer was read out to the troops of the German army by their commanding officers.

TO THE ARMED FORCES:

The Polish government, unwilling to establish good neighborly relations, which I have always sought, now wishes to force the issue between us by force of arms.

The Germans in Poland are being persecuted with bloody terror and driven from their homes. Several cases of border violation, which cannot be tolerated by a great power, show that Poland is no longer prepared to respect the frontiers of the Reich. To put an end finally to these mad acts I can see no other way from now on but to meet force with force and fire with fire.

With firm determination the German armed forces will take up the struggle for the honor and vital rights of the German people.

I expect every soldier to be conscious of his high tradition and of his soldierly German qualities, and to do his duty to the last.

Remember always and in all circumstances that you are representatives of National Socialist Greater Germany!

Long live our people and our Reich!

Adolf Hitler

In fact, Germany had not declared war against Poland before marching across the frontier, and never did get around to doing so.

443

Perhaps it was this deliberate breach of international custom which encouraged the Western allies to believe that there was still a way out. No declaration of war, therefore no war, therefore no need to go to the aid of Poland.

But the pact which Britain had signed with Poland on August 25, 1939, and with which France was associated, was plain, simple and to the point. If Poland was attacked, the Allies were bound to come to her aid at once. If Poland was threatened by martial acts, they were also pledged. If Danzig was attacked or its status changed, the immediate support of Britain and France was automatic. All these acts had taken place, and more. There was no way out—or was there?

"Alex [Cadogan] called for me at Eaton Square about 9 [a.m.]" wrote Lord Halifax on September 1, "and told me that he had heard at seven that Danzig had declared its incorporation into the Reich, and a little later that the Germans had crossed the Polish frontier. [Leslie Hore-Belisha, the British Minister for War, had been roused with the news at five o'clock by his Chief of Staff, but apparently no one awakened the Foreign Secretary or the Prime Minister.] On hearing this, I asked the German Chargé d'Affaires and the Polish Ambassador to call on me at Number 10."

Halifax had to confer with Chamberlain before deciding what to say to the German and Polish envoys. He found the Prime Minister in a mood of bitter despair, but not hopeless, even now. Perhaps something could still be done. What about Mussolini? How were his efforts at mediation going? In fact, they were not proceeding at all, and in the next twenty-four hours they became something of a farce; still, they were a straw to clutch at, and Neville Chamberlain in London and Georges Bonnet in Paris went on clutching it to the last.

It was a beautiful day in London and the sun was shining through the windows of the Cabinet Room at No. 10 Downing Street as Count Raczyński, the Polish ambassador, was shown into the Foreign Secretary's presence. The Slav was trembling with great emotion, and a paper in his hand, from which he proceeded to read the latest news from Warsaw, shook violently as he told Halifax that the Germans had bombed Warsaw and Cracow and Katowice, and that their tanks were firing on Polish cities. It was war—a plain case, as provided by the treaty.

444

Halifax nodded. He had no doubt that if the facts were as His Excellency claimed, the British government would take the same view.

And declare war? Raczyński asked.

First they must ascertain the facts, the Foreign Secretary answered.

But there was no doubt about the facts. The British ambassador in Warsaw had already telephoned London to describe a bombing raid near the Polish capital which he himself had witnessed. He followed it with several other calls reporting acts of aggression against all parts of Poland, and added, "The Polish foreign minister, Colonel Beck, has just spoken to me. He was talking from an air-raid shelter because the capital is under attack."

Beck wanted to know two things: When was Britain going to declare war? When would she take action of a military character? Such action by the West was urgently needed to take pressure off the Polish front. The Polish Foreign Minister also repeated these questions to the French.

Meanwhile, having dispatched Raczyński without an answer to his query, Lord Halifax was now talking to Theo Kordt, who was cut off from Berlin and had no information about what was happening. Kordt promised to convey to his government the "very serious view" which the British were taking of the situation, and he too went away in an unhappy frame of mind. As an anti-Nazi who longed to see the British stand up to Hitler at last, he had hoped to hear a prompt declaration of war. But it had not come.

■

The late-summer morning breezes which were cooling the air in London were absent in Berlin; this first day of September was hot, humid and oppressive. Except in the Wilhelmstrasse, where a silent crowd stood outside the Reich Chancellery, the streets of the German capital were almost deserted, as if, having heard of the imminence of war,* the population had gone to ground. When Adolf Hitler drove to the Kroll Opera House at eleven o'clock, there was almost no one in sight to cheer him.

* The German people still naïvely hoped that the operations in Poland would not lead to a major war, but they were beginning to be afraid.

445

But the paid hirelings of the Nazi party rose to acclaim their Führer as he entered, though the sound of their acclamation changed subtly when they saw how he was dressed, as if they realized for the first time what was happening. Hitler had changed from his usual brown shirt and black trousers into the field-gray uniform of the German army. He sat chatting with Göring and Goebbels while some routine government business was dispatched, and then he rose.

". . . For two whole days," Hitler declared, "I sat with my government and waited to see whether it was convenient for the Polish government to send a plenipotentiary or not . . . But I am wrongly judged if my love of peace and my patience are mistaken for weakness or even cowardice . . . I can no longer find any willingness on the part of the Polish government to conduct serious negotiations with us . . ."

Now he dragged in the sordid provocation of Operation *Konserven*. "This night for the first time Polish regular soldiers fired on our own territory. Since five forty-five this morning we have been returning the fire, and from now on bombs will be met with bombs."

At this Göring rose from his seat and began to clap his flabby hands in a signal for general applause, and Goebbels turned around to the Reichstag members and like a conductor urged more and more fervency from them.

Hitler cried, "I have once more put on this uniform which for me is the dearest and most sacred of all. I will not take it off until after the victory which we will secure."

"Victory will come!" Goebbels shouted. "There will never be another 1918!"

While the Führer was speaking, Birger Dahlerus, the human ping-pong ball, was bouncing back again. Göring had summoned him to the Reich Chancellery, and two Berlin policemen escorted him through the crowd in the Wilhelmstrasse. The Swede had spent the early hours of the morning first with Göring on his armored train and later with Henderson at the British embassy. Göring had accused the Poles of starting the war, citing the attack on the Gleiwitz radio station and the destruction of the Dirschau bridge; Henderson was hoping that Dahlerus could get him an interview with the Führer and had cabled Halifax that "Herr Hitler may ask to see me after the Reichstag as a last effort to save the peace."

What peace? It did not seem to occur to the British ambassador that peace had already ceased to exist.

As he walked down the long corridor, Dahlerus passed the usual milling throng of gabbling Nazi courtiers awaiting the appearance of the Führer. Presently Göring came out of Hitler's study and clapped the Swede on the back. "Have you heard that the Führer has nominated me as his heir?" he said. "Does it not indicate his confidence in me? But it does nothing to change my aims. Peace, that is what I want! Tell me, Dahlerus, are you still sure that England wants to reach a reasonable and peaceful agreement with us?"

Dahlerus was now out of touch with London but suspected that he could not go wrong if he indicated that they were. "But circumstances have changed," he added. "I see only a faint chance of averting a world war now. But can't we try to bring about a meeting— between you, say, and some members of the British government?"

The Field Marshal vanished into Hitler's study. He soon reemerged and beckoned to Dahlerus, and then led him into a small reception room where the Führer was waiting alone.

Hitler looked calm enough but the Swede got the impression that he was extremely nervous. His hand was pressed tightly against his stomach.

Once more Dahlerus found himself forced—as if he were some sort of international ombudsman—to listen to an impassioned argument of Hitler's case and justification for what was happening at the moment. "I have always known that England doesn't want peace, that her every move has been inspired by her own selfish interests. Herr Dahlerus, you have my thanks for all the efforts you have made to bring about an understanding between the two nations. It is England's fault that they have been in vain. Now it is too late; there is no longer any hope of coming to an agreement."

Göring said, "There are points we must reach in Poland before we pause and—"

Hitler interrupted. "I have reached the conclusion that there is nothing for it but to crush Polish resistance and annihilate the Polish nation. But if England wants a discussion, I will still meet her halfway. But if the British don't understand that it is in their own inter-

447

est to keep out of a fight with me, they will live to repent their folly."

Now the Führer began to work himself up into another frenzy. "If England wants to fight for a year, I will fight for a year; if England wants to fight for two years, I will fight for two years!" He was screaming now, and waving his arms like a madman. "If England wants to fight for three years, I will fight for three years!" He was bending down lower and lower, his face suffused with blood, his eyes bulging, as he all but banged his fist against the floor. "And if necessary, I will fight ten years!"

By this time Göring had turned his back in embarrassment, but Dahlerus' gaze never wavered. Adolf Hitler came closer and closer to him, fixing him with his staring eyes. Suddenly the Swede felt sick. "His breath was so foul," he wrote afterward, "that it was all I could do not to step back."

Birger Dahlerus was to see Göring several times after this interview, and was in touch with Nevile Henderson and with London until the bitter end, indefatigably telephoning and getting through when every line in Europe was supposedly closed down. He never gave up, but this interview with Adolf Hitler on the morning of September 1 was really the end of his own private crusade against war. It had been naïvely conducted but valiantly waged, and never once did he allow stupidity, obstinacy, arrogance, stubbornness or even bad breath to halt him in his efforts.

■

On the afternoon of September 1 the tanks of the 3rd Panzer Division of the XIX Army Corps moved eastward from Gross-Klonia and Zempelburg toward the Brahe River, after a morning spent charging the Polish antitank defenses around these two towns. The Poles had fought well. "[They] scored many direct hits," General Guderian reported. "One officer, one officer cadet and eight other ranks were killed."* But when the tanks moved on, they left no Poles alive behind them. They had fought to the last and been killed.

After a swing around his front, Guderian went forward to the 3rd

---

* Among them, the son of Baron Ernst von Weizsäcker.

448

Panzer Division, whose foremost troops had now reached the Brahe.
There he was angered to discover that orders had been given for
them to rest. The regimental commander did not believe that a passage of the river could be forced that day, and the High Command's
orders that it must be crossed at all costs had been ignored.

While Guderian stalked off angrily to think things over "and
tried to decide what measures I should take to improve this unhappy
state of affairs," a young officer, Lieutenant Felix, came over to him.
He was in his shirt sleeves and his arms were black with powder.
"Herr General," he said, "I have just come from the Brahe. The
enemy forces on the far bank are weak. The Poles set fire to the
bridge at Hammermühle, but I put the fire out with my tank. The
bridge is crossable. The advance has stopped only because there is
no one there to lead it. You must go there yourself, sir."

Guderian decided to follow the young officer's advice. Leading in
his command vehicle, he drove through the oak woods of Hammermühle, along a sandy track strewn with broken and burning Polish
transport and dying Polish horses, to the bank of the river. There,
from behind a stout old oak, German officers were directing fire
against the Polish positions hidden on the opposite bank.

"Stop that idiotic noise!" ordered Guderian. "Can't you see it is
doing no good?"

The General sent a reconnaissance team downstream in a rubber
boat to gain access to the other bank. Then, taking a gamble, he
ordered his tanks over the bridge. One by one they rolled over, and
one by one the Poles came out and surrendered. They were a patrol
of bicycle troops and had already run out of ammunition.

Within an hour the whole 3rd Panzer Division had crossed the
bridge over the Brahe and pushed on to Tuchel Heath and the river
Vistula. The pincers were beginning to close on the Poles.

It was dusk in the House of Commons when Neville Chamberlain
rose to make a statement. The House and galleries were packed—
so much so that the Polish and Russian ambassadors found themselves sitting next to each other and could do nothing about it. The
lights had been dimmed in the corridors but were still gleaming
brightly in the Chamber itself. Outside, along the Thames, barrage
balloons floated in the purple evening sky and workmen were con-

structing sandbag walls around the government offices in Whitehall.

As soon as prayers were over and the chaplain had ended with the word "Let us this day pray for wisdom and courage to defend the right," the Prime Minister rose. His speech was in a low key, but his emotion was visible enough. He reminded the House of how he had strived to avoid war and how he had prayed that it would never fall upon him to accept war's "awful arbitrament." "I fear that I may not be able to avoid that responsibility," he added. Suddenly he hit his fist on the dispatch box in front of him. "The responsibility for this terrible catastrophe lies on the shoulders of one man, the German Chancellor, who has not hesitated to plunge the world into misery in order to serve his own senseless ambition."

Chamberlain then went on to recount the negotiations which had taken place, and in a sudden access of animation and anger mentioned the sixteen-point plan which Hitler had produced for the Poles. "The Führer says that it was rejected by the Poles. It was never even communicated to them!"*

There was a pause, and the House waited. Was it coming now—the declaration of war, the fulfillment of the pledge to the Poles, the aid for which a beleaguered ally was now pleading?

No, it was not. There would be no ultimatum that night. Instead, the British and French governments, Chamberlain announced, were sending Adolf Hitler "a warning."

In Warsaw, Ambassador Léon Noël went to see the Polish Foreign Minister. He found him in bed looking desperately ill, and his wife, her eyes showing signs of recent tears, sitting beside him.

The French envoy informed Colonel Beck that the Italian government had proposed a conference to settle the differences between Germany and Poland. At first it had been suggested that Britain, Germany, France and Italy should attend, but France had insisted that Poland should be included too. He had come to reassure the Foreign Minister that this would not be the occasion for another Munich.

Beck looked at him in astonishment. This was no time to talk of conferences, he answered. What Poland needed now was mutual aid

* He did not mention that the British knew of the plan well in advance, thanks to Dahlerus and Kordt, but had not passed it on to the Poles either.

in resistance to aggression. Everyone was asking why there had been no declaration of war by Britain and France. Everyone wanted to know not about conferences but how quickly and effectively the alliance could be effected.

Noël took his leave sheepishly. He did not tell Beck that the initiative for a conference had come not from the Italians but from the French, who had asked Ciano to conceal this fact from the Poles and the British. As he drove back to the embassy through the darkened streets, the crump of bombs could be heard in the distance. There had been fifteen raids near Warsaw by German planes that day and the reek of cordite and burning wood was in the air.

In London, there were those who could still smell the reek of appeasement. Harold Nicolson, a member of the Churchill-Eden "ginger group" which had always opposed Chamberlain's policies, left the House of Commons puzzled. The Prime Minister had read out the terms of the warning which he said was being presented to the Germans by the British and French ambassadors that evening. But why a warning and not an ultimatum, since both countries were bound to aid Poland? And if it had to be a warning, why was there no time limit attached to it?*

That evening Nicolson dined at the Beefsteak Club and chanced upon an old friend, the Duke of Devonshire. A self-confessed snob, Nicolson thought to himself: "I must say I do admire a man like that, who must realise that all his grandeur is gone for ever, not showing the slightest sign of gloom or apprehension." Then he went on to meet Harold Macmillan and Ronald Tree, two other Members of Parliament belonging to the "ginger group," and they hung around waiting for Anthony Eden to arrive. He was their leader; he would tell them how Chamberlain could be galvanized—or kicked out. But this evening Eden did not join in their complaints against the Prime

---

* The warning which Henderson handed to Ribbentrop on the evening of September 1 ended with the words: "I am accordingly to inform Your Excellency that unless the German Government are prepared to give His Majesty's Government satisfactory assurances that the German Government have suspended all aggressive action against Poland and are prepared promptly to withdraw their forces from Polish territory, His Majesty's Government in the United Kingdom will without hesitation fulfill their obligations to Poland." The French made a similar submission.

451

Minister and his clique. It soon became apparent that Eden, though with them, was no longer one of them.

Eighteen months before, Chamberlain had got rid of Anthony Eden by a series of deceptions and shabby tricks. This evening, as if nothing had happened, he had decided to ask Eden to enter the Cabinet again. The Prime Minister's position at this moment was a parlous one; even his staunchest right-wing supporters were beginning to murmur against him, and all his chickens were coming home to roost—not yet, though; not if he could help it. There is something to be said for the arrogance of Neville Chamberlain and his knowledge of the vanity of men; Eden had listened and had decided to accept.

And not only Eden. The man Neville Chamberlain loathed most at Westminster was Winston Churchill, but now he needed Churchill's burly belligerency to bolster his position. Past master in the art of swallowing his pride when it was politically expedient, the Prime Minister sent for Churchill. Would he too join the Cabinet?

Churchill too agreed. Amid all his troubles, Neville Chamberlain could afford to smile. His two bitterest and strongest political opponents had been bought off. Whatever else was in danger, he was safe; no one could get rid of him now.

XXI

At Last

Throughout Saturday, September 2, the rulers of Britain and France —Chamberlain and Halifax in London, Daladier and Bonnet in Paris —wriggled desperately in an effort to escape from the trap they had set for themselves. There was no way out, but they could not see that yet. They cocked their ears eagerly for any whisper of mediation from Rome and firmly plugged them against the noise of bombs and shells in Poland.

Early on that last afternoon of what the British and French governments were still calling "peace," François-Poncet was summoned to see Count Ciano and was soon joined by Sir Percy Loraine, the British ambassador. The Italian Foreign Minister questioned them closely about the warnings which their colleagues in Berlin had handed to Hitler the previous day. "Can you assure me that they in no way amount to ultimatums?" he asked.

The envoys nodded their heads vigorously.

"I would like confirmation of that," Ciano said. "It is important."

Loraine asked his embassy to send him a copy of Halifax's instructions to Henderson, and François-Poncet telephoned Bonnet. Each gave the confirmation demanded of him: it was definitely not an ultimatum.

"Herr Hitler has asked me for information on this point," the

Italian Foreign Minister stated. "He wishes to have until Sunday noon to work out and consider the question of an armistice and a conference."

When Bonnet was told the news, he was overjoyed. In London they were somewhat more wary. By this time Neville Chamberlain knew that the ice on which he was skating was becoming dangerously thin. The country was growing restless. "We gave our bloody word to the bloody Poles," shouted a speaker at Hyde Park Corner, "and what are we bloody well doing for them? Bloody nothing!" There were demonstrations in Trafalgar Square, and M.P.'s were being besieged by angry constituents who urged them to force the government to take action. The Prime Minister knew he had an increasingly uneasy House of Commons to face and handle.

Hence, when Ciano telephoned Halifax after his conversation with the two ambassadors, the Foreign Secretary took a circumspect stance. No, he said, he was not against a conference, but a prerequisite for it was the withdrawal of German troops from Poland.

Ciano was skeptical; he knew Hitler too well by now. It was unlikely, he said, that the Germans would withdraw, but they would probably stay where they were after the declaration of an armistice, and then call a conference for Monday, September 4.

Bonnet was hopping mad when he heard the British condition. "Let's get the conference going!" he declared. "What does it matter about withdrawal of troops? The only important thing is to have the Poles included among the representatives at the conference."

The French Foreign Minister refused point blank to consider putting a time limit to the warning or to follow it with an ultimatum. He gave a variety of reasons: a meeting of the Chamber of Deputies was required before an ultimatum could be given, and it had only just started its session; besides, Ciano had persuaded him to wait while Mussolini mediated; French plans for evacuating women and children were not completed yet; in any case, the French armed forces were still mobilizing.

To be sure, the Chamber of Deputies was given a stirring speech by Edouard Daladier, insisting that France must honor her obligations. "Were France to admit of such aggression," the French Premier said, "it would earn her contempt, isolation and discredit . . . At the price of our honor we would be purchasing a precarious and revokable peace, and when the time came for us to fight, having lost the

454

esteem of our allies and of other nations, we should be a wretched people, doomed to defeat and enslavement."

But the moment the speech was over, Daladier was back supporting Bonnet to the hilt. He was in favor of delaying any ultimatum to the Germans for twenty-four to forty-eight hours—during which time something might turn up.

All through Saturday afternoon, like snakes approaching a mesmerized rabbit, the tank columns of the German army moved into Poland from the west, east and south. Danzig was quiet again, save for the crump of the *Schleswig-Holstein*'s shells landing methodically in Westerplatte, where the Poles still held out. On the horizon, smoke rose from the port of Gdynia, which the Luftwaffe was in the process of pounding to rubble.

Every German unit was urged to speed its progress and show no mercy to the enemy. The orders came from Hitler himself. If the British and French were going to be stupid enough to have a conference, he would be willing—provided that his armies were allowed to stay where they were when the armistice was called. Which was why he wanted as much territory as possible; the more he had, the more he would keep, for there would be no withdrawal.

At four-thirty on the afternoon of September 2, General Karl Bodenschatz sent a message to Luftwaffe commanders in the field: "Specific military targets have now been satisfactorily neutralized. With this achieved, Field Marshal Göring will allow more discretion to local commanders in the choice of targets. Where a military or political result is likely to be obtained, specific towns as well as specific targets may now be attacked."

An hour later, bombs were being loaded in the Dornier 17's for their first raid on the center of Warsaw and its civilian population. That Saturday night the city was literally set alight.

■

When the British Cabinet met in emergency session at four-thirty on Saturday afternoon, Chamberlain and Halifax at once sensed that their colleagues were angry. At last they were beginning to react to the furious discontent and dismay surging through the British people over the procrastination of their elected leaders. The newspapers were full of reports of Poland's agony; their editorials were headed: "WHY ARE WE WAITING?"

Halifax carefully excused the indecision which he and the Prime Minister were showing by blaming the French. "The trouble is that the French don't want to press any ultimatum until noon tomorrow [Sunday, September 3], and then give the Germans a forty-eight-hour time limit."

"All that will achieve is to allow the Germans to capture more territory and kill more Poles!" Hore-Belisha declared. "In any case, what does it matter what the French do? It is for Britain to fulfill her pledges."

There were murmurs of approval from around the table. In freezing tones Chamberlain suggested that it would be "unfortunate" if the British and French ultimatums could not be synchronized. Several ministers vigorously shook their heads in disagreement at this, but reluctantly consented to a statement which Halifax would read in the House of Lords and the Prime Minister in the House of Commons that evening. Members had been waiting for it since two forty-five.

Halifax was the first to rise and explain the government's position, and the assembled peers in the House of Lords listened to him in polite silence. "It went down quite well," he said later.

It is an indication of Halifax's personality, and how divorced from reality he was on this last day of peace for England, that afterward he did not bother to report to Neville Chamberlain or to the Foreign Office—where he might have learned that Warsaw had just been bombed—but instead strode across Green Park and past Buckingham Palace to his townhouse in Eaton Square. After a leisurely bath, he put on his dinner jacket; it was his wife's birthday, and it never occurred to him to cancel his plan to take her out for dinner. He and Lady Halifax were just going down the steps of the house at eight-thirty when the butler came running after them. "The telephone, sir," he said. "It's the Prime Minister."

Chamberlain was very agitated. Could Halifax come over at once? There had been some trouble in the House of Commons, he said. "I have never heard the Prime Minister so disturbed," Halifax wrote later.

There had indeed been trouble. The same statement as Halifax's, which had flowed like water off the backs of the peers of the realm,

456

had infuriated the Members of the House of Commons. Chamberlain's haughty manner did not help things. His voice showed "some emotion as if he is sickening for a cold," noted Harold Nicolson. "He is a strange man. We expected one of his dramatic surprises. But none came. It was evident when he sat down that no decision had been arrived at. The House gasped for one moment in astonishment. Was there to be another Munich after all?"

Then Arthur Greenwood, acting leader of the Labour opposition, rose to his feet. To his amazement, not only did his own side cheer him but the Tories, who had listened to their own leader in freezing silence, cheered him too.

"You speak for England!" cried Robert Boothby, a Tory.

Which Greenwood promptly did. Why this delay? What about their pledge to Poland? They had vacillated for twenty-four hours. What did it mean?

Even Chamberlain's supporters were cheering Greenwood now. The Prime Minister's face had gone gray, and the Cabinet ministers sitting on the front bench looked as if an earthquake had struck.

Immediately after the session, Alfred Duff Cooper, always an anti-appeaser and contemptuous and suspicious of Chamberlain, rushed to Winston Churchill's apartment near the House of Commons.

Churchill was in a thundering rage. He had been tricked: the night before, he had been asked to join the Cabinet and had agreed; now his hands were tied. He had wanted to speak out this evening in Commons and attack Chamberlain, but how could he, now that he was a member of the Cabinet? Sipping his brandy and puffing at his cigar, he huffed like an angry rhinoceros.

Now Boothby entered the apartment and urged Churchill to break with the Prime Minister at once. If you back him now, he pointed out, you will save him. But break with him now, and tomorrow you can take his place leader of Britain.

The two men left Churchill hunched in his armchair, trying to decide what to do.

The future for Britain and for the world might have been brighter in the months to come had Winston Churchill decided that night to break with Chamberlain. But as it happened, there was no need for

457

him to make the decision, for while he was discussing the situation with Duff Cooper and Boothby, five members of Chamberlain's Cabinet* had assembled in the Chancellor's room in the House of Commons and announced that they had gone on strike.

Sir John Anderson sat at the head of the table, with the others grouped around him. Through Sir Horace Wilson they had let it be known that they did not propose to leave the room until Britain had declared war. There was a telephone on the table by Sir John Anderson's side, and they waited for it to ring.

"As we sat there and waited by the telephone," Dorman-Smith recalled later, "and nothing happened, I felt like a disembodied spirit. It didn't seem real. We were on strike . . . There were no words of recrimination. But there was a feeling of great emotion. All of us were getting back to our natural selves. I became more Irish and Hore-Belisha more Jewish—talking of rights and indignities and so on."

At ten o'clock the phone rang. After a moment's pause Anderson answered it, listened, and then said, "Yes, Prime Minister. At once." They had been summoned to No. 10 Downing Street.

The five men walked down Whitehall under a heavily clouded sky to the Prime Minister's residence a quarter of a mile away. They had been sitting around for a long time "and we were all really scruffy and smelly" when they were shown into the Cabinet Room; therefore they were shaken when they saw Halifax, Sir Alexander Cadogan and Sir Horace Wilson standing before them, all in immaculate evening dress. The Prime Minister was still in the suit he had worn in the House of Commons.

All of them took their places around the table and the meeting began. Chamberlain looked calm, almost remote, and his voice was icy cold as he explained the reason for the delay: the reluctance of the French; his own fears that once war was declared, Paris—"that lovely city"—would be bombed immediately.

When he finished he waited for some comment from the striking ministers, but none came. No recriminations, either; just silence. Once Neville Chamberlain had complained to Hitler that he was

* Sir John Anderson (Lord Privy Seal), Leslie Hore-Belisha (Minister of War), W. S. Morrison (Chancellor of the Duchy of Lancaster), Malcolm MacDonald (Minister for the Colonies) and Sir Reginald Dorman-Smith (Minister of Agriculture).

458

being faced with a *Diktat*. This was a *Diktat* too, from his own ministers. He sighed, and then spoke very quietly. "Right, gentlemen, this means war."

Just as he spoke the Cabinet Room was lit by a flash of lightning and there was a heavy clap of thunder, like a roar of surprise from the cosmos that at last Neville Chamberlain had faced up to reality.

There was still a little way to go before Sir Horace Wilson reached the same conclusion. Once the meeting in the Cabinet Room had begun, he slipped away to his office. There Fritz Hesse was waiting for him. He had come, he said, with a proposal from the Foreign Minister in Berlin for another bilateral meeting between Britain and Germany. Hitler was eager to receive a distinguished British statesman and talk the whole thing over. "And I mean the whole situation, everything between us, heart to heart," Hesse said.

By now Wilson was far too wary to be caught by this sort of ploy, but he was lagging behind his master in recognizing that it was all over; he still thought that world peace could be saved. He said that he was sure things could be arranged, provided that Hitler ordered his troops back from Poland. "Then we might be prepared to let bygones be bygones," he said.

There was a pause; Sir Horace obviously thought that this was too much of a concession, for he added hurriedly, "Provided Herr Hitler apologizes too, of course."

■

Sir Nevile Henderson delivered the British ultimatum to the German Foreign Ministry at 9 A.M. on September 3, 1939. It gave the German government until 11 A.M. to announce the withdrawal of the German army from Poland. If it did not, Britain and Germany would be at war.

Hitler was so surprised that the Chamberlain worm had turned at last and Ribbentrop was so furious that his confidence in British cowardice had been confounded that they refused to see the British envoy. He was forced to present the note to Dr. Paul Schmidt, the interpreter, who had been hurriedly called in for the chore.

But after Henderson had gone and Schmidt entered with the piece

459

of paper in his hand, Hitler had a momentary spasm of doubt and fear. To Ribbentrop he said fiercely, "What do we do now?"

In the anteroom, where Göring, Hess, Goebbels, Frick and other Nazi satraps were waiting, the Field Marshal answered for them all. "If we lose this war," he said, "then God have mercy on us!"

At 10:30 A.M. in London, the great bell of Big Ben tolled the half-hour from the tower of the Houses of Parliament. The deadline issued to the German government was thirty minutes away; thereafter Britain would go to war unless Germany complied.

But as the sound reached the Prime Minister's study in No. 10 Downing Street, there was no calm acceptance of the fact, only confusion and doubt, for a messenger had just arrived from the Foreign Office with news that the inextinguishable and indomitable Dahlerus had done it again. His mission was in fact dead, but he refused to let it rest. Regardless of the fact that all frontiers in Europe were shut tight and all communication lines blocked, he had got through to London on the telephone once again. This time he was speaking from an extension in the kitchen car of Göring's operational train. He had a message of urgent importance, he said. "I have spoken to Göring. He has consulted the Führer. The Führer has agreed. Göring is so desperately anxious to prevent a war between Germany and the West that he is prepared to fly to London at once. His plane is standing by. He will leave German territory before eleven A.M. Will the Prime Minister accept his offer?"

In the room next to Chamberlain's study Alvar Liddell of the British Broadcasting Corporation sat before a microphone, waiting to introduce the Prime Minister before he announced to the nation that they were at war. As he stared through the window at the Sunday morning strollers walking down the Horse Guards Parade, a secretary bustled in. "Big things going on!" she whispered.

Liddell wondered what was happening. He had been waiting in this room now for two days. At the moment his announcement was scheduled for 11:15. Would it be postponed again?

In the Prime Minister's study Neville Chamberlain sat with his head in his hands. He looked ill and tired. A few yards away Sir Horace Wilson stood by, an expression of concern and compassion on his face. He must have guessed what was troubling his master:

should he make yet another try to save the peace? Should he accept Göring's offer?

The minutes ticked by. Suddenly the hour struck. It was 11 A.M. and officially war had begun. But still Chamberlain did not move.

He did not stir for another ten minutes, when suddenly he turned to his secretary and said, "Tell the announcer that the broadcast is postponed."

It was 11:13 when Liddell was informed. What on earth was happening now? They were at war, weren't they? Why not tell the nation and the world?

What went on in Neville Chamberlain's mind as he sat for those long moments at his desk, and in the sixty seconds after he ordered the postponement of his broadcast, will never be known, for he told no one, not even Sir Horace Wilson.

At 11:14 the Prime Minister changed his mind again. With a sigh he rose to his feet. The broadcast was on again. He walked into the adjacent room and took his place at the microphone.

"His shoulders were hunched and he was very, very serious," recalled Liddell. "I leaned over his shoulder and made the announcement. He began to speak. He looked crumpled, despondent and old."

"This is a sad day for all of us," Neville Chamberlain said, "and to none is it sadder than to me."

War between Britain and Germany had begun at last.

■

For the moment Hermann Göring did not have to worry about Germany losing the war. France had not yet declared her entry, which presupposed a deep division between the Allies, and in Poland all was going well for the Wehrmacht.

As the last minute of the British ultimatum ticked away on the morning of Sunday, September 3, and as the air-raid sirens began to sound over London,* Poland's most famous cavalry brigade, the Pomorska, was preparing for battle on Tuchel Heath at the neck of the Polish Corridor.

The tanks, armored vehicles and motorized infantry of General Heinz Guderian had moved fast overnight from the Brahe River, and

---

* A false alarm, it turned out. A French air attaché flying back from Paris had failed to identify himself clearly enough.

461

were now prodding hard for the banks of the Vistula. "The panic of the first days of fighting are past," Guderian noted in his diary. "They are making rapid progress. We will soon be at the Vistula. Trap snapped!"

To prevent its closing was the job of the Pomorska Brigade. They were an elite corps of hand-picked men with superb horses and were trained to perfection in the art of cavalry warfare. In bravery and skill with their mounts and swords and lances they were unparalleled, and they had not been equaled since the cavalry withstood the Sudanese fanatics at Omdurman in the 1880's. Now they faced their test. They had gathered in the woods to the east of Tuchel Heath to await the enemy in the early hours on the morning of September 3. Just after noon they saw their foe. Heinz Guderian had prepared his approach well. First came a thin line of unarmored patrol cars and a flanking support of advancing infantry. To the horsemen on their neighing, impatient mounts, it looked like just the target for which, in their fervor and patriotism, they had been waiting in order to demonstrate Poland's determination to throw the enemy back into the ordure where he belonged.

Slowly, in orderly formation, the cavalry moved out of the trees, maneuvered into long lines and then proceeded at walking pace. As more German infantrymen advanced across the plain and more German cars spilled from the copses, the order roared out: "Unsheath!"

With a simultaneous *slurr-yupp!,* which must have drawn a nod of admiration from the Germans, swords came out of their scabbards. Officers cocked revolvers; side riders shouldered their lances. The brigade moved to a canter and then into a gallop while from the shelter of the woods, small Polish field guns suddenly opened up, firing ahead of the galloping cavalrymen at the German infantrymen and vehicles—all of which suddenly turned tail and retreated.

The Poles jabbed their horses' flanks and increased their speed, convinced that the enemy was on the run. It was at this moment that Guderian's tanks appeared. Slowly, methodically, they came out in formation, trundling ponderously across the heath like complacent slugs. In truth, they did not need to advance at all; had they stood still and waited, the result would have been the same. The horses came on unhesitatingly; the swords and lances of their riders slashed unavailingly at the armored sides of the tanks, and revolver bullets bounced off them.

462

For the Germans it was just a matter of turning their guns on the target and letting fly. It took exactly forty minutes; by then the plain was a litter of men and writhing horses.* By nighttime the panzers were on their way again.

"The Corridor is pierced," reported Guderian. "The Poles are trapped. We are available for fresh employment."

While this message was on its way to the German Army High Command on the afternoon of September 3, France's ultimatum was running out. It had been presented at 10:20 that morning by Ambassador Coulondre and was due to expire at 5 P.M.

Unlike Henderson, the French envoy was accorded the dubious privilege of handing his ultimatum to Ribbentrop himself. He pointed out that there had been no reply to his warning of September 1, and that now the moment of truth had come. By 5 P.M. France would be at war.

"Then France will be the aggressor," Ribbentrop said sourly.

"Of this history will be the judge," Coulondre answered.

World War II had begun at last. It was Adolf Hitler's war, but the men whose weakness, stupidity, ignorance and maladroitness had done so much to encourage him still held the reins of power in Britain and France, and it would be a phony war until the German Chancellor made it a real one. But that was more than half a year away, and in the meanwhile Britain and France allowed the Republic of Poland to be crushed out of existence, turning no hand to help her.

To be sure, this was what they had made eminently clear many months before, during the Anglo-French military staff talks in London, but they had never told the Poles. Adolf Hitler had taken his greatest risk in western Germany, where he manned his defenses with a thin force of untrained troops, gambling that the Allies would never dare attack him—sure that, declarations of war or not, they were still terrified of him. He was quite right.

The idealist might wish that the British and French could have been honest enough to tell the Poles that they would not come to

---

* That evening Guderian sent out a squad to dispatch the animals and collect the wounded men.

463

their aid, instead of lying to them and promising massive attacks from the West when the holocaust came. On the other hand, considering the arrogance and recklessness of the Poles, the cynic might say that it wouldn't have made any difference. The Poles were that kind of people; they would have fought the Germans anyway.

There was rejoicing in Warsaw when news reached the people that Britain and France had declared war on Germany. Even Colonel Beck, who was now in great pain and drinking heavily to ease it, managed to conjure up a smile. Everyone waited for news of the first British bombing raids on Germany.

When there were none, the Polish air attaché was dispatched, on orders from Warsaw, to see the British Air Minister, Sir Kingsley Wood, and ask that the R.A.F. immediately bomb German airfields and industrial areas. He was brushed off with the excuse that matters of higher strategy were now under discussion and that no decisions had yet been made.

Shortly afterward Leopold Amery, an influential Tory M.P., saw Kingsley Wood and suggested that the R.A.F. fly across Germany and set fire to the Black Forest with incendiary bombs, depriving Germany of timber.

"Oh, you can't do that," Kingsley Wood answered. "That's private property. You'll be asking me to bomb the Ruhr next." That was private property too.

Epilogue

Day after day, Poland suffered and began painfully to die. But on the western front all was quiet. A thin screen of twenty divisions of ill-prepared, half-trained German troops were filtering into the West Wall fortifications, where some of the recently constructed concrete and cement bunkers were still drying. The German generals on this front had received direct orders from Adolf Hitler to let the enemy make the first move and not to provoke it. Therefore they waited with some apprehension, for they were weak and vulnerable and they knew it.

Opposite them, eighty divisions of the French army were now assembled behind the Maginot Line. There they waited for orders. They went on waiting. As long as Hitler was engaged in Poland they were the masters, but they did not move.

The inhabitants of Whitehall and the Quai d'Orsay had plugged their ears to the cries of the dying Poles. The phony war had begun for the Allies in the West, and it would continue for another eight months, until Nazi tanks and bombs shattered their complacency.

On September 19, 1939, troops of the Red Army moved into Poland from the Soviet Union to pick up the spoils assigned to them under the terms of the secret clause in the Russo-German pact. The ragged and defeated Polish armies fled before them, as did thousands of civilians.

On September 22 Andrei Vishinsky, Deputy People's Commissar for Foreign Affairs, summoned the Polish ambassador to the Kremlin to receive a note from the Soviet government. Shrewdly anticipating what was in it, the ambassador asked that the nature of it be revealed to him before he accepted it.

It was a proclamation of the government of the U.S.S.R. that in view of recent events, the Republic of Poland had now ceased to exist, Vishinsky replied.

"Poland will never cease to exist!" the ambassador cried, and he refused to receive the message.

Vishinsky insisted, and handed it over. The ambassador flung the note back on the desk. "Never!"

For ten minutes the document was passed back and forth, until at last the ambassador angrily stomped out of the room. But by the time he reached his embassy, a messenger had arrived and was waiting for him with the note in his hand. He promptly sent the man back with it to the Kremlin.

Nothing happened for another twenty-four hours, and then the Kremlin had an inspiration. The note was dropped in a Moscow mailbox and sent to the recalcitrant Poles by ordinary post.

Sources
and Notes

Sources

Abbreviations for the most frequently used references in the Notes are indicated by the symbols listed in the left-hand column.

1. Microfilm.

German records filmed at Alexandria, Va.; in the National Archives, Washington, D.C.

GFC	*Records of German Field Commands.* Parts I–IV.
GFMA	*German Foreign Ministry Archives,* particularly Series T-120 (Czechoslovakia and England). See also Vols. 2005, 2791, 5841H in the Foreign Office Library, London.
	Records of the Nationalsozialistische Deutsche Arbeiterpartei (National Socialist Party). Parts I–III.
OKH	*Records of the Oberkommando des Heeres* (Army High Command). Parts I–III.
OKL	*Records of the Oberkommando der Luftwaffe* (Air Force High Command).
OKM	*Records of the Oberkommando der Kriegsmarine* (Navy High Command).
OKW	*Records of the Oberkommando der Wehrmacht* (Armed Forces High Command). Parts I–IV.
RLFM	*Records of the Reichsluftfahrtsministerium* (Reich Air Ministry).
MVP	*Records of the Reichsministerium für Volksaufklärung und Propaganda* (Ministry for Public Enlightenment and Propaganda).
RFSS	*Records of the Reichsführer-SS und Chef der deutschen Polizei* (Reich Leader of the SS and Chief of the German Police). Parts I–III.

469

Sources

2. Published Documents.

BFP   *Documents on British Foreign Policy, 1919–1939*. Edited by E. L. Wood-
        ward and Rohan Butler. Third Series, Vols. I–IX (March 1938–Septem-
        ber 1939). London: His Majesty's Stationery Office, 1947–.
GFP   *Documents on German Foreign Policy, 1918–1945*. Series C, Vols. I–III;
        Series D, Vols. I–XI. London: HMSO, 1949–.
        Dokumente der deutschen Politik, 1933–1940. Berlin, 1935–1943.
        *Documents and Materials relating to the Eve of the Second World War,
        1937–1939*. 2 vols. Moscow: Foreign Languages Publishing House,
        1948.
        The Dirksen Papers. Moscow, 1948.
DDI   *I documenti diplomatici italiana*. Vols. XI–XIII. Rome: Libreria della
        Stato, 1952–1953.
FRUS   *Foreign Relations of the United States*. Diplomatic papers. Washington:
        State Department.
        Hitler e Mussolini—Lettere e documenti. Milan: Rizzoli, 1946.
LJF   *Le Livre Jaune Français. Documents diplomatiques, 1938–1939*. Paris:
        Ministère des Affaires Etrangères. (*French Yellow Book*.)
        Nazi Conspiracy and Aggression. 10 vols. Washington: State Department,
        1948.
        Nazi-Soviet Relations, 1939–1941. Documents extracted from the German
        Foreign Ministry Archives. Washington: State Department, 1948.
NDHM   *New Documents on the History of Munich*. Prague: Orbis, 1958.
IMND   Nuremberg documents, affidavits and interrogations, not used in evidence.
        Washington: National Archives.
PWB   *Official Documents concerning Polish-German and Polish-Soviet Rela-
        tions, 1933–1939*. London: Hutchinson, 1939. (*Polish White Book*.)
        Polish Military Records, Warsaw.
        History of the Polish September Campaign, 1939. Written and edited by
        Colonel Adam Sawczynski. Vols. I, II, III and V. London: The Polish
        Institute and Sikorski Museum.
IMT   *Trial of the Major War Criminals before the International Military
        Tribunal*. Transcript and documents used in evidence. 42 vols. Pub-
        lished at Nuremberg, 1947–1949.
NMT   *Trials of War Criminals before the Nuremberg Military Tribunals*. Tran-
        script and documents used in evidence. 15 vols. Washington: U.S.
        Government Printing Office, 1949–1952.

3. Unpublished or Partly Published Documents.

        "Estimate of Lindbergh's Services to the Office of Military Attaché, Berlin,
        July 1936–January 1939." Truman Smith. Microfilm of unpublished
        MS. in Yale University Library, New Haven, Conn.
        Microfilm of the Grynzspan Case in the Bibliothèque Nationale, Paris.
CAMFA   Documents on Czech foreign relations at the time of Munich. Prague:
        Archives of the Ministry of Foreign Affairs.
CAOPR   Documents concerning Beneš, Syrový and Hácha. Prague: Archives of
        the Office of the President of the Republic.
CMA   Documents on the activities of the Czech army at the time of Munich and
        after, until March 15, 1939. Prague: Military Archives.
CSAB   Documents in the Czechoslovak State Archives, Bratislava.
        Documents on the activities of the Czech Communist party at the time of
        Munich and after. Prague: Archives of the Institute of History of the
        Communist Party.

470

4. Interviews and/or Correspondence.

Lord Avon (Anthony Eden)
General André Beaufre
General Karl Bodenschatz, Munich
Charles E. Bohlen
Lord Coleraine, London
Birger Dahlerus
Edouard Daladier, Paris
David Dilk
Paul Emrys-Evans, Market Drayton and London
General Adolf Galland, Cologne
Earl of Hardwicke, London
Major E. Hinterhoff, London
Viscount Kemsley of Dropmore, Monte Carlo
Erich Kordt
Stanislaw Kostarski, Warsaw
Dr. Karel Kratky, Prague
Alvar Liddell, London
Captain E. Lubomirski, London
Dr. Jaroslav Pospisil, Prague
Colonel M. Prothsewicz, Paris
General Paul Stehlin
Lord Strang
Baron Ernst von Weizsäcker
Sir Horace Wilson

5. Biographies, Diaries, Memoirs, Studies of History.

Adam-Jukasz-Kerekes, *Allianz: Hitler-Horthy-Mussolini*. Budapest: Akademiai Kiado, 1966.

Amery, Leopold S., *My Political Life*, Vol. III, *Unforgiving Years, 1929–1940*. London: Hutchinson, 1955.

Ashton-Gwatkin, F. T. A., *The British Foreign Office*. Syracuse, N.Y.: Syracuse U. Press, 1949.

Avon, Earl of, *The Memoirs of Anthony Eden*, Vol. I, *Facing the Dictators*. London: Cassell, 1962 (Boston: Houghton Mifflin, 1962); Vol. III, *The Reckoning*. London: Cassell, 1965 (Boston: Houghton Mifflin, 1965).

Beaufre, André, *1940: The Fall of France*. London: Cassell, 1968 (New York: Alfred Knopf, 1968).

Beck, Józef, *Dernier Rapport*. Brussels: La Baconnière, 1951 (*Final Report*; New York: Robert Speller, 1958).

Sources

Beneš, Eduard, *Memoirs of Dr. Eduard Beneš: From Munich to New War and New Victory*. London: Allen & Unwin, 1954 (Boston: Houghton Mifflin, 1954).

Birkenhead, Earl of, *The Life of Lord Halifax*. London: Hamish Hamilton, 1965 (Boston: Houghton Mifflin, 1966).

Blum, John M., *From the Diaries of Henry Morgenthau, Jr.*, Vol. I, *Years of Crisis 1928–1939*; Vol. II, *Years of Urgency 1938–1941*. Boston: Houghton Mifflin, 1959 and 1965.

Bonnet, Georges, *De Munich à la guerre*. Paris: Plon, 1967.

Boothby, Robert, *I Fight to Live*. London: Gollancz, 1947.

Bullock, Alan, *Hitler: A Study in Tyranny*. Rev. ed. London: Penguin Books, 1962 (New York: Bantam Books, 1961).

Burckhardt, Carl J., *Meine Danziger Mission, 1937–1939*. Munich, 1960.

Butler, J. R. M., *Lord Lothian*. London: Macmillan, 1960 (New York: St. Martin's Press, 1960).

Celovsky, C., *Das Münchner Abkommen von 1938*. Stuttgart, 1958.

Channon, Sir H. "Chips," *The Diaries of Sir Henry Channon*. R. R. James, ed. London: Weidenfeld & Nicolson, 1967.

Churchill, Winston S., *The Second World War*, Vol. I, *The Gathering Storm*. London: Cassell, 1948 (Boston: Houghton Mifflin, 1948).

Ciano, Galeazzo, *Ciano's Hidden Diary, 1937–1938*. Trans., and with notes by, Andreas Mayor. Intro. by Malcolm Muggeridge. London: Methuen, 1952 (New York: Dutton, 1953).

————, *Ciano's Diaries 1939–1943*. Hugh Gibson, ed. Intro. by Sumner Welles. London: Heinemann, 1947 (New York: Doubleday, 1946).

Colvin, Ian, *Vansittart in Office: The Origins of World War II*. London: Gollancz, 1965 (New York: Doubleday, 1965).

Cooper, Diana, *The Light of Common Day*. London: Hart-Davis, 1959 (Boston: Houghton Mifflin, 1959).

Coulondre, Robert, *De Staline à Hitler*. Paris: Hachette, 1950.

Dahlerus, Birger, *The Last Attempt*. Trans. by A. Dick. London: Hutchinson, 1948.

Dalton, Hugh, *The Fateful Years 1931–1945*. London: Muller, 1957.

Daluces, Jean, *Le Troisième Reich*. Paris, 1950.

Davies, Joseph E., *Mission to Moscow*. London: Gollancz, 1942 (New York: Simon & Schuster, 1941).

The Defence of Poland: September 1939. M. Norwid-Neugebauer, ed. London: Kolin, 1942.

Destiny Can Wait: A History of the Polish Air Force in the Second World War. Foreword by Viscount Portal of Hungerford. Ed. by M. Lisiewicz, trans. by A. Truscoe. London: Heinemann, 1949.

Douglas, Sholto, *Years of Command*, Vol. II. London: Cassell, 1966 (New York: Simon & Schuster, 1966).

Duff Cooper, Alfred, *Old Men Forget*. London: Hart-Davis, 1953 (New York: Dutton, 1954).

Einzig, Paul, *World Finance, 1938–1939*. London: Routledge and Kegan Paul, 1939 (New York: Macmillan, 1939).

————, *Appeasement: Both Before and After the War*. London: Macmillan, 1941 (New York: Macmillan, 1942).

————, *In the Centre of Things*. London: Hutchinson, 1960.

Feiling, Keith, *The Life of Neville Chamberlain*. London: Macmillan, 1946 (New York: St. Martin's Press, 1946).

Förster, Wolfgang, *Ein General kämpft gegen den Krieg* (The General Beck Papers). Munich, 1949.

472

François-Poncet, André, *The Fateful Years: Memoirs of a French Ambassador in Berlin, 1931–1938*. Trans. by Jacques Le Clercq. London: Gollancz, 1949 (New York: Harcourt, 1949).

Gafencu, Grigore, *Last Days of Europe*. London: Muller, 1948 (New Haven, Conn.: Yale U. Press, 1948).
Gamelin, Maurice, *Servir les armées françaises de 1940*. 3 vols. Paris: Plon, 1946–1949.
Gedye, G. E. R., *The Fallen Bastions: The Central European Tragedy*. London: Gollancz, 1939 (*Betrayal in Central Europe; Austria and Czechoslovakia: The Fallen Bastions*; New York: Harper, 1939).
Gilbert, Martin, *The Roots of Appeasement*. London: Weidenfeld & Nicolson, 1967 (New York: New American Library, 1967).
Gilbert, Martin, and Richard Gott, *The Appeasers*. London: Weidenfeld & Nicolson, 1963 (Boston: Houghton Mifflin, 1963).
Guderian, Heinz, *Panzer Leader*. Trans. by Constantine Fitzgibbon. London: Michael Joseph, 1952 (New York: Dutton, 1952).

Halder, Franz, *Hitler as Warlord*. London: Putnam, 1950.
Hassell. Ulrich von, *The Von Hassell Diaries, 1938–1944*. London: Hamish Hamilton, 1948 (New York: Doubleday, 1947).
Henderson, Nevile, *Failure of a Mission*. London: Hodder & Stoughton, 1940 (New York: Putnam, 1940).
Hesse, Fritz, *Das Spiel um Deutschland*. Munich, 1953.
Hitler, Adolf, *Mein Kampf*. London: Hurst & Blackett, 1938 (Boston: Houghton Mifflin, 1942).
Hofer, Walther, *Die Entfesselung des zweiten Weltkrieges*. Frankfurt am Main, 1964.
Hossbach, Friedrich, *Zwischen Wehrmacht und Hitler*. Hanover, 1949.

Ickes, Harold L., *The Secret Diaries of Harold Ickes*, Vol. II, *The Inside Struggle: 1936–1939*. New York: Simon & Schuster, 1954.

Jacobsen, Hans-Adolf, *Dokumente zur Vorgeschichte des Westfeldzuges 1939–1940*. Göttingen, 1956.
Jones, Thomas L., *A Diary with Letters, 1931–1950*. London: Oxford U. Press, 1954.

Keitel, Wilhelm, *Field-Marshal Keitel's Memoirs*. Trans. by David Irving, ed. by Walter Görlitz. London: William Kimber, 1965 (New York: Stein & Day, 1966).
Kennan, George F., *Memoirs 1925–1950*. Boston: Atlantic- Little, Brown, 1967.
Kirkpatrick, Ivone, *The Inner Circle*. London and New York: Macmillan, 1959.
Kordt, Erich, *Nicht aus den Akten: Die Wilhelmstrasse in Frieden und Krieg, 1928–1945*. Stuttgart, 1950.
————, *Wahn und Wirklichkeit*. Stuttgart, 1947.

Liddell Hart, B. H., *The Memoirs of Captain Liddell Hart*, Vol. I, *1895–1938*; Vol. II, *The Later Years*. London: Cassell, 1965 (*The Liddell Hart Memoirs*; New York: Putnam, 1965).
Litvinov, Maxim, *Notes for a Journal*. London: Deutsch, 1955 (New York: Morrow, 1955).
Lochner, Louis P., *What about Germany?* New York: Dodd, Mead, 1942.

Macleod, Iain, *Neville Chamberlain*. London: Muller, 1961 (New York: Atheneum, 1962).
Maczek, Stanislaw, *Avec mes blindes*. Paris: Presses de la Cité, 1968.
Minney, R. J., *The Private Papers of Hore-Belisha*. London: Collins, 1960 (New York: Doubleday, 1960).

Sources

Moffat, Jay Pierrepont, *The Moffat Papers*. Selections from [his] diplomatic journals, 1919–1943. Nancy Harrison Hooker, ed. Cambridge, Mass.: Harvard U. Press, 1956.
Monzie, Anatole de, *Ci-devant*. Paris: Flammarion, 1942.
Morgenthau, Henry, Jr., *see* Blum, John M.
Muggeridge, Malcolm, *The Thirties*. London: Collins, 1967.

Namier, Lewis B., *Diplomatic Prelude, 1938–1939*. London and New York: Macmillan, 1948.
————, *Europe in Decay, 1936–1938*. London and New York: Macmillan, 1950.
————, *In the Nazi Era*. London: Macmillan, 1952 (New York: St. Martin's Press, 1952).
Nicolson, Harold, *Diaries and Letters*. Nigel Nicolson, ed. Vol. I, *1930–1939*. London: Collins, 1966 (New York: Atheneum, 1966); Vol. II, *The War Years, 1939–1945*. London: Collins, 1967 (New York: Atheneum, 1967).
Noël, Léon, *L'Agression allemande contre la Pologne*. Paris: Flammarion, 1949.
Noguères, Henri, *Munich*. Trans. by Patrick O'Brian. London: Weidenfeld & Nicolson, 1965 (New York: McGraw-Hill, 1965).

O'Neill, Robert, *The German Army and the Nazi Party, 1933–1939*. London: Cassell, 1967.

Reith, J. C. W., *Into the Wind*. London: Hodder & Stoughton, 1949.
Ribbentrop, Joachim von, *Zwischen London und Moskau: Erinnerungen und letzte Aufzeichnungen*. Stuttgart, 1955.
Ritter, Gerhard, *Karl Goerdeler und die deutsche Widerstandsbewegung*. Bonn, 1954 (*German Resistance*; trans. by R. T. Clark. New York: Praeger, 1959).
Rowse, A. L., *All Souls and Appeasement*. London: Macmillan, 1961 (*Appeasement: A Study in Political Decline*; New York: Norton, 1961).

Schacht, Hjalmar, *My First Seventy-six Years*. Trans. by Diana Pyke. London: Wingate, 1955 (*Confessions of the Old Wizard;* Boston: Houghton Mifflin, 1956).
Schellenberg, Walter, *The Schellenberg Memoirs*. Trans. by Louis Hagen. London: Deutsch, 1956 (*The Labyrinth*; New York: Harper, 1956).
Schlabrendorff, Fabian von, *Revolt against Hitler*. Gero von S. Gaevernitz, ed. London: Eyre & Spottiswood, 1948 (*They Almost Killed Hitler*; New York: Macmillan, 1947).
Schmidt, Paul, *Hitler's Interpreter*. London: Heinemann, 1951 (New York: Macmillan, 1951).
Schuman, Frederick L., *Europe on the Eve: The Crises of Diplomacy, 1933–1939*. New York: Knopf, 1939.
Seabury, Paul, *The Wilhelmstrasse: A Study of German Diplomats under the Nazi Regime*. Berkeley: U. of Calif. Press, 1955.
Selby, Walford, *Diplomatic Twilight, 1930–1940*. London: Murray, 1953 (Hollywood, Fla.: Transatlantic, 1953).
Shirer, William L., *Berlin Diary*. New York: Knopf, 1941.
————, *The Rise and Fall of the Third Reich*. New York: Simon & Schuster, 1960.
Slessor, John, *The Central Blue*. London: Cassell, 1956.
Stehlin, Paul, *Témoignage pour l'histoire*. Paris: Robert Laffont, 1964.
Strang, Lord, *At Home and Abroad*. London: Deutsch, 1956.
————, *Britain in World Affairs*. London: Faber-Deutsch, 1961 (New York: Praeger, 1961).
Symons, Julian, *The Thirties*. London: Cresset, 1960 (Chester Springs, Pa.: Dufour, 1960).

Taylor, A. J. P., *The Origins of the Second World War*. London: Hamish Hamilton, 1961 (New York: Atheneum, 1962).

Taylor, Telford, *Sword and Swastika*. London: Gollancz, 1953 (New York: Simon & Schuster, 1952).

————, *The March of Conquest*. London: Hulton, 1959 (New York: Simon & Schuster, 1958).

Toynbee, Arnold and Veronica, eds., *The Eve of the War 1939*. Royal Institute of International Affairs. London and New York: Oxford U. Press, 1958.

Toynbee, Arnold and F. T. A. Ashton-Gwatkin, eds., *The World in March 1939*. Royal Institute of International Affairs. London and New York: Oxford U. Press, 1939.

Trevor-Roper, H. R., *The Last Days of Hitler*. London and New York: Macmillan, 1947.

Watt, D. C., *Breach of Security*. London: William Kimber, 1968.

Weizsäcker, Ernst von, *Memoirs*. London: Gollancz, 1951 (Chicago, Ill.: Regnery, 1951).

Whalen, Richard J., *The Founding Father: The Story of Joseph P. Kennedy*. London: Hutchinson, 1966 (New York: New American Library, 1964).

Wheeler-Bennett, John, *Munich: Prologue to Tragedy*. London: Macmillan, 1948 (New York: Duell, Sloan & Pearce, 1948).

————, *The Nemesis of Power: The German Army in Politics, 1918–1945*. London: Macmillan, 1953 (New York: St. Martin's Press, 1954).

Woolton, Lord, *Memoirs*. London: Cassell, 1959.

Wrench, John Evelyn, *Geoffrey Dawson and Our Times*. London: Hutchinson, 1955.

Zay, Jean, *Souvenirs et solitude*. Paris: Julliard, 1954. (Diaries previously published as *Carnets secrets de Jean Zay*. Paris: Edition de France, 1942.)

6. Articles

a) from various periodicals including
Foreign Affairs, New York
Vierteljahrshefte für Zeitgeschichte, Munich
La Revue d'Histoire de la Deuxième Guerre Mondiale
Hansard, London
Keesing's Contemporary Archives

and b) newspaper files at
British Museum, London
Wiener Library (Institute of Contemporary History), London
Bibliothèque Nationale, Paris
Institut für Zeitgeschichte, Munich
Department of Political Science, Institute for International Politics and Economics, Prague
Polish Archives (Western Europe), Cracow
New York Public Library, New York
The *New York Times,* New York

Notes

3 The description of the incident at Eger is taken from the author's own notes, written at the time and subsequently turned into dispatches for Kemsley Newspapers, London, for which he was chief correspondent in Germany; these notes were supplemented by comments in the diary of Dr. Anton Dryak, military judge for the Eger district, and the daybook of police headquarters in Eger. The author subsequently followed Karl Hermann Frank to Konrad Henlein's headquarters in Asch and then accompanied the two Sudeten leaders to Bayreuth, across the frontier in Germany.

7 The first quotation from Hitler about the Abyssinian war was repeated by the late Baron Ernst von Weizsäcker to Dr. Erich Kordt, Ribbentrop's *chef de cabinet*. Dr. Kordt, who now lives in Düsseldorf, repeated it during talks there with the author. Kordt also deals with Hitler's and German reactions to the Abyssinian crisis in his *Nicht aus den Akten* (hereafter referred to as KORDT), pp. 109–16. The second quotation on the same subject comes from remarks made by Captain Fritz Wiedemann during interrogations in Washington, San Francisco and Nuremberg (see IMND, particularly interrogation by Colonel Howard A. Brundage, Oct. 9, 1945). Fritz Wiedemann commanded the company in which Adolf Hitler served as corporal in World War I, and was invited to join the Nazi party when he fell on hard times in 1934. In 1935 he became Hitler's adjutant and was often an outspoken critic of his policies; as a result of his opposition to Hitler's plans for Czechoslovakia in 1939 he was dismissed but, as an old comrade, not punished but sent to San Francisco as consul general.

10 Randolph Churchill in conversation with the author helped to clarify his father's position vis-à-vis Chamberlain.

11 The Winston Churchill quote is from *The Gathering Storm*.

Notes

11 The general background sketches of Neville Chamberlain, Anthony Eden, Sir Horace Wilson, Edouard Daladier and Georges Bonnet are based on talks with their old colleagues (and in some cases with some of them talking about each other), and on official British, French, Italian and German records, all of which will be specified in Notes for later chapters.

12 The removal of Robert Vansittart from his central position at the Foreign Office is described in Ian Colvin's *Vansittart in Office* (hereafter referred to as COLVIN), and the circumstances were elaborated for the author's benefit by the Earl of Avon (Anthony Eden).

14 Roosevelt's offer is to be found in FRUS (Jan. 12, 1938), and Chamberlain's reaction to it (and the subsequent brushing off) is documented in FRUS (Jan. 17) and in BFP, Vol. II (Jan. 17).

15 The intrigue behind the scenes has been described in various sources, including COLVIN, WHEELER-BENNETT and NAMIER (see bibliographical listing), and its atmosphere was colored in for the author by several observers, including the late Sir Reginald Leeper and Paul Emrys-Evans, a close associate of Anthony Eden's at the time. It is interesting to note that when the British government recently declassified documents pertaining to these events, the papers regarding the subsequent Cabinet meetings (see p. 21) were "missing."

16 Eden's remarks to Sir Horace over the sabotage of the Roosevelt offer were recalled by Paul Emrys-Evans.

16 Sir Horace Wilson's own feelings as quoted in this chapter come from the author's conversations with him.

16 Churchill quote, *op. cit.*

17 For details of the activities of Sir Joseph Ball and the Downing Street meeting, see *Ciano's Hidden Diary* (Feb. 18–19); *I documenti diplomatici italiani* (referred to as DDI), Vol. XI (Feb. 17–19); and COLVIN.

19 The assessment of Chamberlain comes from Lord Strang's *Britain in World Affairs*.

19 The Duff Cooper quote is from his *Old Men Forget*, p. 214.

II Prophets of Armageddon

21 Lord Strang's comment on Lord Halifax was made in a letter to Lord Birkenhead, Halifax's biographer.

23 Sir Horace Wilson summed up Chamberlain's views of the Czechs in a conversation with the author.

24 The Beneš-Masaryk conversations are mentioned in KORDT (p. 261), and under GFMA (Series T-120) some examples are to be found of intercepted reports from the Forschungsamt der Luftwaffe (see paragraph nos. 1023–34, 1977, 2043–49, etc.). Göring had created this "research institute" in 1933, when he was, among other things, Reich Commissioner for Aviation and head of the Prussian secret police (forerunner of the Gestapo). Although he subsequently had to turn over his police organization to Himmler, he never relinquished control of this wiretapping service, since it provided him with a useful instrument in the Nazi top-echelon power play.

24 For details of Sir Horace Wilson's interference with the activities of the British Broadcasting Corporation and his comments to Sir John Reith on the character of the BBC's reports on Anglo-German and Anglo-Czech relations, see Reith's *Into the Wind*; there is, however, no sign that Wilson ever really succeeded in persuading Reith, a dour and fearless Scot, that he must toe the pro-Chamberlain line.

24 The press secretary who aroused Sir Horace's wrath was Mr. (later Sir) Reginald Leeper. (See BIRKENHEAD, *The Life of Lord Halifax*: letter from Leeper.)

25 The sketch of General Vuillemin's character and record emerged from conversations between the author and General Paul Stehlin. Captain Stehlin
was really much more than an assistant air attaché, as references to him
later in the narrative and these Notes will make clear. He has described
the Vuillemin visit in his absorbing book, *Témoignage pour l'histoire*
(hereafter referred to as STEHLIN), which is overdue for publication in
the English language.

28 Harold Ickes' account of Ambassador Bullitt is in his *Secret Diary*, Vol. II
(hereafter referred to as ICKES), pp. 408–10.

28 The account of the dinner party at Chantilly comes from a report to Premier
Edouard Daladier from Guy La Chambre, and from Bullitt's own dispatch to the State Dept. (FRUS, Sept. 10, 1938).

29 Joseph P. Kennedy's close relationship with Neville Chamberlain is referred
to by his biographer, Richard J. Whalen, in *The Founding Father*, where
he points out that Kennedy "was one of the few men to whom the austere
Prime Minister granted the privilege of first-name informality. And no
other foreigner was favoured with so many confidences." Their closeness
was maliciously commented upon both by Ickes and by Roosevelt. ("Who
would have thought that the English [the Cliveden set] could take into
camp a redheaded Irishman?" the President asked Cordell Hull and Henry
J. Morgenthau. Quoted in Blum's *From the Diaries of Henry Morgenthau,
Jr.*, Vol. I.)

29 The account of what happened to the Aberdeen speech, in the *New York
Times*, Sept. 3.

30 German doubts about the efficacy of their own air force was voiced by leading members of the Luftwaffe at this time, notably by General Erhard
Milch. They were set out in some detail in a report prepared for the
General Staff on Aug. 23, 1938, which said in part: "The prime responsibility of the German air force in the present situation must be to help
the armed forces, immobilized opposite a fortified front, to achieve operational freedom" (IMND, 375 PS). This is very different from the devastating bombing raids on cities which Lindbergh forecast, and Britain and
France feared.

30 The journey of Kleist-Schmenzin to London is mentioned in many accounts
of the period (NAMIER, WHEELER-BENNETT, KORDT, CELOVSKY, etc.), and in
BFP, Vol. II.

31 Henderson's attempt to dupe him, as well as Kleist's visit to Churchill, in *ibid*.

32 Chamberlain's perfunctory remark to Halifax comes from the same source.

32 The activities of Erich and the late Theo Kordt often came up at the trials
of the German war criminals at Nuremberg, where they both appeared as
defense witnesses for their friend (see NMT, "Trial of Ernst von Weizsäcker"). No one has challenged the fact that they were both anti-Nazis
and worked against Hitler, Ribbentrop and the party while holding official
positions in the German diplomatic service, nor has anyone denied that
they several times risked their lives to inform the British government of
Nazi plans in an attempt to galvanize British opposition to them. For
political reasons, however, and because of the climate prevailing twenty-
odd years ago, there was a tendency to obscure their endeavors and refuse
them the recognition they deserve; I hope this account will do something
to rectify this. Dr. Erich Kordt has written about his and his late brother's
feelings and actions in two books, *Nicht aus den Akten (op. cit.)* and *Wahn
und Wirklichkeit*, neither of which has been published in the English language, though they should be; their visits are referred to and their conversations repeated (as though they were merely "visits" or "conversations"
and not the risky undertakings they really were) in BFP (Vol. II) and
Kordt himself has talked and written at length in reply to questions from

the author. He has read this account and points out that though he and his brother knew Vansittart before the period referred to in this chapter, it was not until after the Munich Pact that they became close to him. Their more intimate association came about as the result of a suggestion from Lord Halifax, who thought that they would attract less attention to themselves and run less risk if they had private meetings with Vansittart rather than try to communicate their information (and their fears) to the Foreign Secretary himself. One suspects that Halifax, who didn't really want to know, was brushing them off, but this they would have refused to believe. It is significant that the name Kordt appears only once in BIRKENHEAD (official biography of Halifax), and then only in connection with an official encounter at the Foreign Office.

33 Details of the conspiracy against Hitler come from conversations with Erich Kordt, from several books on the subject (see CELOVSKY, WHEELER-BENNETT, Schlabrendorff's *They Almost Killed Hitler*), and particularly O'Neill's *The German Army and the Nazi Party, 1933–1939* (pp. 151–70).

34 Halifax's feelings, and Chamberlain's, toward Czechoslovakia are well described in BIRKENHEAD (pp. 380–84), and in chapter after chapter of Feiling, *The Life of Neville Chamberlain*, and McLeod, *Neville Chamberlain*. Sir Horace Wilson also told the author at length what Chamberlain really thought of Czechoslovakia as a country and as a liability in 1938.

34 Burckhardt's conversation with Weizsäcker and his subsequent journey to Switzerland is described in his *Meine Danziger Mission 1937–1939*, and in BFP, Vol. II, Appendix IV (Sept. 8).

34 Halifax's message to Henderson is in *ibid.* (Sept. 9), and is referred to in HENDERSON (*Failure of a Mission*).

35 The British ambassador's physical discomforts and mental state were observed by correspondents on the spot (including the author) at Nuremberg and are referred to in COLVIN.

35 The diary entry of the First Lord of the Admiralty is in Duff Cooper, *op cit.*

36 The quote regarding Chamberlain and Wilson is from Nicolson, *Diaries and Letters*, Vol. I (hereafter referred to as NICOLSON).

37 The description of the Berchtesgaden meeting comes from a long account given to the author by Sir Horace Wilson, from contemporary newspaper reports, from observers present at the time (including the author), from the recollections of Dr. Paul Schmidt and Dr. Erich Kordt, and from the official German transcript in GFP (par. no. F5-0017-0001).

III The Antipathetic Alliance

43 Chamberlain's description of his Berchtesgaden visit as recounted to the Cabinet comes from Duff Cooper, *op. cit.* (pp. 228–40).

44 Liddell Hart's comment on Kingsley Wood's falsification of the German air force figures comes from his *Memoirs*, Vol. II (pp. 170–71).

44 Roosevelt's remark about Chamberlain is in ICKES.

44 The general background of Anglo-French relations at this time is based on discussions with both participants and observers at the time, including Lord Strang, Edouard Daladier, Sir Horace Wilson and Lord Avon.

45 The Anglo-French statement of Sept. 19 is in BFP, Vol. II (same date) but not in LJF (the *French Yellow Book*).

46 Bonnet's intrigues behind the scenes, particularly his telephone calls to Lacroix in Prague are not reported there either, but the French Minister of Education, Jean Zay, wrote in his diary on Sept. 19 (see his *Carnets secrets de Jean Zay* [*Souvenirs et solitude*]): "They say that Bonnet, contrary to the declaration of the Council of Ministers, has advised Prague that in

case of a refusal we will abandon them." At the same time Sir Eric Phipps cabled London (on Sept. 20) about an interview with Bonnet in which the French Foreign Minister told him that he had telephoned Lacroix to press capitulation on Beneš. He appealed for Chamberlain's help to back him (BFP, Vol. II, Sept. 20). Chamberlain, nothing loath, backed the so-called *"Dawn Démarche."* Bonnet still maintains that the Czechs did, in fact, ask for this ultimatum so that they could present a *fait accompli* to their people and excuse their capitulation. This has always been strenuously denied by the Czechs; Premier Milan Hodža did so until the day of his death, maintaining that far from asking for an "ultimatum" from the French, the Czechs were asking them to make up their minds to support them against Germany. See CELOVSKY (p. 352), and Hodža's letter to Dr. Hubert Beuve-Méry, *Le Temps'* correspondent in Prague, on Oct. 10 (cited in CELOVSKY). On Jan. 20, 1939, Beneš wrote to Lacroix: "I have never asked anyone for any ultimatum or anything of the kind that could be used by us to swing us into accepting the Franco-British Plan. If one or other magazine or one or other book published in France speaks along these lines, then it is a shameless slander." (Cited in *ibid.*) See also NDHM.

47 Regarding Beneš' meeting with Gottwald, see "The Triumph and Disaster of Eduard Beneš," by E. Taborsky, in *Foreign Affairs*, Vol. 36 (July 1958), p. 672.

48 The description of the Godesberg meeting is based on contemporary accounts (including those of the author, who was there), BFP, GFP, recollections of Dr. Paul Schmidt and Dr. Erich Kordt.

49 Hitler's statement regarding his ambitions to occupy Czechoslovakia was made to General Keitel on June 18, 1938: "I shall only decide on any action against Czechoslovakia when I am absolutely sure, as when I occupied the demilitarized zone and invaded Austria, that France will not march and England will not interfere." (In NMT.)

50 Roosevelt's suggestion for a conference, in FRUS.

50 Reactions inside the British Cabinet come from recollections and memoirs, particularly those of Duff Cooper.

51 The dispatch of Sept. 24 from Sir Eric Phipps is reprinted in BFP, Vol. II (same date).

51 Ambassador Bullitt's reaction to Georges Bonnet's visit on Sept. 24 is contained in a telegram to Washington on Sept. 25 (FRUS, same date).

52 The Anglo-French conversations of Sept. 25–26 in London have always seemed to be well documented, and I have relied for the general exchanges on the account of Lord Strang in his *At Home and Abroad* (hereafter referred to as STRANG) supplemented by a talk with him in 1967. The conversation as reported seems to me to have been bitter and angry enough, but the words used may have been even more rancorous. I showed the account in this book to M. Daladier himself, whose comments were that *"l'atmosphère de cette conférence est exactement décrite dans le texte que vous m'avez adressé,"* but so far as the verbal exchange went, *"il me paraît plus vigoureux."*

58 In a talk with the author, Sir Horace Wilson himself described his visit to Hitler; this was supplemented by GFMA (Series T-120).

60 The footnote re Horace Wilson's mission is from Duff Cooper, *op. cit.*

62 Thomas Jones's remark comes from his *Diary with Letters.*

63 See also NICOLSON.

64 Chamberlain's comment on the failure of Wilson's mission to Berlin was repeated by Sir Horace to the author.

65 Bonnet's remarks to Bullitt are taken from FRUS (dispatch of Sept. 30), and

Masaryk's to Halifax from BFP (Vol. II) and NDHM; the comments on them are from Sir Horace Wilson to the author.

66 Of the Munich meeting there are many accounts (see CELOVSKY, WHEELER-BENNETT, KORDT, Schmidt's *Hitler's Interpreter*, etc.). The conversations between Sir Horace Wilson and Dr. Voytech Mastny, and between Frank Ashton-Gwatkin and Dr. Mastny, come from CELOVSKY and WHEELER-BENNETT. See also BFP, Vol. II (note by Sir Horace Wilson); Gedye, *The Fallen Bastions* (p. 483); and contemporary accounts by correspondents who were there, including the author.

68 Ambassador Kennedy's comment on President Roosevelt's cable, see the *World-Telegram & Sun*, Apr. 1, 1960. See also Whalen, *op. cit.*

68 Masaryk's own account of his and Mastny's encounter with Chamberlain and Daladier after the *fait accompli* comes from his report to correspondents at Munich, which he subsequently expanded into a report for his government (see NDHM).

70 The conversation between Léger and Stehlin was recounted by General Stehlin to the author.

PART TWO

IV "How Long Will This Burlesque Last?"

77 The account of General von Reichenau's stay in Karlsbad and subsequent activities in Czechoslovakia is based on the diaries of Major (later Colonel) Hans Grosscurth, who died at Stalingrad. These diaries, which reflect the cool, civilized reactions of a cultured German toward the excesses and arrogance of his fellow countrymen in victory, will one day be published in full. Meanwhile, see the *Grosscurth Papers* (Grosscurth diaries, and Grosscurth letters and reports to Colonel Oster of the Abwehr, Berlin, Oct.–Nov. 1938), in GFMA. Grosscurth was known to many correspondents who reported the march of the German army into Czechoslovakia in 1938, and they remember him as a man who never looked over his shoulder while conveying his contempt for the hatemongers in Berlin and their lackeys on the spot. For Reichenau's background, see Wheeler-Bennett's THE NEMESIS OF POWER; also *Records of the Oberkommando der Wehrmacht*, Part II (p. 184).

80 The state of mind in which Eduard Beneš found himself after Munich has been pieced together from the statements he made later to friends in London and Washington (e.g., Lord Avon, Duff Cooper, Harold Ickes and Erika Mann) and from observations on the spot, at the time. I have no doubt in my own mind, after talking to him later, that he felt he had let his people down by accepting the Munich *Diktat* (the cynics of today would say that he did no such thing; by capitulating when he did, he ensured that Prague was the only capital in Europe which, threatened to be bombed, remained undamaged at the end of World War II). His liberal political outlook prevented him from accepting Soviet aid when Franco-British aid was refused him, and like many another liberal he afterward cast doubts on the reality of the Russian help that was offered.

82 The figures indicating Russia's readiness to help Czechoslovakia come from the archives of the Soviet Ministry of Defense and were released in the summer of 1968.

82 Robert Coulondre, the French ambassador in Moscow, reported to Paris about the activities of Fierlinger in Sept. 1938. Later he quoted his dispatch in his book, *De Staline à Hitler*: "He [Fierlinger] has obtained the immediate delivery of sixty bombers. Twenty have already landed at

the airfield of Užhgorod in Slovakia. It is thus proved that Russian planes can land in the less immediately threatened part of the country. On their side the Russians have laid out a great airfield at Vinnitsa, considerably nearer the frontier west of Kiev. The Užhgorod airfield, where the work had to be held up because of a German press campaign, is not yet finished and it still has to be supplied with the spare parts and fuel storage needed for the Russian planes."

82n   While the Munich negotiations were going on, the French reported that there were around two hundred Russian planes on Czechoslovak airfields (see NDHM), and General Delmas, the French military attaché in Bucharest, reported the incident about the forced landing in Rumania (*ibid.*).

82 For the Beneš-Alexandrovsky meeting, and for details of the Soviet protest to Poland over its aggressive intentions toward Czechoslovakia, see *ibid.*

83 Beneš' reasons for accepting the Polish ultimatum were set out by him in a letter to Sir Lewis Namier dated Apr. 20, 1944 (see Namier's *Europe in Decay*, Appendix). He sent Namier the chief diplomatic documents, previously unpublished, relating to the actions taken by Poland against Czechoslovakia in 1938 and added: "The letter to President Mościcki of 22nd September I sent him when I signed the decree for our mobilisation; I believed that within two or three days it would come to war with Germany and I wanted therefore to secure at least the neutrality of Poland. . . ."

84 The comment about the Poles moving into Teschen comes from François-Poncet's *The Fateful Years.*

84 The description of Beneš' farewell meeting comes from contemporary Czech newspaper reports (see CAOPR).

85 The account of the sessions of the International Commission have been pieced together from accounts given by François-Poncet and Stehlin (see also STEHLIN); and reports by Dr. Mastny (in CAMFA).

88 Details of the offer of a house to Neville Chamberlain come from the files of *Paris-Soir* (Oct. 1–3) in the Bibliothèque Nationale. Daladier's feelings and his reaction to Cardinal Verdier's refusal to ring the bells of Notre Dame come from Daladier.

89 Details of the circumstances of the Chamberlain-Hitler meeting after Munich come from WHEELER-BENNETT (*Munich: Prologue to Tragedy*), CELOVSKY, NAMIER and STRANG. The story of Chamberlain's arrival home is from the *Times* of London and other newspapers, including the *N.Y. Times*, of Oct. 1.

91 For the full account of what Czechoslovakia lost at Munich, see WHEELER-BENNETT, NDHM, CAMFA and CAOPR.

92 Though it was Eisenlohr who presented the plan for returning Sudeten and other refugees to Germany, the actual terms were drawn up by Dr. Hans Globke (see BFP, appendices to Vol. III).

92 The account of Werner Jaksch's visit to London was reported in the *News Chronicle* and other newspapers, Oct. 24 and on; re his visit to Lord Runciman, see Gedye (*op. cit.*) and CAMFA.

92 The visit of Sir Harry Twyford and John Wheeler-Bennett to Prague is told in WHEELER-BENNETT.

93 Himmler and Heydrich's visit to the Sudetenland was reported by Major Grosscurth in a letter from Reichenberg (German for Liberec), dated Nov. 1, to his chief, Colonel Oster; and the report of the visit to Hirschberg is also in this letter. (See GFMA, *Grosscurth Papers.*) The actual visit is mentioned in RFSS, Part II.

93 The description of how the inspections were carried out comes from Walter Schellenberg's *The Labyrinth*, as does the profile and proclivities of Heydrich.

94 Hitler's remark about being cheated of his entry into Prague was repeated

by Hjalmar Schacht, head of the Reichsbank (see IMT, Vol. XII). Schacht, always anxious not to get involved, said it wasn't *said* to him, but that he heard it. He was the man who was always within earshot.

94 For reports of Adolf Hitler's speech at Saarbrücken, see the *N.Y. Times* for Oct. 10. Chamberlain's reaction to the Saarbrücken speech comes from Sir Horace Wilson.

95 Hitler's second visit to the Sudetenland is recounted by Major Grosscurth. The date of the diary entry is not specified but appears to have been Oct. 19–20. (See GFMA, *Grosscurth Papers.*)

97 The report of Hitler's third inspection, in *ibid.* (where Grosscurth mentions Rundstedt's *Narrentheater* remark to Canaris), and from General Walter Warlimont's remarks to interrogators at Nuremberg (see IMND, Warlimont affidavit. Oct. 12, 1945 interrogation).

100 Senator Nye's speech quoted in the Washington *Post* (Sept. 28).

100 Roosevelt's remarks to the Cabinet on Oct. 8, from ICKES.

100 Re State Dept. clearance of Ambassador Kennedy's speech, see *The Moffat Papers.*

101 Ambassador Kennedy's speech of Oct. 19 was reported in the *N.Y. Times* the following day.

101 Cordell Hull's reactions to the speech were recorded in *The Moffat Papers (op. cit.).*

102 The account of François-Poncet's visit to Hitler comes from STEHLIN and. François- Poncet, *op. cit.*

V "Don't You See?... It's the German Insurance Companies That Will Have to Pay!"

105 Re Himmler's worry about not having sufficient space for apprehended "criminals," see Warlimont interrogation (NMT).

106 Himmler's letter to Hitler and accounts of the hanging of Bargatzy come from RFSS (Part II) and IMT (782 PS).

108 The account of the assassination of Baron Vom Rath and the subsequent arrest of Herschel Grynszpan was assembled from documents in the Bibliothèque Nationale (files of contemporary newspapers).

111 The Beer Hall meeting was described in Julius Streicher's *Der Stürmer* of Nov. 15, 1938, and in a report for Hermann Göring (in RLFM).

114 The instructions to the police come from RFSS (messages of Nov. 10–12, signed Müller, Nebe, Beutel and Heydrich).

116 The account of the pogrom has been assembled from contemporary reports (see the *N.Y. Times* for Nov. 10–12), including those by the author, and from an official report by Consul Raymond H. Geist (see NMT, 1759 PS).

118 For further details of Göring's interview with Hitler and his subsequent conference, see IMT, 1816 PS.

125 Neville Chamberlain's comment on the Germans and the pogrom was made to the late Sir Kingsley Wood.

125 For Harold Nicolson's comments on the Jews, see NICOLSON, Vol. II.

125 For an account of Hore-Belisha's feelings, see Minney's *Private Papers of Hore-Belisha.*

126 Dean Inge had expressed his opinion in an article in the *Evening Standard* in July 1938.

126 Chamberlain's letter was published in the *Times* and other newspapers in the week of Nov. 14.

126 For French apologies and reactions to the Vom Rath attack, see GFMA; for the aftermath, see Zay, *op. cit.*

128 The December 6 declaration is in GFMA and in LJF.

VI Hitler over Bohemia

PAGE
129 The account of the atmosphere at the Kabarett der Komiker is an amalgam of the impressions of General Paul Stehlin and the author, both of whom used to frequent it.
130 The description of Stehlin's sojourn as assistant air attaché in Berlin, and of his relations with the Luftwaffe generals and Göring's sister, is based on conversations with him and on STEHLIN.
132 Bodenschatz's remarks were subsequently reported by Stehlin to Paris, and
134   his own recall there and his interviews with Guy La Chambre are recounted in *ibid.* and were expanded in conversations with the author.
138 Ambassador Kennedy's conversation with Halifax comes from FRUS.
139 The attitudes and activities of the Earl of Perth are based on a study of the documents in BFP and DDI; Ciano, *Hidden Diary* (*op. cit.*); and a private report from one of Perth's former secretaries.
140 DDI; BFP, Vol. III (Jan. 12, 1939); and *Ciano's Diaries 1932–1943* (hereafter referred to as CIANO), are the basis for the description of Chamberlain's Italian visit, plus a report in BIRKENHEAD.
141 Bullitt's report on France comes from FRUS and ICKES; the truth about the
142   Franco-Italian situation, from GFMA (Mackensen dispatch of Feb. 4).
145 The recital of events in Slovakia comes from NDHM, CAMFA, CMA and CSAB, plus interviews in Prague and Bratislava and talks at the Institute for International Politics and Economics, Prague (Dr. Karel Kratky).
147 Göring's stay at San Remo comes from RLFM; the *Giornale d'Italia* (Feb. 5–9); and other Italian papers.
148 For the letter to Göring from Hitler, see NMT, Vol. IX (p. 292).
149 Keitel's remarks are in his *Memoirs*.
150 KORDT (and interviews) is the source for the reactions of Canaris, Oster and Halder to Keitel's memorandum.
151 The British Secret Service source will not be identified.
152 The events in Slovakia are based on NDHM, CAMFA, CSAB and the reports of the U.S. military attaché in Prague, Major Percy G. Black (see IMND, 3618–19 PS) and the British minister, Sir Basil Newton (IMND, 112–13).
154 The telegram to the German legation in Prague is in GFMA (Mar. 14).
154 The Chvalkovský-Hácha dialogue is from CAMFA and CSAB.
155 Chamberlain's state of mind at this time is based on the reactions of Lobby (House of Commons) correspondents to whom he spoke (see the *Daily Telegraph*, Mar. 12–13).
156 The Tiso-Hitler conversations are taken from GFMA (Mar. 14).
157 The Hungarian plans were revealed in a letter from Admiral von Horthy to Hitler on Mar. 13 (IMT, 2816 PS).
159 The account of Hácha's visit to Berlin comes from GFMA, NDHM, CAOPR; Keitel (*op. cit.*), Kordt (interview), Mrs. Radlova (statement in CAOPR), Dr. Josef Klement (*ibid.*); and from the interrogation of Hermann Göring (see IMT, Oct. 10, 1945, interrogation by Colonel John H. Amen).
160 Re Keitel's part in the events, see Keitel, *op. cit.*

PART THREE

VII The Führer Is Sick

175 The account of the climate of sociological thought in England is based on newspaper reports, recollections of those who were there, and accounts of such observers as Malcolm Muggeridge (*The Thirties*), NICOLSON, "Chips" Channon (*Diaries*) and Thomas Jones, *op. cit.*

PAGE

176 Lady Winterton's remark was reported in the *Daily Telegraph* and cited in a book also entitled *The Thirties*, by Julian Symons. It is also quoted in Muggeridge, *op. cit.*

177 Parliamentary statements come from *Hansard.*

179 Halifax's reaction to Chamberlain's statement in Parliament comes from NAMIER (*Diplomatic Prelude*).

180 Halifax's statement to Ambassador von Dirksen is in BFP (Vol. IV) and GFMA (Mar. 15) — but without the stammer.

181 The text of the Birmingham speech comes from the Manchester *Guardian* (Mar. 18).

182 Bonnet's actions and his relations with Léger come from Zay, *op. cit.*

183 The Berlin interview between Coulondre and Weizsäcker is from GFMA and LJF.

184 American reactions are from FRUS, ICKES and the *N.Y. Times* of Mar. 19–21.

185 The unsavory squabble over the Czech gold is principally based on material in Paul Einzig's autobiography, *In the Centre of Things*, and his book *Appeasement: Both Before and After the War*, plus the records in CAMFA.

189 The account of Hitler's Memel trip comes from the recollections of Admiral Raeder, the notes of Colonel Schmundt, and the interrogations of Ribbentrop and Weizsäcker (NMT, Aug. 24, 1945, and IMND, Mar. 1946), plus the recollections of Kordt.

190 Details of the negotiations with Lithuania are in GFMA (Mar. 17–20, 1939).

VIII The Panic Pact

195 *Who gave lunch to Tilea on March 16, 1939?* is still a favorite after-dinner question in the houses of aging Foreign Office officials, as is the reason for his sudden panic. This version comes from a source who had at the time no official connection with the Foreign Office but a most complete knowledge of what was going on inside it; he would rather not be identified.

196 Details of Tilea's interviews with Orme Sargent and Halifax come from BFP, Vol. IV (Mar. 16–18).

197 Bonnet's remark is from his *De Munich à la guerre*, and Gafencu's repudiation of Tilea in BFP, Vol. IV (Mar. 18–19).

198n The quote from D. C. Watt is in his *Breach of Security.*

199 The description of the state visit to London comes from contemporary newspaper accounts.

199 Chamberlain's remark to Hore-Belisha is in Liddell Hart (*op. cit.*), Vol. II, Chap. 6. His remark about Hitler comes from Bonnet, *op. cit.*

200 For the exchanges with Poland, see BFP, Vol. IV (Mar. 18–).

201 The background of Józef Beck's character comes from NAMIER, CELOVSKY, CAMFA and French sources.

201 Lady Diana Cooper's remarks about him are from her book, *The Light of Common Day.*

205 The Colonel Beck quote is from his instructions to Ambassador Lipski (see PWB).

206 For the exchanges between Poland and Germany, see GFMA (Jan. 1939 and Mar. 21, 1939) and IMT (2505 PS).

206 Chamberlain's evaluation of Russia comes from Feiling, *op. cit.*, and Halifax's, as expressed to Kennedy, from FRUS.

207 Beaverbrook's note is given in Liddell Hart, *op. cit.*

208 The exchanges and circumstances of the British offer to Beck come from BFP, Vol. IV (Mar.–Apr. 1939).

208 Ian Colvin's reports of imminent German action and his interview at the Foreign Office and with Neville Chamberlain are recounted in COLVIN and in BFP.

209 BFP also sets out the course of the subsequent Polish-British conversations in London (Vol. IV, Apr. 1939).

211 The remarks of Duff Cooper are in his book (*op. cit.*); Daladier's in Namier, *Europe in Decay (op. cit.)*; Gafencu's were made to the French ambassador in Bucharest, who sent them on to Bonnet; and Liddell Hart's in his book (*op. cit.*).

IX Hitler Briefs His Generals

213 Mussolini's complaint about Hitler is in CIANO.

214 The Duce's reaction to King Victor Emmanuel's attitude comes from a report by Perth (in BFP).

214 Chamberlain's reaction to Mussolini's taking Albania is in Feiling, *op. cit.*

214 Sir Horace Wilson's remark to Chamberlain was repeated in an interview with the author.

214 Roosevelt's appeal to Hitler on April 15 is taken from contemporary newspaper releases and FRUS.

214 Ickes' reaction to FDR's messages is in ICKES.

215 Hitler's conviction that the Poles would compromise is described in Baron von Weizsäcker's *Memoirs.*

216 The account of Hitler's speech is based on reports and commentaries made at the time (UP, INS, the *Times* of London, the *N. Y. Times*, Manchester *Guardian*), including the author's own.

219*n* The exchange between the French ambassador and Potemkin is in Coulondre, *op. cit.*

220 Joseph Davies' remarks are from his *Mission to Moscow,* both about the negotiations in Moscow and his contacts with Churchill and Kennedy in England.

221*n* Wilson repeated his remark to Chamberlain in a talk with the author.

222 Davies' cable to Roosevelt is in FRUS.

223 Litvinov's offer is in BFP, Vol. V (Apr. 18).

223*n* Vansittart's suspicions of his chiefs are mentioned in COLVIN.

224 David Lloyd George's speech and exchange in the House of Commons were reported in *Hansard* (May 20).
Chamberlain's reaction was related by Sir Horace Wilson.

224 The Stehlin-Bodenschatz conversations, which were later to appear in LJF with Stehlin as Mr. Y and Bodenschatz as Mr. X, are set out more fully in STEHLIN and were expanded and explained by Stehlin to the author. He also discussed his abortive visit to Paris and the letter which followed.

229 The fact that the United States had the same information even earlier was revealed to the author by Charles E. Bohlen. How he came by his startling news will not be revealed here.

230 The report of the Goebbels-Ribbentrop encounter was "leaked" to Berlin newspapermen by Dr. Karl Boehmer, a Propaganda Ministry liaison man with the foreign press, and no great lover of his chief. Such was the antagonism at this time between the two Reich ministers that they even sent gangs of SS men to sabotage each other's headquarters, fusing electric points and machines, spilling ink over files and documents (see KORDT).

231 The account of the signing of the Pact of Steel comes from GFMA, DDI and CIANO.

234 The account of the May 23 conference comes mainly from the *Halder Diary* (GFMA) and the notes kept by Colonel Schmundt (IMND, L. 79).

236 The Milch-Bodenschatz exchange comes from Milch's interrogation; his account of the Milch-Hitler conversation from NMT (Vol. IX) and from remarks he has since made in expansion of this. In view of British fears

of being bombed in 1939, and of Franco-British inertia owing to this fear during the attack on Poland in September 1939, it is interesting to note Milch's statement that "in my opinion the Luftwaffe was not prepared for a major war in 1939."

237 The background to the situation in Danzig is based on eyewitness reports from correspondents, on dispatches from the British consul general, on reports to Warsaw from the Polish commissioner in Danzig, and on observations by the author.

239 The remarks about the appeasers are in NICOLSON.

239 Drummond-Wolff's visit to Germany is in GFMA (May 11–14).

240 Dirksen's cable is in *ibid.* (July 10).

240 Dr. Boehmer's outburst was a talking point among foreign correspondents in Berlin within hours after it occurred; Coulondre's dispatch was sent the same evening (May 27).

241 The Keitel-Brauchitsch exchanges with Hitler came after the meeting on May 23 and were reported to Otto Dietrich (*ibid.*, May 25).

241 The cable to Paris comes from Coulondre, *op. cit.*

242 Daladier's comment is in Zay, *op. cit.*, and has since been confirmed by the former Premier.

242 Eden describes his activities in his memoirs (Vol. III, *The Reckoning*), and the background is filled in by interviews with him and Paul Emrys-Evans.

244 The arrival of William Strang in Moscow comes from STRANG; from BFP, Vol. VI (June 15–); and an interview with the author.

245 The background to the Weizsäcker-Gaus activities comes from Weizsäcker, *op. cit.;* Gaus interrogations and affidavit in Nuremberg (IMND); and GFMA (May 27–29).

246 Strang's cable is in BFP, Vol. VI (June 15).

247 Ribbentrop's cable to Schulenburg is in GFMA (May 30).

X The Conspirators Are Worried

249 Details of conditions in the German Foreign Ministry come from interviews with Erich Kordt, who also recounted his meetings with his co-conspirators.

252 Kordt's account of his visit to London is supplemented by BFP, Vol. VI (June 16–, 1939). (Kordt, by the way, is still amazed at the lack of discretion shown by the British government in publishing details of the activities of himself and his brother in London in the British *Blue Book* issued after the outbreak of the war. He is still joyfully relieved at the obtuseness of the Gestapo in failing to guess what had been going on. He owed his life to it.) For further details, see also KORDT (pp. 313–19).

257 Churchill's sonorous comments are quoted in NICOLSON (p. 403).

258 The reports of the Franco-Polish military talks come from NAMIER, which gives a detailed account of the negotiations and the atmosphere in which they took place on May 14–15. See also documents in the Bibliothèque Nationale and in the Polish Archives (Western Document Center), Cracow.

259 The report to the Chief of the British Air Staff is in Slessor's memoirs, *The Central Blue.*

260 The British ambassador's views and statements are taken from HENDERSON and BFP, Vol. V (June 1939).

261 The Wohltat-Wilson conversations are based on BFP, talks with Sir Horace Wilson (who denies contentions in the *Dirksen Papers* that he was "conspiring" with Wohltat or gave him a memorandum), and GFMA (June 1939). The picture given here should also be studied against an account

263 of this period from Wohltat's point of view given by H. Metzmacher,

working on the *Wohltat Papers,* in the *Vierteljahrshefte für Zeitgeschichte* for October 1966 (pp. 369–412); regarding Wilson's suggestion for secret negotiations, see p. 599 *(ibid.)*

264 As to the *Daily Express* item about Hudson's offer to lend money to Germany, Sir Horace Wilson, in a talk with the author, blamed Hudson himself for the leak.

XI "You Must Think We Are Nitwits and Nincompoops!"

267 For the sources of the Anglo-French-Russian conversations, see BFP, Vol. VI (June 19–, 1939), and STRANG; these were reinforced by a conversation between the author and Lord Strang.

270 The reports of the celebrations and speechmaking in Danzig and Poland are taken from contemporary eyewitness accounts, including those of the author; also see the *Völkischer Beobachter* for June 19–20.

272 Coulondre's report was sent to Paris and used in LJF.

272 Bullitt's comments come from ICKES (June 17).

273 Colonel Beck's remarks are from NAMIER (July 5).

274 Stehlin's report on his conversation with Bodenschatz is from STEHLIN (and interview).

275 Mrs. von Ribbentrop's remark was repeated by Kordt.

276 The *Pravda* article appeared on June 29.

276 Ribbentrop's conversation with Forster is from GFMA (July 19), and its clarification from the author's own notes and investigations made in Danzig at the time. Gerald Shepherd was subsequently posted to Amsterdam as consul general, where one of his last tasks, just before the city fell to the Germans in May 1940, was to help the author escape from Holland. He was knighted in 1946 after service in the United States, Iceland and Bermuda, and died in Ontario in 1968, at the age of eighty.

279 Re Bonnet's note to Ribbentrop, see LJF (telegram dated June 27).

279 The description of Göring's party and Karinhall is based on the author's previous visits and his presence there on July 6, though he must confess he had no knowledge at the time that Birger Dahlerus was a fellow guest.

280 Re Göring's state of mind, see GFMA.

281 What happened between Göring and the Swedish emissary is described in DAHLERUS *(The Last Attempt)* and in interviews at Nuremberg, where Dahlerus was a defense witness for Göring.

285 Strang's report of his negotiations in Moscow are reprinted in STRANG.

288 Schnurre's conversations are in GFMA (July 18), and the background was filled in by an interview with Kordt. See also KORDT and IMND (interrogation of Ribbentrop, Aug. 29–31, by Colonel Howard A. Brundage).

XII Slow Boat to Leningrad

291 Stehlin's conversations in Berlin and Paris come from STEHLIN (and interviews).

294 Information about the code-breaking orgy during the last two years before the war, and of the espionage activities in connection with it, is from a private source which cannot be identified even by nationality.

295 The activities of Schnurre are in GFMA (July 27, 1939) and KORDT.

297 For the complete text of Ribbentrop's cables to Schulenburg, see GFMA (July 29–30).

PAGE
298 The inspection tour of the West Wall is described in Keitel, *op. cit.*, and also in IMT (Göring interrogation.)
298 For a full account of the British ambassador's trip to Bayreuth, see HENDERSON. The author was in Bayreuth at the same time in anticipation of a meeting with Hitler which Lord Kemsley, proprietor of the *Sunday Times* and other Kemsley newspapers, would shortly be having.
299 Information about Frau Wagner and Miss Unity Mitford came from Dr. Karl Boehmer.
299 Harold Denny's dispatch from Moscow appeared in the *N.Y. Times* on Aug. 1.
301 Strang's letter to Sir Orme Sargent is in BFP, Vol. VI (July 20).
301 Details of the formation of the French and British military delegation are from General André Beaufre's *1940: The Fall of France*, and correspondence with him, as is the description of the voyage to Leningrad.
302 Molotov's remarks are from STRANG.
304 The telegrams from Welczeck and Dirksen come from GFMA (July 28 and Aug. 1), and Ribbentrop's urgent message to Schulenburg is in *ibid.* (Aug. 3).
305 The Anglo-French delegation's arrival and its first meeting in Moscow are from contemporary reports and BEAUFRE.

PART FOUR

XIII The Walrus

311 The Stehlin-Riegele exchange was revealed by the former in an interview (see also STEHLIN), and he clarified Göring's state of mind at this time, as did the Swedish emissary in interviews. See also DAHLERUS, and evidence at Nuremberg (NMT, Vol. IX).
312 The situation in Danzig was reported by an international corps of correspondents, including the author.
313 The cable from the British consul general is in BFP, Vol. VI (July 1, 1939; see also messages dated July 8, 10 and 25).
313 Cartilleri's report is in IMND (3595 PS).
314 For details of the crisis in Danzig, see GFMA (Aug. 4–7); Burckhardt, *op cit.*; and BFP, Vol. VI (Aug. 5–7).
315 Beck's reactions were revealed to correspondents in Danzig by Chodacki, and Ribbentrop's reaction by KORDT (pp. 421–22).
316 Hitler's tantrum after he read the press clippings was described by Dr. Dietrich (NMT, interrogation by Colonel John H. Amen, Oct. 1945).
317 The substance of Hitler's outburst to Forster was leaked to correspondents in Danzig by Greiser and confirmed later by Göring in conversation with his Swedish friend (see DAHLERUS; also NAMIER).
317 For the Schleswig-Holstein meeting, see DAHLERUS.
319 The Hitler-Göring telephone conversations are in GFMA.
320 Interviews and correspondence with Kordt, as well as KORDT, are the source of Hitler's nickname and Canaris' remarks.
320 The Aug. 8 meeting with Csáky is in GFMA (same date); see also Adams-Jukasz-Kerekes, *Allianz: Hitler-Horthy-Mussolini*, and NMT (2814 PS).
320 The Hitler-Burckhardt interview is in GFMA (Aug. 11) and in Burckhardt, *op. cit.*

XIV Stalin Makes Up His Mind

323 The account of the meetings of the military delegations comes from BEAUFRE (and interviews), supplemented by STRANG and reports by Strang and Seeds in BFP, Vol. VII (Aug. 12, et seq.).

325 The gist of the Stalin-Molotov conversation comes from a report sent to the State Department by Ambassador Laurence Steinhardt on Aug. 12, as coming from reliable informants. (In 1939 the U.S. embassy in Moscow was remarkably well informed on Soviet affairs, and was often first with news about future German moves. In one unguarded moment in a night club in Istanbul in 1942, Steinhardt, who was then ambassador to Turkey, boasted to the Soviet ambassador, Sergei Vinogradov, and the British ambassador, Sir H. M. Knatchbull-Hugessen, that he knew everything both their governments had been planning in Moscow in 1939. At the same table were Ray Brock of the *N. Y. Times* and the author.)

327 The Ciano meetings of Aug. 11, 12 and 13 come from GFMA (same dates); DDI (same dates); CIANO (Aug. 10–13); and NMT (1871 PS).

333 The Halifax-Beck exchange is in BFP.

333 The proceedings of the Moscow talks are based on STRANG (and interview); BEAUFRE; BFP, Vol. VII (Aug. 14); and LJF (same date).

336 Doumenc's telegram of Aug. 14 comes from BEAUFRE.

336 Details of the Stalin-Molotov exchange were sent by Ambassador Steinhardt to the State Department on Aug. 16.

XV Hitler Takes a Hand

339 The military conference called by Adolf Hitler on Aug. 14, 1939, is recorded in the *Halder Diary* (GFMA). See also NMT (789 and 1014 PS.)

340 General Thomas wrote about his intervention in "Gedanken und Ereignisse," *Schweizerische Monatshefte* (Dec. 1945); this was supplemented by the interrogation of General Keitel (IMND, Aug. 2, 1945).

341 Ribbentrop's cable of Aug. 14 is from GFMA (same date), and KORDT (plus interview) amplifies the circumstances.

342 Schulenburg's interview with Molotov is in GFMA (Aug. 15).

343 Ambassador Steinhardt's conversation with Molotov is in FRUS (Aug. 16).

343 Re Steinhardt's cable to Sumner Welles, see FRUS (Aug. 17).

344 Lord Avon's recollection regarding the British ambassador's cable to the Foreign Office was quoted by Bohlen in interview with author.

344 Stehlin's message from Bodenschatz and the circumstances of his surveillance are from STEHLIN (as well as interviews and correspondence).

345 Coulondre's interview with Weizsäcker is in GFMA and LJF (both Aug. 15).

347 The quote about British reaction to world events is from Churchill, *op. cit.*

348 Conditions in the Reich Foreign Ministry are described in KORDT (and in interviews).

349 Ribbentrop's telegram to Schulenburg is in GFMA (Aug. 16), as are details of
350   the Schulenburg-Molotov interview (Aug. 17) and the Ribbentrop telegrams of that and the following day.

351 General Doumenc's words to his colleagues are remembered by BEAUFRE, as are details of the conference of Aug. 17.

353 Doumenc's telegram of Aug. 17 is in BEAUFRE, as are details of his own mission to Warsaw.

355 The Bonnet-Lukasiewicz exchanges are from Bonnet, *op. cit.*

356 Details of the atmosphere at Berchtesgaden come from IMND (interrogation and affidavit of Friedrich Gaus, Aug. 1945; it was not used for fear of offending Russian susceptibilities).

357 Schulenburg's telegram from Moscow is in GFMA (Aug. 19).

XVI Ribbentrop's Hour of Triumph

359 Halifax's message to Chamberlain is in BFP, Vol. VII (Aug. 19, 1939).

PAGE

360 Hitler's message to Stalin is in GFMA (Aug. 20), and the atmosphere at Berchtesgaden was described by Gaus and reported in KORDT.

362 Daladier's telegram is in LJF (Aug. 21) and BEAUFRE.

362 The Voroshilov-Doumenc encounter on Aug. 22 was issued verbatim by the Soviet government in *Documents and Materials relating to the Eve of the Second World War,* and is in BFP, Vol. VII, Appendix II. Also reprinted in BEAUFRE.

365 The telegram from Stalin is in GFMA (Aug. 21), and Hitler's reactions were recounted by Gaus.

365 Details of Göring's plan to fly to London come from BIRKENHEAD; the *Hickleton Papers* (in possession of Lord Halifax's family), "A Record of Events before the War"; General Karl Bodenschatz; and RLFM (Aug. 20).

367 Canaris' remarks come from KORDT (as well as interview).

368 The Aug. 22 conference at Berchtesgaden is reported in several documents; this account is based on notes taken by General Halder (GFMA entry Aug. 22, *Halder Diary*) and Admiral Boehm (NMT, Vol. XII). An account was also leaked to Louis Lochner, Berlin correspondent of the Associated Press, and this version—though overextravagant in its language—was an astounding exclusive which he was unable to use (see his book *What about Germany?*). Details of the atmosphere are also contained in a two-part unsigned memorandum found by American troops in a dump of army documents in the Tyrol (NMT, 798 PS).

374 The description of the signing of the Russo-German pact and the atmosphere in which it was conducted comes from an unsigned memorandum in GFMA (Aug. 24), probably by Gaus or Hilger.

374 Charles E. Bohlen told the author about his adventure inside the German embassy in Moscow.

376 The text of the secret clause to the Russo-German pact comes from GFMA (Aug. 23). See also IMND (F 19 182).

378 The remark made to correspondents at the British embassy by the press secretary were passed on by Mr. Bohlen and confirmed by Sir John Russell.

378 The meeting of the French Cabinet on Aug. 23 is taken from NAMIER; Bonnet, *op. cit.;* and General Gamelin's *Servir les armées françaises de 1940.*

381 Chamberlain's letter is in BFP, Vol. VII (Aug. 23).

382 The Henderson interview with Hitler is in *ibid.* (Aug. 24) and GFMA (same date).

385 The meeting between Sir Horace Wilson and Joseph Kennedy is in FRUS (Aug. 24), though Wilson's name is not mentioned but was revealed by A. J. P. Taylor in his book *The Origins of the Second World War.*

385 Roosevelt's reaction is recorded in Moffat, *op. cit.*

386 Information about Chamberlain's determination to resign comes from several sources. See particularly NICOLSON (p. 413).

PART FIVE

XVII Mussolini Reneges

391 For the full text of President Roosevelt's message, see FRUS (Aug. 24, 1939).

391 The full text of Pope Pius' broadcast of Aug. 24 is in the *Osservatore Romano* of the following day.

392 The description of the Reich Chancellery is from KORDT (and interviews).

392 Hitler's letter to Mussolini is in GFMA (Aug. 24). See also NMT (2834 PS).

392 The circumstances of Dahlerus' meeting with Göring and his proposed flight to England are recounted in DAHLERUS (and interview). See also NMT (Vol. IX).

393 Nevile Henderson's call to Ambassador Lipski is in HENDERSON and in BFP, Vol. VII (Aug. 25), as are details of his interview with Hitler on the same day. See also GFMA (Aug. 25).

394n Ambassador Noël's dispatches are in LJF.

395 Dahlerus' movements and his interview with Halifax, as well as his conversation with Göring, are in DAHLERUS.

396 The details of the signing of the Anglo-Polish treaty of mutual assistance are in BFP, Vol. VII (Aug. 25).

397 Mussolini's state of mind is described in CIANO (see entries for Aug. 24–26).

397 The messages between the Duce and the Führer are in GFMA and DDI (both Aug. 26); see also *Hitler e Mussolini: Lettere e documenti*.

398 Hitler's decision to postpone the invasion of Poland is described in Keitel, *op. cit.* (and interrogation at Nuremberg; IMND, Aug. 2, 1945). See also NMT (TC 90) for Göring's telephone talk with Hitler.

XVIII The Indefatigable Swede

399 Coulondre's message to Daladier about Hitler's state of mind is reproduced in STEHLIN.

400 For Kordt's diary entry, see KORDT.

400 Ribbentrop's telegram to Rome is in GFMA (Aug. 27, 1939). See also IMND (1832 PS).

400 The activities of Dahlerus on Aug. 26 come from DAHLERUS (and interview). See also NMT (Vol. IX).

407 Lord Halifax's telegram to Sir Percy Loraine is in BFP, Vol. VII (Aug. 26), as are his telegram to Kennard, Phipps's telegram to Halifax, and Loraine's reply to Halifax.

408 Hesse's telegram to Ribbentrop is in GFMA (Aug. 26). See also Hesse's *Das Spiel um Deutschland*.

408 Ciano's telegram to Attolico is in DDI (Aug. 26).

409 The exchanges between Hitler and Mussolini are in GFMA and DDI (both Aug. 27).

409 Daladier's message to Hitler and the Führer's reply, as well as Coulondre's remarks, are in LJF.

411 Notes on the Pope's intervention are in the Polish Archives (Western Documents Center). See also BFP, Vol. VII (Aug. 30).

411 The activities of the Swedish peace negotiator are described in DAHLERUS. See also BFP, Vol. VII (Aug. 28).

413 Forbes's reaction to his first encounter with Dahlerus was later described by Forbes to colleagues in the Foreign Office.

414 The Henderson-Hitler conversation of Aug. 28 is in BFP, Vol. VII (same date). See also HENDERSON.

415 Vansittart's reaction is in BFP, Vol. VII.

XIX Operation "Canned Goods"

418 The account of the Henderson-Hitler encounter of Aug. 29, 1939, is in BFP (Vol. VII) and GFMA (both of same date); see also HENDERSON, and his dispatch on Aug. 30 in BFP, Vol. VII.

419 To what extent was General Halder in Hitler's confidence? Since he is now an old man, it is difficult for him to remember or to answer questions. But a close study of his replies to a series of private interrogations at Nuremberg in 1945, together with those of other witnesses and defendants, reveal that he was never much more than an interpreter for the army of Hitler's directives, which were often so vague that the officers were unsure of what

the Führer intended to do next. "I had been chosen as a companion for Hitler so that if something was to be discussed that Von Brauchitsch should know about, I would be there," Halder said. "That is because Von Brauchitsch was constantly worried that Hitler would adopt some military measure without informing him...We knew that Hitler was not very conscientious with the truth." (Reply to questions by Colonel John H. Amen during interrogation at Nuremberg on Oct. 27, 1945.) But that Hitler suspected Halder's role as a member of the anti-Hitler conspiracy as well as his function as a Wehrmacht spy—and took precautions accordingly—seems certain. As his speech to his generals on Aug. 2, 1939, indicated, Hitler knew much more about them and their clandestine activities than they had hitherto suspected. (See NMT, 789 PS.) "It was completely senseless to think about anything that Hitler liked," Halder said. "Every time he said something else...It is my personal impression only that Adolf Hitler always tried to see how far he could go and how much he could get. Now, that had been the case with Austria and Czechoslovakia and thus it was our opinion that the same thing would happen in the case of Poland." (Interrogation by Colonel Amen, Nuremberg, Oct. 27, 1945.)

420 The military commentator's memorandum is reprinted from Liddell Hart (*op. cit.*), Vol. II.

421 Further attempts to save the peace are described in DAHLERUS (details also based on an interview) and NMT (Vol. IX).

425 The Aug. 30–31 encounter between Henderson and Ribbentrop is in BFP, Vol. VII (Aug. 31), GFMA and HENDERSON. See also interrogation of Ribbentrop by Colonel Howard A. Brundage (IMND, Oct. 10, 1945).

426 For Weizsäcker's instructions to Theo Kordt, see GFMA (Aug. 30). Kordt's brother, Erich, appears to believe that these instructions reached Theo *after* they had been given to Henderson (or, in Henderson's version, "gabbled" at him) by Ribbentrop. "The transcript of the 16 points had been handed over already by Göring to Ambassador Henderson when my brother received it," Dr. Erich Kordt writes to the author. What in fact happened was that Göring had handed over the transcript to Dahlerus, who subsequently passed it on to Henderson, who in turn sent it to London. But in the meantime Dahlerus had already sketched out the offer the Germans were making to the Prime Minister and Lord Halifax in London, and through Weizsäcker, the text had been cabled to Theo Kordt in London to "hold." For the time being the source of the statement that he did not do so must be withheld. But it is wrong to suggest that either Chamberlain and Halifax or Vansittart were ignorant of the nature of the German offer, if not its exact text. Erich Kordt says, somewhat enigmatically: "When my brother received it [the 16-point offer] I believe that Vansittart had not yet any knowledge *at least of its wording* [my italics]." But he certainly knew what the Germans were offering, and one of the departments in the Foreign Office was in possession of the full text. (See also William Shirer, *The Rise and Fall of the Third Reich*, Chap. 16.)

427 Kennedy's remark about Chamberlain is in FRUS (Aug. 23).

427 For Colonel Beck's attitude, see Kennard to Halifax and Noël to Bonnet in BFP, Vol. VII (Aug. 31); PWB; LJF.

427 The Henderson-Lipski encounter is in BFP, Vol. VII (Aug. 31) and HENDERSON.

428 The interview with Lipski comes from DAHLERUS (and interview), and BFP (*loc. cit.*).

429 The details of the Polish telegram are in GFMA (Aug. 31), DAHLERUS and the emasculated version in PWB.

430 Details of the operations in Upper Silesia during Aug. 31–Sept. 1 are all to be found in NMT: interrogations of Alfred Helmut Naujocks at Nurem-

berg by Colonel Howard A. Brundage (Sept. 11–12, 1945) and by Lieutenant Colonel Smith Brookhart (Oct. 9, 1945); Naujocks' affidavit of Nov. 19, 1945; an interrogation by George Sawicki, prosecuting attorney for Poland (Mar. 2, 1946); the interrogation of General Erwin Lahousen of the Abwehr (June 1945), when he quoted from Admiral Canaris' diary about Operation "Canned Goods" (which Canaris and Lahousen called "Secret Operation Himmler"); from the interrogation of SS Major (Sturmbannführer) Geissler (June 7, 1945).

434 Signor Attolico's interview with Hitler is in GFMA (Sept. 1, 1939).

435 The Loraine-Ciano encounter is in CIANO (Aug. 31–Sept. 1).

436 The background for the German operations in Poland on Sept. 1 comes from OKW, OKL and OKM; and particularly from GFC; from an interview with General Heinz Guderian in *Signal* magazine (published by MVP); and from Guderian's book, *Panzer Leader.*

437 Polish details come from archives in the Polish Institute and Sikorski Museum (London), Polish Military Records (Warsaw), and several books on the Polish campaign, including *Destiny Can Wait* and *The Defence of Poland.*

438 For additional information about Russo-German co-operation in the first days of the attack on Poland, see GFMA (Sept. 1–9).

PART SIX

XX Common Action—or Another Conference?

443 Hitler's proclamation to the German armed forces is in NMT (GB 73, Sept. 1, 1939).

444 Halifax's statement is quoted in BIRKENHEAD.

445 Raczyński's remarks are in BFP, Vol. VII (Sept. 1), as is Kennard's telephone call to London and Halifax's talk with Theo Kordt.

446 For the complete text of Hitler's speech, see the *N.Y. Times* (Sept. 2).

447 The Dahlerus-Göring encounter is in DAHLERUS, as is his subsequent talk with Hitler.

448 The operations of the 3rd Panzer Division of the XIX Army Corps are detailed in *Signal;* GFC; and in Guderian, *op. cit.*

450 Chamberlain's speech of Sept. 1 is in *Hansard* of the following day, as are the interjections.

450 Noël's account of his interview with Colonel Beck is in his *L'Agression allemande contre la Pologne.*

451n Henderson's warning is in BFP, Vol. VII (Sept. 1), and Nicolson's reactions in NICOLSON.

XXI At Last

453 For the meetings of Loraine and François-Poncet with Ciano on Sept. 2, as well as Ciano's conversation with Halifax, see BFP (Vol. VII) and DDI (same date).

454 The French Foreign Minister discusses his own part during these days in Bonnet, *op. cit.*

455 For details of the activities of the *Schleswig-Holstein* against Westerplatte, see OKM (Sept. 1–6) and reports of Verb. Gruppe OKW Ausland in their *Tagebuch* of the same dates (GFC).

455 Bodenschatz's message is in OKL (Sept. 2).

455 Re the Cabinet meeting on Sept. 2, see Minney *(op. cit.);* BIRKENHEAD; Duff
Cooper *(op. cit.);* Amery, *My Political Life;* and *Hansard.* It was originally
believed that Amery was the M.P. who called out "You speak for
England!" but Lord Boothby has confirmed that it was he who raised the
rallying cry. See NICOLSON entry for Sept. 2, and footnote, for more details.

457 Churchill's dilemma in having been "trapped" into Chamberlain's Cabinet,
and his reactions to the situation, were set out at some length by him at
a later date. According to his biographer, the late Randolph Churchill,
with whom the author had several talks over various aspects of this book,
the situation will be dealt with at some length in the appropriate section
of the official biography.

458 The sit-down strike by members of the British Cabinet was elaborated upon
in a memorandum written sometime afterward by Sir Reginald Dorman-
Smith and subsequently published in the London *Sunday Times* (Sept.
6, 1964). See also the *Hickleton Papers, op. cit.*

459 The Air Ministry weather records in London confirm that there were lightning
flashes while the Cabinet meeting was taking place. As a result of severe
electrical storms, barrage balloons hoisted over London against German
bombers were lowered to "safe heights," but according to one squad
member, "still barged around the sky like drunken elephants."

459 For details of Sir Horace Wilson's interview, see Hesse, *op. cit.* Sir Horace
appears to have been out of touch with his master's thinking about this
time. That at least was the conclusion reached by the late Lord Morrison
of Lambeth (then Sir Herbert Morrison), who in Sept. 1939 was head
of the London County Council and responsible for evacuating women
and children from London. He saw Sir Horace repeatedly and pleaded for
permission to get them out of the metropolis but was told each time by
an increasingly adamant Sir Horace that "this would only encourage Herr
Hitler to believe that we seriously wanted war." Lord Morrison went into
great detail about these "distressing meetings," as he called them, in conversations with the author in 1959; they were subsequently published in
the London *Sunday Express* (Aug. 9–30, 1959).

459 The account of Henderson's reception at the Foreign Ministry is in Schmidt,
op. cit.

460 The final attempts to restore peace are in DAHLERUS.

460 The scene in the Cabinet Room at No. 10 Downing Street was described
in an interview with Alvar Liddell, published in the London *Daily Express*
on Sept. 3, 1967, and elaborated upon in a letter to the author.

461 The reports of the charge of the Pomorska Brigade come from GFC; *History
of the Polish September Campaign, 1939;* and Guderian, *op. cit.*

463 Re Ambassador Coulondre's meeting with Ribbentrop, see LJF.

Epilogue

466 The account of the last interview between the Polish ambassador in Moscow,
Dr. Waclaw Grzybowski, and Andrei Vishinsky was described to the
author by Charles E. Bohlen, who had heard it from the ambassador
himself in Moscow.

Index

Bund Deutscher Mädel, 110
Bürckel, Josef, 146-47, 152-53
Burckhardt, Carl F., 34, 238, 315, 436n
  Hitler and, 320-22, 326
Burgess, Guy, 344
Burnett, Air Marshal Sir Charles, 302
Butler, Richard Austin, 209, 302

Cadogan, Sir Alexander, 12, 15, 209,
  444, 458
  Dahlerus and, 411, 413
  during invasion of Czechoslovakia,
  151, 156
Campinchi, César, 127, 378n
Camrose, Lord, 126
Canaris, Admiral Wilhelm, 78, 99, 320,
  341, 367
  in German officers plot (*q.v.*)
  Hitler and, 368, 370, 373
Chamberlain, Sir Austen, 10, 13
Chamberlain, Joseph, 10
Chamberlain, Neville, 33-35, 250-51,
  319, 333, 346, 359
  and Anglo-Polish agreement (*q.v.*)
  anti-Communism of, 176-77
  anti-Semitism and, 125-26, 198n
  anti-workingclass attitude of, 175
  antipathy to Czechs of, 22-24, 182
  background of, 10-11
  Colonel Beck and, 206-12
  Bonnet and, 45, 50-51, 55, 199
  Cabinet and Parliament opposition
  to, 178-80, 455-58
  Churchill and, 10, 14, 16, 90, 95, 224
  Dahlerus and, 401-2, 411-12, 424
  Daladier and, 51-56
  declaration of war and, 461
  hesitations, 449-50, 453-54
  dismissal of German officers plot by,
  31-32
  on German-Soviet pact, 380-82
  Göring and, 366-67, 380, 460, 461
  Hitler and, 59, 261, 294, 459
    Bad Godesberg meeting, 47-57
    Berchtesgaden meeting, 5, 36-42, 45
  Kennedy and, 29-30, 44, 305
  loan offer to Germany of, 263-65
  Munich Conference and, 66-69, 88,
    102, 138, 142
  "peace in our time" document, 89-91
  plans for, 61-64
  Mussolini and, 13, 18, 62, 64, 214, 360
    Rome meeting, 139-41
  offered resignation of, 386
  post-Munich outlook of, 137-38, 151,
    154-56

refusal of visas for Sudetens by, 92
reshuffling of Foreign Office by, 11-19
Rumania and, 195-200, 206, 208-12
Soviet Union and, 199, 200, 206, 222,
  287, 301, 335
underhandedness of, 43-44, 181-82
verbal abuse of, by Beneš and
  Masaryk, 23, 24, 46
Cheb, *see* Eger
Chodacki, M., 238, 314-16, 436
Churchill, Winston, 11, 12n, 63, 257-58,
  319, 333
  anti-appeasement group led by, 10,
    44n
  Beneš and, 184
  in Cabinet, 452, 457, 458
  Chamberlain and, 10, 14, 16, 90, 95,
    224
  Davies and, 220-21
  German officers plot and, 31
  on loss of Czechoslovak assets, 188
  visit to Maginto Line by, 346-48
Chvalkovský, Dr. František, 81, 144, 152
  Hácha and, *see* Hácha
Ciano, Edda, 140
Ciano, Count Galeazzo (foreign minister),
  18, 139, 213, 408, 412, 451
  in attempted Franco-Italian
  rapprochement, 142-43
  diary entries of, 13n, 141, 397
  Hitler and, 233, 327-31
  at Munich conference, 66
  passing of information to British by,
    333, 359, 392, 435, 453-54
  Ribbentrop and, 327-29
  in signing of Pact of Steel, 230-32
City of Exeter (ship), 303-5, 352
Colvin, Ian, 208, 209
Conwell-Evans, Dr. Philip, 253
Cooper, Lady Diana, 201-2
Corsica, Italian claims to, 132n, 141
Coulondre, Ambassador Robert, 219n,
  240-42, 399-400, 409, 463
  Stehlin and, 133, 136, 228, 272, 345
  Weizsäcker and, 183-84, 345-46
Cracow, 316, 438, 444
Crewe, Lord, 221n
Csáky, Count István (foreign minister),
  320, 322n
Czas (Cracow newspaper), 316
Czechoslovakia, 251
  air force of, 27, 29n, 44n
  demobilization of, 76
  friendship pact with Poland, 83, 201
  loss of assets abroad of, 185-87
    Churchill on, 188

Index

Index

509

ABOUT
THE AUTHOR

Born in Manchester, England, in 1913, LEONARD MOSLEY
left school at the age of seventeen and sailed aboard a cattle
boat for Canada. There he worked briefly for a Montreal
newspaper, then came to New York, where he had an even
briefer fling as assistant stage manager at Minsky's Forty-
second Street burlesque theater, before securing a job on
Fortune and later a position as a Hollywood screen writer.

Back in Great Britain, Mr. Mosley became a columnist
for one of the newspapers of the Kemsley (now Thomson)
chain and traveled the world for them. He covered the
Spanish Civil War (and was expelled by both sides), left
Berlin the day Hitler marched into Poland, and was on the
spot in Holland when German troops invaded in 1940. In
East Africa he traveled behind the Italian lines with Emperor
Haile Selassie, and in the Western Desert he covered the
great battles which culminated in El Alamein. Thereafter,
in his role as war correspondent, he parachuted into Yugoslavia and the Dodecanese Islands, and on D-Day in 1944
was dropped into Normandy with the 6th British Airborne
Division. His subsequent dispatches gave the world the first
eyewitness account of the invasion.

In 1946 Mr. Mosley joined the London *Daily Express* as
a roving correspondent, and he now serves as their film critic.
The author of five novels and twelve works of nonfiction,
Mr. Mosley now lives in France.